PC Magazine 1996 Computer Buyer's Guide

PC Magazine
1996
Computer
Buyer's Guide

Ziff-Davis Press

Emeryville, California

Edited by John C. Dvorak

Copy Editor	Margo Hill
Technical Reviewer	David Farrell
Project Coordinator	Ami Knox
Proofreaders	Madhu Prasher and Jeff Barrash
Cover Photograph	Robert Songroth
Cover Design	Ken Roberts
Book Design	Laura Lamar/MAX, San Francisco
Technical Illustration	Cherie Plumlee Computer Graphics & Illustration, Steph Bradshaw, and Dave Feasey
Word Processing	Howard Blechman and Cat Haglund
Page Layout	Russel Stolins
Indexer	Carol Burbo

Ziff-Davis Press, ZD Press, and the Ziff-Davis Press logo are licensed to Macmillan Computer Publishing USA by Ziff-Davis Publishing Company, New York, New York.

Ziff-Davis Press imprint books are produced on a Macintosh computer system with the following applications: FrameMaker®, Microsoft® Word, QuarkXPress®, Adobe Illustrator®, Adobe Photoshop®, Adobe Streamline™, MacLink® *Plus*, Aldus® FreeHand™, Collage Plus™.

If you have comments or questions or would like to receive a free catalog, call or write:
Macmillan Computer Publishing USA
Ziff-Davis Press Line of Books
5903 Christie Avenue
Emeryville, CA 94608
800-688-0448

ISBN 1-56276-343-1

Manufactured in the United States of America
10 9 8 7 6 5 4 3 2 1

CONTENTS AT A GLANCE

TABLE OF CONTENTS

TABLE OF CONTENTS

TABLE OF CONTENTS

TABLE OF CONTENTS

TABLE OF CONTENTS

TABLE OF CONTENTS

TABLE OF CONTENTS

TABLE OF CONTENTS

TABLE OF CONTENTS

TABLE OF CONTENTS

TABLE OF CONTENTS

ACKNOWLEDGMENTS

AS THIS BOOK continues to be the definitive buyer's guide that can be used by experienced users and novices alike, I have to thank all those who made it possible. First of all, Mimi Dvorak gets the credit for fine-tuning the readability. When you write about computers all the time, it's very easy to forget that the average user (not to mention the newcomer) doesn't automatically know all the buzzwords and concepts that come packaged with today's computer system. Mimi has a knack for handling this oversight and making the writing approachable to all users.

Credit also goes to the staff of *PC Magazine*, along with the contributing editors, especially Winn Rosch, whose ability to explain difficult technologies is unexcelled. Also a great thanks to Alfred Poor, Matt Ross, Charles Petzold, Robin Raskin, Chris Barr, Carol Levin, Don Wilmott, Rick Ayres, Bill Machrone, Jim Seymour, Bill Howard, Tom Stanton, Bruce Brown, Frank Bican, Ed Mendelson, Bill O'Brien, and Mitt Jones. Special thanks go to PC Labs for their neverending testing of the equipment and their help in doing the tables found in this book. Since this book is based on material that first appeared in *PC Magazine*, I have to thank Michael Miller and the editors of the magazine for letting this project continue and evolve. Special thanks go to *PC Magazine* publishing director Jim Stafford for producing one of the greatest magazines in history.

Thanks also to the crew at *PC Magazine UK*. In England there is nothing to match the quality of *PC Magazine UK*.

Finally, I also want to thank the staff at ZD Press for getting this book out in time and making it look terrific.

INTRODUCTION

WELCOME to *PC Magazine 1996 Computer Buyer's Guide.*

This is a book designed to help you make smart buying decisions. You can use it as both an introduction to computer hardware and a reference tool. The first part of the book takes you through every hardware technology that you need to be familiar with. You will learn what the experts think and you will be carefully guided past the traps and pitfalls that newcomers and experts both encounter.

The idea for this book came along one day when a shelf of carefully organized *PC Magazines* collapsed a solid oak bookshelf from their massive weight. I thought it might be a good idea to condense the material found in all those older issues and put the information in a concise book: a buyer's guide. This book is the result of that effort. While the book is no substitute for a subscription to *PC Magazine*, you'll find that it is a handy reference.

In this book you'll learn how a computer works. You'll learn what components are needed in a system that is just right for you. You'll become fluent in computerese—the awful language they speak on the computer store sales floor. No chance of being tricked into making a bad decision once you read this book. You'll learn how modems work and how you can link your computer to other computers. You will understand how different printers work and which one is best for you. In short, you'll become an instant expert after reading this book. I now tell people that if they want to get a job in the computer industry, they can get one if they read this book. I hope you enjoy it.

A Quick Tour of the Chapters

The first two chapters of this book give you the building blocks for making an informed buying decision. Chapter 1, "Basics for Beginners," describes in simple terms what a PC is and what the different components are that make up a typical PC system. Chapter 2, "Smart PC Shopping," gives you the inside story on how and where to shop. Common sense rules, hints on mail-order purchasing, and tips on buying a used computer are just a few of the useful topics in this chapter.

The heart of the book is in Chapters 3–12. Here you'll find all the information you need on each of the components of a typical PC system. Chapter 3 covers the basics of software buying, including tips on getting the best price and a guide to the many types of programs available. Chapter 4 covers computers—everything from the earliest, most primitive PCs to the current power-user machines. Monitors of every type are discussed in Chapter 5, and information about video cards and graphic display standards is found in Chapter 6. Chapter 7 gives you the lowdown on printers—ink-jet, laser printers, and more—and teaches you how to decide which is the right one for you. Chapter 8 covers multimedia—this chapter

INTRODUCTION

has been thoroughly revised, updated, and expanded. Chapter 9 discusses backup and storage devices, including hard disks, tape drives, and CD-ROM drives. Chapter 10 covers input devices. You'll learn about keyboards and mice, as well as some interesting and unusual alternatives to the two. Modems are discussed in Chapter 11. You'll find a handy guide to the ever-changing terminology of modems and telecommunications, a discussion of how modems work, and a survey of the different types of modems now available. Chapter 12 discusses computer accessories such as power strips, diagnostic software, and other recommended utilities that will help breathe life into your PC system.

The next part of the book is Comparison Charts A–J. These are elaborate condensed specifications for machines tested in the comparative reviews done in *PC Magazine*. Included are the famous *PC Magazine* Editor's Choices, which are determined at the time of testing by the project leaders and various editors. I have also included Dvorak's Picks, which are products that I personally have familiarity with and would recommend to others. You should note that these selections are subjective and open to debate. Many times the best product for you, the buyer, is something else.

The appendix is a directory of computer equipment manufacturers. Hundreds of names, addresses, phone numbers, and fax numbers are listed here so you can easily contact the manufacturers of the products mentioned in this book. And let's not forget the glossary. It's your guide to the always mercurial and sometimes confusing terms you'll encounter as you investigate computer equipment and make your buying decisions.

CHAPTER

BASICS FOR BEGINNERS

BUYING YOUR FIRST COMPUTER can be a very frustrating experience. Often salespeople at computer stores don't know how to guide you to the right system, or they have a system they're "pushing." The lack of material written for the computer novice compounds the frustration. And nothing's more aggravating than being told to "take a class" to learn the basics.

BASICS FOR BEGINNERS

CHAPTER 1 IS DESIGNED to help a beginning computer user learn some of the terms, concepts, and buzzwords of PC computing. Once you grasp the language and phrases, much of the gibberish will begin to make sense. You'll gain the ability to ask the right questions and make an intelligent purchase.

What Is a PC?

A PC (short for personal computer) is a machine. Like other machines, it has basic functions, and these functions can be applied to certain tasks.

A PC has four basic functions:

- To store and display information, or *data*

- To do calculations

- To talk to other computers (online) and share information

- To control the operations of another machine, such as a printer

These functions can be directed toward many tasks. A PC may be used to control a robotic arm, calculate a spreadsheet, play a game, or compose music. But a computer cannot do any of these things without instructions. These instructions are called *software programs* or *applications*. These sets of instructions tell the different elements of the computer to do something, such as perform a mathematical function, word-process, create a picture, connect to a telephone line, and more. There is good software and bad software, great software and dismal software. Badly written software will not perform well no matter how good the computer.

A minimum amount of programming (that is, software) is already in the computer when you buy it. This lets the computer know it's a computer and not a microwave oven, or simply a doorstop. The machine needs instructions for everything, no matter how simple.

What Are the Different Parts of a PC?

The computer system is made up of several different parts: a keyboard, a video screen, a box, and various cables. The box may also be called the system unit, central processing unit (CPU), or simply the computer. Additional parts may include a printer, a modem, and a mouse. All of these pieces are collectively referred to as the system *hardware* (see Figure 1.1).

It is a common misconception among beginners that all of these pieces of hardware must "go together"—in other words, that they must be made by one manufacturer and sold as a package.

The different components must be *compatible* (designed to work together). The issue of compatibility has changed over the last few years.

BASICS FOR BEGINNERS

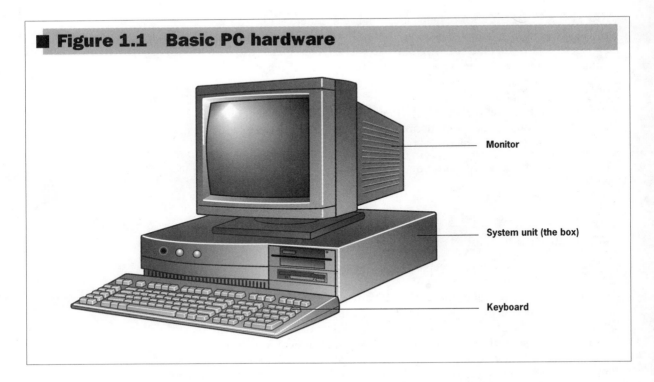

■ **Figure 1.1   Basic PC hardware**

Monitor

System unit (the box)

Keyboard

Historically, making computer components compatible was a big headache. It was a maze of "what-ifs" and exceptions to try to make different parts work correctly. With today's computers, this is almost a moot point. Manufacturers have worked very hard to correct the problems and the quirks of incompatibility. Now you can shop around for the different pieces of your computer system. Feel free to purchase your computer at one store, the printer at another, a keyboard through a mail-order company, and the monitor and video card at yet another outlet.

The System Unit

The box part of the computer contains a whole world of hardware unto itself. The system unit is a case which holds a number of different components (see Figure 1.2). The box may be opened. There are usually four screws located on the back of the unit. Unscrew these and the entire case can be lifted off to reveal the innards of the computer. (Warning: The computer must be unplugged from the electrical outlet.)

A Dvorak tip: If you have young children, familiarize yourself with how to remove the cover of the machine and the disk drive because toddler-sized kids love to put pennies and other small objects into the

BASICS FOR BEGINNERS

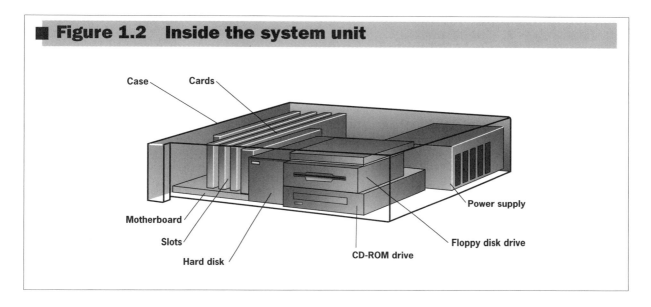

■ Figure 1.2   Inside the system unit

open slot. Service time will add up if you rely on a serviceperson to pull out packages of Kool-Aid from the disk drive unit.

Inside the computer are the *cards* (also called boards). The cards are flat, rigid pieces of a hard, plastic-like green resin. They have different objects, square and rectangular raised pieces, called chips, and maybe a set of little rocker switches soldered onto them. These cards plug into a panel. The panel is called a *bus* and the places where the card plugs in are called *slots*.

The bus is on the computer's *motherboard*, which is the biggest card in the computer. The *processor chip*, the bus, and the memory chips are all attached to the motherboard. The *processor chip* is the main chip—the brains of the computer. It oversees all the functions of the computer and processes all the data. (For a full discussion of the different processor chips, see Chapter 4.) In addition, the motherboard has open connectors for single in-line memory modules (SIMMs) so you can add more memory cheaply. You can buy SIMMs at any time to add more main memory, which is also known as random-access memory (RAM).

Other cards which may be added to the box include a modem card, video card, small computer systems interface (SCSI) card, bus mouse card, joystick card, sound card, and Windows accelerator card, among others. The box also houses a fan to cool the unit and a power supply to regulate electricity to the whole machine. The hard or floppy disk drives are inside the system unit, too. We'll discuss these in detail in a moment.

BASICS FOR BEGINNERS

■ Thanks for the Memory

Memory is like money—what you have is never enough. The more memory your computer has, the better, but only to a point. Random-access memory (RAM) is short-term, temporary memory. If there is a power outage or if you turn off the machine, whatever is in the short-term memory will be lost. (For instance, if you're writing the great American novel and forget to save your work, it will become a bittersweet memory.)

Let's say you turn on your computer and see the C > prompt on the screen. When you type in the code or word that runs a program, that program is read from permanent memory on the hard disk to this RAM memory. That's why when you turn off the computer and turn it back on again, you'll see the C > prompt but not the word processing program. This short-term memory may be referred to as dynamic RAM (DRAM) or static RAM (SRAM). These terms are inconsequential to the user. They're just techie terms to describe the exact, precise, detailed way the chips work.

Flash memory, a brand-new kind of memory, is not widely available yet. This flash memory differs from RAM in that the data is not lost when the machine is powered down. Currently, it is used in mobile computers and other tiny hand-held devices. Someday it may be found in the big, desktop computers.

Read-only memory (ROM) is the real brains behind the machine's operations. ROM, which cannot be overwritten, is permanently encoded programming that tells the computer how to operate. This includes the basic input/output system (BIOS). The input/output information governs how data is moved through the system—from the keyboard to the computer, from the computer to the monitor, and so on. It also governs how the machine boots (starts up) the system, and other operations as well. ■

The Keyboard

A keyboard is usually included when you purchase the system. If you don't like a keyboard, if it stops working, or if you spill your cola on it, you can purchase a different one. We cover input devices in Chapter 10.

The keyboard looks a lot like a typewriter's, as shown in Figure 1.3. It's flatter, and there are extra keys on it, usually across the top and on the left, which are labeled F1 through F10 or F12. These *function keys* may be programmed for special functions. A number of different software programs will use these keys for specific commands. A keyboard may also have a numeric keypad, which is arranged much like a ten-key calculator.

The Monitor

The monitor is a video screen. It looks like a television set in many ways. It may have vertical and horizontal control adjustment knobs and color adjustment knobs if it's a color monitor. The monitor "reports" the results of your commands and will display requested information. Monitors are either monochrome or color. *Monochrome* designates a two-color display: black and white, amber and white, or even green and black. *Color* screens typically display from 16 to over 16 million different colors, depending on the video card installed.

BASICS FOR BEGINNERS

Figure 1.3   Typical keyboard layout

The Video Adapter Card

You can't just hook a monitor to a computer. It won't work. You need to
purchase a video card. Many computers don't even have a place to plug the
monitor in—it's on the video card. Video cards come in different varieties:
VGA, SVGA, and XGA. Most cards used today in high-performance
systems are designed to plug into a special "local bus" slot. This can be
either the PCI bus or the VL bus. There are some compatibility problems
between monitors and video adapter cards: A monochrome monitor won't
work with a color video card, and a high-end advanced card may require an
expensive, specialized monitor. The differences and conflicts between
monitors and video cards are covered in Chapter 6.

The Disk Drive

The disk drive is also called the *floppy drive*. Floppy disks come in two
sizes: $5\frac{1}{4}$- and $3\frac{1}{2}$-inch, although the $5\frac{1}{4}$-inch disk drives are less
prominent and are now considered practically obsolete. The smaller disk
is encased in rigid plastic, while the larger is in a flimsy, thin plastic case
(see Figure 1.4). Disks must be used in the appropriately sized disk drives.
Obviously, trying to use a $5\frac{1}{4}$-inch disk in a $3\frac{1}{2}$-inch disk drive is like
shoving a quarter into the nickel slot of a parking meter. The issue of a
$5\frac{1}{4}$-inch drive is a moot point, as manufacturers have moved to a single
$3\frac{1}{2}$-inch drive. In fact, the only way you'll find a new computer with both
drive formats would be if you had a clone builder make one for you.
(Which would only be a good choice if you had a number of programs
and archived data on the larger disks.) Nowadays, very little new software
comes on $5\frac{1}{4}$-inch disks.

BASICS FOR BEGINNERS

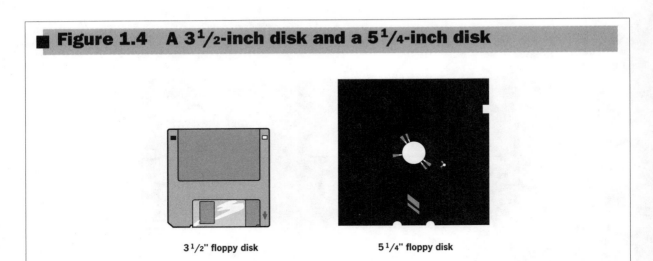

■ **Figure 1.4   A 3^1/$_2$-inch disk and a 5^1/$_4$-inch disk**

3^1/$_2$" floppy disk   5^1/$_4$" floppy disk

Today most computers sold are "multimedia-ready," which means there is a CD-ROM drive built in. They lack a sound card and speakers for full multimedia action, although often they are available as add-on options. The most common box configuration on the market is a 3^1/$_2$-inch drive and a CD-ROM drive. The CD-ROM drive usually looks like a little pop-out drawer that the CD-ROM platter lays in, although there are a few other, less popular variations. (For more information on CD-ROMs and multimedia, go to Chapter 8.)

The Floppy Disk

Inside the plastic cover of a floppy disk is a thin plastic wafer coated with a magnetic oxide. The coating can be magnetized in small sections. The magnetized patterns can be read as information by your computer's disk drive. The wafer is fragile, which is why a protective cover is placed over it. Inside, the disk is spun very quickly by the disk drive, like a record on a phonograph. The disk drive has *read heads* and *write heads*, which find data by reading the patterns or store data by magnetizing the disk's coating. Dirt, grit, and oily fingerprints can damage a disk and render it "unreadable" and "unwriteable."

Back in the "olden days" before hard disks, floppy disks held programs and stored data until you were ready to use them. A user would have a pile of disks on the desk and would have to sort through them to find the right program disk and then the right data disk. But since the emergence of hard disks, floppies have fallen into a lesser role. There are probably some computer users who have never even used a

BASICS FOR BEGINNERS

■ Computer Cheat Sheet

If you're shopping for your first PC, it would be a good idea to know a few basic computer terms.

■ **Application**   A specific task a computer performs. Other words for this include software, program, or instructions.

■ **Bit**   The smallest piece of information a computer can process. Think of it as an electronic Morse code in which a bit is one dot or dash. Eight of these equal a *byte*. A *kilobyte* (K) is around a thousand bytes, a *megabyte* (Mb) is about a million bytes, and a *gigabyte* (G) is a billion bytes.

■ **CD-ROM (Compact Disc, Read Only Memory)**   This is a silver plastic disc which looks identical to an audio music CD, except it holds data for your computer instead of songs. The data on the CD-ROM may be only the machine instruction for a computer program, or computer-readable audio, video, still pictures, text, or some combination of these. A computer which can produce audio, video, and text (that is, sound and moving pictures) is now referred to as a *multimedia computer*.

■ **Chip**   A very tiny square or rectangular sliver of material (usually silicon) with electrical components built into it. Some of the chips in a computer help to control the flow of information. Others help the computer to remember information. The most important chip is the microprocessor, which is the 8088, 286, 386, 486, Pentium, and so on, that every salesperson will speak of when talking about a specific machine's features.

■ **CPU (central processing unit)**   Also known as the system or the box, this is the functional "brain" of the computer.

■ **Data**   Another word for the information manipulated by a computer.

■ **DOS (disk operating system)**   A widely used operating system which gives the computer instructions. These instructions, along with the BIOS, enable the computer to work. Examples of DOS functions include displaying characters on the screen, reading and writing to a disk, printing, and accepting commands from the keyboard.

■ **Function**   An operation; a set of tasks for a computer to do.

■ **Hardware**   The various components of the computer you need to lug to your car after purchasing them. These include the CPU, keyboard, printer, and any other peripherals.

■ **Multimedia**   A computer equipped with a CD-ROM drive, speakers, a sound card, and a good quality monitor/video card. A multimedia computer can produce audio, video, and text.

■ **Software**   The other stuff you need to buy to make a computer usable. Software instructs the computer to perform specific tasks. Word processing, games, spreadsheets, databases, and telecommunications programs are all software you may want to consider. Software can also be referred to as the application.   ■

BASICS FOR BEGINNERS

floppy, except to copy a program onto their hard disks. (Retail software programs come on floppies.) But floppy disks are very valuable in a few key ways. For instance, if your hard disk gets clogged up with too many files—some important and others simply copies—you can move the files to a floppy disk and remove them from your hard disk. This will give you extra hard-disk space or make room for a new program. Also, it's a good idea to back up important files by copying them to a floppy disk and keeping the disk in a safe place, just in case an accident or catastrophe occurs. For more on data storage and security, refer to Chapter 9, which covers backup and storage.

The Hard Disk

The hard disk functions like a floppy disk. The only difference is the hard disk can hold vast amounts of data. A hard disk allows you to store many different programs and data on your computer. This speeds things up considerably from back when a program had to be read off floppy disks in a disk drive for the program to work. Many software programs are so large that one floppy disk wouldn't hold enough instructions to allow the program to run. The trend is toward programs becoming so large it just isn't feasible to use floppies at all. As a convenience, software makers are starting to use CD-ROMs to hold their programs. This speeds the transfer to your hard disk, and has the added benefit of protecting the program better (floppies are more susceptible to damage and prone to being erased, or having one of the set misplaced). A hard disk is mandatory for today's personal computers.

There are both internal and external hard disks. An internal disk is a necessary part of any computer system. External disks are for storing even more data or for specific needs like backing up data. Backing up data involves copying everything from the internal hard disk to a second location for security. This is common in the business world, but most home computer users just back up important data by making a copy to a floppy disk, called a *backup disk*. External hard disks are covered in Chapter 9.

Conclusion

These are the basics. There are many other details about computers which you can learn before you go out and buy one. Some of this information is important, but much of it isn't. What you have learned in this chapter and what you'll learn throughout the rest of this book will provide you with the knowledge base you'll need to be a wise consumer.

CHAPTER

SMART PC SHOPPING

2

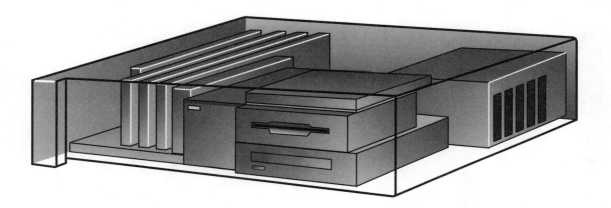

WHEN YOU WALK into a computer store as a novice buyer, you can easily become overwhelmed by all the choices. The seemingly simple purchase of one peripheral—like a printer— becomes a massive undertaking. It's unnerving. The salesperson will speak in fancy high-techie terms like NLQ (near letter quality), ppm (pages per minute), ink-jet, laser, and dot matrix. Just reading the sales literature is like deciphering hieroglyphics or translating Finnish into English.

SMART PC SHOPPING

YOUR FIRST STEP in buying a new computer is to bone up on this kooky "foreign" tongue: computerese. The best way to learn is to have a very patient friend (ideally, one who knows a lot about personal computers). Failing that, read, read, read. This book is a good start. Then go on to the magazines: *PC Magazine* and *PC/Computing*. Find out about user's groups in your area; usually a local computer store can point you in the right direction. And, of course, ask a lot of questions at the store.

Dvorak's Golden Rules

There are five things to keep in mind when shopping for a computer: Parts is parts; faster is better; little things add up; buy the newest technology you can afford; and shop, shop around. Don't let a salesperson sway you or persuade you to purchase a machine because "the parts are better," or "it will be fast enough for you," or even "you won't find a lower retail price anywhere."

Rule #1: Parts Is Parts

A PC clone is a PC clone is a PC clone. Most of the hundreds of different brands of PC clones use the same Taiwanese manufactured parts mixed with American microprocessors and hard disks. Software programmers are very cautious, so most software works on a compatible clone just as well as on an IBM or Compaq machine. The most important thing to research when choosing a clone is whether the company has a reasonable maintenance program and good technical assistance. Your machine will be useless to you if getting it repaired is an impossible chore or getting the answer to a simple question involves calling Hong Kong.

In the past, IBM and Compaq had a head start in marketing the newest and fastest technology. It often took up to a year for clone makers to produce machines similar to the latest from the big computer companies. Nowadays, however, compatible computers appear at the same time as the major computer companies release their latest models. That means the prices on machines begin to drop as soon as the computers appear at the store. And this competition is a good thing for the computer buyer.

Today, the IBM standard for compatibles and the machines produced by IBM have diverged slightly. In 1987, IBM introduced the PS/2 (Personal System 2), which featured a new Micro Channel bus to help the computer's various expansion cards work together more efficiently. PS/2s can run IBM-compatible software, but the expansion cards a PS/2 uses differ from the ones used by other IBM-compatible computers.

The clone manufacturers continued to refine the IBM system, introducing faster and better machines without the Micro Channel technology. More manufacturers are making expansion cards for the

SMART PC SHOPPING

compatibles than for the IBM PS/2, so the PS/2 did not become the new standard. Instead, IBM compatibles with the old type of expansion cards have continued to be the IBM standard.

This means that there are certain advantages to owning a clone instead of the latest from IBM, including a wider (and cheaper) choice of expansion cards.

Rule #2: Faster Is Better

Purchase the fastest, most powerful unit you can afford. It should have a big, fast hard disk with at least 540Mb. The more memory, the better. It might sound like overkill, but memory is like money: You always wish you had more.

If you have a specific software program that you must use on your new machine, find out what chip it requires to run. If it requires a 486 chip, the software won't run on an old 286. Most well-written software written for an earlier chip (such as a 286) will run on a new machine (such as a 486 or Pentium). This isn't a hard and fast rule, but is usually the case. Otherwise, as far as chips go, a good, fast 386 is functional but slow when compared to a 486 or Pentium. It all depends on the price you can afford and your individual requirements.

Rule #3: The Little Things Add Up

A competitive price is an important factor when buying, but your decisions also must be based on personal variables. What do you plan to do with the system? Do you need the vendor's warranty and support? In your haste to save money, don't forget these easily overlooked options.

The documentation that comes with a PC reveals something about the quality of a system. If the manual includes generic descriptions of components, this means the vendor uses whatever parts are available or cheapest at the moment. Because the system's components keep changing, there isn't any time to revise the documentation.

Specific documentation and a limited but adequate number of options (say, five or six hard-disk choices) usually guarantee a better overall quality. They also indicate higher compatibility, because the number of variables is controlled. A PC manufacturer that uses only one or two motherboard designs per processor type is in a better position to obtain Class B FCC ratings, and the machine will probably have greater compatibility with the computer peripherals.

Rule #4: Buy the Newest Technology You Can Afford

Computers become outdated in a very short time. What was top of the line six years ago is old and sluggish by today's standards. You might get a great deal on a "really cheap" 386 PC, and it might serve you well, but it

SMART PC SHOPPING

is already outdated. And if for some reason you use a friend's 486 or your office gets a new Pentium, you will instantly become very unhappy with your painfully slow 386.

Rule #5: Shop, Shop Around
First of all, know what you want. Do some comparative shopping. Visit dealers to ask about the services they provide. Pick up a copy of *PC Magazine* and start calling the direct marketers. What are their services and prices? Do you know the applications you'll want to run? What do they require? What video performance do you expect? What are your expectations for the speed and capacity of the disk? Put in the legwork up front, and you'll be happier with your system.

When considering price, remember that the list price and street price differ greatly. The list price is the manufacturer's suggested retail price, which has almost no basis in fact. (Well, perhaps a few government purchasing agents have paid the list price.) The *street price* is the discounted cost after the price wars between the discount computer chains, the direct-sales dealers, and special offers from the manufacturers themselves. The list and street prices can differ by as much as 40 percent.

Where Should You Purchase Your PC?
If you want a sandwich, you go to the deli. If you want a book, you go to the bookstore. But if you want to buy a new PC, things can get complicated. The options are endless. The large superstore with boxes piled high competes with the local computer store, which offers hands-on help and service. Then there's the mail-order house, where price is everything. If you want to get funky, go to the local computer swap meet. You can even buy a computer through the home shopping channel.

Those are just a few places to buy a computer or peripheral. You could also buy a used computer through a newspaper ad or a notice on a bulletin board. A relative or friend might give you an old, idle one. There is no one right place to buy your computer equipment. Let's examine some of the options and alternatives to see what's best for you.

Local Retail Stores
If you are a grass-green newcomer to computer ownership, you should purchase a new unit from a reliable source. This, for many users, means a local retail store. These stores can range from a nationwide chain to a mom-and-pop storefront clone builder. The key is they are local. This is convenient if something goes wrong, if you have a question, or if you need help hooking the computer up.

The prices may be 30 percent higher than a mail-order house's advertised price, but the local store will give you the support you're sure to need in

SMART PC SHOPPING

the beginning. It's much easier to lug a computer back to the store if something goes wrong than to pack it and ship it off to who-knows-where. In addition, if it's a minor connection problem or an intermittent one, the inconvenience and expense of shipping the computer back several times can eat up any savings you may have realized. Some direct-sales companies offer on-site service, it's true, but they don't offer the on-site handholding the first-time buyer sometimes needs. However, if you have friends who know the ropes, they can help you set up and run a mail-order machine. In fact, there is no one right way or one right place to buy your computer equipment.

The Clone Builders   These are guys with a screwdriver who know how to turn it to the right. They assemble computers from all the various parts to make a custom computer. A hot trend around the country is the "clone store." You walk in, figure out which components you want your machine made up of, and the clone builder slaps it together while you wait. One advantage to this—if you know what you're doing—is that you get some control over the components. If you aren't secure in your knowledge of computer parts and don't want to know (or care about) the details of every little thing, you might as well just purchase an already assembled clone from another type of vendor.

Computer Superstores   These giant stores focus on office supplies and computers. They have piles and piles of software, hardware, and peripherals, as well as office paper, pens, and other supplies. There are specials and "sale" tags on every item, and there's a quantity discount for everything. The problem with these stores is they've cropped up so quickly that few of the employees or the buyers have any experience with computers. While the store may have a variety of choices, these may not be well selected. The employees rarely know much about the products they're selling, which is an advantage of sorts; you can browse around without a pesky salesperson trying to help.

Mass-Market Superstores   These are the "membership" warehouse chains piled high with boxes and boxes of the same stuff. You can buy tires, beans, and toilet paper, as well as books, office supplies, and computers. You can't get in to shop—or get the best deal—unless you're a member. The places are crammed with everything, and forklifts run up and down the aisles dodging people. They seem to offer a wide variety of computers, when in fact, there's only a lot of the same thing. The problem with these superstores is you're not able to do any comparison shopping. The price they quote as less than "retail" may not be such a significant savings. They rarely quote the street price—the price the item may actually be selling

SMART PC SHOPPING

for through most of the retail channels. (Computers, their peripherals, and software rarely sell for the retail price. The street price is often lower, occasionally lower by a significant amount.)

And Furthermore... Don't buy a computer from any retail store with snooty help. If they try to make you feel like a complete dweeb and act like your questions are the stupidest ones they've ever heard, don't put up with it. There is no reason for a computer store to make you feel ill at ease. Look around for a computer store with a friendly, knowledgeable staff.

Mail-Order Houses

Mail-order houses can offer some great deals at low prices. If you know what you are purchasing, this can be a good way to go. Things to look for in a mail-order house include a toll-free order number, round-the-clock service, a money-back guarantee, an extended warranty, and speedy shipping.

Mail-Order Hints Here are some hints for purchasing mail-order equipment:

- Pay by credit card instead of by check. With a credit purchase you can stop payment, and the bank will act as your agent if there is a problem. Even if the amount has already been billed, you can dispute a charge, refuse to pay, and let the bank work out the dispute. Contact your credit card's issuing bank to clarify their policies before you start looking through the ads.

- When buying by mail order, insist on a firm shipping date and find out the method of delivery the mail-order dealer uses. You need to know so you'll have a good idea of when your equipment will arrive.

- Confirm the exact configuration of the machine—right down to the make and model number of internal components such as hard disks. Shifting relationships between suppliers, fluctuations in the prices of components, and the constant revision and renaming of components mean vendors often make changes in their machines' internal configurations. Some vendors' ads will not reflect these changes, which affect both prices and shipping dates.

- Don't order anything from a mail-order company you or your friends have never heard of without checking out the operation. Check with your local users' group and find out what companies are on their hit and miss lists. Ask friends about their satisfaction with a company they have used. You might want to call the Better Business Bureau and ask what they know about a specific company.

SMART PC SHOPPING

■ Don't fall for a very low price accompanied by high-pressure phone tactics. If the price in the ad seems too incredible to be true, it probably is. When you see an amazingly low price on a machine, question the salesperson about the company's return policy (which should be a minimum of 30 days/money back). Check older issues of the magazine where you saw the ad and see if the company has been advertising for a fairly long time.

■ If it's not right, send it back.

If you are a novice buyer trying out mail-order dealers, make sure you have friends who know the ropes. Your friends can help guide you through the difficulties during setup and teach you how to use your mail-order machine. Check out a mail-order company's technical support before you purchase your PC. Many of these tech support groups are very good.

VARs (Value-Added Resellers)

VARs are dealers who specialize in selling a PC in a package complete with specialty software. If you are a real estate broker, for instance, you might want to look for a VAR selling a complete system with real estate software. The software packages are the "value added" to the computer system. Most computer buyers never deal with VARs, but they may prove useful to you in the future.

Television Shopping Shows

Recently, some television shopping shows have broken into the direct-sales computer market. The machines they sell are usually older design versions of PC clones. These machines are cheap, but unless you know exactly what you are buying, it's likely the machine won't be what you'd hoped for. Keep in mind that the telephone order takers know even less about their computer merchandise than the computer mail-order house order takers. These well-meaning people can lead you astray.

Another drawback is they offer only a 30-day guarantee. If a problem develops after the warranty period, you must take the problem up with the manufacturer. The manufacturer might be an obscure clone maker on the other side of the country—or the world. A simple computer malfunction can become a complicated matter if you have to ship the entire unit to Taiwan.

Used Computers

For the budget minded, some great bargains can be found in the used-computer market. A used computer doesn't have a guarantee or warranty, however, which is a drawback. On the other hand, electronic equipment either works or it doesn't—if the computer works, it's likely to continue

SMART PC SHOPPING

working for a long time. If the machine fails, don't fret. Few of the replacement parts are very expensive—power supplies and keyboards cost around a hundred dollars each.

Don't pay much for these older, used machines. Even if the computer cost thousands of dollars new, the retail value isn't more than 20 percent of the original cost, at most. If a friend or relative purchased an IBM AT in 1985 for $3,000, he or she can't expect to sell the machine for $1,500 or even $1,000.

Think about it: If you pay $1,000 for the machine, you'll still need to upgrade it. That IBM AT probably has a 40Mb hard disk (too little memory by today's standards). It may have a keyboard with a few sticking keys and may be missing its monitor. A new 520Mb hard disk will cost about $250, the keyboard $100, and a monitor another $350—which all adds up to a whopping $1,700 for a used piece of equipment.

Why buy the machine at all? You could purchase a new machine for that much money without all the time spent on the upgrades. If, however, you took that old unit off your friend's hands for $200 and then added on the $700 in upgrades, you'd have a useable machine at a bargain price.

As for all the accumulated software that goes along with the used machine—don't pay for it. It should be thrown in for free. Software loses its value faster than hardware. Some of it might be useful, but the $150 spent in 1985 is worth about $1.50 today. It doesn't add to the machine's retail value any more than if you purchased a used car with an eight-track stereo system. An eight-track may have cost a mint way back when, but who cares?

Before you jump in and buy a used gem, shop around. Look at comparable new units, price replacement parts, call a few of the local computer repair and upgrade shops—find out everything you can. Read this book!

Whatever you do, don't fall for a pressure sale. Maybe there are a zillion people already interested in the deal, but so what? Remember, it's just like a used car purchase—buyer beware. Know what you want to buy and don't be in a rush.

Don't get talked into anything, either. An old CP/M computer might still work, but unless you have a museum or an old computer collection, or need a good sturdy conversation-piece doorstop, don't buy it. Software is almost impossible to find. Repairs are costly. Your friends will laugh at you.

What If It Breaks?

Service has always been an important feature—and selling point—for the pricey dealers and resellers. They can custom configure a system for large corporate accounts, and their service people usually show up quickly if anything goes wrong. Customers have grown tired of inadequately equipped

SMART PC SHOPPING

■ Support Costs Money

Is the era of free customer support drawing to a close? Software vendors are increasingly offering multiple levels of support, most at a price.

The most recent support scheme is a 900 number that charges the user on a per-call or per-minute basis. The worst aspect of this idea is that if you work in a large corporation, the 900 number may be blocked from your telephone system. Turning support into a revenue center encourages companies to produce inferior products that need support. This adds to the bottom line at the customer's expense. Not good.

With third-party, on-site service contracts, you get all the service you need for one flat fee. More and more, you will find on-site service contracts bundled with systems, included as part of the warranty (usually lasting a year), or available as an insurance policy to protect your system. An added option will extend the warranty of your system for an extra year or two, or as long as you choose to pay for the extra coverage.

With any service contract, find out up front what's covered: Who does the support? How far are you from the people responsible for the service? Are they familiar with this system? Undoubtedly, the areas of service and support are key to any would-be PC buyer. Check into the options; you'll be better off in the long run.   ■

dealers who charge high prices for service and repairs. It's enough to make customers look for other options.

For the individual, the mail-order manufacturers have outperformed the large, dealer-distributed companies in service and price. This accounts for the overall success of mail-order business over the last few years.

Mail-order companies have discovered that buyers want faster and more convenient technical service. If the vendor can't resolve a problem over the phone, many will provide on-site service (provided the product is still under warranty). A number of direct marketers use the policy of mirror shipment. (The vendor returns your repaired PC by the same delivery method you used to send it.) If you need the computer back in a rush, ship it overnight. After a day or two of repairs, it's rushed back. If you're not so pressed, you can send it by ground delivery. (An important tip: Save your computer boxes, just in case you need to ship the system out for repairs.)

Some companies make provisions to ship parts to you by overnight express. They don't wait until the broken component is received. Once tech support determines that a faulty monitor needs replacing (from your frantic telephone call), the new part is on the way.

The amount of coverage and the degree of technical service varies from company to company (not to mention dealer to dealer). Some direct dealers offer free technical support over the phone, in the form of a toll-free number, for as long as you own the computer. Some provide 24-hour phone support and supplement support methods through a dedicated electronic bulletin board system (BBS) or a national service

SMART PC SHOPPING

such as CompuServe. The service provided on these on-line forums usually includes answers to commonly asked questions and the posting of additional driver files.

Beware, there are still those fly-by-night companies that offer few or no fix-it services. Some of these companies may be on the up-and-up, but they might sacrifice technical support in order to offer the lowest price. To paraphrase the old saying: "Penny-wise, dollar-foolish." Saving a buck up front with these firms may end up costing more in the long run.

Now that you know a little about your options for purchasing a computer, you can begin checking out various dealers. If you have a question that hasn't been answered yet, read a little further in the book. Good luck!

CHAPTER  3

BUYING SOFTWARE

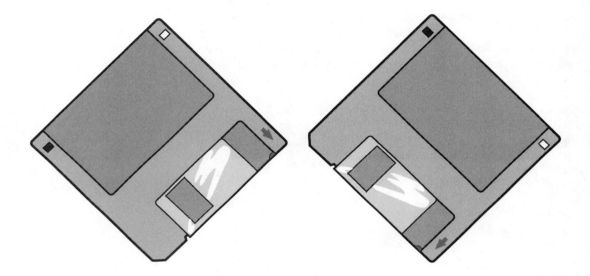

AFTER YOU PURCHASE your first computer (or even your tenth!), you have to get software for it. Software, also called computer programs or applications, is what makes computers compute. Without it they'd be large, cumbersome doorstops, or landfill. Software is a set of instructions that tell a computer how to carry out a specific job. The trend nowadays is for the computer maker to "throw in" some software—an operating system, for example. The operating system is what controls the communications between the processor, all its peripherals

BUYING SOFTWARE

(hard disk, keyboard, memory, printer, and so on), and the user. It also coordinates the activity of the installed application whether it be a word processor, a spreadsheet, or some other off-the-shelf software package. To fully understand this process, we recommend you purchase the books *How Computers Work* and *How Software Works* (Ziff-Davis Press).

This chapter discusses the different types of software available and explains how they can help you with your computing tasks. You'll also find some tips on how to shop for software.

Operating Systems

You have a number of choices when it comes to operating systems (OS). The most popular is Windows 3.1 and its variants, Windows for Workgroups 3.11 and Windows NT. More recently, a new variant called Windows 95 was released and it is expected to be the primary operating system for most computers by the end of 1995. Other operating systems include DOS, the original OS found on the PC (much modified since 1982), and OS/2, which is probably the most advanced and interesting OS of them all for these small machines. Other also-ran operating systems are available, including Novell DOS, NextStep, and others. Large, powerful systems might also be able to run variants of UNIX—a minicomputer operating system that was ported to the PC some years ago. A free version called Linux can be downloaded from many online services and the Internet. Most users will find a version of Windows on their computer when they purchase it. There are books available from Ziff-Davis Press regarding all these operating systems. I recommend that you look at many operating systems before deciding which is right for you.

Development Software

These are primarily programming languages. You can compare programming your computer to "programming" your dishwasher. Dishwashers have a selection of buttons and/or dials to set your dishwashing preference. Let's say the dishwasher has five buttons on the left: rinse, light wash, regular wash, heavy wash, and pot scrubber. On the right are three buttons: dry off, dry, and sani-steam. If you choose regular wash and dry, you're programming the dishwasher. The washing and drying buttons are selected and the program instructions read "off, off, on, off, off" and "off, on, off," respectively. The dishwasher is an electromechanical device, and it performs what it has been designed to do based on the on/off combinations of switch settings. The computer is similar but more sophisticated. Programs outline for the computer a series of steps for it to do. Programming languages make developing the program easy.

BUYING SOFTWARE

■ Multiple Operating Systems

The product, System Commander, allows you to boot 42 different operating systems on a single machine: 16 versions of DOS and 26 other Intel-compatible operating systems. This is a bit more interesting than those boot managers that allow you to load different CONFIG.SYS files. It's perfect for small developers who have to test their software against Windows, Windows NT, OS/2, UNIX, DOS, and whatever else is targeted. But be sure you have a large hard disk! The company to contact is V Communications, 4320 Stevens Creek Blvd., San Jose, CA, phone (408) 296-4224; the price is $99.95. ■

When people talk about coding, they are talking about using a programming language. The most popular languages used by professionals are Pascal, C, and C++. You may also have heard of assembly language programming, which is much more difficult. Some professionals and many amateurs use a language called BASIC or Visual Basic. BASIC is an easy-to-use, easy-to-learn language that is very powerful. Most languages can make the computer do just about anything. Choosing one language over another becomes a personal preference developed after working with the different languages.

Along with the languages there are various debugging aids and other helpful utilities that might be classified as development software.

Application Software

This type of software is the most widely used. These are the programs to do things such as word processing, spreadsheets, database management, and telecommunications. Application software also includes music software, educational software, and games.

Word Processing Programs

Word processing on a computer beats pounding on a typewriter. You can delete mistakes (saving money on correction fluid), rearrange your sentences, and fix spelling errors, all without wasting time and paper. For simple letters or long, multipage documents, word processing is one good reason to own a computer. A host of additional software programs can help to make your pages perfect. These include spelling checkers, grammar checkers, thesauruses, and other writing aids.

But in today's world, it's not enough to use a word processor to create perfectly spelled, grammatically correct prose. It has to look sharp, too. People used to call it *WYSIWYG* (wizzy-wig) for "What You See Is What You Get."

BUYING SOFTWARE

■ A Book for Software Developers

If you're in the mood to develop software, you should spend a little time with a new book ($44.95) from Nolo Press (950 Parker St., Berkeley, CA 94710, phone 510-549-1976, fax 510-548-5902). It's called *Software Development: A Legal Guide* by Stephen Fishman. It's a tremen- dous resource and includes sample contracts on disk. I've learned more than I wanted to know by plowing through this book. Also, if you want to learn about patents and copyrights, this is the book for you. Highly recommended. ■

What you see on your screen is—pretty much—what you'll see on the paper when you print it out. Most word processors have a multitude of formatting options. You can arrange the text with either left or right justification, or centered on the page. And you can change, rearrange, and change again, the format of a page or a line of type.

Most word processors also can offer special characters—foreign letters, mathematical and scientific symbols, bullets, and underlines—and let you mix typefaces, sizes, and styles of letters. (For even fancier document handling, you can move to a desktop publishing program, also called a page layout program.

One thing you're likely to want is a variety of fonts. Fonts are the computer data needed to draw a specific looking typeface, as designed by a professional font maker, or a type foundry. A font is a collection of all the letters within this design parameter. Some examples are "Helvetica," "American Typewriter," and "Garamond." There are literally thousands of type fonts available in both PostScript and TrueType formats. (For more information on these formats, please refer to Chapter 7, "Printers.")

Business Software

Spreadsheets, graph programs, and databases all have a multitude of business uses. Spreadsheets track every business cent earned and spent. Graph programs can make detailed visual representations. Databases can hold thousands of records, which may be searched with ease. These are routinely used for mailing lists because names, addresses, and other vital information can quickly be searched by zip code, type of business, or other key information.

Personal information managers (PIMs) are a hot business item these days. With a PIM you can schedule your week, plan your time, and log your minutes.

BUYING SOFTWARE

■ Windows, Windows...

The newest version of Windows is Windows 95, once referred to as Chicago. It introduces new features similar to those found in OS/2 and the Macintosh, including the use of folders to organize files and the ability to run more than one program at once (multitasking). This new version of Windows will run old Windows programs. (Programs especially written to take advantage of the new conventions will not run on older versions of Windows.)

Windows 95 does not require DOS to run; rather, it incorporates a DOS-like operating system within its code in the same way OS/2 and Windows NT do.

It remains to be seen how well accepted the new system will be and whether it will generate enough interest to have special programs written for it. OS/2, which has many similar fancy features, did not draw much of a crowd when it came to special applications designed to take advantage of its features. The same holds true for Windows NT. ■

Other useful software includes business-specific programs such as CAD/CAM programs (computer-aided design/computer-aided manufacturing), multimedia programs, and accounts receivable/accounts payable billing programs.

Personal and Home Computing Programs

These programs include personal and household financial managers, income tax programs, educational software, and, of course, games.

Personal and financial managers help you to balance your checkbook, pay bills, and track your money. They make it easy to set up a household budget and figure out how to achieve your long-term financial goals.

Check-writing programs are often integral to home money-management software. This software can balance your checkbook and track where your money goes (besides just "away"). If you keep the information current (by noting automated teller withdrawals, deposits, and recently written checks), this software can also generate reports, graphs, and charts, and provide a method for long-range planning.

Income tax programs are very popular in the home software market. All you do is plug in the right numbers, and the computer calculates the amount of tax you owe. These packages are good for calculating estimated taxes, which is especially helpful for self-employed people who must calculate a realistic quarterly payment.

BUYING SOFTWARE

■ Font Publication

Some years back, the famous graphic designer Herb Lubalin began a publication called *U&lc*, which was a tabloid highlighting the typeface designed by International Typoeface Corporation. Over the years, ITC would dream up remarkable typefaces and use them in all sorts of creative ways in the magazine. Anyone interested in fonts would get numerous ideas from this publication. Most of today's modern typographical design began with Lubalin and his type pals in New York and elsewhere. Lubalin died a few years back and much of the energy in the type world scattered.

I've always hoped other type companies would take the hint and produce a publication akin to the early *U&lc* publication. Adobe has taken a few cracks at it but seemed to miss the mark. Now there's something called *X-Height* from Font Haus. It contains interesting and entertaining articles about type, and highlights the use of type in pleasant ways. Worth a look for any of you out there that are addicted to playing with type fonts. A subscription is $18 a year. For more information, call Font Haus in Westport, CT, at (203) 846-6988 or fax them at (203) 849-8527. ■

Music Software

Music programs teach people to play music, help professionals synthesize music, create new sounds, and perform other specialized functions.

The leading magazine on the subject is *Electronic Musician*. If your bookstore doesn't carry it, contact

Cardinal Music Entertainment
6400 Hollis #12
Emeryville, CA 94608
(510) 653-3307

Educational Software and Games

Educational programs are wonderful if you have kids around the house. They have all the appeal of games but inspire none of the parental guilt associated with letting the kids waste time—because with educational programs the kids learn while they play.

Games have a certain charm and addictive quality. They require more mental power than watching television, and you are able to achieve a sense of accomplishment when you improve your score. These programs often are very popular with all members of a household. They are many people's first introduction to using a computer, since they can be less threatening than more "serious" programs. And they are more familiar, owing to the proliferation of video game machines. Keep in mind that most of the really great games today are on CD-ROM. This is because the complexity of the games has increased to the point that it is no longer practical to use floppy disks.

BUYING SOFTWARE

■ Caller ID, Anyone?

One of the finest products I've seen is Caller ID+Plus from Rochelle Communications (8906 Wall St., #205, Austin, TX, 78754, (512) 339-8188). This $149 gem of a product works with local phone systems that utilize the premium phone service called Caller ID, which lets phone users see the phone number from which they are receiving phone calls. Caller ID virtually eliminates crank calls and stops anonymous harassment. But it has additional benefits when used in conjunction with Caller ID+Plus.

Caller ID+Plus routes the phone line through the computer and when an incoming call is received, the Caller ID system alerts the computer, which then looks up the person calling. Once the database of associates is searched, you can expect to see the caller's name pop up on your screen as the phone rings. You'll also see whatever information you might have in the database. Unknowns are entered on the fly, too. The system also logs all calls in and out, and the user can make notes about each call, with the information going into a master log. This is a killer program for any salesperson. ■

Due to the success of some extremely popular shareware games (such as Doom), a number of games are offered through bulletin boards as shareware. (See more about shareware a little later in this chapter.) All you need is a fast modem, lots of available hard-disk space, and about an hour to download the games. (Some of these games may take as long as an hour to transfer to your computer.)

Utility Programs

Often called simply "utilities," these programs support the operation of your computer. Though many of these support functions are supplied with the operating system, you may find you need additional utilities. For example, a utility program can enable you to recover a disk file if it is accidentally deleted, use enhanced file management functions, and check the health and performance of your computer with diagnostic and measurement programs.

Utilities can be purchased off the shelf or even downloaded with your modem from electronic bulletin boards. You can find lots of interesting and valuable utility software on the market, not the big applications programs but the small accessory programs, which are helpful for more humble computing tasks. (They're like purchasing a vase for the living room; it's not a major purchase like a piece of furniture, but it's nice to have around.)

BUYING SOFTWARE

What to Look for When Buying Software

Each major category of program has a number of companies with products vying for your hard-earned dollar. Each one claims to be the best. Each one seems to have even more features than the one before. It can be confusing.

Software for tasks such as word processing may have a bunch of different products which all seem to do the same thing. What do you shop for? Price? Name recognition? Package design? It's not clear-cut. The best thing would be to sit down and try every one, but that's just too time-consuming.

Avoid the tendency to shop for features. Just because a program seems to be able to "do it all" doesn't mean it's the best choice. The larger and more complex a program is, the harder it may be to learn and the more memory it will chew up on your computer. Don't buy a word processing program, for example, which will do graphing and has a mini-spreadsheet and a calculator, if you only need a word processing program.

On the side of each software box there should be a small listing telling you the system requirements. Always read this listing before buying anything. Make sure you have what is required on the box.

Buying Through Mail Order versus Stores

A lot of Users are confused by the variety of places where you can purchase software. In the trade these are called *channels*. The direct channel is where you call the vendor directly and buy from the source. When you do this, you are assured of getting the latest version. Software versions change so often that many people prefer this method.

The other major channel is the retail store. This can be a superstore, a small computer store, or a store specializing in software. The advantage of many retail outlets is that they sell software at a price lower than the vendor's price. This is a curiosity in the world of retail. Normally, mail-order and direct sales are associated with discounts. With computer software the opposite is usually the case.

When people talk about computer software prices, they seldom talk about the retail price—they talk about the "street price" as if it were a drug deal. That's because it has become a tradition to lower the manufacturer's suggested retail price by about 25 percent and sell software at a competitive street price. This began when a chain of software-only stores sold all software at a discount. Nowadays software companies price their products with the eventual street price in mind.

Good hunting!

BUYING SOFTWARE

■ Joe's Solution

Joe Uhrmacher is an old-time clone builder who was frustrated with an inability to locate the addresses and phone numbers of vendors. His solution was to develop the Computer Vendors Directory. He's been selling his labor of love for a few years now. It currently contains the names and numbers of about 110,000 computer-related companies worldwide. There's also a short description of what they do. Updated monthly, every company is verified over an 18-month cycle. It's available on 10 high-density floppies and is about

130 megabytes worth of compressed data; Joe will provide it in dBase, Paradox, or Q&A format. The price is $49.95. This database is worth ten times more! And if you send the disks back within a year, he'll update you FREE! It's a great product. Write:

Computer Vendors Directory
908 - 1st Avenue NW
Minot, North Dakota 58701
(701) 838-5395   ■

Shareware and Free Software

Not to be overlooked is the enormous amount of high-quality software that is sold as shareware. This is software you obtain for free; then if you like the software, you buy it. There are various kinds of shareware, ranging from fully functional programs to programs that only have a few limited features. When you buy the whole package, you get all the features. Whatever the case, there is a lot of variety and it's usually inexpensive. In fact, some programs are free!

Exec-PC

The best way to collect and examine shareware is by using a modem to call a computerized bulletin board. Start with the biggest and best—Exec-PC, an enormous system in Elk Grove, Wisconsin. It has virtually every shareware program ever written.

Exec-PC has 280 phone lines going into the system, and it contains over 650,000 files. Here are three numbers you can call to get access to Exec-PC. Their nominal fee is money well spent. For a 2400 baud modem, call (414) 789-4210 and for V.32bis (14.4 kbps) call (414) 789-4360. They even have an ISDN connection at (414) 341-2074.

What's a Computer Virus?

Computer viruses are programs written by some crazed people as a way of leaving their mark on the world. Usually, their only purpose is to annoy you and disrupt your work. Some virus programs are irksome, and others are outright malevolent.

BUYING SOFTWARE

■ Dvorak Recommends

A friend of mine called to tell me that he had made the mistake of booting his machine on a Sunday when that old Michelangelo virus would activate. It did. No backups, either. Integrity Master from Stiller Research is the current state-of-the-art anti-virus package on the market. In a side-by-side comparison, this product beats everything on the market.

Not only will it find every known virus with its built-in scanner, but it also has the ability to handle polymorphic and other odd virus types. It's $39.95 in the United States and $44.50 elsewhere. Shipping and handling is included in the price. The product can be purchased through AST Distributors, at (314) 256-3130 or (800) 788-0787 ■

The virus program will attach itself, like a leech, to another program, and become part of that program. When the program runs, it also allows the virus program to run. Most of these virus programs have only two instructions—copy and execute. First, the virus copies itself wherever it can (onto other programs, other parts of a network, and so on), ensuring that it becomes firmly entrenched in the system. Then it executes whatever bad stuff it has been programmed to do—chew up memory, erase disks, or other weird stuff.

The better-designed the virus, the better it can hide itself—and the longer it remains undetected, the better its chance of infecting more programs and other systems.

When the program is executed, it may display a silly picture on the screen or play a little ditty to advertise the fact that you've been had—which seems innocent enough. But meanwhile, the program may be erasing your disk boot sectors (the instructions telling the computer how to start up), or doing some other destructive act.

There are many computer viruses and strains. They're divided by the experts into several categories: bombs, logic bombs, worms, stealth, polymorphic, and multipartite viruses. Every virus has a name, too. Some of the better known ones are Frodo, Michelangelo, the Tequila, and the FLip.

The trend is toward more and more sinister virus programs. There are estimated to be more than 1,500 active viruses in existence, and at least a hundred are virulent—these are fairly common and widespread.

However, it's not hopeless. There's a software "medicine" for these computer viruses called *anti-viral software*. It works in one of two ways: either by scanning software or by catching the virus "in the act." Scanning is the better method, as it detects the virus before it can do much damage. It looks inside the programs on your computer for telltale signs of embedded code (the virus), and then it checks for symptoms. The thing to keep in

BUYING SOFTWARE

■ Piracy

Finally, remember to carefully read your warranty card that comes with the software to see what the vendor is allowing in terms of copying and backing up your software. It's usually illegal to copy software and give it to a friend. It's also wrong to sell old software that has since been updated. Software is usually licensed, not sold outright, and different laws regarding ownership apply. ■

mind about anti-viral software is that the programs are only effective if they're up to date. This means you can't rely on some program your buddy bought two years ago to be effective against today's computer viruses.

CHAPTER

COMPUTERS

PEOPLE TALK ABOUT COMPUTERS the way they talk about cars. It's not enough to just say that you have a computer, or that you have a car. The variables are what you need to discuss. With cars, the number of cylinders, the cubic inches, and the amount of horsepower are the objects of clarification. You can describe the model type (sedan or coupe, hatchback, station wagon, or ATV). With computers you describe the operating system, the bus, the chip, the megahertz (MHz), and whether you've got a laptop or a desktop. This chapter is

COMPUTERS

about all of the variables—present and historical—of the basic box, the computer.

A Short History of the Microcomputer

The history of microcomputers doesn't compare with the history of ancient China. Microcomputers have only been around for about a decade and a half, but in those few years, there have been some milestones (and mill stones). It's good to have some knowledge of this short history to give you perspective on where we really are today.

Early Desktop Computers

The very first microcomputer machines were about as exciting as a do-it-yourself Heathkit Radio set—a thrill if you were an enthusiast, but just a pile of junk if you weren't. The early computers of the late 1970s were functional, but crude by today's standards. The little machines couldn't outperform the large mainframes and minicomputers that dominated the computing scene, but they were a lot more fun.

In the 1980s we witnessed an explosive growth of the personal computer scene. Early personal computers (or microcomputers, as they were originally dubbed) lacked a clear standard. The computer chip makers—Intel, Motorola, and Zilog—all competed in the microprocessor market in a rash of different computers from different manufacturers. None were compatible with any others. Perhaps the closest thing to a standard was the operating system CP/M (control program for microprocessors). In its day it was a great little operating system. As a matter of fact, much of DOS is based on the old CP/M program. Way back when DOS was first introduced, the die-hard CP/M aficionados swore that DOS was doomed to failure.

The real problem in the microcomputer scene was a lack of acceptance. "Big Business" was still reluctant to purchase any of those tabletop computers. Most corporations had been sold on the idea of giant mainframe CPUs, and smaller companies had a minicomputer stashed behind a Herman Miller partition. The attitude of the businesses was, "But we have a real computer. Why would we want a silly little micro?" So none of the PC manufacturers were able to get their foot in the door.

Enter IBM

IBM's introduction of the IBM PC in August 1981 opened the eyes of many. IBM had scores of sales representatives well entrenched in corporations and businesses all across the country. The sales staff—used to selling big-ticket items and invoicing hundreds of thousands of dollars—were dressed in three-piece suits, accustomed to a casual lunch with a corporate president. This was a big advantage over the other microcomputer

COMPUTERS

companies. Most of those guys had never been in a corporate president's waiting room or even owned a decent suit. Furthermore, they couldn't have cared less.

In their inimitable style, IBM opened their own stores selling all IBM equipment as well as their own brand of software. The software had been written by other companies but adapted for PC-DOS (IBM's proprietary operating system). IBM insisted all the software be packaged in the same standard plain white boxing and identical labeling. (It was very similar to the trend toward generic packaging of house-labeled items at grocery stores.) Distributors grumbled. Software manufacturers grumbled. The IBM PC was a success, as was the PC/XT that followed it.

The CP/M machines just couldn't compete with IBM. Because IBM had chosen Intel's 8088 processor, CP/M's Z-80 chip was essentially dead. The 8088 chip had a larger address space that would accommodate bigger, more involved software programs than the Z-80 could. (Intel subsequently developed the 80286, 80386, and 80486 chips, which now dominate the PC marketplace.)

A number of companies began to produce machines that used the MS-DOS (Microsoft DOS) operating system. In the beginning, they were similar to PC-DOS machines but were not truly compatible—software for PC-DOS would seldom run on an MS-DOS machine, and vice versa. It is not exactly clear when PC-DOS and MS-DOS merged, but today there is little distinction (if any) between the two. IBM-compatible clones and genuine IBM computers all run the same software.

IBM kept the pressure on with its next system release, the 6 MHz PC/AT, the first machine to use Intel's next-generation 80286 chip. The power-user computer was born, with improved EGA graphics (capable of 640-by-350 lines of resolution and 16 colors), an I/O and memory bus capable of moving data to and from the processor 16 bits at a time, and more internal hard-disk storage (at least 20Mb). Like every new generation of PCs, the AT quickly became a best-selling machine.

However, these first-generation ATs were plagued by frequent hard-disk failures. Without any warning, a user's disk would fail and data would be lost. The problem was widespread enough that IBM clone manufacturers started to erode IBM's dominance as early as the spring of 1986 with their own faster (8, 10, and 12 MHz), more reliable systems.

Bring in the Clones

The IBM PC/AT's hard-disk failures allowed the PC-compatible makers to gain a foothold in the market. The AT clones were more reliable than IBMs—a fact that was quickly pointed out in numerous magazine articles.

IBM tried to knock the clone makers back with an improved offering later in 1986. IBM raised the 80286 clock speed to 8 MHz and began to

COMPUTERS

use hardier, IBM-manufactured 30Mb hard disks. The AT 339 became the most popular IBM-made PC ever, and one of the most reliable.

But the clone competition continually improved PCs. PC clones were cheaper than IBM's machines, with larger hard disks (from 40Mb to 100Mb). Greater memory became standard, and options such as built-in serial and parallel ports were added to system boards. Clones often included displays, display adapters, and software in attractively priced bundles.

The PC/AT continued to sell well, but IBM's market share began to fall, even though it was selling more machines than ever. Other clone manufacturers (Compaq and Advanced Logic Research, for example) moved quickly on Intel's next big microprocessor evolution, the 32-bit 80386. In a daring move, IBM vied to win back dominance in the PC market by trying to change the standard.

PS/2

In 1987, IBM introduced its PS/2 line of PCs. Some say it was to avoid competition with the by now well-entrenched clone makers; other say it was to increase the performance of PCs. In any case, the PS/2 machines were characterized by an all-new proprietary input-output bus, which IBM termed Micro Channel architecture (MCA). The PS/2 lineup included the 80286-powered desktop Model 50 and the floor-standing Model 60. Both systems were slow performers, however. The Model 50 sold reasonably well because of its smaller footprint (the total space taken up on the desk by the CPU). The competition quickly caught on to that strategy and started to produce 286-powered PCs in smaller cases. These small-footprint machines occupied less desk space and were shorter in height than older machines like the AT. IBM later followed these machines with more powerful 386-based Model 70s. Unfortunately, while the PS/2 was a well-designed machine, it failed in the marketplace and IBM went back to a more old-fashioned design based on the original PC/AT. (Microchannel machines are still made for specialized applications.)

OS/2

In 1987, IBM announced a new operating system, OS/2. Unlike the PS/2, there is no machine associated with this new standard: OS/2 will run on an IBM machine or any clone. OS/2 is like the Macintosh operating system in that it relies on a desktop as the base of operations. There are folders, icons, and other Mac-like features, but there are also command-line capabilities. It's really a hybrid of the DOS and Macintosh operating systems.

After its introduction, early versions (1.0 and 1.3) met with little success. But with the release of 2.0, 2.1, and most recently WARP, many users have warmed up to OS/2. It's estimated that over 5 million copies are in use today. For multi-tasking multiple DOS programs, OS/2 is the

COMPUTERS

superior operating system. Its user interface is better than the Windows offerings—so much so that Microsoft adopted many of the innovations in Windows 95.

The most obvious drawback to OS/2 (which has probably done the most to hurt sales) is its lack of native applications and drivers. IBM has recognized this as a problem, but as yet has been unable to overcome the obstacle.

Windows

Soon after the introduction of the IBM PC/AT and the Apple Lisa (Apple's first attempt at the Macintosh, which was expensive and unpopular), Microsoft promised a new graphical user interface (GUI) called Windows. This was largely a response to the promise of a product from VisiCorp called Visi-On, which was a graphical system of sorts. Microsoft believed that the GUI was the wave of the future and began to release versions of the Windows environment, each with distinct improvements. Currently, the most prominent version is Windows 3.11.

Windows 95

Windows 95 has become the new standard for desktop computing, supplanting Windows 3.11 (which still has a following). The new Windows has a totally new interface, with *plug-and-play* capabilities (allowing the computer to self-configure, which means the hardware attached will be obvious to the computer. The user ideally won't have to install drivers or go through complex processes to install a peripheral or add-on device). Windows 95 has genuine multi-tasking capability, which is the ability to run more than one program at the same time.

Among the drawbacks are problems with potential software bugs (because it's new), the multi-tasking isn't as well designed or developed as either OS/2 or Windows NT, and it's not as crash-proof, either. But, overall, Windows 95 and Windows 3.11 are the most common operating systems installed today.

Desktop Computer Talk

Times have changed from way back about 14 years ago when you could say, "I want an IBM," and the only computer available was an IBM PC. Now there is more to consider than just deciding you want a computer. Unfortunately, it's tough to know what's what, especially if you're a beginner. Walk into a computer store and the salesperson will overwhelm you with numbers and other computerese gibberish. It's like wandering into a foreign country. Let's try to make this easier for you by discussing some of the basic things you should know about a computer.

COMPUTERS

■ **Figure 4.1 A microprocessor chip—the brains of every computer**

Chip Chat: Some Basic Information about Chips

The key component of any computer system is the microprocessor, or central processing unit (CPU). The actual "brain" of the machine is a little chip like the one shown in Figure 4.1. The "legs" of the chip are the connectors, which allow the chip to be either snapped into place or soldered onto the card.

A special chip socket called the Zero Insertion Force (ZIF) socket is a way for a user to easily maneuver a chip out of the motherboard and insert a newer chip, instantly upgrading the computer. The ZIF socket has a lever that releases the chip's pins and then locks in a new chip's pins, a simple maneuver that makes the switch effortless.

Each CPU's designation (8088, 80286, 80386, and so on) is like a model number. Sometimes the number is expanded to denote speed and other attributes. For example, consider the 486SX-20 and the 486DX-25. *SX* designates the complexity of the chip (SX is simpler than DX), and *20* and *25* are the clock speeds in megahertz.

MHz (for megahertz) is the measurement of millions of cycles per second. It's used to gauge the speed at which a chip operates. We measure our own performance in seconds, minutes, and hours. A chip is measured in cycles per second. When we say a chip is operating at 20 MHz, it is

COMPUTERS

running at 20 million cycles per second. The bigger the number, the faster the chip performs. Magazine articles often describe the difference between chip speeds as a percentage that measures how much faster one chip runs than another. For example, a 20 MHz chip is said to run about 20 percent faster than the 16 MHz version.

People often speak of the chip number when they talk about their PCs. They will say something like "My 486 is faster than my old 8088." This is similar to car buffs talking about the power of their vehicles' engines, but it's not quite the same. The speed of a very fast car usually depends on more variables than engine size. The model may have a high performance cam shaft, a specially geared transmission, special tires, and other racing features. If they're describing a stock car, they also discuss whether the vehicle has two or four doors, an automatic transmission or five-speed, a convertible or hard top, and on and on.

When it comes to computers, the question of speed is simple: It's the chip. The chip *is* the computer. A fast chip makes a fast computer, while a slow chip makes a sluggish computer. (Other attributes to take into consideration are the hard-disk size, video/graphics speed, the I/O bus, and possibly the cache, but for now, we'll stick to chips.) When you go into a computer store, the first question you'll hear is always "What machine do you have?" The answer to this question isn't the manufacturer's name, but instead, is the chip number. While there are a slew of computer makers, they all rely on only a few types of chips.

Big manufacturers such as IBM, Hewlett-Packard, and Zenith make computers with their name appearing boldly across the front. However, manufacturers often sell computers to retailers, who then put their own names on the machines and sell them. (These are referred to as original equipment manufacturer, or OEM, machines.) Then there are the various clone builders. This could be someone assembling a computer in a garage for resale or a big factory in Taiwan spewing out thousands of machines a day.

The types of computers also vary. A manufacturer may make a variety of different machines to appeal to different segments of the market. So, purchasing a machine is not as simple as just saying "I want an IBM."

Users should note the dominant processor manufacturer is Intel, but Cyrix, AMD, and Texas Instruments all make clones of the Intel chips. These clones seem to function flawlessly and it isn't apparent to the user if a clone or an Intel chip is inside the box. Because of this, Intel has pushed ahead with its technology and marketing in an attempt to maintain its lead. Users will continue to see ad campaigns such as "Intel Inside" which promote the company.

The following sections briefly summarize the different chips which are the heart and guts of the computers on the market.

COMPUTERS

■ Chip-Naming Confusion

Intel is the main provider of CPUs for these computers, and they've managed to confuse the market by changing their naming scheme over the years. For example, what we like to call the 486 might also be referred to as the 80486 in one catalog or the iAPX486 in another. These are all the same chip. The American Micro Devices (AMD) version of the chip is usually called the AMD486, but it's also called the 80AMD486 or the 80AM486. Don't let all these names for the same thing confuse you. Most writers use 80486 interchangeably with 486 and 80386 with 386. Little attention is paid to the manufacturer of the chip unless the chip has some special attribute. The courts have decided the numbering scheme is public domain. Intel decided to drop the numbering scheme and go with the trademarked names, thus the Pentium.   ■

8088: The Dodo Bird of Microprocessors   The 8088 is slow by today's standards, but 14 years ago it was a hot item. Compared to the newer chips, it's like racing a moped against a Kawasaki Ninja motorcycle.

8088-based systems are still available, but for a few extra dollars you can buy a 386. The 8088-based systems are almost always made from Taiwanese components in a mix-and-match fashion. An 8088 may be functional as a simple word processor or terminal, but there is no longer any reason to consider one in a personal computer.

80286: The Brain-Dead Microprocessor   A 286 is about three to four times faster than an 8088, but it's still slow. The biggest problem with a 286 chip is that it doesn't handle memory as well as a 386. It has a different instruction set (the programming telling a chip what to do), which is just slightly incompatible with the 386. These differences make the 286 almost completely incompatible with new software, which spelled its doom.

80386SX and DX   Few 386 machines are on the market today. They've been replaced by the 486 and Pentium machines. But, in its day, the 386 chip was a revolutionary change in personal computing.

Compared to a 286, the 386 had a huge amount of addressable memory. The 386 came in two basic flavors—SX and DX—and in a whole range of speeds. The SX was a bridge between the 16-bit and the 32-bit chips.

Higher clock speeds certainly boosted performance, but the most notable change was the move from 16-bit to 32-bit computing. When that occurred, performance was doubled immediately, since twice as much data could be moved and used. (It's like comparing a small child's hand grabbing 16 Reese's pieces with a larger child's hand grabbing 32 of them. The bigger the handful, the more that can be grabbed at a time.)

COMPUTERS

■ Don't Forget The Government: What FCC Ratings Mean

The FCC (Federal Communications Commission) approves two classes of computers, Class A and Class B.

Class A approval signifies that a computer has sufficiently low radio frequency emissions for operation in a business locale. A Class A machine is more likely to act as a transmitter of interference, and therefore is unsuitable for the home or anywhere else that a TV, stereo, or AM/FM radio might be affected.

The more stringent Class B rating allows for home use as well, where computers are likely to be placed near radios and TVs. The Class B rating is much harder for a manufacturer to meet. The PC must be inspected first by an independent testing lab, and then it must be submitted to the FCC itself for direct approval. Class A machines merely conform to a published list of specifications, so Class A approval is a self-regulated process.

While a Class B rating is mandatory for any electronic devices operating in the home, it makes sense to get Class B-rated equipment for the office, too. This rating means that the system is less likely to send out emissions which might interfere with other electronic devices around the workplace. A machine with the Class B rating is also better protected from incoming electrical interference, which is a factor in offices where many computers and other electronic equipment are close to one another. Finally, Class B machines are generally better designed and engineered, and will likely prove to be more dependable over time. ■

Today, all this seems old hat and commonplace, since all 486 and Pentium machines are 32-bit.

80486   The 486 is a more efficient design than a 386. It incorporates a built-in 8Kb cache and cache controller, a math coprocessor (see the section "What about Coprocessors?" later), and better architecture and memory management for 32-bit operations. The cache gives a boost to overall performance while still using relatively inexpensive dynamic random-access memory (DRAM)—a volatile type of main memory. (A *cache*, in simple terms, is a way to help speed up the computer. The cache anticipates the next instruction based on what you're doing and stores it in a hiding place in memory. Then when the instruction or data is needed, it's retrieved from the hiding place more quickly than it could have been otherwise.) A 486 can process complex 32-bit instructions faster than any 386. DOS and most of today's software don't take advantage of this, because many applications and DOS itself were written with older 8- and 16-bit processing designs. OS/2, a multitasking operating system developed by IBM and Microsoft, and Windows are able to take full advantage of the 486's features.

80486DX2   The 486DX2 is a peculiar chip that runs internally twice as fast as the external system. In other words, if a machine were designed to run a 25 MHz 486, you could put in the 50 MHz 486DX2 and it would

COMPUTERS

work fine without any major changes to the rest of the computer. It would not run as fast as a 50 MHz 486DX, though. Only the innards of the CPU are running fast on a DX2 chip—the rest of the computer is running at the speed designed around the 25 MHz chip. This is a little confusing, but suffice it to say that a 50 MHz 486DX has more performance than a 50 MHz 486DX2. Currently the clock-doubled 33MHz 486, better known as the 486DX266, is the most popular chip on the market. It is the top-end workhorse desktop machine.

80486SX   The 486SX is a slowed-down 486—it runs at 16, 20, and 25 MHz—with the math coprocessor circuitry disabled. This chip is not recommended.

80486DX3   IBM has a license to build 486 chips, and it now ships clock-tripled 486 chips running at 75 MHz and 99 MHz (which everyone calls 100 MHz). Meanwhile, Intel makes a version of the same chip, the DX4. AMD and Cyrix ship clock-tripled chips also.

Pentium   This chip should have been dubbed the 586, but instead was named the Pentium and was first shown publicly at COMDEX in late 1992. Intel initially announced two clock speeds of 60 and 66 MHz, and has since shipped 90 and 100 MHz models. Currently they ship chips with speeds of 90, 100, 120, 133, and 150 MHz. The faster chips are a slightly different design, they're smaller and run cooler than the original. They're the recommended chips and are the standard for high-performance desktop computing.

PowerPC   The latest change in the industry is the introduction of the radically new microprocessor called the PowerPC. It was developed as a joint venture between IBM, Motorola, and Apple. It employs a new design concept called RISC, which is used in the chips found in more expensive computer workstations. It's about half the price of a comparable Pentium and delivers the same amount of power. IBM hopes this chip will supersede all the chips and the current architecture. Anyone considering the purchase

■ Pentium Bug

Users should be aware of the fact that the early Pentiums (typically the 60 to 66 MHz) were shipped with a flawed mathematics function. This is no longer a problem, but buyers of used machines should keep this in mind. Intel has offered to swap old chips for newer chips, but the process is arduous, according to those who have tried to get new chips.   ■

COMPUTERS

of a number of computers with the expectation they will remain usable for a long time should keep an eye on this technology. Early indications are that this machine will increase in importance as the year progresses. Apple was the first to employ this microprocessor in its line of PowerMac computers.

Upgradable PCs

In 1994, a fad of "upgradability" appeared on the market. Supposedly, an upgradable PC could stave off obsolescence, save money, and boost productivity over the years. Many of the promises up upgradability were never realized.

In reality, nearly any PC is upgradable if you're willing to replace the motherboard or pry out the microprocessor chip and plug an upgraded board in its place. The result is a workable, but confused, mess. One key advantage that an "upgradable" PC has over a "regular" one is the ZIF (zero insertion force) socket on the motherboard. This allows you to easily pop off the current microprocessor and stick a more up-to-date one on the motherboard.

With the ZIF socket, you can upgrade as many times as you like. Because it's an easy socket to insert and extract a CPU from, you can perform as many upgrades as your pocketbook and the technology allows.

In the case of the non-ZIF upgrade socket, there are two sockets. This is the case where putting the new chip into the upgrade socket disables the other chip in the non-upgrade socket. Also, it's not true that you can only upgrade once. True, once you have put the chip into the non-ZIF socket, it's hard to remove it, but certainly not impossible if you have the right tools.

A number of machines called upgradable really aren't. Let's say a computer is said to be a 486, it runs at 50 MHz, and the salesperson says you can upgrade it. If you ask what chip is in the machine, the reply is, "A 486DX2." This means it's really a 25 MHz 486 with a clock doubler. This doubler makes the chip run twice as fast. But that's not the same as a true upgradable 50 MHz 486 machine.

This upgrading trend has a lot of "gotchas," since the specifications for the chips of the future keep changing, and although Intel says it keeps vendors apprised of the future architecture, it can't guarantee anything. It's possible that the "upgradable" PC you buy won't be upgradable after all.

What about Coprocessors?

When the early IBM PC was invented, the microprocessor did not incorporate something called a "floating point processor." Thus, to do complex mathematics used in photo rendering and CAD/CAM (as well as most graphics), the machine required something called a coprocessor.

COMPUTERS

This was designed by Intel with an ending digit of "7" instead of a "6" as the chip number: 8087, 80287, and 80387. With the advent of the 486, the coprocessor was built into the chip itself and separate coprocessors were no longer necessary. This was until Intel itself brought out a crippled chip called the 486SX which had the coprocessor disabled so the company could sell a dubious chip called the 487 coprocessor. Suffice it to say that this idea wasn't a good one and all new microprocessors designed today will always incorporate a math coprocessor and users should no longer be concerned with this issue. A so-called 586 chip from Nexgen was released without math coprocessing capability and it is not recommended because of that. I doubt if we'll see any other chips without built-in coprocessing.

The Computer Bus

Once you start looking around at computers, the issue of "which bus?" will arise (not which bus to take to the computer store, but which bus to put into your computer). The *expansion bus* is a data highway for information to travel on; the *bandwidth* is the number of lanes. The bigger the bandwidth the more data that can be sent. As examples, a 16-bit bandwidth means data can be sent in 16-bit chunks, and a 32-bit bandwidth sends data in 32-bit chunks.

An expansion bus is where cards connect to the computer. Cards have a connector edge, which fits snugly into the bus much like an electrical plug fits into a wall socket.

When cards are plugged into the bus, they communicate with the system, sometimes through the BIOS and other times not. (The *BIOS* is the basic input/output system that tells the computer how to move data from the different components.) The 16- or 32-bit bandwidth is an important consideration due to the communication time between the cards. Let's say you have a 32-bit 486 machine, and it's pumping out data at 32 bits; your video card (which connects to the monitor and is discussed in Chapter 5) is also 32 bits. If you have a 16-bit bus, it will become a bottleneck. It's like a four-lane highway connected to another four-lane highway by way of a two-lane connector. At rush hour, traffic movement will be sluggish.

You have the choice of four types of expansion bus: ISA, MCA, EISA, and Local Bus (VL or PCI). There are some performance differences between the buses—and often a lot of discussion about them at gatherings of computer techno-nerds. Newer buses offer increased performance over the older technology buses. This performance is important in regard to networks and the newer multitasking operating systems (OS/2, Windows, Windows NT, and so on) which demand higher throughput. Generally speaking, the average user buying a first computer should buy the most common bus: ISA. But there are exceptions to this rule, like almost every other rule in the computer world. (One such exception: If you buy an

COMPUTERS

IBM PS/2 machine, you will get an MCA bus, since that's the only one they put in those machines.)

Industry Standard Architecture (ISA)   For most 386s, you can stick with the original AT bus, also called the ISA bus. This expansion bus originated in the IBM PC at an 8-bit bandwidth. IBM improved on the design with the PC/AT, raising its bandwidth to 16 bits. In an old 16-bit computer, it's a fine match, but for today's system, it won't do. You'll need an additional bus, such as a PCI bus.

Micro Channel Architecture (MCA)   386-based computers raised computing power on the desktop to the 32-bit level, leaving the expansion bus suddenly lagging behind the processor in performance. IBM introduced MCA in April 1987, forsaking its older architecture for a new 32-bit design. Not only did it offer a wider data path, but the process of bus-mastering was unveiled. *Bus-mastering* is a way to speed I/O transfers without losing processor performance. Intelligent peripherals on the expansion bus can take control of the bus to transfer information across it without the processor's having to arbitrate the process. An intelligent hard-disk controller can move data into memory without involving the CPU. It can continue to perform an instruction and have information it needs ready without controlling the movement of data. Performance is improved by task sharing. Unfortunately, this bus never became popular.

Extended Industry Standard Architecture (EISA)   The MCA introduction was not well received by other manufacturers. A "Gang of Nine" consortium (including Compaq, Zenith, Hewlett-Packard, and several others) decided to create their own expansion bus architecture. It would be 32-bit, include bus-mastering, and remain compatible with older expansion cards.

The EISA connector was designed for full backward compatibility with ISA boards. All the connectors on the ISA bus are present in their ordinary positions, but a new, lower row of contacts is added to link up the advanced functions of the bus. The developers linked these new contacts to the expansion board circuitry by interleaving their connecting traces between the ISA contacts on the card, as shown in Figure 4.2.

Micro Channel, on the other hand, forgoes hardware compatibility and guarantees only software compatibility with classic AT-bus computers. Thus, the MCA designers were free to alter the ISA layout completely, rearranging the functions of the contacts to minimize interference and to promote higher-speed operation. They added new functions as well. The result is that Micro Channel boards work only in Micro Channel slots. EISA slots will accommodate both ISA and EISA expansion boards, but this is a one-way compatibility: EISA boards cannot be used in ISA expansion slots.

COMPUTERS

■ Figure 4.2   Bus connectors

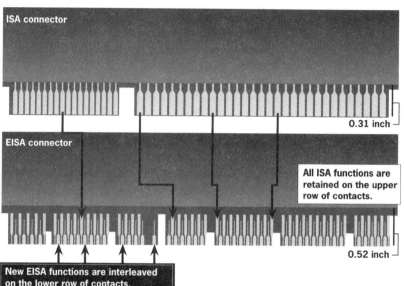

ISA connector

EISA connector

0.31 inch

All ISA functions are retained on the upper row of contacts.

0.52 inch

New EISA functions are interleaved on the lower row of contacts.

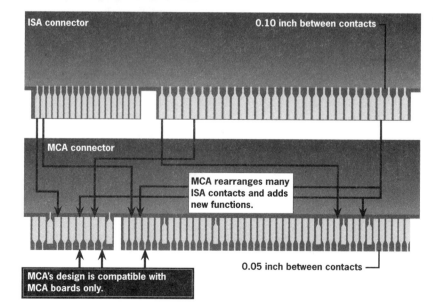

ISA connector

0.10 inch between contacts

MCA connector

MCA rearranges many ISA contacts and adds new functions.

MCA's design is compatible with MCA boards only.

0.05 inch between contacts

COMPUTERS

When it was announced in August 1988, the extended industry standard architecture (EISA) promised too much. With its wealth of system-enhancing technologies, EISA promised to accelerate the performance of any peripheral through its bus-mastering, interrupt sharing, 32-bit bus width, high-speed transfer modes, and automated setup. But its success did not come easily.

Only recently have EISA systems come close to delivering on the promises the vendors made. Its original costs were disproportionately high: The first EISA machines demanded a $2,000 premium over their ISA kin. The premium still hovers around $500.

Despite the demonstrable improvements in performance made by this technology, the best advantages of the better bus design still lie ahead. EISA is a bundle of technologies, and most of today's quicker controllers cash in on only a single performance-improving aspect of the standard: EISA's 32-bit bandwidth. Future applications should implement EISA's higher-speed modes and allow data-transfer rates of up to 33Mb per second. (The AT bus is limited to about one-quarter of that speed.) The true power of bus-mastering, also, won't be realized until a new generation of software becomes available. This will include software drivers capable of bringing the advanced modes to life and versions of operating systems able to take advantage of this technology. The multitasking abilities of OS/2, Windows NT, and UNIX make EISA versions of these operating systems possible, but none of these are here yet.

Nevertheless, EISA outperforms the AT bus. Those performance-enhancing capabilities should soon migrate into peripherals other than disk controllers. Vendors including Cogent Data Technologies, Mylex, 3-Com, and Proteon already manufacture EISA network adapters, and 32-bit coprocessed graphics boards are on the way, promising even faster video performance.

VL Bus   As the popularity of Windows increased, users discovered the video boards hooked to the machine via the ISA bus were running too slowly. They were bogged down by the graphical requirements of Windows. Engineers noted that with the advent of the 486 in particular, it was quite easy to talk to the processor directly (and at high speeds) over the processor's so-called local bus. A committee called the Video Electronics Standards Association formed to develop something called the VL bus. Its members defined the connector and electronics of a high-speed bus that could be used to make video cards work faster. The VL bus was generically known as the local bus and most new 486 machines employ it. Most video card makers have a VL-bus version of their display adapter. Other kinds of adapters such as joysticks and serial port cards have also used this bus.

COMPUTERS

■ What's an Mb?

Mb is short for megabyte. A megabyte is a million bytes, plus some change (1,048,576, or 1,024 times 1,024). Megabytes are used to measure the size of a hard or floppy disk and the total amount of RAM in the computer. Another term coming into common usage is a gigabyte (Gb), which is roughly a billion bytes. And looming on the horizon is the still larger terabyte (Tb), which is one trillion bytes.

When Mb describes a disk size, as in a 1.44Mb 3$\frac{1}{2}$-inch floppy drive, the 1.44 is just a more exact convention. In reality, 2Mb of RAM or 60Mb of hard disk should be more accurately written to two decimal places, but they just aren't. ■

PCI Bus When the Pentium chip was released, Intel saw the need for a more general purpose local bus that could eventually supplant the ISA/EISA and VL-bus designs completely. So it invented the Personal Computer Interconnect bus, or the PCI bus. It's now considered a standard on most Pentiums. It has even been adopted by Apple for its latest PowerMac computers. Most observers believe this is now the bus of choice for a new computer. For the next few years, most machines will have both a PCI and ISA bus incorporated into the motherboard. Eventually the ISA will disappear.

A Look at Some Typical Desktop Systems

The following sections briefly discuss some of the more common systems you can use as standards with which to compare your needs.

The Home Computer

This is a machine that will probably be used by everyone in the family. You will use it to play games, run educational programs, word process, and handle family finances. The ideal system would be an inexpensive 100 MHz 486-DX/4 machine with a 540Mb hard disk, a CD-ROM drive, a VGA color card, and a 14-inch color monitor.

For a printer, the home computer user will find an ink-jet printer a perfect accompaniment. (See Chapter 7 for a full discussion of printer basics.)

Look for these specifications in a home computer:

- 100 MHz 486DX/4 computer

- 8Mb of RAM

- 1.44Mb 3$\frac{1}{2}$-inch floppy drive

- 540Mb hard disk

COMPUTERS

■ A Word about Floppy Drives

You may want your computer to have two floppy disk drives: one 5¼-inch 1.2Mb drive and one 3½-inch 1.44Mb drive. This is especially handy if you have a lot of old software or data stored on 5¼-inch disks. Most software now appears in the smaller disk drive size. If you have just one size floppy drive and the disks are not the size you need, you'll have to convert the disks to the proper size. While this inconvenience can be tolerated by some, it's a terrible inconvenience for the person who doesn't have the time to fuss with finding a friend or service to do this. When both drives are available, you'll never have a problem. It's also handy since you can put data or software on either size drive to exchange with a friend or colleague.

If you are going to purchase a system and want the two disk drive sizes, be sure to have the 3½-inch drive as drive A and the larger 5¼-inch disk as drive B. You'll need this arrangement because most of today's software comes with only 3½-inch disks. Newer software expects to be booted from drive A. If you have the smaller drive as drive B, the software won't be able to locate the disk and may not run.   ■

- CD-ROM drive
- Super VGA video card
- Standard 14-inch VGA color monitor

The Home Office Computer

This is similar to the home computer, but it has more power. Although a 80386-based machine may have sufficed a year ago, it's now silly to buy anything less than a Pentium machine. A 540Mb hard disk is the minimum, although a larger hard disk would be more practical. An SVGA card is recommended, along with a 15-inch VGA monitor. The home office needs a high-quality color ink-jet printer or a laser printer.

Look for these specifications in a home office computer:

- 100 MHz Pentium computer
- 8Mb of RAM
- 1.44Mb 3½-inch floppy drive
- 540Mb–1.2Gb hard disk
- Double-speed CD-ROM drive
- Super VGA video card
- 15-inch VGA color monitor
- Mouse
- High-quality color ink-jet printer or laser printer

COMPUTERS

The Business Computer

The business computer should be able to run all available business software with speed. This means any Pentium computer will do. When you're paid by the hour, time shouldn't be wasted waiting on the computer. Much of today's business software is bloated and takes up a lot of disk space. Your best bet is to buy a minimum of 1.2Gb of hard-disk capacity or, ideally, as much as you can afford.

The business computer system should also include a high-quality laser printer.

A business computer system should meet these specifications:

- 100MHz Pentium computer

- 16Mb of RAM

- 3 $1/2$-inch 1.44Mb floppy drive

- 1/2–1.6Gb hard disk

- Quad-speed CD-ROM drive

- Super VGA video card (PCI Bus)

- 17-inch super VGA color monitor

- Mouse

- Laser printer

The Engineering PC Workstation

This is the machine needed to do CAD/CAM work. It requires as much processing power as possible. This means a Pentium that incorporates a floating-point chip within the CPU. Since most CAD/CAM files use large amounts of disk space, at least a 1.2Gb hard disk is necessary. One major consideration is that CAD/CAM demands the best video you can afford. Super VGA and a 21-inch multifrequency monitor is the minimum for accommodating higher resolutions.

An engineering PC system should have the following:

- 133 MHz Pentium

- 16–32Mb of RAM

- 3 $1/2$-inch 1.44Mb floppy drive

- 1.2Gb hard disk or larger

- Quad-speed CD-ROM drive

- Super VGA video card (PCI Bus)

COMPUTERS

- Multifrequency 21-inch VGA color monitor

- Mouse

- Laser printer

The Power-User Computer

An additional type of computer system is available for the class of user called the power user. It's not much different than the engineering PC workstation. Programmers will use such a system to do compilations. Show-offs who want the fastest, best machine will also want this kind of system. Intensive users of graphics software, desktop publishing software, and large spreadsheets and databases will also benefit from a powerful, fast computer.

A power-user system should meet these specifications:

- 150MHz Pentium

- 32Mb of RAM

- 3 1/2-inch 1.44Mb floppy drive

- 1.6Gb hard disk or larger

- Quad-speed CD-ROM drive

- Super VGA video card (PCI Bus)

- Multifrequency, multiscan 21-inch SVGA color monitor

- Mouse

- Laser printer

Mobile Computers

The trend today is toward computers you can carry around with you. You know, the ones the airlines ask you not to use during takeoff and landing. Those things you see carried around by business- and salespeople instead of the old, traditional briefcase. The mobile computer has become the badge of productivity. Everyone wants one.

In the past, a mobile computer could only be a substitute for a desktop unit. It was neither as versatile nor as powerful as an office or home personal computer. But these mobile units are beginning to blur the lines. These machines can have regular monitors and keyboards plugged into them when they're "home" to be used as a "real" desktop computer, with every bit as much power as a regular unit.

Over the past few years, mobile computers have gone through a number of trends, some of which have fallen into obscurity. For a while "palmtop"

COMPUTERS

computers were the rage. These were very small, calculator-sized computers with tiny keyboards and screens, which weighed about a pound at most. The outlook, just a few years ago, was that these machines would be a major element of personal computing. A number of manufacturers were producing them. But the fad faded, and today there are still palmtops. These are mostly from Casio and Sharp, with a limited market appeal as "organizers" or computerized notepads and date books.

In the not-so-distant past, mobile computers were divided into rough categories which depended on the dimensions and weight of the machine. These dubious categories included notebook, subnotebook, laptop, portable, and transportable. But the technology has leveled out. These units vary in weight from four to seven pounds (a far cry from the days when mobile computer weights varied from four to 12 pounds).

Ideal Mobile Computer Requirements

If you could have everything you wanted in a mobile computer, you would probably want 16Mb RAM; an active matrix color screen (or the newer 800×600 screen resolutions); a 28,800 bps, V.34 bis data/fax modem; about 540Mb or more of hard-disk space; a 486 DX4/100 or Pentium processor; two PCMCIA slots; a floppy drive; a trackpoint pointing device (or some mouse or mouse substitute); a serial port, parallel port, VGA output port, and SCSI port, as well as a keyboard port and separate mouse port; four to six hours of battery life; and a CD-ROM drive built in. Since no one machine offers all these features, you'll have to decide for yourself which ones you really need. Just make sure it comes as close as possible to mimicking your desktop machine.

Expansion Options for Mobile Computers

Other expansion options will depend on what you need access to, but an important one to keep in mind is an external expansion port. If you plan to use your unit as a dual-purpose desktop/travel machine, or if you need regular access to a network, you'll probably need a docking station or expansion unit. You'll pay a premium for these pricey add-ons. The expansion unit has room for the add-on cards and storage units that just won't fit in a portable computer. It allows you to quickly connect to and disconnect from those same options by providing a single connection that tells your portable computer what it's attached to when you plug it in. If you do buy a docking station, make sure it's self-configuring.

A better choice is a port replicator which costs a few hundred dollars. A port replicator attaches to a special connector on the back of the mobile machine and adds all the I/O (input/output) functionality of a desktop machine. (Toshiba, IBM, and other companies make these.) From one connector on the mobile computer you add a printer port, an external

COMPUTERS

■ FCC Class B Certification

A note of warning about portable computers: Pay attention to FCC Class B certification. Portable computers must have this certification, which ensures that the machine has adequate radio frequency emission shielding. This keeps the portable from interfering with television and radio reception and, most importantly, an airplane's navigational equipment.

Unlike desktop computers, no portable computer of any type can be legally sold without that FCC certification. Beware of oddball portable computers sold at swap-meets, through dubious mail-order firms, or by other shifty-eyed, fly-by-night merchandisers. FCC Class B certification stickers can be, and are, counterfeited. When in doubt, you can call the FCC to check. (FCC is listed in the federal government pages of the telephone book.) Just give the manufacturer's name and the model number of the machine to verify a Class B certification.   ■

floppy, serial port, Super VGA port, mouse, and keyboard port. Some have additional ports such as a SCSI and network connectors. These units are lightweight and can travel with you.

What to Shop for: Features

There are a number of real and imagined features to consider when it comes to mobile computers. Understand the trade-offs and your real requirements before you shop.

VGA Compatibility

Most laptops offer a high-resolution, readable Super VGA display with a gray scale. Monochrome VGA graphics are available on most mobile computers. Color VGA graphics are available on many mobile computers.

Screen Size

Look for a screen size of at least 8–10 diagonal inches. Anything smaller is impossible to read without a magnifying glass. Try to buy the largest screen size you can afford. There is nothing worse than straining to read a display—it's frustrating, causes headaches, and results in the computer being left home and unused more often than not.

Screen Lighting

The screen lighting for monochrome mobile computers is either back lighting or reflective lighting. The type that's best for you is a matter of personal choice. (A display that I don't like, my wife thinks is terrific.)

Back-lit displays use battery power to run, which limits the amount of computing time available. A back-lit screen is impossible to see in direct sunlight, so if you plan to do most of your computing on your yacht or at the beach, you'll probably be happier with a reflective display.

COMPUTERS

Reflective displays depend on the available light to reflect characters on the screen. Reflective screens are particularly hard to read in rooms lit with energy-saving fluorescent lights. If you'll be using your portable mainly in airport lobbies, on airplanes, in hotel rooms, and in other makeshift indoor offices, a back-lit screen may work best for you. However, reflective screens have the advantage of requiring less battery power, so your computing time is less limited in this regard.

The best way to find out which screen lighting works for you is to compare the displays of a number of machines. Try them out in sunlight and in the darkest part of the store until you find one that meets your needs.

Hard-Disk Drives

Hard-disk drives aren't a new feature in portable computers. The early Compaq had double floppy-disk drives for $5^1/_4$-inch floppies. The size of the drives contributed to the excessive weight of these early lap squishers (in the 20-pound range). Of course, these early attempts at "take-along" computing also had a video display tube, a case made of metal, and significantly larger components than their counterparts today. Later, the portables added the weighty and cumbersome $5^1/_4$-inch hard drives to their units.

When the $3^1/_2$-inch hard drives became commonplace in computer manufacturing, they were added to portables. The innovation made a significant dent in the weight of the laptop computers—a reduction of more than a pound.

As manufacturers have increased the density of data per square inch on the platter of the hard disk, the costs have fallen. Also the size of hard disks has decreased from $5^1/_4$" to $3^1/_2$" to $2^1/_2$", lowering the cost per megabyte to the end user. The first drives held about 20Mb, but at the time of this writing, the newest evolution is in the 1.2Gb and higher range.

The new feature of the lightweight computers is a small, $2^1/_2$-inch fixed-disk drive. These petite drives weigh no more than a pack of playing cards, and their capacity ranges from 80Mb to more than 800Mb. These small drives have cropped up in some of the machines, which has resulted in a downturn of weight.

Internal Modem

Your portable should have at least a 14.4-bps internal modem so that you can transfer files and connect with MCI Mail or another e-mail service, but a 28.8 is preferred. This, combined with a good file-transfer program (such as Lap Link, Brooklyn Bridge, or FastLynx), eliminates the need for a built-in floppy-disk drive.

COMPUTERS

PCMCIA Slot(s)
Most new mobiles contain at least one PCMCIA card slot for holding various add-in devices and extra memory. Originally designed to be used for ROM containing large programs, now the card can be anything from a network adapter to a small hard disk. The most popular use is for modems. Be careful: Many of these devices have delicate connectors that are easily broken.

Port Replicator Units
These units will give all the functionality of a desktop computer in a mobile computer. So if you move from site to site, you can have a regular keyboard, monitor, and printer at each location—and just carry a little mobile computer around. No need to have replicated desktop machines at each site. The units are reasonably priced and lightweight.

Battery Life
Battery life is still the major limitation with mobile computers. While you shouldn't accept a machine that provides less than two hours of intensive computing time, be aware that many machines are now able to operate six hours or more.

Keyboard
One item to consider when choosing a portable—and the most subjective—is the keyboard. Because of the tight space limitations of mobile computers, you can expect some variation of the QWERTY layout, with tighter key spacing (.75 inch or less). The layout of function, cursor, PgUp, PgDn, Home, and End keys will vary even within a manufacturer's product line.

This is another good reason to invest in a port replicator. With it, you can use your mobile computer for some "serious" typing by adding a *real* keyboard.

Weight
If you're considering a mobile computer, weight is probably a major concern for you. Most likely you plan to carry this computer with you extensively and don't feel like going into weight training to do so. While you probably won't notice the difference of a pound in weight, you should try to get the lightest machine that has the features you need. Remember, along with the computer itself, you're going to be carrying the battery in the machine, a spare battery, a recharger/wall adapter, a carrying case, and probably some manuals and floppy disks. Eventually it adds up to quite a bit more than the weight the manufacturer advertises.

COMPUTERS

Try Before You Buy

The only way to decide what's right for you is to try out any computer before you buy it. Any good retailer is willing to let you tap on the keys to your heart's content. Remember, you're going to have to live with the miserable keyboard that's permanently attached to that dreamy mobile computer, so pay attention not only to the layout and special key combinations needed to perform normal operations, but also to the feel of the keys themselves. If you hate it, then don't buy it. (On the other hand, it's amazing what you can get used to.)

One last thing to keep in mind when comparing machines, particularly concerning price and weight, is to make sure that you compare the same configuration. That means adding in the price and weight of an internal modem (if it does not come as standard equipment) and any extra memory you will need.

Convenience on the Go

Computing while on the road is becoming more commonplace. As you gain experience with mobile computing, the missing pieces you take for granted at your desktop computer may become desirable to you in your travels. You may want to have a mobile printer, scanner, modem, fax machine, external hard disk, tape drive, mouse, or even a convenient way to use the computer and printer in your car.

Portable Printing

Printing while you are away from your office can be inconvenient—at best—when you need to hook up to a client's printer. For those who don't want to annoy their hosts, or who visit printerless offices (or homes), mobile printers are just the thing.

The minimum requirements for mobile printers are small size and light weight. Battery operation is handy, but not always crucial; it depends upon your needs.

External Hard Disks: Data Luggage

External hard disks serve multiple purposes for mobile computers. When paired with mobile computers without a hard disk, external units hold programs and data that can be carried along for access when AC power is available. If your computer already has an internal hard disk, you can use an external one as a secondary large-capacity storage device or as a fast data backup unit.

Road Trackballs

The popularity of GUIs (graphical user interfaces), especially Windows, has brought about the need for mobile pointing devices. The most common

COMPUTERS

style of these pointing devices is a very small trackball that clips to the side of the laptop's keyboard. You use your thumb to move the cursor. (Some machines are now incorporating a variety of other mouse substitutes in their keyboard layouts. The most notable is the Trackpoint, which is discussed in Chapter 10.)

Other Products

A number of other products are available for mobile computing. These include modems (covered in Chapter 9), some of which connect with cellular or other wireless systems. Extra add-ons include screen enhancers, lightweight plastic keyboard overlays and covers (to keep crumbs out of the keys), fancy carrying cases in nylon and leather, joysticks, and other specialty products.

As with any buying decision, you'll have to prioritize your wants and needs in order to find the machine and the peripherals that are best for you.

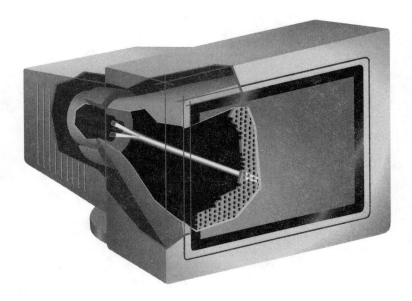

MONITORS ARE AN INTEGRAL PART of today's computer scene. They come in a variety of sizes, prices, and screen resolutions, some sharper than others. Back in 1977, it was as easy to purchase a monitor as it was a television set: "Yep, that one looks like it will work; won't clash with my wallpaper." Now specialized monitors are designed for explicit applications, and with them comes a multitude of compatibility issues, such as which specialty cards go with which monitors. (A monitor won't work without a video card,

MONITORS

which fits into the bus within your computer's case. The video card is the "middleman" which interprets the computer's data and sends it to the monitor. Chapter 6 covers these video cards in detail, and yes, some are built into the motherboard.)

The monitor is called by many names, including the video display terminal (VDT), the video display unit (VDU), the computer screen, or even outdated terms such as the cathode-ray tube (CRT) or the terminal.

How a Monitor Works

The main difference between the picture quality of a television and a monitor is the resolution. A monitor's screen display should be stable and of good quality, since you will sit very close to the monitor and will spend many hours reading the display. If the images are fuzzy (low resolution) or waver constantly, you'll have a raging headache and watering eyes in no time. (Although employing similar technology, a monitor is a better-built piece of equipment than a TV.)

Monitors have knobs to adjust for clarity. These include a brightness knob which adjusts the illumination of the entire screen, and a contrast knob which makes the letters lighter or darker in relation to the background screen. Particular monitors may have other adjustments, and color monitors may have a way to adjust the colors.

Color

A typical color screen works in much the same way as a color television. The inside of the picture tube is coated with three different phosphors: red, green, and blue. Phosphors are special chemical compounds that glow with characteristic colors when they are bombarded by a stream of electrons. The phosphor gets "excited." Thanks to the additive properties of colored light, you can use combinations of these three primary colors to produce every shade in the rainbow. When all three colors are mixed together in equal quantities, your eye perceives white light (see Figure 5.1).

This approach has its limitations. Since each type of phosphor must be excited by electrons fired from a different gun than the other two, the tubes must be constructed to fine tolerances. No matter how small the dots or how high the screen resolution, a little crispness and detail at the edge of a white line will be lost where a final row of one color pixel or another gives the edges of images a faint color tint. (Monochrome monitors have it much easier than their color cousins. They use one color phosphor which is uniformly coated across the inside of the screen. The precise placement of specific dots isn't an issue.)

The sharpness of a color monitor's image is determined by three factors: the monitor's bandwidth, its dot pitch, and the accuracy of its convergence. Although the bandwidth and dot pitch are important to determine a good monitor, convergence is the real measurement.

MONITORS

■ Video Talk: A Guide to Video Terms

Discussions of monitors involve a particular kind of lingo. While most of these terms are computerese, many of them do describe the characteristics of a monitor. Here are some of the video terms you will come across in magazines, when you try to talk to a salesperson, and even as you read this book:

- **Aspect ratio**   The aspect ratio is the ratio of a pixel's width to its height. In VGA and Super VGA mode, this ratio is 1:1, which means the pixels are as tall as they are wide.

- **Autosizing**   True autosizing occurs when a monitor can maintain a constant image size when moving across low and high resolutions. Many monitors use preprogrammed factory settings to achieve a similar effect, but only for certain resolutions, usually VGA and Super VGA. Some manufacturers also provide user-determined settings. Autosizing is especially important for the newer multitasking operating systems, such as Windows and OS/2.

- **Barrel distortion**   Barrel distortion occurs at the edges of the screen and is the inverse of *pincushioning*. The sides of an image afflicted with this type of distortion seem to bow out, resembling a barrel.

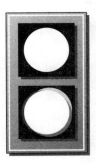

- **Convergence**   Theoretically, each of the beams that generate the three color dots (red, green, and blue) should converge at appropriate distances from one another. When all three dots are being excited simultaneously and their relative distance is perfect, the result is pure white. Serious deviation from this harmony (mainly due to the relationship of the electron beams to each other) results in poor convergence. This can cause white pixels to show bits of color and can also decrease both picture sharpness and resolution.

- **Dot pitch**   Dot pitch describes the distance between the holes in the *shadow mask;* it therefore also indirectly describes how far apart the individual dots are on screen. The smaller the dot pitch, the finer the image's "grain." Some color monitors, such as the Sony Trinitron, use an aperture grille which is perforated by strips, not holes, in the shadow mask. In this case, the dots are arranged linearly, and their density is called *striped dot pitch.* (Monochrome monitors do not use a shadow mask and therefore do not have a dot pitch.)

- **Drift**   *Drift, jitter,* and *swim* are all terms that relate to an unwanted motion of a line. The only difference between the three terms is the amount of time used to measure on-screen wavers. A perfect image should be rock-steady on the screen.

- **Horizontal scan frequency**   This is the frequency per second at which a monitor repaints the horizontal lines that make up an image. Horizontal scan frequency is measured in kHz (kilohertz). A standard VGA signal requires a 31.5 kHz horizontal scan frequency capability.

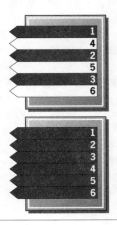

- **Interlaced and noninterlaced scanning**   There are two basic schemes for painting an image on the screen: interlaced and noninterlaced. Interlaced scanning takes two passes, painting every other line on the first pass and filling in the rest of the lines on the second pass. Noninterlaced scanning paints all the lines in one pass and

Continued on next page

MONITORS

■ Video Talk: A Guide to Video Terms

Continued from previous page

then paints an entirely new frame. Noninterlaced scanning is preferable because it reduces screen flicker. However, it is more expensive.

- **Pincushioning** Pincushioning describes an unwanted curve of an image which usually occurs at the edges of the screen. The sides of the image appear to curve inward.

- **Pixel** A pixel is the smallest information building block of an on-screen image. On a color-monitor screen, each pixel is made of one or more triads. Resolution is usually expressed in terms of the number of pixels comprising the width and height of a complete on-screen image. In VGA, the resolution is 640×480 pixels; in Super VGA, it is 800×600 pixels or higher.

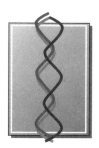

- **Roping** Roping describes an image distortion that gives solid straight lines a helical or twisted appearance. This problem is caused by poor convergence.

- **Shadow mask** A shadow mask is inside the monitor just behind the screen. It is drilled with small holes, each of which corresponds to a *triad*. The shadow mask helps guide the electron beam so that each beam hits only one phosphor dot in the triad.

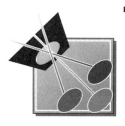

- **Slot mask** The slot mask, also known as the aperture grille, serves the same function as a shadow mask. The slot mask is made up of vertical wires stretched behind the screen. The spacing of these wires (or the slots between them) determines the finest detail that the monitor can display horizontally. The dot pitch for such a display measures the space between these slots.

- **Triad** A triad contains three phosphor-filled dots—one red, one green, and one blue—arranged in a triangle. Each of the three electron guns is dedicated to one of these colors (for example, the red gun excites only a triad's red phosphor dot). As the guns scan the screen, each active triad produces a single color. Which color it is depends on the combination of excited color dots and how active each dot is.

- **Vertical refresh rate** The vertical refresh rate, also called the vertical scan frequency, is related to horizontal sweeps in that once an image has been entirely repainted (by horizontal sweeps), it has been vertically scanned or refreshed. Slow vertical refresh rates will increase screen flicker. Standard VGA has a vertical scan frequency of 60 Hz or 70 Hz, and Super VGA vertical refresh rates vary from industry guidelines of 56 Hz and 60 Hz to the official standard of 72 Hz.

- **Video bandwidth** Video bandwidth represents the highest input frequency a monitor can handle. It determines the monitor's resolution capabilities. Video bandwidth is measured in MHz (megahertz). ■

MONITORS

■ Figure 5.1   Making white with phosphors

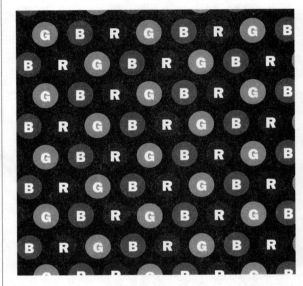

Close-up of the phosphors of an RGB color monitor

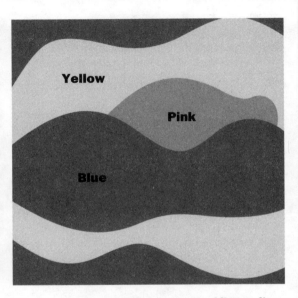

Close-up of the phosphors of a paper-white monitor

Bandwidth   The *bandwidth* of a monitor is the range of signal frequencies that its circuits can handle. This frequency range determines what resolution the monitor can display. Most bandwidth figures do not represent absolute capabilities, but rather indicate the range at which the monitor achieves optimal operation. The visual effect of modestly exceeding the rated bandwidth is a slight softening of the sharp edges of each pixel (see Figure 5.2).

To estimate the minimum bandwidth a monitor must display to attain a given graphics standard, you need to know the number of pixels and the frame rate associated with the standard. The bandwidth is equal to the total number of pixels (the number of horizontal pixels multiplied by the number of vertical pixels) multiplied by the frame rate. (This calculation assumes that each pixel represents a signal pulse.)

In the case of 800×600-pixel graphics and a frame rate of 60 Hz, this calculation (800×600×60) would give a bandwidth of 28.8 MHz. This is a low figure—in reality, such a resolution requires some overhead for *horizontal and vertical retrace*. This refers to the time it takes the monitor's

MONITORS

■ Figure 5.2   Bandwidth

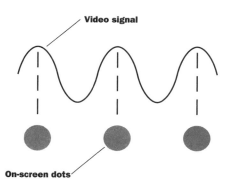

Video signal

On-screen dots

Bandwidth indicates the range of frequencies that can be handled by a multiscanning monitor. This directly relates to how closely dots can be spaced on the screen.

---

circuitry to shift from the end of a line to the beginning of the next line, and from the bottom of one frame to the top of the next. A 30 MHz system would be barely adequate for 800×600-pixel graphics.

Dot Pitch   All monitors come with *dot pitch* specifications, a measure of pixel spacing given in millimeters (see Figure 5.3). Each pixel on a color screen consists of a trio of dots with each dot glowing in one of the primary colors of light: red, green, or blue. The pitch is determined by the spacing of the holes in what is called the *shadow* (or *slot*) *mask* of the monitor's CRT. The smaller a monitor's dot pitch rating, the sharper the on-screen image it can display.

■ Figure 5.3   Dot pitch

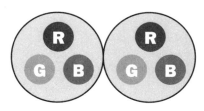

An effective dot pitch

Every pixel on the screen is made from three dots of color, sorted out by the shadow mask of the picture tube. The dot pitch is determined by the spacing of holes in the shadow mask.

MONITORS

Convergence Convergence defines how accurately each of the three colored dots in a pixel is placed in relation to the other two (see Figure 5.4). In theory, the three electron beams should converge on a single point as they scan the inside of the CRT to create the monitor's image. In reality, they must be offset somewhat because the three phosphor colors of the tube are next to, rather than on top of, each other.

When convergence is perfect and all three guns are exciting the phosphor, the result is a pixel that appears perfectly white, but a number of factors conspire against this perfection: small irregularities in the electronics that control each color gun, tiny differences in the alignment of the guns, and variations in the magnetic fields that guide the electron beams. The result is that one or two colors may stray from ideal positioning, which gives the pixels a distinctly two- or three-color look. Because of the spread of the dot trios, the image also loses sharpness and resolution. The misconvergence results in a loss of true white (and black) on screen, causing text to appear fuzzy.

Convergence problems do not result from monitor design flaws, but rather from real-world imperfections. For this reason, the convergence of monitors of the same make and model varies. Convergence may even vary across the face of a screen. (Electron beams are more difficult to control near the corners of the image, so convergence problems usually arise there.)

Convergence errors are often the chief limitation on a particular monitor's resolution. For example, a monitor may have a rated maximum convergence error of 0.6 mm—twice the dot pitch of the CRT tube. This would cause a very poor image quality, particularly at higher resolutions when more information is sent to the screen.

■ Figure 5.4   Convergence

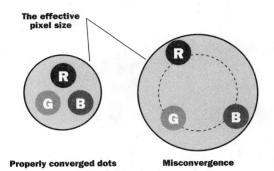

The effective pixel size

Properly converged dots

Misconvergence

Convergence is a measure of how precisely the colored dots composing each pixel meet at the same point. When these dots don't converge properly, the pixels are enlarged (often doubled in size) and the image is blurred.

MONITORS

■ Trinitron—What's in a Name?

A new color picture tube technology developed by Sony Corporation has become public domain. The technology uses an *aperture grille* instead of a shadow mask. Most manufacturers are now using this aperture grille technology, but they still cannot use the trademarked name, Trinitron. This has caused some confusion in the marketplace. ■

Most monitors use a shadow mask to align the electron beams. The exceptions are the monitors that utilize Trinitron technology. The Trinitron uses an aperture grille, which is a series of vertical wires held tight in a frame. The curved screen has a series of horizontal stripes of phosphor coating (coded red, green and blue). The Trinitron monitors have a sharper image and fewer color errors than monitors that use a dot-perforated shadow mask.

A Little Monitor History

Until the early 1980s, most monitors were terminals. These were boxy video display terminals (VDTs) combined with an attached keyboard. A terminal could be configured to work with just about any computer on the market (not that there was a wide selection of personal computers to choose from). Terminals were attached to computers by a serial interface. In those days, the VDT was commonly referred to as a CRT (cathode-ray tube).

Before DOS, the dominant operating system for 8-bit computers was CP/M (control program for microprocessors). Early CP/M machines were originally designed to use separate memory-mapped video display devices and discrete keyboards that plugged into the machines—not unlike the video display cards used today. The most well-known was the VDM-1. Terminal manufacturers recognized this "lost market" and began to market mainframe and mini-style terminals to the CP/M community. The sales pitch of "just like a real computer" paid off: CP/M computers soon used terminals almost exclusively.

Apple II computers and the early game machines (such as those made by Atari) hooked to a monitor, not a terminal. (The Apple II was built with a keyboard as part of the system. All that was missing was a monitor.) These monitors—unlike terminals—looked like television sets without the tuner. In some cases they *were* television sets. (Many early computers could be used with any television set with a special RF adapter that hooked to the antenna.) Then IBM came out with PC-DOS computers, which were dubbed "three-piece" computers because they included three main components: the monitor, the keyboard, and the "box."

MONITORS

■ Terminals versus Monitors

A "terminal" usually means a keyboard/monitor combination (often as one "blended" unit). Many terminals are semi-smart machines and can perform functions on their own. Some of the old Tele-Video terminals could print directly from the screen to the printer—without going through the computer. (However, there are also dumb terminals which are little more than a keyboard and a monitor.) A terminal can also store information in a queue until it is *polled* (asked for information from a computer).

This is different from a monitor which can do nothing except display on the screen the information given to it by the computer. The monitor cannot store or queue information, nor can it request or answer a poll on its own. It is just a video display tube which is then hooked to a CPU. The keyboard is also hooked to the CPU.   ■

Ironically, when the IBM PC-DOS computers arrived on the scene—with separate monitor and keyboard—the monitor connected directly to the computer (just like the earliest personal computers) through a display device connection. These new monitors used video cards that were either IBM monochrome (MDA), IBM color graphics adapter (CGA), or Hercules (the first third-party add-on card) cards.

Meanwhile, about the time these early personal computers were gaining some momentum, the big computers—mainframes—at large corporations were adding some pretty dazzling terminals. Compared to a terminal connected to a mainframe computer, the first monitors for personal computers were crude and unattractive. The early monitors predominantly had green or black and bluish-white displays. They were 40-column monitors, which meant that 40 characters could appear on the screen before the text wrapped to a new line. The Apple II had a 40-column, all uppercase display.

The next generation of personal computer monitors had 64 columns in stylish "eye-ease" amber. Add-in video cards would eventually change the display to a whopping 132 columns.

The Evolution of Resolution

The most dramatic technical advances in monitor development have been made in the area of resolution—the sharpness of the screen image. Early CGA monitors had a resolution of about 320×200 pixels; the standard noninterlaced monitors produced today usually have a resolution of 1,024×768 pixels (a resolution of 1,280×1,024 is also not uncommon). Current trends indicate that we can expect even greater improvements in resolution technology.

CGA (1981)   CGA (color graphics adapter) was one of the two display adapters IBM introduced for its original PC. CGA offered a palette of 16 colors in two modes: 320×200 resolution in four colors and 640×200 in

MONITORS

two colors. The second adapter, MDA (monochrome display adapter), was less expensive. It offered higher resolution (720×350 pixels) but could display only text—no more than 25 lines of 80 characters each—in a single color. By 1982, power users were employing both adapters, MDA for text and CGA for then-new Lotus 1-2-3 graphics.

Hercules (1982)   The Hercules graphics adapter card was invented by Van Suwannukul (founder of Hercules Computer Technology) so he could use a standard PC and monitor to produce his doctoral thesis using his native Thai alphabet.

Before VGA (video graphics array), monochrome graphics meant one thing: the Hercules graphics adapter. Fully compatible with IBM's monochrome display adapter (MDA) for displaying text, the Hercules board added graphics capabilities to ordinary digital monochrome displays. Along the way, it brought the highest graphics resolution available to standard PC monitors before VGA—720×400 pixels.

For nearly five years, the Hercules card was the standard for monochrome graphics. Dozens of programs were rewritten to take advantage of its capabilities, including the one that confirmed the success of the Hercules card—Lotus 1-2-3. But in 1987, the introduction of the VGA standard challenged Hercules's dominance.

EGA (1984)   Although today the standard EGA configuration is a card with 256K of DRAM, which can provide 16 out of 64 colors at 640×350 resolution, the EGA card originally produced by IBM offered only 64K, enough to display only 16 colors at 320×200 resolution. Before long, the optional 192K memory addition was considered mandatory, even though it nearly doubled the cost of the card. Competitive EGA board makers offered 256K as a standard configuration.

At the same time it introduced EGA, IBM released PGC, the professional graphics controller. The PGC card was slow and expensive, so despite its 640×480 resolution, it failed to become a graphics standard.

Multiscanning Monitor (1985)   The first multiple-frequency (multiscanning) monitor, MultiSync from NEC Home Electronics (USA), could work with CGA, EGA, and PGC adapters.

VGA (1987)   The video graphics array adapter, introduced with IBM's PS/2 line, offered a palette of 262,144 colors. VGA provided 256 colors at 320×200 resolution or 16 at full 640×480 resolution. Though originally VGA was available only for Micro Channel machines, within a year, board manufacturers successfully created standard cards using the new VGA standard.

VGA improved the resolution above the Hercules standard only modestly. The text mode was slightly sharper at 720×400, due to two

MONITORS

additional vertical dots in the matrix from which each character is made. In graphics mode, the VGA system can deliver 640×480 resolution, which is about 20 percent sharper than the 720×348 delivered by the Hercules board—not too dramatic an improvement. However, VGA held an important advantage over Hercules: It was compatible with color graphics software.

With VGA, monochrome and color were united under a single standard; the only operational difference between the two display modes (for which programmers need to allow) was the number of colors available on the screen. A color VGA system would show CGA and EGA graphics on its screen; a monochrome VGA system would do likewise, without the special drivers.

In addition, VGA monochrome displays used analog signals, so they had the potential to offer a near-infinite number of shades of gray. (MDA and Hercules display systems were limited to three levels—black, white, and highlighted—although with clever programming some video boards squeezed out up to 16 gray levels.)

Super VGA (1988) Promoted by a consortium of monitor and graphics-board manufacturers called the Video Electronics Standards Association (VESA), Super VGA (also called extended VGA or VGA Plus) offered 800×600 graphics resolution and 56 percent more on-screen pixels than VGA. It used 16 colors out of a palette of 256, which may not have satisfied serious graphics users, but should have sufficed for Microsoft Windows and text-mode users. Adapters capable of displaying 256 colors were readily available but were not addressed by VESA. Super VGA adapters cost little more than regular VGA adapters.

Today's Super VGA monitors provide all the resolution of the original release, a palette of colors (some have over 16 million), and fast screen updates with high-speed 24-bit graphics adapters. They can adapt to any IBM video standard and graphics adapter, and some will even accommodate Apple II and Macintosh computers.

Keep in mind that one difference between older types of SVGA monitors and the most up-to-date designs is the scanning frequency. Originally, the VESA specification for SVGA specified a vertical refresh rate of just 56 Hz, but in recent years we've come to expect a flicker-free 72 Hz display, or faster.

Noninterlaced 1,024×768 (1989) Beginning in 1989, Compaq promoted noninterlaced 1,024×768 resolution, targeting high-end graphics users such as CAD/CAM aficionados. Its boards offered 256 colors with a 512K memory addition.

Meanwhile, in the same market, IBM promoted interlaced 1,024×768 resolution with its 8514/A adapter, introduced in 1987 with the PS/2 line. The board came with 500K of memory, which allowed 16 colors to be

MONITORS

displayed simultaneously. The interlaced display, however, was more likely to produce flicker. At present, not much software exists to support either adapter.

XGA (1991) XGA (extended graphics array) has never been widely accepted in the market. The current XGA design has a screen resolution of up to 1,024×768 with 256 colors. (At the lower resolution of 640×480 pixels, the color palette is 64,000 colors.) Future versions will include so-called "true color" (16 million simultaneous colors) and resolution of up to 4,000×4,000 pixels. It is downward compatible with the VGA standard.

Monitors in the Market

There are a number of different monitors on the market. The most common are VGA and Super VGA. If you go out shopping, these will be the ones you will most likely encounter.

All VGA and Super VGA monitors are divided into general classes, discussed below, according to the way they react to the synchronizing signals generated by your PC's VGA circuitry. These signals are used by the monitor to lock the screen image in place so that it doesn't roll like a 1950s television on the fritz.

Fixed-Frequency Monitors

Fixed-frequency monitors, such as the IBM and Compaq captive displays, are designed to lock onto a very narrow frequency range. These monitors demand that the signals from your VGA adapter be close to its nominal value—31.5 kHz for horizontal sync signals and both 60 and 70 Hz for vertical sync signals. Usually, you would choose a fixed-frequency monitor if you purchased your computer and monitor as a "package" deal. The monitors are designed to work only with the computer, and vice versa.

Multiple-Frequency Monitors

Multiple-frequency (or multiple-fixed-frequency) monitors are designed to operate at two or more frequency settings, each of which has a narrow band of acceptance like that of a fixed-frequency display. The best known of these monitors is IBM's 8514, a 16-inch monitor that accepts horizontal sync frequencies of either 31.5 kHz (for MCGA and VGA signals) or 35.5 kHz (for IBM's proprietary 1,024×768 interlaced graphics standard).

Multiscanning Monitors

Multiscanning monitors are specially designed for high-resolution graphics. To display graphic images, a monitor must be able to handle the two synchronizing frequencies used to form them: the horizontal scanning frequency (the rate at which one line is drawn across the width of the

MONITORS

■ Oh My Achin' Eyes

As personal computer usage grows, computer-related eyestrain is approaching epidemic proportions. In 1991, a Harris poll cited computer-related eyestrain as the number one office-related health complaint in the United States. A study the same year by the National Institute of Occupational Safety and Health (NIOSH) indicated that of the 66 million people who work at computers for more than three hours a day, 88 percent—nearly 60 million—suffer from symptoms of eyestrain.

Because most optometrists, ophthalmologists, and opticians have assumed that reading a computer screen was identical to the printed page, there was no "cure," or aid. So users relied on "folk remedies" such as adjusting ambient light levels, moving the monitor farther away, and so on.

Our eyes respond well to most printed material, which is characterized by dense black characters with well-defined edges. These edges contrast markedly from their light background, which makes it easy to focus on the printed page.

Characters on a computer screen don't have this contrast or the well-defined edges. They're a series of dots (pixels), brightest at their centers and diminished in intensity toward their edges. Our eyes are unable to maintain a fixed focus as we gaze at a monitor. Instead, the focus drifts out to a point—the *resting point of accommodation* (RPA)—which is somewhere *behind* the computer screen. Our eyes constantly move to the RPA and then strain to regain focus of the screen. The constant flexing of the eyes' focus creates fatigue and eyestrain.

Now, a company called PRIO has a solution: a test to determine the position of your RPA. The PRIO VDT Vision Tester is a tool for eye specialists. With a PRIO tester, an examining doctor can generate a specialized eyewear prescription, which allows the computer user's eyes to focus naturally on the computer screen, rather than behind it. The prescription will fill the *lag of accommodation* (the distance between the computer screen and the eyes' natural resting point on the screen) to keep your focus on the same plane as the computer screen. This specialized prescription cannot be generated using the doctor's "typical" printed black-on-white vision targets. The PRIO tester generates a prescription for glasses which are able to correct the computer-screen-induced lag of accommodation.

There are currently five wholesale optical labs supplying a network of nearly 200 doctors from coast to coast. The PRIO VDT Vision Tester is a patented, FDA market-approved Class 1 Medical Device. For more information, contact PRIO in Lake Oswego, OR, or call (800) 621-1098, or (503) 636-3707. ■

screen) and the vertical scanning frequency, also called the refresh or frame rate (the rate at which a complete screen is filled with an image). Each graphic standard requires a different combination of these scan rates; multiscanning monitors are so named because they can scan a range of horizontal and vertical frequencies.

It's important for the multiscanning monitor to operate within its limits, which means it requires a compatible video adapter card. (See Chapter 6 for a more complete discussion of video adapter cards.) If a video card puts out higher horizontal and vertical frequency rates than the monitor can handle, there may be problems. The frequency-handling limits determined by a monitor's manufacturer are noted to ensure safe operation (for example, to keep the operating temperatures of inductive

MONITORS

components such as flyback transformers and semiconductors within acceptable limits) and long machine life; most monitors can exceed these limits within reason. But significantly higher scanning frequencies stress critical circuits more than lower frequencies do, which causes the circuits to produce more heat.

When you set a multiscanning monitor to display each different resolution graphics standard, the image is likely to appear in a different spot on the screen at first. Horizontal and vertical position controls allow you to move the image around. The controls help ensure that no part of the image is cut off and that the black dead space around the image is equal on all four sides of the tube. Ideally, these controls should allow you to move the image beyond the edge of the screen on all four sides.

Specialty Monitors

There are some specialty monitors on the market designed for specific applications, such as desktop publishing, CAD/CAM, video editing, and illustration and graphic arts, among others. The monitors are expensive and often very large. They include 1,600×1,200 monitors, paper-white monitors, and other big-screen monitors.

1,600×1,200 Monitors   These monitors, including big-screen and paper-white monitors, are specialty devices. Desktop publishing experts and those who use CAD/CAM programs like these monitors because their size and high resolution provide a crisp, legible display and because they can accommodate a two-page layout.

Paper-White Monitors   These monitors are designed for desktop publishing, CAD/CAM, and other specific uses. They have crisp white-and-black displays. This white light is displayed in a variety of ways, all of which involve color.

It may be surprising to discover that even these paper-white displays still rely on phosphors to produce different colors. Although we tend to refer to the display as white, close inspection reveals that the images are made up of a mixture of different colors. Most monitors use combinations of blue and yellow, and some use pink as well.

As you shop for a monitor, you may notice that some paper-white monitors have a blue tinge and some have a distinctly warmer tone. This is because some monitors are assembled by manufacturers and sold to OEMs (original equipment manufacturers). These OEMs purchase equipment components to sell under their own names and may shop through samples of varying phosphor mixtures to determine the exact shades they want for their products. Thus, the difference in shades is simply a matter of the buyer's personal taste and doesn't reflect the quality or cost of the monitor.

MONITORS

■ Monitor Emissions

No discussion of monitors would be complete without covering the subject of monitor emissions. For years, a debate has been raging over how monitors can affect our health. Several medical studies from different angles have implicated electromagnetic emissions from computer monitors as the cause of health problems. They've been blamed for everything from miscarriages and birth defects to cancer. Although there's no concrete scientific proof—nothing conclusive—there has been enough concern to warrant further investigation. The next few years may yield an answer.

In the meantime, customer demand has created a market for low-emissions monitors, and many manufacturers have products with reduced low-frequency electromagnetic emissions. Currently, the largest market for these products is Europe, especially Sweden (where the standards for manufacturers were developed). In the United States, large corporations, government agencies, and a segment of the general population (mostly in California) have generated a great deal of interest in low-emission monitors.

VLF (Very Low Frequency) and ELF (Extremely Low Frequency)

Nearly all electrical appliances emit electromagnetic energy over a wide range of frequencies. Some of these emissions are regulated by law. Televisions, for example, emit very low levels of radiation, but it's absorbed by shielding and the glass in the screen. These emissions are stringently regulated because of the known carcinogenic effects. Lower-frequency emissions in communications broadcasting are regulated by the FCC, but not for health reasons—it's so household equipment doesn't interfere with aircraft navigation or your neighbor's TV reception. Emissions that are still lower than the broadcast frequencies are called VLF (very low frequency) and ELF (extremely low frequency). These were considered safe—until recently.

These are the frequencies addressed by the Swedish monitor-emission standard. ELF and VLF are not considered radiation, as true radiation—x-rays—ionizes molecules, which can bombard the DNA in your genes. The ELF range in monitors is about 30 to 300 Hz. ELF signals have been associated with a variety of negative health effects, both in laboratory experiments and epidemiological surveys. These effects include increased cancer rates, changes in sleep patterns, and laceration of nerve-cell physiology. The studies have shown increased cancer rates for people living near power lines and using electric blankets, both of which produce excessive electrical and magnetic ELF fields. But it is still debatable whether these fields are truly dangerous.

Magnetic and Electric Fields

Electromagnetic energy is made up of both magnetic and electric fields. At high frequencies the two are one and the same, but at lower frequencies they behave differently. There has been some research to indicate that ELF magnetic emissions are more likely to cause health problems than are VLF emissions. A possible explanation is that magnetic fields are biologically active in that they interact with the natural electric activity of the cells, modifying ion balances across cell membranes, growth rates, and nerve-cell behavior. While ELF has been used to speed bone-tissue healing, it has also been blamed for promoting the growth of cancerous cells in some studies.

Continued on next page

MONITORS

▊ Monitor Emissions

Continued from previous page

Monitor-Emission Guidelines

The Swedish National Board for Measurement and Testing (MPR) established guidelines for monitor-emission levels in 1987. The standard was adopted worldwide. The first set of MPR guidelines covered magnetic fields in the VLF range—defined as 1 kHz to 300 kHz—and static electric fields. MPR recently revised its guidelines to include a strict set of emissions standards for magnetic and electric fields in both VLF and ELF frequency ranges. MPR now defines ELF as the frequencies from 5 Hz to 2,000 Hz (2 kHz) and VLF as the frequencies from 2 kHz to 400 kHz. The new recommendations are officially known as SWEDAC MPR 1990:8 (the date of release was in August 1990). The standard is also referred to as MPR II. The standard has been adopted by the Institute of Electronic and Electrical Engineers (IEEE), a U.S. standards organization, and by the European Economic Community.

When Shopping for a Monitor

Don't just ask for a low-emissions monitor. Find out if the monitor limits specific types of emissions, and if so, which ones (particularly ELF magnetic fields). Ask if the monitor complies with MPR II. Many monitor manufacturers offer products that comply, but you'll pay a premium.

If you decide not to invest the extra money to protect against a danger that has not been fully proven, there are a few things you can do to hedge your bet: Stay at least an arm's length (28 inches) from the front of your monitor (if you're nearsighted, wear your glasses!). The electromagnetic field's strength is lessened by distance. At a distance of a few feet the emission level drops to that of a fluorescent light. Keep at least three feet away from the sides and back of a monitor; this is where the emissions are highest. (And keep in mind, this rule applies to other electronic office equipment—especially copier machines—that have high ELF emissions.) Turn off your monitor whenever you're not using it. (Just dimming the display doesn't diminish the emissions.)

When we're talking about health and monitors, let's not forget the proven health risks and stress causers—screen glare, flicker, and long-duration computer keyboard pounding. Take regular breaks, get a good chair, and make sure your lighting is adequate (ideally, use an incandescent desk lamp to reduce glare). ▪

MONITORS

Big-Screen Monitors

Large-screen monitors measure at least 19 inches diagonally. You'll find fewer and fewer 19-inch monitors, since the manufacturers are making 21-inch monitors in volume. You need at least 20 inches to produce a full 17-inch-wide image—enough to show two 8 1/2-inch sheets side by side.

Keep in mind that despite the high resolutions offered by these larger tubes, you can still end up with a surprisingly low dots-per-inch (dpi) image. If you have 1,200 pixels spread across a 17-inch line, you get a display with only about 70 dpi—roughly the same resolution as a cheap dot-matrix printer. Still, it's actually not the dpi that counts as much as the large viewing area over which those 1 or 2 million pixels are spread.

One thing to keep in mind about the large-screen monitors is that monitor packages that offer total large-display solutions are preferable to the normal component approach, because many of the generic video cards don't have the right specs for the monitor, especially if you want 1,600×1,200 resolution. Video cards are finicky about which monitors they will cooperate with, and you must carefully match the monitor to the card. Chapter 6 covers video cards in detail.

Dvorak's Recommendations

When shopping for a monitor, you might be disappointed if you purchase the cheapest model. You should buy a monitor with the ability to adapt to different scanning frequencies. The buzzwords to look for are multiscanning and multiple frequency. These will give you the most flexibility in compatibility. This type of monitor will also allow you to upgrade your video card to keep up with the newer standards as they come along. Consider what you are going to use your computer for. Obviously, if you intend to do CAD/CAM or demand high-end graphics, you won't be happy or able to function with a low-end monitor.

Keep in mind that with the right choice, your monitor can have a longer usable life than your computer. It's not unusual to purchase a monitor for one machine—say, a 486—and keep it through an upgrade to a Pentium or beyond. A versatile monitor can keep up with technological improvements.

CHAPTER

VIDEO CARDS 6

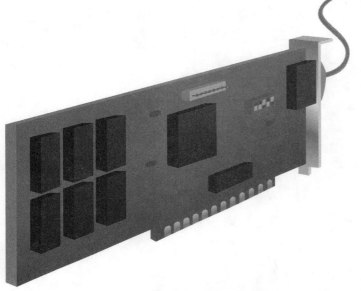

IF YOU HAVE a computer and a monitor, but no video display card, you're not going to have much luck using your machine. You must have a display adapter or video card to have any data appear on the screen. A computer seller will rarely bundle the monitor and the card as a package; they are usually purchased separately.

VIDEO CARDS

VIDEO CARDS, ADAPTER CARDS, OR ADD-IN BOARDS—whatever name you want to call them—run the gamut from an inexpensive monochrome display card (around $50) to a state-of-the-art graphics coprocessor that does everything but make coffee (with a price to make even the Department of Defense wince).

Card Basics

Add-in cards come in three basic flavors: 8-bit, 16-bit, and 32-bit. These terms refer to the number of data bits the card sends out at one time. Ideally, a 16-bit video card sends an image to the monitor in half the time it would take for an 8-bit version to do so. It's important to know what kind of card your machine accepts. The older PCs and XTs usually have an 8-bit or PC bus, which accepts only the 8-bit cards. The newer machines use a PCI bus combined with ISA (Industry Standard Architecture).

In addition to the ISA bus, there is typically an auxillary bus such as the VL-bus or the newer PCI bus, which were designed for video cards so they could operate at a faster speed. The PCI bus, though, looks as if it may become an all-purpose bus. Another bus called EISA was going to become the next industry standard but instead was used almost exclusively on servers. Some machines can still be found with the EISA bus.

An important point to remember here is that EISA is backward-compatible to ISA (an ISA card will fit into an EISA bus). ISA is backward-compatible with 8-bit cards (8-bit cards fit into ISA and EISA slots), but MCA will not work with either of the other two standards. (*Backward-compatible* means that the device works with all previous hardware technology, but it will not necessarily work with any new iterations.) In other words, if you move up to an EISA bus computer, the cards from your ISA bus computer will work in the new machine. If you move up to IBM's MCA machines, you're out of luck if you want to use your old cards. Now, the most popular bus for video cards is the PCI Bus. This was developed especially for the high-performance video cards on the market.

Many video cards manufactured today are available in AT-ISA, PCI, and VL Bus. Newer computers come equipped with either a couple of VL slots or some PCI slots. If your machine supports PCI Bus—*use it!* (See Chapter 4 for a more complete discussion of computer buses.)

Add-in cards are also described in terms of length—$^1/_2$-length, $^3/_4$-length, and full-size. This, along with the less common XT height, refers to the physical size of the card. These terms are loosely applied. There are no accepted standard sizes.

VIDEO CARDS

■ Video Terms

As you shop for a video card, you'll come across an array of terms and jargon that can make a difficult task even harder. Here's a quick guide to some of the more commonly used video terms:

- **Alpha channel**   The upper 8 bits of the 32-bit data path in some graphics adapters. The alpha channel is used by some software for controlling the color information in the lower 24 bits.

- **BitBLT (bit-block transfer)**   An operation in which the pixel data residing in one area of the frame buffer is copied directly to another area of the frame buffer, and vice versa. By performing bit-block transfers, graphics coprocessors can dramatically improve video display speeds, since a displayed object is treated as one unit rather than as many individual pixels.

- **DAC (digital-to-analog converter)**   A chip that converts the binary numbers representing particular colors to analog red, green, and blue signals that the monitor displays.

- **DRAM (dynamic RAM)**   The most commonly used type of memory, found on video boards as well as on PC system boards. DRAM is usually slower than VRAM, since it has only a single data pathway.

- **Flicker**   Describes two different effects. True flicker, where the screen seems to blink rapidly on and off, is caused by a slow refresh rate, also called low vertical frequency. This means the screen isn't rewritten quickly enough to fool the eye into seeing a steady image. The second kind of flicker, which looks more like a jiggling of horizontal lines, is caused by interlacing. To avoid both kinds of flicker you need a high vertical frequency (at least 60 Hz, but often more) and a noninterlaced video scheme—currently an expensive combination.

- **Frame buffer**   A large section of memory used to store an image to be displayed on screen, as well as parts of the image that lie outside the limits of the display.

- **Graphics coprocessor**   Similar to a math coprocessor in concept, this is a programmable chip that speeds video performance by carrying out graphics processing independently of the CPU. It can speed up performance in two ways: by taking over tasks the main processor would lose time performing and by optimizing for graphics. Video adapters with graphics coprocessors are expensive compared with those without them, but they speed up graphics operations considerably.

- **Horizontal frequency**   Measures how long it takes a monitor to draw one horizontal line across the screen. Monitors are designed and rated for one or more specific horizontal (and vertical) frequencies. Similarly, video modes are designed for specific frequencies. When you choose a graphics adapter and monitor, the frequencies of both must match. Horizontal frequencies are usually given in kHz.

- **Interlaced display**   A display created by drawing images on screen in two passes. The first pass draws the odd-numbered lines, while the second pass draws the even-numbered lines. Interlaced displays tend to flicker noticeably.

- **JPEG (Joint Photographic Experts Group)**   The image compression standard developed by an international committee of the same name. JPEG was developed to compress large, still images, such as photographs, single video frames, or scanned pictures, to reduce the amount of memory required to store them.

- **MPEG (Motion Picture Experts Group)**   An alternative compression standard to JPEG for full motion video.

Continued on next page

VIDEO CARDS

■ Video Terms

Continued from previous page

- **Noninterlaced display** The opposite of an interlaced display. All the lines are drawn in one pass rather than two. This reduces the appearance of flicker.

- **Pass-through VGA** A method of handling VGA display that passes a VGA signal from another graphics board through a cable attached to the high-resolution adapter and out to the monitor. Other methods of handling VGA include on-board VGA (where a VGA controller is mounted on the high-resolution board) and daughter-card VGA (where the VGA controller and memory reside on a small daughterboard that plugs into the high-resolution board).

- **TMS 34010** A popular graphics coprocessor from Texas Instruments and one of the leading choices for coprocessed video boards. It is only the first generation in a promised series. In fact, the second generation—the 34020—is already available on some boards.

- **Vertical frequency** Also called the refresh rate. Indicates how long it takes to draw an entire screenful of lines from top to bottom. Monitors are designed for specific vertical (and horizontal) frequencies. Vertical frequency is a key factor in image flicker. Given a low enough vertical frequency (53 Hz, for example), virtually everyone will see a flicker because the screen isn't rewritten quickly enough. A high vertical frequency (70 Hz on a 14-inch monitor) will eliminate the flicker for most people.

- **VESA (Video Electronics Standards Association)** A consortium of manufacturers formed to establish and maintain industry-wide standards for video cards and monitors. VESA is responsible for establishing the Super VGA recommendations that many manufacturers follow today.

- **VGA pass-through** A feature present on the 8514/A and some other high-resolution boards. The VGA signal literally passes through the board. The VGA signal originates on a VGA board or system board-mounted VGA system and goes to a monitor connected to the high-resolution board. This feature lets you use a single monitor for both VGA and high-resolution levels.

- **VLSI (Very Large Scale Integration)** A bunch of different chips and their functions jammed onto a single silicon chip. Over 100,000 transistors can be integrated into one, and the amazing thing is that as one chip they consume little power and can perform extremely complex functions.

- **VRAM (video RAM)** Special-purpose RAM with two data paths for access, rather than the one path in conventional RAM. The two paths let a VRAM board handle two functions at once: display refresh and processor access. VRAM doesn't force the system to wait for one function to finish before starting the other, so it permits faster operation for the video subsystem. ■

VIDEO CARDS

Graphic Display Standards and Compatibility

Not everyone needs the same resolution in a monitor. Some applications do require high resolution for a really sharp color display and crisp letters. For this you will need to purchase an expensive monitor and proprietary display adapter. Others, including most home users, can do just fine with a monochrome monitor and a plain-vanilla VGA card. The trick is to select the right video card for your monitor. There are a number of different video display schemes and standards on the market.

EGA Cards

The EGA (enhanced graphics adapter) was an IBM invention that started the migration toward higher-resolution color displays. Before the EGA, the display offerings were either monochrome or a four-color CGA (color graphics adapter) which was both crude and hard on the eyes. The EGA had a 640×350 resolution and 16 colors. The key difference, and main drawback, is that the EGA scheme was digital. The EGA, although it's still around, was never wholeheartedly accepted by the computer-buying masses. Compared to the widespread VGA, EGA cards are rare. Also, few monitors will work with an EGA video card since most monitors are analog. Although it's possible to locate a monitor which is switchable between digital and analog, the option can be pricey. For the most part, the EGA will continue to fade until it is simply a footnote in history.

VGA Cards

VGA, which stands for video graphics array, is simply a descriptive name for the circuitry used to bring the chip to life. IBM uses a large VLSI (very large scale integration) chip containing a huge number of logic gates—a "gate array" chip—to implement the video circuitry. The result is an image, in graphics mode, that is 640×480×16. In other words, there are 640 picture elements (or pixels) in every row and 480 pixels in every column, and the screen can display 16 simultaneous colors from a palette of 262,144. The difference from the EGA standard (640×350×16) may seem slight, but VGA's wider palette and sharper image produces a much more realistic and pleasing display.

With the introduction of VGA, you could still run software written for the older standards, but you couldn't use the same monitor. The only exceptions to this were multiscanning monitors, which were capable of handling the horizontal and vertical frequencies required by the new standard.

VIDEO CARDS

Super VGA

Super VGA often refers to any enhancements—such as more colors or greater resolution—that ensure VGA compatibility. The original VESA recommendation called for 800×600 resolution and 16 colors. Today manufacturers produce boards with 256 colors or higher, and may even refer to boards that offer 1,024×768 resolution as Super VGA.

The problem, however, is the astounding number of graphic display standards. The VGA standard itself incorporates 17 video modes— different methods to display an image on the monitor. Most of these provide backward compatibility to the most important of the earlier standards: the color graphics adapter (CGA), enhanced graphics adapter (EGA), and monochrome display adapter (MDA).

Even discounting the earlier standards, that leaves us with Super VGA (the nonstandard standard), IBM's 8514/A adapter for MCA machines, and IBM's new extended graphics array (XGA) standard. All of these standards deliver more colors or higher resolution than VGA. That doesn't include the adapters that make use of new continuous edge graphics (CEG) chips, which promise to put over 740,000 colors on your screen simultaneously. Even more specialized are the 1,600×1,200-resolution cards that can offer millions of colors.

Before you race out and buy any of these enhanced video adapters, keep one thought in mind: software. Most new software includes support for the standard VGA modes. With the other video cards, you can only hope the manufacturer includes drivers for the software. This is probably not a problem if you use Lotus 1-2-3, AutoCAD, Windows, or Ventura Publisher. Other than that, you'll want to make sure the manufacturer supplies the drivers you need before you buy a new card. This changes daily, so always ask if the driver is included.

Another important issue is whether the monitor you have can support the higher resolutions the card offers. If you have a CGA- or EGA-compatible monitor, chances are you'll need a new monitor to take advantage of a VGA or better video board. Older monitors used a digital interface, while the VGA specification requires an analog interface. Only the multiscanning monitors allow you to use both a digital and an analog system. But not every multiscanning monitor will work with a VGA card. The monitor must be able to work within the horizontal and vertical scanning frequencies required by the standard you intend to use. (For more information on monitors and their requirements, see Chapter 5.)

The 8514/A Card

The 8514/A card and 8514 monitor were introduced in 1987 by IBM as their high-end video hardware. The 8514/A offered 256 colors, a 640×480 resolution, and an interlaced 1,024×768 resolution with either 16 or 256

VIDEO CARDS

■ Buying a Plain-Vanilla VGA Card

Since 1990 the guts of the VGA circuitry have been incorporated into various VLSI chips, and the cards are now inexpensively made by most board makers. Dozens of them are cranked out in Taiwan. A plain VGA card costs less than $100. Many of the newest computer systems actually incorporate the VGA circuitry on the machine's motherboard. This will become more and more common in future systems. Each time a new VLSI chip is released, these cards are redesigned. This makes testing the cards impractical.

Unfortunately, few low-end VGA cards or on-board systems are completely compatible with the original specification. This basic problem still exists with many of the newest, most inexpensive VGA cards. I recommend testing your favorite applications and demo programs on a card before buying it. Make sure you are offered a money-back guarantee when you do buy one. By the time all the cards discussed are perfectly compatible, XGA will be old-hat, and we'll have a new scheme. Meanwhile, we have to live with this situation. ■

colors. Technically, 8514/A refers to the card and 8514 refers to the monitor, but the "/A" is often dropped when discussing the card. IBM is clearly aiming to replace the 8514/A standard with XGA in the Micro Channel world. Still, 8514-compatible boards may survive for some time on the ISA bus.

XGA Cards

XGA is IBM's latest high-resolution video scheme. XGA was introduced along with the PS/2 Models 90 and 95, and it puts 8514-level and VGA-level resolutions on the same board. The current IBM implementation is interlaced, but the specification does include support for noninterlaced modes. The XGA is expected to become the next standard and should be considered as boards are announced.

Super VGA (SVGA) for Windows

Until recently you probably have not given much thought to your graphics adapter. Whatever card came in your PC is probably the one you are using today. After all, it ran fine under DOS. But if you have moved into the Microsoft Windows arena, you need a faster board to get around the new graphics-intensive neighborhood.

But choosing the best video card for Windows is more complicated than simply shopping for the best price. Today's Super VGA marketplace is filled with tantalizing possibilities. It's all very exciting, but it is also confusing. Is the right video controller a frame buffer, a graphics accelerator board, or a coprocessor board? Is one chip set faster than the rest? Let's try to answer these questions.

VIDEO CARDS

The VL Bus

If you use any graphical application (including Windows and OS/2), you may want to buy a video card that runs on the local (VL) bus. This card is fast and modern, but requires a VL-bus slot in your computer.

Look for a 72 Hz vertical refresh rate. The *refresh rate* refers to the number of times the screen is redrawn each second. The higher the rate, the less flicker you will see. For Super VGA modes, VESA has defined 72 Hz as its official standard vertical refresh rate. It has also defined 56 and 60 Hz as its manufacturer's guidelines (VGA has a vertical refresh rate of 60 or 70 Hz).

The reason VESA chose 72 Hz—not 75 Hz or any other number—is because the same video bandwidth produces a 1,024×768-pixel mode at 60 Hz.

Get 1Mb of display memory. For a 1,024×768 resolution with 256 colors, you need 1Mb (actually, you need only 786,432 bytes, but since memory doesn't come in that configuration, look for 1Mb). With 512K you can go to only 16 colors in the high-resolution mode. Most 512K boards cannot handle the 72 Hz Super VGA refresh rate.

Weigh price against performance carefully. Super VGA boards are getting cheaper all the time. DRAM boards are less expensive than VRAM, but the latter is faster.

Faster, Faster

You can speed up Microsoft Windows either with software or hardware. The software approach means writing a driver that is optimized for the environment. Microsoft has recently begun to emphasize the role that hardware can play. To get the best video performance under Windows, buy a board with a fully programmable graphics coprocessor. A graphics coprocessor offers two advantages: It is specifically designed for video functions, and it lightens your CPU's workload. In most resolutions/color combinations, coprocessed boards outperform frame buffers (which have no built-in intelligence). The only downside to coprocessed boards is the price—they are expensive.

Graphics accelerator chips, which contain specific Windows functions such as bitBLTs, area filling, and line drawing, also promise performance gains.

PRINTERS

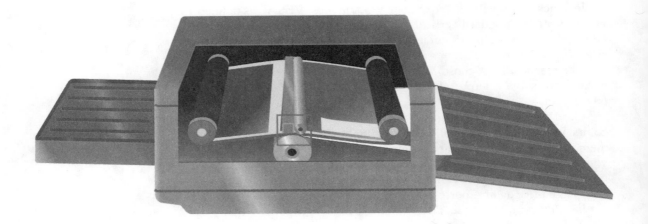

PRINTERS ARE HIGH on new computer users' wish lists. Long before modems or speed-up cards or even a new desk, new computer owners want a printer. With a printer you can show people what you've done. You can print letters and memos, charts and spreadsheets, mailing labels for Christmas cards, and much more.

PRINTERS

PRINTERS COME IN A WIDE VARIETY: plain laser, dot-matrix, color dot-matrix, ink-jet, color ink-jet, color laser, and PostScript laser printers —not to mention the tangle of fonts, drivers, and printer supplies. Beyond the standard array of printer choices, you'll also find some less desirable options, such as thermal-paper and daisy-wheel printers. The printer you choose will depend upon your needs and your pocketbook.

Print quality will ultimately affect your buying decision. Look for a consistent, deep black print with little or no white showing through. For simple home uses, a modest dot-matrix printer will suffice, but if you want to print graphics and other high-quality, "wow" output, then consider one of the laser printers.

Laser Printers

The laser printer (also called a page printer) is the printer everyone wants to own. It produces high-quality output quickly and uses regular, single sheet paper. It's quiet, too.

The new standard for laser printers is 600-by-600 dpi (dots per inch). The number of pages produced ranges from 4 to 15 ppm (pages per minute), with 8 being the typical speed.

Font Formats

When you begin your search for a laser printer, you will find that there are a few different font and page imaging technologies. The three formats are PCL (Printer Control Language), PostScript, and TrueType. Unless you're in a mixed Macintosh/PC enviroment, the combination of PCL and TrueType is all that most PC users will ever need. PCL 5, a recent release, has two major advantages over other font formats on the market—it's less costly and the print quality is excellent. Those with specialized needs, such as proofing documents that will go to a Linotronic device, imagesetter, or regular offset print shop will probably need to use PostScript. Advanced users and OS/2 users should also consider a PostScript printer.

How a Laser Printer Works

The printer is more accurately called *electrophotographic*. An image is made by a beam of light (hence the term *laser*) focused on a photoconductive drum which is uniformly electrically charged over its surface. The light beam causes a localized conductivity, in the pattern of the light beam, on the drum's surface. The charged pattern attracts pigment—the toner particles. (The background repels the toner particles.) The image is then transferred to the paper by pressing the paper against the drum. The toner particles are fixed to the paper by intense heat and pressure. The technology is very similar to that used in office copiers. For a close-up of how a laser printer works, see Figure 7.1.

PRINTERS

■ Figure 7.1 How a laser printer works

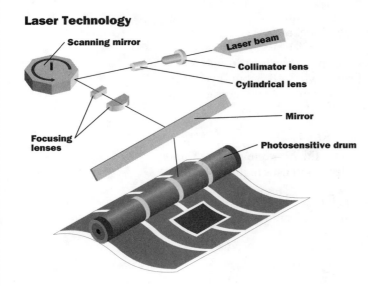

Laser Technology

- Scanning mirror
- Laser beam
- Collimator lens
- Cylindrical lens
- Mirror
- Focusing lenses
- Photosensitive drum

In a typical laser printer, a single laser beam is focused on a rotating polygon mirror. As the mirror spins, the beam is deflected through a focusing lens and scans across the rotating drum, which accepts the image line by line.

Laser Printer History

In 1984, PC Labs tested one laser printer for the annual *PC Magazine* printer issue. Not surprisingly, it was the Hewlett-Packard LaserJet. This was the printer that broke the dam and opened desktop computing to the superb quality and silent operation of laser printing. The only other page printer reviewed that year was the soon-to-be forgotten Diablo EPM-1 thermal transfer printer. Daisy-wheel printers, which ruled the letter-quality printing roost, were doomed once the laser printer appeared.

People didn't expect lasers to be hooked up to individual PCs when the LaserJet was introduced. At $3,495 plus font cartridges, it cost as much as or more than most PC configurations, and besides, not much software existed to support the then new PCL codes embodied in the Canon-made engine's driver. Local area networks seemed a more logical target for these expensive but speedy and quiet machines. Wrong: People prefer their own printer and will pay extra for the privilege if they have to.

The LaserJet took off like a shot. Office workers were tired of the hammering daisy-wheel printers and whining dot-matrix printers. The

PRINTERS

LaserJet's price didn't seem much to pay for a little peace and quiet and a lot of speed. The drawback? The inconveniences of the early LaserJet.

For example, the original Canon engine had space for only 100 sheets of paper in its input bin and output tray. In response, sheet feeders that could handle large capacities, multiple bins of paper, and even envelopes began showing up early in the laser game. Some units came with collators that could assemble multiple copies of reports into the correct page sequence (the original LaserJet couldn't assemble even one copy into its correct sequence); some even put letters together with their properly addressed envelopes.

Printer-sharing devices began to be touted as low-cost (non-LAN) answers to the high cost of laser printing. Many of them came with print-queuing and spooling capabilities that put mainframe operating systems to shame.

Software incompatibility provided a wide playing field for innovators. Third-party utilities that magically transformed output designed for other printers into LaserJet format started popping up everywhere. Third-party vendors also produced LaserJet printer drivers compatible with popular software products, especially word processors and spreadsheets.

Similar fixes and patches became available both in user groups and on bulletin boards, where the price certainly was right. PC add-on cards appeared, and they too worked magic by transforming the LaserJet into something else. Boards that replaced the LaserJet's controller also came on the scene. Unfortunately, the LaserJet sometimes was transformed into something equally foreign to your software.

Software vendors were likewise excited by the new laser technology, and sooner than many people expected, word processing and graphics vendors caught up with the LaserJet and began to ship compatible products, as well as fixes for existing products. That meant the LaserJet had come of age, and users could rely on supported compatibility from original software vendors rather than add-on products.

As software support spread, LaserJet clones came along, stiffening the competition for Hewlett-Packard. The challenge was quickly met by the LaserJet Plus, which accommodated more memory for graphics and downloadable fonts to replace or supplement the company's expensive font cartridges.

The clones kept coming anyway. Most met the capabilities of the LaserJet Plus, and many added more features. Some of them offered more memory and a better selection of fonts, while others increased paper capacity and even envelope handling. Still others had faster print engines and alternative printer emulations so the printer could be used with software that still didn't support the LaserJet. And many of those capabilities were offered at a lower price.

PRINTERS

Getting the Most Out of Your Laser Printer

If your laser printer has ceased to amaze you, maybe it's time to push its limits. You can buy enhancement boards which plug into your computer to improve the quality of your laser's text and graphics. And while these boards add new features and capabilities to your printer, they take nothing away from the functions it already provides. Most of them will work on any printer built around a Canon laser engine. You can even add PostScript to your laser printer.

What Is PostScript?   PostScript is generally acknowledged to be the most versatile page description language (PDL) available, and it has set the standard for desktop publishing and many graphics applications.

Although the Hewlett-Packard LaserJet line of printers can handle the majority of desktop publishing tasks of a typical business, PCL (the LaserJet's native Printer Control Language) has its limitations. There are certainly occasions that call for PostScript. If you find that your business needs PostScript, don't chuck your LaserJet and start over with a new printer. There are a number of solutions—both hardware and software-based—to bring PostScript to your LaserJet. For example, a few products now can even turn a LaserJet into a PostScript printer.

Adding PostScript to a Laser Printer   Most of the add-ins are composed of the same components: a board that you install in an unused expansion slot in your computer, another smaller board that fits into the expansion slot on your printer, a custom cable that connects these two cards, and special software drivers that allow them to work together. Some packages use genuine PostScript (licensed from Adobe Systems, the developer of the page description language). Other manufacturers use clone products. These clones do well overall with only minor incompatibilities.

PostScript capabilities can be added to your laser printer by using add-on boards, emulation software, or emulation cartridges. Add-in products may differ significantly in their operation, depending on how the PostScript code is treated. Most of the systems can be configured to take over one of your DOS printer ports (LPT1 through LPT3) to allow for direct use by any application that can send a stream of PostScript code to a printer. Another, less convenient approach is to print your PostScript code to a disk file. It's processed by a separate PostScript interpreter program to produce a printed page. For the most part, these boards are fast.

Printer Enhancement Boards   By far the best thing you can do to a page printer is to attach it to a printer enhancement board. With an enhancement board, text resolution can be improved almost to the quality

PRINTERS

Color Laser Printers

A color laser printer is similar to a regular laser printer, except that within the device are multiple drums (cyan, magenta, yellow, and black—CMYK) used to print the various colors. These printers are extremely expensive, starting at $5,000—and up, which prohibits their entry into the general business or personal market. A common mistake in the general marketplace is to call any color page printer a color laser printer. This is inaccurate, as few color printers use laser technology. ∎

of low-end typesetters. Unfortunately, most of the boards cannot increase the resolution of 300-dpi laser printers. Although most do not change the text print speed, graphics printing can be up to ten times faster. Enhancement boards come with their own printer drivers and scalable fonts that are usually compatible with PostScript printers. These enhancement boards can be costly, however, which might be their only drawback.

The add-in boards have a custom connection between the computer and the printer. The standard parallel or serial port connection is still in place. This means that the printer can still be used as a LaserJet without the PostScript.

These boards work by processing the regular LaserJet commands faster than the printer's controller. These products also give you features beyond the scope of PCL and support high-speed output from desktop publishing programs through proprietary drivers.

In either case, although you won't be able to print from the same PostScript files your large typesetting machine uses, you should be able to print desktop publishing or presentation graphics pages much faster than with an unmodified LaserJet.

Some of the boards do not work with network servers, and those that do can be limited in the types of networks they support. The nonstandard cables these products use may also create a problem. They may not be able to hook into a printer switchbox.

Emulation Software   But you don't have to buy an add-in board to print PostScript pages on a non-PostScript page printer. You can simply buy emulation software packages—if you have 1.5Mb of extended memory to spare. They work by printing PostScript files to a disk and then using the software to send the files to the printer.

Emulation Cartridges   These cartridges are another way to add PostScript to your laser printer. An emulation cartridge plugs into an open, external slot (normally for fonts) on a laser printer. The cartridge makes the laser printer behave like a PostScript printer. Hewlett-Packard

PRINTERS

◼ Heat Fusion Printers

Heat fusion technology is a relatively new offering in the printer market. It has the pluses of the ink jet, but eliminates the ink jet's tendency to smear (especially on certain kinds of paper). Instead of squirting droplets of ink that soak into the paper, the heat fusion printers use a polyester-resin-dye-impregnated ribbon. This polyester-resin dye is fused to the paper surface with heat (much like the way a thermal transfer printer such as a low-end fax machine works). These ribbons are very similar to a typewriter or dot-matrix printer ribbon, and are contained within cartridges. The print result is a very sharp, clear, and well-defined image with no bleeding.

These printers are slightly more expensive than regular ink jets, but they're certainly more cost-effective than laser printers (especially color laser printers). But color output may take significantly longer, and requires a frequent change of ribbons.

Currently, only a few manufacturers employ this technology. ◼

sells a cartridge such as this to answer the PostScript problem. It's not the best solution, but it is one solution.

Color Page Printers

Color printing is a rapidly evolving scene. Until recently, the market was populated with expensive high-quality devices and cheap dot-matrix and ink-jet machines, but very little in the middle.

At the low end, the best ink-jet printers can print on plain paper or overhead film at 300 dots per inch (dpi), making them a good choice for producing business graphics and charts. But the limited range of seven to eight colors offered by ink-jet technology makes them less suitable for the reproduction of complex, continuous-tone images such as scanned photographs. Another drawback of the ink jet is the tendency of the ink to soak into the paper and spread slightly, resulting in a loss of definition. Many manufacturers recommend the use of high-quality coated paper for best results (although coated paper may cause the ink to smear). Even so, the overall cost per page makes the ink jet the most cost-effective choice for business presentations.

The difference is minor between the "workings" of an ink-jet printer that can print color and one that prints only black. The printer's "intelligence" is the main distinction, along with the different ink cartridges loaded into the machine. For a close-up of how an ink-jet printer works, refer ahead to Figure 7.5.

Thermal Wax Transfer

The higher end of the market—for high-quality graphics applications—was, until recently, dominated by *thermal wax transfer* printers (see Figure

PRINTERS

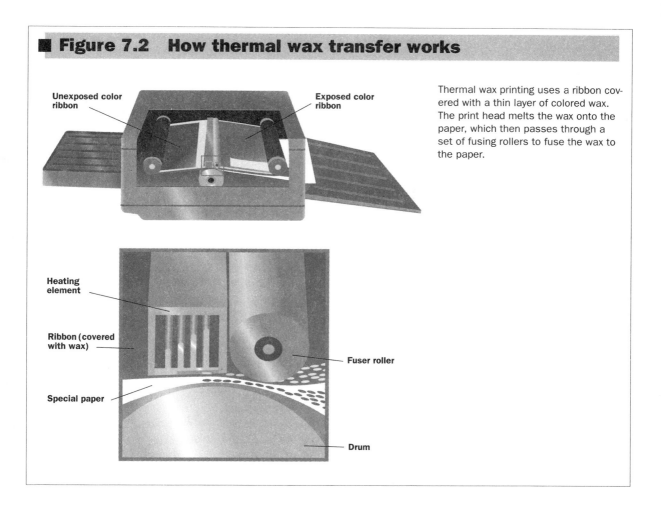

■ Figure 7.2   How thermal wax transfer works

Unexposed color ribbon

Exposed color ribbon

Thermal wax printing uses a ribbon covered with a thin layer of colored wax. The print head melts the wax onto the paper, which then passes through a set of fusing rollers to fuse the wax to the paper.

Heating element

Ribbon (covered with wax)

Special paper

Fuser roller

Drum

7.2). These machines use colored wax on a backing sheet that is melted by heating elements and deposited in small droplets onto paper. A resolution of 300 dpi is common with these printers, and though only the four process colors of wax are used—cyan, magenta, yellow, and black (CMYK)— a technique called dithering overlaps different colored dots of wax to give a much wider range of colors.

Thermal wax transfer technology was dominant in early color printers. Prices have dropped significantly since their emergence in the very early 1990s. Competition among manufacturers has brought down the prices somewhat—although for professionals the quality is as important as the price. In addition, thermal wax printers normally use paper with a special coating designed to hold the wax drops. This makes the per-page cost

PRINTERS

New Technology

Last year Tektronix introduced a printer called the Phaser 340. It's a thermal wax color printer that uses technology similar to that used in photo off-set lithography printing presses. It uses four *crayon-style* solid wax ink sticks (in cyan, magenta, yellow, and black) and four ink-jets which melt and squirt the ink. The ink is deposited, not on the paper, but on a rotating drum for transfer to paper. This technique speeds up the printing process and

reduces costs while producing a stunning image. A typical page of color graphics takes about 45 seconds to print. The output resolution is 300 dpi and users are able to employ a variety of halftone settings. The Phaser 340 can also print transparencies. It uses Adobe PostScript Level 2, as well as PCL 5 and HPGL emulations. There are parallel and Ethernet interfaces and a SCSI port for fonts. The printer was introduced at just under $5,000. ■

high. And while output quality is higher than that of ink-jet printers, the inability of most wax transfer printers to use plain paper limits their use for creating reports or other types of documents that need to be presented on plain paper. (A graph or chart printed on the thick coated paper is distracting in a business report.) They do, however, produce very good results on overhead film.

Dye-Transfer

Even better results can be obtained by using a technology called *dye-transfer* or *dye-sublimation* (see Figure 7.3). This process has become more popular since the technology has matured and the price has fallen. Superficially similar to thermal wax, it uses a ribbon coated with colored dyes rather than the wax pigments used in thermal wax printers. These printers also use a special paper that reacts to the dyes and can produce results akin to photographic images. Print speed is slow—even a simple image can take several minutes to print—but the composition of the dyes and the printer's ability to deposit precise amounts allow the printer very close control over the amount of each color used, producing much better results for continuous-tone images.

As a result, dye-transfer printers have carved out a niche in the professional publishing and graphics market. But their high initial cost and their need for special paper makes the price per page costly. Because of this, dye-transfer printers have not made a major impact on the mainstream business market.

Mass-Market Color Printers   The color printer market is changing rapidly. Hewlett-Packard has driven ink-jet technology forward by improving speed and print quality while using its mass-market expertise and mass-production techniques to keep prices low. At the same time,

PRINTERS

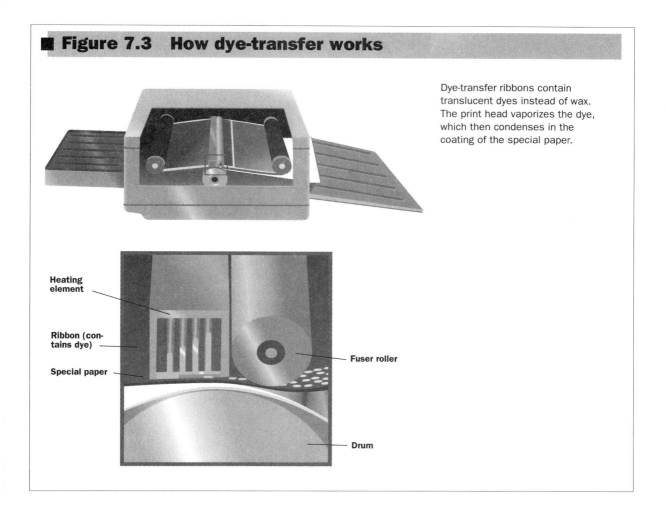

■ Figure 7.3   How dye-transfer works

Dye-transfer ribbons contain translucent dyes instead of wax. The print head vaporizes the dye, which then condenses in the coating of the special paper.

Heating element

Ribbon (contains dye)

Special paper

Fuser roller

Drum

thermal wax and dye-transfer printers have begun to change from complicated devices needing constant attention into reliable products that can be used by nonspecialists. Manufacturers, with one eye firmly on the bottom line of the booming ink-jet market, have brought prices down. (The prices are close to half of what they were when the printers were first introduced.)

The different technologies are converging in terms of price and quality, and a large middle market is emerging where high-quality ink jets will compete with thermal wax and dye-transfer printers.

Other factors have driven the ascendancy of the color printers. Windows has been a big influence. It has attracted powerful desktop publishing and

PRINTERS

graphics applications such as QuarkXPress and Adobe Photoshop to the PC from the Macintosh, opening up the PC's graphics potential to a wider user base than before. To keep up with the greater sophistication of Windows graphics software, both Hewlett-Packard and the IBM subsidiary Lexmark have made further innovations by producing their first PostScript-compatible ink-jet printers—the HP DeskJet 1200C and the Lexmark IBM JetPrinter PS4079. These PostScript printers output onto plain paper and produce higher-quality continuous-tone images than was previously possible with ink-jet technology.

Other major players are Tektronix and Dataproducts, which make printers that use a solid wax technology. The solid wax process is a variation on the thermal wax process that can, in theory, offer the best of both worlds—high-quality color output on plain paper. However, as with dye-transfer a year or so ago, it's too early to predict whether this promising technology will find a wide market. Table 7.1 outlines the pros and cons of the four major printer categories.

Dot-Matrix Printers

A dot-matrix printer is one of the simplest, most rugged, and most serviceable machines in the computer industry. It consists of a plastic case containing only three or four moving parts and a small computer that communicates with your PC and controls the printing mechanism at the behest of the PC's commands. Dot-matrix printers are workhorses. They perform their job very well. Dot-matrix printers have one real advantage over all the other kinds of printers. They can print on almost any kind of paper, including multipart forms and very wide papers. It's a sensible choice if you need a real low-maintenance, high-volume workhorse.

The dot-matrix market has broken itself into three distinct segments. The extremely high-volume models (for corporations, banks, billing, and so on) demand prices in the $10,000 range; the high-volume models (for businesses with high output demands) have prices close to $1,000; and the personal models sell for under $250.

The inexpensive, lightweight personal models are just as durable and versatile as their bigger counterparts. The 24-pin personal desktop printers have far overshadowed the 9-pin models, and many have color capabilities.

How a Dot-Matrix Printer Works

A dot-matrix printer creates each character from an array of dots. The basic printing mechanism of a dot-matrix printer is simple: A print head houses one or more vertical rows of tiny metal rods called pins, and each pin is carefully positioned in a tube-like track (see Figure 7.4). The pins are held back from the ribbon and paper by springs. When a pin's electromagnet is charged, the magnet forces the pin into the ribbon,

PRINTERS

■ Table 7.1 Print Technologies: How to Decide

These comments apply to most printers within each category; some will fall outside. High-end color ink-jet printers such as the HP DeskJet 1200C should also be considered color printers. The cost per page does not include paper cost (which normally runs about a penny a sheet). The speeds of laser and dot-matrix printers are not directly comparable, but a rough rule of thumb is that 1 page per minute (ppm) from a laser printer equals 30 characters per second (cps) printing a full page of double-spaced text, or 60 cps printing single-spaced text.

	Dot Matrix	Ink Jet	Personal Laser	Color
Pros	Inexpensive, with low-cost output. Can handle multipart forms and wide paper.	Quiet, compact, inexpensive. $150 to $200 less than the cheapest laser. Some print up to 17 by 22 inches.	High print quality, very quiet. Under-$500 prices for basic models, meaning you can have one on every desktop.	High-quality color output at high resolutions. Ideal for business graphics. Output can sometimes approximate color photographs.
Cons	Noisy. Average print quality; graphics show banding. Few built-in fonts.	High per-page costs. Occasional streaking and smudging.	Significantly higher per-page cost than with dot-matrix printers.	Bulky, extremely slow. High hardware and per-page costs. Output not quite photographic quality.
Speed	Personal models, 25 to 200 cps; forms printers, to 300 cps. Printing in quality mode reduces speed.	30 to 100 cps. Quality-mode speed decrease is less than that of dot matrix.	Personal models, 4 to 6 ppm; desktop models, 6 to 10 ppm. Need RISC processors for fast graphics performance.	Usually 1 ppm or slower.
Cost	Personal models, $100 to $500; heavy-duty models, $500 to $2,000; line printer emulators, $5,000 to $10,000.	Monochrome and portable models, $275 to $500; color models, $600 and up. Prices are falling fast.	Personal models, $500 to $1,500; desktop models, $1,500 to $3,000. PostScript adds $200 to $500.	Ink-jet models, $600 to $3,500; thermal wax, thermal dye, solid-ink models, $3,000 to $10,000.
Cost per page	Under 1 cent.	4 to 8 cents (some as low as 2 cents).	1 to 5 cents (3 cents is typical).	$0.50 to $1.00 (thermal dye is more expensive).
Output quality	24-pin quality mode, moderately good; 9-pin mode, fair. Quality falls off as ribbon ages.	Almost laser quality.	Excellent text, good graphics. Many offer 600-dpi resolution and resolution enhancement.	Vibrant ink-jet and thermal wax output, saturated thermal dye output. May have trouble printing fine lines.
Color	Inexpensive upgrade or special version.	Some models.	Not available.	Standard.
Noise	Loud; slow in quiet mode.	Virtually silent.	Quiet.	Quiet.
Size	Narrow-carriage models fit easily on desktop. Some small enough to take on the road.	Very small, except for some models with horizontal paper trays.	4- to 6-ppm models, footprint slightly larger than letter-size paper. 8–12-ppm models may be too large for desktops. Internal paper trays reduce footprint.	Very bulky and can overwhelm a small office.
Paper	Tractor-feed or continuous multipart forms, cut sheets.	Cut sheets, overhead transparencies, labels, envelopes. Porous stock not recommended.	Cut sheets, overhead transparencies, labels, envelopes.	Best results on coated stock or transparencies.
Common options	Cut-sheet feeder, color upgrade. Mylar ("carbon") single-strike ribbon.	None.	Second paper cassette, envelope feeder, duplexer, PostScript.	Network interfaces.
Energy efficiency	Naturally efficient.	Most energy-efficient printing technology.	Some meet Energy Star spec (under 30 watts when idle). Others use 30 to 100 watts.	Typically idle at about 50 watts. Power-saving modes rare.

PRINTERS

■ Figure 7.4 Dot-matrix printer engine

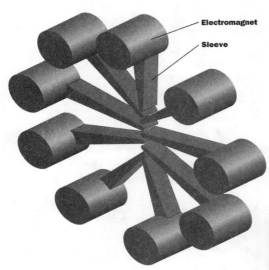

Electromagnet

Sleeve

The 9-pin dot-matrix heads usually arrange all nine pins in a single vertical column, while 24-pin heads usually have three offset columns of eight pins each. In order to fit all of these pins in close proximity, the magnets are often arranged in a radial pattern. To put a dot on a page, a dot-matrix printer sends a pulse of current through the electromagnetic coils, making the pin shoot forward. The pin strikes the paper through the inked ribbon and transfers the ink to the paper. A spring quickly retracts the pin so that it is ready to fire again.

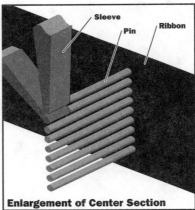

Sleeve   Pin   Ribbon

Enlargement of Center Section

coloring a spot on the paper positioned between the printer's platen and the ribbon, then the spring retracts the pin to its original position.

Pins are typically arranged in a single vertical row in 7- or 9-pin print heads; 18-pin models have two rows of nine pins, while 24-pin models have three vertical rows of eight pins each, usually arranged in a staggered pattern. The basic pin action is the same regardless of the number of pins in the print head. The 24-pin models are the most popular in today's market.

The print head is mounted on a track so it can slide back and forth across the paper surface. The pins form characters on the paper by

PRINTERS

■ Some Dot-Matrix Printing Terms

- **Burst**   To separate track paper at the perforations to make standard-sized pieces of paper.

- **Paper-parking device**   A mechanism that allows you to print on a single sheet while fanfold paper is still loaded in the printer. Instead of taking out the track paper, feeding in a single sheet, and then reloading the track paper, you use the paper-parking device. It moves the track paper out of the way (with the press of a button), and you can feed in a single sheet. Once you're done, the printer will move the track paper back into place.

- **Sheet feeder**   An optional piece of hardware that enables a dot-matrix printer to use multiple single sheets of paper. Most printers will let you use a single sheet of paper, but you must feed

each sheet in—one after another—much like a manual typewriter. The sheet feeder automates the process.

- **Tractor-feed paper**   Also called computer paper, fanfold paper, tractor paper, or simply track paper. The paper is in one long sheet, and perforations divide it into standard-sized sheets. Tractor-feed paper has a gutter along the edges in which regularly spaced holes appear. This gutter may be easily detached. The holes fit onto a pair of sprockets in the printer. The sprockets pull the paper through the printing mechanism.

- **Zero tear-off**   The printer advances the track paper so finished output can be removed, and then backs up the paper to begin printing the next job at the top of the page. ■

coloring an appropriate pattern of dots within a character box of horizontal and vertical dot positions in a rectangular or matrix pattern. The number of positions in the character box depends on the resolution of the printer. For better quality printing, the print head may pass over the character a number of times, each time filling in gaps between the dots. Lower-quality printing often has voids and scalloped edges, and occasionally the dots can be detected.

Tractor-feed Paper   When you print with a dot-matrix printer, most of the time you will use tractor-feed paper. Tractor-feed (or continuous-feed) paper has vertical holes on both sides of the page. These holes fit onto sprockets on the printer roller, which pull the paper through. The paper is perforated to make 8½-by-11-inch sheets. The part of the paper that has the holes is also perforated so it can be easily detached—the paper looks like "real" paper when it's "burst apart" (separated).

This paper tractor-feed device was invented for the mainframe environment. Mainframe computers crank out zillions upon zillions of bank statements, bills, and itemized reports and need a surefire way to feed paper through the printers with a minimum of paper jams.

Tractor-feed paper can be purchased by the box, which can be economical. A number of stationery stores have "home office" tractor-feed

PRINTERS

paper packages available. These aren't as economical as commercial packaging, but they are available in a greater variety than commercial paper. They include high-quality, colored papers and tractor-feed envelopes, as well as traditional white paper. Tractor-feed forms, labels, checks, and other specialty products are also available through stationery stores and mail-order houses.

Tractor-feed paper sometimes misfeeds when it is run through the printer. This is usually caused by the stack of unprinted-on paper behind the printer. If the printer cable is in the way or if the paper isn't in line with the printer, the paper will pull to one side and jam in the printer.

Tractor-feed paper is hardy. It isn't affected by the environment as much as laser printer paper is. It won't go bad over time, so you can buy it in bulk to save money. As long as it's kept dry and stored indoors, it shouldn't have any problems running through your printer. As a matter of fact, I've had a box of tractor-feed paper for about ten years. It sits in a storage room, and when I need a handful I get some. It's fine.

Improvements in Dot-Matrix Printers   Paper handling, once the bane of every printer user, has been redesigned. It's much easier to load paper on the newer dot-matrix printers. Paper can be loaded from the front, back, or bottom, depending on the printer. There's even automatic paper loading; just stick the end of the tractor-feed paper into a slot and press a button—the printer takes care of the rest. Some have an output tray that holds the printed paper away from the paper being fed into the printer (to avoid those ferocious paper jams).

A sheet feeder can be attached to the newer dot-matrix printers to allow single-sheet printing. Some printers allow multiple bins for distinctive second sheets or even envelopes. This is a wonderful add-on if you've never liked the ragged-edge look of bursted, perforated, fanfold, tractor-feed computer paper. Even the high-cost paper still has the telltale fuzzy edges.

Dot-matrix printers are also quieter than they used to be. The head and traveler mechanisms which move them are now designed to run more smoothly, constructed of better materials, and assembled with greater emphasis on quality. Printers that aren't quieted by mechanical means are soundproofed. Other advances include easy-to-lift-off covers that stay put when you replace them, custom-built stands, and simple operating panels and switches.

Color printing, which used to require a special printer, is now just another feature requiring only a special ribbon. Mylar ribbon is commonplace; it enhances the output quality of matrix printers, especially the 24-pin models.

Many of these improvements are included with the printer, while others must be bought separately. The ones you choose will depend on your needs. A sheet feeder is worth paying for if your correspondence

PRINTERS

must be on the company letterhead. Add-on features must be weighed—cost versus benefit. With printers, as with all purchases, it's best to shop around and familiarize yourself with all the available options. One printer will stand out as the best choice for you.

Color Dot-Matrix Printers

Color printing with dot-matrix printers includes the production of business graphs and charts as well as hard-copy presentation materials such as text charts with clip art, and it can also be used to create colorful overhead transparencies.

Another valuable use for color dot-matrix printing is in the creation of drafts of output that will later be generated by a color page printer. Although color page printers have dropped in price, they are still significantly more expensive than a color dot-matrix printer.

Two factors should affect your buying decision: print quality and color-control command set compatibility. High-quality color printout should have clear color differentiation, deep, saturated colors with little or no white showing through, and true colors rather than off-shades.

The color-control command set is a group of instructions that allows for communication between the software and the printer. The software's print drivers and the printer's internal command set must be compatible. If they aren't, you'll end up with screwball colors in strange and inappropriate places.

Your color printer may produce gorgeous images, but if the printer doesn't have a common color-printer compatibility, your application software is less likely to have printer drivers able to take advantage of the printer's capabilities. The major color-control command sets are for Epson and IBM color printers.

Don't expect color printing to be fast, especially if the print head has to make more than one pass to blend the colors.

Some mono-color dot-matrix printers can be modified to add color-print capability. This is surprisingly inexpensive. The necessary four-color ribbons of black, yellow, red, and blue bands allow the printer to blend dots to produce up to seven different colors. These ribbons cost two to three times as much as black fabric ribbons—more expensive, but not an intimidating premium.

If you use color only occasionally, it's a good idea to use a black ribbon and swap it for a four-color ribbon when you need the color. The color portions of ribbons dry out, which results in faded shades. To prevent this, store the color ribbons in a plastic bag when not in use.

PRINTERS

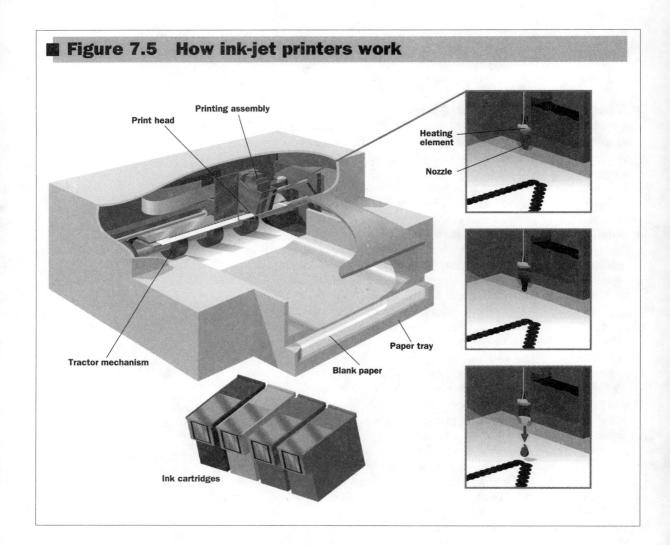

■ **Figure 7.5   How ink-jet printers work**

Print head

Printing assembly

Heating element

Nozzle

Tractor mechanism

Paper tray

Blank paper

Ink cartridges

Ink-jet Printers

An ink-jet printer (see Figure 7.5) forms letters and graphics by projecting squirts of ink onto the paper. The technology is very similar to the dot matrix, except there isn't any contact with the paper (no pins striking the paper), so the image looks smoother. The resolution is much finer than that of a dot-matrix printer, and the quality can approach that of a laser printer.

Ink jets aren't a new technology; they have been in use for many years in the data-processing industry (since the 1960s) in a number of

PRINTERS

different devices. In 1976, IBM's 6640 ink-jet printer became a popular, reliable device which enjoyed widespread use.

One of two types of technological designs is employed in ink jets: pulsing jet and continuous stream.

The first is when the ink is sprayed in a pulsing jet. There may be one or more of these jets mounted in the print head (usually more than one). Each jet ejects a single squirt at the page. Characters are printed as a matrix array, much like a dot-matrix printer. Print speeds may be as great as 400 characters per second. Printers with a greater number of jets offer a higher resolution and a crisper, more even print quality.

The second design is a print head with a single jet, which shoots out in a continuous stream at a constant velocity. The characters are made as the ink shoots out of the jet and is passed through electrode plates. These plates alter the jet of ink, deflecting it in the necessary direction towards the paper (much like placing your thumb over the end of a hose to change the spray pattern of the water). This is a slower process, printing up to 100 characters per second.

The ink jet is finding most of its popularity in portable printer applications, as well as in home "desktop" use. The printers are lightweight and small. They produce very good print quality for a relatively low price. Most of the ink-jet printers, however, are not suitable for high volume use, and a number of the lower-priced printers on the market require you to hand-feed sheets of paper into the printer—a drawback for multiple pages and/or high volume. In addition, ink cartridges are expensive (around $20) and tend to run out pretty quickly. But if you want quality approaching that of a laser printer for a low price, these ink jets are an excellent choice.

Other Printers

When shopping for a printer, you will most likely buy an ink-jet or laser printer. However, there are a couple other types of printers you should be aware of.

Thermal Paper Printers

Thermal paper printers require a special kind of a paper that is sensitive to heat. The paper has a thermosensitive coating made up of two different colorless chemicals. When heated, one of the chemicals melts and combines with the second chemical to make a visible mark. (Many facsimile machines use thermal paper technology.)

Thermal paper printers are quiet and inexpensive, but are slow and have a very limited ability to print graphics. The print quality has a cheap, fuzzy look. Another significant drawback is that thermal paper tends to fade over time or if it's left in direct sunlight.

PRINTERS

Daisy-wheel Printers

Daisy-wheel printers were one of the early computer peripherals. Introduced by Diablo Systems in 1972, they had a whopping speed of 30 cps (characters per second). At their introduction, they were an impressive improvement over the low-speed typewriter-based printers in use. (Some of these were actually typewriters with special adapters and could be used either with a computer or manually.)

The main component of the daisy-wheel printer is the print device, a spoked wheel with each spoke ending in a character or number (a variation of and improvement over the old IBM Selectric "golf ball"). To change fonts, you remove the wheel and replace it with a different one.

The daisy-wheels went through a number of improvements. Speeds eventually rose to 65 cps. They produced a crisp, good-quality typewriter-style print, but were unable to print graphics or on envelopes or single sheets of paper.

Daisy-wheel printers once were one of the best choices for home printing needs, but they have limitations that have been overcome by the newer printers. The ink-jet printer is a better choice for basic printing needs.

Portable Printers

If you travel, the advantage of a portable printer is either obvious or it's not. If you're a salesperson, the ability to print out a job bid or contract can instantly close the sale.

A portable printer is light enough to bring along with you on the road. But the weight in the portable category can range from 2.5 pounds to a barely luggable 8.5 pounds, with most in the 5- to 7-pound range. Portable printers use a variety of technologies ranging from ink jet and thermal fusion (also known as thermal transfer) to carbon transfer.

A traveling printer should come in a small, light package and use a battery with enough life to crank out a few pages. (An AC adapter shouldn't be the only power source.) But these printers really aren't adequate for use as full-time desktop office printers. They're too slow, and generally the quality just isn't impressive. Another drawback is the cost of supplies—portable printers use proprietary ribbons, and some use special papers.

Paper Is Paper, Right? Wrong

When you go into a stationery store, the paper selection can be confusing and baffling. You'll find laser paper in a wide variety of colors; with cotton and linen rag content; and in reams labeled "long grain," "hi-speed," and "xerographic." Some papers are called copier paper, while others are called laser paper. There's premium paper, coated and uncoated paper, exotic paper, opaque paper, presentation paper, onion skin, and vellum.

PRINTERS

There's paper weight (by the pound) and recycled paper. How do you choose? First you need to know a little about printer paper.

Factors to Consider When Choosing Paper   The first step is to understand the printing process. Laser printers rely on an electrical charge to hold the toner to the paper, and then heat and pressure to fuse the toner to the page. So it stands to reason that good laser paper will have special electrical- and heat-resistant properties, just as copier machine paper does.

Brightness is rated according to the amount of light reflected by the paper. A sheet with a brightness rating of 90 percent reflects 90 percent of the light striking it; a high brightness rating makes for a high contrast between the page and ink. Colored paper may be misleading as to brightness, because a dark purple sheet doesn't reflect light as well as a light tan of the same rating.

Electrical resistance results from a number of factors in the papermaking process. Paper manufacturers can either add resistant chemicals to the surface of the paper or mix them into the paper itself. The moisture content of the paper also has a significant impact on paper's resistance, which is why print quality can vary with humidity.

Moisture affects another aspect of the laser printing process: paper feeding. The greater the moisture content of paper, the more likely it is to curl. And if a page has too much curl, it can be more prone to jamming. As a result, it is important that you store paper carefully and take care to close the packaging on partial reams.

The paper-making process creates paper that has two distinctly different sides, though the difference is not always obvious to the eye or touch. The top is called the felt side, and the bottom is called the wire side—the rule is to print on the wire side first. Look at the label on the front of the ream wrapper for an arrow indicating the wire side, and keep this in mind when loading your printer's paper trays. And be aware of whether your printer's tray loads face-up or face-down.

Another factor that affects paper jamming is the weight of the paper. Basis weight is a standard measure based on 500 sheets of paper. Most paper is rated at 20 pounds, though some higher-quality paper is rated at 24 pounds or more. Paper that is too light or too heavy is more likely to jam.

Many people assume that "weight" means the same as "thickness" and "stiffness." In fact, the three measures tend to correlate, but they are not directly related. Stiffness is a measure of how much a page resists bending, while thickness describes the physical dimension. It is quite possible to have three sheets of different 20-pound paper, one significantly stiffer than the other two, and one noticeably thicker.

Cotton bond paper, as its name suggests, has cotton fibers mixed with the wood pulp that forms the paper. Paper with this mixture often has a

PRINTERS

high-quality feel and typically is stamped with a watermark as part of the manufacturing process.

There are other factors that affect print quality. *Wax pick* is the strength of the paper's surface; cheap (water) papers can leave lots of lint inside your printer, compromising print quality and shortening engine life. *Opacity* describes how well a page prevents print on the back from showing through to the front. *Smoothness* measures the texture of the page; rough surfaces such as classic laid bonds often do not take toner evenly, but toner doesn't fuse well to very smooth surfaces either and is prone to flaking and falling off.

Types of Laser Printer Paper

Laser printers have special paper needs. It's no wonder that supply catalogs list dozens of types of laser printer paper; each manufacturer offers at least a half-dozen varieties of its own. How should you choose which paper to use?

Premium Papers   These are the highest quality papers available. They are made of the same fibers (wood, cotton and/or linen) as regular office paper, but the difference lies in the way the raw paper products are handled. In premium papers, the paper-making machines are slowed down to a crawl, which gives the paper pulp more time to "knit" the fibers and for water to drain off. The process is well inspected and controlled.

Premium papers may be either coated or uncoated. Coated paper is glossy, and is usually used in color brochures and slick magazine pages. Uncoated paper is used in all types of printing, from letterhead to books and posters.

Laser-Printer Papers   Laser-printer papers are very smooth and have a high brightness rating—about 85 percent or above. The moisture content for laser printer papers is lower than for many other grades of paper. Bond and xerographic papers will work in laser printers and look similar, but they are designed for copiers. They may not look as good or perform as well (expect jamming or smearing) because they were designed for a different purpose.

Xerographic Paper   The commonplace copy machines have a specific grade of papers designed just for them: xerographic grade. These, like laser papers, have less moisture to resist curling and are flexible enough to move through the copier innards. The main difference is they are not as smooth as laser-grade papers.

Bond   Bond, the standard business paper, was designed for use with pen and ink or in typewriters. It is heavy and durable, as well as thick and

PRINTERS

impressive. It feels good to hold. Bond can usually run through a laser printer pretty well without too much jamming. Most paper manufacturers are moving toward adding some of the xerographic and laser qualities to bond paper.

Recycled Papers   The trend towards recycled paper, as opposed to all-virgin stock, is becoming fairly commonplace, as well as ecologically correct. There are two advantages to recycled papers from a technical perspective: They lay flatter and are easier to fold. However, these same attributes are negative for high-speed copiers and laser printers. In these machines, the paper follows a curved path. Recycled paper is less stiff and has less curl than virgin paper, and when the static electricity and heat build up, the more malleable paper is prone to jamming inside the machine. (Paper manufacturers are attempting to solve this problem by making recycled stock designed specifically for laser printers.)

Specialty Papers   When you leave the realm of blank paper and start looking at special supplies, the laser printer paper world gets even more complex.

A number of "handmade" papers will perform very well in a laser printer. The possibilities are endless. We've used some spectacular Japanese and Italian marbled handmade papers (cut to $8^{1}/_{2}$-by-11 inches) with impressive results. A number of manufacturers are rising to the demand with some beautiful granite-look, marbled, or simulated handmade papers designed to be used in laser printers. It's fun to experiment with different papers for different effects.

If you wish to add color to your standard black-and-white output, you have a number of options. You can get pages that have been preprinted in another color. (Don't try to run raised-ink printing through your laser, however; the thermographic ink will melt in the fuser. Embossing also does not travel well through the heat and pressure of the fusing rollers.)

There are many colored papers and preprinted forms available for use with page printers. New products specifically designed for lasers are introduced all the time. These range from clear plastic "overhead" transparencies to prescored and preperforated mailers, and even die-cut Rolodex cards.

Laser-Printer Envelopes   Envelopes tend to cause some of the biggest headaches for page printers. Hewlett-Packard has run extensive tests on envelopes and recommends those with diagonal seams and standard gummed flaps. This style results in the fewest layers of paper. Another tip from HP for reducing envelope printing problems is to make certain that the leading edge of the envelope has a sharp crease.

PRINTERS

Labels Labels also have special requirements. Since the fusing rollers can be as hot as 200° or more, you must be sure that the label adhesive can withstand the heat. Labels for copiers are designed to handle these temperatures, but many labels designed for impact printers can't take the punishment.

Dvorak's Printer Buying Tips

Most people buy printers based on price. They find out if a particular printer is reliable, and then they search for the cheapest price.

Unfortunately, neither PC Labs nor anyone else has really given all printers a serious torture test. Most reliability questions are answered by word-of-mouth. This is yet another reason for joining a users' group.

I would suggest you go to a dealer or store that carries a lot of different printers from which you can get a printout. The quality of the print varies enormously. When you find a printer you like, try to put price considerations aside and buy it.

Among laser printers, I prefer those with the Canon engine, such as the HP and the Apple LaserWriter. A wide variety of toner cartridges is readily available for Canon-based laser printers. If you buy a Hashimoto X55 with a Sumo 10 print engine, you've bought something you'll never find supplies for. Ricoh, Panasonic, and others have good distribution, but Canon has great distribution.

CHAPTER

MULTIMEDIA AND CD-ROM

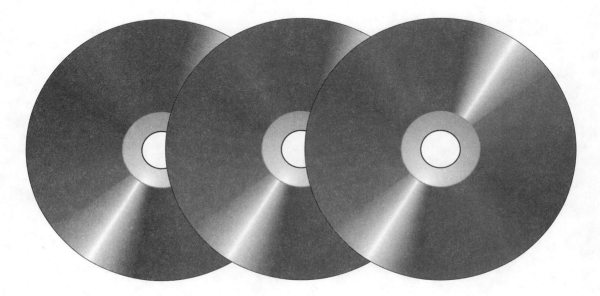

WHAT IS THIS THING called multimedia? For some, the word inspires visions of computer utopia; for others, it's no big deal. Multimedia, for the most part, is a combination of a lot of available technology. Take a computer, add a sound card and a CD-ROM drive, and that's the basic multimedia setup.

MULTIMEDIA AND CD-ROM

MULTIMEDIA, by definition, is a tangle of text, video, graphics, and audio. But multimedia is also a catchall term. Multimedia has been talked about in connection with many quasi-mythical technologies, which have been looming on the horizon like the mirage of water on a highway on a hot summer's day. These technologies include ISDN (Integrated Services Digital Network), video-on-demand, text-on-demand, video desktop teleconferencing, voice recognition, the merging of voice mail and e-mail, and the fabled "paperless office."

The promise of ISDN, for example, has been kicking about since before there were home computers. It's a digital telephone line that would eliminate the need for modems, provide a clearer data channel, and give us all sorts of wondrous capabilities (some of which we've been hearing about since Disney/Monsanto's Home of the Future display). ISDN could actually give us real-time video telephones, just like on the Jetsons.

Multimedia merges several current technologies. The results are pretty impressive. Your computer can read aloud passages of text, or play a synchronized video/audio clip of Martin Luther King, Jr., giving his famous "I have a dream" speech. It's hard to not sound all golly-gee-whiz, but it does satisfy a lot of people's dreams about what computers should do. And it will keep the kids occupied for hours in parental-guilt-soothing educational pursuits (a relief from the angst felt by most parents when the kids play video games for hours). Perhaps someday more technology will be merged in, but for now, we'll just discuss the real nuts and bolts: the computer, sound board, and CD-ROM drive.

Sound Boards

Sound cards range from inexpensive kazoolike models to high-end models designed for the professional musician. These cards are becoming more important as business tools with the proliferation of CD-ROMs. The large storage capacity allows the developer to incorporate large voice files so the computer can "talk" to the user. This is impossible without a sound card. Almost any sound card (from the cheapest to the most expensive) will reproduce digitized voice accurately.

CD-ROM Drives

CD-ROM drives are selling like hotcakes. Although the actual numbers haven't been tallied yet, the 1995 projection called for sales of over 25 million units—more than the totals sold in *both* 1993 and 1994. It's getting to the point where you're left out if you don't add one to your system.

Drives come in single speed (yawn), double-speed, triple-speed, quadruple-speed, and the speed demon of the lot: 6X speed. Quite obviously, the quad-speed is faster than the single-speed. Single-speed

MULTIMEDIA AND CD-ROM

drives are very slow, and in the low-end market, have been almost entirely replaced by double-speed units as the bargain-hunters' choice (under $150). The most desirable units are the quad-speed and 6X units, because the performance gain is noticeable. This means you'll spend less time waiting. Programs and database searches will load faster.

In general terms the CD-ROM throughput (double-speed, quad-speed, and so forth) is a good indicator of how well a drive will perform. In most instances a quad speed will outperform double- and triple-speed units. But in actual use, the drive will be affected by the "real" world. Things such as the adapter card, the driver, and the size and efficiency of the buffer will affect the actual access and retrieval speed. Keep in mind also that the speed of a drive is determined by its speed compared to the performance of a single-speed CD-ROM drive. A double-speed is twice as fast as a single-speed; a quad-speed is four times as fast as a single-speed, and so on. So performance comparisons between a quad-speed and a triple-speed unit may not be very noticeable or stunning if the units were run side by side.

CD-ROM (which stands for compact disc, read-only memory) is a trend that's been slow in coming. For almost a decade it's been heralded as the next "big thing," but it has fallen short of expectations. To put it mildly, CD-ROM technology has taken a while to build up a head of steam.

CD-ROM is useful in a number of ways. It's terrific for games, presentation graphics files, sound clips, and video clips—all of which need massive amounts of storage space. For the kids, it's easier to have the entire encyclopedia set on CD-ROM than it is to try to store a 30-volume set of books. The sheer amount of reference data found on CD-ROM is astounding, and it's inexpensive compared to the bound, hardcover book.

Games are also a hot commodity on CD-ROM. The graphics are sharper, the games more involved and more complex, which make them even closer to what's offered on the dedicated game machines, such as the 3DO, Sega, Nintendo, and so on.

How a CD-ROM Works

A data CD-ROM is similar in many ways to an audio CD. Data is read with a laser beam, which sees a "spot" on the shiny surface. Data bits are represented by shiny spots alternating with flat spots. The CD-ROM is pressed like a record, so the cost of manufacture is very inexpensive. There are some writeable CD-ROM drives that use a laser to "burn" a disk, but these are very expensive. A regular drive cannot be made into a writeable drive.

CD-ROMs can store an enormous amount of information, but they are slower than hard disks in retrieving data. There are a couple of reasons for this. First, a CD-ROM's sectors are arranged in a continuous spiral

MULTIMEDIA AND CD-ROM

track, which is ideal for reading large blocks of sequential data, such as music. The spiral track also allows CD-ROM makers to take advantage of the equipment and infrastructure developed for mastering, pressing, and playing audio CDs. But it makes for slower random-access times than the concentric tracks used by hard disks (see Figure 8.1), whose sectors can be located faster because they are always found on a given track at a fixed distance from the center.

The other reason for their slow access rates lies in the way sectors are arranged along the tracks. Hard disks use a *constant angular velocity* (*CAV*) encoding scheme, in which the disk spins at a constant speed and each sector occupies the area subtended by a fixed angle. Sectors are placed at maximum density along the inside track of the disk; moving outward, however, the sectors must spread to cover the increasing track circumference, leading to wasted space between and within them.

To make use of this space, CD-ROMs use the *constant linear velocity* (*CLV*) encoding scheme, in which the length of a sector is constant regardless of whether it's located on the inside or the outside of the disc. This means the rotation speed of the disc must vary inversely with the radius; the motor must slow down the disc to read sectors located toward the outside of the disc and speed it up to read sectors loaded toward the inside. Doing this requires a more complicated drive mechanism that can overcome the inertia of the disc when accelerating and the momentum when decelerating, which slows the drive's random-access times. But this encoding scheme also allows data to be packed at maximum density over the entire disc.

Compatibility and Speed

Many of the CD-ROM drives on the market have SCSI interfaces. This is certainly true in the higher end of the market and marks a distinct change from the not-so-distant past when every drive unit had its own quirky proprietary interface. The interface standards are changing, however, with two distinct interface schemes emerging: SCSI and EIDE/ATAPI.

Many of the CD-ROM drives on the market will use a standard SCSI interface, which may come complete with its own SCSI adapter card or the drive maker will offer it as an option. Some drives will require you to go out and purchase a card on your own. One such card is the industry-standard Adaptec AHA-1542CF SCSI adapter.

Other units may use the ATAPI (AT Attachment Packet Interface) standard introduced in 1994 as part of the Enhanced IDE by Western Digital. The EIDE/ATAPI allows you to plug your IDE CD-ROM right into an IDE connector on your system's motherboard. Proponents of this standard cite ease of use as the main feature, with the drives easier

MULTIMEDIA AND CD-ROM

■ Figure 8.1 How a CD-ROM holds data

CD-ROM disk: Data stored in a continuous spiral track

Hard disk: Data stored in concentric tracks

MULTIMEDIA AND CD-ROM

to install, configure, and better performance. Others argue that the performance isn't notably different from that of an SCSI interface drive.

There are two choices for a CD-ROM drive to be attached to a laptop computer: either a parallel connection or a PCMCIA SCSI connection. If a parallel port is used, it's just like hooking up any external unit. Plug it in and then install the drivers. The parallel port is not a very sophisticated interface: It's slow, and no matter how fast the drive unit may be, performance is affected by the parallel bottleneck. If your notebook has a type II PCMCIA slot, you can connect the CD-ROM drive by connecting it to a PCMCIA SCSI adapter card. Due to the performance considerations, this is preferable to using the parallel port.

The average speed of drives has improved greatly over the years. If you go shopping you'll see single-speed, double-speed, triple-speed, quadruple-speed, and 6X-speed drives. This speed refers to the minimum sustained transfer rate and access time, which is expressed as the amount of data (K) transferred per second (sec). In essence, the higher the speed, the faster the disc spins.

The MPC (Multimedia PC) Marketing Council has set minimum sustained data transfer rates for multimedia-compatible CD-ROM drives. The original MPC Level 1 standard was 153K/sec; Level 2 is more rigorous. The newer standards take into account improvements in the drive mechanisms. For example, a double-spin drive must have an average rate of 300K/sec.

If speed is your buying criterion, note that currently the fastest drives on the market are the 6X-speed drives. But software products are emerging that can cache the data. For example, Norton Speedcache may improve the actual speed, depending on the application and the drive.

Reliability and Compatibility   Dust is an enemy of data CD-ROM. It's not as important that music CDs have a dustless environment—unless you're a real audiophile, you probably wouldn't notice a slight skip because of dust. But with synchronized data and video every bit is an important bit, and skips will not go unnoticed. This is why the disc loading method is important. The Sony/Philips-type caddie, in which the CD is encased in a plastic case which you purchase for about $5.00 each and looks like a big floppy disk, is in use by many manufacturers. The CD is less prone to pick up fingerprints and other dirt and grime, since you don't handle it as often. Portable units and some desktop drives use a tray loading system like that used by a regular audio CD player, which is less hygienic for the CD-ROM. The caddieless drive is fine for most home uses, but keep in mind that in most cases such a drive cannot function when the unit is turned on its side.

CD-ROMs can be cleaned with a soft cloth and a little soap and water or Windex. There are also cleaning kits available at most record stores.

MULTIMEDIA AND CD-ROM

But the bigger problem is getting dirt inside the drive itself. You don't want a glob of goo on a CD-ROM to get transferred to the laser source of a CD-ROM drive. Probably the best advice: Don't let your toddler eat peanut butter and banana sandwiches and play with your CD-ROMs.

Things to Consider

Quad-speed drives are quickly becoming the standard because most of the CD-ROM applications demand more speed. This need for speed is even more pronounced when it comes to motion video. There have been some strides in compression techniques to store more video more efficiently, but the demad of consumers is toward longer and more involved video capability. Today's multimedia programs have been designed to run on double-speed drives, which limit the motion-video clips to about 15 frames per second, with 256-color and screen-size frames. Larger video use will require larger video windows. Games are already on the market which require triple-speed (Rebel Assault and Wing Commander 3), and quad-speed games are in development. For this reason, it's prudent to purchase the fastest drive you can afford, especially if your kids will be using the unit.

It's a good idea to make sure any drive you select is compatible with Kodak's multisession PhotoCD standard. This is a format for storing digitized photographs on CD. *Multisession* means digitized photos can be recorded in multiple sessions. But the CD-ROM XA standard that a salesperson may tout is still not a big deal for most users. (The XA standard is a scheme for interleaving sound, but it hasn't been totally accepted yet.) Other format standards to take into consideration when purchasing a unit are the ability for continuous read and an average access time below 300 milliseconds.

Compatibility Woes

If you already have a computer and want to add a CD-ROM player, follow this rule: **Make sure you get a money-back guarantee.** This way, if it works, it works; if it doesn't, you can bring it back.

The problem lies in the multiplicity of possible configurations. Some "cute" device you've added on and can't live without might interfere with the functionality of something you want to add on later. There may be various internal conflicts that you can't easily foresee or avoid. For example, a scanner, the printer port, and a given sound card may all require the exact same resources of the computer. Thus, all three cannot work together. To make things even more confusing and frustrating, these difficulties may be more pronounced in new machines than in older ones.

So, if you already have a machine, you may be able to add a CD-ROM drive, but don't drive yourself crazy: Unfortunately, no matter what you

MULTIMEDIA AND CD-ROM

■ CD-ROMs Are Accepted as Entertainment

On April 22, 1994, *Entertainment Weekly*, a general interest publication devoted to covering the entertainment industry—movies, television, and music—boldly introduced a new section in its magazine, called simply "Multimedia." They explained the move by saying:

"Imagine that this magazine had existed 15 years ago, and imagine that we had indulged in a little bold prophecy: 'In the next decade, you will buy all your music on shiny little discs, rent movies on tape to watch at home, and have 50 TV channels to choose from.' You would have laughed. You would have pshawed. Maybe you would have bought a different magazine.

"We're not indulging in prophecy now, though the coming decade promises to bring more techological change more quickly than any other. Instead, we intend to give our readers the latest information about the brave new multimedia world and to serve as their consumer guide to its products. In EW's new Multimedia review section you'll find answers to questions like: Which CD-ROMs are worthy of my time and money? Is 'virtual reality' more virtual than real? What's the latest news about online services? Who are the stars of this new age?" ■

do, sometimes the CD-ROM drive just won't work. Make sure you have an iron-clad money-back guarantee, and then give it a go.

Here's the best advice if you are going to purchase a new machine: If a CD-ROM drive is an option, buy it! Or have a CD-ROM player included in the machine purchase and let the retailer set it up. A double-speed drive is generally an excellent choice for the home user.

Frills

A CD-ROM drive and sound card can be hooked to a stereo amplifier and regular floor speakers if you want to play regular music CDs, or have house-shaking sounds accompany your favorite game on your computer. But for most people, a set of special multimedia shielded speakers sitting on the desktop is adequate. It's important that the speakers be magnetically shielded—otherwise, if they're placed anywhere near the monitor they will distort the image severely and could damage the monitor.

CD-ROM Software

It's becoming more common to purchase a software package and find that instead of a stack of floppy disks, there's one nice, shiny, silver CD-ROM. Delivering a product on CD-ROM is less expensive (with less chance of disk errors or faulty disks) for the vendor and much easier for the buyer to install. Instead of feeding floppies in one disk at a time, you just pop a CD in the drive and let it install without further attention. Support for the program is on the CD-ROM itself instead of on an expensive, bulky printed manual. CD-ROM drives also offer a way for users to save space

MULTIMEDIA AND CD-ROM

by installing only regularly used software on their hard drive, loading in the infrequently used ones on CD as needed. It's only a matter of time before these advantages will become a necessity as application programs grow in size and complexity.

Some Recommended CD-ROMs

There are hundreds of good CD-ROMs. This is just a sampling of a few I like.

Digital Directory has a set of CD-ROMs containing all the phone numbers in the country. Called *PhoneDiscs*, these CD-ROMs also include a "reverse directory" so you can look up an address or a phone number and see who it belongs to. There are both residential and business sets of discs. The plain-vanilla (no reverse capability) residential two-disc set of 80 million households is just $99. The business directory, with 9.5 million businesses listed, is on one disc and also sells for $99. If you can afford it, the five-disc reverse directory of 90 million businesses, residential addresses, and phone numbers is a great tool for $349 (information overload, here we come). These CDs are updated quarterly, so the information is as good as it gets. For more information contact: Digital Directory, Inc. (617) 639-2900; fax: (617) 639-2980.

Grolier Publishing produces the *New Grolier Multimedia Encyclopedia*. It's $199 and an outstanding encyclopedia for everyday use. The CD version contains text and images from the 21-volume *Grolier Academic American Encyclopedia*; 330,000 subjects are covered. Included are live video photo and audio tracks to enhance the research experience. It's perfect for families.

Microsoft Bookshelf (1996 edition) is a must-have CD-ROM for anyone who does more than play games on their computer. It works better than ever and is highly recommended. It contains the contents of *The American Heritage Dictionary of the English Language* (which pronounces many of the words out loud—including a few obscene ones, much to the amusement of kids), *The Columbia Dictionary of Quotations, The Original Roget's Thesaurus, The Concise Columbia Encyclopedia, The Hammond World Atlas,* and *The World Almanac and Book of Facts 1996.* The 1996 edition of Microsoft's encyclopedia, *Microsoft Encarta*, includes more than eight hours of digital recordings, as well as 200 natural sounds of birds and animals and more than 1,500 geographic pronunciations. Text entries, based on Funk & Wagnall, are often brief.

The *McGraw-Hill Multimedia Encyclopedia of Science & Technology* is at the other end of the bargain spectrum. At $1,300, it pretty much covers everything you'll ever need to know about science and technology in great detail. The CD contains 20 full volumes of books. Contact McGraw-Hill directly at (800) 233-1128 for more information. Another excellent reference tool is the 1996 version of *Compton's Interactive Encyclopedia*. This is a

MULTIMEDIA AND CD-ROM

■ Club Kidsoft

A new trend in software retailing is the inclusion of demoware, crippleware (software that gives you a taste of how it works, but isn't the full program—parts of it have been disabled), and sampleware on a CD-ROM. Some are full packages you can unlock by calling an 800 number and paying to get a code.

The newest CD-ROM-related sales tool is actually going after the kids. It's called Club Kidsoft and it's lucky it's an outstanding product—despite the fact that it's supposed to be a sales tool. The product is sold on a subscription basis: The $9.95 subscription fee gets you four large format kids' magazines with plenty of projects inside, plus four CD-ROMs per year. The CDs have stand-alone games and some storytelling along with promotional demos for a variety of children's software. The disc runs under both Windows and the Mac.

The good news: My son spent hours with the disc and book and didn't ask me to buy anything. (The disc seemed to be entertaining enough.) The bad news: The company will lose money if all the kids are like mine.

Call Club Kidsoft for a subscription at (800) 354-1033, fax (408) 354-1033.   ■

detailed pictorial timeline of U.S. and world history which puts things in perspective.

Job Power Source from Infobusiness is an interesting disc for people who are looking for work, but as was pointed out in *PC Magazine*, who has money to buy a CD-ROM if they're looking for work? Whatever the case, it contains 11 books and training videos to help you get the perfect job. Call Infobusiness at (801) 221-1100.

Broderbund Software's Living Book Series are fun and funny educational programs for children from 6 through 10. Children can hear and see objects on the screen by clicking on them with a mouse. The popular titles include Arthur's Teacher Troubles and Arthur's Birthday party. Call Broderbund for more information: (800) 521-6263.

Another excellent series of children's CD-ROMs is the line from Humongus Entertainment which includes *The Farm*, a talking introduction to agrarian life for kids from 3 through 8. The animals explain how everything on a farm works. And the Putt Putt series (Putt Putt is a car), kept our younger son glued to the computer for weeks. Call Humongus at: (206) 485-1212.

To entertain the adults, Monty Python's Complete Waste of Time is a break from the mundane. The disc includes over 30 video clips, games, and new material from the original cast members—not to mention the "useful" stuff like Python wallpaper and screensavers. Contact 7th Level, Inc. at: (214) 437-4858.

CHAPTER

BACKUP AND STORAGE

9

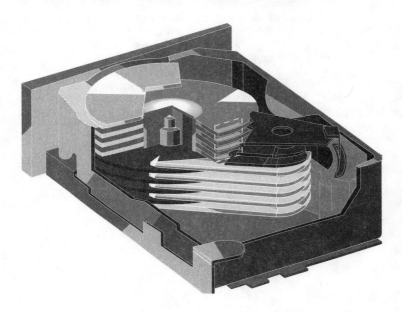

A HARD DISK is a necessity. It's no longer possible to try and make do without one. At one time in the not-too-distant past, you could run software off floppy disks. But today, software programs are too large and encompass many disks (sometimes more than ten). The programs simply aren't designed to work without a hard disk.

BACKUP AND STORAGE

HOWEVER, some programs do contain all their information on a CD-ROM disc. They put minimal set-up information on the hard disk, then go to the CD-ROM to access the needed information. But even this requires a hard disk to hold the set-up information.

Hard-disk sizes have been zooming through the roof in their capacities to hold data. Just a few years ago, 200Mb was a huge, expensive investment, but today, 1,000Mb (commonly called 1 gigabyte) can be had for about $300. These drives are not only bigger, but faster and more reliable. The trend is toward even bigger drives.

What may seem like a huge amount of hard-disk storage when you purchase your machine will become dinky and confining after just a few months. In today's market, it's inevitable. The space will soon become filled with programs, files, and utilities.

But just because your computer has a small hard disk doesn't mean that you should toss out the machine and buy a new one. You can upgrade the hard disk. And, if the hard disk in your machine is beginning to fail, you can replace it. This chapter will give you enough information to guide you through the purchase of the next drive and to find the best buy. Along with hard disks, this chapter will also take a look at some alternative methods of backing up your data, including tape backups and optical drives.

Hard Disks: How They Work, How They Break

In simple terms, a hard disk is much like a record player (see Figure 9.1). There is a spinning disk (the record) and a read/write head (the old phonograph needle). The read/write head hovers over the disk and reads the data off the disk.

The disk, or platter, spins at very high speeds. The read/write head floats over the platter on a thin film of air without ever touching it. It's like a 747 airplane flying 700 miles an hour one inch over the ground. The data is magnetically encoded so the read/write head can detect these positive and negative magnetic patches and read data without ever coming in contact with the platter. When someone is said to have a *disk crash*, the read/write head has bumped into the hard disk and destroyed the disk's media, or surface. Although this is becoming a rare occurrence, it is not a repairable failure. Hard disks may have other problems. Many of these concern drive circuitry.

Disk Controllers

The disk controller is the brains of the hard disk. It's the part that tells the hard disk how to work, when to work, and what it should look for. It's the interface between the hard disk and the computer's brains—the microprocessor. Until recently the disk controller was a separate card that fit into the motherboard, but now, it's usually built into the hard disk, and a cable interface connects it to the motherboard.

BACKUP AND STORAGE

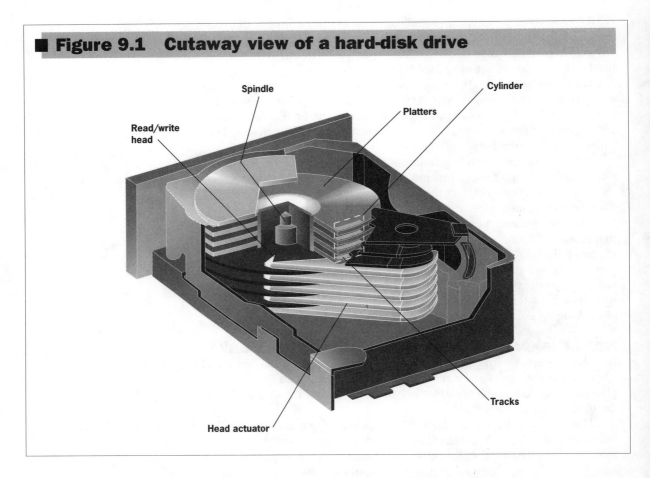

■ Figure 9.1   Cutaway view of a hard-disk drive

The disk controller may develop some hardware problems that can be repaired. These problems usually occur suddenly, as do most hardware errors. If your hard disk just doesn't work and it's had no previous problems, you probably have a disk controller problem.

Do You Have a Bad Disk?

A hard disk may begin to fail because the material magnetically coded on the platter begins to lose its ability to hold a magnetic charge. These bad areas—called *sectors*—are unable to work properly, and you'll begin to see odd errors and discover that data is missing. Disk failure is most often caused by poor manufacturing. There is little you can do to prevent a bad hard disk from total failure. The best option is to replace the entire drive unit with a new one.

BACKUP AND STORAGE

It is difficult to manufacture a 100-percent-perfect hard disk. Most hard disks have a few bad sectors. These are detected when the hard disk is formatted (most come formatted from the manufacturer). The bad sectors are mapped and blocked off so data cannot be written to them. Programs that check a disk for accuracy may find a few bad sectors, and these will also be blocked off. If you begin to see new bad sectors showing up, this is not a good trend. It indicates a failing disk. Although it seems logical to reformat a hard disk to extend its life, it's not a good computing practice to entrust any unbacked-up data to a failing hard disk. Sooner or later it will fail completely (usually when you least expect it).

Sometimes hard-disk failure is a complete surprise, but other times it's a creeping problem. If it's a gradual process, you can reboot the machine a few times and then it will begin to work fine. This is not just a minor quirk, however. It's a warning to back up your valuable data and begin to shop for a new hard disk. These things just don't fix themselves.

If your disk begins to fail, you will have some symptoms. These can range from error messages (which say "Drive not ready" or "Drive not found" to total disk failure at start-up, when the machine won't boot at all. If you begin to see the ominous "number 17" error codes, be prepared. (In IBM code schemes, error messages prefaced with 17, such as 1701, indicate a problem in your hard-disk system.) Read this chapter and start pricing a new hard disk. The good news is that bigger hard disks are cheaper than ever!

Good hard disks have few errors, and they aren't regular occurrences. Most hard disks are extremely reliable. Out of the dozens of computers I've used, only one hard disk died, and that was due to a bad bearing. The data was all recoverable. Hard-disk failure is something to be aware of and plan for even if it never happens. If you should have one of the rare lemons that is unstable, look into a replacement. Contrary to popular thought, disk drives don't wear out with overuse or "go bad" if you leave the machine on overnight. If a hard disk works, it works, and it will continue to do so for a very long time.

Unfortunately, you can no more predict the failure of your drive than you can predict the weather next January or a runaway truck hitting your house, so prepare for the worst and back up your data. While there is no foolproof way to gauge how long hard disks will last, manufacturers rate their products using a *mean time between failures* (*MTBF*) measurement. Statistically, the MTBF is the best estimation of how long your hard disk will run before it crashes. Your hard disk, however, will probably become obsolete long before it fails. Furthermore, warranties generally run out before the MTBF. For example, a drive with an advertised 50,000-hour MTBF typically carries a one-year warranty, which equals 8,760 hours.

BACKUP AND STORAGE

Troubleshooting Problems Your drive may give you a few hints of impending problems. For example, if you start to get an increased number of disk errors, you can be certain something is going wrong. Commercial disk-testing software can help locate and even minimize the effects of these errors on your files. These include:

- SpinRite 3.1 from Gibson Research Corp., (800) 736-0637

- Mace Utilities and Norton Utilities from Symantec, (800) 441-7234 (customer service)

- PC Tools from Central Point Software, (800) 445-4208

If sectors start going bad on your drive, you can no longer depend on it. It is time to consider a replacement.

Some hard-disk failures are easy to repair. If you start noticing problems, make sure a dead battery isn't the cause of your problems.

Your computer has a small lithium battery to power a little chip called a CMOS. This chip holds a small amount of vital information to which the computer needs to refer when it's powered up. (This battery also powers the clock/calendar.) Included in this information is what kind of disk drive is contained in the machine. If the battery wears out (it has about a two-year life span), the CMOS chip doesn't do its job: It loses its memory and must be reprogrammed. This reprogramming is done on 211the computer by entering the set-up program during bootup. Refer to your computer's manual for specific instructions about this.

Then check your controller to ensure that it is properly seated in its socket, and that all the cables between the controller and your drive are fully plugged in at both ends. Those quick experiments are all most people can do to repair an ailing drive. For anything more serious, you'll need a soldering iron, the knowledge to use it, and an environmentally controlled chamber, all of which is beyond the scope of this book.

You could send your old drive out for repair, but face it: You'll get back a piece of hardware that is not more reliable than it was before the failure. New drives are lower priced, higher capacity, and faster than the older ones.

These are the points to remember:

- Always back up

- Replace instead of repair

- Upgrade instead of tolerating a shrinking hard disk

Users should note that some viruses, when activated, mimic a bad hard disk to make the user think something is wrong with the computer and disk drive. Always check for viruses before jumping to conclusions (see Chapter 3).

BACKUP AND STORAGE

■ Glossary of Hard-Disk Terms

■ **Areal density** The amount of data that can be stored in one area of a disk.

■ **ATAPI** A system-level interface designed for CD-ROMs. It is a competitive interface to the SCSI standard.

■ **Average access time** The time in milliseconds that the drive takes to find the right track in response to a request (the *seek time*) plus the time it takes to get to the right place on the track (the *latency*).

■ **Back up** To make a copy of a file, a group of files, or the entire contents of a hard disk. This ensures that you have a copy to "restore" lost files in the event of some terrible event—the hard disk crashing and dying, a fire, or the theft of a computer.

■ **Buffer** An area of RAM (usually 512 bytes plus another 16 for overhead) in which DOS temporarily stores data.

■ **Cluster** A group of sectors; the smallest storage unit recognized by DOS. On most modern hard disks, four 512-byte sectors make up a cluster, and one or more clusters make up a track.

■ **Cylinder** A three-dimensional stack of vertical tracks from multiple platters. The number of cylinders in a drive corresponds to the name of different positions to which the read/write heads can be moved.

■ **Device** Also known as a level interface, it uses an external controller to connect drives to the PC. Among its other functions, the controller converts the serial stream of data read from the drive into parallel data for the host computer's bus. ST-506 and ESDI are device-level interfaces.

■ **Drive array** A storage system composed of several hard disks in which data is divided among the different drives for greater speed and higher reliability.

■ **ESDI (enhanced small device interface)** A device-level interface designed as a successor to ST-506 but with a higher transfer rate (1.25Mb–2.5Mb per second). Never used nowadays.

■ **Fast ATA** A system-level interface which is used with most Seagate drives. It is a different standard from its main competitor, EIDE, and which standard will dominate is not clear at this writing.

■ **GCR (group coded recording)** A storage process in which bits are packaged as groups, each of which is assigned to and stored under a particular code; used by RLL drives.

■ **Head actuator** The mechanism that moves the read/write head radially across the surface of the platters of a disk drive.

■ **IDE (integrated drive electronics)** A system-level interface that conforms to ANSI's AT Attachment standard. This standard uses a variation on the AT expansion bus to connect a disk drive to the CPU, the maximum transfer rate being 4Mb per second. Originally, IDE was a generic term for any system-level interface (one that integrates controller electronics onto the drive).

■ **Interface** The connection between the disk-drive mechanism and the system bus. The interface defines the way signals pass between the system bus and the hard disk, which in turn determines the speed at which information can be transferred between them. Examples are EIDE, SCSI, and FAST ATA.

■ **Interleaving** A method of arranging disk sectors to compensate for relatively slow computers. Instead of sectors being arranged consecutively, they are spread apart. For example, 3:1 interleaving means your system reads one out of every three tracks on one rotation. The time required for the extra spins lets the read/write head catch up with the disk drive, which might otherwise outpace the head's ability to read the data. Thanks to track buffering and the speed of

Continued on next page

BACKUP AND STORAGE

■ Glossary of Hard-Disk Terms

Continued from previous page

today's PCs, interleaving is obsolete. Look for "1:1 interleaving" (which actually indicates a non-interleaved drive).

■ **MFM (modified frequency modulation)** A method of magnetically encoding information that creates a one-to-one correspondence between data bits and flux transitions (magnetic changes) on a disk. It uses smaller storage densities and lower transfer speeds than RLL.

■ **Platter** The actual disk inside a hard-disk drive; this is what carries the magnetic recording material. All but the thinnest disk drives have multiple platters, most of which have two sides that can be used for data storage.

■ **Read/write head** The part of the hard-disk drive that writes data to or reads data from a platter. It functions like a coil of wire that reacts to a changing magnetic field by producing a minute current that can be detected and amplified by the electronics of the disk drive.

■ **Restore** To replace files on a disk from a backup copy.

■ **RLL (run length limited)** A method of encoding information magnetically that uses GCR to store blocks instead of single bits of data. It allows greater storage densities and higher transfer speeds than MFM.

■ **SCSI (small computer system interface)** A system-level interface, designed for general-purpose applications, that allows up to seven devices to be connected to a single host adapter. It uses a parallel connection that produces a transfer rate faster than other currently available drive technologies. The term is pronounced "scuzzy." There are a number of variations of SCSI on the market (SCSI-2; wide SCSI-2; Ultra SCSI; Ultra-SCSI-wide) each with its own strengths. As yet, one "standard" hasn't emerged as the leader.

■ **Sector** The basic data storage unit on hard disks. On most modern hard disks, sectors are 512 bytes each, four sectors make up a cluster, and 17 to 34 sectors make up a track. Newer drives may have different numbers of sectors.

■ **Spindle** The part of a hard-disk drive around which the platters rotate.

■ **ST-506** A device-level interface; the first interface used with PCs. It provides a maximum data-transfer rate of less than 1Mb per second (625K per second with MFM encoding or 984K per second with RLL encoding).

■ **System-level interface** A connection between the hard disk and its host system that puts control and data-separation functions on the drive itself (and not on the external controller). SCSI and EIDE are examples of system-level interfaces.

■ **Track** The circular path traced across the spinning surface of a disk platter by the read/write head. The track consists of one or more clusters.

■ **Track buffer** Memory sometimes built into disk drive electronics, sufficient to store the contents of one full track. This allows the drive to read the entire track quickly in one rotation and then slowly send the information to your CPU. It eliminates the need for interleaving and can speed up drive operation.

■ **Transfer rate** The speed at which a disk drive can transfer information between its platters and your CPU. The transfer rate is typically measured in megabytes per second. The ST-506 interface has a transfer rate below 1Mb per second; today's SCSI drives can reach about 5Mb per second.

Continued on next page

BACKUP AND STORAGE

■ Glossary of Hard-Disk Terms

■ **Winchester disk drive** A nickname for a hard disk with a spinning platter. IBM's original hard disk stored 30Mb on each side of a platter and was called a 3030, which reminded people of the Winchester 30-30 rifle.

■ **Zone-bit recording** A storage process that arranges more sectors on the longer outer tracks of the disk but maintains a constant spin rate. It is designed to get more data on the disk, but can be used only with intelligent interfaces. ■

The Only Reason to Repair The only compelling reason to repair a failed hard disk is when you have important files on it and you failed to back them up. Then, your best bet is to contact a data recovery service. In the yellow pages these are listed under "Computer Service and Repair." You'll need to make a few calls to find out if they are able to do data recovery. Unfortunately, this service is expensive.

If there are no businesses in your area that are capable of data recovery, you can ship your drive to a service that specializes in it. One such service is Ontrack Data Recovery. You'll need to pull out the disk drive from your machine, pack it up, and ship it to them. They charge a flat fee to diagnose the disk's ailment (within 24 hours) and an additional charge to restore the data. It can cost two or three times as much (or more) as a new hard disk. If your data is valuable, it's a necessary expense to get your files back. But for those prices, a good data backup system would be a better choice. (Keep in mind, they're making money on people's laziness—always a good business.)

Contact Ontrack Data Recovery at (800) 872-2599, (612) 937-5161 in Minnesota, or on the West Coast in Irvine, California, at (714) 263-9245. Their address is 6321 Bury Drive, Ste. 15-19, Eden Prairie, MN 55346, or 2400 Main Street, Ste. 200, Irvine, CA 92714.

Choosing a New Hard Disk

When you select a new hard-disk drive, there are several factors to consider: whether to get an internal or external disk, what kind of interface to get, how big a disk to get, and more.

Capacity

An important feature to consider is capacity. No one makes 10Mb or 20Mb drives anymore. Full-size 5 1/4-inch drives storing 20Mb are as obsolete as your DOS 2.0 system disks.

BACKUP AND STORAGE

The smallest drive you'll want will likely have a capacity of between 540Mb and 1.2G (although 1.2G is most in demand). These drives can be found for between $200–$4500 through mail-order channels. (The thing to remember with hard disks is the bigger the better. It's like money: You never have enough.)

Interfaces: ST-506, ESDI, IDE, or SCSI?

The interface for hard disks has changed over the years. In the early PCs, the interface was a full-size card, much like the old video adapter cards. But the trend has been toward moving most of the controller logic to the disk drive itself. The interface is now small, often no more than just a couple of chips and a connector (more accurately called a *host adapter*). The only possible exceptions to this little-card trend are a few of the specialized drives, SCSI, for example. The interface hooks into the motherboard. (You've probably gotten the drift by now—everything hooks into the motherboard at some point.) The interface determines the speed at which data can be transferred between the drive and the motherboard.

ST-506 and ESDI

The device-level ST-506 and ESDI (enhanced small device interface) fell from fashion years ago. No new drives use either one because they hinder the speed and capacity expected from a modern unit. The data-transfer rates of ST-506 and ESDI interfaces are relatively slow; they actually impede the performance of 486- and Pentium-based machines.

IDE/ATA and SCSI

Two interfaces—IDE (integrated drive electronics), sometimes called ATA for AT Attachment, and SCSI (small computer system interface)—have been around for a while. Originally, IDE was a generic term for any system-level interface, but most people use it to mean a system-level interface that conforms to ANSI's AT Attachment standard (based on the PC/AT expansion bus) and that matches the bus in its potential throughput. IDE's and SCSI's higher-level connection allows them to use all the latest technologies to increase capacity and speed.

EIDE, Fast ATA, and Future SCSI

In retrospect, IDE/ATA were thought to be essentially the same interface. The world of interfaces seemed pretty tame, predictable, and standardized. But in mid-1995, all bets were off regarding disk interfaces as Western Digital came up with a new specification called EIDE (Enhanced IDE), while Seagate promoted a similar technology called Fast ATA. The ANSI standards committee then released ATA-2, while yet another group

BACKUP AND STORAGE

produced ATAPI, which was designed for CD-ROMs. The SCSI people were promoting SCSI-2, Wide SCSI-2, and something called Ultra-SCSI.

At this point, it appears the complexity in the disk-drive world is actually increasing with all these competing standards and specifications. It's now anyone's guess what the final "dominant" standard will be. Because of all the confusing, all-too-technical differences in the interface, one thing must be noted: In the next few years it will be more important than ever to understand what kind of disk drives are in your machine. While none of these standards should affect your purchase, it will be important if you ever want to upgrade the box. There is no reason to recommend one technology over the other unless you are seeking the highest possible performance (in that case, look into Ultra-SCSI Wide), but there is good reason to recommend that you find out which technology is employed.

What Are Your Options?

If your PC is six or more years old, the hard disk probably uses an ST-506 interface, and its performance alone is good reason to upgrade. There are no ST-506 drives on the market. If you bought your PC more recently, it probably uses a more advanced interface—enhanced IDE or SCSI-2— which will allow you to upgrade your hard disk without making a costly change of interface. The Enhanced IDE and Fast ATA interfaces put the controller electronics on the drive, so the "controller card" you buy is really just a host adapter for connecting the drive to your PC. Nowadays, most PC motherboards have the controller built in.

If you've got one of the advanced interfaces, stick with it. You will save yourself money (because you won't have to buy a new controller or host adapter) and some minor headaches (such as switching from IDE to SCSI, which might require tinkering with your PC to disable the IDE circuitry built into your system board).

Check your manual or invoice to determine what kind of drive is inside your PC. That is the easiest and most reliable indication of drive type. For example, you can't just tell by looking at a drive whether it uses an EIDE, Fast ATA, or which variation of SCSI interface; all the cables and connections appear the same. To guard against future problems, you should label any new drive you get with its interface type, its capacity, and the drive type number your PC's setup program uses for it.

Optimizing Your Hard Disk

Even when your hard disk is operating perfectly, there are still a few things you can do to optimize its performance, including defragmenting the data on the disk, adding a disk cache, and compressing the data.

BACKUP AND STORAGE

■ Don't Forget about Floppy Drives

When upgrading hard disks, don't forget about your floppy disk drives. Disk controllers for middle-aged computers, from the AT to the last generation of PCs, have combined the hard disk and floppy drive controllers. Earlier machines used separate boards for each; current machines are likely to use IDE interfaces on the system board. If you have one of these middle-aged machines and want to upgrade it, you will have to be sure to get floppy-disk control circuitry on your new host adapter controller or get a dedicated controller board for your floppy disk drives to accompany your new host adapter.

In some cases, you'll find combination cards (such as the Western Digital Paradise Board) that combine the newest IDE specifications and can control both floppies and hard disks along with parallel and serial interfaces. ■

Defragment Your Disk

Every time you use your hard disk, it gets a little slower. This is because DOS was written when capacity was more important than speed. It tries to pack files on disk as conservatively as possible, dividing them into clusters and squeezing them as tightly as possible wherever there is a smidgen of room. Even the newest version of Windows and OS/2 may use this old disk format.

Whenever you erase (or delete) a file, a space is made on the disk. Then, when you save something new, this space can be filled with new data. If the space left is bigger than the new data, a little gap will remain. The next time you save something, some data will get squeezed into that opening, and the rest will be put in other little voids. Sometimes, when you've erased and saved data repeatedly, the data gets scattered over wide areas—a little here, a little there. But file clusters saved in this way cause DOS (and your hard disk's read mechanism) to search all over the disk for errant clusters. In addition, if something should happen to your hard disk, it makes complete file recovery difficult.

You can reorganize your disk by putting all of each file's clusters next to one another, so DOS and your disk drive do not have to search for them. You can do this easily with a special disk optimizer program (also referred to as a *disk defragmenter* or *disk compactor*). These programs are often included in hard-disk utility packages.

The cheap way to reorganize your hard disk is to back up (make a copy of everything on the disk), reformat, and restore all your files (copy them back onto the disk). It's a long, tedious job, but it's beneficial to the life of your hard disk and also reduces access time. A side benefit is a current backup of your hard disk.

BACKUP AND STORAGE

Add a Disk Cache

The most effective software acceleration you can give your hard disk is a disk cache. This cache dynamically duplicates part of the contents of your hard disk in fast RAM so it can be read (and sometimes written to) at RAM speed. Unlike buffers, the disk cache has a memory management scheme that attempts to anticipate your program's requests for disk data, typically by retaining the data you've most recently accessed under the assumption that this is what you are most likely to need next. Disk caches are generally more versatile than RAM disks because they are larger. However, software disk caches may demonstrate incompatibilities with some applications.

Compress Your Data

Data compression is a way to take out extra spaces and repetitive characters in order to squeeze a file into the smallest possible amount of space on your hard disk. Data compression was originally used only in telecommunications, to shorten the transmission time (which lowered telephone bills), but soon moved into the realm of data storage for squeezing out every last bit of precious hard-disk space. It's a cheap way to double your disk capacity.

Today, you can buy software-based or combined hardware-and-software systems, such as Stacker or SpeedStor, to add data compression to existing PC systems. The newest version of DOS from both IBM and Microsoft contain a program to do this. A hardware compression, or "internal compression," of a hard disk will render any add-on compression systems completely useless. Once a file is compressed, it cannot be compressed further. If you already have a hard disk that compresses data, don't waste your money on a software-based compression program in hopes of a further gain in storage capacity.

The major selling point of compression—both software- and hardware-based —is the promise of doubling the amount you can store on your hard disk. This is an impressive gain. On the other hand, one dark and dreary drawback to disk compression is that the data cannot be recovered if the disk fails. This is because the data is not recognizable as data—it's encrypted. It cannot be pulled out and pieced back together as regular uncompressed data. It is unrecoverable, a complete loss. Users should be aware that compressed hard disks perform poorly. Some programs are twice (or more) as slow to execute and run. This is why we don't recommend them.

If you are religious about backup, and do it on a regular basis, a disk failure won't pose much of a problem. A compressed disk and the extra storage it offers may be the way to go. But if you're like most people, the threat of an unrecoverable failed disk makes you blanch. It's a decision only you can make.

BACKUP AND STORAGE

File Backup

It can't be said often enough: Back up your important files. It may be both time-consuming and bothersome, but there are tools that make it less boring.

One good reason to back up important files is to avoid the heartache that will result if you inadvertently erase the file, or you have some major catastrophe—fire, theft, a virus, or a failed hard disk. It's not all that important to back up everything on your computer, but it is vital that you get into the habit of backing up important files. One bad loss usually remedies bad habits.

The most inexpensive, common, and readily available media to use for backup are floppy disks. Almost everyone begins by backing up data to floppies. However, this is tedious and time-consuming. If you must back up your entire hard disk on a regular basis, or if you have many files to keep secure, the only solution is a dedicated hardware backup device.

Ways to Back Up

Once you decide to back up, you must also decide on a method or strategy and how often to implement it: every day, once a week, or once a month. To back up whenever the "whim" strikes is a poor strategy. Another decision is what kind of backup you will do. A good backup system isn't just hardware, but a hardware and software combination that partially "automates" the system. Some software will work with a tape backup system to allow you to back up while you're absent. Software offers different choices for backup, including mirror, incremental, archival, and selective backups.

Mirror Backup   This involves making a copy of everything on the hard disk. In high-volume situations (large inventory control systems, accounts payable/receivable), this often means there are two recording media— such as two hard disks or a hard disk and a tape backup system—and all the data is recorded on both at the same time. This provides an immediate "mirror" of the data.

A single mirror backup can also be done on floppy disks (you'll need a bunch of them). You can make a copy of everything on the hard disk—files, software, and so on. This is commonly done before reformatting a hard disk.

Incremental Backup   This is useful only for updating the files that have changed since the last backup. Software backup programs do this automatically, by comparing the date and time of the last backup to the dates and times of files on the disk. The new version of the file will replace the previous version. The software also looks for files that have been deleted since the last backup.

BACKUP AND STORAGE

Archival Backup   This will make a copy of an updated file, but it won't delete the previous version. In this way, you'll have a trail of files, each one more current than the last. It's useful if you need to go back and check a previous version of a file for historical data (for instance, during an audit). A drawback to this system is that you'll need to have more and more backup media and storage for it. (Some companies have set aside storage for three years, and then reuse the media.)

Selective Backup   This is when just a few files, usually the important ones, are backed up. This is usually how you'd do it if you were using a floppy disk to make a simple backup. Some software backup programs let you select the files to be backed up.

Backup Hardware

Adding a backup system to your machine is easy. The problem you may face is in the selection of the system. A number of different backup hardware options are available: tape, WORM, DAT, and disk. Some of these devices are technically excellent, while others are really "in" temporarily (with a great sales pitch).

Vendor stability is the key phrase. It's an important factor in choosing any system. There are so many choices and no effective standards. Because different systems use different media, and so much is "proprietary," few systems are compatible with any others. Look for a company that has been in business for a while and has a large installed base. If you have a popular, widely used system, you'll have a better chance of walking into a computer store after some catastrophic event and saying, "Here's my backup data tape. Now please build a computer system around it for me." Table 9.1 shows the date of introduction for the major categories of systems.

Dvorak's Rule: Consider the selection of a backup device by its popularity. Ask around. Price should not be the sole consideration.

Tape Backup   This backup is fairly inexpensive and it does the job. A tape backup unit may cost from $300 to $2,000 (for a DAT backup unit).

The data is stored on the magnetic tape in a sequential, linear way, which makes finding a particular file difficult if only one file on your system is damaged. (Most other storage devices operate more like a disk drive, so a file can be located quickly.) But tape backup is a tried-and-true way to store data. It has been used on mainframes for years, and there are a number of different sizes of tapes to choose from. These tapes look much like standard cassette audio tapes. The popular tape formats include $1/2$-inch magnetic tape, $1/4$-inch magnetic tape and cartridge, and 4-mm digital audio tape.

One of the oldest tape drive storage devices is $1/2$-inch magnetic tape. The $1/2$-inch, open-reel tapes were developed for mainframes in the 1950s.

BACKUP AND STORAGE

■ **Table 9.1   From Floppy to Magneto-Optical:
A Guide to Storage**

Nobody has invented a storage solution that will satisfy all PC business users, so any choice you make will involve trade-offs among capacity, cost, and speed. To help you make the best choice for your applications, we have rated each medium, from the floppy disk to the magneto-optical disk, on its ability to perform the following functions: primary storage (for programs and data that must be available online, when maximum speed for reading and writing is essential), secondary storage (for programs and data that you want on hand, but when speed is not a critical factor), and backup (for backing up the contents of your primary storage area for safety and archival purposes).

The ratings (excellent, good, poor, or inappropriate) are based on the needs of the mainstream business user, but you may have a niche application that turns a normally poor choice into an excellent one. For example, an optical disk's removability may be more important to you (if you want your data securely locked overnight in a safe) than a hard disk's faster access times. And in a harsh environment, the rewritable optical disk's invulnerability to head crashes may be more important than a hard disk's faster speed for primary storage.

The table is organized in reverse chronological order.

	Date of Introduction	Primary Storage	Secondary Storage	Backup
Magneto-optical and phase-change disks	1988	Poor	Excellent	Good
4-mm digital audio tape cartridge	1988	Inappropriate	Inappropriate	Excellent
8-mm helical scan tape cartridge	1987	Inappropriate	Inappropriate	Excellent
WORM disk	1985	Poor	Good	Poor
$^1/_4$-inch tape, DC-2000 minicartridge	1984	Inappropriate	Inappropriate	Excellent
Removable cartridge (Bernoulli box)	1983	Good	Good	Good
Hard disk (Winchester)	1974	Excellent	Inappropriate	Good
$/_4$-inch tape, DC-6000 cartridge	1972	Inappropriate	Inappropriate	Excellent
Floppy disk	1971	Poor	Inappropriate	Poor

For microcomputers, a smaller tape enclosed in a plastic cartridge is more common. The main difference between the regular magnetic audio tapes and data tapes is in the way the tape is pulled. The data cartridge is designed differently. The tape sits on a big flat spool, and the outer rim hub of the spool is rotated. This means the tape is pulled onto the spool at a constant speed no matter how much tape is on either side of the reel.

An audio tape is wound in like a fishing line onto a reel, around and around a center hub. The more tape on the hub, the faster the tape is wound on. Although the variance in speed is minimal, it's just enough to cause problems with data storage. For this reason, magnetic audio tapes are not recommended or used in tape backup.

BACKUP AND STORAGE

Magnetic Cartridge Standards   Many different tape/cartridge combinations can be found on the market, the naming of which meets some conventional standards adopted by ANSI (American National Standards Institute). One such standard is DC, which stands for data cartridge. A number of $1/4$-inch magnetic tape cartridge sizes are on the market, including DC 600, DC 1000, DC 2000, DC 2000XL, and DC 6000. The numbers following the DC have little rhyme or reason. For instance, the DC 600 has 600 feet of tape, while the DC 1000 has 185 feet of tape.

Another variation in magnetic cartridges is the QIC (Quarter Inch Cartridge) standard for tape drives. QICs use a minicartridge tape (referred to as a DC2000 cartridge) based on the dual-hub system developed by the 3M Corporation two decades ago.

There are two sizes of cartridges—3.5 inch and 5.25 inch. Capacities range from 120Mb to 5G. The blank tape costs more than DAT, but in tradeoff, the QIC drive unit is cheaper and has cross-vendor compatibility.

DAT   DAT (Digital Audio Tape), developed and patented by Sony, is an audio recording medium that can also be used for data. As an audio tape, it records the sound digitally, which eliminates any noise caused by the inherent problems of the tape and produces a superior, clean recording. As a data storage tape, it is excellent. DAT is said to be better suited to computer storage because it was originally created as a high-capacity digital medium. DAT has been capable of holding up to 1.3G of uncompressed data from its inception, and units with 5G and more (uncompressed) capacity are now available.

DAT technology has two important strengths: access speed and capacity. The 4-mm DAT medium was designed for rapid access to information; hence, a file can be located in about 15 seconds. This speed is generally more critical for restorations than for backups.

DAT is packed into 3-inch-by-2-inch cassettes that measure about $1/4$-inch thick. You can buy these tapes in either 60- or 90-meter lengths, and they list for about $30 and $60, respectively.

DAT uses a type of recording method called *helical scan*. It is similar to the technology used by video recorders. The tape travels about 90 degrees around a drum spinning at 2000 rpm. The drum is at an angle of about 5 to 6 degrees to the tape. As the drum spins, the data is recorded in long diagonal strips across the tape, which create sections of a spiral helix of recorded data. The spinning drum has two read and two write heads, so data can be read and recorded at the same time. "Crossover" between the two recorded tracks is reduced, because each track is actually recorded at different *azimuth* angles. The two tracks make up a "frame" of 8K of data. The scheme efficiently uses the tape surface for about 60K per inch of

BACKUP AND STORAGE

storage capacity. Two principal data formats for 4-mm tape are DDS (digital data storage) and DAT.

Optical Drives

Optical drives come in three major categories: compact disc read-only memory (CD-ROM); write-once/read-many (WORM) drives; and magneto-optical drives. Optical drives use lasers instead of magnetic fields to read and write data. These drives can pack data tighter, squeezing as much as 650Mb on an optical disk smaller in size than a regular floppy disk. Optical drives can access data randomly rather than sequentially, just as a regular hard disk does, with access times below 30 milliseconds. With the use of a mechanical optical disk changer (like a jukebox), it is possible to have hundreds of gigabytes of data online.

CD-ROM Drives   A data CD-ROM is read-only, which makes it unusable for backup. Some service bureaus will convert data from regular floppies or backup tapes to CD-ROM for a permanent historical backup, but this is expensive. CD-ROM is used as a resource for bringing vast quantities of data—virtual libraries—to your fingertips. A number of publishers of CD-ROM information offer everything from encyclopedias to nationwide telephone numbers, copies of newspapers, and old out-of-print books. (For more information, see Chapter 8.)

The newest innovation—appropriate for backup—is the writeable CD-ROM. This device, which costs about $3,000, can create a CD-ROM using a special writeable disc that costs about $25 and cannot be erased and rewritten. This is perfect for archiving data, but impractical for the small-time user who uses the same media over and over. A writeable CD-ROM drive can also function as a normal CD-ROM player. Users should note that a normal CD-ROM player can NOT be turned into a writeable CD-ROM drive. Some jokers on the Internet tried to pass off a software program claiming to do this. Instead, the user got a virus that erased the hard disk.

WORM (Write-Once/Read-Many) Drives   These drives are much like CD-ROM drives, but they have a write laser. They can burn information onto the CD-ROM disc, but they can only do it once. The write lasers aren't as powerful as the ones which master CD-ROMs, but they do the job. A WORM drive is usable for backup, and the backed-up copy is permanent.

Magneto-Optical (MO) Disks   This technology (also referred to as erasable optical drives) relies on both laser and magnetic technology. A laser beam heats a small area of the disk's surface. Then a magnetic write head magnetizes the area. When the area cools, the spot becomes stable. The entire idea is based on a screwy oddity of physics, namely, the *Kerr*

BACKUP AND STORAGE

Effect. When a laser is aimed at the spot, the reflection will show a detectable polar rotation based on the polarity of the magnetic media. When the spot is reheated, it can be rewritten to or erased. Vendors claim that this may be done up to a million times with no ill effects on the data.

Early magneto-optical drives had a tendency to do something called a soft write, which was never fully readable later. A soft write may be a temperature-related anomaly that causes the MO disk to improperly record data on scattered, random sectors. (Possibly the disk does not heat up enough for the data to "stick.") The data appears to be readable when copied, but then the next time the disk is accessed, the data is missing. When this soft write was done within the file allocation table that controlled the contents of the disk, all the data would be lost. Unfortunately, even the newer drives are slow to write data, which makes it a questionable choice for data backup.

CHAPTER 10

INPUT DEVICES

THERE ARE A LOT OF WAYS for the user to communicate directly with the computer. The most common is the keyboard, but there are also the joystick, the graphics tablet, and the mouse. Today, almost every new computer is sold with a keyboard and a mouse. With the move toward graphic-based operating systems, it's become a necessity to have a mouse. This is a change from the recent past when a mouse was an accessory, to be added on by the user.

INPUT DEVICES

Keyboards

Most new computer users think of the keyboard as a fixed part of the computer. It's like owning an old Royal typewriter with a sticking L key; you get used to it. (It's cheaper than getting it fixed or buying a new typewriter.)

If your computer keyboard has keys that stick or don't feel right, there's an easy solution: Get a new keyboard. This may sound decadent (how many people have you known to buy a new typewriter because the "feel" was wrong?), but it's not. There is a keyboard out there for you, but they aren't all alike.

Keyboard History

Most keyboards conform—with minor variations—to the IBM Enhanced 101 Key keyboard which IBM decreed as the standard in 1987. In fact, the Enhanced design was IBM's third keyboard standard for PCs.

The original IBM PC and XT keyboard had 83 keys (see Figure 10.1); ten function keys appeared on the left, and a combined number pad and cursor pad appeared on the right. The Ctrl, Left Shift, and Alt keys were arranged in a line next to the function keys; Esc was to the left of the numbers in the top row. To the right of the Right Shift key, an unshifted asterisk key let you type *.* without acrobatics. Between the tiny Left Shift and Z keys was a Backslash/Vertical key. The Enter key was narrow, vertically aligned, and easy to miss. The design was a mixture of sensible and absurd layout decisions combined with a splendidly positive touch that many users believe no other manufacturer has equaled.

IBM's next design was the original AT keyboard. This was incompatible with the PC/XT design, but could be programmed through the MODE command and other utilities to change both the rate at which a held-down key was repeated and the delay before the first repeat. The AT keyboard again had ten function keys on the left, but exiled Esc and the unshifted asterisk to the number pad. The Enter key was L-shaped, and the Backslash key (which occupied the spot that used to be the left half of the Backspace key) was reduced to the width of a single alpha key.

When IBM upgraded the AT, it introduced the Enhanced model, which was compatible with the original AT model, but had a drastically different layout. The Esc key and 12 function keys were now along the top, the number pad was moved to the right, and a new cursor pad was placed between the alpha keys and number pad. The cursor pad (which was actually split into two sets of keys) consisted of four arrow keys in an inverted T at the bottom and a separate bank of six keys at the top: Ins and Del, Home and End, and PgUp and PgDn. Computer users started pressing Del when they meant End, sometimes with disastrous results (for example, when a large block of text happened to be defined on

INPUT DEVICES

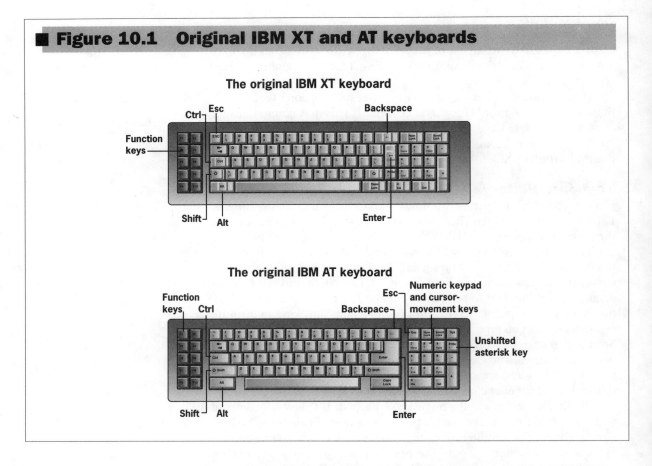

Figure 10.1   Original IBM XT and AT keyboards

The original IBM XT keyboard

The original IBM AT keyboard

screen at the time). The Backspace returned to its original double width. The Backslash replaced the upper part of the two-row AT Enter key, and the Enter key now occupied a single row. Caps Lock migrated to the old site of the Ctrl Key, and twin Ctrl and Alt keys flanked the spacebar.

Variations on the Standard   Like it or not, the Enhanced layout has become the unshakable corporate standard, although many replacement keyboards alter this standard slightly by restoring the original AT's two-row L-shaped Enter key, single-width Backspace, and top-row Backslash key. Your keyboard preference will depend on whether you press the wrong key more often when aiming for a single-width Backspace or when aiming for a single-row Enter key. Some keyboards also let you reverse Ctrl and Caps Lock, and some let you remove an IBM-standard

INPUT DEVICES

■ Keyboard Key Talk

In any discussion of a keyboard, the description of the individual keys comes up. If you've never used a computer before, this may be confusing. We've compiled a list of the more common keys and their common abbreviations.

- **Alternate (Alt)** This is similar to the Control key. It is also like a Shift key in that when used in conjunction (simultaneously) with another key, it executes a command, or in certain applications, creates a graphics character. The Alt key is more common in telecommunications programs and TSR (terminate-and-stay-resident) programs than in regular application programs. It is used often in multitasking environments.

- **Arrow keys (Right, Left, Up, Down)** The arrow keys move the cursor up and down, left and right.

- **Control key (Ctrl)** This is like the Shift key or Alt key in that when used in conjunction (simultaneously) with another key, it makes a new graphics character or executes a command.

- **Delete (Del)** In most word processing programs, this will delete the characters to the right of the cursor. The longer you hold down the Delete key, the more characters are "sucked up." The cursor itself does not move. (It is different from the Backspace key, which does move the cursor.)

- **Enter (also called the Return key or Rtn key)** This key lets the computer know a command has been issued; in a word processing document, it adds a line feed similar to a typewriter.

- **Escape (Esc)** Usually it backs you out of a command, menu, dialog box, or program.

- **Function key (F-key)** Usually numbered from 1 to 12 (F1, F2, and so on), they perform special functions. They are also used to standardize software interfaces. For example, F1 in most software will produce a help screen. They also make word processing and other applications easier to use, because function keys are linked to common commands. So instead of typing in a command or using a number of control key/key combinations, you can just use a function key as a shortcut.

- **Home, End** Home is supposed to move the cursor to the upper-left corner of an application document. In reality, it does a number of variable things depending on the software program. In some programs, Home will move the cursor to the top of the current page, while in others it does nothing. The End key, in theory, should bring you to the bottom right of a document, but often it does nothing. Sometimes these keys must be used in conjunction with a Ctrl or Alt key to function properly.

- **Insert (Ins)** In many applications, this key is a "toggle" for Insert mode, meaning that if you depress the key, it will turn Insert mode on or off. If you turn off Insert mode, move your cursor into a line of text, and type, you will write over existing text instead of inserting text. With Insert mode on, you would thrust new text between the existing text.

- **Page Up, Page Down (PgUp, PgDn)** PgUp moves the cursor up 25 lines or a page (depending on the software). PgDn moves the cursor down 25 lines or a page. In a telecommunications program, these keys may be used to begin to send or receive files. ■

INPUT DEVICES

annoyance by locking the period and comma keys so that their shifted states generate a period and comma instead of angle brackets. All these keyboards are functionally equivalent to Enhanced keyboards despite differences in layout (see Figure 10.2).

■ Figure 10.2 Variations on a theme

The **IBM Enhanced 101 Key** keyboard is the keyboard that all the others imitate, with more or less minor modifications. The single-row Enter key and double-width Backspace are the features most likely to be modified in other layouts.

The **Northgate OmniKey/Ultra-T** improvises on the standard IBM design by including a double complement of function keys. It lets you modify IBM's layout by rearranging the Ctrl and Caps Lock keys so that the Ctrl, Shift, and Alt keys are in a vertical line, as in the original IBM-XT and -AT layouts.

The **Microsoft Natural Keyboard** has a split, sloped key arrangement with soft, tactile key switches. The built-in palm rest and *Wrist Leveler* help to promote a more comfortable and straight wrist position. The numeric keypad can be used like a mouse to navigate the pointer on the screen.

INPUT DEVICES

How a Keyboard Works

The secret to the click of a keyboard is in the key-switch technology it uses. The four key-switch technologies commonly found inside PC keyboards are mechanical, capacitive, conductive rubber-dome, and membrane switches. All but the last one are hidden under key caps, but you can't tell much about a keyboard's switch technology just by popping off the cap. (Be careful if you do try—some keyboards can be broken if the key caps are removed.)

Although you might expect a keyboard's touch to be directly related to its switch technology, this is not always the case. Keyboards with mechanical switches tend to have the positive clicky touch you would expect, but keyboards that use capacitive, conductive rubber-dome, or membrane technology aren't always mushy.

Note that keyboards can differentiate up to about 300 characters per second—more than any human hands can produce. The computer can't always process the signals that quickly, however. In order to ensure that keystrokes can be saved for future execution, all of these keyboards send their signals into a special buffer on the motherboard that can hold up to 16 characters. The presence and activity of this buffer are unrelated to the key-switch technology a keyboard uses.

The switch technology a vendor uses is governed by how and where the keyboard will be used, how reliable it needs to be, and how much it will cost. Several vendors sell keyboards with a variety of switch technologies to cater to customer preference or application.

Mechanical Switches   Mechanical switches are one of the most popular technologies. Keyboards that use mechanical key switches tend to have a positive, tactile touch, which is produced by the spring tension used to return the key. These keyboards generate audible clicks when keys are depressed. The feel and sound result from the contact that occurs between conductive materials on the plunger; the conductors are often made of gold, gold alloy, or mylar with silver-carbon overlay.

One drawback to mechanical switches is the greater number of parts they require, which increases the cost. A mechanical-switch keyboard may use as many as three times the parts of a membrane-switch model (See Figure 10.3). Mechanical switches are reliable and have a relatively long life expectancy.

Capacitive Switches   Capacitive key switches don't make a mechanical contact between conductive elements (see Figure 10.4).

A mechanical contact between conductive elements is like a Rube Goldberg design: An act triggers another act. It functions like a typewriter key struck by the finger: As the key moves down, the arm moves up, strikes the ribbon, and leaves an inked impression on the paper. It relies on motion and force. A capacitive key switch uses another design.

INPUT DEVICES

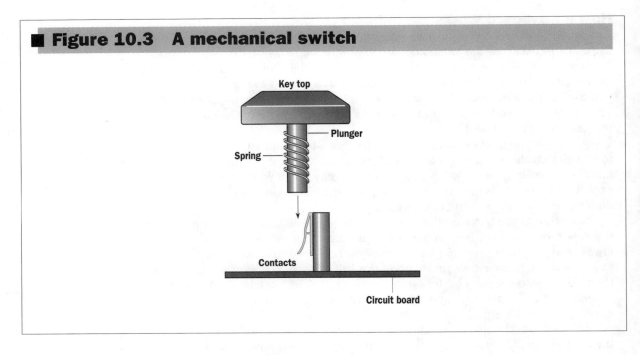

Figure 10.3   A mechanical switch

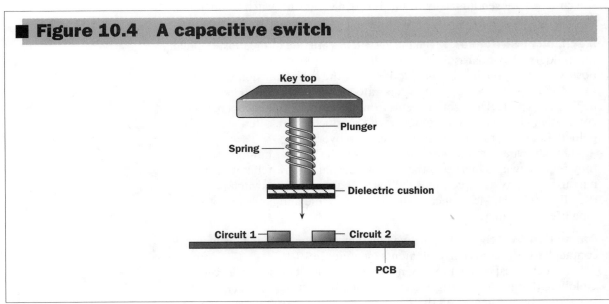

Figure 10.4   A capacitive switch

INPUT DEVICES

Capacitive key switches are designed to detect a change in the electrical impulse of a circuit. The circuit—in true electric form—is either opened or closed (that is, on or off). When a keyboard key is pressed, it presses down a dielectric cushion (*dielectric* means the pad does not transfer electricity). This dielectric cushion forces the conductive elements farther apart or closer together—depending on the design—to create a change in the electric impulse of the circuit. This change in the circuit is what signals the computer to "recognize" the depressed key.

Keyboards with capacitive switches are expensive to design. The electronics are relatively complex, but they also offer high reliability and a long life. (These keyboards may have problems in harsh environments, especially in dusty or very humid workplaces.) Traditionally, capacitive switches use springs on the plunger to control stroke pressure and feel; the IBM Enhanced-style keyboards use this design. Other keyboards use capacitive switches with a rubber-domed sheet to control pressure and feel. (This differs from a conductive rubber-dome key switch.)

Conductive Rubber-Dome Switches   In conductive rubber-dome technology, each switch has a carbon dot under the center of a raised rubber dome. When a key is pressed, the dome collapses, pushing the carbon dot down to complete a circuit between two contact pads (see Figure 10.5). This type of switch is very quiet and can have a good feel, depending upon the composition of the rubber that is used. The rubber domes themselves may be individual pads under separate keys or, more commonly, may be arranged on a single, thin sheet of rubber.

Conductive rubber-dome switches are relatively inexpensive and easy to assemble. Single-sheet rubber-dome keyboards give you some protection

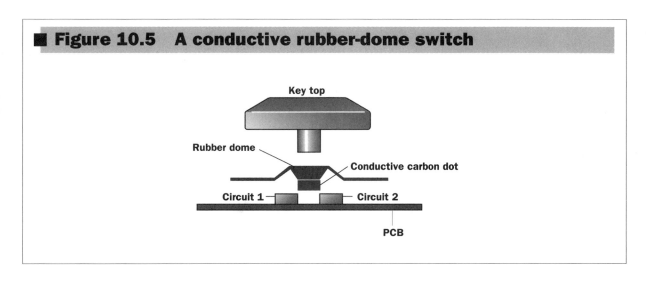

■ Figure 10.5   A conductive rubber-dome switch

INPUT DEVICES

against spills, but if one part of the sheet goes bad, the whole thing must be replaced. Not surprisingly, conductive rubber-dome keyboards typically have a rubbery feel.

Membrane Switches   Membrane switches are now among the most popular technologies. Once the least reliable keyboard technology with the shortest life expectancy, current versions of membrane-switch keyboards are among the most reliable of all. Membrane switches use a very small number of parts, and current materials are durable and resistant to environmental changes.

Membrane switches consist of two layers of polyester film, each with a silk-screened pattern of conductive silver-carbon ink. A layer of insulation between the two membranes has small holes in strategic locations. When you press a key, a cushion—sometimes an inverted rubber dome—squeezes the conductive membranes, causing them to make contact and close the circuit (see Figure 10.6).

There are other implementations. IBM uses a buckling spring and a pivot plate. When pushed, the spring causes the plate to rotate, which closes the circuit. The spring can be adjusted to return the key to its "up" position, similar to conductive rubber-dome technology.

Another point in favor of membrane switches is that they need not have a stiff mechanical touch. While some of the membrane entrants offer little better than slightly muted mechanical clicks, the current IBM and Tandy models provide the full clickiness of their capacitive-based

■ Figure 10.6   A membrane switch

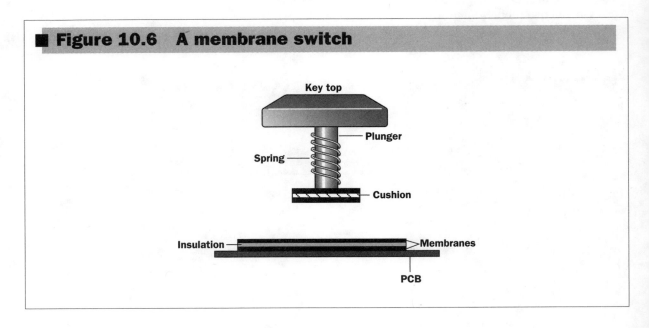

INPUT DEVICES

predecessors. Like the IBM, the Tandy keyboard maintains its particular feel by employing the same kind of spring actuators used in its older models to trigger the membrane switches. IBM's keyboard technology is patented, so the Tandy can't exactly match its feel, but it comes close.

Buying a Keyboard

Replacement keyboards range in price from $50 to $150. All you have to do is plug them into the computer. Some computers still use a 5-pin DIN connector for the keyboard cable, and almost all replacement keyboards have the 5-pin connector attached (see Figure 10.7).

But the primary connector now is the PS/2 6-pin mini-DIN connector. The 5- to 6-pin adapters are readily available; however, 6-pin to 5-pin adapters are harder to find.

Try It Out To choose a keyboard, sit down and type. It needs to feel just right for you—a subjective thing. The top-of-the-line, gold-plated, pricey keyboard might not feel as good as a more modestly priced one. It might not perform any better, either.

Don't buy a used keyboard at a swap meet. It's possible to get a good one, but what's the point? Keyboards fail, they get gunk between the keys, a spring on a key gets broken, the connections get loose—all of which may not be apparent at first. There is nothing worse than trying to "make do" with a faulty keyboard.

■ Figure 10.7   A 5-pin DIN and 6-pin mini-DIN connector

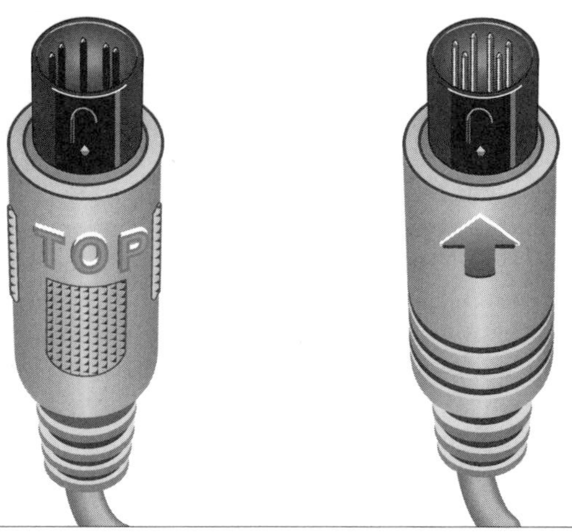

INPUT DEVICES

Things to Consider   Keyboards vary. If you compare computer keyboards from different makers, you'll note that the Ctrl, Caps Lock, Num Lock, and Shift keys appear in different locations. The "throw" (the distance the finger travels to make a letter on the screen) and the key spacing would range from comfortable to alien, depending on personal tastes.

I'll give you an example. You have a keyboard at the office that's perfect—it fits like a glove. You've used the office computer for years and know the keyboard well. Then, you purchase a home computer. The computer doesn't "feel" right. You make mistakes. You fumble for the Ctrl key. You type half the page in caps. The home computer is frustrating; using it isn't a pleasurable experience.

Then you realize that it's not the computer at all—it's the keyboard. It's completely different from the one you use at work. The Caps Lock and Ctrl keys are switched. And that's not all: The keyboard feels mushy and your little finger can barely reach the Delete key. It's time to replace the keyboard.

The placement of the function keys might seem like a minor point, but it isn't. It's as important as the H key being next to the G key. Touch typing is a habit. Move one key and it's like going on a hike with a pebble in your boot.

When it comes to keyboards, there is no absolute best choice, just as there is no one perfect car for everyone. Individual taste, comfort, and habit are the guidelines for choosing a keyboard that suits you.

Touch and Technology   The touch of a keyboard can be divided into two basic categories: those with a positive (or tactile), hard clicky touch versus keyboards with a relatively nontactile, silent (or soft clicky) feel. Mail-order dealers report that user preferences divide more or less evenly between the two categories.

IBM's keyboards are the leading examples of a clicky, tactile response. When you press an IBM key top, pressure builds until the contact is complete—or, as keyboard engineers say, the key is "made." At that point the user receives aural feedback through a loud mechanical click and positive tactile feedback by way of an abrupt drop in pressure. An audible click is far less important than precise tactile feedback, and you should probably avoid third-party keyboards that generate an annoying electronic click or add mechanisms solely to produce noise beyond that caused by the switch itself.

Compaq's desktop keyboards, with some recent exceptions, offer the most famous examples of silent, soft, and imprecise tactile feedback. Keyboards of this kind give less positive feedback and often have a soft, pliable feeling at the bottom. This feeling tells you when you've made the key, but it doesn't tell you precisely. Some users find these keyboards

INPUT DEVICES

■ The Dvorak Keyboard Layout

There is a dedicated following for the famous Dvorak layout (no relation). The keys are laid out differently from the standard QWERTY configuration (named for the first six alphabetic keys at the upper-left corner). QWERTY was originally devised to slow down typists. Back in 1868, when the first workable typewriter was introduced, typewriters had a tendency to jam, especially with a speedy operator. So to keep the keys from piling up, they were arranged so the most common letters were spread apart and different fingers were called upon, with the most common letters on the left side of the keyboard. (Just think about touch typing: The little finger of the left hand hits the letter A, and the middle finger of the left hand must also travel up to hit E.) It was designed to be inefficient.

Modern technology has eliminated jams. The Dvorak keyboard was designed with a different key placement for more efficient typing, but the Dvorak is old hat now. You can get keyboards with this arrangement from a variety of sources, and there are even public-domain and shareware programs that will remap your keyboard to give you a Dvorak layout.　■

Qwerty

Dvorak

INPUT DEVICES

more restful, because there is none of the sharp, exact response you get from an IBM-style design.

Ergonomic Concerns (OUCH! My Aching Wrists!)

The hand-to-keyboard relationship is the most strained interface between you and your PC. Typing can be more than just a bothersome task; it can cause permanent damage to your hands and wrists. A study conducted by the South Australian Health Commission in 1984 found that 56 percent of keyboard operators had recurring symptoms of keyboard-caused injury, 8 percent of them so seriously that they had to contact a health-care provider. In 1989 there were 147,000 cases of CTS (carpal tunnel syndrome) reported in the United States, and in 1991 Worker's Compensation claims for CTS were tallied at $26 million. In 1992, there were 281,000 cases reported to the Bureau of Labor Statistics. Clearly, the number of injuries associated with keyboard use is rising steadily.

The most serious health problem associated with keyboard use is the same ailment suffered by chicken pluckers and meat packers. The formal name for the ailment is *repetitive strain injury* (RSI). The name explains the cause: Straining to perform the same hand movements over and over again eventually leads to physical damage. The most common manifestation of RSI among typists is CTS. A similar ailment, wrist tendonitis, has also been associated with keyboard use.

The carpal tunnel is a narrow passageway in your wrist through which the median nerve passes; it carries sensations for your entire hand (see Figure 10.8). It also affects the finger flexor tendons, which link your fingers to the muscles in your lower arm. The tunnel is formed by walls of solid bone on three sides with the bottom enclosed by the transverse carpal ligament, a tough, inelastic cartilage.

CTS occurs when the tendons protect themselves from overuse. Each tendon is surrounded by a thick, fluid-filled sac called a synovial sheath, which swells with extra fluid to protect the tendon. Scientifically, this swelling is called tendonitis. When these sacs swell in the carpal tunnel, they can pinch the median nerve against the bones or the carpal ligament. The result can be loss of sensation in the hand and debilitating pain.

Although the problem develops over a period of years, the onset of pain caused by CTS is often sudden. Some sufferers have no symptoms at night and wake up the next morning in excruciating pain, unable to work, possibly for months. In most cases those afflicted with CTS have ignored all the pain warning signs: a minor pain in the wrist after a day of typing or some numbness in the thumb or fingers.

People have been typing for over 100 years, yet CTS appears to be a recent phenomenon. The diagnosis is not new, and the condition is not caused by a recently evolved virus or bacterium. People's typing habits have actually changed.

INPUT DEVICES

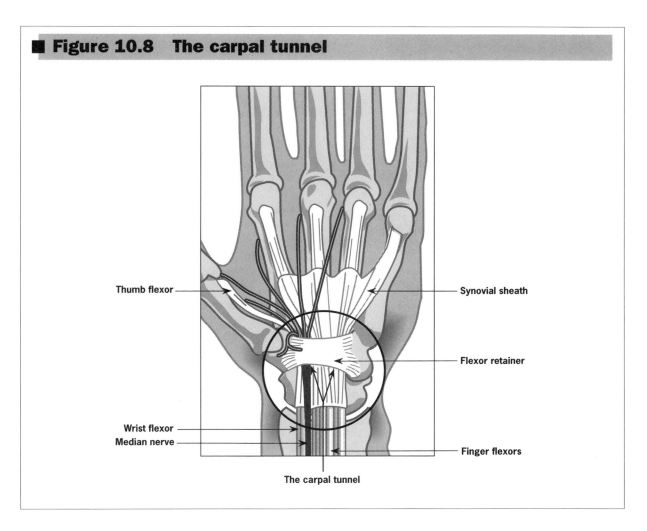

Figure 10.8   The carpal tunnel

Thumb flexor

Synovial sheath

Flexor retainer

Wrist flexor

Median nerve

Finger flexors

The carpal tunnel

Today, a typist's or word processor's fingers stay as close to the home row on the keyboard as possible. A simple press of the pinkie is all that's needed to issue a carriage return. Old typewriters required a definite change of position and a resounding right hook to send the carriage back to the left after each page, and at the end of the page, the typist had to extract one sheet and roll a new one into the typewriter. All of these simple, necessary acts added variation to the typing process. Computers encourage extended use, resulting in hour upon hour of entering and editing text and data.

These differences between classic typing and modern keyboarding hint at one way of avoiding CTS: Take frequent breaks.

INPUT DEVICES

■ RSI (Repetitive Strain Injury)

You can replace your keyboard, but not the hands you use for typing. It's important to take care of them. A growing number of office workers are being diagnosed with ailments that stem from long hours at the computer. Repetitive strain injury (RSI) results from executing the same motions over and over, and the much talked about carpal tunnel syndrome (CTS) is caused primarily by bad keying habits. They progress from irritating (numbness and shooting pains in the arms) to debilitating (permanent inability to use the hand). Wrist surgery to repair the damage caused by CTS is the second most frequently performed surgical procedure in the United States.

RSI develops gradually and is often ignored until it becomes chronic. The symptoms of RSI include restricted joint movement and swelling of soft tissues. RSI can affect a keyboard user's nerves, tendons, and neurovascular structures. The most common disorders include CTS, De Quervain's disease, tendonitis, and ganglionic cyst.

Frequent work breaks can help to prevent the onset of these injuries; however, use of a traditional keyboard requires inherently stressful postures. According to the Kinesis Corporation (whose alternative keyboard will be discussed in a moment), the postures to be avoided include:

- **Ulnar deviation** The wrist is bent outward in the direction of the little finger.

- **Abduction** The hands and arms are angled together in front of the body rather than at shoulder width.

- **Flexion** The wrist is bent down such that the fingers are lower than the wrist joint.

- **Extension** The wrist is bent up and back such that the fingers are higher than the wrist joint.

- **Pronation** A forearm and hand position in which the hand is open, palm down and parallel with the flat surface of the desk or floor.

- If you must operate a keyboard for the entire workday, you can take some simple steps to lower your risk significantly:

  - Try to keep your wrists straight while typing.

  - Adjust your chair so that as you type, your elbows are at the same height as your wrists.

  - Resting your wrists is important. If the center of your keyboard is less than two inches thick and you have enough room, rest your wrists on the desk as you type. Special contoured wrist-rest pads, which attach to the front of the keyboard, are also available.

  - Every hour, rest your hands and wrists for five minutes.   ■

Products claiming to increase keyboarding comfort and decrease the risk of CTS have proliferated, but like the words "diet" and "lite," "ergonomic" is often only an advertiser's catchy marketing hype. Most experts agree that if a product aims to promote the ideal keyboard posture, that posture is the one that takes the least effort to hold.

Ergonomic (Specialty) Keyboards A wild variety of ergonomic keyboards has been designed, some of which are on the market and some of which aren't. (Thank goodness!) One model which came and went was a pole-shaped device that stood upright on your desk. You'd wrap your hands around it like a giant oboe.

INPUT DEVICES

Ergonomic keyboards have a dedicated following, but it's a matter of personal taste. Some people have had amazing relief of hand and wrist disorders and swear by their ergonomic keyboards. Others think they're awkward and silly looking.

The basic designs of these ergonomic keyboards focus on moving the hands further apart (straight with the shoulders) and keeping the wrists straight.

The Comfort Keyboard   The three sections of the Comfort Keyboard (left-hand, right-hand, and numeric keypad) can be independently separated, raised, lowered, rotated, and tilted into an infinite number of positions (see Figure 10.9). This can remove barriers to computer access and use for people with a variety of physical disabilities, including arthritis, spinal cord injuries, and orthopedic conditions such as CTS. Specific adjustability applications are numerous. For example, the keyboard can accommodate orthopedic conditions, including those requiring the use of splints and braces; it can also adjust for use in a standing position to assist people with back problems. A person with cerebral palsy or arthritis might have hands that are angled, so the keyboard sections could be adjusted away from the body or arranged for one-handed use. In addition, quadriplegics can vary the angle of each section so a head-wand can be used comfortably and effectively.

■ Figure 10.9   The Comfort Keyboard

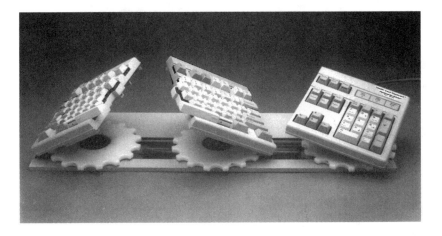

INPUT DEVICES

The keyboard uses a standard QWERTY key arrangement. For more information, contact:

Health Care Keyboard Company, Inc.
N82 W15340 Appleton Ave., Suite L
Menomonee Falls, WI 53051
(414) 253-4131; Fax: (414) 253-4177

The Kinesis Keyboard   This keyboard (see Figure 10.10) resembles a regular keyboard, except there are separated, concave, alphanumeric keypads for each hand. The separation is to minimize strain and stretching. The user's arms and hands are positioned at shoulder width, and the wrists remain straight.

The hands are raised at the thumb relative to the little finger, further reducing stress. Thumb keypads redistribute the workload from the relatively weak little fingers to the stronger and more flexible thumbs. The Kinesis keyboard uses thumb keys for such heavily used keys as Enter, Space, Backspace, and Delete. As a result, the workload is more evenly distributed and the lateral motions required to reach peripheral keys are reduced.

■ **Figure 10.10   The Kinesis keyboard**

INPUT DEVICES

Keys are arranged in columns to reflect the natural motion of the fingers, and the keypads are sculpted and concave to fit the varying lengths of fingers. Palm supports with optional, self-adhesive pads increase comfort and reduce static postural effort. They also prohibit stressful wrist extension.

The key switches are engineered to provide mechanical and audible feedback with a minimal force and activation distance. The audible click is user-selected. The layout retains the standard QWERTY configuration (although a Dvorak configuration is planned). An optional numeric/cursor keypad can be positioned for right- or left-hand use. For more information, contact:

Kinesis Corporation
22232 17th Ave. S.E.
Bothell, WA 98021
(206) 402-8100; Fax: (206) 402-8181

The Microsoft Natural Keyboard   Microsoft spent millions of dollars (the exact amount hasn't been disclosed by the company) and 19 months developing its answer to the ergonomic keyboard. Research for the keyboard was exhaustive. It included runnng marketing groups and focus groups, talking to ergonomic consultants for design guidelines, testing prototypes at corporations in the United States and Europe, and even delaying the release date of the product to wait for test findings by a leading ergonomics researcher from the University of California at San Francisco. But it has been an overwhelming success. More than 100,000 units were sold within the first two months. The retail price is just under $100. This keyboard is pictured in Figure 10.2.

Special Keyboards and Aids for the Disabled

Some of the most innovative and unusual keyboards and input devices are special-purpose models for people with special needs. Nowhere is the PC's tremendous power more apparent than in the burgeoning field of assistive technologies.

The available types of assistive input devices are as various as the disabilities they overcome. There are customized keyboards for those who have difficulty with the size or tension of the standard keyboard. There are keyboards that range from regular keyboard layouts with enlarged keys, to braille keyboards, to programmable membrane surfaces, to single-switch entry systems that display a keyboard on screen, as well as other innovative solutions for almost every need. (For more information, contact Furalletech Systems of North Liberty, Iowa; EKEG Electronics of Vancouver, British Columbia; Polytel Computer Products of Tulsa, Oklahoma; and Koala Technologies of Santa Clara, California.)

INPUT DEVICES

The EyeTyper from Sentient Systems Technology of Pittsburgh, Pennsylvania, offers an alternative for the severely physically disabled user. The user briefly focuses on a tiny light on the desired key cap, and the letter is "typed" by a camera embedded in the keyboard.

Other companies specialize in custom systems that use infrared scanning technology and a sensitive visor to interpret input from a single brow or head movement, or eye blinks and eye movements. (For information, contact Words Plus of Sunnyvale, California, and Pointer Systems of Burlington, Vermont.)

Add-on speech synthesis units, such as Personal Reader (Kurzweil Computer Products of Cambridge, Massachusetts) and the Arkenstone Reader (Arkenstone of Santa Clara, California) actually speak the text.

Pioneer technologies, such as voice recognition, have a long way to go before they can be truly useful in the general market. Some voice-recognition devices are currently on the market, however. At best, they have an accuracy of 98 percent, with a vocabulary of up to 150 user-selected words.

For information about these products or for help in building a customized solution, contact the IBM National Support Center for People with Disabilities at (800) 426-4832 or Apple Computer's Office of Special Education and Rehabilitation at (800) 600-7808. Or try the American Speech Language and Hearing Association at (301) 897-5700.

Keyboard Accessories

A variety of wrist supports are available for your keyboard. These help you maintain the best typing position. When typing at your workstation, your wrists should be naturally in line with your arms; flexing them forward or extending them backward for long periods of time will injure them. Forearms should be parallel to the floor (not half-raised as they are at most desks, which are generally three inches too high). And neither the wrists nor forearms are designed to support body weight, as they do when you rest them on your desk.

The simplest keyboard enhancements are wrist rests. The most readily available and cheapest rest can be fashioned out of a hand towel (rolled and rubber-banded). Commercial wrist rests are padded bars the same height as the keyboard; the wrists rest on them flatly, neither flexing nor extending. Most computer-supply sources offer wrist rests for desktop use or PC "pillows" for those who plop the keyboard in their laps. One such pillow is the CTS-Pillow from:

Ergo-Nomic Inc.
4102 E. 7th St., Suite 260
Long Beach, CA 90804-5310

Since the wrists should be kept straight, the angled keyboard supports offered by many vendors might not be useful for you; some authorities

INPUT DEVICES

even recommend the keyboard lie flat on the typing surface. The Wrist Pro, from the company of the same name, is a wrist support system with an adjustable stairstep design. It supplies "neutral" wrist support (neither extended nor flexed) and lets you position the board comfortably beneath your fingers. MicroComputer Accessories's Keyboard Platform is another combination keyboard platform and wrist support.

If you've already done serious damage to your hands from keyboarding, you may need the full-body approach of the Compu-Rest Arm Support from Ergonomics Unlimited, Inc. This is an arm rest attached to a desktop on either side of the computer; it allows users to move their hands across the keyboard without moving their wrists or putting excessive strain on the arms and shoulders. It is designed for people with advanced CTS.

The Wrist Trolly from MicroComputer Accessories consists of two padded platforms on a rolling track attached to the edge of the desk. It also allows hand movements without wrist action, but it sells for under $100. Fox Bay Industries makes the CarpalRest, which supports the wrists, hands, and upper body on a padded contoured surface. It retails for about $60.

For more information, contact:
Fox Bay Industries
4150 B Place NW #101
Auburn, WA 98001
(800) 874-8527 or (206) 941-9155

Ergonomics Unlimited, Inc.
422 Larkfield Center Ste. 251
Santa Rosa, CA 95403
(707) 544-3020

Wrist Pro
16100 N. Outer Forty, #250
St. Louis, MO 63017
(800) 348-8633 or (314) 532-2827

Mice

Mice are said to be intuitive devices. It ain't necessarily so. Take the case of the new clerk whom I was showing how to use a Macintosh. I thought it would be an easy machine for her to learn, but I turned around to see her waving the mouse in the air in a vain attempt to get the cursor to move. I was stunned. I've heard stories about people who have mistaken the mouse for a foot pedal (like a sewing machine pedal), plopped it onto the floor and stepped on it, hoping the machine would turn on and go. In fact the mouse is anything but intuitive. Most of the things we call "intuitive" only seem natural after we've learned to use them.

INPUT DEVICES

■ Wrist Roller and Mouse Arm

A number of small companies have arrived on the scene with various products to aid the wrists. Some are pads; some are platforms. All have their promoters and followers. Propably a rolled-up towel would be just as good for keeping your wrists straight and supported. But for most people, it's just not "cool" enough. An old bath towel just doesn't have the visual or tactile appeal necessary. Why have a high-tech computer and a low-tech wrist rest?

One add-on wrist rest for your keyboard with a fanatic "word-of-mouth" following is the Wrist Roller. Its innovative design is a series of beads which roll (and massage) your wrists to stimulate circulation. (And you could pick it up and use it to massage most any area, too.) They are manufactured for D Cubed Workspace Solutions at the Austin State School Vocational Rehabilitation Center in Austin, Texas (a sheltered workshop for mentally impaired adults).

It sells for around $256. Contact D Cubed Workspace Solutions at (512) 441-2960, or leave a message on CompuServe at 72644,2307, or write them at 2701 Wilson, Austin, TX 78704.

As for sufferers of "mouse arm" (a debility like tennis elbow, but from using the mouse), there's a solution. If your arm and shoulder are sore after a long day of computing and pushing that darn mouse all over the desk, there is a preventative measure: Attach a Mouse Arm to your chair's armrest. One end of the device supports your arm with a sturdy resing place, while the other end widens to provide a platform for you to roll your mouse on. With a handy place for your mouse, your hand position and posture will become more natural. The makers of this product claim it will decrease fatigue and reduce the chances of developing carpal tunnel syndrome, too. The price is around $40. Contact Ring King Visibles for information on the Mouse Arm at (800) 272-2366, or (319) 263-8144, or fax them at (800) 272-2382. ■

INPUT DEVICES

A mouse is an add-on peripheral. Its function is to move the cursor around and execute commands—both of which can be done by the keyboard. The mouse is a "nice break" for some people, a way to get their hands off the keyboard. Others hate mice.

The device is a box with a ball on the bottom. As you roll the ball the cursor moves. Buttons on the mouse execute commands and "place" the cursor.

Some mice deliver on the promise of graphic computing environments better than others. To help you distinguish among the good, the bad, and the ugly, there are a few mouse basics you should be aware of. Most of this information applies to trackballs as well, since trackballs are essentially upside-down mice.

Serial Mouse versus Bus Mouse

There is no appreciable difference in performance between a serial and a bus mouse, so the choice depends on your system's port availability.

A *serial mouse* uses one of the two serial ports MS-DOS provides (four in MS-DOS 3.3 and up), which may cause problems if you have a mouse, a modem, and a serial printer. A *bus mouse* takes up one half-slot but may cost more. Many systems now come with a built-in mouse port.

Most serial mice include a short connector that lets you use either a 9- or 25-pin serial port.

Two or Three Buttons?

Most mice have either two or three buttons. The number of buttons determines the number of possible choices that can be programmed for any given action. A two-button mouse offers three choices, which makes it easy to learn but may necessitate several steps to complete an action. Except for CAD programs, most software requires only two buttons.

The three-button mouse offers seven choices, which makes it more difficult to learn but may provide greater flexibility in applications. A three-button mouse can, however, be used as a two-button mouse, so there's no disadvantage there, except that the case is somewhat wider and less comfortable to handle.

Mouse Tracking Systems

The tracking system determines how accurately you can position the mouse cursor. There are three types of tracking systems; each has its pluses and minuses. The three are mechanical, optomechanical, and optical.

Mechanical Tracking   Mechanical tracking uses a hard rubber ball or wheels to turn rollers that send signals to move the cursor. Drawbacks to mechanical tracking are that the balls and rollers pick up hair and dirt. (Sugar-laden liquids can do terrible damage.) The moving parts wear out,

INPUT DEVICES

and performance is affected. This system is usually used on a firm rubber pad to help cushion the mouse ball assembly, and therefore prolong life.

Optomechanical and Optical Tracking   The optomechanical mouse uses the same tracking mechanism, but the rollers use optical elements to send signals.

The high end of the mouse market is the optical mouse. An optical tracking system has no internal moving parts; instead, it bounces a light beam off a highly reflective pad with a grid pattern. Its strong point is accuracy, which is critical in CAD and high-end desktop publishing applications, though not particularly noticeable in mainstream Windows applications. One drawback to the optical mouse is the space needed for the reflective pad.

Trackballs

Trackballs use the same technology as mice, but instead of rolling the mouse ball around on the desk, you move the ball with your fingers. They are stationary, which makes them easier to find on a cluttered desktop. Trackballs are not as popular as mice. They have their fans and their foes. Some people find the trackball easier to use because it doesn't involve as much arm movement.

A new category of trackballs and mice has emerged specifically for notebook and laptop computers. These include tiny trackballs (about the size of a matchbox), scaled down mice, and even a small joystick for games.

Another new "mouse device" is a TrackPad. (It's currently offered on the Macintosh Powerbook 540c mobile computer and on some PC notebooks.) The TrackPad is a two-inch square, sensitive, flat panel with a button directly below it. It's essentially a small touch screen. When you move your finger over the panel, the cursor moves. Undoubtedly, there will be even more new mouse devices in the coming years.

Other Pointing Devices

A light pen is an add-on device which you use with the screen, to point and to execute commands. It is connected in much the same way as a mouse, but a light pen is the size of a fat ballpoint pen—so it often gets lost in mounds of paper. Light pens, while they may not be as versatile as mice, come closest in function and design to the most intuitive of all pointing devices: the human finger. The light pen is a natural for specialized menu-oriented database software. Hospital record keeping, point-of-sale operations, and automotive maintenance are the biggest markets for these pens. The light pen's main drawback arises from constantly holding

INPUT DEVICES

■ Mouse History

Like so many developments now common on PCs, the mouse had its origins in the innovative work done more than two decades ago at the Xerox Palo Alto Research Center (PARC). The PARC mouse had two rollers for horizontal and vertical motion and a single button. The decidedly boxy shape was favored by many developers at PARC and has persisted throughout various mouse incarnations. New mice from other manufacturers have broken out of the box, led by the Microsoft mouse.

Microsoft Mice

Microsoft mice have always had an ergonomic design (even before ergonomics was fashionable). The first Microsoft mouse had a broad teardrop shape with two buttons. The original green-buttoned model had a steel ball that spawned an industry in foam mouse pads. The next iteration had larger buttons, a larger body, and a rubber-coated ball.

When Microsoft decided the mouse needed to be redesigned, it turned to Matrix Design of San Francisco. Mike Nuttal, one of Matrix Design's founders, was intrigued by Microsoft's project: reshaping the exterior without altering the internal mechanism.

Matrix did change one internal element: the position of the mouse ball. "Almost the first thing we tried was to move the ball forward," Nuttal says. "In the older design, the ball sits under the palm, and there's a tendency to put your weight on your palm and the ball. By moving it forward, you can achieve greater accuracy, even though the mechanical resolution was the same."

"We knew the buttons had to be bigger," Nuttal said. "We tried several button sizes, and in the process of designing, we ended up incorporating the buttons into the body of the mouse." Another change was in relative button size. "We felt the left button should be larger, and when we tested it, the results were better than we had expected, particularly with left-handed users. By making the left button larger, finger position is no longer a factor, so the index finger can curve from lower-left to upper-right (vice versa for lefties), as it does naturally." Rubber-dome switches were replaced with microswitches that had a short travel depression and better tactile feedback.

Matrix built more than 100 conceptual prototypes using surfboard foam. Fourteen working prototypes were tested over a nine-month period by ex-PARC staffer Bill VerPlank and Kate Oliver, associates of IDTwo, another San Francisco industrial design firm.

Nuttal says the design of the new mouse was shaped in part by products outside the computer industry. Nuttal eschewed textured surfaces for high-gloss white plastic on the body because it's easier to clean and doesn't show fingerprints. The rounded heel that fits so well into the palm of your hand (it feels like an electric razor), the large buttons, and the smooth edges all have roots in that most universal of electrical/electronic products— the telephone. It turns out that Nuttal and Matrix Design worked on telephones before mice.

Logitech Responds

Logitech's first mouse was an international effort. Professor Niklaus Wirth of the University of Lausanne, Switzerland, spent a year on sabbatical at Xerox PARC in 1970 and returned to Europe to test mouse designs, working closely with Inria, a French design center for office automation products. The final design was a round mouse with front-mounted buttons. Much argument ensued over the position of the buttons, and the front position won out over the top.

However, Logitech soon found that the buttons on the front made the mouse jump backward slightly when clicked. The design was abandoned in favor of a wedge shape, followed by the rectangular shape used today, which features the buttons on top. Pierluigi Zappacosta, president of Logitech, believes mouse improvements spurred by technology and industry experience are more important than a new design. "We are in the mouse business, nothing else," says Zappacosta. "If we had received lots of requests for a new design, you would've seen it. But if consumers like the new (Microsoft) shape, we'll respond." ■

INPUT DEVICES

■ Trackpoint II Keyboard

The IBM Trackpoint II incorporates the unique Trackpoint cursor-moving mouse substitute used on the IBM Thinkpad notebook computer. It's been described as looking like a little nipple or a pencil's eraserhead. The little nub is a very sensitive, small projection in the center of the keyboard (between the *G* and the *H*), which doesn't interfere with touch typing but is conveniently located, allowing you to activate mouselike functions without taking your hands off the home keys. It's the perfect keyboard for people who want to be able to switch between mouse and keyboard with ease.

The keyboard is a standard IBM 101 layout, and is also used by Toshiba. IBM markets the computer under their Lexmark logo. It's Lexmark part #92G7461.   ■

it up to a computer screen, which can be tiring to your arm. These pens prove cumbersome in data entry applications.

A digitizing tablet is a grid with sensors (about the size of an Etch-A-Sketch) which you write or draw on with a special stylus. Their application is mostly for graphics and CAD uses. As for recognizing human writing and storing it as digitized text—the digitizing tablets have a ways to go.

Using a touch screen is much like using a light pen, except that the screen itself is sensitized. When you touch a command it is executed. There is *no* practical application for home use of touch screens, but they are great for ATMs and marketing tools.

In the past few years, there have been a number of new twists: the IsoPoint, a below-the-spacebar rolling cylinder; GRiDPad's "electronic pen," which recognizes handwritten characters; CalComp's Wiz Mouse System, which bundles an electromagnetic mouse-like device with application-specific templates; foot pedals (as a stand-alone product in the case of PC Pedal, and as an adjunct to a trackball in the case of the Kraft Trackball); DataDesk's modular keyboard, which can be configured with different devices including a trackball; and Home Row, a technology being licensed to keyboard vendors that modifies the J key, turning it into a miniature trackball-like device.

Finally, we have to mention that there are a number of computer makers trying to make stylus- or pen-based computers work for the

INPUT DEVICES

general user. So far these have been niche products and probably will remain so a little longer.

Scanners

We're not talking about heads exploding, but instead about a machine that allows you to enter graphics, photos, or text into your computer. Two common types of optical scanners are hand-held (which looks like a big lint-roller), and flatbed (which looks like a copy machine). Scanners work by shining a very bright light at the original image. Photoreceptors, called CCDs (charge-coupled devices), detect the amount of light reflected back from the image and interpret it as an electrical signal that the computer can store. The scanner resolution is determined by the number of photoreceptors—CCDs—in the array.

Most flatbed scanners have a 300, 400, or 600 dpi (dots per inch) resolution range. But keep in mind, these resolutions are for the horizontal range, perpendicular to the scanning direction. To get parallel resolution, a stepper motor moves the scan head back and forth. Costwise, it's easier to boost vertical resolution with small movements of the stepper motor than it is to increase horizontal CCD density. This is why most scanners have a resolution range of 300 by 600, 400 by 800, or 600 by 1,200 dpi, and so on: The first number refers to the horizontal resolution, the second to the vertical resolution. It may be misleading, but manufacturers often quote the higher number as the actual scanner resolution.

Scanners can translate an image into a TIFF (Tagged Image File Format) or a text file. (For graphic images, other formats besides TIFF may be used. These include: PCX, BMP, PIC, EPS, and GIF.) Text is translated into regular, readable, text files by OCR (optical character recognition) software. OCR software "figures out" what letters correspond to the scanned images.

OCR technology has made leaps forward in the last few years. More fonts are now recognized, though even the best OCR software will occasionally throw in a strange character or letter, or may even get stumped completely and give you a line or paragraph of gibberish. But if you need to reproduce an old typed or typeset document, scanning—even with a few errors—is faster and less labor-intensive than rekeying the entire thing. (OCR for handwritten documents is still not a feasible reality.)

How you will use the scanner and what you will scan are the determining factors in what you should look for in a scanner. Obviously, if all you're going to do is scan in text, the requirements aren't as rigorous as they would be if you were going to scan in photographs.

The speed of scanning depends on the resolution, type of image, and model of scanner. The higher the resolution, the longer the scan takes. Hand-held scanners use the human hand as the scanner motor, and

INPUT DEVICES

therefore are best used for text scanning. You need a very steady hand to scan a page, and since your hand's speed isn't exact, reproductions of large images won't be very good.

Flatbed scanner motors make from one to three passes at an image to gather the data. A single-pass scanner is like a copy machine; the head will read the image once. A triple-pass scanner will go over, and over, and over the image. But triple-pass scanners are not necessarily slower than single-pass ones. Some single-pass scanners move very slowly, and some triple-pass scanners may speed along.

For black-and-white images, inexpensive gray-scale scanners have up to 16 shades of gray, while the higher priced ones may support up to 256 shades. A *halftone scanner* simulates gray-scale values by varying the size of the dots making up the image. For a color scanner, color filters are placed in front of the array of CCDs to create up to 16.7 million variations on the RGB (red, green, blue) color model.

Some scanners use a sheet-feeder mechanism to move the image, one page after another, automatically through the scanner. This is a very good labor-saving device for multiple pages of text. You can do many scans without the accompanying boredom of standing over the machine feeding in one sheet at a time. The drawback is that books or manuscripts must be detached from their bindings, which will destroy an old or valuable book.

Scanners can't rely on their hardware alone; most have some software to "read between the lines." This software is referred to as interpolation software. The scanner does its stuff and the software inserts new pixels between existing ones, determines their color value by looking at the surrounding pixels in an image, and sort of fudges; it averages pixel color values to "guess" the color or intensity. This can be very good for scanning line art, as it can smooth out the jagged edges. For photographs the quality depends on the interpolation algorithms used by the software.

While scanners seem like a luxury to many users, in fact, they are handy input devices with many uses. I recommend that users consider adding a scanner to their current computer configuration.

INPUT DEVICES

■ Digital Cameras

Like scanners, digital cameras use CCD photoreceptors to convert an image to a computerized file. You use a digital camera like a regular one—walk around, point it at something, and click the button. The only difference is what's inside. There's no film. The camera translates the image into digital information for your computer's use. With image editing software you can alter the photo. Then you can print the image with your regular printer.

Manufacturers of digital cameras include:

Apple Computer, Inc. (408) 996-1010
Dycam, Inc. (818) 998-8008
Digital Vision, Inc. (617) 329-5400
Eastman Kodak Co. (716) 724-4000
Leaf Systems, Inc. (508) 460-8300
Logitech, Inc. (510) 795-8500
Nikon, Inc. (516) 547-4200   ■

CHAPTER

MODEMS

11

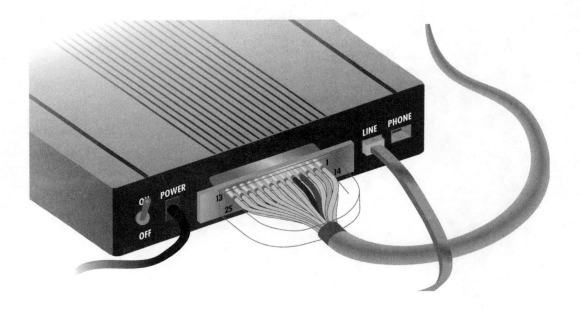

IF YOU WANT TO GET on the Information Superhighway, you need a modem. Modems are an add-on (a peripheral) to your computer system or built into your computer. A modem lets you "talk" through the keyboard with remote users, either directly or through an on-line service. You can search through vast libraries or on-line databases. It's easy to send and transmit files, memos, and letters either directly or through an E-mail system (such as MCI or CompuServe).

MODEMS

THERE ARE NUMEROUS bulletin boards for special interest groups where you can obtain *shareware* and *freeware* (software at nominal or no cost).

What Is a Modem?

Telephone lines are designed to carry sounds. Computers are digital. They emit silent electronic impulses. A *modem* translates these electronic impulses into sound, so that the transformed impulses can be sent over the telephone lines. At the other end, a modem decodes the sounds and reinterprets them as electronic impulses. In technical jargon, this is known as *mo*dulation and *dem*odulation, hence the name of the device: modem.

Modems are either internal or external. Internal modems reside on a card which fits snugly into your computer's bus. External ones come in their own containers and sit on the desk next to the computer; these connect to the serial port of your computer and come in all sizes—from the size of a bar of soap to large shoe-box size devices.

A variety of specialty modems are now on the market. These include cellular modems (which connect and transmit over the cellular telephone system) and wireless modems (which connect by means of special RF radio relay systems). Pocket modems for on-the-road telecommunications and fax/modem combination cards (which will allow you to send files either to another computer modem or to a fax machine) are other examples of specialty modems.

What Modems Do

A modem converts digital bits from your PC to analog tones, which are more suitable for telephone lines (the ear-shattering "beep-beep-deet-beep-whistle-tweet" that you hear when you dial a line to which a modem or fax is connected). The receiving modem then converts the tones back to digital bits for subsequent processing by a PC.

When you make a voice call, the person at the receiving end usually answers "Hello." You respond with your name, and the conversation begins. Modems work in much the same way to establish communication. This initial exchange is called *handshaking*. When your modem calls another, the second modem responds with a set of answer tones. The two modems then "negotiate" to find out how to communicate with each other. The underlying procedure, called a *renegotiation protocol*, helps the modems determine which signaling, error-correction, and data compression protocols to follow.

The Protocol

Protocol is to modems what language is to humans. If someone answers the telephone, "Allô, allô. Parlez-vous français?" you respond (if you're bilingual) in French. If the caller doesn't speak English and you don't speak French, but you both speak Spanish, you will communicate that way. For

MODEMS

■ Modem Talk—a Few Common Terms

■ **AT Command Set** An industry standard set of commands communications (also known as the Hayes Command Set). The computer uses these commands to control the modem. But, in reality, communications software is also required because the AT Command Set is limited. If a modem is called "Hayes-compatible," it uses the AT Command Set. Most modems use the AT Command Set and are Hayes-compatible.

■ **ASCII** American Standard Code for Information Interchange. This standard way of transmitting characters is used internationally by all computers, from big mainframes to small hand-held ones. It's the computers' universal character set.

■ **Baud rate** The rate symbols are transmitted per second. This is often used interchangeably with *bps* (bits per second), although technically, this is incorrect.

■ **BBS (bulletin board system)** A computer set up to receive calls and act as a host system. These computers often have messages, shareware software, games, and other special-interest information.

■ **Bps (bits per second)** The number of data bits sent per second between a pair of modems. Speeds of 2,400 bps, 9,600 bps, 14.4 kbps (14,400 bits per second), and 28.8 kbps are common. The higher the number, the faster the modem. The faster the modem, the shorter the telephone call.

■ **COM (1, 2, 3, and so on)** Short for communications port. Printers, mice, modems, scanners, and so on, all connect to a COM port. COM 1 (meaning the first communications port, also known as the first *serial port*) is usually "hardwired" to the motherboard. Subsequent ports are numbered 2 through 4, currently. In the near future, COM ports 2 through 8 will be available.

■ **Communications parameters** These settings define how your communications software will handle incoming data and transmit outgoing data. Parameters include bits per second, parity, data bits, and stop bits.

■ **Data bits** The bits sent by a modem. These bits make up the characters of the message being sent and don't include the bits which make up the communications parameters.

■ **Download** To receive a copy of a file from another modem/computer to your computer. Opposite of *upload*.

■ **Electronic mail (e-mail)** The exchange of messages via a bulletin board, on-line service, or local area network (LAN).

■ **Handshaking** The way one modem asks another "Are you there?" and the other one answers "I am here."

■ **Host system** Very generally, this refers to the system to which you are connected when you call a bulletin board system (BBS) or a large on-line service (such as CompuServe).

■ **Local area network (LAN)** A group of computers hooked together by cables in a confined area—an office, building, or group of adjacent buildings. Larger networks—encompassing a larger area—are called WANs (wide area networks).

■ **Logoff/logon** The first means to disconnect from another computer; the second, to connect to it. When you call an information service such as CompuServe or a BBS (bulletin board system), you will be asked to "logon." The host computer is asking you if you want to begin a session. To do this you must type in a user code (like a membership number) and possibly a personal password. Once this is done, you can then move through the host computer system and download files, receive and send e-mail, log on to conferences, and so on. Then, when you want to end the session, you must "logoff." This tells the host computer that you are hanging up. Since many on-line services and BBSs charge a

Continued on next page

MODEMS

■ Modem Talk—a Few Common Terms

Continued from previous page

monthly fee for on-line time, the logon/logoff is needed to accurately calculate the charges.

■ **Modem** A combination of the words *"modulate/dem*odulate." A modem is a device that allows a computer to communicate with other computers over telephone lines.

■ **On-line/off-line** The modem state of being. When connected to another computer via modems and telephone lines, a modem is on-line. When disconnected, it's off-line.

■ **Parity** An unsophisticated means of error checking. After a set of bits is sent, an additional bit is sent to make the total number of bits sent either even or odd. Parity can be set to even, odd, or no parity. No parity is the most common setting for personal computer telecommunication.

■ **Protocol** A set of rules which governs a modem's transfer of information. It's much like playing poker—you must adhere to the set of rules of the particular game of poker you're playing. There are a number of different protocols (Kermit, Zmodem, Xmodem, Lynx, and so on), each of which has its own attributes. The most popular protocol right now is Zmodem.

■ **Serial port** (also called a COM port) This is a "male" connector (usually DB-9 or DB-25) located at the back of your computer. It sends out data one bit at a time. It is used by modems and, in years past, for daisy-wheel and other types of printers.

■ **Stop bit** Signals the end of a string of bits.

■ **Telecommunications** Another way to say modem communications. ■

modems, signaling is the "allô, allô," "hello, hello." The entire process is the handshake. Error correction is analogous to when a transatlantic telephone line gets static and suddenly you cannot hear what the other person said. You respond, "What? Repeat that? Pardon?"

The Handshake

When modems handshake, they go through a series of questions and answers to establish what kinds of modems they are and then what transfer rate (the speed at which modems can transmit) they are going to use. The transfer rate (also called the send rate, the signal rate, or the transmit rate) is measured in terms of bits per second (bps).

The handshake will find the fastest transfer rate between different-speed modems. This rate is usually the fastest speed of the slowest modem—the highest common rate. Noise on the telephone line may lower the transfer rate further. The transfer rate can be as slow as 110 bps, but this is uncommon.

Two modems of different speeds are able to communicate because this handshake establishes a common transfer rate. Next, the modems check to see if a hardware error-correction protocol is available. They use the highest common protocol level for error correction and data compression. Then the modems transfer control to the telecommunications software.

MODEMS

Telecommunications Software

Modems need instructions, and telecommunications programs provide them. The software tells the computer to send a set of characters (called a configuration string) to the modem. This tells the modem how to communicate with your computer, your phone line, and other modems. Usually the Hayes Standard AT Command Set or a derivative is used as the configuration string.

The program will then, at your command, direct the modem to open the telephone line and dial, connect, read or send mail, send files, receive files, and disconnect. If you are uploading or downloading a file, the program will give you options for the possible types of file transfers. This is called a transfer protocol.

Transfer Protocol

A protocol ensures that the information sent by the modem and the information received are the same. There are many different schemes for doing this, but most protocols use a form of *error correcting* in which extra data is attached to the beginning or end of a block of text being sent. This extra data must be verified as having been received intact at the other end for the block of text to be successfully transmitted. If the receiving computer detects changes in the verification data, it requests that the block of text be re-sent until the extra data is received intact. Errors may actually be transmitted in the block of text itself, but as long as the verification data is correctly transmitted, the block is accepted. This is how most telecommunications protocols work.

Protocol Types   A number of error-correcting file transfer protocols have been introduced over the years, but fewer than a dozen have met with any real acceptance. Each of the major telecommunications programs will offer a wide selection of these popular protocols, so the selection of one is up to you. There is no "one right" protocol. Some work better with some types of files, some better with some modems, some are slow, and some are *proprietary* (only supported by one telecommunications package, so they require that each end of the connection use the same program).

Some of the more popular protocols include

- Kermit

- Xmodem

- Ymodem

- Zmodem

- Lynx

MODEMS

Hayes Commands

You can send Hayes commands directly to your modem through your computer to place and answer phone calls. However, the commands are limited to basic modem functions, such as:

- Dial the line (pulse or tone)
- Redial a busy line
- Auto-redial
- Connect
- Force a connection if the modem hasn't answered a ringing (incoming) line
- Hang up
- Switch parity (on, off, or none)

- Turn Echo on and off (it's usually set to off)
- Turn the modem speaker on and off

With the AT Command Set, you can communicate with another party over your modem. If you want to do any "higher level" functions, such as transferring files over the modem line, you will need telecommunications software.

If you travel with a portable computer, it's handy to have available a list of the AT Command Set. In this way, you can enable and disable modem features in awkward situations, such as at a hotel with a strange "in-house" dial tone which the modem cannot accept.

- Telelink
- CIS-B

Most telecommunications packages will offer a variety of different file transfer protocols. The important thing to remember is that the sender and receiver must use the same protocol, so you must find one which is common to both telecommunications packages. (There should be a number of choices.) Zmodem is a good one to start with when you are first learning to transfer files. It has a number of automatic options and is easy to use.

Data Compression

Data compression is a way to squeeze more data into a smaller unit. When you compress a file, the redundant or empty sections are removed. The transmission time is decreased, and a shorter transmission time means less possibility of telephone line errors (and a lower telephone bill).

Most compression schemes use a combination of two approaches. One simple (and obvious) way to compress data is to remove all the spaces from a document. Another is to assign a character in place of common words, much like shorthand.

Several file compression utilities are available, the most popular of which are Lharc and PKZIP. They can be acquired through many users' groups and shareware services. You use them to compress files before you

MODEMS

send them. The person who receives the files will need to decompress them in order to view them.

Most computer bulletin board systems store their files in compressed form. A word of warning: If you are using an MNP 5–compatible modem, turn off MNP 5 before downloading compressed files. (Precompression only confuses this protocol, which will then expand the file instead of compressing it.) There are no disadvantages to V.42bis.

The Need for Speed

PC users deserve credit for demanding technological improvements in modems. Way back before personal computers, there was only one modem company to speak of: Bell Telephone. Their two modems were the Bell 103 and Bell 212, at 300- and 1,200-baud, respectively. (Other manufacturers existed, but not in force.) These modems had no extra features, and were big, ugly, and expensive. But at the time, the only customers using modems were companies with large mini- and mainframe-computers. The telephone company had no motivation to make a faster modem. After all, the longer the line was being used to transmit data, the more money they raked in. They had the market coming and going.

Then with the break up of Big Bell into a number of Baby Bells and with the deluge of PC hardware, modem manufacturers figured out pretty quickly that the market demanded faster modem speeds. And PC hardware and software systems kept evolving. Files became bigger, and modems had to perform increasingly complex tasks.

Almost ten years ago, Rockwell International Corporation and other manufacturers made chip sets available for modems following the international V.22bis standards. (See the next section for a description of V.x standards.) This increased the maximum transfer rate to 2,400 bps.

As PC users moved an ever-increasing volume of data through modems, they demanded even higher transfer rates. Hayes Microcomputer Products, Microcom, and U.S. Robotics rose to the challenge. They offered faster modems and proprietary transfer protocols. These early high-speed modems worked their magic when communicating with a twin modem, but they regressed to the standard 2,400 and 1,200 bps when a modem from another manufacturer answered at the other end.

With the advent of the international standards, the proprietary protocols fell by the wayside. Manufacturers changed to these international standards, and modems became "truly" high-speed. Today, a fast modem can communicate with other fast modems with no difficulty. This means you can send larger files faster, which saves on connect charges and your time.

MODEMS

Compatibility Issues

Even though the Hays Command Set is a de facto standard, compatibility between modems is occasionally a problem. For example, very fast modems sometimes cannot communicate with very slow modems. (Think of it as a slow-talking Texan with a drawl, trying to carry on a long, involved, technical conversation with a high-strung, nontechnical, hyper New Yorker.)

Modems made by different manufacturers may be incompatible for reasons that are not always apparent, but the finger often points to seemingly insignificant differences in timing or performance thresholds in the initial handshake. Each vendor uses its own method and sequence for conducting the protocol handshake, and some offer additional proprietary protocols. Since the handshake method and order of the protocols may influence the final protocol agreement, we strongly recommend that you purchase modems which adhere to the ITU standards: V.32, V.32bis, V.42, V.42bis, and V.34.

What's All This ITU Stuff?   ITU stands for *International Telephony Union*. (This group used to be known as CCITT, which was short for the *Comité Consultatif Internationale Téléphonique et Télégraphique*. Quite an improvement, isn't it?). This agency of the United Nations was established in the early 1970s to address the worldwide questions of modem compatibility and to create coordinated standards. This is a French group, so the naming standards are, well, very French. When a standard has been introduced and a second, improved version is released, the second is dubbed bis. If a third is released, it has the suffix *ter*, for third. You should be at least slightly familiar with the ITU's "V-dot" standards when you are out shopping for a modem. There are five important standards applicable for today's modems. Let's look at each of them in turn.

V.32   The V.32 standard is the forerunner of all standards. Introduced in 1985 to avert the creation of an electronic Tower of Babel by manufacturers with incompatible proprietary standards, the V.32 standard enables transmissions up to 14,400 bps, which was necessary for higher speed modems (faster than 300 bps) to communicate. The V.32 standard describes how modems should talk to each other using two-way signaling at 4,800 and 9,600 bps over dial-up telephone lines.

Unfortunately, the V.32 standard did not provide a method for error control. V.32 signaling is more sensitive to noise on the telephone line than lower-speed protocols are.

MNP and MNP5   MNP (Microcom Networking Protocol) is an independent standard created by Microcom, a modem manufacturer,

MODEMS

to improve data transfer. Versions of MNP are now available in a variety of modems and communications software packages. MNP 4 (an error-correcting scheme) and MNP 5 (a compression method) are compatible with, but not supported by, the ITU. However, many modem manufacturers use both MNP 4 and V.42 standards for the best possible combination of error detection and correction.

Microcom led the industry by introducing the MNP Class 5 data-compression protocol. It soon became a feature in many modems and some application programs. Software supporting the MNP 5 protocol can compress files to half their original size during transmission.

V.42 and V.42bis   In 1989, the ITU issued a hardware-implemented error-correction standard called V.42, which describes two error-correction schemes. The primary protocol is named *link access procedure for modems* (LAPM). The secondary (or support) protocol is functionally the same as MNP Class 4. If you want to communicate between two modems that are V.42 compliant, you should connect them with the LAPM protocol. LAPM offers slightly better error recovery and reliability than MNP 4.

In late 1989, the ITU issued the V.42bis standard, which describes how to implement data compression in hardware. Using the Lempel-Ziv compression algorithm, the new V.42bis protocol offers much greater data compression than MNP 5. For a 9,600-bps modem, there is a potential transfer of 38,400 bps for compressable files. For most file transfers, however, you can expect transfers of around 19,200 bps for files not previously compressed through other means.

V.32bis   In early 1991, the ITU approved a revision of the V.32 standard. V.32bis adds 7-, 200-, 12,000-, and 14,400-bps transfer rates and a faster renegotiation protocol. V.32bis is able to renegotiate the protocol in less than 100 milliseconds.

On the 2,400-bps side, note the recent availability of V.22bis modems with 2,400-bps signaling and V.42bis data compression. Most new 2,400-bps modems should be V.42bis compatible.

V.34/V.Fast   In the last few years, a new high-speed standard loosely called V.Fast or V.Fast Class has been in development. The standard has been finalized as V.34. This allows a 28,800-bps data transfer rate. Modems will be released thoughout the year utilizing this new standard.

Types of Modems

Common modem speeds on the market today include 2,400 bps, 2,400/9,600-bps modem/fax combos, 9,600 bps, 14,400 bps, and 28,800 bps. These modems may be internal cards, external, pocket modems, or one of the new wireless kind—cellular or radio.

MODEMS

■ Is Your UART Chip a Weak Link?

Even with the fastest modem in town, you might not be ready to burn up the phone lines yet. There is another potential weak link in the communications chain.

Most serial cards have a chip that controls the serial port. These are called UART (universal asynchronous receiver/transmitter) chips. They come in two flavors: 8250 (8-bit) or 16450 (16-bit). During modem communications, the PC's UART and the CPU transfer a great deal of information. Unfortunately, if the communications program asks the CPU to manage large changes on the screen or to move data to and from the hard disk, the UART on the receiving side may drop bits, particularly if it runs under a multitasking environment like Windows or OS/2.

The new 16550 UART solves the problem by creating a FIFO (first in, first out) buffer stack. (A buffer is like a queue: Data stacks up and waits its turn.) This buffer allows the UART to save any incoming data while it's waiting for the CPU. Although the 16550 can directly replace the 8250 and 16450, it needs communications software that initializes it to implement its FIFO stack. Luckily, most modern communications programs do this.

If your old 8250 or 16450 UART still occupies a socket, you can purchase a new 16550 and replace the chip for less than $15. Anyone interested in high-speed modem communications (including those running a 2,400-bps modem under a multitasking environment) will find this a worthwhile investment. ■

Some modems are "feature heavy," while others are "bare bones." The feature-heavy modems may have extensions of the basic AT Command Set. To fully access all of these features, you might need to consult both the modem vendor and the vendor of your communications software to correctly initialize all of the modem's features.

External versus Internal Modems

Internal and external modems display few differences beyond their physical configuration. Your choice between an internal or external modem should be based solely on your needs and preferences. There are no differences in terms of efficiency or transfer rate.

Internal Modems   Internal modems have some advantages. You don't have to hassle with the proper configuration of an RS-232 connecting cable, the modem doesn't clutter desktop space, and you don't need a free AC wall plug. Internal modems don't have cabinets and power supplies. This means they are a little less expensive than their external kin. Once they've saved money on these items, manufacturers can afford to throw in a perk or two. One common bundled-in extra is a communications software package.

External Modems   The external models are more entertaining because most of them have lights installed on the front panels that show when the modem is in operation. There are lights for carrier detect, read data, and

MODEMS

terminal ready, among other functions. In addition, an external modem can be moved among PCs or used between a PC and an Apple Macintosh. (To move internal modems between PCs is a project, and an internal PC modem is unusable on an Apple Macintosh.)

Modem/Fax Combos

Most modems sold today are modem/fax combos. Unlike in the past, they have both fax and data components interlinked. In fact, very few modems are not fax modems as well as regular data transfer modems. In purchasing a modem, look for fax modems that send at 14,400 bps.

Pocket (Portable) Modems

You can take pocket modems on the road if your laptop or notebook computer lacks an internal modem. The power needs of the pocket modems vary. Some use a single 9-volt battery, while others are self-powered; they suck the juice out of the portable computer to establish the connection and then draw power from the telephone line to continue operations.

These may be used with a regular computer as well, but can easily get lost on the desk if your paperwork piles up. The speeds of the self-powered modems are limited. The circuits are low-powered, and high-speed modem circuitry has not been developed to take advantage of these advanced power tricks.

Wireless Modems

Cellular and radio technologies create a wireless communications path. They use radio waves instead of phone lines to communicate. Modems are still needed, but the modems are specialized to either broadcast radio waves or use the existing cellular services.

Cellular Modems   Cellular phones use a series of transmitters/receivers (called *cells*) that work together to provide coverage over a large geographic area. The system can automatically pass calls from one cell to another as you travel from one destination to the next. This changing of cells is almost seamless, although occasionally you do hear noises. Many cellular companies have joined together to create "roam" service and to allow a client of one service to call a client of another service.

Cellular modems are now available to connect to cellular telephones (some handheld models optionally come with a female telephone connector (RJ11) to plug a modem into). The downside of telecommunications by cellular phones is that the technology was designed primarily for voice; cell changes may disrupt data transmissions.

MODEMS

Wireless Communications—What's The Connection?

There are three types of wireless communications in the marketplace today: one-way radio, two-way radio, and two-way cellular.

- **One-Way Radio** This is most commonly used in those annoying and common personal pagers (beepers). A message is sent out to the receiving unit, which will beep and deliver a simple message, such as a telephone number or "Call Your Mom." There are also some "adva1nced" styles of receivers that can be connected to a laptop or palmtop computer, and larger amounts of data—like e-mail or reports and contracts—can be received.

- **Two-Way Radio** The transceivers can be hooked to a computer and will receive data as well as send it. The data can be sent to a salesman or delivery person in the field, or just across an office for a LAN (local area network) without the wires to trip on. Ardis and RAM Mobil Data (discussed in this chapter) are two companies that offer two-way radio service to the general public for field communications.

- **Two-Way Cellular** Cellular modems are able to convert any size portable computer into one for the road. The cellular technology is familiar to many people, because voice cellular is pretty common everywhere. Currently, there is no service catering exclusively to the data cellular market. ∎

Radio Modems Radio modems use RF signals much like a ham radio does. The modem transmits these signals, which are then picked up by a base station. The station then either relays the signal to another base station or transmits the data to regular telephone lines. Finally, the information is carried by telephone lines to its destination. These radio networks were developed for and limited to data transmissions for a fairly reliable data exchange. Unlike cellular technology, which is available to anyone, these systems are proprietary.

Buying a Modem: Dvorak's Tips

Now that you have some background on modems and a slew of terms at your disposal, what should you buy? If you want to go out and buy a modem today that would serve you well for the next few years, I'd say that you should get a 28,800-bps modem with V.34 and V.42bis. Most modems with these two specifications will also feature various MNP protocols and a few other features. You might also consider buying a modem from U.S. Robotics which incorporates its proprietary HST protocol; this protocol is still used by many of the computerized bulletin board systems (BBSs).

You can expect to pay around $250 for V.34. A slow 2,400-bps modem can be purchased for less than $100. The price difference is meaningless considering the difference in speed. It is just silly to buy a slow modem nowadays. If these are long-distance calls, the modem will pay for itself in no time at all.

C H A P T E R

ACCESSORIES

12

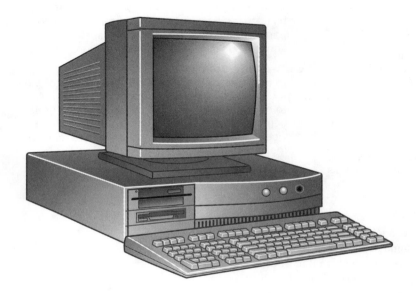

ONCE YOUR COMPUTER is up and running, it's always

fun to find new accessories to add. There is always some new

thing on the market that is both useful and needed. Copy

holders, mouse pads, computer dust covers, sound boards,

and the like are just the beginning. Here are just a few

Dvorak recommendations.

ACCESSORIES

Preventing Crashes:
Power Supply Accessories and Diagnostics

Computers crash for a variety of reasons. If your computer is crashing frequently, chances are you have a hardware problem. Power surges, overheating, bad wiring, and bad chips are all common problems that cause computers to crash. Here are some accessories to deal with these problems.

Power Strips

A power strip is a power shop standby. It's a simple way to turn your one wall outlet into enough plugs for the four, five, or six electrical plugs you need without rewiring the house. Power strips come in a number of different varieties.

Most of these outlets have a power switch to turn on the entire strip at once. One drawback to the toggle switch is most people put the power strip on the floor under their computer—and invariably, at one time or another, your foot will accidentally hit the switch and turn off the computer. (This, of course, only happens when you've been working on a long word-processed document and have neglected to save your work, thereby wiping out hours of work.)

The plain power strips sold in computer stores and hardware stores are essentially the same. And if you're shopping by price, the hardware store prices are usually better. But not all power strips are plain. Some higher-priced models have surge protection. A *surge* refers to a fluctuation in the electrical current, which rarely flows steadily. When the refrigerator kicks on or someone turns on the vacuum cleaner, there will be a momentary drop in the power current. (You can often see this when the light dims for an instant as an appliance is turned on.) When the appliance motor is switched off, the current surges—a *spike*. Spikes and drops in current are more common than you might think. Computers are designed to handle these power fluctuations, but only to a point.

The ebb and flow of electricity can be greater, due to a problem at the power company, a bolt of lightning hitting a power line, or after a "brownout." Then a big gush of electricity rushes through the line. (It's like unkinking a hose!) The computer's circuitry could be damaged. The surge protector guards against such damage. Instead of the spike hitting the computer, it blows out the fuse in the power strip, so instead of buying a new computer, you just have to shell out the cash for a new power strip.

All about Electrical Surge Suppressors

Surges are a particular kind of anomaly on the power line that are part of a wider class called overvoltages, which occur when more than the

ACCESSORIES

expected voltage appears on your power lines. Not all surge overvoltages are the same: They differ in intensity, duration, and mode. The various facets of a surge influence its capability to damage your PC and the kind of protection that you require.

Voltage is one factor in characterizing surge intensity. PC power supplies are designed to deal with moderate overvoltages—of 5 to 10 percent nominal—and automatically compensate to keep the electricity going to your computer within acceptable limits.

PCs are vulnerable to surges ranging from 800 to 6,000 volts. Typical PC power supplies can handle surges below 800 volts unassisted, though certainly the lower the voltage, the better the power supply's chance of surviving a surge. Surges in excess of 6,000 volts arc over the wiring (short out) before reaching the computer. Allowing for a margin of safety, surge suppressors should not let more than 500 volts pass through. Regardless, if your building suffers a direct lightning hit, you might suffer catastrophic damage to any electronic device, even with a surge suppressor connected.

Because of the low resistance of power lines, high voltages are inevitably linked to high currents, and the resulting surges can contain huge amounts of power. Surges cause damage when this energy rushes through semiconductor circuits faster than they can dissipate it. Silicon junctions fry in microseconds (millionths of a second). The job of the surge suppressor is to absorb or reroute the surge energy before it reaches your PC.

Modern electrical wiring involves three conductors: hot, neutral, and ground. (If you think of this in terms of home wiring, hot is the live, black wire; neutral is the white, return wire; and ground is the third, green wire.) The hot wire carries the power; neutral provides a return path; and the ground provides safety protection. The ground lead is ostensibly connected directly to the earth. A surge can occur between any pairings of conductors: hot and neutral, hot and ground, or neutral and ground. The first pairing is termed *normal mode*. It reflects a voltage difference between the power conductors used by your PC. When a surge arises from a voltage difference between hot or neutral and ground, it is called *common mode*.

Most surge suppressors on the market, but not all, have a common-mode surge suppression. Some manufacturers don't believe that there is enough energy behind common-mode surges to do the damage that a normal-mode surge can do. But this is an arguable point. You should look for a unit equipped with common-mode suppression.

It's little wonder that surge suppressors are so compelling. These inexpensive plug-in creations can halt the worst surges before they reach our PC, stopping them dead in their tracks and keeping your hardware and data alive.

ACCESSORIES

Not all PC vendors believe surge suppressors are necessary; Compaq Computer, for instance, states that all of its PCs are built to withstand surges. According to Compaq, adding an external surge suppressor to one of its systems may cause more damage than not using one, and therefore, does not recommend the use of external surge suppressors with its PCs.

Many surge suppressor manufacturers tout EMI (electromagnetic interference) noise reduction circuitry as an additional feature of their products. However, external noise reduction is essentially irrelevant to PCs. All PCs must pass FCC class B certification (for home use) or Class A verification (for business use). Both standards require PCs to prevent the noise and interference they generate from reaching the power line.

Some of the surge suppressors on the market complement their protection indicators with LEDs that show the condition of your outlet power. Although these little flashing lights won't help in protecting your PC from surges, they will help guarantee your own safety. Surge suppressor prices range from $12.95 to $265. Most manufacturers back their products with generous warranties that include not just the device but also the equipment plugged in. However, many of the warranties are carefully worded and quite restrictive, requiring strict compliance with their terms; proving the damage to your equipment may be a difficult task.

The toughest decision about surge suppression is whether you need any such device at all. Surges powerful enough to damage electrical equipment are, in fact, rare. But the effects are so devastating that the small cost of a surge protector can be inexpensive insurance. You can't predict surges, and you can't prevent them. But at least you can stop them before they reach your PC.

Uninterruptible Power Supply (UPS)

A UPS offers the ultimate in power peace-of-mind. These devices are battery backups into which you plug your computer. If the power suddenly fails, you'll hear a warning beep to alert you that the power isn't coming in. Then you'll have at least enough time to save your files and turn off your computer. The benefit of the UPS is you'll never be caught in the middle of a program at the mercy of a power outage. A UPS is also an excellent device to guard against electrical surges. It is well worth the investment if you're in an area with frequent outages.

A backup power system will supply electricity to a PC when the main current fails. It bridges fraction-of-a-second power pauses that inevitably crash systems, and keeps you running during utility outages many minutes long. Properly installed, a backup power system will keep you running until its reserves grow weak. Then it will warn you to save your work and let you shut down until reliable power is restored.

How long a backup power system needs to work depends on your needs. If all you require is enough time to save your work and shut down,

ACCESSORIES

as little as five minutes should be sufficient. If you want to keep working for hours or days after an outage, you should buy an emergency generator that runs on gasoline or natural gas.

Most users require just enough time to keep trains of thought on track and make a rational decision about the prognosis of an outage and the need for shutting down. An inadvertently thrown power switch can be fixed in seconds; hurricanes take longer to abate. Some of the backup systems on the market can give power for more than half an hour, but the more backup energy available, the more costly the unit.

Traditionally, backup systems have been divided into two classes: true uninterruptible power supplies (UPSs), which deliver a constant current to your PC without even the briefest interruption; and standby power supplies (SPSs) which switch from utility to battery power and briefly interrupt their output. This interruption is so short that nearly all PCs ignore it and continue operating as though the electrical supply were continuous. The term UPS is often used for both uninterruptible and standby devices (Underwriters Laboratories, for example, uses UPS to mean both types of systems). Technology also is smoothing over the differences; the short switching times of commercial standby systems are now fast enough (by a great margin) to keep any current PC running without interruption.

Not all UPSs are the same in their ability to control voltage. Some backup systems regulate in discrete steps by automatically altering transformer taps or similarly compensating for input variations. These allow voltage to drift within a range; should the voltage drift too far afield, the unit will switch to backup operation. Other units control their output voltage only after their inverters switch into operation, affecting control as an all-or-nothing affair. The output voltage from these units can rise or dip dramatically before a switchover. As long as the backup system maintains the voltage within the range your PC can tolerate, you have nothing to worry about.

All UPSs depend on batteries for their power reserves. Most use sealed lead-acid batteries or variations of this technology (lead-calcium or lead-cadmium) because of the low battery cost, relatively long life, and maintenance-free operation. Essentially, these are car batteries in miniature. The only down side to sealed lead-acid batteries is that they are heavy and require more mass for every joule they store.

The number of available models of sealed lead-acid batteries is small, so many backup power systems from different manufacturers use the same battery model. To gain greater reserves backup power systems makers add more batteries. Connecting multiple batteries in series yields a higher voltage input to the backup system's inverter, which adds efficiency because higher voltage circuits need to handle less current at a given

ACCESSORIES

power level. Most of these systems link four 12-V batteries together to make a 48-V supply.

Batteries are rated in ampere-hours; at their rated voltage, each can store a distinct quantity of energy measured in *joules*—the product of voltage (volts), current (amps), and time (hours) for backing up your PC. The conversion circuitry of a backup power system operates at less than 100 percent efficiency. More efficient backup systems pull more life from a given size of battery. (Keep this in mind if you intend to add external batteries for longer operation during failures; a more efficient unit will make an expansion less costly.) This isn't as great a concern to a home user as it is to a business user, but it is something to keep in mind.

All chemical battery cells suffer general aging, and after three to five years they may not run through a power failure. Unfortunately, there is no outward sign of this battery deterioration. Backup power system makers use a variety of strategies to cope with this problem. The most common one is a means to monitor battery condition to check the battery voltage. This gives a general indication of the state of charge. But capacity and charge are not necessarily the same. Since battery failure is inevitable, you need to consider the ease and affordability of battery replacement.

To guard against power problems, an ounce of prevention really is worth a pound of cure. The right backup power system can eliminate one source of disaster and ensure that your utility company's problems don't become your own.

Wire Testing

If you have a lot of unexplained crashes with your computer, the problem might be improper AC wiring and grounding. Many buildings, especially older ones, aren't wired correctly. Little mistakes here and there contribute to computer problems. A power strip with a surge protector won't help you with these wiring anomalies. You could hire an electrician to come and check each socket in your home or office for one of a multitude of possible errors: open neutrals, ground shorts, reversed polarity, ground and hot reversals, and all sorts of other problems, but that's expensive, given the number of sockets the average building has.

There is a device you can buy to check the sockets yourself: the Accu-Test II wiring integrity tester, from Ecos Electronics in Oak Park, Illinois (retail $198). You plug this hand-held device into the socket, and a panel of lights will diagnose any problems and isolate where the problems are. (Then you can call an electrician to fix it.) It's an excellent device and will pay for itself when it finds just one defective outlet. For more information, they can be reached at (708) 383-2505.

ACCESSORIES

Heat problems? Moi?

Put your finger on a powered-up 50-MHz 486. It's hot. The DX2 version of the 486 is even hotter, so hot that the 66 MHz version of the chip might actually contribute to global warming. While the manufacturers are aware of the heat problem, the users aren't. Many report unusual crashes (especially when running processor-intensive Windows and OS/2 operating systems) and other screwy problems that will make you begin to think you're going crazy. You're not, it's just the processor overheating. (The Intel heat specification for the chip tops out at 185 degrees Fahrenheit.) When the heat of summertime comes, the problem may become more serious. You should expect to see manufacturers redesign the computer's box to better dissipate heat—someday.

In the meantime, there's a quick fix. From Norm Bailey comes the CPU Kooler. This is a $39.95 package consisting of a milspec (military specification) fan hooked to a heat sink. The fan is glued onto the top of the 486 chip with a special thermal compound, which transfers most of the heat to the heat-sink fan. It's plugged into the power supply. According to the company, "A surface temperature of 170.2 degrees Fahrenheit was measured on a 80486-33 after one hour's operation. This reduces the life of the most costly component in the PC. With the CPU Kooler installed, the temperature increased only 7 degrees above ambient room temperature to 87.6 degrees."

For more information call PCubid Computer Technology in Sacramento, California, at (916) 338-1338 or fax them at (916) 725-0230.

Hardware Helper

There are diagnostic tools and there is PocketPOST, a $199 minicard that pops into any PC or ISA slot. Included with the card is a complete diagnostic system that can pinpoint any PC failure (including boot failure). It comes with a comprehensive book with hundreds of error codes that can crop up on the PocketPOST digital display and LED read outs. The product comes from Data Depot (1525 Sandy Lane, Clearwater, FL, 34615, (813) 446-3402). When combined with the company's Remote RX software ($100 when purchased with PocketPOST), there is no problem that can't be resolved. The software can even isolate a single bad memory chip and specifically show you what chip to pull. This is an amazing system that is equaled only by equipment selling for thousands of dollars. You'll be a hero in your company if you own PocketPOST and Remote RX from Data Depot. If you have anything to do with maintenance or repair, call these guys immediately. Also ask the company about their inexpensive (but outstanding) PC Certify—a program that certifies compatibility. I give the highest recommendation for the entire product line.

ACCESSORIES

Superior Cables

Granite Digital, 3101 Whipple Rd., Union City, CA 94587 (phone 510-471-6442, fax 510-471-6267) makes legendary cables that I highly recommend for everyone using SCSI connections. Specializing only in SCSI cables and terminators, these cables are specially made to protect the Acknowledge and Request lines with special insulation. Special high dielectric PVC covers the cables. Internally there are loads of special shielding and ferrite beads. When you see one of these black beauties, you immediately say "Wow!" The cables all have LEDs indicating they are "live." The company also makes a terminator that has a series of LEDs to indicate the daisy chain is live, active, and working. These are very cool cables. The company also makes special internal SCSI cables that are unlike anything you've ever seen: They are gold plated and impedance matched. SCSI errors and retries will fall to zero once you use these marvelous cables and terminators.

PC Security

Once you have the perfect computer system, it's time to think about the perfect way to protect it. Secure-It has one concept in computer security: the Kablit security cabling system. For about $35, you get a 10-foot cable/fastener set that will attach your computer and keyboard to your desk. The cable threads through each fastener and wraps around a leg or your desk (or uses special glue-on fasteners). Contact Secure-It at (800) 451-7592 or (413) 525-7039, or fax them at (413) 525-8807.

Get an Angle on the Tangle

Are your power cords in a tangle behind your desk? It's time to round up the masses of coils with American Power Conversion's PowerManager. The unit keeps cords stored and coiled neatly under a cover. It also provides surge protection and power control for up to five devices, with an available socket on the side to plug in a mobile computer or desktop lamp. The PowerManager comes with a $25,000 equipment protection policy that guarantees repair or replacement if anything is damaged by a power surge or lightning strike. The unit costs around $120. For more information contact American Power Conversion at (800) 800-4272 or (401) 789-5735, or fax them at (401) 789-3710.

Overseas Telecommunications Helpers

When you travel overseas, you will run into many situations where you cannot connect your mobile computer's modem directly to the local telephone system. Every foreign telephone system has its own standard. Either the phone plug is a different size or shape, or the local system uses pulse instead of tone. There are some tools to overcome these problems.

ACCESSORIES

The first trick in the overseas telecommunications bag is an acoustic coupler. This is a set of rubber cups which attach to the mouth- and ear-piece of the telephone handset. The cups press directly onto the handset and a velcro strap holds them there. It can operate at speeds up to 14.4 kbps, and uses the signal from your mobile computer's modem. This handy device costs about $150. The one I use is the Konexx 204 coupler, available from Unlimited Systems. Call them at (619) 622-1400.

The Executive TeleKit ($105) is a bag of tricks. Inside its lightweight vinyl bag is a variety of tools to help you get connected overseas. The tools included are TeleClips (a standard RJ-11 phone plug attached to a pair of alligator clips) to let you connect your modem to a phone receiver (by taking off the screw-on cover); TeleDaptors, a set of some 40 or so customized foreign telephone plugs; TeleTester, a device to determine if you have a good phone connection (a green light indicates the line is working); and a set of mini-screwdrivers to remove wall covers and examine wiring. As if that wasn't enough, the kit also has a collapsible pocket phone and a tone dialer, a custom flashlight (which will sit on the floor at a 90-degree angle to help you remove the phone's wall bracket in that hard-to-reach location—which always seems to be behind the bed).

Contact TeleAdapt, Inc. at (408) 370-5105.

Multimedia Add Ons

With today's high performance PC, it's nuts not to have a good sound card and a couple of speakers. Many software packages and all games have sound. Let's face it: For "real" multimedia (and to keep the kids happy), you'll need to buy some speakers. But who wants to spend a mint on speakers if it's just for the annoying sound effects for some kids' games. (Face the fact: That's what's it all about anyway.) Sony has come into the market with low prices and deep discounts, going for market share of their new entry-level audio products: the SRS-PC20 Active Speaker System and their MDR-009VPC Headphones.

Let's talk prices. At $40, Sony's SRS-PC20 speakers are a steal. They list for half the price of the PC30s which were formerly the firm's bottom line. The new 1.5 ounce MDR-009VPC headphones at $20, on the other hand, cost twice as much as Sony's old MDR-007PC, but they have their own volume control.

Each SRS-PC20 speaker weighs less than a pound and is rated at 1 watt; a 2-watt amplifier in the left speaker takes four AA batteries. The magnetically shielded speakers offer 85dB sensitivity and a 150Hz–20,000Hz frequency-response range. They're very listenable for computer-generated sounds, if less so for CD-audio output, since they have neither speaker-to-speaker volume balancing nor tone controls. They may be just right, though, for modest multimedia applications, and will keep the kids happy.

ACCESSORIES

The right speaker plugs into the left one with a relatively short (57-inch) cable, which makes wide placement and good stereo separation questionable. The cable from the left speaker to your PC's sound card is 49 inches— barely long enough to reach around the back of the desk from a tower-cased system.

The MDR-009VPC headset connects to your PC's audio source with an L-shaped stereo mini plug. Sony has applied its extensive experience in small headphone design well: The wide, ergonomically designed headband distributes pressure evenly for greater comfort during long listening sessions, and adjusts from big heads to little heads.

Like other budget speakers, the SRS-PC20s are too small and weak to satisfy a real audiophile, but at the price, who cares? Picky users will want to look to Sony's next steps up—the 3-watt PC30s or the 5-watt PC50s—and pay two to three times as much. But for a family PC, the PC20s are just the ticket. But consider the worthwhile investment in headphones. There is nothing worse than listening to the game sounds— over and over and over and over.

For information, contact:
Sony Electronics, Inc.
1 Sony Dr.
Park Ridge, NJ 07656
800-342-5721

Portable Innovations

Using a mobile computer in a car can be quite a challenge. The steering wheel is in the way, for one, and unless you are the Great Contortini the Human Pretzel, it's nearly impossible to get comfortable. DVX Company has devised one way to overcome the problem, the MobilDesk. This device creates a portable aluminum desk which hangs off the steering wheel (and can be used for those on-the-road meals, too). The desk, which weighs less than five pounds, is designed for safety and stability. (By the way, it is impossible to drive while it's in place.) The price is around $80. For more information, contact the DVC Company at (508) 747-6471, or fax them at (508) 747-6450.

Fun Stuff and Gift Ideas

There is a lot of fun stuff on the market for PCs that makes the computer seem like less of a tool and more of a toy. There are gadgets to stick onto the computer that look like a big wind-up key, a big tongue sticking out of the small disk drive, and other silly items. Let's face it, computers don't have to be dull. Keep your eyes open for the occasional good, useful (but silly) gift items, interesting specialty catalogs, small utility software programs, and the occasional "conversation piece." They're fun.

ACCESSORIES

The latest in computer accessories comes from the rock 'n' roll institution the Grateful Dead. It's merchandise like this that helped put the Dead at the top of Forbes' list of highest-paid entertainers. Digital Deadheads have their choice of dancing bears, strutting skeletons, or the steal-your-face design on mouse pads ($8), mouse pads with wrist rests ($13), and keyboard wrist rests ($15). There's even a desk set for the tie-dyed executive ($25, complete with coasters). All are available through Grateful Dead Merchandising at (800) 225-3323, The Music Stand (800) 515-5010, or Deadhead computer stores.

The Corvette Mouse

How can anyone resist a product like the Corvette Mouse! Actually it's a little Corvette model that fits over a Macintosh or Microsoft mouse. The user presses on the hood of the 'Vette to activate the mouse button underneath. The company says, "Instead of having a boring-looking mouse on your desk, you are driving a hot Corvette!" Cheap thrills at only $19.95. To order one of these nifty covers, contact:

Suntime
7817 N. Cameron Ave.
Tampa, FL 33614
(813) 886-1145

MotorMouse

Another interesting gizmo is the MotorMouse, a switchable two- or three-button mouse in the shape of a Lamborghini or a Corvette. You push down on the hood to get the button action. The mouse comes in red, white, and yellow. The red Corvette looks great! The U.S. list price is $65.99. This is a perfect gift for the person who has everything. The company can be reached by calling (604) 681-6062, or writing:

MotorMouse
126 Garden Avenue
North Vancouver, BC V7P 3H2

or

P.O. Box 9754, 3873 Airport Way
Bellingham, WA 98227-9754

ACCESSORIES

■ Genuinely Interesting Mail

Computer mail-order catalogs usually fall into two categories: the software catalog in which, in many cases, the vendors have to pay for inclusion, which creates a mish-mosh of ever-changing products; and the hardware catalog selling the same old cables and connectors. But a new generation of specialty catalogs is emerging.

Specialty Paper

One excellent specialty catalog is from a company called Paper Direct. It specializes in something new: laser printer paper. Not just any laser printer paper, mind you, but exotic stuff like the Shimizu line that appears to be handmade Japanese one-of-a-kind paper. They also sell a strange foil that you can put through your laser printer to create a foil-stamped letterhead. The product line doesn't end there. There are recycled papers, tri-fold brochures, and greeting cards which will all run through your laser printer with ease. Get their catalog and you won't regret it. The company can be reached at (201) 507-5488, or fax them at (201) 507-0817 and ask for a catalog.

Price Trend Newsletter

If you like to watch computer price trends, there's a new and interesting newsletter available called *The PC Street Price Index*. It's 25 pages of price data reflecting street prices of everything from 386SX machines to AskSAM software. Not cheap at $195, the newsletter is a must-have for large corporations and vendors who want to know the real price of their competitor's products. The publisher is Metro Computing of Gibbsboro, New Jersey. Contact them at (609) 784-8866 for more information or a subscription.   ■

Key to Comparison Charts A–J

The tables in the following charts were compiled from the last four years'
worth of *PC Magazine*s. Because prices change quickly, we will specify
the general price range to which each product belongs rather than specify-
ing original list prices. Price ranges are denoted by dollar signs, as follows:

$	= $1400 or less
$$	= $1401–$2400
$$$	= $2401–$4000
$$$$	= $4001–$6000
$$$$$	= over $6000

The tables also use the following symbols and abbreviations:

N/A = Not applicable (the product does not have this feature)

INA = Information not available

● = Yes

○ = No

PC MAGAZINE = *PC Magazine* Editor's Choice

= Dvorak's Pick

COMPUTER SYSTEMS

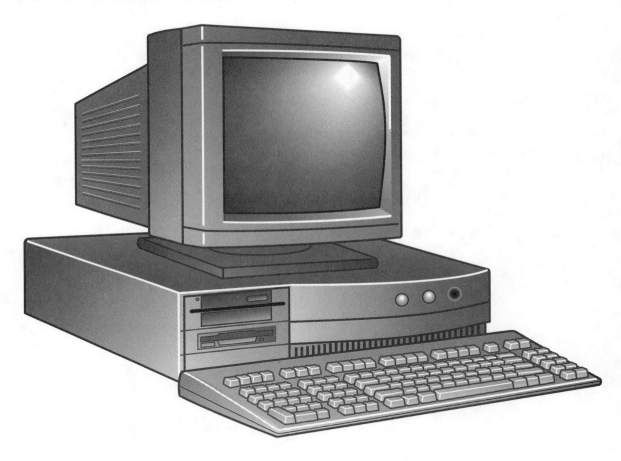

A.1   Pentium and 486 Buyers' Guide

(Products listed in alphabetical order by company)	AcerPower DX2/66	AcerPower 60MHz Pentium	AcerPower 90MHz Pentium	ACMA Desktop 486DX2/66	ACMA P66 Tower
List price (tested configuration)	$$	$$$	$$$	$$	$$$
Processor	Intel 486DX2/66	Intel Pentium/60	Intel Pentium/90	Intel 486DX2/66	Intel Pentium/66
Installed/maximum motherboard RAM	8Mb, 64Mb	16Mb, 128Mb	16Mb, 128Mb	8Mb, 64Mb	16Mb, 128Mb
Installed/maximum external RAM cache	256K, 512K	256K, 256K	256K, 256K	256K, 512K	256K, 256K
Motherboard manufacturer	Acer	Acer	Acer	FCT	Intel
Chip set manufacturer	ALI	Intel	Intel	SIS	Intel
BIOS manufacturer and version (or date)	Acer (6/24/94)	Acer 1.2R1.4	Acer 1.2R1.4	Award 4.50G	AMI (4/15/94)
Flash BIOS/16550 UART chip	●/●	○/●	●/●	○/○	●/●
Expansion-bus slots	5 ISA, 3 PCI, 1 VL	5 ISA, 3 PCI	5 ISA, 3 PCI	5 ISA, 3 VL	5 ISA, 3 PCI
Parallel, serial, mouse ports	1, 2, 1	1, 2, 1	1, 2, 1	1, 2, 0	1, 2, 0
Graphics adapter (and memory)	ATI Graphics Pro Turbo (2Mb)	ATI Graphics Pro Turbo (2Mb)	ATI Graphics Pro Turbo (2Mb)	Diamond Stealth 64 (1Mb)	Diamond Stealth 64 (2Mb)
Hard-disk capacity and interface	527Mb IDE	528Mb IDE	810Mb IDE	503Mb IDE	503Mb IDE
CD-ROM drive (and speed)	Matsushita CR-562-B (2x)	Matsushita CR-562-B (2x)	Matsushita CR-562-B (2x)	Chinon CDS-535 (2x)	Chinon CDS-535 (2x)
Modem/Network adapter/Audio	●/○/●	●/○/●	●/○/●	○/○/●	○/○/●
Accessible drive bays (5.25", 3.5")	3, 2	3, 2	3, 2	3, 1	4, 2
Internal drive bays (5.25", 3.5")	0, 1	0, 2	0, 2	0, 2	2, 3
Power supply (and number of connectors)	145W (4)	200W (3)	200W (3)	250W (6)	250W (6)
Monitor (and diagonal screen size)	Acer AcerView 56L (15")	Acer AcerView 76i (17")	Acer AcerView 76i (17")	MAG Innovision DX15F (15")	MAG Innovision MXI5F (15")
System software	DOS 6.22, Windows 3.1	DOS 6.22, Windows 3.11	DOS 6.22, Windows 3.1	DOS 6.22, WfWG 3.11	DOS 6.22, WfWG 3.11
Warranty on parts/labor	1 year/1 year	1 year/1 year	1 year/1 year	1 year/1 year	1 year/1 year
On-site service	Included (1 year)	Included (1 year)	Included (1 year)	Included (1 year)	Included (1 year)

●—Yes   ○—No   N/A—Not applicable   INA—Information not available

Table Continues →

Pentium and 486 Buyers' Guide

	ACMA P90 Tower	Alaris Leopard Plus EnergySmartPC 486SLC2 66	Alaris Cougar EnergySmartPC 486BL3X 75	AMAX 486DX2 66 PowerSaver	AMAX 66 PowerStation
List price (tested configuration)	$$$	$$	$$	$$	$$$
Processor	Intel Pentium/90	IBM 486SLC2/66	IBM BL 25/75	Intel 486DX2/66	Intel Pentium/66
Installed/maximum motherboard RAM	16Mb, 128Mb	8Mb, 64Mb	16Mb, 64Mb	8Mb, 32Mb	16Mb, 128Mb
Installed/maximum external RAM cache	256K, 256K	512K, 512K	256K, 512K	256K, 256K	256K, 256K
Motherboard manufacturer	Intel	Alaris	Alaris	Impression	Intel
Chip set manufacturer	Intel	OPTi	OPTi	USA	Intel
BIOS manufacturer and version (or date)	AMI 1.00.06.AX1	Microid 1.61	Microid 1.53	AMI (8/8/93)	AMI 1.00.07.AF2
Flash BIOS/16550 UART chip	●/●	●/●	●/●	●/●	●/●
Expansion-bus slots	5 ISA, 3 PCI	5 ISA, 3 VL	5 ISA, 2 VL	6 ISA, 2 VL	5 ISA, 3 PCI
Parallel, serial, mouse ports	1, 2, 0	1, 2, 0	1, 2, 0	1, 2, 0	1, 2, 0
Graphics adapter (and memory)	Diamond Stealth 64 (2Mb)	Alaris SkyEagle (1Mb)	Alaris SkyEagle (1Mb)	Diamond Stealth 64 (1Mb)	Diamond Stealth 64 (2Mb)
Hard-disk capacity and interface	1GB IDE	425Mb IDE	503Mb IDE	541Mb IDE	540Mb IDE
CD-ROM drive (and speed)	Chinon CDS-535 (2x)	Mitsumi FX001D (2x)	Toshiba XM-3401B (2x)	Chinon CDS-535 (2x)	Chinon CDS-535 (2x)
Modem/Network adapter/Audio	●/●/●	●/●/●	●/●/●	●/●/●	●/●/●
Accessible drive bays (5.25", 3.5")	4, 2	3, 2	5, 2	2, 2	4, 0
Internal drive bays (5.25", 3.5")	2, 1	0, 0	1, 2	0, 0	2, 2
Power supply (and number of connectors)	300W (6)	200W (4)	300W (4)	250W (3)	250W (3)
Monitor (and diagonal screen size)	MAG Innovision DX17F (17")	IBM 6324 (14")	IBM 6324 (14")	Impression DCM-1588 (15")	Impression DX-17F (17")
System software	DOS 6.22, WfWG 3.11	DOS 6.22, WfWG 3.11	DOS 6.2, WfWG 3.11	DOS 6.22, WfWG 3.11	DOS 6.22, WfWG 3.11
Warranty on parts/labor	1 year/1 year	3 years/3 years	3 years/3 years	1 year/1 year	1 year/1 year
On-site service	Included (1 year)	$79 (1 year)	$79 (1 year)	$39 (1 year)	$39 (1 year)

●—Yes ○—No N/A—Not applicable INA—Information not available

Pentium and 486 Buyers' Guide ▪

	AMAX 90 PowerStation	American Multisystems InfoGold 486DX2/66	American Multisystems InfoGold Pentium/66	American Multisystems InfoGold Pentium/90	AST Bravo LC 4/66d
List price (tested configuration)	$$$	$$	$$$	$$$$	$$ (estimated)
Processor	Intel Pentium/90	Intel 486DX2/66	Intel Pentium/66	Intel Pentium/90	Intel 486DX2/66
Installed/maximum motherboard RAM	16Mb, 128Mb	8Mb, 64Mb	16Mb, 192Mb	16Mb, 128Mb	8Mb, 64Mb
Installed/maximum external RAM cache	256K, 256K	256K, 256K	256K, 512K	256K, 256K	64K, 256K
Motherboard manufacturer	Intel	FCT	Asus	Intel	AST
Chip set manufacturer	Intel	SIS	Intel	Intel	VLSI
BIOS manufacturer and version (or date)	AMI 1.00.06.AX1	Award 4.50G	Award 4.5	AMI 1.00.03.AX1Z	AST Bravo 1.0
Flash BIOS/16550 UART chip	●/●	○/○	●/○	●/●	○/○
Expansion-bus slots	5 ISA, 3 PCI	4 ISA, 3 VL	5 ISA, 3 PCI	5 ISA, 3 PCI	3 ISA, 1 VL
Parallel, serial, mouse ports	1, 2, 0	1, 2, 0	1, 2, 0	1, 2, 0	1, 2, 1
Graphics adapter (and memory)	Diamond Stealth 64 (4Mb)	Diamond Stealth 24 (1Mb)	Diamond Stealth 64 (2Mb)	Diamond Stealth 64 (2Mb)	Integrated Cirrus Logic GD5428 (1Mb)
Hard-disk capacity and interface	1GB IDE	494Mb IDE	494Mb IDE	1.7GB SCSI	404Mb IDE
CD-ROM drive (and speed)	NEC CDR-510 (3x)	Sony CDU 33A (2x)	Sony CDU 33A (2x)	Toshiba XM-3401B (2x)	Sony CDU 33A (2x)
Modem/Network adapter/Audio	●/●/●	○/○/○	○/○/○	○/○/○	○/○/○
Accessible drive bays (5.25", 3.5")	4, 0	2, 2	3, 1	4, 0	2, 1
Internal drive bays (5.25", 3.5")	2, 2	0, 2	0, 4	0, 3	0, 2
Power supply (and number of connectors)	300W (3)	200W (5)	300W (3)	250W (3)	145W (3)
Monitor (and diagonal screen size)	Impression DX-17F (17")	Everware Technology DM-1448 (14")	Everware Technology DM-1448 (14")	Antec CM-15GS (15")	AST Vision 5L (15")
System software	DOS 6.22, WfWG 3.11	DOS 6.22, Windows 3.1	DOS 6.22, Windows 3.1	DOS 6.22, Windows 3.1	DOS 6.2, Windows 3.1
Warranty on parts/labor	1 year/1 year	1 year/1 year	1 year/1 year	1 year/1 year	3 years/3 years
On-site service	$39 (1 year)	None	None	None	Included (1 year)

●—Yes   ○—No   N/A—Not applicable   INA—Information not available

Table Continues →

■ Pentium and 486 Buyers' Guide

	AST Bravo MS P/60	AST Premmia MX 4/66d	AST Premmia MX 4/100t	AST Premmia GX P/90	AT&T Globalyst 550
List price (tested configuration)	$$$ (estimated)	$$$ (estimated)	$$$ (estimated)	$$$$ (estimated)	$$$
Processor	Intel Pentium/60	Intel 486DX2/66	Intel DX4/100	Intel Pentium/90	Intel 486DX2/66
Installed/maximum motherboard RAM	16Mb, 128Mb	8Mb, 128Mb	16Mb, 128Mb	16Mb, 192Mb	8Mb, 64Mb
Installed/maximum external RAM cache	256K, 256K	256K, 256K	256K, 256K	256K, 512K	256K, 256K
Motherboard manufacturer	AST	AST	AST	AST	AT&T
Chip set manufacturer	VLSI	Intel	Intel	Intel	OPTi
BIOS manufacturer and version (or date)	AST 1.00.26	AST 1.00.27	AST 1.00.27	AST Shasta 1.01	Phoenix 1.01-02
Flash BIOS/16550 UART chip	●/●	●/●	●/●	●/●	●/●
Expansion-bus slots	3 ISA, 2 PCI	4 ISA, 3 PCI	4 ISA, 3 PCI	5 EISA, 2 PCI	3 ISA, 2 PCI
Parallel, serial, mouse ports	1, 2, 1	1, 2, 1	1, 2, 1	1, 2, 1	1, 2, 1
Graphics adapter (and memory)	Integrated Cirrus Logic GD5434 (2Mb)	ATI Graphics Pro Turbo (2Mb)	ATI Graphics Pro Turbo (2Mb)	ATI Graphics Pro Turbo (4Mb)	Integrated S3 Vision864 (2Mb)
Hard-disk capacity and interface	514Mb IDE	404Mb IDE	731Mb IDE	697Mb SCSI-2	341Mb IDE
CD-ROM drive (and speed)	Sony CDU 33A (2x)	Sony CDU 55E (2x)	Sony CDU 55E (2x)	Toshiba XM-3401B (2x)	Sony CDU 561 (2x)
Modem/Network adapter/Audio	○/○/○	○/○/○	○/○/○	○/●/○	○/○/○
Accessible drive bays (5.25", 3.5")	1, 1	2, 1	2, 2	2, 1	1, 1
Internal drive bays (5.25", 3.5")	1, 1	0, 2	0, 2	0, 2	0, 1
Power supply (and number of connectors)	145W (4)	230W (4)	230W (4)	230W (4)	150W (3)
Monitor (and diagonal screen size)	AST Vision 5L (15")	AST Vision 5L (15")	AST Vision 5L (15")	AST Vision 5L (15")	NCR CAM630Z (15")
System software	DOS 6.21, Windows 3.11	DOS 6.21, Windows 3.1	DOS 6.21, Windows 3.1	DOS 6.21, Windows 3.11	DOS 6.21, WfWG 3.11
Warranty on parts/labor	3 years/3 years	3 years/3 years	3 years/3 years	3 years/3 years	3 years/3 years
On-site service	Included (1 year)	Included (1 year)	Included (1 year)	Included (1 year)	Included (1 year)

●—Yes   ○—No   N/A—Not applicable   INA—Information not available

Pentium and 486 Buyers' Guide ■

	AT&T Globalyst 590	AT&T Globalyst 600	Austin Communications Manager 486DX2-66	Austin Communications Manager P66	Austin Edutainer
List price (tested configuration)	$$$$	$$$$	$$	$$$	$$
Processor	Intel Pentium/66	Intel Pentium/90	Intel 486DX2/66	Intel Pentium/66	Intel 486DX2/66
Installed, maximum motherboard RAM	16Mb, 128Mb	16Mb, 128Mb	8Mb, 128Mb	16Mb, 128Mb	8Mb, 64Mb
Installed, maximum external RAM cache	256K, 256K	256K, 256K	256K, 256K	256K, 256K	128K, 128K
Motherboard manufacturer	Intel	Intel	Intel	Intel	BCM
Chip set manufacturer	Intel	Intel	Intel	Intel	OPTi
BIOS manufacturer and version (or date)	AMI 1.00.09.A	AMI 1.00.03.BF0B	AMI 1.00.02.AY0	AMI 1.00.07.AF2	Phoenix 4.03
Flash BIOS/16550 UART chip	●/●	●/●	●/●	●/●	●/○
Expansion-bus slots	5 ISA, 2 PCI	6 ISA, 2 PCI	4 ISA, 3 PCI	4 ISA, 3 PCI	5 ISA
Parallel, serial, mouse ports	1, 2, 1	1, 2, 1	1, 2, 0	1, 2, 0	1, 2, 1
Graphics adapter (and memory)	ATI Graphics Wonder (2Mb)	ATI Graphics Pro Turbo (2Mb)	Diamond Stealth 32 (2Mb)	Diamond Stealth 64 (2Mb)	Integrated Cirrus Logic GD5428 (2Mb)
Hard-disk capacity and interface	527Mb IDE	1GB SCSI-2	341Mb IDE	540Mb IDE	340Mb IDE
CD-ROM drive (and speed)	NEC CDR-260 (2x)	Sony CDU 561 (2x)	Sony CDU 33A (2x)	Sony CDU 33A (2x)	Sony CDU 33A-01 (2x)
Modem/Network adapter/Audio	○/○/○	○/○/○	○/○/●	○/○/●	○/○/●
Accessible drive bays (5.25", 3.5")	2, 1	2, 1	2, 0	3, 2	2, 1
Internal drive bays (5.25", 3.5")	0, 4	0, 3	1, 3	1, 2	0, 1
Power supply (and number of connectors)	200W (5)	180W (3)	200W (3)	250W (4)	200W (3)
Monitor (and diagonal screen size)	NCR CAM630Z (15")	NCR CAM630Z (15")	KFC MN2404 (14")	KFC MN2409 (15")	KFC MN2404 (14")
System software	DOS 6.21, WfWG 3.11	DOS 6.21, Windows 3.11	DOS 6.21, WfWG 3.11	DOS 6.21, Windows 3.11	DOS 6.21, WfWG 3.11
Warranty on parts/labor	3 years/3 years	3 years/3 years	3 years/3 years	3 years/3 years	3 years/3 years
On-site service	Included (1 year)	Included (1 year)	Included (1 year)	Included (1 year)	Included (1 year)

●—Yes   ○—No   N/A—Not applicable   INA—Information not available

Table Continues →

■ Pentium and 486 Buyers' Guide

	Austin Edutainer Plus	Austin Power System 60	Austin Power System 90	CAF Gold G66	CAF Lightning P6
List price (tested configuration)	$$$	$$$	$$$	$$	$$$
Processor	Intel Pentium/60	Intel Pentium/60	Intel Pentium/90	Intel 486DX2/66	Intel Pentium/66
Installed, maximum motherboard RAM	16Mb, 128Mb	16Mb, 128Mb	16Mb, 128Mb	8Mb, 128Mb	16Mb, 128Mb
Installed, maximum external RAM cache	256K, 256K	256K, 256K	256K, 256K	256K, 512K	512K, 512K
Motherboard manufacturer	Intel	BCM	Intel	Aquarius	TMC
Chip set manufacturer	Intel	OPTi	Intel	ALI	OPTi
BIOS manufacturer and version (or date)	AMI 1.00.03.AF2	Phoenix 4.03	AMI 1.00.05.AX1	Phoenix (4/26/94)	AMI (12/15/93)
Flash BIOS/16550 UART chip	●/○	●/●	●/●	●/○	●/○
Expansion-bus slots	5 ISA, 3 PCI	3 ISA, 3 PCI, 2 VL	5 ISA, 3 PCI	2 ISA, 3 PCI, 2 VL	3 ISA, 3 PCI, 3 VL
Parallel, serial, mouse ports	1, 2, 0	1, 2, 0	1, 2, 0	1, 2, 0	1, 2, 0
Graphics adapter (and memory)	Diamond Stealth 32 (2Mb)	Diamond Stealth 64 (2Mb)	Diamond Stealth 64 (2Mb)	Diamond Stealth 64 (2Mb)	Diamond Stealth 64 (2Mb)
Hard-disk capacity and interface	514Mb IDE	540Mb IDE	1GB IDE	546Mb IDE	540Mb IDE
CD-ROM drive (and speed)	Sony CDU 33A (2x)	Sony CDU 33A-01 (2x)	Teac CD 55A (4x)	Philips LMS CR940 (2x)	Philips LMS CR940 (2x)
Modem/Network adapter/Audio	○/○/●	○/○/●	○/○/●	○/○/○	○/○/○
Accessible drive bays (5.25", 3.5")	2, 0	2, 2	3, 2	2, 1	3, 2
Internal drive bays (5.25", 3.5")	1, 3	0, 0	1, 2	0, 2	0, 1
Power supply (and number of connectors)	200W (4)	200W (3)	250W (4)	150W (5)	200W (4)
Monitor (and diagonal screen size)	KFC MN2409 (15")	KFC MN2409 (15")	KFC MN2410 (17")	Sceptre CC-615GL (15")	Sceptre CC-615GL (15")
System software	DOS 6.21, WfWG 3.11	DOS 6.21, WfWG 3.11	DOS 6.21, WfWG 3.11	DOS 6.2, Windows 3.1	DOS 6.2, Windows 3.11
Warranty on parts/labor	3 years/3 years	3 years/3 years	3 years/3 years	1 year/1 year	1 year/1 year
On-site service	Included (1 year)	Included (1 year)	Included (1 year)	None	None

●—Yes   ○—No   N/A—Not applicable   INA—Information not available

Pentium and 486 Buyers' Guide ■

	CAF Lightning P9	Compaq Deskpro XL 466 Model 535/CDS	Compaq Deskpro XL 566 Model 535/CDS	CompuAdd C466D Desktop	CompuAdd CP60p Desktop
List price (tested configuration)	$$$	$$$ (estimated)	$$$$ (estimated)	$$$	$$
Processor	Intel Pentium/90	Intel 486DX2/66	Intel Pentium/66	Intel 486DX2/66	Intel Pentium/60
Installed, maximum motherboard RAM	16Mb, 128Mb	8Mb, 128Mb	16Mb, 144Mb	8Mb, 64Mb	16Mb, 128Mb
Installed, maximum external RAM cache	512K, 512K	256K, 256K	256K, 256K	256K, 256K	256K, 256K
Motherboard manufacturer	Aquarius	Compaq	Compaq	Micronics	Micronics
Chip set manufacturer	OPTi	Intel	Intel	Micronics	Intel
BIOS manufacturer and version (or date)	AMI (12/15/93)	Compaq (7/19/94)	Compaq (7/19/94)	Phoenix 0.1	Phoenix 1.03
Flash BIOS/16550 UART chip	●/●	●/●	●/●	●/●	●/●
Expansion-bus slots	3 ISA, 4 PCI, 2 VL	4 EISA, 2 PCI	4 EISA, 2 PCI	5 ISA, 1 VL	5 ISA, 3 PCI
Parallel, serial, mouse ports	1, 2, 0	1, 2, 1	1, 2, 1	1, 2, 1	1, 2, 0
Graphics adapter (and memory)	Diamond Stealth 64 (2Mb)	Compaq QVision 2000 (2Mb)	Compaq QVision 2000 (2Mb)	ATI Graphics Wonder (2Mb)	Hercules Dynamite (2Mb)
Hard-disk capacity and interface	1GB SCSI-2	536Mb SCSI-2	504Mb SCSI-2	424Mb IDE	541Mb IDE
CD-ROM drive (and speed)	Philips LMS CR940	Matsushita CR-503-B (2x)	Matsushita CR-503-B (2x)	Mitsumi FX001D (2x)	Mitsumi FX001D (2x)
Modem/Network adapter/Audio	○/○/○	○/●/●	○/●/●	○/○/○	○/○/○
Accessible drive bays (5.25", 3.5")	3, 2	3, 0	3, 0	2, 1	3, 2
Internal drive bays (5.25", 3.5")	0, 1	0, 1	0, 1	0, 1	0, 1
Power supply (and number of connectors)	200W (4)	245W (6)	245W (6)	200W (4)	200W (3)
Monitor (and diagonal screen size)	Sceptre CC-615GL (15")	Compaq 171FS (15")	Compaq 171FS (15")	CompuAdd TE1564M (15")	CompuAdd TE1564M (15")
System software	DOS 6.2, Windows 3.11	DOS 6.2, Windows 3.1	DOS 6.2, Windows 3.1	DOS 6.2, WfWG 3.11	DOS 6.2, WfWG 3.11
Warranty on parts/labor	1 year/1 year	3 years/3 years	3 years/3 years	1 year/1 year	1 year/1 year
On-site service	None	Included (1 year)	Included (1 year)	Included (1 year)	Included (1 year)

●—Yes ○—No N/A—Not applicable INA—Information not available

Table Continues →

Pentium and 486 Buyers' Guide

	CompuAdd CP90p Mini-Tower	Comtrade PCI Best Buy 466	Comtrade PCI Best Buy 566	Comtrade PCI CAD/Publishing 566	Comtrade PCI CAD/Publishing 590
List price (tested configuration)	$$$	$$	$$$	$$$	$$$
Processor	Intel Pentium/90	Intel 486DX2/66	Intel Pentium/66	Intel Pentium/66	Intel Pentium/90
Installed, maximum motherboard RAM	16Mb, 128Mb	8Mb, 112Mb	16Mb, 128Mb	16Mb, 128Mb	16Mb, 128Mb
Installed, maximum external RAM cache	256K, 256K	256K, 256K	256K, 256K	256K, 256K	256K, 256K
Motherboard manufacturer	Intel	MicroStar	Intel	Intel	Intel
Chip set manufacturer	Intel	ALI	Intel	Intel	Intel
BIOS manufacturer and version (or date)	AMI 1.00.08.AXI	AMI (5/23/94)	AMI 1.00.07.AF2	AMI 1.00.07.AF2	AMI 1.00.07.AF2
Flash BIOS/16550 UART chip	●/○	○/○	●/●	●/●	●/●
Expansion-bus slots	5 ISA, 3 PCI	3 ISA, 3 PCI, 2 VL	5 ISA, 3 PCI	5 ISA, 3 PCI	5 ISA, 3 PCI
Parallel, serial, mouse ports	1, 2, 0	1, 2, 0	1, 2, 0	1, 2, 0	1, 2, 0
Graphics adapter (and memory)	Hercules Dynamite (1Mb)	Diamond Stealth 64 (2Mb)	Diamond Stealth 64 (2Mb)	Diamond Stealth 64 (4Mb)	Diamond Stealth 64 (4Mb)
Hard-disk capacity and interface	1GB SCSI-2	503Mb IDE	540Mb IDE	1GB IDE	1GB IDE
CD-ROM drive (and speed)	Mitsumi FX001D (2x)	Mitsumi FX001D (2x)	Mitsumi FX001D (2x)	Mitsumi FX001D (2x)	Mitsumi FX001D (2x)
Modem/Network adapter/Audio	○/○/○	○/○/○	○/○/○	○/○/○	○/○/○
Accessible drive bays (5.25", 3.5")	3, 1	3, 2	3, 2	3, 2	3, 2
Internal drive bays (5.25", 3.5")	0, 3	0, 3	0, 3	0, 3	0, 3
Power supply (and number of connectors)	200W (6)	230W (4)	230W (5)	230W (5)	230W (5)
Monitor (and diagonal screen size)	CompuAdd TE1564M (15")	CTX 1562GM (15")	CTX 1562GM (15")	MAG Innovision DX-17F (17")	MAG Innovision DX-17F (17")
System software	DOS 6.2, WfWG 3.11	DOS 6.22, WfWG 3.11	DOS 6.22, WfWG 3.11	DOS 6.21, WfWG 3.11	DOS 6.21, WfWG 3.11
Warranty on parts/labor	1 year/1 year	1 year/1 year	1 year/1 year	1 year/1 year	1 year/1 year
On-site service	Included (1 year)	$50 (1 year)	$50 (1 year)	$50 (1 year)	$50 (1 year)

●—Yes   ○—No   N/A—Not applicable   INA—Information not available

Pentium and 486 Buyers' Guide ■

	Cornell PCI Power Workstation	Cornell PCI/EISA Ultima Workstation	DataStor 486-66DX2VESA	DataStor P5-66	DataStor P5-90
List price (tested configuration)	$$$	$$$$	$$$	$$$	$$$$
Processor	Intel Pentium/66	Intel Pentium/90	Intel 486DX2/66	Intel Pentium/66	Intel Pentium/90
Installed, maximum motherboard RAM	16Mb, 192Mb	16Mb, 192Mb	8Mb, 32Mb	16Mb, 128Mb	16Mb, 128Mb
Installed, maximum external RAM cache	256K, 512K	512K, 512K	256K, 256K	256K, 256K	256K, 256K
Motherboard manufacturer	Asus	Asus	Elite Group	Intel	Intel
Chip set manufacturer	Intel	Intel	UMC	Intel	Intel
BIOS manufacturer and version (or date)	Award 4.5	Award 4.50G	AMI (11/11/92)	AMI 1.00.07.AF2	AMI 1.00.03.AX1Z
Flash BIOS/16550 UART chip	●/●	●/●	●/○	●/●	●/●
Expansion-bus slots	5 ISA, 3 PCI	4 EISA, 4 PCI	4 ISA, 2 VL	5 ISA, 3 PCI	5 ISA, 3 PCI
Parallel, serial, mouse ports	1, 2, 0	1, 2, 0	1, 2, 0	1, 2, 0	1, 2, 0
Graphics adapter (and memory)	STB Powergraph Pro (2Mb)	Diamond Stealth 64 (2Mb)	STB LightSpeed (2Mb)	STB LightSpeed (2Mb)	STB LightSpeed (1Mb)
Hard-disk capacity and interface	541Mb SCSI-2	1.1GB SCSI-2	345Mb SCSI	1GB SCSI-2	1GB SCSI-2
CD-ROM drive (and speed)	NEC CDR-510 (3x)	Plextor 4-Plex PX-43CH (4x)	Toshiba XM-3401B (2x)	Toshiba XM-3401B (2x)	Toshiba XM-3401B (2x)
Modem/Network adapter/Audio	○/○/○	○/○/○	○/○/○	○/○/○	○/○/○
Accessible drive bays (5.25", 3.5")	6, 0	6, 0	3, 2	6, 0	6, 0
Internal drive bays (5.25", 3.5")	0, 5	0, 5	0, 0	0, 5	0, 3
Power supply (and number of connectors)	300W (4)	300W (4)	250W (5)	300W (4)	300W (6)
Monitor (and diagonal screen size)	ADI MicroScan 4GP (15")	ADI MicroScan 4GP (15")	Viewsonic 15E (15")	Philips 7BM749074I	ViewSonic 15E (15")
System software	DOS 6.22, WfWG 3.11	DOS 6.22, WfWG 3.11	DOS 6.22, WfWG 3.11	DOS 6.21, WfWG 3.11	DOS 6.21, WfWG 3.11
Warranty on parts/labor	3 years/3 years	3 years/3 years	3 years/3 years	3 years/3 years	3 years/3 years
On-site service	Included (1 year)	Included (1 year)	$50 (1 year)	$50 (1 year)	$50 (1 year)

●—Yes ○—No N/A—Not applicable INA—Information not available

Table Continues →

■ Pentium and 486 Buyers' Guide

	Dell Dimension XPS P60	Dell Dimension XPS P90	Dell OmniPlex 560	Dell OmniPlex 590	Dell OptiPlex 4100/Le
List price (tested configuration)	$$$	$$$	$$$$	$$$$	$$$
Processor	Intel Pentium/60	Intel Pentium/90	Intel Pentium/60	Intel Pentium/90	Intel DX4/100
Installed, maximum motherboard RAM	16Mb, 128Mb	16Mb, 128Mb	16Mb, 192Mb	16Mb, 192Mb	16Mb, 64Mb
Installed, maximum external RAM cache	256K, 256K	256K, 256K	256K, 256K	256K, 256K	128K, 128K
Motherboard manufacturer	Intel	Intel	Dell	Dell	Dell
Chip set manufacturer	Intel	Intel	Intel	Intel	VLSI
BIOS manufacturer and version (or date)	AMI (11/11/92)	AMI (11/11/92)	Phoenix 1.00 A	Phoenix 1.00 A	Phoenix 1.10 A
Flash BIOS/16550 UART chip	●/●	●/●	●/●	●/●	●/●
Expansion-bus slots	5 ISA, 3 PCI	5 ISA, 3 PCI	5 EISA, 2 PCI	5 EISA, 2 PCI	3 ISA
Parallel, serial, mouse ports	1, 2, 1	1, 2, 1	1, 2, 1	1, 2, 1	1, 2, 1
Graphics adapter (and memory)	Number Nine #9GXE64 (2Mb)	Number Nine #9GXE64 (2Mb)	Integrated ATI Mach32 (2Mb)	Integrated ATI Mach32 (2Mb)	Integrated Cirrus Logic GD5429 (1Mb)
Hard-disk capacity and interface	527Mb IDE	1GB IDE	502Mb SCSI-2	1GB SCSI-2	540Mb IDE
CD-ROM drive (and speed)	Matsushita CR-563-B (2x)	Matsushita CR-563-B (2x)	NEC CDR-510 (3x)	NEC CDR-510 (3x)	Matsushita CR-563-B (2x)
Modem/Network adapter/Audio	○/○/●	○/○/●	○/○/○	○/○/○	○/○/○
Accessible drive bays (5.25", 3.5")	3, 0	3, 1	3, 0	3, 0	2, 0
Internal drive bays (5.25", 3.5")	0, 2	0, 2	0, 1	0, 2	0, 1
Power supply (and number of connectors)	200W (3)	200W (5)	225W (5)	225W (5)	145W (4)
Monitor (and diagonal screen size)	Dell UltraScan V1528U (15")	Dell UltraScan V1528U (15")	Dell UltraScan 15ES (15")	Dell UltraScan 15ES (15")	Dell UltraScan 15ES (15")
System software	DOS 6.2, WfWG 3.11	DOS 6.2, WfWG 3.11	DOS 6.2, WfWG 3.11	DOS 6.2, WfWG 3.11	DOS 6.2, WfWG 3.11
Warranty on parts/labor	3 years/3 years	3 years/3 years	3 years/3 years	3 years/3 years	3 years/3 years
On-site service	Included (1 year)	Included (1 year)	Included (1 year)	Included (1 year)	Included (1 year)

●—Yes   ○—No   N/A—Not applicable   INA—Information not available

Pentium and 486 Buyers' Guide ■

	Dell OptiPlexXM590	Diamond Blaze 486DX2/66	Diamond Tornado P66	Diamond Hurricane P90	DECpc XL 466d2
List price (tested configuration)	$$$$	$$	$$$	$$$	$$$
Processor	Intel Pentium/90	Intel 486DX2/66	Intel Pentium/66	Intel Pentium/90	Intel 486DX2/66
Installed, maximum motherboard RAM	16Mb, 128Mb	8Mb, 64Mb	16Mb, 128Mb	16Mb, 128Mb	8Mb, 192Mb
Installed, maximum external RAM cache	256K, 256K	128K, 256K	256K, 256K	256K, 256K	256K, 256K
Motherboard manufacturer	Dell	Diamond	Intel	Intel	Digital
Chip set manufacturer	Intel	Bioteq	Intel	Intel	Intel
BIOS manufacturer and version (or date)	Phoenix 1.1	AMI (4/4/93)	AMI 1.00.07.AF2	AMI 1.00.06.AX1	Phoenix A44100
Flash BIOS/16550 UART chip	●/●	○/○	● /●	●/●	●/●
Expansion-bus slots	5 ISA, 2 PCI	4 ISA, 3 VL	5 ISA, 3 PCI	5 ISA, 3 PCI	4 ISA, 3 PCI
Parallel, serial, mouse ports	1, 2, 1	1, 2, 0	1, 2, 0	1, 2, 0	1, 2, 1
Graphics adapter (and memory)	Integrated S3 Vision864 (2Mb)	Hercules Dynamite (2Mb)	Diamond Stealth 32 (2Mb)	Diamond Stealth 64 (2Mb)	Diamond ViperPCI (2Mb)
Hard-disk capacity and interface	1GB IDE	502Mb IDE	810Mb IDE	810Mb IDE	535Mb SCSI-2
CD-ROM drive (and speed)	Matsushita CR-563-B (2x)	Mitsumi FX001D (2x)	Mitsumi FX001D (2x)	Mitsumi FX001D (2x)	Toshiba XM-4101B (2x)
Modem/Network adapter/Audio	○/○/○	○/○/○	○/○/○	○/○/○	○/○/○
Accessible drive bays (5.25", 3.5")	3, 0	3, 2	3, 2	3, 2	3, 1
Internal drive bays (5.25", 3.5")	0, 1	0, 2	0, 0	0, 3	0, 1
Power supply (and number of connectors)	150W (4)	230W (3)	230W (3)	250W (5)	300W (4)
Monitor (and diagonal screen size)	Dell UltraScan 15ES (15")	Sceptre 6Y (14")	Sceptre 6EY (14")	Sceptre 62N (14")	Digital FR-PCXBV-PE (14")
System software	DOS 6.2, WfWG 3.11	DOS 6.2, Windows 3.1	DOS 6.2, Windows 3.1	DOS 6.2, Windows 3.1	DOS 6.21, Windows 3.1
Warranty on parts/labor	3 years/3 years	3 years/3 years	3 years/3 years	3 years/3 years	3 years/3 years
On-site service	Included (1 year)	$30 (1 year)	$30 (1 year)	$30 (1 year)	Included (1 year)

●—Yes ○—No N/A—Not applicable INA—Information not available

Table Continues →

Pentium and 486 Buyers' Guide

	DECpc XL 566	DECpc XL 590	DTK Feat-62	DTK Quin-32	Duracom 486DX2/66
List price (tested configuration)	$$$	$$$$	$$	$$$	$$
Processor	Intel Pentium/66	Intel Pentium/90	Intel 486DX2/66	Intel Pentium/60	Intel 486DX2/66
Installed, maximum motherboard RAM	16Mb, 192Mb	16Mb, 192Mb	8Mb, 64Mb	16Mb, 128Mb	8Mb, 64Mb
Installed, maximum external RAM cache	256K, 256K	256K, 256K	128K, 256K	256K, 512K	128K, 256K
Motherboard manufacturer	Digital	Digital	DTK	Datatech	DEI
Chip set manufacturer	Intel	Intel	SIS	OPTi	OPTi
BIOS manufacturer and version (or date)	Phoenix 1.01	Phoenix A34958	AMI (8/8/93)	Award 4.50G	AMI 1.02.09
Flash BIOS/16550 UART chip	●/●	●/●	○/○	○/○	●/●
Expansion-bus slots	4 ISA, 3 PCI	4 ISA, 3 PCI	3 ISA, 2 VL	5 ISA, 2 VL	6 ISA, 2 VL
Parallel, serial, mouse ports	1, 2, 1	1, 2, 1	1, 2, 1	1, 2, 0	1, 2, 0
Graphics adapter (and memory)	Diamond Stealth 64 (2Mb)	Diamond Stealth 64 (4Mb)	Cardex 9208-90 (1Mb)	DTK PTI-X16VESA (2Mb)	Number Nine #9GXE64 (2Mb)
Hard-disk capacity and interface	535Mb SCSI-2	1GB SCSI-2	360Mb IDE	541Mb IDE	340Mb IDE
CD-ROM drive (and speed)	Toshiba XM-4101B (2x)	Toshiba XM-4101B (2x)	Mitsumi FX001D (2x)	Matsushita CR-562-B (2x)	Sony CDU 33A (2x)
Modem/Network adapter/Audio	○/○/○	○/○/○	○/●	○/●	○/○/○
Accessible drive bays (5.25", 3.5")	3, 1	3, 1	2, 2	5, 0	3, 1
Internal drive bays (5.25", 3.5")	0, 1	0, 1	0, 0	0, 0	0, 2
Power supply (and number of connectors)	300W (4)	300W (4)	200W (2)	200W (3)	200W (3)
Monitor (and diagonal screen size)	Digital FR-PCXBV-PE (14")	Digital FR-PCXAV-EA (16")	DTK DUA-1528G (15")	DTK DUA-1528G (15")	3G (15") ADI MicroScan
System software	DOS 6.21, Windows 3.1	DOS 6.21, Windows 3.1	DOS 6.21, Windows 3.1	DOS 6.2, WfWG 3.11	DOS 6.2, WfWG 3.11
Warranty on parts/labor	3 years/3 years	3 years/3 years	2 years/2 years	2 years/2 years	1 year/1 year
On-site service	Included (1 year)	Included (1 year)	$50 (1 year)	$50 (1 year)	$75 (2 years)

●—Yes   ○—No   N/A—Not applicable   INA—Information not available

Pentium and 486 Buyers' Guide ■

	Duracom 586/66	Duracom FilePro 586/90	Dyna System 466	Dyna System 590	Epson Endeavor VL DX2/66
List price (tested configuration)	$$$	$$$$	$$	$$$	$$
Processor	Intel Pentium/66	Intel Pentium/90	Intel 486DX2/66	Intel Pentium/90	Intel 486DX2/66
Installed, maximum motherboard RAM	16Mb, 128Mb	16Mb, 128Mb	8Mb, 64Mb	16Mb, 128Mb	8Mb, 40Mb
Installed, maximum external RAM cache	256K, 256K	256K, 256K	256K, 1Mb	512K, 2Mb	None, 256K
Motherboard manufacturer	Intel	Intel	Addonics	Shuttle	Epson
Chip set manufacturer	Intel	Intel	SIS	OPTi	SIS
BIOS manufacturer and version (or date)	AMI 1.00.07.AF2	AMI 1.00.03.AX1Z	Award 4.50G	Award (6/27/94)	AMI (11/2/92)
Flash BIOS/16550 UART chip	●/○	●/●	○/○	●/●	○/○
Expansion-bus slots	4 ISA, 3 PCI	5 ISA, 3 PCI	5 ISA, 2 VL	3 ISA, 4 PCI, 2 VL	2 ISA, 2 VL
Parallel, serial, mouse ports	1, 2, 0	1, 2, 0	1, 2, 0	1, 2, 0	1, 2, 1
Graphics adapter (and memory)	Number Nine #9GXE64 (2Mb)	Number Nine #9GXE64 (2Mb)	Cardex Cobra (2Mb)	Diamond Stealth 64 (2Mb)	Cirrus Logic GD5426-based (1Mb)
Hard-disk capacity and interface	540Mb IDE	1GB SCSI-2	426Mb IDE	1GB SCSI-2	426Mb IDE
CD-ROM drive (and speed)	Sony CDU 33A (2x)	Plextor DM-3028 (2x)	Sony CDU 33A-01 (2x)	Plextor DM-3028 (2x)	Mitsumi FX001D (2x)
Modem/Network adapter/Audio	○/○/○	○/○/○	○/○/○	○/○/○	○/○/○
Accessible drive bays (5.25", 3.5")	3, 3	4, 0	3, 1	3, 2	2, 0
Internal drive bays (5.25", 3.5")	0, 0	0, 3	0, 1	0, 1	0, 1
Power supply (and number of connectors)	220W (4)	250W (6)	200W (5)	200W (3)	145W (4)
Monitor (and diagonal screen size)	ADI MicroScan 3G (15")	ADI MicroScan 4G (15")	Addonics 152GLR (15")	Addonics 172GLR (17")	Epson CG1428N (14")
System software	DOS 6.22, WfWG 3.11	DOS 6.22, WfWG 3.11	DOS 6.22, Windows 3.1	DOS 6.22, Windows 3.1	DOS 6.21, Windows 3.1
Warranty on parts/labor	1 year/1 year	1 year/1 year	1 year/1 year	1 year/1 year	1 year/1 year
On-site service	$75 (2 years)	$75 (2 years)	$49 (1 year)	$49 (1 year)	Included (1 year)

●—Yes ○—No N/A—Not applicable INA—Information not available

Table Continues →

■ Pentium and 486 Buyers' Guide

	Epson Endeavor P60	EPS 4-DX2/66 Media-Pro	EPS P60 Phantom	EPS P90 Predator	Gain Master DX2/66
List price (tested configuration)	$$	$$	$$$	$$$	$$$
Processor	Intel Pentium/60	Intel 486DX2/66	Intel Pentium/60	Intel Pentium/90	Intel 486DX2/66
Installed, maximum motherboard RAM	16Mb, 128Mb	8Mb, 128Mb	16Mb, 192Mb	16Mb, 512Mb	8Mb, 128Mb
Installed, maximum external RAM cache	256K, 256K	256K, 512K	512K, 512K	512K, 512K	256K, 256K
Motherboard manufacturer	Intel	GBT	GBT	GBT	AMI
Chip set manufacturer	Intel	Intel	Intel	Intel	SIS
BIOS manufacturer and version (or date)	AMI 1.00.07.A	AMI 2.1	Award 4.50G	Award 4.50G	AMI (12/15/93)
Flash BIOS/16550 UART chip	●/●	○/●	○/●	●/●	●/●
Expansion-bus slots	3 ISA, 2 PCI	4 ISA, 4 PCI	4 ISA, 4 PCI	4 ISA, 4 PCI	5 ISA, 2 VL
Parallel, serial, mouse ports	1, 2, 1	1, 2, 0	1, 2, 0	1, 2, 0	1, 2, 0
Graphics adapter (and memory)	ATI Graphics Wonder (1Mb)	Diamond Stealth 64 (2Mb)	Diamond Stealth 64 (2Mb)	Diamond Stealth 64 (4Mb)	AMI Fast View VLB (2Mb)
Hard-disk capacity and interface	527Mb IDE	425Mb IDE	528Mb IDE	528Mb IDE	527Mb IDE
CD-ROM drive (and speed)	Mitsumi FX001D (2x)	Mitsumi FX001D (2x)	Mitsumi FX001D (2x)	Mitsumi FX001D (2x)	Toshiba XM-3401B (2x)
Modem/Network adapter/Audio	○/○/○	○/○/●	○/○/○	○/○/○	○/●/○
Accessible drive bays (5.25", 3.5")	2, 1	2, 2	2, 2	2, 2	3, 2
Internal drive bays (5.25", 3.5")	0, 1	2, 0	2, 0	2, 0	0, 2
Power supply (and number of connectors)	145W (4)	200W (3)	200W (3)	200W (3)	250W (3)
Monitor (and diagonal screen size)	Epson T1189U (15")	ADI SM5515CP (15")	ADI SM5515CP (15")	ADI SM5515CP (15")	IDEK 8617 Vision Master (17")
System software	DOS 6.21, Windows 3.1	DOS 6.21, WfWG 3.11	DOS 6.21, WfWG 3.11	DOS 6.21, WfWG 3.11	DOS 6.22, WfWG 3.11
Warranty on parts/labor	1 year/1 year	3 years/3 years	3 years/3 years	3 years/3 years	1 year/1 year
On-site service	Included (1 year)	Included (1 year)	Included (1 year)	Included (1 year)	Included (1 year)

●—Yes   ○—No   N/A—Not applicable   INA—Information not available

Pentium and 486 Buyers' Guide ■

	Gain Master P560	Gateway 2000 4DX2-66 Family PC	Gateway 2000 P5-60 Family PC	Gateway 2000 P5-90 Family PC	Gateway 2000 P4D-66
List price (tested configuration)	$$$$	$$	$$$	$$$	$$
Processor	Intel Pentium/60	Intel 486DX2/66	Intel Pentium/60	Intel Pentium/90	Intel 486DX2/66
Installed, maximum motherboard RAM	16Mb, 192Mb	8Mb, 32Mb	16Mb, 128Mb	16Mb, 128Mb	8Mb, 128Mb
Installed, maximum external RAM cache	256K, 512K	128K, 256K	256K, 256K	256K, 256K	128K, 256K
Motherboard manufacturer	AMI	TI	Intel	Intel	Intel
Chip set manufacturer	Intel	VLSI	Intel	Intel	Intel
BIOS manufacturer and version (or date)	AMI (12/15/93)	Phoenix 1.00.06.AC0	AMI 1.00.08.AF2	Phoenix 1.00.09.AX1	Phoenix 4.03
Flash BIOS/16550 UART chip	●/○	○/○	●/●	●/●	●/●
Expansion-bus slots	4 ISA, 3 PCI	5 ISA	5 ISA, 3 PCI	5 ISA, 3 PCI	5 ISA, 3 PCI
Parallel, serial, mouse ports	1, 2, 0	1, 2, 1	1, 2, 1	1, 2, 1	1, 2, 1
Graphics adapter (and memory)	Diamond Stealth 64 (2Mb)	Integrated Cirrus Logic GD5428 (1Mb)	STB LightSpeed (1Mb)	STB LightSpeed (2Mb)	STB LightSpeed (1Mb)
Hard-disk capacity and interface	1.8GB SCSI-2	425Mb IDE	539Mb IDE	731Mb IDE	730Mb IDE
CD-ROM drive (and speed)	Toshiba XM-3401B (2x)	Philips LMS CM206 (2x)	Philips LMS CM206 (2x)	Philips LMS CM206 (2x)	NEC CDR-260 (2x)
Modem/Network adapter/Audio	○/○/○	●/●/●	●/●/●	●/●/●	○/○/○
Accessible drive bays (5.25", 3.5")	4, 0	2, 1	3, 1	3, 1	3, 1
Internal drive bays (5.25", 3.5")	4, 0	0, 1	0, 3	0, 3	0, 3
Power supply (and number of connectors)	300W (4)	145W (5)	145W (5)	145W (5)	145W (5)
Monitor (and diagonal screen size)	IDEK 8617 Vision Master (17")	Gateway 2000 CrystalScan 14SVGA (14")	Gateway 2000 CrystalScan 1572DG (15")	Gateway 2000 CrystalScan 1572FS (15")	Gateway 2000 CrystalScan 1572DG (15")
System software	DOS 6.22, WfWG 3.11	DOS 6.22, WfWG 3.11	DOS 6.22, WfWG 3.11	DOS 6.22, WfWG 3.11	DOS 6.22, WfWG 3.11
Warranty on parts/labor	1 year/1 year	3 years/1 year	3 years/1 year	3 years/1 year	3 years/1 year
On-site service	Included (1 year)	Included (1 year)	Included (1 year)	Included (1 year)	Included (1 year)

●—Yes   ○—No   N/A—Not applicable   INA—Information not available

Table Continues →

■ Pentium and 486 Buyers' Guide

	Gateway 2000 P5-60	Gateway 2000 P5-90 XL	Hertz 486D66X2e	Hertz P66e	Hertz P9e
List price (tested configuration)	$$	$$$	$$	$$$	$$$
Processor	Intel Pentium/60	Intel Pentium/90	Intel 486DX2/66	Intel Pentium/66	Intel Pentium/90
Installed, maximum motherboard RAM	16Mb, 128Mb	16Mb, 128Mb	8Mb, 32Mb	16Mb, 128Mb	16Mb, 128Mb
Installed, maximum external RAM cache	256K, 256K	256K, 256K	256K, 256K	256K, 512K	256K, 512K
Motherboard manufacturer	Intel	Intel	Hertz	Super Micro	Super Micro
Chip set manufacturer	Intel	Intel	SIS	OPTi	OPTi
BIOS manufacturer and version (or date)	AMI 1.00.08.AF2	AMI 1.00.09.AX1	AMI (4/4/93)	AMI AB5960722	AMI (12/15/93)
Flash BIOS/16550 UART chip	●/●	●/●	○/○	●/●	●/●
Expansion-bus slots	5 ISA, 3 PCI	5 ISA, 3 PCI	5 ISA, 2 VL	5 ISA, 4 PCI, 2 VL	3 ISA, 4 PCI, 2 VL
Parallel, serial, mouse ports	1, 2, 1	1, 2, 1	1, 2, 0	1, 2, 0	1, 2, 0
Graphics adapter (and memory)	STB LightSpeed (1Mb)	ATI Graphics Pro Turbo (2Mb)	Cirrus LogicGD5426-based (1Mb)	Diamond ViperPCI (2Mb)	Diamond Viper PCI (2Mb)
Hard-disk capacity and interface	514Mb IDE	1GB IDE	452Mb IDE	545Mb SCSI-2	1GB IDE
CD-ROM drive (and speed)	NEC CDR-260 (2x)	NEC CDR-260 (2x)	Sony CDU 33A (2x)	Sony CDU 33A (2x)	NEC CDR-510 (3x)
Modem/Network adapter/Audio	○/○/○	●/●/●	●/●/●	●/●/●	●/●/●
Accessible drive bays (5.25", 3.5")	3, 1	4, 1	3, 2	3, 2	3, 2
Internal drive bays (5.25", 3.5")	0, 3	0, 4	0, 1	0, 1	0, 1
Power supply (and number of connectors)	145W (5)	200W (4)	200W (4)	200W (5)	200W (3)
Monitor (and diagonal screen size)	Gateway 2000 CrystalScan 1572DG (15")	Gateway 2000 CrystalScan CS1776LE (17")	MAG Innovision DX15FK (15")	MAG Innovision DX15F (15")	MAG Innovision MX15F (15")
System software	DOS 6.22, WfWG 3.11	DOS 6.22, WfWG 3.11	DOS 6.22, WfWG 3.11	DOS 6.22, WfWG 3.11	DOS 6.22, WfWG 3.11
Warranty on parts/labor	3 years/1 year	3 years/1 year	1 year/1 year	1 year/1 year	1 year/1 year
On-site service	Included (1 year)	Included (1 year)	$495 (1 year)	$495 (1 year)	$495 (1 year)

●—Yes   ○—No   N/A—Not applicable   INA—Information not available

Pentium and 486 Buyers' Guide ▨

	HP Vectra VL2 4/66	HP Vectra XU 5/90C	HiQ Neptune II P66/PCI	HiQ Neptune II P90/PCI	IBM ValuePoint 466DX2/Sp
List price (tested configuration)	$$$	$$$$	$$$	$$$	$$$
Processor	Intel 486DX2/66	Intel Pentium/90	Intel Pentium/66	Intel Pentium/90	Intel 486DX2/66
Installed, maximum motherboard RAM	8Mb, 64Mb	16Mb, 256Mb	16Mb, 128Mb	16Mb, 128Mb	8Mb, 128Mb
Installed, maximum external RAM cache	256K, 256K	512K, 512K	256K, 256K	256K, 256K	256K, 256K
Motherboard manufacturer	HP	HP	Intel	Intel	IBM
Chip set manufacturer	VLSI	Intel	Intel	Intel	OPTi
BIOS manufacturer and version (or date)	HP CA.04.01	HP GC.05.03	AMI 1.00.07.AF2	AMI 1.00.06.AX1	IBM SurePath 0.02
Flash BIOS/16550 UART chip	○/●	●/●	●/●	●/●	●/●
Expansion-bus slots	4 ISA	4 ISA, 2 PCI	5 ISA, 3 PCI	4 ISA, 3 PCI	2 ISA, 1 VL
Parallel, serial, mouse ports	1, 2, 1	1, 1, 1	1, 2, 0	1, 2, 0	1, 2, 1
Graphics adapter (and memory)	Integrated Cirrus Logic GD5428 (1Mb)	Matrox MGA Ultima Plus (2Mb)	Diamond Stealth 64 (2Mb)	Diamond Stealth 64 (2Mb)	Integrated S3 Vision864 (2Mb)
Hard-disk capacity and interface	341Mb IDE	1GB SCSI-2	520Mb IDE	1GB IDE	365Mb IDE
CD-ROM drive (and speed)	HP D2886-60001 (2x)	Toshiba XM-4101B (2x)	Matsushita CR-562-B (2x)	Matsushita CR-563-B (2x)	Matsushita CR-563-B (2x)
Modem/Network adapter/Audio	○/○/○	○/●/○	○/○/●	○/○/●	○/○/●
Accessible drive bays (5.25", 3.5")	1, 1	2, 1	3, 2	4, 0	1, 1
Internal drive bays (5.25", 3.5")	0, 2	0, 1	0, 2	0, 3	0, 1
Power supply (and number of connectors)	100W (4)	160W (4)	200W (3)	250W (4)	100W (5)
Monitor (and diagonal screen size)	HP D2804A (14")	HP D2807A (17")	ADI MicroScan 3GP (14")	ADI MicroScan 3GP (14")	IBM 9527 (17")
System software	DOS 6.2, WfWG 3.11	DOS 6.2, WfWG 3.11	DOS 6.2, WfWG 3.11	DOS 6.22, WfWG 3.11	IBM PC DOS 6.3, WfWG 3.11
Warranty on parts/labor	3 years/3 years	3 years/3 years	1 year/2 years	1 year/2 years	3 years/3 years
On-site service	Included (1 years)	Included (1 year)	None	None	Included (1 year)

●—Yes ○—No N/A—Not applicable INA—Information not available

Table Continues →

■ Pentium and 486 Buyers' Guide

	IBM ValuePoint 100DX4/Dp	ITI DX2-66	ITI M54PI-90	Insight 486DX2-66 MM	Insight PCI P66 MM
List price (tested configuration)	$$$$	$$	$$$	$$	$$$
Processor	Intel DX4/100	Intel 486DX2/66	Intel Pentium/90	Intel 486DX2/66	Intel Pentium/66
Installed, maximum motherboard RAM	16Mb, 128Mb	8Mb, 64Mb	16Mb, 192Mb	8Mb, 96Mb	16Mb, 128Mb
Installed, maximum external RAM cache	256K, 256K	256K, 256K	256K, 512K	128K, 256K	256K, 256K
Motherboard manufacturer	IBM	Micronics	Micronics	FIC	Intel
Chip set manufacturer	OPTi	Micronics	Intel	VIA	Intel
BIOS manufacturer and version (or date)	IBM SurePath 0.02	Phoenix 0.1	Phoenix (5/15/94)	Award 3.03	AMI 1.00.07.AF2
Flash BIOS/16550 UART chip	○/●	●/●	●/○	○/●	●/●
Expansion-bus slots	4 ISA, 1 VL	5 ISA, 2 VL	5 ISA, 3 PCI	5 ISA, 2 VL	5 ISA, 3 PCI
Parallel, serial, mouse ports	1, 2, 1	1, 2, 0	1, 2, 0	1, 3, 0	1, 2, 0
Graphics adapter (and memory)	Integrated S3 Vision864 (2Mb)	Diamond Speedstar Pro (1Mb)	Diamond Viper PCI (2Mb)	Boca Research VGAXL1M (1Mb)	Diamond Stealth 64 (4Mb)
Hard-disk capacity and interface	540Mb IDE	342Mb IDE	810Mb SCSI-2	425Mb IDE	526Mb IDE
CD-ROM drive (and speed)	Matsushita CR-563-BBZ (2x)	Matsushita CR-563-B (2x)	NEC MultiSpin 3Xi (3x)	Sony CDU 33A (2x)	Matsushita CR-563-B (2x)
Modem/Network adapter/Audio	○/○/●	○/○/○	○/○/○	●/○/●	●/○/●
Accessible drive bays (5.25", 3.5")	2, 1	3, 2	3, 2	3, 2	4, 1
Internal drive bays (5.25", 3.5")	0, 1	0, 2	0, 2	0, 0	0, 8
Power supply (and number of connectors)	205W (6)	200W (4)	200W (4)	230W (4)	230W (7)
Monitor (and diagonal screen size)	IBM 9527 (17")	Standard Technologies 428C-Vesa (14")	NEC JC-1535VMA (15")	CTX 1562GM (15")	MAG Innovision DX17F (17")
System software	IBM PC DOS 6.3, WfWG 3.11	DOS 6.22, Windows 3.1	DOS 6.2, WfWG 3.11	DOS 6.21, WfWG 3.11	DOS 6.21, WfWG 3.11
Warranty on parts/labor	3 years/3 years	1 year/1 year	1 year/1 year	1 year/1 year	1 year/1 year
On-site service	Included (1 year)	None	None	None	None

●—Yes ○—No N/A—Not applicable INA—Information not available

Pentium and 486 Buyers' Guide ■

	Insight PCI P90 MM	Micro Express MicroFLEX-VL/66	Micro Express MicroFLEX-VL/P66	Micron 466PCI Magnum	Micron 4100PCI Magnum
List price (tested configuration)	$$$$	$$	$$$	$$	$$$
Processor	Intel Pentium/90	Intel 486DX2/66	Intel Pentium/66	Intel 486DX2/66	Intel DX4/100
Installed, maximum motherboard RAM	16Mb, 128Mb	8Mb, 128Mb	16Mb, 128Mb	8Mb, 128Mb	16Mb, 128Mb
Installed, maximum external RAM cache	256K, 256K	256K, 512K	512K, 512K	256K, 256K	256K, 256K
Motherboard manufacturer	Intel	Micro Express	Micro Express	Micronics	Micronics
Chip set manufacturer	Intel	SIS	OPTi	Intel	Intel
BIOS manufacturer and version (or date)	AMI 1.00.08.AX1	AMI (8/8/93)	AMI (12/17/93)	Phoenix 1.03	Phoenix 1.03
Flash BIOS/16550 UART chip	●/●	●/●	●/●	●/●	●/●
Expansion-bus slots	5 ISA, 3 PCI	5 ISA, 3 VL	5 ISA, 3 VL	6 ISA, 3 PCI	6 ISA, 3 PCI
Parallel, serial, mouse ports	1, 2, 0	1, 2, 0	1, 2, 0	1, 2, 0	1, 2, 0
Graphics adapter (and memory)	Diamond Stealth 64 (4Mb)	ATI Graphics Pro Turbo (2Mb)	ATI Graphics Pro Turbo (2Mb)	Diamond Stealth 64 (2Mb)	Diamond Stealth 64 (2Mb)
Hard-disk capacity and interface	1GB IDE	341Mb IDE	541Mb SCSI-2	527Mb IDE	527Mb IDE
CD-ROM drive (and speed)	Plextor 4-Plex PX-43CH (4x)	Sony CDU 33A (2x)	Toshiba XM-3401B (2x)	Mitsumi FX001D (2x)	Mitsumi FX001D (2x)
Modem/Network adapter/Audio	●/○/●	○/○/●	○/○/●	○/○/○	○/○/○
Accessible drive bays (5.25", 3.5")	4, 1	3, 2	3, 2	3, 0	3, 0
Internal drive bays (5.25", 3.5")	0, 8	0, 2	0, 2	0, 3	0, 3
Power supply (and number of connectors)	230W (7)	250W (4)	250W (4)	200W (4)	200W (4)
Monitor (and diagonal screen size)	ViewSonic 17 (17")	Micro Express FM590 (15")	Micro Express FM590 (15")	MAG Innovision DX15F (15")	MAG Innovision DX15F (15")
System software	DOS 6.21, WfWG 3.11	DOS 6.21, Windows 3.1	DOS 6.21, Windows 3.1	DOS 6.21, WfWG 3.11	DOS 6.22, WfWG 3.11
Warranty on parts/labor	1 year/1 year	2 years/2 years	2 years/2 years	1 year/1 year	1 year/1 year
On-site service	None	$50 (1 year)	$50 (1 year)	Included (1 year)	Included (1 year)

●—Yes   ○—No   N/A—Not applicable   INA—Information not available

Table Continues →

■ Pentium and 486 Buyers' Guide

	Micron P90PCI PowerStation	MicroTech Ultima XVC/66	MicroTech Ultima MP5/90	MidWest Micro Elite DX2-66 PCI	MidWest Micro Elite P5-66
List price (tested configuration)	$$$	$$$	$$$$	$$	$$$
Processor	Intel Pentium/90	Intel 486DX2/66	Intel Pentium/90	Intel 486DX2/66	Intel Pentium/66
Installed, maximum motherboard RAM	16Mb, 192Mb	8Mb, 64Mb	16Mb, 192Mb	8Mb, 128Mb	16Mb, 128Mb
Installed, maximum external RAM cache	512K, 512K	256K, 256K	256K, 512K	256K, 512K	256K, 256K
Motherboard manufacturer	Micronics	Micronics	Micronics	Elite Group	Intel
Chip set manufacturer	Intel	Micronics	Intel	Intel	Intel
BIOS manufacturer and version (or date)	Phoenix (7/21/94)	Phoenix 0.1	Phoenix 4.03	Phoenix 4.03	AMI 1.00.07.AF2
Flash BIOS/16550 UART chip	●/●	●/●	●/●	●/●	●/●
Expansion-bus slots	5 ISA, 3 PCI	5 ISA, 2 VL	5 ISA, 3 PCI	4 ISA, 3 PCI	5 ISA, 3 PCI
Parallel, serial, mouse ports	1, 2, 0	1, 2, 0	1, 2, 0	1, 2, 0	1, 2, 0
Graphics adapter (and memory)	Diamond Stealth 64 (2Mb)	Diamond Speedstar Pro (1Mb)	ATI Graphics Pro Turbo (2Mb)	Hercules Stingray S801 (1Mb)	Hercules Dynamite (2Mb)
Hard-disk capacity and interface	1GB IDE	324Mb IDE	1GB SCSI-2	503Mb IDE	503Mb IDE
CD-ROM drive (and speed)	Mitsumi FX001D (2x)	Sony CDU 33A (2x)	NEC MultiSpin 3Xi (3x)	Mitsumi FX001D (2x)	Mitsumi FX001D (2x)
Modem/Network adapter/Audio	○/○/○	○/○/●	○/○/○	○/○/○	●/○/○
Accessible drive bays (5.25", 3.5")	3, 0	4, 0	4, 0	3, 2	3, 2
Internal drive bays (5.25", 3.5")	0, 3	2, 2	2, 2	0, 3	0, 3
Power supply (and number of connectors)	200W (4)	250W (4)	250W (4)	230W (3)	230W (5)
Monitor (and diagonal screen size)	MAG Innovision DX15F (15")	Synco CM-15GS (15")	Synco CM-17GS (17")	Infotel SCR 1501P (15")	Infotel SRC 1501 P (15")
System software	DOS 6.22, WfWG 3.11	DOS 6.21, WfWG 3.11	DOS 6.21, WfWG 3.11	DOS 6.22, WfWG 3.11	DOS 6.21, WfWG 3.11
Warranty on parts/labor	1 year/1 year	1 year/1 year	1 year/1 year	3 years/3 years	3 years/3 years
On-site service	Included (1 year)	None	None	None	None

●—Yes   ○—No   N/A—Not applicable   INA—Information not available

Pentium and 486 Buyers' Guide ■

	MidWest Micro Elite P5-90	Mitsuba i486DX2-66	Mitsuba i486DX4-100	Mitsuba Fileserver-P-90	NMC Pro-System 466
List price (tested configuration)	$$$	$$	$$$	$$$	$$
Processor	Intel Pentium/90	Intel 486DX2/66	Intel DX4/100	Intel Pentium/90	Intel 486DX2/66
Installed, maximum motherboard RAM	16Mb, 128Mb	8Mb, 64Mb	16Mb, 64Mb	16Mb, 128Mb	8Mb, 96Mb
Installed, maximum external RAM cache	256K, 256K	256K, 256K	256K, 256K	256K, 256K	256K, 512K
Motherboard manufacturer	Intel	Mitsuba	Mitsuba	Intel	Elite Group
Chip set manufacturer	Intel	OPTi	OPTi	Intel	ALI
BIOS manufacturer and version (or date)	AMI 1.00.06.AX1	AMI (6/1/94)	AMI (6/1/94)	AMI (6/16/94)	Phoenix (4/26/94)
Flash BIOS/16550 UART chip	●/●	○/●	●/○	○/●	○/○
Expansion-bus slots	5 ISA, 3 PCI	3 ISA, 3 PCI, 2 VL	3 ISA, 3 PCI, 2 VL	5 ISA, 3 PCI	4 ISA, 3 VL
Parallel, serial, mouse ports	1, 2, 0	1, 2, 1	1, 2, 1	1, 2, 0	1, 2, 0
Graphics adapter (and memory)	Hercules Dynamite (2Mb)	Hercules Dynamite (1Mb)	ATI Graphics Pro Turbo (4Mb)	Tseng VGA Mentor (1Mb)	STB LightSpeed (2Mb)
Hard-disk capacity and interface	1GB SCSI-2	401Mb IDE	810Mb IDE	1GB IDE	528Mb IDE
CD-ROM drive (and speed)	Mitsumi FX001D (2x)	Mitsumi FX001D (2x)	Mitsumi FX001D (2x)	Toshiba XM-4101B (2x)	Matsushita CR-562-B (2x)
Modem/Network adapter/Audio	●/○/○	●/○/○	●/○/○	○/○/○	○/○/●
Accessible drive bays (5.25", 3.5")	5, 1	2, 2	3, 2	3, 2	3, 0
Internal drive bays (5.25", 3.5")	0, 5	0, 1	0, 2	0, 2	0, 3
Power supply (and number of connectors)	250W (6)	200W (3)	200W (3)	230W (3)	200W (3)
Monitor (and diagonal screen size)	Infotel SRC 1501P (15")	Mitsuba E462 (14")	Mitsuba E462D (14")	Mitsuba E462D (14")	ADI MicroScan 4GP (15")
System software	DOS 6.21, WfWG 3.11	DOS 6.22, WfWG 3.11	DOS 6.22, WfWG 3.11	DOS 6.22, WfWG 3.11	DOS 6.2, WfWG 3.11
Warranty on parts/labor	3 years/3 years	2 years/2 years	2 years/2 years	2 years/2 years	1 year/2 years
On-site service	None	$39 (1 year)	$39 (1 year)	$39 (1 year)	$39 (1 year)

●—Yes ○—No N/A—Not applicable INA—Information not available

Table Continues →

■ Pentium and 486 Buyers' Guide

	NMC Expert-System P66	NMC Expert-Server+ DP90	NEC PowerMate 466D	NEC PowerMate P60D	NEC Ready 466D
List price (tested configuration)	$$$	$$$$	$$	$$$	$$$
Processor	Intel Pentium/66	Intel Pentium/90	Intel 486DX2/66	Intel Pentium/60	Intel 486DX2/66
Installed, maximum motherboard RAM	16Mb, 192Mb	16Mb, 192Mb	8Mb, 128Mb	16Mb, 80Mb	8Mb, 128Mb
Installed, maximum external RAM cache	256K, 256K	256K, 512K	256K, 256K	256K, 256K	256K, 256K
Motherboard manufacturer	Elite Group	Asus	NEC	Intel	NEC
Chip set manufacturer	Intel	Intel	C&T	Intel	VLSI
BIOS manufacturer and version (or date)	Award (4/21/94)	Award 4.5	Phoenix 4.06.6	AMI 1.00.1.BC0K	Phoenix 4.03.6
Flash BIOS/16550 UART chip	○/●	●/●	●/●	●/●	●/●
Expansion-bus slots	5 ISA, 3 PCI	4 EISA, 4 PCI	4 ISA, 1 VL	4 ISA, 1 PCI	4 ISA, 1 VL
Parallel, serial, mouse ports	1, 2, 0	1, 2, 0	1, 2, 0	1, 2, 1	1, 2, 1
Graphics adapter (and memory)	STB LightSpeed (2Mb)	STB LightSpeed (2Mb)	Integrated C&T F64300 (1Mb)	Integrated Cirrus Logic GD5434 (1Mb)	Integrated C&T F64300 (1Mb)
Hard-disk capacity and interface	528Mb IDE	1.7GB SCSI-2	503Mb IDE	514Mb IDE	404Mb IDE
CD-ROM drive (and speed)	Plextor 4-Plex PX-43CH (4x)	Plextor 4-Plex PX-43CH (4x)	NEC CDR-260 (2x)	NEC MultiSpin 3Xi (3x)	NEC CDR-260 (2x)
Modem/Network adapter/Audio	○/○/○	○/●/○	○/○/●	○/○/●	●/○/●
Accessible drive bays (5.25", 3.5")	3, 1	5, 0	2, 1	2, 1	2, 1
Internal drive bays (5.25", 3.5")	0, 2	0, 4	0, 2	0, 1	0, 1
Power supply (and number of connectors)	200W (4)	250W (3)	145W (3)	145W (3)	145W (5)
Monitor (and diagonal screen size)	ADI MicroScan 4GP (15")	ADI MicroScan 4GP (15")	NEC MultiSync 2V (14")	NEC MultiSync 2V (14")	NEC MultiSync 17 (17")
System software	DOS 6.2, WfWG 3.11	DOS 6.22, WfWG 3.11	DOS 6.22, Windows 3.1	DOS 6.22, Windows 3.1	DOS 6.22, Windows 3.1
Warranty on parts/labor	1 year/2 years	1 year/2 years	3 years/3 years	3 years/3 years	3 years/3 years
On-site service	$39 (1 year)	$39 (1 year)	Included (1 year)	Included (1 year)	Included (1 year)

●—Yes   ○—No   N/A—Not applicable   INA—Information not available

Pentium and 486 Buyers' Guide ■

	NETiS N466P Best Buy	NETiS N566 Best Buy	NETiS N566 PowerStation	NETiS N590 PowerStation	Olivetti M4-464
List price (tested configuration)	$$$	$$$	$$$	$$$	$$$
Processor	Intel 486DX2/66	Intel Pentium/66	Intel Pentium/66	Intel Pentium/90	Intel 486DX2/66
Installed, maximum motherboard RAM	8Mb, 128Mb	16Mb, 192Mb	16Mb, 192Mb	16Mb, 128Mb	8Mb, 64Mb
Installed, maximum external RAM cache	256K, 512K	512K, 512K	256K, 512K	512K, 512K	256K, 256K
Motherboard manufacturer	Asus	Asus	Asus	Super Micro	Olivetti
Chip set manufacturer	Intel	Intel	Intel	OPTi	UMC
BIOS manufacturer and version (or date)	Award 4.5	Award 4.5	Award 4.5	AMI (12/15/93)	AMI 1.1
Flash BIOS/16550 UART chip	○/○	●/●	●/●	●/●	●/●
Expansion-bus slots	4 ISA, 3 PCI	5 ISA, 3 PCI	5 ISA, 3 PCI	3 ISA, 4 PCI, 2 VL	4 ISA, 2 VL
Parallel, serial, mouse ports	1, 2, 0	1, 2, 0	1, 2, 0	1, 2, 0	1, 2, 1
Graphics adapter (and memory)	ATI Graphics Pro Turbo (2Mb)	ATI Graphics Pro Turbo (2Mb)	ATI Graphics Pro Turbo (2Mb)	ATI Graphics Pro Turbo (2Mb)	Integrated Cirrus Logic GD5428 (1Mb)
Hard-disk capacity and interface	427Mb IDE	528Mb IDE	515Mb SCSI-2	1GB SCSI-2	407Mb IDE
CD-ROM drive (and speed)	Mitsumi FX001D (2x)	NEC CD-ROM:500 (3x)	NEC CD-ROM:500 (3x)	NEC CD-ROM:500 (3x)	Sony CDU 33A (2x)
Modem/Network adapter/Audio	○/○/○	●/○/●	●/○/○	○/○/○	○/○/○
Accessible drive bays (5.25", 3.5")	3, 2	3, 2	3, 2	6, 0	2, 1
Internal drive bays (5.25", 3.5")	0, 0	0, 3	0, 0	0, 5	0, 3
Power supply (and number of connectors)	250W (4)	230W (4)	230W (4)	250W (5)	200W (6)
Monitor (and diagonal screen size)	View Magic CA-1565 (15")	View Magic CA-1565 (15")	ViewSonic 1564 (15")	ViewSonic 1564 (15")	Olivetti CDU 1764/SA01 (17")
System software	DOS 6.22, WfWG 3.11	DOS 6.22, WfWG 3.11	DOS 6.22, WfWG 3.11	DOS 6.22, Windows 3.11	DOS 6.2, Windows 3.1
Warranty on parts/labor	1 year/1 year	1 year/1 year	1 year/1 year	1 year/1 year	3 years/1 year
On-site service	Included (1 year)	Included (1 year)	Included (1 year)	Included (1 year)	Included (1 year)

●—Yes   ○—No   N/A—Not applicable   INA—Information not available

Table Continues →

Pentium and 486 Buyers' Guide

	Olivetti M4-82	PC Express EXP66	PC Express EXP100	PC Express EXP90	PCG BurStar 466
List price (tested configuration)	$$$$	$$	$$	$$$	$$
Processor	Intel Pentium/60	Intel 486DX2/66	Intel DX4/100	Intel Pentium/90	Intel 486DX2/66
Installed, maximum motherboard RAM	16Mb, 128Mb	8Mb, 64Mb	16Mb, 64Mb	16Mb, 128Mb	8Mb, 128Mb
Installed, maximum external RAM cache	256K, 256K	256K, 512K	256K, 1Mb	256K, 256K	256K, 1Mb
Motherboard manufacturer	Intel	Firenze	Asus	Intel	ATC
Chip set manufacturer	Intel	SIS	SIS	Intel	Intel
BIOS manufacturer and version (or date)	AMI 1.00.06.AF2	Award 4.50G	Award 4.50G	AMI 1.00.03.AX1Z	Award 4.50G
Flash BIOS/16550 UART chip	●/●	○/○	○/○	○/●	●/●
Expansion-bus slots	5 ISA, 3 PCI	5 ISA, 3 VL	5 ISA, 2 VL	5 ISA, 3 PCI	4 ISA, 3 PCI
Parallel, serial, mouse ports	1, 2, 1	1, 2, 0	1, 2, 0	1, 2, 0	1, 2, 0
Graphics adapter (and memory)	Matrox MGA-PCI (2Mb)	Hercules Dynamite (1Mb)	Hercules Dynamite (1Mb)	Diamond Viper PCI (2Mb)	Photon Torpedo864 (2Mb)
Hard-disk capacity and interface	503Mb IDE	425Mb IDE	503Mb IDE	942Mb SCSI-2	540Mb SCSI-2
CD-ROM drive (and speed)	Sony CDU 33A (2x)	Sony CDU 33A (2x)	Sony CDU 33A (2x)	Sony CDU 33A (2x)	Toshiba XM-3401B (2x)
Modem/Network adapter/Audio	○/○/○	○/○/○	○/○/○	○/○/○	○/○/○
Accessible drive bays (5.25", 3.5")	2, 1	3, 1	3, 1	5, 0	2, 1
Internal drive bays (5.25", 3.5")	0, 3	0, 1	1, 2	1, 4	0, 1
Power supply (and number of connectors)	200W (6)	200W (5)	230W (5)	250W (6)	200W (3)
Monitor (and diagonal screen size)	Olivetti CDU 1764/SA01 (17")	CTX 1451ES (14")	CTX 1562GM (15")	Nokia 447X058 (17")	MAG Innovision MX15F (15")
System software	DOS 6.2, WfWG 3.11	DOS 6.22, WfWG 3.11	DOS 6.22, WfWG 3.11	DOS 6.22, WfWG 3.11	DOS 6.22, WfWG 3.11
Warranty on parts/labor	3 years/1 year	4 years/4 years	4 years/4 years	4 years/4 years	3 years/3 years
On-site service	Included (1 year)	Included (1 year)	Included (1 year)	Included (1 year)	Included (1 year)

●—Yes ○—No N/A—Not applicable INA—Information not available

Pentium and 486 Buyers' Guide ■

	PCG BurSTar P60	PCG BurSTar P90	Poly 486-66VP	Poly DX4-100P	Poly 590IP
List price (tested configuration)	$$$	$$$$	$$	$$$	$$$$
Processor	Intel Pentium/60	Intel Pentium/90	Intel 486DX2/66	Intel DX4/100	Intel Pentium/90
Installed, maximum motherboard RAM	16Mb, 128Mb	16Mb, 256Mb	8Mb, 128Mb	16Mb, 128Mb	16Mb, 128Mb
Installed, maximum external RAM cache	256K, 512K	256K, 512K	256K, 512K	256K, 512K	256K, 256K
Motherboard manufacturer	FCI	Intel	Prima	ECS	Intel
Chip set manufacturer	Intel	Intel	Intel	Intel	Intel
BIOS manufacturer and version (or date)	AMI (12/15/93)	AMI 1.00.03.AX1Z	AMI (8/8/93)	Phoenix 1.03	AMI 1.00.03.AX1Z
Flash BIOS/16550 UART chip	○/○	●/●	●/●	○/●	●/●
Expansion-bus slots	5 ISA, 4 PCI	5 ISA, 3 PCI	2 ISA, 4 PCI, 3 VL	4 ISA, 3 PCI	5 ISA, 3 PCI
Parallel, serial, mouse ports	1, 2, 0	1, 2, 0	1, 2, 0	1, 2, 0	1, 2, 0
Graphics adapter (and memory)	Diamond Stealth 64 (2Mb)	Diamond Stealth 64 (2Mb)	Actix Graphics Engine 64 (1Mb)	ATI Graphics Pro Turbo (2Mb)	ATI Graphics Pro Turbo (4Mb)
Hard-disk capacity and interface	540Mb SCSI-2	1GB SCSI-2	341Mb IDE	527Mb IDE	1.1GB SCSI-2
CD-ROM drive (and speed)	Plextor DM-3028 (2x)	Toshiba XM-3401B (2x)	Optics Storage Dolphin AT (2x)	Philips LMS CR328A (2x)	Plextor DM-3028 (2x)
Modem/Network adapter/Audio	○/○/○	○/○/○	○/○/○	○/○/○	○/○/○
Accessible drive bays (5.25", 3.5")	3, 2	3, 2	3, 1	3, 2	8, 0
Internal drive bays (5.25", 3.5")	1, 3	0, 3	0, 1	0, 3	2, 0
Power supply (and number of connectors)	250W (3)	250W (5)	230W (4)	230W (3)	300W (7)
Monitor (and diagonal screen size)	MAG Innovision MX15F (15")	MAG Innovision MX17F (17")	Optiquest 1000S (14")	Optiquest 1000S (14")	ADI MicroScan 4GP (15")
System software	DOS 6.22, WfWG 3.11	DOS 6.2, WfWG 3.11	DOS 6.2, WfWG 3.11	DOS 6.22, WfWG 3.11	DOS 6.22, WfWG 3.11
Warranty on parts/labor	3 years/3 years	3 years/3 years	2 years/5 years	2 years/5 years	2 years/5 years
On-site service	Included (1 year)	Included (1 year)	$75 (1 year)	$75 (1 year)	$75 (1 year)

●—Yes ○—No N/A—Not applicable INA—Information not available

Table Continues →

■ Pentium and 486 Buyers' Guide

	Precision 486-VIP	Precision PTI-66	Precision PTI-90	Robotech Cobra RS-DX2/66	Robotech Cobra RS-DX4/100
List price (tested configuration)	$$	$$$	$$$	$$	$$$
Processor	Intel 486DX2/66	Intel Pentium/66	Intel Pentium/90	Intel 486DX2/66	Intel DX4/100
Installed, maximum motherboard RAM	8Mb, 128Mb	16Mb, 128Mb	16Mb, 128Mb	8Mb, 128Mb	16Mb, 128Mb
Installed, maximum external RAM cache	256K, 1Mb	256K, 256K	256K, 256K	256K, 1Mb	256K, 1Mb
Motherboard manufacturer	Precision	Intel	Intel	Robotech	Robotech
Chip set manufacturer	Contaq	Intel	Intel	Contaq	Contaq
BIOS manufacturer and version (or date)	Award 4.50G	AMI 1.00.03.AF2	AMI 1.00.08.AX1	AMI (8/8/94)	AMI (8/8/93)
Flash BIOS/16550 UART chip	●/○	●/○	●/●	○/○	○/○
Expansion-bus slots	2 ISA, 4 PCI, 2 VL	5 ISA, 3 PCI	5 ISA, 3 PCI	5 ISA, 3 VL	5 ISA, 3 VL
Parallel, serial, mouse ports	1, 2, 0	1, 2, 1	1, 2, 0	1, 2, 0	1, 2, 0
Graphics adapter (and memory)	Diamond Viper PCI (2Mb)	Diamond Viper PCI (2Mb)	ATI Graphics Pro Turbo (4Mb)	Genoa Hornet 8300 (1Mb)	Genoa Hornet 8300 (1Mb)
Hard-disk capacity and interface	345Mb IDE	539Mb IDE	1GB SCSI-2	430Mb IDE	527Mb IDE
CD-ROM drive (and speed)	Sony CDU 33A (2x)	NEC CDR-510 (3x)	NEC CDR-510 (3x)	Matsushita CR-563-B (2x)	Matsushita CR-563-B (2x)
Modem/Network adapter/Audio	○/○/●	○/○/○	○/○/○	○/○/●	○/○/●
Accessible drive bays (5.25", 3.5")	2, 1	2, 1	2, 1	3, 1	3, 1
Internal drive bays (5.25", 3.5")	1, 2	1, 2	1, 2	0, 1	0, 1
Power supply (and number of connectors)	200W (5)	250W (5)	250W (5)	230W (4)	230W (4)
Monitor (and diagonal screen size)	Viewsonic 17 (17")	ViewSonic 17 (17")	ViewSonic 17 (17")	Robotech Cobra RS 1428NI (14")	Robotech Cobra RS 1428NI (14")
System software	DOS 6.22, WfWG 3.11	DOS 6.22, WfWG 3.11	DOS 6.22, WfWG 3.11	DOS 6.2, WfWG 3.11	DOS 6.2, WfWG 3.11
Warranty on parts/labor	1 year/1 year	1 year/1 year	1 year/1 year	2 years/2 years	2 years/2 years
On-site service	$50 (1 year)	$50 (1 year)	$50 (1 year)	None	None

●—Yes ○—No N/A—Not applicable INA—Information not available

Pentium and 486 Buyers' Guide

	Robotech Cobra RS-P90	Royal 486/66 Media Master III	Royal P/66 Media Master IV	Royal P/90 Ultra Media	Seanix ASI 9000 486DX266/08L
List price (tested configuration)	$$$$	$$	$$$	$$$	$$$
Processor	Intel Pentium/90	Intel 486DX2/66	Intel Pentium/66	Intel Pentium/90	Intel 486DX2/66
Installed, maximum motherboard RAM	16Mb, 128Mb	8Mb, 128Mb	16Mb, 128Mb	16Mb, 128Mb	8Mb, 64Mb
Installed, maximum external RAM cache	256K, 256K	256K, 512K	256K, 512K	256K, 256K	256K, 256K
Motherboard manufacturer	Intel	Genoa	Microstar	Intel	Seanix
Chip set manufacturer	Intel	Intel	Intel	Intel	OPTi
BIOS manufacturer and version (or date)	AMI 1.00.03.AX1Z	Award 4.50G	Award 4.50G	AMI 1.00.03.AX1Z	Microid 1.6
Flash BIOS/16550 UART chip	●/●	○/○	○/○	●/●	○/○
Expansion-bus slots	5 ISA, 3 PCI	5 ISA, 4 PCI	5 ISA, 4 PCI	5 ISA, 3 PCI	5 ISA, 2 VL
Parallel, serial, mouse ports	1, 2, 0	1, 2, 0	1, 2, 0	1, 2, 0	1, 2, 0
Graphics adapter (and memory)	Genoa Phantom 64 (2Mb)	ATI Graphics Pro Turbo (2Mb)	ATI Graphics Pro Turbo (2Mb)	ATI Graphics Pro Turbo (2Mb)	Seanix ASI Rocket-VL (1Mb)
Hard-disk capacity and interface	730Mb IDE	527Mb IDE	1GB SCSI-2	772Mb IDE	365Mb IDE
CD-ROM drive (and speed)	Plextor 4-Plex PX-43CH (4x)	Mitsumi FX001D (2x)	NEC CDR-510 (3x)	NEC CDR-510 (3x)	Mitsumi FX001D (2x)
Modem/Network adapter/Audio	○/○/●	○/○/●	○/○/●	○/○/●	○/○/○
Accessible drive bays (5.25", 3.5")	4, 1	3, 2	3, 2	3, 2	3, 2
Internal drive bays (5.25", 3.5")	0, 4	0, 3	0, 3	0, 3	0, 2
Power supply (and number of connectors)	230W (6)	230W (4)	230W (4)	230W (5)	230W (5)
Monitor (and diagonal screen size)	Tatung Omniscan CM-20MKR (20")	KFC CA1507 (15")	KFC CA1507 (15")	MAG Innovision DX17F (17")	KFC CA1505 (15")
System software	DOS 6.2, WfWG 3.11	DOS 6.2, WfWG 3.11	DOS 6.2, WfWG 3.11	DOS 6.2, WfWG 3.11	DOS 6.21, WfWG 3.11
Warranty on parts/labor	2 years/2 years	1 year/lifetime	1 year/lifetime	1 year/lifetime	3 years/3 years
On-site service	None	$45 (1 year)	$45 (1 year)	$45 (1 year)	None

●—Yes ○—No N/A—Not applicable INA—Information not available

Table Continues →

■ Pentium and 486 Buyers' Guide

	Seanix ASI 9000 486DX499/16L	Sidus Formula SCI966DC256DT	Sidus Formula SCI9P590PDT	Sys Business P66	Sys Performance P90
List price (tested configuration)	$$$	$$$	$$$	$$$	$$$
Processor	Intel DX4/100	Intel DX4/100	Intel Pentium/90	Intel Pentium/66	Intel Pentium/90
Installed, maximum motherboard RAM	16Mb, 64Mb	16Mb, 64Mb	16Mb, 128Mb	16Mb, 192Mb	16Mb, 768Mb
Installed, maximum external RAM cache	256K, 256K	256K, 256K	256K, 256K	256K, 512K	256K, 512K
Motherboard manufacturer	Seanix	Micronics	Intel	GBT	GBT
Chip set manufacturer	OPTi	Micronics	Intel	Intel	Intel
BIOS manufacturer and version (or date)	Microid 1.6	Phoenix 0.1	AMI 1.00.08.AX1	Award 4.50G	Award 4.50G
Flash BIOS/16550 UART chip	○/○	●/●	●/●	●/●	●/●
Expansion-bus slots	5 ISA, 2 VL	5 ISA, 2 VL	5 ISA, 3 PCI	4 ISA, 4 PCI	4 ISA, 4 PCI
Parallel, serial, mouse ports	1, 2, 0	1, 2, 0	1, 2, 0	1, 2, 0	1, 2, 0
Graphics adapter (and memory)	Seanix ASI Rocket-VL (1Mb)	ATI Graphics Wonder (2Mb)	ATI Graphics Pro Turbo (2Mb)	Diamond Stealth 32 (2Mb)	ATI Graphics Pro Turbo (2Mb)
Hard-disk capacity and interface	548Mb IDE	527Mb IDE	730Mb IDE	503Mb IDE	1GB IDE
CD-ROM drive (and speed)	Mitsumi FX001D (2x)	Sony CDU 33A (2x)	Sony CDU 33A-01 (2x)	Sony CDU 33A (2x)	Sony CDU 33A (2x)
Modem/Network adapter/Audio	○/○/○	○/○/○	○/○/○	○/○/○	○/○/○
Accessible drive bays (5.25", 3.5")	3, 2	2, 1	2, 1	3, 0	3, 1
Internal drive bays (5.25", 3.5")	0, 2	1, 1	1, 1	0, 2	0, 2
Power supply (and number of connectors)	230W (5)	200W (3)	200W (3)	200W (4)	200W (4)
Monitor (and diagonal screen size)	KFC CA1505 (15")	Sidus SID 1500N (15")	Sidus SID 1500N (15")	KFC CA1507 15")	KFC CA1507 (15")
System software	DOS 6.21, WfWG 3.11	DOS 6.21, WfWG 3.11	DOS 6.22, WfWG 3.11	DOS 6.21, WfWG 3.11	DOS 6.21, WfWG 3.11
Warranty on parts/labor	3 years/3 years	1 year/1 year	1 year/1 year	1 year/1 year	1 year/1 year
On-site service	None	$25 (1 year)	$25 (1 year)	None	None

●—Yes   ○—No   N/A—Not applicable   INA—Information not available

Pentium and 486 Buyers' Guide ■

	Tagram Thunderbolt ZR	Tagram Thunderbolt XL	Tangent DX2/66	Tangent DX4/100	Tangent PCI590
List price (tested configuration)	$$	$$$	$$	$$$	$$$
Processor	Intel 486DX2/66	Intel DX4/100	Intel 486DX2/66	Intel DX4/100	Intel Pentium/90
Installed, maximum motherboard RAM	8Mb, 64Mb	16Mb, 64Mb	8Mb, 64Mb	16Mb, 64Mb	16MB, 128MB
Installed, maximum external RAM cache	256K, 512K	256K, 512K	256K, 512K	256K, 512K	256K, 256K
Motherboard manufacturer	Tagram	Tagram	FCT	FCT	Intel
Chip set manufacturer	OPTi	OPTi	SIS	SIS	Intel
BIOS manufacturer and version (or date)	AMI (8/8/93)	AMI (8/8/93)	Award 4.50G	Award 4.50G	AMI 1.00.03.AX1Z
Flash BIOS/16550 UART chip	●/●	●/●	●/○	●/●	●/●
Expansion-bus slots	4 ISA, 1 VL	5 ISA	5 ISA, 3 VL	5 ISA, 3 VL	5 ISA, 3 PCI
Parallel, serial, mouse ports	1, 2, 1	1, 2, 1	1, 2, 0	1, 2, 0	1, 2, 0
Graphics adapter (and memory)	Integrated Tseng ET4000/W32P (2Mb)	Integrated Tseng ET4000/W32P (2Mb)	Ark 1000VL2M (2Mb)	Diamond Stealth 64 (2Mb)	Diamond Stealth 64 (2MB)
Hard-disk capacity and interface	503Mb IDE	503Mb IDE	405Mb IDE	504Mb IDE	1GB IDE
CD-ROM drive (and speed)	Mitsumi FX001D (2x)	Teac CD 55A (4x)	Sony CDU 33A (2x)	Sony CDU 33A (2x)	Sony CDU 33A (2x)
Modem/Network adapter/Audio	○/○/○	○/○/○	○/○/○	○/○/○	○/○/○
Accessible drive bays (5.25", 3.5")	2, 2	3, 1	3, 2	3, 0	3, 0
Internal drive bays (5.25", 3.5")	0, 0	0, 2	0, 0	0, 3	0, 3
Power supply (and number of connectors)	200W (3)	250W (3)	250W (4)	200W (4)	200W (4)
Monitor (and diagonal screen size)	Proton DH1448 (14")	Optiquest 2000DS (15")	Tangent SM-5515CP (15")	ADI MicroScan4GP (15")	Tangent SM-5515GP (15")
System software	DOS 6.22, WfWG 3.11	DOS 6.22, WfWG 3.11	DOS 6.2, WfWG 3.11	DOS 6.22, WfWG 3.11	DOS 6.22, WfWG 3.11
Warranty on parts/labor	3 years/3 years	3 years/3 years	1 year/1 year	1 year/1 year	1 year/1 year
On-site service	$30 (1 year)	$30 (1 year)	Included (1 year)	Included (1 year)	Included (1 year)

●—Yes ○—No N/A—Not applicable INA—Information not available

Table Continues →

■ Pentium and 486 Buyers' Guide

	Tri-Star Tri-CAD 486DX2/66	Tri-Star Tri-CAD Pentium 66	Tri-Star Tri-CAD Vigor	Unitek UT-486DX2/66LB	Unitek UT-P60
List price (tested configuration)	$$	$$$	$$$$	$$	$$
Processor	Intel 486DX2/66	Intel Pentium/66	Intel Pentium/90	Intel 486DX2/66	Intel Pentium/60
Installed, maximum motherboard RAM	8Mb, 64Mb	16Mb, 128Mb	16Mb, 128Mb	8Mb, 128Mb	16Mb, 128Mb
Installed, maximum external RAM cache	256K, 512K	256K, 256K	256K, 256K	256K, 256K	256K, 256K
Motherboard manufacturer	GBT	Intel	Intel	Shuttle	Intel
Chip set manufacturer	SIS	Intel	Intel	VIA	Intel
BIOS manufacturer and version (or date)	Award 4.50G	AMI 1.00.08.AF2	AMI 1.00.06.AX1	AMI (6/6/92)	AMI 1.00.06.AF1
Flash BIOS/16550 UART chip	○/○	○/●	●/●	○/●	●/●
Expansion-bus slots	4 ISA, 3 VL	5 ISA, 3 PCI	5 ISA, 3 PCI	5 ISA, 3 VL	5 ISA, 3 PCI
Parallel, serial, mouse ports	1, 2, 0	1, 2, 0	1, 2, 0	1, 2, 0	1, 2, 0
Graphics adapter (and memory)	ATI Graphics Wonder (2Mb)	ATI Graphics Pro Turbo (2Mb)	ATI Graphics Pro Turbo (4Mb)	ATI Graphics Pro Turbo (2Mb)	ATI Graphics Pro Turbo (2Mb)
Hard-disk capacity and interface	341Mb IDE	540Mb IDE	1GB SCSI-2	425Mb IDE	541Mb IDE
CD-ROM drive (and speed)	Sony CDU 33A (2x)	Sony CDU 33A (2x)	Sony CDU 33A (2x)	Sony CDU 33A (2x)	Sony CDU 33A (2x)
Modem/Network adapter/Audio	○/○/○	○/○/○	○/○/○	○/○/○	○/○/○
Accessible drive bays (5.25", 3.5")	3, 2	3, 2	4, 0	2, 2	3, 1
Internal drive bays (5.25", 3.5")	0, 2	0, 2	2, 0	0, 1	0, 1
Power supply (and number of connectors)	200W (3)	200W (3)	250W (4)	230W (3)	230W (3)
Monitor (and diagonal screen size)	ADI MicroScan 4GP (15")	ADI MicroScan 5EP (15")	ViewSonic 2182-1 (21")	Optiquest 2000DS (15")	Optiquest 2000DS (15")
System software	DOS 6.22, WfWG 3.11	DOS 6.21, WfWG 3.11	DOS 6.22, WfWG 3.11	DOS 6.22, WfWG 3.11	DOS 6.22, WfWG 3.11
Warranty on parts/labor	2 years/lifetime	2 years/lifetime	2 years/lifetime	1 year/1 year	1 year/1 year
On-site service	None	None	None	$45 (1 year)	$45 (1 year)

●—Yes ○—No N/A—Not applicable INA—Information not available

Pentium and 486 Buyers' Guide ▓

	Unitek UT-P90	Vektron Edutainment Multimedia/486DX 266	Vektron PCI Professional Multimedia/Pentium 60	Vektron PCI Multimedia Ultimate/Pentium 90	Vektron Windows Power Station/486DX266
List price (tested configuration)	$$$	$$	$$$	$$$	$$
Processor	Intel Pentium/90	Intel 486DX2/66	Intel Pentium/60	Intel Pentium/90	Intel 486DX2/66
Installed, maximum motherboard RAM	16Mb, 128Mb	8Mb, 64Mb	16Mb, 192Mb	16Mb, 128Mb	8Mb, 64Mb
Installed, maximum external RAM cache	256K, 256K	128K, 1Mb	256K, 512K	256K, 512K	128K, 1Mb
Motherboard manufacturer	Intel	Asus	Asus	TMC	Asus
Chip set manufacturer	Intel	SIS	Intel	OPTi	SIS
BIOS manufacturer and version (or date)	AMI 1.00.03.AX1Z	Award 4.50G	Award 4.5	AMI G4ZZ	Award 4.50G
Flash BIOS/16550 UART chip	●/●	○/○	●/○	●/●	○/○
Expansion-bus slots	5 ISA, 3 PCI	5 ISA, 2 VL	5 ISA, 3 PCI	3 ISA, 4 PCI, 2 VL	5 ISA, 2 VL
Parallel, serial, mouse ports	1, 2, 0	1, 2, 0	1, 2, 0	1, 2, 0	1, 2, 0
Graphics adapter (and memory)	ATI Graphics Pro Turbo (4Mb)	Diamond Speedstar Pro (1Mb)	Hercules Stingray S801 (1Mb)	Diamond Stealth 64 (2Mb)	Diamond Speedstar Pro (1Mb)
Hard-disk capacity and interface	1GB IDE	341Mb IDE	541Mb SCSI-2	1.1GB SCSI-2	341Mb IDE
CD-ROM drive (and speed)	Sony CDU 33A (2x)	Mitsumi FX001D (2x)	NEC CDR-510 (3x)	Plextor 4-Plex PX-43CH (4x)	Mitsumi FX001D (2x)
Modem/Network adapter/Audio	○/○/○	●/○/●	●/○/●	●/○/●	○/○/○
Accessible drive bays (5.25", 3.5")	4, 1	2, 2	3, 2	3, 2	2, 2
Internal drive bays (5.25", 3.5")	4, 0	0, 1	0, 3	0, 2	0, 1
Power supply (and number of connectors)	230W (4)	250W (4)	250W (3)	250W (3)	250W (4)
Monitor (and diagonal screen size)	Optiquest 2000DS (15")	ADI MicroScan 3GP (14")	ADI MicroScan 4GP (15")	ADI MicroScan 4GP (15")	ADI MicroScan 4GP (15")
System software	DOS 6.22, WfWG 3.11	DOS 6.21, WfWG 3.11	DOS 6.21, WfWG 3.11	DOS 6.21, WfWG 3.11	DOS 6.21, WfWG 3.11
Warranty on parts/labor	1 year/1 year	3 years/lifetime	3 years/lifetime	3 years/lifetime	3 years/lifetime
On-site service	$45 (1 year)	Included (1 year)	Included (1 year)	Included (1 year)	Included (1 year)

●—Yes   ○—No   N/A—Not applicable   INA—Information not available

Table Continues →

■ Pentium and 486 Buyers' Guide

	Vektron PCI Power Station/Pentium 60	Vektron PCI Power Ultimate/Pentium 90	Xinetron X/LAN 486/66	Xinetron X/LAN P66	Xinetron X/LAN P90
List price (tested configuration)	$$	$$$	$$	$$$	$$$$
Processor	Intel Pentium/60	Intel Pentium/90	Intel 486DX2/66	Intel Pentium/66	Intel Pentium/90
Installed, maximum motherboard RAM	16Mb, 192Mb	16Mb, 128Mb	8Mb, 32Mb	16Mb, 128Mb	16Mb, 128Mb
Installed, maximum external RAM cache	256K, 512K	256K, 512K	256K, 256K	512K, 512K	512K, 512K
Motherboard manufacturer	Asus	TMC	J. Bond	Super Micro	Super Micro
Chip set manufacturer	Intel	OPTi	SIS	OPTi	OPTi
BIOS manufacturer and version (or date)	Award 4.5	AMI G4ZZ	AMI (9/26/93)	AMI (12/15/93)	AMI (12/15/93)
Flash BIOS/16550 UART chip	●/○	●/○	○/○	●/●	●/●
Expansion-bus slots	5 ISA, 3 PCI	3 ISA, 4 PCI, 2 VL	2 ISA, 2 VL	3 ISA, 4 PCI, 2 VL	3 ISA, 4 PCI, 2 VL
Parallel, serial, mouse ports	1, 2, 0	1, 2, 0	1, 2, 0	1, 2, 0	1, 2, 0
Graphics adapter (and memory)	Hercules Stingray S801 (1Mb)	Diamond Stealth 64 (2Mb)	Tseng ET4000/W32P-based (1Mb)	ATI Graphics Pro Turbo (2Mb)	ATI Graphics Pro Turbo (2Mb)
Hard-disk capacity and interface	528Mb IDE	1.1GB SCSI-2	345Mb IDE	540Mb SCSI-2	1.7GB SCSI-2
CD-ROM drive (and speed)	Mitsumi FX001D (2x)	Mitsumi FX001D (2x)	Mitsumi FX001D (2x)	Toshiba XM-3401B (2x)	Toshiba XM-3401B (2x)
Modem/Network adapter/Audio	○/○/○	○/○/○	●/●/○	○/●/○	○/○/○
Accessible drive bays (5.25", 3.5")	3, 2	3, 2	2, 2	2, 2	4, 0
Internal drive bays (5.25", 3.5")	0, 2	0, 3	0, 0	0, 1	3, 0
Power supply (and number of connectors)	250W (4)	250W (3)	230W (3)	230W (4)	250W (5)
Monitor (and diagonal screen size)	ADI MicroScan 4GP (15")	ADI MicroScan 4GP (15")	SOCOS DM-1488 (14")	SOCOS DM-1488 (14")	SOCOS DM-1488 (14")
System software	DOS 6.21, WfWG 3.11	DOS 6.21, WfWG 3.11	DOS 6.22, Windows 3.11	DOS 6.2, Windows 3.11	DOS 6.2, Windows 3.11
Warranty on parts/labor	3 years/lifetime	3 years/lifetime	1 year/3 years	1 year/3 years	1 year/3 years
On-site service	Included (1 year)	Included (1 year)	$125 (1 year)	$225 (1 year)	$225 (1 year)

●—Yes ○—No N/A—Not applicable INA—Information not available

Pentium and 486 Buyers' Guide ■

	ZDS Z-Station 500	ZDS Z-Station EX	ZEOS Pantera 486DX2-66	ZEOS Pantera Pentium-66	ZEOS Pantera Pentium-90
List price (tested configuration)	$$$	$$$$	$$	$$$	$$$
Processor	Intel 486DX2/66	Intel Pentium/90	Intel 486DX2/66	Intel Pentium/66	Intel Pentium/90
Installed, maximum motherboard RAM	8Mb, 128Mb	16Mb, 128Mb	8Mb, 128Mb	16Mb, 192Mb	16Mb, 384Mb
Installed, maximum external RAM cache	256K, 512K	256K, 256K	256K, 256K	256K, 512K	256K, 512K
Motherboard manufacturer	Zenith	Intel	ZEOS	ZEOS	ZEOS
Chip set manufacturer	Intel	Intel	Intel	Intel	Intel
BIOS manufacturer and version (or date)	Phoenix 1.03	AMI 9.99.99.BF0U	Phoenix 4.03	Phoenix 4.03	Phoenix 4.03
Flash BIOS/16550 UART chip	●/●	●/●	●/○	●/●	●/●
Expansion-bus slots	3 ISA, 2 PCI	3 ISA, 2 PCI	5 ISA, 3 PCI	5 ISA, 3 PCI	5 ISA, 3 PCI
Parallel, serial, mouse ports	1, 1, 1	1, 2, 1	1, 2, 0	1, 2, 0	1, 2, 0
Graphics adapter (and memory)	Integrated ATI Mach32 (1Mb)	Integrated ATI Mach64 (2Mb)	Diamond Stealth 64 (2Mb)	Diamond Stealth 64 (2Mb)	Diamond Stealth 64 (2Mb)
Hard-disk capacity and interface	340Mb IDE	729Mb IDE	545Mb IDE	1GB IDE	1GB IDE
CD-ROM drive (and speed)	Toshiba XM-4101B (2x)	Mitsumi FX001DE (2x)	Mitsumi FX001D (2x)	Mitsumi FX001D (2x)	Mitsumi FX001D (2x)
Modem/Network adapter/Audio	○/●/○	○/●/○	○/○/○	○/○/○	○/○/○
Accessible drive bays (5.25", 3.5")	2, 1	2, 1	2, 2	2, 2	4, 0
Internal drive bays (5.25", 3.5")	0, 1	0, 1	1, 1	1, 1	2, 4
Power supply (and number of connectors)	150W (4)	145W (3)	200W (4)	200W (4)	200W (3)
Monitor (and diagonal screen size)	Nokia ZCM-1740-UT (17")	Nokia ZCM-1740-UT (17")	ZEOS 15 (15")	ZEOS 15 (15")	ZEOS 15 (15")
System software	DOS 6.21, WfWG 3.11	DOS 6.2, WfWG 3.11	DOS 6.21, WfWG 3.11	DOS 6.21, WfWG 3.11	DOS 6.21, WfWG 3.11
Warranty on parts/labor	3 years/3 years	3 years/3 years	1 year/1 year	1 year/1 year	1 year/1 year
On-site service	Included (1 year)	Included (1 year)	$59 (1 year)	$59 (1 year)	$59 (1 year)

●—Yes   ○—No   N/A—Not applicable   INA—Information not available

E n d ■

■ A.2   Home PCs

(Products listed in alphabetical order by company name)	**AcerPower 9812TG**	**ACMA P60 MPC**	**ALR Multimedia Express M466D**	**AT&T Globalyst 360 TPC**	**Blackship Atlantis**
List price (tested configuration)	$$$	$$$	$$	$$	$$
Processor	Intel Pentium/60	Intel Pentium/60	Intel 486DX2/66	Intel 486DX2/66	Intel 486DX2/66
Installed/maximum motherboard RAM	8Mb, 128Mb	8Mb, 128Mb	8Mb, 136Mb	8Mb, 64Mb	8Mb, 64Mb
Installed/maximum external RAM cache	256K, 256K	256K, 256K	128K, 256K	None, 256K	256K, 256K
Motherboard manufacturer	Acer	Intel	ALR	AT&T	Blackship
Chip set manufacturer	Intel	Intel	ALI	SIS	SIS
BIOS manufacturer and version (or date)	Acer (8/25/94)	AMI (4/15/94)	IBM (8/18/94)	Award (7/27/94)	Award (7/26/92)
Flash BIOS/16550 UART chip	●/○	●/●	●/○	○/○	○ ●
Expansion-bus slots	5 ISA, 3 PCI	5 ISA, 3 PCI	3 ISA	4 ISA, 2 VL	4 ISA, 3 VL
Parallel, serial, mouse ports	1, 2, 1	1, 2, 0	1, 2, 1	1, 2, 0	1, 2, 0
Graphics adapter (and memory)	ATI Mach32-based (2Mb)	Diamond Stealth 64 (1Mb)	Integrated Cirrus Logic CL-GD5428 (1Mb)	AT&T PWA-MVGA-542X (1Mb)	Cirrus Logic GD5428-based (1Mb)
Hard disk capacity and interface	546Mb IDE	540Mb IDE	424Mb IDE	424Mb IDE	426Mb IDE
CD-ROM drive (and speed)	Mitsumi CRMC-FXOOIDE (2x)	Panasonic CR-562-B (2x)	Wearnes CDD-110 (2x)	Sony CDU 33A (2x)	IBM/Panasonic CR-562 (2x)
Speakers	Acer Speakers	ACMA 80-Watt	MIDI Land MLi 168	AT&T Talkback	QuickShot Sound Mate 4
Audio/Microphone/Headphones	●/○/○	●/●/○	●/○ ○	●/●/○	●/○/○
Modem/TV board/Radio	●/○/○	●/○/○	●/○/○	●/○/○	●/○/○
Box-topper/Getting-started video/Windows front end	●/○/●	●/○/●	●/○/●	●/●/●	○/○/○
Labeled ports/Color-coded cables	●/○	●/○	●/○	●/○	●/○
Accessible drive bays (5.25, 3.5)	3, 2	3, 2	1, 1	2, 2	2, 2
Internal drive bays (5.25, 3.5)	0, 2	0, 1	1, 1	0, 1	0, 2
Power supply (and number of connectors)	200W (3)	250W (6)	125W (3)	200W (5)	235W (3)
Monitor (and diagonal screen size)	Acer View 56L (15)	Impression 5528NG (15)	MAG Innovision Dx15F (15)	AT&T/NCR CAM630Z (14)	MGC 1588VA (15)
System software	DOS 6.22, Windows 3.11	DOS 6.22, WfWG 3.11	DOS 6.22, Windows 3.11	DOS 6.22, Windows 3.11	DOS 6.22, WfWG 3.11
Dealers/Direct-distribution channel	○/●	●/●	●/●	●/●	○/●
Warranty on parts/labor	1 year/1 year	1 year/1 year	1 year/1 year	1 year/1 year	1 year/1 year
On-site service (1 year)	Included	Included	$9.95	Included	Included

●—Yes   ○—No   N/A—Not applicable   INA—Information not available

Home PCs ■

	Compaq Presario CDS 520 Model 420	CompuAdd C466D	Data Storage Delta 75VL	Dell Dimension 466/V	EPS Mega Multi-Media
List price (tested configuration)	$$	$$	$$	$$	$$
Processor	AMD Am486SX2-66	Intel 486DX2/66	IBM BL 25/75	Intel 486DX2/66	Intel 486DX2/66
Installed/maximum motherboard RAM	8Mb, 64Mb	8Mb, 64Mb	8Mb, 64Mb	8Mb, 64Mb	16Mb, 512Mb
Installed/maximum external RAM cache	None, None	128K, 256K	256K, 256K	None, 256K	256K, 512K
Motherboard manufacturer	Compaq	Micronics	IBM	Dell	EPS
Chip set manufacturer	VLSI	Micronics	OPTi	OPTi	UMC
BIOS manufacturer and version (or date)	Compaq (8/5/94)	Phoenix (1/15/88)	IBM (10/24/93)	AMI/Dell (11/11/92)	Award (8/18/94)
Flash BIOS/16550 UART chip	●/●	●/●	○/●	○/○	○/●
Expansion-bus slots	2 ISA	5 ISA, 2 VL	5 ISA, 2 VL	3 ISA, 2 VL	2 ISA, 4 PCI, 2 VL
Parallel, serial, mouse ports	1, 1, 1	1, 2, 0	1, 2, 0	1, 2, 1	1, 2, 0
Graphics adapter (and memory)	Integrated Cirrus Logic CL-GD5424 (512K)	Western Digital Paradise (1Mb)	Diamond SpeedStar Pro (1Mb)	Integrated Cirrus Logic CL-GD5428 (512K)	ATI WinTurbo 64 (2Mb)
Hard disk capacity and interface	422Mb IDE	424Mb IDE	405Mb IDE	528Mb IDE	528Mb IDE
CD-ROM drive (and speed)	Matsushita CR-571-C (2x)	Mitsumi Fx001D (2x)	Aztech CDA-268-01a (2x)	Panasonic CR-563-x (2x)	Mitsumi FX001D (2x)
Speakers	Integrated Compaq/Panasonic	LabTec MCS-600	Aztech AZT18	Peavey MediaVoice 200A	LabTech CS-1400
Audio/Microphone/Headphones	●/●/○	●/●/○	●/●/○	●/●/○	●/●/○
Modem/TV board/Radio	●/○/○	●/○○	●/○/○	●/○/○	●/○/○
Box-topper/Getting-started video/Windows front end	●/●/●	○/○/●	●/○/○	○/○/●	●/○/○
Labeled ports/Color-coded cables	●/○	○/○	○/○	○/○	●/○
Accessible drive bays (5.25, 3.5)	1, 1	3, 2	3, 2	3, 0	2, 2
Internal drive bays (5.25, 3.5)	0, 1	0, 2	0, 0	0, 2	2, 0
Power supply (and number of connectors)	150W (3)	200W (5)	250W (4)	150W (3)	200W (3)
Monitor (and diagonal screen size)	Integrated Compaq 177018.001 (14)	CompuAdd TE1564M (15)	ViewSonic/Data Storage 6E (14)	Dell VS15 (15)	Hitachi SuperScan 15s (15)
System software	DOS 6.2, Windows 3.1	DOS 6.2, WfWG 3.11	DOS 6.22, WfWG 3.11	DOS 6.2, Windows 3.1	DOS 6.22, WfWG 3.11
Dealers/Direct-distribution channel	●/○	○/○	●/●	○/●	●/●
Warranty on parts/labor	3 years/3 years	1 year/1 year	3 years/3 years	1 year/1 year	3 years/1 year
On-site service (1 year)	Included	Included	$50.00	Included	Included

●—Yes ○—No N/A—Not applicable INA—Information not available

Table Continues →

■ Home PCs

	FutureTech System 4414	Gateway 2000 P5-60 Family PC	IBM Aptiva 530 PC Model 530	Insight PCI P60 MM	Micron P90 Home MPC
List price (tested configuration)	$$	$$$	$$	$$$	$$$
Processor	Intel 486DX2/66	Intel Pentium/60	Intel 486DX2/66	Intel Pentium/60	Intel Pentium/90
Installed/maximum motherboard RAM	8Mb, 128Mb	8Mb, 128Mb	8Mb, 128Mb	8Mb, 128Mb	8Mb, 192Mb
Installed/maximum external RAM cache	256K, 512K	256K, 256K	None, 256K	256K, 256K	256K, 512K
Motherboard manufacturer	Asus	Intel	IBM	Intel	Micronics
Chip set manufacturer	SIS	Intel	OPTi	Intel	Intel
BIOS manufacturer and version (or date)	Award (4/26/94)	AMI (5/18/94)	IBM (8/16/94)	AMI (4/15/94)	Phoenix (8/25/94)
Flash BIOS/16550 UART chip	●/○	●/●	●/●	●/●	●/●
Expansion-bus slots	5 ISA, 2 VL	5 ISA, 3 PCI	3 ISA, 1 VL	5 ISA, 3 PCI	5 ISA, 3 PCI
Parallel, serial, mouse ports	1, 2, 0	1, 2, 1	1, 2, 1	1, 2, 0	1, 2, 1
Graphics adapter (and memory)	Jax Tech VI-41 (2Mb)	STB 5430 (1Mb)	Integrated Cirrus Logic CL-GD5430 (1Mb)	ATI Mach32-based (2Mb)	Diamond Stealth 64 PCI (2Mb)
Hard disk capacity and interface	341Mb IDE	729Mb IDE	424Mb IDE	428Mb IDE	527Mb IDE
CD-ROM drive (and speed)	Mitsumi FX001d2 (2x)	NEC CDR-260 (2x)	IBM/Mitsumi CRMC-FXNO1DE (2x)	Panasonic CR-563-B (2x)	Mitsumi FX001D (2x)
Speakers	Hi-Tex CP-18	Yamaha YST-M10	Jazz Hipster J-590 AV	Reveal RS380	Koss HD/4
Audio/Microphone/Headphones	●/○/○	●/○/○	●/●/○	●/●/●	●/○/○
Modem/TV board/Radio	●/●/○	●/○/○	●/○/○	●/○/○	●/○/○
Box-topper/Getting-started video/Windows front end	○/○/○	●/○/●	●/○/●	●/○/●	●/○/●
Labeled ports/Color-coded cables	●/○	●/○	●/○	●/○	●/○
Accessible drive bays (5.25, 3.5)	3, 2	3, 1	1, 1	3, 2	3, 1
Internal drive bays (5.25, 3.5)	2, 0	0, 0	0, 2	0, 1	0, 2
Power supply (and number of connectors)	250W (5)	145W (5)	145W (3)	200W (4)	200W (4)
Monitor (and diagonal screen size)	Socos DCM-1588 E (15)	Gateway 2000 CS1572DG (14)	IBM 15R MS (14)	MAG Innovision DX15F (15)	MAG Innovision LX1450LG (14)
System software	DOS 6.2, Windows 3.11	DOS 6.22, WfWG 3.11	IBM PC DOS 6.3, Windows 3.11	DOS 6.22, WfWG 3.11	DOS 6.22, WfWG 3.11
Dealers/Direct-distribution channel	○/●	○/●	●/●	○/●	○/●
Warranty on parts/labor	15 months/15 months	3 years/3 years	3 years/3 years	1 year/1 year	1 year/1 year
On-site service (1 year)	$49.00	N/A	N/A	N/A	Included

●—Yes   ○—No   N/A—Not applicable   INA—Information not available

Home PCs ■

	MidWest Micro Elite Home PC P5-90	NEC Ready P60M	NETiS Pentium N566 Best Buy	Packard Bell 486DX2/66 Multimedia System
List price (tested configuration)	$$$	$$$	$$$	$$
Processor	Intel Pentium/90	Intel Pentium/60	Intel Pentium/66	Intel 486DX2/66
Installed/maximum motherboard RAM	8Mb, 128Mb	8Mb, 136Mb	8Mb, 192Mb	8Mb, 64Mb
Installed/maximum external RAM cache	256K, 256K	256K, 256K	256K, 512K	None, 512K
Motherboard manufacturer	Intel	NEC	Asus	Packard Bell
Chip set manufacturer	Intel	Intel	Intel	OPTi
BIOS manufacturer and version (or date)	AMI (7/22/94)	AMI (6/22/94)	Award (7/7/94)	Phoenix (6/23/94)
Flash BIOS/16550 UART chip	●/●	●/●	●/●	●/●
Expansion-bus slots	5 ISA, 3 PCI	4 ISA, 2 PCI	5 ISA, 3 PCI	3 ISA
Parallel, serial, mouse ports	1, 2, 0	1, 2, 1	1, 2, 0	1, 2, 1
Graphics adapter (and memory)	ATI WinTurbo (2Mb)	Integrated Cirrus Logic CL-GD5434 (1Mb)	ATI WinTurbo (2Mb)	Integrated Cirrus Logic CL-GD5428 (1Mb)
Hard disk capacity and interface	428Mb IDE	425Mb IDE	424Mb IDE	539Mb IDE
CD-ROM drive (and speed)	Mitsumi FX001D (2x)	NEC MultiSpin 3Xi (3x)	Mitsumi FX001D (2x)	Panasonic CR-563-B (2x)
Speakers	Altec Lansing Multimedia ACS 50	Labtec CS-150	Media Active SP-690	Packard Bell SPK-229
Audio/Microphone/Headphones	●/○/○	●/●/○	●/○/○	●/○/○
Modem/TV board/Radio	●/○/○	●/○/○	●/○/○	●/●/○
Box-topper/Getting-started video/Windows front end	○/○/○	○/●/●	●/○/○	●/○/●
Labeled ports/Color-coded cables	●/○	●/○	●/○	●/●
Accessible drive bays (5.25, 3.5)	3, 2	3, 1	3, 2	1, 1
Internal drive bays (5.25, 3.5)	0, 2	0, 2	0, 0	0, 1
Power supply (and number of connectors)	230W (6)	200W (4)	250W (5)	150W (3)
Monitor (and diagonal screen size)	Infotel SRC1502 (15)	NEC 3V (15)	ETC CA-15CG (15)	Packard Bell 1511SL (15)
System software	DOS 6.22, WfWG 3.11	DOS 6.22, Windows 3.1	DOS 6.22, WfWG 3.11	DOS 6.2, WfWG 3.11
Dealers/Direct-distribution channel	●/●	●/●	●/●	●/○
Warranty on parts/labor	3 years/3 years	3 years/3 years	1 year/1 year	1 year/1 year
On-site service (1 year)	N/A	Included	Included	Included

●—Yes ○—No N/A—Not applicable INA—Information not available

Table Continues →

ZIFF-DAVIS PRESS

■ Home PCs

	PC Express Family Multimedia System	Robotech Cobra RS Home Runner p60	Tagram Platinum I	USA Flex Family Edition
List price (tested configuration)	$$	$$$	$$$	$$
Processor	Intel 486DX2/66	Intel Pentium/60	Intel Pentium/60	Intel 486DX2/66
Installed/maximum motherboard RAM	8Mb, 64Mb	16Mb, 128Mb	8Mb, 128Mb	8Mb, 64Mb
Installed/maximum external RAM cache	128K, 256K	512K, 2Mb	256K, 512K	256K, 512K
Motherboard manufacturer	Asus	Robotech	BCM	USA Flex
Chip set manufacturer	SIS	Forex	Intel	SIS
BIOS manufacturer and version (or date)	Award (4/26/94)	Award (7/19/94)	Phoenix (9/16/93)	Award (3/23/94)
Flash BIOS/16550 UART chip	○/○	●/○	○/●	○/●
Expansion-bus slots	5 ISA, 2 VL	4 ISA, 3 VL	5 ISA, 3 PCI	4 ISA, 3 VL
Parallel, serial, mouse ports	1, 2, 0	1, 2, 0	1, 2, 0	1, 2, 0
Graphics adapter (and memory)	Hercules Stingray VL-1 (1Mb)	Genoa Hornet VGA 8300VL (1Mb)	Diamond Stealth 64 PCI (2Mb)	Hercules Stingray VL-1 (1Mb)
Hard disk capacity and interface	427Mb IDE	404Mb IDE	528Mb IDE	425Mb IDE
CD-ROM drive (and speed)	Sony CDU 33A (2x)	Panasonic CR-563 (2x)	Mitsumi FX0001D (2x)	Sony CDU 33A (2x)
Speakers	Laser Station S80GT	Creative Labs SBS38	Integrated Proton GM-1563M	Micro Innovations MM40P
Audio/Microphone/Headphones	●/●/○	●/●/○	●/●/○	●/○/●
Modem/TV board/Radio	●/○/○	●/○/○	●/○/○	●/○/○
Box-topper/Getting-started video/Windows front end	○/○/●	●/○/●	●/●/●	○/○/○
Labeled ports/Color-coded cables	●/○	●/○	●/○	●/○
Accessible drive bays (5.25, 3.5)	3, 2	3, 1	2, 1	3, 2
Internal drive bays (5.25, 3.5)	0, 3	0, 1	1, 2	0, 2
Power supply (and number of connectors)	230W (4)	230W (4)	250W (5)	200W (3)
Monitor (and diagonal screen size)	CTX 1451ES (14)	Tatung CM15VBE (15)	Proton GM-1565M (15)	CTX 1562GM (15)
System software	DOS 6.22, WfWG 3.11	DOS 6.22, WfWG 3.11	DOS 6.22, WfWG 3.11	DOS 6.22, WfWG 3.11
Dealers/Direct-distribution channel	●/●	●/●	●/●	○/●
Warranty on parts/labor	5 years/5 years	2 years/2 years	3 years/3 years	3 years/3 years
On-site service (1 year)	$79.00	Included	$30.00	$49.00

●—Yes ○—No N/A—Not applicable INA—Information not available

End ■

A.3 File Servers

(Products listed in alphabetical order by company name)	AcerAltos 7000	Axik NetPower Enterprise Server Series-I	Compaq ProLiant 1000 486DX2/66	Dell PowerEdge SP590	DECpc XL Server 566
Price (tested configuration)	$$$$$	$$$$$	$$$$$	$$$$$	$$$$$
PROCESSOR AND MEMORY					
Processor	Intel Pentium/90	Intel DX4/100	Intel 486DX2/66	Intel Pentium/90	Intel Pentium/66
Processor location	ZIF socket on processor card	ZIF socket on motherboard	Standard socket on motherboard	Standard socket on processor card	Socket on processor card
Maximum number of CPUs supported	1	1	1	1	1
External RAM cache	256K–1Mb	256K–1Mb	256K	256K	256K
Installable system RAM	16Mb–256Mb	1Mb–128Mb	16Mb–128Mb	8Mb–192Mb	8Mb–256Mb
RAM supports error correction	○	○	○	●	○
EXPANSION BUSES					
Bus architecture (primary, secondary)	EISA, VL-Bus	EISA, VL-Bus	EISA	EISA, PCI	EISA, PCI
ISA, EISA, MCA slots	0, 6, 0	0, 6, 0	0, 7, 0	0, 6, 0	0, 5, 0
VL-Bus, PCI, proprietary local-bus slots	2, 0, 0	2, 0, 0	0, 0, 0	0, 2, 0	0, 3, 0
Other proprietary slots	1 CPU	None	None	1 CPU	1 CPU
Number of bus-mastering slots	8	6	7	8	8
DISK SUBSYSTEM					
Number and capacity of installed hard disks	Four 1Gb	Four 1.7Gb	Four 1.05Gb	Four 1Gb	Four 1Gb
Mirroring implementation	Hardware	Software	Hardware, software	Hardware, software	Hardware
Disk controller hardware cache	16Mb	None	4Mb	1.5Mb	4Mb
RAID levels supported by disk controller	1, 5	1	1, 4, 5, 10	1, 4, 5, 10	1, 5
Tested configuration supports hot-swapping	●	○	●	●	○
Drive bays in provided case	12	9	8	8	9
OPERATING-SYSTEM SUPPORT					
Compatible with DOS, NetWare, and Unix	●	●	●	●	●
Other compatible operating systems	Altos/SCO Unix, Microsoft Windows NT, OS/2, SCO Unix	Microsoft Windows NT, Microsoft Windows NTAS	Microsoft Windows NT, Microsoft Windows NTAS, OS/2, SCO Open Server, SCO Unix, VINES	Coactive Connector, LANtastic, Microsoft Windows NT, Microsoft Windows NTAS, NeXTStep, OS/2, SCO Unix, Solaris, VINES	Microsoft Windows NT, Microsoft Windows NTAS, NeXTStep, OS/2, Pathworks, SCO Unix, UnixWare, VINES

●—Yes ○—No N/A—Not applicable INA—Information not available

Table Continues →

■ File Servers

	Duracom FilePro 586/66	EPS Super Server Goliath P5-66 SSBKP	GAIN Vector 90ER	HR Mission Critical	HP NetServer 486/LF
Price (tested configuration)	$$$$$	$$$$$	$$$$$	$$$$	$$$$$
PROCESSOR AND MEMORY					
Processor	Intel Pentium/66	Intel Pentium/66	Intel Pentium/90	Intel Pentium/66	Intel 486DX2/66
Processor location	ZIF socket on motherboard	ZIF socket on motherboard	Standard socket on motherboard	ZIF socket on motherboard	ZIF socket on processor card
Maximum number of CPUs supported	1	1	2	1	1
External RAM cache	128K–256K	256K–512K	512K	256K	256K
Installable system RAM	2Mb–128Mb	8Mb–192Mb	16Mb–384Mb	1Mb–128Mb	8Mb–136Mb
RAM supports error correction	○	●	●	○	○
EXPANSION BUSES					
Bus architecture (primary, secondary)	ISA, PCI	EISA, PCI	EISA	ISA, PCI	EISA, PCI
ISA, EISA, MCA slots	5, 0, 0	0, 5, 0	0, 8, 0	5, 0, 0	0, 7, 0
VL-Bus, PCI, proprietary local-bus slots	0, 3, 0	0, 3, 0	0, 0, 0	0, 3, 0	0, 2, 0
Other proprietary slots	None	None	1 CPU, 1 RAM	None	1 CPU
Number of bus-mastering slots	3	6	6	4	7
DISK SUBSYSTEM					
Number and capacity of installed hard disks	Four 1Gb	Four 1Gb	Five 1.75Gb	Two 1.8Gb, two 1.4Gb	Four 535Mb, two 1Gb
Mirroring implementation	Software	Hardware	Hardware	Hardware, software	Hardware, software
Disk controller hardware cache	None	8Mb	16Mb	None	None
RAID levels supported by disk controller	1	1, 5	1, 5, 6	1, 5	1, 5, 6
Tested configuration supports hot-swapping	○	○	○	○	●
Drive bays in provided case	7	16	12	8	9
OPERATING-SYSTEM SUPPORT					
Compatible with DOS, NetWare, and Unix	●	●	●	●	●
Other compatible operating systems	Microsoft Windows NT, OS/2, SCO Unix, Solaris, UnixWare	Microsoft Windows NT, SCO Unix, SCO Xenix GT, VINES	Microsoft Windows NT, Microsoft Windows NTAS, OS/2, SCO Unix Open Desktop and Multiprocessor Extension, SecureWare Trusted Unix, VINES	Microsoft Windows NT, OS/2, SCO Unix, UnixWare, VINES	Microsoft Windows NT, OS/2, VINES

●—Yes ○—No N/A—Not applicable INA—Information not available

File Servers ◼

	IBM PS/2 Server 95 Array 566	Poly RAID-586EV	Tangent Just'N Case Server 100	Wyse Series 6000i Model 665	ZDS Z-Server EX DP66E
Price (tested configuration)	$$$$$	$$$$$	$$$$$	$$$$$	$$$$$
PROCESSOR AND MEMORY					
Processor	Intel Pentium/66	Intel Pentium/66	Intel Pentium/66	Intel Pentium/60	Two Intel Pentium/66s
Processor location	Standard socket on processor card	ZIF socket on motherboard	ZIF socket on motherboard	ZIF socket on motherboard	Standard sockets on processor card
Maximum number of CPUs supported	1	1	1	1	2
External RAM cache	256K	256K–512K	256K–512K	256K	256K
Installable system RAM	16Mb–256Mb	8Mb–128Mb	2Mb–192Mb	16Mb–192Mb	4Mb–384Mb
RAM supports error correction	●	○	○	○	●
EXPANSION BUSES					
Bus architecture (primary, secondary)	MCA	EISA, VL-Bus	EISA, PCI	EISA	EISA
ISA, EISA, MCA slots	0, 0, 8	0, 6, 0	0, 4, 0	0, 7, 0	0, 8, 0
VL-Bus, PCI, proprietary local-bus slots	0, 0, 0	2, 0, 0	0, 4, 0	0, 0, 0	0, 0, 0
Other proprietary slots	1 CPU	None	None	None	1 CPU, 1 RAM
Number of bus-mastering slots	8	8	8	7	8
DISK SUBSYSTEM					
Number and capacity of installed hard disks	Four 1Gb	Five 1.2Gb, one 80Mb	Four 1Gb	Four 1Gb	Four 1Gb
Mirroring implementation	Hardware	Hardware	Software	Hardware	Hardware, software
Disk controller hardware cache	4Mb	4Mb	None	16Mb	None
RAID levels supported by disk controller	1, 5	1, 3, 5	1	1, 5	1, 5, 6
Tested configuration supports hot-swapping	●	●	●	○	○
Drive bays in provided case	9	8	8	6	11
OPERATING-SYSTEM SUPPORT					
Compatible with DOS, NetWare, and Unix	●	●	●	●	●
Other compatible operating systems	LanServer, Microsoft Windows NT, OS/2, VINES	Microsoft Windows NT, OS/2, SCO Unix	LanServer, Microsoft Windows NT, OS/2, SCO Open Desktop, SCO Unix	Microsoft Windows NT, OS/2, SCO Unix, Solaris, UnixWare, VINES	Microsoft Windows NT, Microsoft Windows NTAS, OS/2, SCO Open Server Enterprise, SCO Open Server Network, SCO Unix, Solaris, VINES

●—Yes　○—No　N/A—Not applicable　INA—Information not available

E n d ◼

■ A.4 Mobile Computers

	Altima Virage (Active color)	Altima Virage (Dual-scan color)	Ambra N75D	Ambra N100T	AMS SoundPro DX4/75
Price	$$$$	$$$	$$$	$$$$	$$
Processor	DX2/66	DX2/66	DX4/75 SL	DX4/100 SL	Intel DX4/75
Fixed disk size	256	256	340	455	INA
Windows version	Windows 3.1	Windows 3.1	Windows 3.1	Windows for Workgroups 3.11	Windows for Workgroups 3.11
Pointing device	INA	INA	INA	INA	Integrated trackball
Case size (HWD, in inches)	2.3 × 11.5 × 8.5	2.3 × 11.5 × 8.5	2.0 × 11.0 × 8.5	2.1 × 11.0 × 8.5	2.1 × 11.0 × 8.1
Weight/Travel weight (pounds)	6.52/8.15	6.48/8.11	6.75/8.14	6.77/8.3	6.69/7.88
Screen size (LW, in inches)	7.5 × 5.8	7.5 × 5.8	7.5 × 5.6	7.52 × 5.7	7.5 × 5.6
MEMORY AND DISK DRIVES					
Installed/maximum external cache	INA	INA	INA	INA	128K/128K
Installable RAM (minimum–maximum)	INA	N/A	4Mb–20Mb	4Mb–20Mb	8Mb–32Mb
Fixed disk range (minimum–maximum)	120–524	120–524	340	455	245–800
I/O AND EXPANSION					
Parallel, serial, mouse ports	1, 1, 0	1, 1, 0	1, 1, 0	1, 1, 0	INA
Shared keyboard mouse ports	1	1	1	1	INA
Docking station options	●	●	●	●	INA
Expansion bus ports	1	1	1	1	INA
Expansion unit	●	●	●	●	INA
VIDEO					
Screen Mfg	NEC	Sharp	Sanyo	NEC	Hitachi
Color/Monochrome	Color	Color	Color	Color	Color
Illuminated/Active matrix	○/●	○/●	○/○	●/●	INA
Display technology	Active TFT	Other	Dual Matrix	Active TFT	INA
Display lighting	Edgelit	Backlit	Backlit	Backlit	INA
Video chip set manufacturer	WD	WD	C&T	C&T	WD
Video memory size (Mb)	1	1	1	1	1
Maximum internal and external resolution	640 × 480–1,024 × 768	640 × 480–1,024 × 768	640 × 480–1,024 × 768	640 × 480–1,024 × 768	INA
MODEM					
Modem type/Speed	PCMCIA/14,400	PCMCIA/14,400	PCMCIA/2400	PCMCIA/14,400	None
POWER					
Rated battery life (hours)	4	3	4.5	4.5	INA
Charge time while on, off (hours)	4, 1.5	4, 1.5	3, 1.5	3, 1.5	7, 2
Display/hard disk power-down	●/●	●/●	●/●	●/●	●/○
CPU/Peripheral power-down	●/●	●/●	●/●	●/●	●/○
Standby/Hibernation	●/●	●/●	●/●	●/●	●/●

●—Yes   ○—No   N/A—Not applicable   INA—Information not available

Mobile Computers ■

	AMS SoundPro DX4/100	AMS SoundWave	AMS TravelPro 5333	AMS TravelPro 5366	Aquiline Cruiser
Price	$$$	$$$	$$$	$$$	$$$$
Processor	Intel DX4/100	DX4/100	DX/33	DX2/66	Intel DX4/75
Fixed disk size	INA	121	253	253	INA
Windows version	Windows for Workgroups 3.11	Windows for Workgroups 3.11	Windows for Workgroups 3.11	Windows for Workgroups 3.11	Windows 3.11
Pointing device	Integrated trackball	INA	INA	INA	Integrated trackball
Case size (HWD, in inches)	2.3 × 11.0 × 8.1	1.8 × 11.3 × 8.5	2.0 × 11.0 × 8.5	2 × 11 × 8.5	2.3 × 11.5 × 9
Weight/Travel weight (pounds)	6.93/8.13	5.04/6.53	6.62/7.79	6.77/8.23	7.25/8.44
Screen size (LW, in inches)	7.8 × 5.8	5.8 × 7.8	7.5 × 5.6	7.5 × 5.8	6.8 × 5.2
MEMORY AND DISK DRIVES					
Installed/maximum external cache	128K/128K	INA	INA	INA	N/A
Installable RAM (minimum–maximum)	8Mb–32Mb	8Mb–20Mb	4Mb–20Mb	4Mb–32Mb	16Mb–24Mb
Fixed disk range (minimum–maximum)	344–800	121–520	120–520	120–520	523–810
I/O AND EXPANSION					
Parallel, serial, mouse ports	INA	1, 1, 1	1, 2, 0	1, 2, 0	INA
Shared keyboard mouse ports	INA	0	0	0	INA
Docking station options	INA	●	●	●	INA
Expansion bus ports	INA	1	1	1	INA
Expansion unit	INA	●	●	●	INA
VIDEO					
Screen Mfg	NEC	NEC	Hitachi	NEC	Sharp
Color/Monochrome	Color	Color	Color	Color	Color
Illuminated/Active matrix	INA	INA	○/	○/●	INA
Display technology	INA	INA	Dual Matrix	Active TFT	INA
Display lighting	INA	INA	Backlit	Backlit	INA
Video chip set manufacturer	WD	WD	WD	WD	C&T
Video memory size (Mb)	1	1	1	1	1
Maximum internal and external resolution	INA	640 × 480–1,280 × 1,024	640 × 480–1,280 × 1,024	640 × 480–1,280 × 1,024	INA
MODEM					
Modem type/Speed	PCMCIA fax/14,400	PCMCIA/14,400	Integrated/14,400	Integrated/14,400	PCMCIA fax/14,400
POWER					
Rated battery life (hours)	INA	INA	3	3	INA
Charge time while on, off (hours)	7, 2	6.25, 2	8, 2	8, 2	1.5, 1.5
Display/hard disk power-down	●/●	●/●	●/●	●/●	●/●
CPU/Peripheral power-down	●/●	●/●	●/○	●/●	●/○
Standby/Hibernation	●/●	●/●	●/○	●/○	○/●

●—Yes ○—No N/A—Not applicable INA—Information not available

Table Continues →

■ Mobile Computers

	Aquiline Hurricane DX2/66 Multimedia Notebook	Aquiline Hurricane DX4/75 Multimedia Notebook	Aquiline Hurricane DX4/100 Multimedia Notebook	ARMNote TS30ME	ARMNote TS30PS
Price	$$$$	$$$	$$$$	$$$$	$$$$
Processor	DX2/66	DX4/75	DX4/100	Intel DX4/100	Pentium/90
Fixed disk size	340	524	524	INA	INA
Windows version	Windows 3.1	Windows for Workgroups 3.11	Windows 3.1	Windows 3.1	Windows for Workgroups 3.11
Pointing device	INA	INA	INA	Integrated trackball	Integrated trackball
Case size (HWD, in inches)	2.5 × 11.5 × 9.3	2.5 × 11.5 × 9.3	2.5 × 11.5 × 9.3	1.9 × 11 × 8.5	2 × 11 × 8.5
Weight/Travel weight (pounds)	7.6/8.37	7.58 /8.71	7.59/8.72	6.69/7.88	6.5/7.75
Screen size (LW, in inches)	7.5 × 5.8	7.5 × 5.8	7.5 × 5.8	7.6 × 5.6	8.3 × 6
MEMORY AND DISK DRIVES					
Installed/maximum external cache	INA	INA	INA	N/A	256K, 256K
Installable RAM (minimum–maximum)	4Mb–20Mb	4Mb–20Mb	4Mb–20Mb	20Mb–20Mb	24Mb–40Mb
Fixed disk range (minimum–maximum)	120–540	120–540	120–540	527–810	250–720
I/O AND EXPANSION					
Parallel, serial, mouse ports	1, 2, 0	1, 2, 0	1, 2, 0	INA	INA
Shared keyboard mouse ports	1	1	1	INA	INA
Docking station options	●	●	●	INA	INA
Expansion bus ports	1	1	1	INA	INA
Expansion unit	●	●	●	INA	INA
VIDEO					
Screen Mfg	NEC	Sanyo	Hitachi	NEC	Sanyo
Color/Monochrome	Color	Color	Color	Color	Color
Illuminated/Active matrix	○/●	●/○	●/●	INA	INA
Display technology	Active TFT	Dual Matrix	Active TFT	INA	INA
Display lighting	Backlit	Backlit	Backlit	INA	INA
Video chip set manufacturer	WD	WD	WD	C&T	C&T
Video memory size (Mb)	1	1	1	1	1
Maximum internal and external resolution	640 × 480–1,024 × 768	640 × 480–1,024 × 768	640 × 480–1,024 × 768	INA	INA
MODEM					
Modem type/Speed	PCMCIA/14,400	PCMCIA/14,400	PCMCIA/14,400	N/A	N/A
POWER					
Rated battery life (hours)	3	3	3	INA	INA
Charge time while on, off (hours)	10, 1.5	10, 1.5	10, 1.5	3.7, 1.8	2, 1.5
Display/hard disk power-down	●/●	●/●	●/●	●/●	●/●
CPU/Peripheral power-down	●/●	●/●	●/●	●/●	●/○
Standby/Hibernation	●/●	●/●	●/●	●/●	●/●

●—Yes ○—No N/A—Not applicable INA—Information not available

Mobile Computers ◼

	ARM TS38	ARM TS38S	ARM TS38T	Aspen Select	Aspen Select Color
Price	$$	$$$	$$$$	$$$	$$$$
Processor	SX/25	DX/33	DX2/66	DX/33 SL	DX/33 SL
Fixed disk size	128	210	524	340	524
Windows version	Windows 3.1	Windows 3.1	Windows 3.1	Windows 3.1	Windows 3.1
Pointing device	INA	INA	INA	INA	INA
Case size (HWD, in inches)	2 × 11 × 8.5	2 × 11 × 8.5	2 × 11 × 8.5	2 × 11.5 × 8.5	2 × 11.5 × 8.5
Weight/Travel weight (pounds)	6.45/7.81	6.93/8.28	7.18/8.42	5.9/7.64	6.57/7.67
Screen size (LW, in inches)	7.5 × 5.5	7.5 × 5.5	7.5 × 5.5	7.5 × 5.5	7.5 × 5.5
MEMORY AND DISK DRIVES					
Installed/maximum external cache	INA	INA	INA	INA	INA
Installable RAM (minimum–maximum)	4Mb–20Mb	4Mb–20Mb	4Mb–20Mb	4Mb–32Mb	4Mb–32Mb
Fixed disk range (minimum–maximum)	128–320	125–520	125-524	250–520	250–524
I/O AND EXPANSION					
Parallel, serial, mouse ports	1, 1, 1	1, 1, 1	1, 1, 1	1, 1, 0	1, 1, 0
Shared keyboard mouse ports	0	0	0	0	0
Docking station options	●	●	●	●	●
Expansion bus ports	1	1	1	1	1
Expansion unit	●	●	●	●	●
VIDEO					
Screen Mfg	Sharp	Sharp	Toshiba	Sharp	NEC
Color/Monochrome	Monochrome	Color	Color	Monochrome	Color
Illuminated/Active matrix	●/○	●/○	○/●	●/○	●/○
Display technology	TSTN	Dual Matrix	Active TFT	Passive TFT	Dual Matrix
Display lighting	Backlit	Backlit	Backlit	Backlit	Backlit
Video chip set manufacturer	C&T	C&T	C&T	WD	WD
Video memory size (Mb)	1	1	0.512	0.512	0.512
Maximum internal and external resolution	640 × 480–1,024 × 768	640 × 480–1,024 × 768	640 × 480–1,024 × 768	640 × 480–1,024 × 768	640 × 480–1,024 × 768
MODEM					
Modem type/Speed	PCMCIA/14,400	PCMCIA/14,400	PCMCIA/14,400	PCMCIA/14,400	PCMCIA/14,400
POWER					
Rated battery life (hours)	6	5	4	4	3
Charge time while on, off (hours)	4, 2	4, 2	4, 2	4, 2	4, 2
Display/hard disk power-down	●/●	●/●	●/●	●/●	●/●
CPU/Peripheral power-down	●/●	●/●	●/●	●/●	●/●
Standby/Hibernation	●/●	●/●	●/●	●/●	●/●

●—Yes ○—No N/A—Not applicable INA—Information not available   **T a b l e   C o n t i n u e s →**

■ Mobile Computers

	Aspenta 60/66	Aspen Universa E Series	AST Ascentia 800N	AST Ascentia 900N	AT&T Globalyst 200
Price	$$$$	$$$	$$$	$$$$	$$$
Processor	Pentium/66	Intel DX4/100	Intel 486DX2/50	Intel DX4/75	Intel DX4/75
Fixed disk size	INA	INA	INA	INA	INA
Windows version	Windows 3.1	Windows 3.11	Windows 3.1	Windows 3.11	Windows 3.11
Pointing device	Integrated trackball	Integrated trackball	Integrated trackball	Integrated pointing stick	Integrated trackball
Case size (HWD, in inches)	2.5 × 11 × 10.3	2.3 × 11 × 8.8	1.7 × 10.4 × 8.8	2 × 11.5 × 8.5	2.3 × 11 × 9
Weight/Travel weight (pounds)	8.63/9.81	7.13/8.31	5.88/6.5	6.56/7.81	6.5/7.25
Screen size (LW, in inches)	7.5 × 5.7	7.8 × 5.8	7.7 × 5.8	8.4 × 6.3	8.3 × 6
MEMORY AND DISK DRIVES					
Installed/maximum external cache	N/A	128K, 128K	N/A	N/A	N/A
Installable RAM (minimum–maximum)	8Mb–40Mb	8Mb–36Mb	8Mb–20Mb	8Mb–32Mb	8Mb–20Mb
Fixed disk range (minimum–maximum)	344–800	343–800	340–340	477–510	349–810
I/O AND EXPANSION					
Parallel, serial, mouse ports	INA	INA	INA	INA	INA
Shared keyboard mouse ports	INA	INA	INA	INA	INA
Docking station options	INA	INA	INA	INA	INA
Expansion bus ports	INA	INA	INA	INA	INA
Expansion unit	INA	INA	INA	INA	INA
VIDEO					
Screen Mfg	NEC	NEC	Sanyo	Hitachi	AT&T
Color/Monochrome	Color	Color	Color	Color	Color
Illuminated/Active matrix	INA	INA	INA	INA	INA
Display technology	INA	INA	INA	INA	INA
Display lighting	INA	INA	INA	INA	INA
Video chip set manufacturer	Cirrus	Cirrus	WD	WD	WD
Video memory size (Mb)	1	1	1	1	1
Maximum internal and external resolution	INA	INA	INA	INA	INA
MODEM					
Modem type/Speed	PCMCIA fax/14,400	PCMCIA fax/14,400	PCMCIA fax/14,400	PCMCIA fax/14,400	PCMCIA fax/14,400
POWER					
Rated battery life (hours)	INA	INA	INA	INA	INA
Charge time while on, off (hours)	2, 2	N/A, 1.5	2.5, 2.5	1.5, 1	N/A, 2.5
Display/hard disk power-down	●/●	●/●	●/●	●/●	●/●
CPU/Peripheral power-down	○/○	○/○	●/●	●/●	●/●
Standby/Hibernation	○/○	○/○	●/●	●/●	○/○

●—Yes ○—No N/A—Not applicable INA—Information not available

Mobile Computers ■

	AT&T Globalyst 250	Austin Business Audio DX4/100	BSI GN8549D	BSI NP3656T Pentium	BSI NP7549D
Price	$$$$	$$$$	$$$	$$$	$$$
Processor	Intel DX4/75	Intel DX4/100	Intel DX4/100	Pentium/66	Intel DX4/100
Fixed disk size	INA	INA	INA	INA	INA
Windows version	Windows 3.11	Windows for Workgroups 3.11	Windows for Workgroups 3.11	Windows for Workgroups 3.11	Windows for Workgroups 3.11
Pointing device	Integrated trackball	Integrated trackball	Integrated trackball	Integrated trackball	Integrated trackball
Case size (HWD, in inches)	2.2 × 11.5 × 9.3	2.3 × 11 × 8.5	2.1 × 11.3 × 8.4	2.5 × 11 × 10.3	2.5 × 11 × 9.5
Weight/Travel weight (pounds)	6.88/8.25	7/8.25	6.19/7.44	8.88/10	7.06/8.31
Screen size (LW, in inches)	7.5 × 5.8	7.8 × 5.8	7.5 × 5.6	7.5 × 5.8	8.3 × 6
MEMORY AND DISK DRIVES					
Installed/maximum external cache	N/A	N/A	N/A	N/A	N/A
Installable RAM (minimum–maximum)	8Mb–40Mb	10Mb–32Mb	8Mb–32Mb	8Mb–40Mb	8Mb–36Mb
Fixed disk range (minimum–maximum)	540–810	488–704	328–520	340–520	344–520
I/O AND EXPANSION					
Parallel, serial, mouse ports	INA	INA	INA	INA	INA
Shared keyboard mouse ports	INA	INA	INA	INA	INA
Docking station options	INA	INA	INA	INA	INA
Expansion bus ports	INA	INA	INA	INA	INA
Expansion unit	INA	INA	INA	INA	INA
VIDEO					
Screen Mfg	NEC	Hitachi/Sharp	Sharp	NEC	Sanyo
Color/Monochrome	Color	Color	Color	Color	Color
Illuminated/Active matrix	INA	INA	INA	INA	INA
Display technology	INA	INA	INA	INA	INA
Display lighting	INA	INA	INA	INA	INA
Video chip set manufacturer	C&T	WD	WD	Cirrus	Cirrus
Video memory size (Mb)	1	1	1	1	1
Maximum internal and external resolution	INA	INA	INA	INA	INA
MODEM					
Modem type/Speed	Internal fax/14,400	Internal fax/14,400	PCMCIA fax/14,400	PCMCIA fax/14,400	PCMCIA fax/14,400
POWER					
Rated battery life (hours)	INA	INA	INA	INA	INA
Charge time while on, off (hours)	2.5, 1.25	4, 1.75	2, 2	2, 2	2, 2
Display/hard disk power-down	●/●	●/●	●/●	●/●	●/●
CPU/Peripheral power-down	●/●	●/●	●/●	●/○	●/○
Standby/Hibernation	●/●	●/○	●/●	●/○	○/○

●—Yes   ○—No   N/A—Not applicable   INA—Information not available

Table Continues →

■ Mobile Computers

	BSI NP9249D	Commax Smartbook III	AT&T/NCR AT&T Globalyst 200 (DX2/50)	AT&T/NCR AT&T Globalyst 200 (SX/33)	Austin DX/33 DSTN Color
Price	$$$	$$$$	$$$$	$$$	$$$
Processor	Intel DX4/100	Intel DX4/100	DX2/50	SX/33 SL	DX/33 SL
Fixed disk size	INA	INA	250	170	262
Windows version	Windows for Workgroups 3.11	Windows 3.11	Windows for Workgroups 3.11	Windows for Workgroups 3.11	Windows 3.1
Pointing device	Integrated trackball	Integrated trackball	INA	INA	INA
Case size (HWD, in inches)	2.3 × 11 × 8.8	2.3 × 11 × 8.8	2.3 × 11.3 × 8.8	2.3 × 11.3 × 8.8	2 × 11 × 8
Weight/Travel weight (pounds)	6.93/8.13	7.25/8.44	6.31/7.32	6.11/7.32	6.55/7.85
Screen size (LW, in inches)	7.8 × 5.8	7.8 × 5.8	7.5 × 5.6	7.5 × 5.6	7.5 × 5.5
MEMORY AND DISK DRIVES					
Installed/maximum external cache	128K, 128K	128K, 128K	INA	INA	INA
Installable RAM (minimum–maximum)	8Mb–36Mb	16Mb–36Mb	4Mb–20Mb	4Mb–20Mb	4Mb–32Mb
Fixed disk range (minimum–maximum)	343–520	527–540	170–250	170–250	262–524
I/O AND EXPANSION					
Parallel, serial, mouse ports	INA	INA	1, 1, 0	1, 1, 0	1, 2, 0
Shared keyboard mouse ports	INA	INA	1	1	0
Docking station options	INA	INA	●	●	●
Expansion bus ports	INA	INA	1	1	1
Expansion unit	INA	INA	●	●	●
VIDEO					
Screen Mfg	Sanyo	NEC	AT&T	AT&T	Sanyo
Color/Monochrome	Color	Color	Color	Color	Color
Illuminated/Active matrix	INA	INA	●/●	○/○	○/●
Display technology	INA	INA	Active TFT	Dual Matrix	Dual Matrix
Display lighting	INA	INA	Backlit	Backlit	Backlit
Video chip set manufacturer	Cirrus	Cirrus	WD	WD	WD
Video memory size (Mb)	1	1	1	1	1
Maximum internal and external resolution	INA	INA	640 × 480–1,024 × 768	640 × 480–1,024 × 768	640 × 480–1,024 × 768
MODEM					
Modem type/Speed	PCMCIA fax/14,400	PCMCIA fax/14,400	PCMCIA/14,400	PCMCIA/14,400	Integrated/14,400
POWER					
Rated battery life (hours)	INA	INA	3.5	3.5	2.5
Charge time while on, off (hours)	3, 3	N/A, 1.5	N/A, 2.5	N/A, 2.5	N/A, 1.5 hr
Display/hard disk power-down	●/●	●/●	●/●	●/●	●/●
CPU/Peripheral power-down	○/○	●/○	●/●	●/●	●/●
Standby/Hibernation	○/○	○/○	●/●	●/●	●/●

●—Yes ○—No N/A—Not applicable INA—Information not available

Mobile Computers ∎

	Austin DX2/66 Active Matrix Color	Broadax Systems NP846D	Broadax Systems NP846 Mono	Broadax Systems NP846T	Commax Smartbook II Active Matrix
Price	$$$$	$$$	$$$	$$$$	$$$$
Processor	DX2/66	DX2/66	DX2/66	DX2/66	DX2/66
Fixed disk size	340	524	524	512	340
Windows version	Windows 3.1	Windows 3.1	Windows 3.1	Windows 3.1	Windows 3.1
Pointing device	INA	INA	INA	INA	INA
Case size (HWD, in inches)	2.0 × 11.0 × 8.0	2.0 × 11.0 × 9.0	2.0 × 11.0 × 9	2.0 × 11.0 × 9	2 × 11.3 × 8.5
Weight/Travel weight (pounds)	6.5/7.84	6.65/8.18	6.24/7.69	7.7/7.85	6.12/7.68
Screen size (LW, in inches)	7.5 × 5.5	7.5 × 5.8	7.5 × 5.8	7.5 × 5.8	7.5 × 5.6
MEMORY AND DISK DRIVES					
Installed/maximum external cache	INA	INA	INA	INA	INA
Installable RAM (minimum–maximum)	4Mb–32Mb	4Mb–20Mb	4Mb–20Mb	4Mb–20Mb	4Mb–32Mb
Fixed disk range (minimum–maximum)	262–524	120–524	120–524	120–512	120–524
I/O AND EXPANSION					
Parallel, serial, mouse ports	1, 2, 0	1, 1, 0	1, 1, 0	1, 1, 0	1, 1, 0
Shared keyboard mouse ports	0	0	0	0	0
Docking station options	●	●	●	●	●
Expansion bus ports	1	1	1	1	1
Expansion unit	●	●	●	●	●
VIDEO					
Screen Mfg	NEC	Sanyo	Sharp	Toshiba	NEC
Color/Monochrome	Color	Color	Monochrome	Color	Color
Illuminated/Active matrix	●/●	●/●	○/●	○/●	○/●
Display technology	Active TFT	Dual Matrix	Passive TFT	Active TFT	Active TFT
Display lighting	Edgelit	Backlit	Backlit	Backlit	Backlit
Video chip set manufacturer	WD	Cirrus	Cirrus	Cirrus	WD
Video memory size (Mb)	1	0.5	0.512	0.25	1
Maximum internal and external resolution	640 × 480–1,024 × 768	640 × 480–1,024 × 768	640 × 480–1,024 × 768	640 × 480–1,024 × 768	640 × 480–1,024 × 768
MODEM					
Modem type/Speed	Integrated/14,400	PCMCIA/14,400	PCMCIA/14,400	PCMCIA/14,400	PCMCIA/14,400
POWER					
Rated battery life (hours)	2	2	2	2.5	2.5
Charge time while on, off (hours)	N/A, 1.5	2.5, 2.5	2.5, 2.5	2.5, 2.5	1.5, 1.3
Display/hard disk power-down	●/●	●/●	●/●	●/●	●/●
CPU/Peripheral power-down	●/●	●/●	●/●	●/●	●/○
Standby/Hibernation	●/●	●/●	●/●	●/●	●/●

●—Yes   ○—No   N/A—Not applicable   INA—Information not available

Table Continues →

■ Mobile Computers

	Commax Smartbook II Dual Scan	Compaq Contura 400C	Compaq Contura 400CX	Compaq Contura 4/25 Model 120	Compaq Contura 4/25C Model 120
Price	$$$	$$$	$$$	$$$	$$$
Processor	DX/33	Intel 486DX2/40	Intel 486DX2/40	DX/25	DX/25
Fixed disk size	252	INA	INA	120	120
Windows version	Windows 3.1	Windows 3.1	Windows 3.1	Windows 3.1	Windows 3.1
Pointing device	INA	Integrated trackball	Integrated trackball	INA	INA
Case size (HWD, in inches)	2 × 11.3 × 8.5	2 × 11.8 × 9	2 × 11.8 × 9	2.0 × 11.5 × 8.9	2.0 × 11.5 × 8.9
Weight/Travel weight (pounds)	6.12/7.62	5.88/6.56	5.88/6.56	6.82/7.93	6.61/8.81
Screen size (LW, in inches)	7.5 × 5.6	7.6 × 5.7	6.5 × 5.1	7.6 × 5.8	7.5 × 5.8
MEMORY AND DISK DRIVES					
Installed/maximum external cache	INA	N/A	N/A	INA	INA
Installable RAM (minimum–maximum)	4Mb–32Mb	8Mb–20Mb	8Mb–20Mb	4Mb–20Mb	4Mb–20Mb
Fixed disk range (minimum–maximum)	120–524	253–253	255–256	84–209	84–209
I/O AND EXPANSION					
Parallel, serial, mouse ports	1, 1, 0	INA	INA	1, 1, 0	1, 1, 0
Shared keyboard mouse ports	0	INA	INA	1	1
Docking station options	●	INA	INA	○	○
Expansion bus ports	1	INA	INA	0	0
Expansion unit	●	INA	INA	○	○
VIDEO					
Screen Mfg	Sanyo	Compaq	Compaq	Compaq	Compaq
Color/Monochrome	Color	Color	Color	Monochrome	Color
Illuminated/Active matrix	●/○	INA	INA	○/●	○/○
Display technology	Dual Matrix	INA	INA	Passive TFT	Passive TFT
Display lighting	Backlit	INA	INA	Edgelit	Edgelit
Video chip set manufacturer	WD	WD	WD	WD	Compaq
Video memory size (Mb)	1	1	1	0.512	0.512
Maximum internal and external resolution	640 × 480–1,024 × 768	INA	INA	640 × 480–800 × 600	640 × 480–800 × 600
MODEM					
Modem type/Speed	PCMCIA/14,400	None	None	Integrated/14,400	Integrated/14,400
POWER					
Rated battery life (hours)	2.5	INA	INA	3.5	3
Charge time while on, off (hours)	1.5, 1.3	3, 1.5	3, 1.5	1.5, 1	1.5, 1
Display/hard disk power-down	●/●	●/●	●/●	●/●	●/●
CPU/Peripheral power-down	●/●	●/●	●/●	●/●	●/●
Standby/Hibernation	●/●	●/●	●/●	●/●	●/●

●—Yes   ○—No   N/A—Not applicable   INA—Information not available

Mobile Computers ■

	Compaq Contura 4/25CX Model 120	Compaq Contura Aero 4/25 Model 84	Compaq Contura Aero 4/33C Model 170	Compaq LTE Elite 4/50CX Model 340	Compaq LTE Elite 4/75CX Model 340
Price	$$$$	$$	$$$	$$$$	$$$$
Processor	SX/25	SX/25	SX/33 SL	Intel 486DX2/50	Intel 486DX4/75
Fixed disk size	120	84	170	INA	INA
Windows version	Windows 3.1	Windows 3.1	Windows 3.1	Windows 3.1	Windows 3.1
Pointing device	INA	INA	INA	Integrated trackball	Integrated trackball
Case size (HWD, in inches)	2 × 11.5 × 8.9	1.7 × 10.3 × 7.3	1.2 × 10.3 × 7.3	2 × 11.8 × 8.9	2 × 11.9 × 8.9
Weight/Travel weight (pounds)	6.81/7.92	4.49/5.23	4.7/5.44	6.75/6.93	6.75/6.93
Screen size (LW, in inches)	7.6 × 5.8	6.5 × 4.8	6.2 × 4.7	7.6 × 5.7	7.6 × 5.7
MEMORY AND DISK DRIVES					
Installed/maximum external cache	INA	INA	INA	N/A	N/A
Installable RAM (minimum–maximum)	4Mb–20Mb	4Mb–12Mb	4Mb–12Mb	8Mb–24Mb	8Mb–24Mb
Fixed disk range (minimum–maximum)	84–209	84–250	84–250	340–510	340–510
I/O AND EXPANSION					
Parallel, serial, mouse ports	1, 1, 0	1, 1, 0	1, 1, 0	INA	INA
Shared keyboard mouse ports	1	0	0	INA	INA
Docking station options	○	●	●	INA	INA
Expansion bus ports	0	0	0	INA	INA
Expansion unit	○	●	●	INA	INA
VIDEO					
Screen Mfg	Compaq	Compaq	Compaq	Compaq	Compaq
Color/Monochrome	Color	Monochrome	Color	Color	Color
Illuminated/Active matrix	○/●	○/○	○/○	INA	INA
Display technology	Active TFT	Passive TFT	Passive TFT	INA	INA
Display lighting	Edgelit	Backlit	Backlit	INA	INA
Video chip set manufacturer	Compaq	Compaq	Compaq	WD	WD
Video memory size (Mb)	0.512	0.512	0.512	1	1
Maximum internal and external resolution	640 × 480–800 × 600	640 × 480–640 × 480	640 × 480–640 × 480	INA	INA
MODEM					
Modem type/Speed	Integrated/14,400	PCMCIA/14,400	PCMCIA/14,400	None	None
POWER					
Rated battery life (hours)	2.5	3.25	3.25	INA	INA
Charge time while on, off (hours)	1.5, 1	4, 1.5	4, 2.5	1.5, 1	1.5, 1
Display/hard disk power-down	●/●	●/●	●/●	●/●	●/●
CPU/Peripheral power-down	●/●	●/●	●/●	●/●	●/●
Standby/Hibernation	●/●	●/●	●/●	●/●	●/●

●—Yes ○—No N/A—Not applicable INA—Information not available

Table Continues →

ZIFF-DAVIS PRESS

■ Mobile Computers

	CTX EzBook DX4/75	CTX EzBook DX4/100	CTX EzBook 486DX/33	DECpc 425SE (SX/25)	DECpc 425SE Color
Price	$$$	$$$	$$	$$	$$$
Processor	Intel DX4/75	Intel DX4/100	CyrixCx486DX/33	SX/25	SX/25
Fixed disk size	INA	INA	INA	128	128
Windows version	Windows 3.1	Windows 3.1	Windows 3.11	Windows 3.1	Windows 3.1
Pointing device	Integrated trackball	Integrated trackball	Integrated trackball	INA	INA
Case size (HWD, in inches)	2 × 11.1 × 8.5	2 × 11.1 × 8.5	1.7 × 9.9 × 7.6	1.6 × 11.5 × 8.5	1.6 × 11.5 × 8.5
Weight/Travel weight (pounds)	6.19/7.44	6.19/7.44	4.19/6.56	4.65/6.9	6.2/7.38
Screen size (LW, in inches)	7.6 × 5.7	7.1 × 5.7	6.1 × 4.6	7.5 × 5.7	7.5 × 5.7
MEMORY AND DISK DRIVES					
Installed/maximum external cache	N/A	N/A	N/A	INA	INA
Installable RAM (minimum–maximum)	8Mb–32Mb	8Mb–32Mb	8Mb–32Mb	4Mb–20Mb	4Mb–20Mb
Fixed disk range (minimum–maximum)	326–720	512–720	262–340	128–170	128–170
I/O AND EXPANSION					
Parallel, serial, mouse ports	INA	INA	INA	1, 1, 1	1, 1, 1
Shared keyboard mouse ports	INA	INA	INA	0	0
Docking station options	INA	INA	INA	●	●
Expansion bus ports	INA	INA	INA	0	0
Expansion unit	INA	INA	INA	●	●
VIDEO					
Screen Mfg	Sharp	Hosiden	Citizen	Sharp	Sharp
Color/Monochrome	Color	Color	Color	Monochrome	Color
Illuminated/Active matrix	INA	INA	INA	○/●	○/○
Display technology	INA	INA	INA	Active TFT	Dual Matrix
Display lighting	INA	INA	INA	Edgelit	Backlit
Video chip set manufacturer	WD	WD	WD	C&T	C&T
Video memory size (Mb)	1	1	1	1	1
Maximum internal and external resolution	INA	INA	INA	640 × 480–1,024 × 768	640 × 480–1,024 × 768
MODEM					
Modem type/Speed	None	None	None	PCMCIA/14,400	PCMCIA/14,400
POWER					
Rated battery life (hours)	INA	INA	INA	2.5	2
Charge time while on, off (hours)	3, 2	3, 2	3, 2	8, 2	8, 2
Display/hard disk power-down	●/●	●/●	●/●	●/●	●/●
CPU/Peripheral power-down	●/●	●/●	●/●	●/●	●/●
Standby/Hibernation	●/●	●/●	●/●	●/●	●/●

●—Yes ○—No N/A—Not applicable INA—Information not available

Mobile Computers

	DECpc 433SLC Premium	Dell Latitude 450C	Dell Latitude 450CX	Dell Latitude XP 450C	Dell Latitude XP 4100C
Price	$$$$	$$$	$$$	$$$	$$$$
Processor	DX/33	Intel 486DX2/50	Intel 486DX2/50	Intel 486DX2/50	Intel DX4/100
Fixed disk size	210	INA	INA	INA	INA
Windows version	Windows 3.1	Windows for Workgroups 3.11	Windows for Workgroups 3.11	Windows for Workgroups 3.11	Windows for Workgroups 3.11
Pointing device	INA	Integrated trackball	Integrated trackball	Integrated trackball	Integrated trackball
Case size (HWD, in inches)	$2 \times 11.5 \times 8.5$	$2 \times 10.5 \times 8.5$	$2 \times 10.5 \times 8.5$	$2.1 \times 11 \times 8.8$	$2.1 \times 11 \times 8.8$
Weight/Travel weight (pounds)	7.37/8.56	5.88/6.69	6.19/6.93	5.88/6.81	6.06/7
Screen size (LW, in inches)	7.5×5.7	7.5×5.5	7.5×5.5	7.6×5.7	7.6×5.8
MEMORY AND DISK DRIVES					
Installed/maximum external cache	INA	N/A	N/A	N/A	N/A
Installable RAM (minimum–maximum)	4Mb–32Mb	8Mb–20Mb	8Mb–20Mb	8Mb–36Mb	8Mb–36Mb
Fixed disk range (minimum–maximum)	210–340	340–524	340–524	341–524	524–524
I/O AND EXPANSION					
Parallel, serial, mouse ports	1, 1, 1	INA	INA	INA	INA
Shared keyboard mouse ports	0	INA	INA	INA	INA
Docking station options	○	INA	INA	INA	INA
Expansion bus ports	1	INA	INA	INA	INA
Expansion unit	○	INA	INA	INA	INA
VIDEO					
Screen Mfg	Sharp	Dell	Dell	Dell	Dell
Color/Monochrome	Color	Color	Color	Color	Color
Illuminated/Active matrix	○/●	INA	INA	INA	INA
Display technology	Active TFT	INA	INA	INA	INA
Display lighting	Backlit	INA	INA	INA	INA
Video chip set manufacturer	WD	WD	WD	WD	WD
Video memory size (Mb)	0.512	1	1	1	1
Maximum internal and external resolution	640×480–$1,024 \times 768$	INA	INA	INA	INA
MODEM					
Modem type/Speed	PCMCIA/14,400	PCMCIA fax/14,400	PCMCIA fax/14,400	PCMCIA fax/14,400	PCMCIA fax/14,400
POWER					
Rated battery life (hours)	6.5	INA	INA	INA	INA
Charge time while on, off (hours)	1.5, 1	2.5, 2.5	2.5, 2.5	2.5, 2.5	2.5, 2.5
Display/hard disk power-down	●/●	●/●	●/●	●/●	●/●
CPU/Peripheral power-down	●/●	●/●	●/●	●/●	●/●
Standby/Hibernation	●/●	●/●	●/●	●/●	●/●

●—Yes ○—No N/A—Not applicable INA—Information not available

Table Continues →

ZIFF-DAVIS PRESS

■ Mobile Computers

	DTX DTN-4T100P	DTK DCN-4T66M	DTK DCN-4T66P	Duracom 5110	Duracom TravelPro NBAC 486/33DX Active Color
Price	$$$	$$	$$$	$$$$	$$$$
Processor	Intel DX4/100	DX2/66	DX2/66	Intel DX4/100	Cyrix 486DX/33
Fixed disk size	INA	128	128	INA	210
Windows version	Windows 3.11	Windows 3.1	Windows 3.1	Windows for Workgroups 3.11	Windows for Workgroups 3.11
Pointing device	Integrated trackball	INA	INA	Integrated trackball	INA
Case size (HWD, in inches)	2.5 × 11 × 9.3	1.9 × 11.6 × 8.7	1.9 × 11.6 × 8.7	2 × 8.6 × 11	2.0 × 11.0 × 8.5
Weight/Travel weight (pounds)	6.88/8.06	6.12/7.87	6.12/7.91	7.33/8.63	6.62/8.54
Screen size (LW, in inches)	8.3 × 6	7.5 × 5.8	7.5 × 5.8	5.8 × 7.5	7.5 × 5.8
MEMORY AND DISK DRIVES					
Installed/maximum external cache	N/A	INA	INA	N/A	INA
Installable RAM (minimum–maximum)	8Mb–36Mb	4Mb–52Mb	4Mb–52Mb	8Mb–36Mb	4Mb–36Mb
Fixed disk range (minimum–maximum)	343–520	128–340	128–340	340–540	120–520
I/O AND EXPANSION					
Parallel, serial, mouse ports	INA	1, 2, 0	1, 2, 0	INA	1, 1, 0
Shared keyboard mouse ports	INA	0	0	INA	1
Docking station options	INA	●	●	INA	●
Expansion bus ports	INA	1	1	INA	1
Expansion unit	INA	●	●	INA	●
VIDEO					
Screen Mfg	Sanyo	INA	INA	NEC	Duracom
Color/Monochrome	Color	Monochrome	Color	Color	Color
Illuminated/Active matrix	INA	●/○	●/○	INA	○/●
Display technology	INA	TSTN	Passive TFT	INA	Active TFT
Display lighting	INA	Backlit	Backlit	INA	Backlit
Video chip set manufacturer	Cirrus	Cirrus	Cirrus	Cirrus	Cirrus
Video memory size (Mb)	1	0.512	0.512	1	0.5
Maximum internal and external resolution	INA	640 × 480–1,024 × 768	640 × 480–1,024 × 768	INA	640 × 480–1,024 × 768
MODEM					
Modem type/Speed	PCMCIA fax/14,400	Integrated/14,400	Integrated/14,400	PCMCIA data/fax/ 2,400/9,600	PCMCIA/14,400
POWER					
Rated battery life (hours)	INA	3.5	3.5	INA	3.5
Charge time while on, off (hours)	3.5, 2	4.5, 2.5	4.5, 2.5	8, 2	3.5, 2
Display/hard disk power-down	●/●	●/●	●/●	●/●	●/●
CPU/Peripheral power-down	●/○	●/●	●/●	○/○	●/●
Standby/Hibernation	○/○	●/●	●/○	○/○	●/○

●—Yes   ○—No   N/A—Not applicable   INA—Information not available

Mobile Computers ■

	Duracom TravelPro NBC 486/33DX Passive color	Duracom TravelPro NBM 486/33DX Monochrome	Ergo PowerBrick 100	Ergo SubBrick 33	Everex Step Note DX2/50
Price	$$$	$$$	$$$$	$$$	$$$
Processor	Cyrix 486DX/33	Cyrix 486DX/33	Intel DX4/100	Cyrix Cx486DX/33	Intel DX2/50
Fixed disk size	210	210	INA	INA	INA
Windows version	Windows for Workgroups 3.11	Windows for Workgroups 3.11	Windows 3.11	Windows 3.11	Windows 3.11
Pointing device	INA	INA	Integrated trackball	Integrated trackball	Integrated trackball
Case size (HWD, in inches)	2.0 × 11.0 × 8.5	2.0 × 11.0 × 8.5	2.3 × 11 × 8.3	1.9 × 9.8 × 7.5	2 × 11.3 × 8.8
Weight/Travel weight (pounds)	6.18/8.31	6.59/8.21	6.93/8.13	5.44/6.5	6.13/7.31
Screen size (LW, in inches)	7.5 × 5.8	7.5 × 5.8	7.5 × 5.8	6.2 × 4.2	7.6 × 5.7
MEMORY AND DISK DRIVES					
Installed/maximum external cache	INA	INA	N/A	N/A	N/A
Installable RAM (minimum–maximum)	4Mb–36Mb	4Mb–36Mb	8Mb–32Mb	8Mb–20Mb	8Mb–20Mb
Fixed disk range (minimum–maximum)	120–520	120–520	515–720	261–261	340–524
I/O AND EXPANSION					
Parallel, serial, mouse ports	1, 1, 0	1, 1, 0	INA	INA	INA
Shared keyboard mouse ports	1	1	INA	INA	INA
Docking station options	●	●	INA	INA	INA
Expansion bus ports	1	1	INA	INA	INA
Expansion unit	●	●	INA	INA	INA
VIDEO					
Screen Mfg	Duracom	Duracom	NEC	Sony	Hitachi
Color/Monochrome	Color	Monochrome	Color	Color	Color
Illuminated/Active matrix	●/○	●/○	INA	INA	INA
Display technology	Passive TFT	Passive TFT	INA	INA	INA
Display lighting	Backlit	Backlit	INA	INA	INA
Video chip set manufacturer	Cirrus	Cirrus	WD	WD	WD
Video memory size (Mb)	0.512	0.5	1	1	1
Maximum internal and external resolution	640 × 480–1,024 × 768	640 × 480–1,024 × 768	INA	INA	INA
MODEM					
Modem type/Speed	PCMCIA/14,400	PCMCIA/14,400	PCMCIA fax/14,400	PCMCIA data/fax/2,400/9,600	PCMCIA fax/14,400
POWER					
Rated battery life (hours)	2.5	3.5	INA	INA	INA
Charge time while on, off (hours)	2.5, 2	2.5, 2	3.75, 2	5, 3.5	3, 1.5
Display/hard disk power-down	●/●	●/●	●/●	●/●	●/●
CPU/Peripheral power-down	●/●	●/●	●/●	●/●	●/○
Standby/Hibernation	●/○	●/○	●/●	●/●	●/●

●—Yes ○—No N/A—Not applicable INA—Information not available

Table Continues →

◼ Mobile Computers

	FutureTech FutureMate FM366T	FutureTech FutureMate FM910T	FutureTech FutureMate 462nV	Gateway ColorBook DX2-50	Gateway 2000 ColorBook DX4-75
Price	$$$$	$$$	$$$	$$$	$$$
Processor	Pentium/66	Intel DX4/100	DX2/66	Intel 486DX2/50	DX4/75
Fixed disk size	INA	INA	340	INA	260
Windows version	Windows 3.1	Windows 3.11	Windows for Workgroups 3.11	Windows for Workgroups 3.11	Windows for Workgroups 3.11
Pointing device	Integrated trackball	Integrated trackball	INA	Integrated trackball	INA
Case size (HWD, in inches)	2.5 × 11 × 10.3	2.3 × 11 × 8.3	2 × 11 × 8.5	2 × 11.7 × 8.5	1.80 × 11.5 × 8.4
Weight/Travel weight (pounds)	8.88/10.06	7.25/8.44	6.87/8.53	5.88/7.06	5.84/7.18
Screen size (LW, in inches)	7.5 × 5.7	7.5 × 5.8	7.5 × 5.8	8.3 × 6.1	8.2 × 6.0
MEMORY AND DISK DRIVES					
Installed/maximum external cache	N/A	128K, 128K	INA	N/A	INA
Installable RAM (minimum–maximum)	16Mb–40Mb	16Mb–36Mb	4Mb–20Mb	8Mb–20Mb	4Mb–20Mb
Fixed disk range (minimum–maximum)	528–800	343–800	170–520	250–340	120–260
I/O AND EXPANSION					
Parallel, serial, mouse ports	INA	INA	1, 1, 0	INA	1, 1, 0
Shared keyboard mouse ports	INA	INA	0	INA	1
Docking station options	INA	INA	●	INA	0
Expansion bus ports	INA	INA	0	INA	○
Expansion unit	INA	INA	●	INA	0
VIDEO					
Screen Mfg	Toshiba	Toshiba	Sharp	Sanyo	Sanyo
Color/Monochrome	Color	Color	Color	Color	Color
Illuminated/Active matrix	INA	INA	●/●	INA	●/○
Display technology	INA	INA	Active TFT	INA	Dual Matrix
Display lighting	INA	INA	Backlit	INA	Backlit
Video chip set manufacturer	Cirrus	Cirrus	Cirrus	Cirrus	Cirrus
Video memory size (Mb)	1	1	0.512	.5	0.512
Maximum internal and external resolution	INA	INA	640 × 480–1,024 × 768	INA	640 × 480–1,024 × 768
MODEM					
Modem type/Speed	None	PCMCIA fax/14,400	PCMCIA/14,400	PCMCIA fax/14,400	PCMCIA/14,400
POWER					
Rated battery life (hours)	INA	INA	2.5	INA	3
Charge time while on, off (hours)	4, 2	4, 2	2, 2	N/A, 2	N/A, 2
Display/hard disk power-down	●/●	●/●	●/●	●/●	●/●
CPU/Peripheral power-down	○/○	○/○	●/○	●/●	●/●
Standby/Hibernation	○/○	○/○	●/○	●/●	●/●

●—Yes ○—No N/A—Not applicable INA—Information not available

Mobile Computers

	Gateway 2000 HandBook DX2-40	Hertz Z-Optima 486 Notebook PC	HP OmniBook 600C PC	HyperData MB320PEN	Hyundai Neuron 400
Price	$$$	$$$	$$$	$$$	$$
Processor	DX2/40	Intel 486DX2/66	Intel DX4/75	DX2/66	SX/25
Fixed disk size	130	INA	INA	210	170
Windows version	Windows for Workgroups 3.11	Windows 3.11	Windows for Workgroups 3.11	Windows 3.1	Windows 3.1
Pointing device	INA	Integrated trackball	Integrated mouse	INA	INA
Case size (HWD, in inches)	1.6 × 9.8 × 5.9	2 × 11.5 × 8.9	1.6 × 11.1 × 7.3	2.3 × 11.5 × 8.8	1.8 × 11.0 × 8.5
Weight/Travel weight (pounds)	2.87/5.21	6.75/8.06	3.93/5.44	7.38/8.95	5.62/6.87
Screen size (LW, in inches)	6.8 × 3.8	7.5 × 5.7	6.8 × 5.3	7.6 × 5.7	7.6 × 5.7
MEMORY AND DISK DRIVES					
Installed/maximum external cache	INA	N/A	N/A	INA	INA
Installable RAM (minimum–maximum)	4Mb–20Mb	16Mb–16Mb	16Mb–16Mb	4Mb–20Mb	4Mb–20Mb
Fixed disk range (minimum–maximum)	130–130	341–525	171–260	130–520	120–250
I/O AND EXPANSION					
Parallel, serial, mouse ports	1, 1, 0	INA	INA	1, 2, 0	1, 1, 0
Shared keyboard mouse ports	1	INA	INA	0	0
Docking station options	○	INA	INA	○	○
Expansion bus ports	0	INA	INA	0	1
Expansion unit	○	INA	INA	○	○
VIDEO					
Screen Mfg	Sanyo	Sharp	Hitachi	Hitachi	Hyundai
Color/Monochrome	Monochrome	Color	Color	Color	Monochrome
Illuminated/Active matrix	●/○	INA	INA	○/●	●/○
Display technology	TSTN	INA	INA	Dual Matrix	Passive TFT
Display lighting	Backlit	INA	INA	Backlit	Backlit
Video chip set manufacturer	C&T	Cirrus	C&T	Cirrus	C&T
Video memory size (Mb)	0.25	1	1	0.512	0.512
Maximum internal and external resolution	640 × 480–640 × 480	INA	INA	640 × 480–1,024 × 768	640 × 480–1,024 × 768
MODEM					
Modem type/Speed	PCMCIA/14,400	PCMCIA fax/14,400	PCMCIA fax/14,400	PCMCIA/14,400	PCMCIA/2400
POWER					
Rated battery life (hours)	2.5	INA	INA	2	2.5
Charge time while on, off (hours)	2, 2	4, 1	4, 4	2, 1.3	4.5, 1.5
Display/hard disk power-down	●/●	●/●	●/●	●/●	●/●
CPU/Peripheral power-down	●/●	●/●	●/●	●/●	●/○
Standby/Hibernation	●/●	●/●	●/●	●/●	●/●

●—Yes ○—No N/A—Not applicable INA—Information not available

Table Continues →

ZIFF-DAVIS PRESS

■ Mobile Computers

	Hyundai Neuron Lite	IBM ThinkPad 360C	IBM ThinkPad 360P	IBM ThinkPad 755CD	IBM ThinkPad 755C
Price	$$	$$$$	$$$$	$$$$$	$$$$$
Processor	SX/25	SX/33 SL	SX/33 SL	Intel DX4/100	DX4/75
Fixed disk size	120	170	327	INA	540
Windows version	Windows 3.1	Windows 3.1	Windows 3.1	Windows 3.1	Windows 3.1
Pointing device	INA	INA	INA	Integrated pointing stick	INA
Case size (HWD, in inches)	1.5 × 10.5 × 7.8	2 × 11.7 × 8.3	2.0 × 11.7 × 8.3	2.2 × 11.7 × 8.3	2 × 11.7 × 8.3
Weight/Travel weight (pounds)	4.24/6.07	6.12/6.88	6.81/7.68	6.69/8.5	6.36/7.35
Screen size (LW, in inches)	7.6 × 5.7	6.7 × 5.2	7.5 × 5.7	8.4 × 6.3	8.3 × 6.3
MEMORY AND DISK DRIVES					
Installed/maximum external cache	INA	INA	INA	N/A	INA
Installable RAM (minimum–maximum)	4Mb–20Mb	4Mb–20Mb	4Mb–20Mb	8Mb–40Mb	4Mb–36Mb
Fixed disk range (minimum–maximum)	120–170	170–540	170–340	540–810	170–540
I/O AND EXPANSION					
Parallel, serial, mouse ports	1, 1, 0	1, 1, 0	1, 1, 1	INA	1, 1, 0
Shared keyboard mouse ports	0	1	1	INA	1
Docking station options	○	●	●	INA	●
Expansion bus ports	0	1	1	INA	1
Expansion unit	○	●	●	INA	●
VIDEO					
Screen Mfg	Hyundai	Sharp	Toshiba	DTI	DTI
Color/Monochrome	Monochrome	Color	Color	Color	Color
Illuminated/Active matrix	●/○	●/●	○/○	INA	●/●
Display technology	TSTN	Active TFT	Dual Matrix	INA	Active TFT
Display lighting	Backlit	Backlit	Edgelit	INA	Backlit
Video chip set manufacturer	Cirrus	WD	WD	WD	WD
Video memory size (Mb)	0.512	1	1	1	1
Maximum internal and external resolution	640 × 480–1,024 × 768	640 × 480–1,024 × 768	640 × 480–1,024 × 768	INA	640 × 480–1,024 × 768
MODEM					
Modem type/Speed	PCMCIA/2400	PCMCIA/2400	PCMCIA/14,400	internal fax/14,400	PCMCIA/14,400
POWER					
Rated battery life (hours)	2.5	6	5	INA	6
Charge time while on, off (hours)	INA, INA	2, 1.5	2, 1	1.75, 1.25	2, 1.5
Display/hard disk power-down	●/●	●/●	●/●	●/●	●/●
CPU/Peripheral power-down	●/○	●/●	●/●	●/●	●/●
Standby/Hibernation	●/●	●/●	●/●	●/●	●/●

●—Yes ○—No N/A—Not applicable INA—Information not available

Mobile Computers

	Identity Select Series (486DX/33)	Intelligent Executive EchoBook DX4-75	Intelligent Professional EchoBook DX2-50	Intelligent Value EchoBook DX-33	Micro Center WinBook XP DX2/50 4/260 Monochrome
Price	$$$	$$$$	$$$	$$	$$
Processor	DX/33	DX4/75	DX2/50	DX/33 SL	DX2/50
Fixed disk size	340	524	340	210	260
Windows version	Windows for Workgroups 3.11	Windows 3.1	Windows 3.1	Windows 3.1	Windows 3.1
Pointing device	INA	INA	INA	INA	INA
Case size (HWD, in inches)	2 × 11.5 × 8.8	1.7 × 11.2 × 8.8	1.7 × 11.2 × 8.8	1.7 × 11.2 × 8.8	2 × 11.5 × 8.5
Weight/Travel weight (pounds)	6.58/8.22	6.18/7.68	6.12/7.25	6.02/7.35	5.63/6.5
Screen size (LW, in inches)	7.5 × 5.8	7.5 × 5.5	7.5 × 5.5	7.5 × 5.5	7.5 × 5.8
MEMORY AND DISK DRIVES					
Installed/maximum external cache	INA	INA	INA	INA	INA
Installable RAM (minimum–maximum)	4Mb–32Mb	4Mb–20Mb	4Mb–20Mb	4Mb–20Mb	4Mb–32Mb
Fixed disk range (minimum–maximum)	130–525	120–524	120–524	120–524	120–520
I/O AND EXPANSION					
Parallel, serial, mouse ports	1, 1, 0	1, 1, 0	1, 1, 0	1, 1, 0	1, 1, 0
Shared keyboard mouse ports	0	1	1	1	1
Docking station options	●	●	●	●	●
Expansion bus ports	1	1	1	1	1
Expansion unit	●	●	●	●	●
VIDEO					
Screen Mfg	Sanyo (or Sharp)	Toshiba	Toshiba	Toshiba	Hitachi
Color/Monochrome	Color	Color	Color	Monochrome	Monochrome
Illuminated/Active matrix	●/○	○/●	○/○	○/○	○/○
Display technology	Dual Matrix	Active TFT	Dual Matrix	Dual Matrix	Passive TFT
Display lighting	Edgelit	Edgelit	Edgelit	Backlit	Backlit
Video chip set manufacturer	WD	WD	WD	WD	WD
Video memory size (Mb)	0.512	1	1	1	1
Maximum internal and external resolution	640 × 480–1,024 × 768	640 × 480–1,024 × 768	640 × 480–1,024 × 768	640 × 480–1,024 × 768	640 × 480–1,024 × 768
MODEM					
Modem type/Speed	PCMCIA/14,400	PCMCIA/14,400	PCMCIA/14,400	PCMCIA/14,400	Integrated/14,400
POWER					
Rated battery life (hours)	3	3	3	3	3.75
Charge time while on, off (hours)	2, 2	2, 1	2, 1	2, 1	5, 2
Display/hard disk power-down	●/●	●/●	●/●	●/●	●/●
CPU/Peripheral power-down	●/●	●/●	●/●	●/●	●/●
Standby/Hibernation	●/●	●/●	●/●	●/●	●/●

●—Yes ○—No N/A—Not applicable INA—Information not available

Table Continues →

■ Mobile Computers

	Micro Express NB8266	Micro Express NB8266M	Micro Express NB9266	MidWest Micro Elite DX4-100 SoundBook	MidWest Micro Elite Pentium SoundBook Plus
Price	$$$	$$	$$	$$$	$$$$
Processor	DX2/66	DX2/66	Intel 486DX2/66	Intel DX4/100	Pentium/90
Fixed disk size	340	250	INA	INA	INA
Windows version	Windows 3.1	Windows 3.1	Windows 3.11	Windows 3.11	Windows for Workgroups 3.11
Pointing device	INA	INA	Integrated trackball	Integrated trackball	Integrated trackball
Case size (HWD, in inches)	2 × 11 × 8.5	2.0 × 11 × 8.5	2.1 × 11 × 8.7	1.9 × 11 × 8.5	2 × 11 × 8.5
Weight/Travel weight (pounds)	7.31/9.02	4.8/8.21	7.0/8.13	6.69/7.88	6.69/7.88
Screen size (LW, in inches)	7.5 × 5.5	7.6 × 5.8	8.3 × 6	7.6 × 5.5	7.6 × 5.5
MEMORY AND DISK DRIVES					
Installed/maximum external cache	INA	INA	128K, 128K	N/A	256K, 256K
Installable RAM (minimum–maximum)	4Mb–20Mb	4Mb–20Mb	8Mb–36Mb	12Mb–20Mb	16Mb–40Mb
Fixed disk range (minimum–maximum)	200–340	200–340	343–520	525–720	677–720
I/O AND EXPANSION					
Parallel, serial, mouse ports	1, 1, 0	1, 1, 1	INA	INA	INA
Shared keyboard mouse ports	1	0	INA	INA	INA
Docking station options	●	●	INA	INA	INA
Expansion bus ports	1	1	INA	INA	INA
Expansion unit	●	●	INA	INA	INA
VIDEO					
Screen Mfg	Toshiba	Toshiba	NEC	Hitachi	Hitachi
Color/Monochrome	Color	Monochrome	Color	Color	Color
Illuminated/Active matrix	○/●	●/○	INA	INA	INA
Display technology	Active TFT	Passive TFT	INA	INA	INA
Display lighting	Backlit	Backlit	INA	INA	INA
Video chip set manufacturer	Cirrus	Cirrus	Cirrus	C&T	C&T
Video memory size (Mb)	8	0.5	1	1	1
Maximum internal and external resolution	640 × 480–1,024 × 768	640 × 480–1,024 × 768	INA	INA	INA
MODEM					
Modem type/Speed	PCMCIA/2400	PCMCIA/2400	PCMCIA fax/14,400	None	None
POWER					
Rated battery life (hours)	2.5	0	INA	INA	INA
Charge time while on, off (hours)	2, 1.5	2, 1.5	N/A, 3	4, 2	4, 2
Display/hard disk power-down	●/●	●/●	●/●	●/●	●/●
CPU/Peripheral power-down	●/○	○/●	●/○	●/●	●/●
Standby/Hibernation	●/●	●/●	●/○	●/●	○/●

●—Yes ○—No N/A—Not applicable INA—Information not available

Mobile Computers ▪

	Milkyway MyriadBook/466	Mintronix SLic4100	Mitsuba Ninja-Lite	Mitsuba Ninja II TS38M	Mitsuba Ninja II TS38S
Price	$$$	$$$	$$	$$	$$$
Processor	Intel 486DX2/66	Intel DX4/100	Intel 486DX2/66	SX/33	DX2/66 SL
Fixed disk size	INA	INA	INA	120	340
Windows version	Windows 3.11	Windows for Workgroups 3.11	Windows for Workgroups 3.11	Windows for Workgroups 3.11	Windows for Workgroups 3.11
Pointing device	Integrated trackball	Integrated trackball	Integrated trackball	INA	INA
Case size (HWD, in inches)	2.3 × 11 × 8.8	2 × 11 × 8.5	1.9 × 10.5 × 8.3	2 × 11 × 8.5	2 × 11 × 8.5
Weight/Travel weight (pounds)	6.93/8.13	6.81/8.06	5.06/6.06	6.75/8.29	6.91/8.36
Screen size (LW, in inches)	7.8 × 5.8	7.8 × 5.5	7.8 × 5.6	7.5 × 5.5	6.3 × 8.5
MEMORY AND DISK DRIVES					
Installed/maximum external cache	N/A	N/A	N/A	INA	INA
Installable RAM (minimum–maximum)	8Mb–32Mb	8Mb–52Mb	8Mb–20Mb	4Mb–20Mb	4Mb–20Mb
Fixed disk range (minimum–maximum)	343–800	340–540	340–520	120–520	120–520
I/O AND EXPANSION					
Parallel, serial, mouse ports	INA	INA	INA	1, 1, 1	1, 1, 1
Shared keyboard mouse ports	INA	INA	INA	0	0
Docking station options	INA	INA	INA	●	●
Expansion bus ports	INA	INA	INA	1	1
Expansion unit	INA	INA	INA	●	●
VIDEO					
Screen Mfg	Sanyo	Sharp	Sharp	Sharp	Sharp
Color/Monochrome	Color	Color	Color	Monochrome	Color
Illuminated/Active matrix	INA	INA	INA	○/○	○/○
Display technology	INA	INA	INA	TSTN	Dual Matrix
Display lighting	INA	INA	INA	Backlit	Backlit
Video chip set manufacturer	Cirrus	C&T	C&T	C&T	C&T
Video memory size (Mb)	1	1	1	0.512	0.512
Maximum internal and external resolution	INA	INA	INA	640 × 480–800 × 600	640 × 480–800 × 600
MODEM					
Modem type/Speed	PCMCIA fax/14,400	internal fax/14,400	PCMCIA fax/14,400	PCMCIA/14,400	PCMCIA/14,400
POWER					
Rated battery life (hours)	INA	INA	INA	4	4
Charge time while on, off (hours)	N/A, 2.5	2.25, 2.25	3, 2	4, 2.5	4, 2.5
Display/hard disk power-down	●/●	●/●	●/●	●/●	●/●
CPU/Peripheral power-down	○/○	●/●	●/●	●/●	●/●
Standby/Hibernation	○/○	●/●	●/●	○/●	○/●

●—Yes ○—No N/A—Not applicable INA—Information not available

Table Continues →

■ Mobile Computers

	MPC Model 380 (Dual Scan Color)	MPC Model 380 (Monochrome)	MPC CD-Book	NCR Corp AT&T Safari 3181	NEC Versa E Series DX4/75
Price	$$$	$$	$$$	$$$$	$$$$$
Processor	DX2/66	DX2/50	Intel DX4/75	DX2/50	DX4/75
Fixed disk size	210	340	INA	210	340
Windows version	Windows 3.1	Windows for Workgroups 3.11	Windows for Workgroups 3.11	Windows 3.1	Windows 3.1
Pointing device	INA	INA	Integrated pointing stick	INA	INA
Case size (HWD, in inches)	$1.9 \times 11.0 \times 8.5$	$1.9 \times 11.0 \times 8.5$	$2.5 \times 11.5 \times 8.8$	$2.3 \times 11.8 \times 9.5$	$2.3 \times 11.8 \times 9.3$
Weight/Travel weight (pounds)	6.87/8.3	6.34/7.74	6.69/8.44	6.96/8.14	6.93/8.11
Screen size (LW, in inches)	8.3×5.9	7.5×5.6	7.1×5.8	7.5×5.6	7.5×5.8
MEMORY AND DISK DRIVES					
Installed/maximum external cache	INA	INA	N/A	INA	INA
Installable RAM (minimum–maximum)	4Mb–20Mb	4Mb–20Mb	8Mb–64Mb	4Mb–20Mb	4Mb–36Mb
Fixed disk range (minimum–maximum)	120–524	120–524	340–700	210–340	209–528
I/O AND EXPANSION					
Parallel, serial, mouse ports	1, 1, 1	1, 1, 1	INA	1, 1, 1	1, 1, 1
Shared keyboard mouse ports	○	○	INA	○	○
Docking station options	●	●	INA	●	●
Expansion bus ports	1	1	INA	1	1
Expansion unit	●	●	INA	●	●
VIDEO					
Screen Mfg	Sharp	Epson	Hitachi	NEC	NEC
Color/Monochrome	Color	Monochrome	Color	Color	Color
Illuminated/Active matrix	○/●	○/●	INA	○/●	●/●
Display technology	Active TFT	Active TFT	INA	Active TFT	Active TFT
Display lighting	Backlit	Edgelit	INA	Backlit	Backlit
Video chip set manufacturer	C&T	C&T	C&T	WD	WD
Video memory size (Mb)	0.512	0.5	1	1	1
Maximum internal and external resolution	640×480–$1,024 \times 768$	640×480–$1,024 \times 768$	INA	640×480–$1,024 \times 768$	640×480–$1,024 \times 768$
MODEM					
Modem type/Speed	PCMCIA/14,400	PCMCIA/14,400	None	PCMCIA/14,400	PCMCIA/14,400
POWER					
Rated battery life (hours)	2.5	4	INA	4	3
Charge time while on, off (hours)	4, 2.5	4, 2.5	6, 3	2.6, 1.5	2.3, 1.3
Display/hard disk power-down	●/●	●/●	●/●	●/●	●/●
CPU/Peripheral power-down	●/●	●/●	●/●	●/●	●/●
Standby/Hibernation	●/●	●/●	●/●	●/●	●/●

●—Yes ○—No N/A—Not applicable INA—Information not available

Mobile Computers ■

	Panasonic CF-V21P	Panasonic V41	Samsung S3945T DX4/75	Sharp PC-8150T	Sharp PC-8650T
Price	$$$$	$$$$$	$$$$	$$$	$$$
Processor	DX2/50	Intel DX4/100	Intel DX4/75	DX/33	DX/33
Fixed disk size	210	INA	INA	213	213
Windows version	Windows 3.1	Windows 3.1	Windows 3.1	Windows 3.1	Windows 3.1
Pointing device	INA	Integrated trackball	Integrated trackball	INA	INA
Case size (HWD, in inches)	2.5 × 11.6 × 8.5	2.3 × 11.7 × 9.4	2.3 × 11.3 × 8.9	1.75 × 11.25 × 8.8	1.75 × 11.25 × 8.75
Weight/Travel weight (pounds)	6.43/8.19	8.06/9.31	6.44/7.38	6.71/7.86	6.53/7.68
Screen size (LW, in inches)	8.45 × 6.4	8.4 × 6.5	7.6 × 5.8	7.5 × 5.75	6.75 × 5.10
MEMORY AND DISK DRIVES					
Installed/maximum external cache	INA	N/A	N/A	INA	INA
Installable RAM (minimum–maximum)	4Mb–20Mb	8Mb–32Mb	8Mb–20Mb	4Mb–20Mb	4Mb–20Mb
Fixed disk range (minimum–maximum)	210–450	455–680	213–500	213	213
I/O AND EXPANSION					
Parallel, serial, mouse ports	1, 1, 0	INA	INA	1, 1, 0	1, 1, 0
Shared keyboard mouse ports	1	INA	INA	1	1
Docking station options	●	INA	INA	●	●
Expansion bus ports	1	INA	INA	1	1
Expansion unit	●	INA	INA	●	●
VIDEO					
Screen Mfg	Panasonic	Matsushita	Samsung	Sharp	Sharp
Color/Monochrome	Color	Color	Color	Color	Color
Illuminated/Active matrix	○/●	INA	INA	●/○	○/●
Display technology	Active TFT	INA	INA	Dual Matrix	Active TFT
Display lighting	Backlit	INA	INA	Backlit	Backlit
Video chip set manufacturer	WD	C&T	WD	Cirrus	Cirrus
Video memory size (Mb)	1	1	1	512	512
Maximum internal and external resolution	640 × 480–1,024 × 768	INA	INA	640 × 480–1,024 × 768	640 × 480–1,024 × 768
MODEM					
Modem type/Speed	PCMCIA/ N/A	None	PCMCIA fax/14,400	Integrated/14,400	Integrated/14,400
POWER					
Rated battery life (hours)	0	INA	INA	0	0
Charge time while on, off (hours)	N/A, N/A	5.5, 3.5	2.5, 2	INA	INA
Display/hard disk power-down	●/●	●/●	●/●	●/●	●/●
CPU/Peripheral power-down	●/○	●/○	●/●	●/●	●/●
Standby/Hibernation	●/●	●/●	●/●	●/●	●/●

●—Yes   ○—No   N/A—Not applicable   INA—Information not available

Table Continues →

■ Mobile Computers

	Summit Mount Hood	Summit Mount Ranier	TI TravelMate 4000M/50 Dual Scan	TI TravelMate 4000M/75 Dual Scan	TI TravelMate 4000E WindX2/50 DSC
Price	$$	$$$	$$$	$$$$	$$$
Processor	Intel 486DX2/66	Intel DX4/100	Intel 486DX2/50	Intel DX4/75	DX2/50
Fixed disk size	INA	INA	INA	INA	210
Windows version	Windows 3.11	Windows 3.11	Windows for Workgroups 3.11	Windows for Workgroups 3.11	Windows 3.1
Pointing device	Integrated trackball	Integrated trackball	Integrated pointing stick	Integrated pointing stick	INA
Case size (HWD, in inches)	2.5 × 8.5 × 10.5	2.3 × 11 × 9.3	2 × 10.9 × 8.6	2 × 11 × 8.5	2.25 × 11.0 × 8.5
Weight/Travel weight (pounds)	6.93/8.19	7.25/8.5	6.44/7.0	6.31/6.88	6.6/8.22
Screen size (LW, in inches)	8.3 × 6	7.5 × 5.7	7.5 × 5.8	7.5 × 5.8	7.5 × 5.6
MEMORY AND DISK DRIVES					
Installed/maximum external cache	N/A	N/A	N/A	N/A	INA
Installable RAM (minimum–maximum)	8Mb–36Mb	8Mb–36Mb	8Mb–20Mb	8Mb–20Mb	4Mb–20Mb
Fixed disk range (minimum–maximum)	344–540	343–540	340–340	455–455	210
I/O AND EXPANSION					
Parallel, serial, mouse ports	INA	INA	INA	INA	1, 1, 1
Shared keyboard mouse ports	INA	INA	INA	INA	1
Docking station options	INA	INA	INA	INA	●
Expansion bus ports	INA	INA	INA	INA	1
Expansion unit	INA	INA	INA	INA	●
VIDEO					
Screen Mfg	Sanyo	Sanyo	Sanyo	Sanyo	Sanyo
Color/Monochrome	Color	Color	Color	Color	Color
Illuminated/Active matrix	INA	INA	INA	INA	○/○
Display technology	INA	INA	INA	INA	Dual Matrix
Display lighting	INA	INA	INA	INA	Edgelit
Video chip set manufacturer	Cirrus	Cirrus	Cirrus	Cirrus	Cirrus
Video memory size (Mb)	1	1	1	1	1
Maximum internal and external resolution	INA	INA	INA	INA	640 × 480–1,024 × 768
MODEM					
Modem type/Speed	PCMCIA fax/14,400	PCMCIA fax/14,400	PCMCIA fax/14,400	PCMCIA fax/14,400	PCMCIA/14,400
POWER					
Rated battery life (hours)	INA	INA	INA	INA	3
Charge time while on, off (hours)	2, 2	2, 2	3, 3	3, 3	3, 3
Display/hard disk power-down	●/●	●/●	●/●	●/●	●/●
CPU/Peripheral power-down	○/○	●/○	●/●	●/●	●/●
Standby/Hibernation	●/○	●/●	○/●	○/○	●/●

●—Yes ○—No N/A—Not applicable INA—Information not available

Mobile Computers

	TI TravelMate 4000E WinDX2/50 Monochrome	TI TravelMate 4000M	Toshiba T4700CS	Toshiba T4800CT	Toshiba Satellite T1910
Price	$$$	$$$	$$$	$$$$$	$$$
Processor	DX2/50	SX/25	DX2/50	DX4/75	SX/33
Fixed disk size	210	210	213	524	130
Windows version	Windows 3.1	Windows for Workgroups 3.11	Windows for Workgroups 3.11	Windows for Workgroups 3.11	Windows 3.1
Pointing device	INA	INA	INA	INA	INA
Case size (HWD, in inches)	1.80 × 11.0 × 8.5	2.0 × 11.0 × 8.5	2 × 11.5 × 8	2 × 11.5 × 8	2.0 × 11.5 × 8.3
Weight/Travel weight (pounds)	6.55/8.2	6.55/7.24	6.98/8.11	7.24/8.53	6.57/7.51
Screen size (LW, in inches)	7.85 × 5.85	6.8 × 5.2	7.5 × 5.7	7.5 × 5.7	7.6 × 5.7
MEMORY AND DISK DRIVES					
Installed/maximum external cache	INA	INA	INA	INA	INA
Installable RAM (minimum–maximum)	4Mb–20Mb	4Mb–20Mb	8Mb–24Mb	8Mb–24Mb	4Mb–20Mb
Fixed disk range (minimum–maximum)	210	210	200–320	524	120–200
I/O AND EXPANSION					
Parallel, serial, mouse ports	1, 1, 1	1, 1, 0	1, 1, 1	1, 1, 1	1, 1, 1
Shared keyboard mouse ports	0	1	0	0	0
Docking station options	●	●	●	●	○
Expansion bus ports	1	1	1	1	0
Expansion unit	●	●	●	●	○
VIDEO					
Screen Mfg	Sharp for TI	Sanyo	N/A	N/A	N/A
Color/Monochrome	Monochrome	Color	Color	Color	Monochrome
Illuminated/Active matrix	○/○	○/●	●/○	●/●	○/●
Display technology	TSTN	Active TFT	Dual Matrix	Active TFT	Active TFT
Display lighting	Edgelit	Edgelit	Backlit	Backlit	Backlit
Video chip set manufacturer	Cirrus	Cirrus	WD	WD	WD
Video memory size (Mb)	1	1	1	1	1
Maximum internal and external resolution	640 × 480–1,024 × 768	640 × 480–1,280 × 1,024	640 × 480–1,024 × 768	640 × 480–1,024 × 768	640 × 480–1,024 × 768
MODEM					
Modem type/Speed	PCMCIA/14,400	PCMCIA/14,400	PCMCIA/2400	PCMCIA/2400	PCMCIA/14,400
POWER					
Rated battery life (hours)	4	4	0	5	5
Charge time while on, off (hours)	3, 3	3, 3	3, 1.5	3, 1.5	N/A, 2.3
Display/hard disk power-down	●/●	●/●	●/●	●/●	●/●
CPU/Peripheral power-down	●/●	●/○	●/○	●/○	●/○
Standby/Hibernation	●/●	●/●	●/○	●/○	●/●

●—Yes ○—No N/A—Not applicable INA—Information not available

Table Continues →

■ Mobile Computers

	Toshiba Portégé T3600CT	Toshiba T4850CT	Tri-Star MediaBook	Twinhead Slimnote 550S	Twinhead Slimnote 550T
Price	$$$	$$$$$	$$$	$$$	$$$
Processor	Intel 486DX2/50	Intel DX2/75	Intel DX4/100	Intel 486DX2/50	Intel 486DX2/50
Fixed disk size	INA	INA	INA	INA	INA
Windows version	Windows for Workgroups 3.11	Windows for Workgroups 3.11	Windows for Workgroups 3.11	Windows 3.1	Windows 3.1
Pointing device	Integrated pointing stick	Clip-on trackball	Integrated trackball	Integrated trackball	Integrated trackball
Case size (HWD, in inches)	1.9 × 9.9 × 8	2.3 × 11.8 × 8.3	2.3 × 11 × 8.5	2 × 11.6 × 8.9	2 × 11.6 × 8.9
Weight/Travel weight (pounds)	4.5/5.93	7.0/7.93	7.31/8.5	6.25/7.69	6.25/7.19
Screen size (LW, in inches)	6.8 × 5.3	8.3 × 6.2	7.5 × 5.6	7.8 × 5.5	7.5 × 5.8
MEMORY AND DISK DRIVES					
Installed/maximum external cache	N/A	N/A	128K, 128K	N/A	N/A
Installable RAM (minimum–maximum)	8Mb–24Mb	8Mb–24Mb	8Mb–32Mb	8Mb–32Mb	8Mb–32Mb
Fixed disk range (minimum–maximum)	261–261	528–772	339–528	340–520	340–520
I/O AND EXPANSION					
Parallel, serial, mouse ports	INA	INA	INA	INA	INA
Shared keyboard mouse ports	INA	INA	INA	INA	INA
Docking station options	INA	INA	INA	INA	INA
Expansion bus ports	INA	INA	INA	INA	INA
Expansion unit	INA	INA	INA	INA	INA
VIDEO					
Screen Mfg	Toshiba	Toshiba	Sharp	Sharp	Sharp
Color/Monochrome	Color	Color	Color	Color	Color
Illuminated/Active matrix	INA	INA	INA	INA	INA
Display technology	INA	INA	INA	INA	INA
Display lighting	INA	INA	INA	INA	INA
Video chip set manufacturer	WD	WD	Cirrus	WD	WD
Video memory size (Mb)	1	1	1	1	1
Maximum internal and external resolution	INA	INA	INA	INA	INA
MODEM					
Modem type/Speed	None	PCMCIA fax/14,400	PCMCIA fax/14,400	PCMCIA fax/14,400	PCMCIA fax/14,400
POWER					
Rated battery life (hours)	INA	INA	INA	INA	INA
Charge time while on, off (hours)	9, 3	3, 1.5	N/A, 1.5	8, 1.75	N/A, 1.75
Display/hard disk power-down	●/●	●/●	●/●	●/●	●/●
CPU/Peripheral power-down	●/○	●/○	○/○	●/●	●/●
Standby/Hibernation	●/○	●/○	○/○	●/●	●/●

●—Yes   ○—No   N/A—Not applicable   INA—Information not available

Mobile Computers ■

	Twinhead Slimnote 5100T	Twinhead Slimnote 486E 4DX2/66T	WinBook XP 486DX4/100 8/520 Active-Matrix	WinBook XP 486DX4/100 8/520 Dual-Scan Color	ZDS S-Lite
Price	$$$$	$$$$	$$$$	$$$	$$
Processor	Intel DX4/100	DX2/66	Intel DX4/100	Intel DX4/100	Cyrix Cx486DLC-33
Fixed disk size	INA	340	INA	INA	INA
Windows version	Windows 3.11	Windows 3.1	Windows for Workgroups 3.11	Windows for Workgroups 3.11	Windows for Workgroups 3.11
Pointing device	Integrated trackpad	INA	Integrated pointing stick	Integrated pointing stick	Integrated J-key
Case size (HWD, in inches)	2 × 11.6 × 8.9	1.9 × 11.3 × 8.8	2 × 11.4 × 8.9	2 × 11.4 × 8.9	2 × 7.3 × 9.8
Weight/Travel weight (pounds)	6.25/7.19	6.91/8.45	6.44/7.19	6.31/7.13	4.13/5.81
Screen size (LW, in inches)	7.5 × 5.8	7.5 × 6.7	7.6 × 5.7	8.3 × 6	6.3 × 4.5
MEMORY AND DISK DRIVES					
Installed/maximum external cache	N/A	INA	N/A	N/A	N/A
Installable RAM (minimum–maximum)	16Mb–32Mb	4Mb–20Mb	8Mb–32Mb	8Mb–32Mb	8Mb–12Mb
Fixed disk range (minimum–maximum)	520–520	200–500	513–520	505–520	209–340
I/O AND EXPANSION					
Parallel, serial, mouse ports	INA	1, 1, 0	INA	INA	INA
Shared keyboard mouse ports	INA	1	INA	INA	INA
Docking station options	INA	●	INA	INA	INA
Expansion bus ports	INA	1	INA	INA	INA
Expansion unit	INA	●	INA	INA	INA
VIDEO					
Screen Mfg	Sharp	NEC	Hitachi	Sanyo	Sanyo
Color/Monochrome	Color	Color	Color	Color	Color
Illuminated/Active matrix	INA	●/●	INA	INA	INA
Display technology	INA	Active TFT	INA	INA	INA
Display lighting	INA	Backlit	INA	INA	INA
Video chip set manufacturer	WD	WD	WD	WD	C&T
Video memory size (Mb)	1	1	1	1	.5
Maximum internal and external resolution	INA	640 × 480–1,024 × 768	INA	INA	INA
MODEM					
Modem type/Speed	PCMCIA fax/14,400	Integrated/14,400	internal fax/14,400	internal fax/14,400	PCMCIA fax/14,400
POWER					
Rated battery life (hours)	INA	3	INA	INA	INA
Charge time while on, off (hours)	8, 1.75	8, 2	5, 2	5, 2	12, 2
Display/hard disk power-down	●/●	●/●	●/●	●/●	●/●
CPU/Peripheral power-down	●/●	●/●	●/●	●/●	●/●
Standby/Hibernation	●/●	●/●	●/●	●/●	●/○

●—Yes ○—No N/A—Not applicable INA—Information not available

Table Continues →

Mobile Computers

	ZDS Z-LITE 425L	ZEOS Meridian 400A	ZEOS Meridian 400C	ZEOS Meridian 800A	ZEOS Meridian 800C
Price	$$	$$$	$$$	$$$	$$$
Processor	SX/25 SL	Intel DX4/100	Intel DX4/100	Intel DX4/100	Intel DX4/100
Fixed disk size	172	INA	INA	INA	INA
Windows version	Windows 3.1	Windows for Workgroups 3.11	Windows for Workgroups 3.11	Windows for Workgroups 3.11	Windows for Workgroups 3.11
Pointing device	INA	Integrated pointing stick	Integrated pointing stick	Integrated pointing stick	Integrated pointing stick
Case size (HWD, in inches)	1.5 × 9.9 × 9.5	1.7 × 10.2 × 8	1.7 × 10.2 × 8	1.9 × 11.7 × 8.9	1.9 × 11.7 × 8.9
Weight/Travel weight (pounds)	4.23/6.36	4.06/5.93	4.06/5.93	6.31/7.5	6.31/7.5
Screen size (LW, in inches)	6.8 × 5.1	6.3 × 4.8	6.2 × 4.8	7.7 × 5.9	7.7 × 5.9
MEMORY AND DISK DRIVES					
Installed/maximum external cache	INA	N/A	N/A	N/A	N/A
Installable RAM (minimum–maximum)	4Mb–20Mb	8Mb–20Mb	8Mb–20Mb	8Mb–20Mb	8Mb–20Mb
Fixed disk range (minimum–maximum)	120–172	350–350	349–350	350–350	349–350
I/O AND EXPANSION					
Parallel, serial, mouse ports	1, 1, 0	INA	INA	INA	INA
Shared keyboard mouse ports	1	INA	INA	INA	INA
Docking station options	○	INA	INA	INA	INA
Expansion bus ports	0	INA	INA	INA	INA
Expansion unit	○	INA	INA	INA	INA
VIDEO					
Screen Mfg	Sanyo	Toshiba	Sanyo	Toshiba	Sanyo
Color/Monochrome	Monochrome	Color	Color	Color	Color
Illuminated/Active matrix	●/○	INA	INA	INA	INA
Display technology	Other	INA	INA	INA	INA
Display lighting	Backlit	INA	INA	INA	INA
Video chip set manufacturer	C	Cirrus	Cirrus	Cirrus	Cirrus
Video memory size (Mb)	0.512	1	1	1	1
Maximum internal and external resolution	640 × 480–1,024 × 768	INA	INA	INA	INA
MODEM					
Modem type/Speed	PCMCIA/14,400	None	None	None	None
POWER					
Rated battery life (hours)	4	INA	INA	INA	INA
Charge time while on, off (hours)	2, 2	N/A, 1	N/A, 1	N/A, 1	N/A, 1
Display/hard disk power-down	●/●	●/●	●/●	●/●	●/●
CPU/Peripheral power-down	●/●	●/●	●/●	●/●	●/●
Standby/Hibernation	●/●	●/●	●/●	●/●	●/●

●—Yes ○—No N/A—Not applicable INA—Information not available

End ■

A.5 90-MHz Pentium PCs

(Products listed in alphabetical order)	Aberdeen Super P90 VLPCI	ACMA P90 PCI	AMAX 90MHz PowerStation	Ambra TP90PCI	ARES Pentium Pro 90
List price (tested configuration)	$$$	$$$	$$$	$$$	$$$
Hard-disk capacity and interface	546Mb IDE	514Mb IDE	514Mb IDE	731Mb IDE	540Mb IDE
Dealers/Direct-distribution channel	○/●	●/●	●/●	○/●	○/●
Case style	Mini-tower	Tower	Tower	Mini-tower	Tower
Power supply (and number of connectors)	250W (6)	250W (8)	250W (6)	200W (6)	250W (5)
DOS, Microsoft Windows version	DOS 6.2, Windows for Workgroups 3.11	DOS 6.21, Windows for Workgroups 3.11	DOS 6.21, Windows for Workgroups 3.11	DOS 6.2, Windows 3.1	DOS 6.21, Windows for Workgroups 3.11
Warranty	2 years parts, lifetime labor	1 year	1 year	1 year	3 years parts, lifetime labor
On-site service charge	$229.95 (4 years)	Included (1 year)	$39.00 (1 year)	Included (1 year)	Included (1 year)
PROCESSOR AND MEMORY					
Bus architecture (primary)	ISA	ISA	ISA	ISA	ISA
Bus architecture (secondary)	PCI and VL-Bus	PCI	PCI	PCI	PCI
Motherboard manufacturer	Super Micro	Intel	Intel	Intel	Intel
Chip set manufacturer	OPTi	Intel	Intel	Intel	Intel
Processor upgrade path	ZIF	ZIF	ZIF	ZIF	ZIF
BIOS version (or date)	AMI (12/15/93)	AMI (3/23/94)	AMI (3/23/94)	AMI 1.00.1.AX1D	AMI 1.00.03
Flash BIOS/16550 UART support	●/○	●/●	●/●	●/●	●/●
Installable system RAM	2Mb–128Mb	2Mb–128Mb	2Mb–128Mb	4Mb–128Mb	4Mb–128Mb
External RAM cache	128K–512K	256K	256K	256K	256K
Cache architecture	Two-way set-associative	Direct-mapped	Direct-mapped	Direct-mapped	Direct-mapped
Cache write design	Write-through	Write-back	Write-back	Write-back	Write-back
COMPONENTS					
Available hard-disk sizes	210Mb–4Gb	210Mb–2Gb	210Mb–9Gb	420Mb–2Gb	270Mb–2Gb
Disk controller location	VL-Bus card	Motherboard (PCI)	Motherboard (PCI)	Motherboard (PCI)	Motherboard (PCI)
Accessible drive bays (5.25", 3.5")	3, 0	6, 0	4, 0	3, 1	4, 0
Internal drive bays (5.25", 3.5")	0, 2	0, 4	1, 3	0, 2	2, 2
Floppy disk drives	1.44Mb	1.44Mb	1.44Mb	1.44Mb	1.44Mb
CD-ROM drive	Sony CDU-33A-01	NEC CDR-510	Chinon CDS-535	Philips/LMS CDR 206	Mitsumi FX-001D
ISA, EISA, MCA slots	3, 0, 0	5, 0, 0	5, 0, 0	5, 0, 0	4, 0, 0
VL-Bus, PCI, proprietary local-bus slots	2, 4, 0	0, 3, 0	0, 3, 0	0, 3, 0	0, 3, 0
Parallel, serial, mouse ports	1, 2, 0	1, 2, 0	1, 2, 0	1, 2, 1	1, 2, 0
Display circuitry location	PCI card	PCI card	PCI card	PCI card	PCI card
Video chip set manufacturer	ATI	ATI	ATI	Weitek	S3
Video RAM	2Mb–4Mb	2Mb	2Mb–4Mb	2Mb	2Mb–4Mb

●—Yes   ○—No   N/A—Not applicable   INA—Information not availablee

Table Continues →

■ 90-MHz Pentium PCs

	AST Premmia GX P/90 Model 733C	AT&T Globalyst 600	Axik Ace Power 586-90PCI	CAF Lightning P9	Comtrade Professional P5/90
List price (tested configuration)	$$$$	$$$$	$$$$	$$$	$$$
Hard-disk capacity and interface	730Mb SCSI-2	540Mb IDE	525Mb SCSI-2	343Mb SCSI-2	540Mb IDE
Dealers/Direct-distribution channel	●/○	●/●	○/●	●/○	○/●
Case style	Desktop	Desktop	Tower	Desktop	Mini-tower
Power supply (and number of connectors)	230W (5)	180W (5)	250W (6)	200W (4)	230W (6)
DOS, Microsoft Windows version	DOS 6.21, Windows 3.1	DOS 6.2, Windows for Workgroups 3.11	DOS 6.21, Windows for Workgroups 3.11	DOS 6.2, Windows 3.1	DOS 6.21, Windows for Workgroups 3.11
Warranty	3 years	3 years	1 year	1 year	1 year
On-site service charge	Included (1 year)	Included (1 year)	Included (1 year)	N/A	$50.00 (1 year)
PROCESSOR AND MEMORY					
Bus architecture (primary)	EISA	ISA	ISA	ISA	ISA
Bus architecture (secondary)	PCI	PCI	PCI and VL-Bus	PCI and VL-Bus	PCI
Motherboard manufacturer	AST	AT&T	Axik Computer	Aquarius Systems/CAF	Intel
Chip set manufacturer	Intel	Intel	OPTi	OPTi	Intel
Processor upgrade path	ZIF	ZIF	ZIF	ZIF	ZIF
BIOS version (or date)	AST 1.00.11	AMI/Intel (4/11/94)	AMI (5/8/94)	AMI (12/15/93)	AMI 1.00.03 AXIZ
Flash BIOS/16550 UART support	●/●	●/●	●/●	●/○	●/●
Installable system RAM	8Mb–192Mb	8Mb–128Mb	2Mb–128Mb	2Mb–128Mb	4Mb–128Mb
External RAM cache	256K–512K	256K	0–1Mb	256K–512K	256K
Cache architecture	Direct-mapped	Direct-mapped	Two-way set-associative	Direct-mapped	Direct-mapped
Cache write design	Write-back	Write-back	Write-back	Write-back	Write-back
COMPONENTS					
Available hard-disk sizes	365Mb–730Mb	270Mb–1Gb	340Mb–4Gb	170Mb–540Mb	210Mb–4Gb
Disk controller location	Motherboard (PCI)	Motherboard	PCI card	PCI card	Motherboard (PCI)
Accessible drive bays (5.25", 3.5")	2, 1	2, 1	5, 0	2, 1	3, 2
Internal drive bays (5.25", 3.5")	0, 2	1, 1	4, 0	0, 1	0, 2
Floppy disk drives	1.44Mb	1.44Mb	1.44Mb	1.44Mb	1.44Mb
CD-ROM drive	Toshiba XM-3401 TA	Sony CDU-561	NEC CDR-510	Panasonic CR-562-B	Mitsumi FX001D
ISA, EISA, MCA slots	0, 5, 0	6, 0, 0	5, 0, 0	3, 0, 0	5, 0, 0
VL-Bus, PCI, proprietary local-bus slots	0, 2, 0	0, 2, 0	2, 4, 0	2, 4, 0	0, 3, 0
Parallel, serial, mouse ports	1, 2, 1	1, 2, 1	1, 2, 0	1, 2, 0	1, 2, 0
Display circuitry location	PCI card	Motherboard (PCI)	PCI card	PCI card	PCI card
Video chip set manufacturer	ATI	ATI	S3	S3	S3
Video RAM	2Mb–4Mb	2Mb	1Mb–2Mb	1Mb	2Mb–4Mb

●—Yes ○—No N/A—Not applicable INA—Information not available

90-MHz Pentium PCs ∎

	Dell Dimension XPS P90	Diamond DT 586-90	EPS P90 Explorer	FCS Green Pentium 90	FutureTech System 5490P
List price (tested configuration)	$$$	$$$	$$$$	$$$	$$$
Hard-disk capacity and interface	1Gb IDE	345Mb SCSI-2	540Mb SCSI-2	541Mb SCSI-2	425Mb IDE
Dealers/Direct-distribution channel	○/●	●/●	○/●	○/●	●/●
Case style	Desktop	Desktop	Desktop	Tower	Tower
Power supply (and number of connectors)	200W (5)	230W (6)	300W (5)	250W (9)	300W (10)
DOS, Microsoft Windows version	DOS 6.21, Windows for Workgroups 3.11	DOS 6.21, Windows 3.11	DOS 6.2, Windows 3.1	DOS 6.2, Windows 3.11	DOS 6.2, Windows 3.11
Warranty	1 year	3 years	3 years parts, 1 year labor	2 years parts, lifetime labor	15 months
On-site service charge	Included (1 year)	Included (1 year)	Included (1 year)	Included (1 year)	Included (1 year)
PROCESSOR AND MEMORY					
Bus architecture (primary)	ISA	ISA	ISA	ISA	ISA
Bus architecture (secondary)	PCI	PCI and VL-Bus	PCI and VL-Bus	PCI and VL-Bus	PCI and VL-Bus
Motherboard manufacturer	Intel/Dell	Super Micro	EPS	Super Micro	Mars Technologies
Chip set manufacturer	Intel	OPTi	OPTi	OPTi	OPTi
Processor upgrade path	ZIF	ZIF	ZIF	ZIF	ZIF
BIOS version (or date)	AMI/Dell A03	AMI (5/2/94)	AMI (12/15/93)	AMI (12/15/93)	AMI (5/2/94)
Flash BIOS/16550 UART support	●/●	●/●	●/○	●/●	●/○
Installable system RAM	8Mb–128Mb	2Mb–128Mb	1Mb–128Mb	2Mb–128Mb	2Mb–256Mb
External RAM cache	256K	128K–512K	64K–1Mb	256K–1Mb	256K–512K
Cache architecture	Direct-mapped	Direct-mapped	Two-way set-associative	Direct-mapped	Direct-mapped
Cache write design	Write-back	Write-through	Write-back	Write-through	Write-back
COMPONENTS					
Available hard-disk sizes	340Mb–1.1Gb	345Mb–4Gb	270Mb–3Gb	420Mb–3.3Gb	212Mb–4Gb
Disk controller location	Motherboard (PCI)	VL-Bus card	PCI card	VL-Bus card	PCI card
Accessible drive bays (5.25", 3.5")	3, 0	3, 2	2, 2	5, 2	5, 2
Internal drive bays (5.25", 3.5")	0, 2	0, 1	2, 0	3, 0	0, 3
Floppy disk drives	Dual 1.2Mb/1.44Mb	Dual 1.2Mb/1.44Mb	1.44Mb	1.44Mb	1.44Mb
CD-ROM drive	Panasonic CR563	Toshiba TXM3401B	Plextor DM-3028	NEC 3Xi	Mitsumi FX-001
ISA, EISA, MCA slots	5, 0, 0	3, 0, 0	3, 0, 0	5, 0, 0	3, 0, 0
VL-Bus, PCI, proprietary local-bus slots	0, 3, 0	2, 4, 0	2, 4, 0	2, 4, 0	2, 4, 0
Parallel, serial, mouse ports	1, 2, 1	1, 2, 0	1, 2, 0	1, 2, 0	1, 2, 0
Display circuitry location	PCI card	PCI card	PCI card	PCI card	PCI card
Video chip set manufacturer	S3	S3	S3	ATI	ATI
Video RAM	2Mb–4Mb	2Mb–4Mb	2Mb–4Mb	2Mb	2Mb–4Mb

●—Yes ○—No N/A—Not applicable INA—Information not available

Table Continues →

■ 90-MHz Pentium PCs

	Gateway 2000 P5-90	Hewitt Rand HR P5-90 Panther	HP Vectra XU 5/90C	Initiative Technology ITI 590 Pi	Insight PCI P90 SCSI
List price (tested configuration)	$$$	$$$	$$$$	$$$$	$$$$
Hard-disk capacity and interface	540Mb IDE	515Mb SCSI-2	540Mb IDE	545Mb IDE	2.1Gb SCSI-2
Dealers/Direct-distribution channel	○/●	●/○	●/○	●/○	○/●
Case style	Tower	Desktop	Desktop	Desktop	Tower
Power supply (and number of connectors)	300W (6)	200W (6)	160W (4)	400W (5)	250W (6)
DOS, Microsoft Windows version	DOS 6.21, Windows for Workgroups 3.11	DOS 6.21, Windows for Workgroups 3.11	DOS 6.2, Windows for Workgroups 3.11	DOS 6.21, Windows for Workgroups 3.11	DOS 6.21, Windows for Workgroups 3.11
Warranty	3 years parts, 1 year labor	2 years	3 years	1 year	1 year
On-site service charge	Included (1 year)	$39.00 (1 year)	Included (1 year)	N/A	N/A
PROCESSOR AND MEMORY					
Bus architecture (primary)	ISA	ISA	ISA	ISA	ISA
Bus architecture (secondary)	PCI	PCI	PCI	PCI	PCI
Motherboard manufacturer	Intel	Intel	Hewlett-Packard	Micronics	Intel
Chip set manufacturer	Intel	Intel	Intel	Intel	Intel
Processor upgrade path	ZIF	ZIF	ZIF	ZIF	ZIF
BIOS version (or date)	AMI 1.00.05.AX1	AMI (11/11/92)	Phoenix (5/13/94)	Phoenix (5/15/94)	AMI 1.00.05.Ax1
Flash BIOS/16550 UART support	●/●	●/●	●/●	●/●	●/●
Installable system RAM	16Mb–128Mb	2Mb–128Mb	8Mb–256Mb	8Mb–192Mb	1Mb–128Mb
External RAM cache	256K	256K	256K–512K	256K–512K	256K
Cache architecture	Direct-mapped	Direct-mapped	Direct-mapped	Direct-mapped	Direct-mapped
Cache write design	Write-back	Write-back	Write-back	Write-back	Write-back
COMPONENTS					
Available hard-disk sizes	340Mb–1Gb	250Mb–9Gb	270Mb–1Gb	215Mb–2Gb	40Mb–4Gb
Disk controller location	Motherboard (PCI)	PCI card	Motherboard (PCI)	Motherboard (PCI)	PCI card
Accessible drive bays (5.25", 3.5")	4, 1	3, 2	2, 1	3, 2	4, 1
Internal drive bays (5.25", 3.5")	0, 4	0, 0	0, 0	3, 3	0, 8
Floppy disk drives	1.44Mb	1.2Mb, 1.44Mb	1.44Mb	Dual 1.2Mb/1.44Mb	1.44Mb
CD-ROM drive	NEC 2X IDE	Toshiba	Toshiba XM 4101 XM-3401TA	NEC 3Xi	Plextor TX3028
ISA, EISA, MCA slots	5, 0, 0	5, 0, 0	4, 0, 0	5, 0, 0	5, 0, 0
VL-Bus, PCI, proprietary local bus slots	0, 3, 0	0, 3, 0	0, 2, 0	0, 2, 0	0, 3, 0
Parallel, serial, mouse ports	1, 2, 0	1, 2, 0	1, 1, 1	1, 2, 1	1, 2, 0
Display circuitry location	PCI card	PCI card	PCI card	PCI card	PCI card
Video chip set manufacturer	ATI	ATI	Matrox	Weitek	Matrox
Video RAM	2Mb	2Mb–4Mb	2Mb–4Mb	1Mb–2Mb	2Mb

●—Yes ○—No N/A—Not applicable INA—Information not available

90-MHz Pentium PCs ■

	Mega Impact P90PCI/VLB+	Memorex Telex Celerria LP90	MicroFLEX-VL/ Pentium/90	Micron P90PCI PowerStation	Mitsuba Premier System-90
List price (tested configuration)	$$$	$$$$	$$$	$$$	$$$
Hard-disk capacity and interface	519Mb SCSI-2	522Mb IDE	541Mb IDE	527Mb IDE	525Mb IDE
Dealers/Direct-distribution channel	●/●	○/●	○/●	○/●	●/○
Case style	Desktop	Slimline	Tower	Desktop	Desktop
Power supply (and number of connectors)	250W (5)	145W (5)	250W (8)	230W (5)	200W (5)
DOS, Microsoft Windows version	DOS 6.2, Windows 3.1	DOS 6.2, Windows for Workgroups 3.11	DOS 6.21, Windows 3.1	DOS 6.21, Windows for Workgroups 3.11	DOS 6.21, Windows for Workgroups 3.11
Warranty	1 year	1 year	2 years	1 year	2 years
On-site service charge	N/A	Included (1 year)	$50.00 (1 year)	Included (1 year)	$40.00 (1 year)
PROCESSOR AND MEMORY					
Bus architecture (primary)	ISA	ISA	ISA	ISA	ISA
Bus architecture (secondary)	PCI and VL-Bus	PCI	VL-Bus	PCI	PCI and VL-Bus
Motherboard manufacturer	Super Micro	Intel	Micro Express	Micronics	Mitsuba Corp.
Chip set manufacturer	OPTi	Intel	OPTi	Intel	OPTi
Processor upgrade path	ZIF	ZIF	ZIF	ZIF	ZIF
BIOS version (or date)	AMI (12/15/93)	AMI (5/2/94)	AMI (11/11/92)	Phoenix (4/12/94)	AMI (12/15/93)
Flash BIOS/16550 UART support	●/○	●/●	●/○	●/●	●/○
Installable system RAM	4Mb–128Mb	1Mb–128Mb	4Mb–128Mb	8Mb–192Mb	4Mb–128Mb
External RAM cache	256K–512K	256K	256K–1Mb	256K–512K	256K–1Mb
Cache architecture	Direct-mapped	Direct-mapped	Direct-mapped	Direct-mapped	Four-way set-associative
Cache write design	Write-back	Write-back	Write-back	Write-back	Write-back
COMPONENTS					
Available hard-disk sizes	340Mb–8Gb	200Mb–1Gb	300Mb–2.8Gb	420Mb–2Gb	525Mb–2.1Gb
Disk controller location	PCI card	Motherboard	ISA card	Motherboard	Motherboard
Accessible drive bays (5.25", 3.5")	2, 1	2, 1	3, 2	3, 0	3, 2
Internal drive bays (5.25", 3.5")	2, 2	0, 1	4, 3	0, 2	3, 3
Floppy disk drives	1.44Mb	1.44Mb	1.44Mb	Dual 1.2Mb/1.44Mb	Dual 1.2Mb/1.44Mb
CD-ROM drive	Sony CDU-33A-01	NEC 3Xi	Sony CDU-33A-01	Mitsumi CRMC-FX00ID	Toshiba XM-4101B
ISA, EISA, MCA slots	3, 0, 0	3, 0, 0	5, 0, 0	5, 0, 0	3, 0, 0
VL-Bus, PCI, proprietary local-bus slots	2, 4, 0	0, 2, 0	3, 0, 0	0, 3, 0	2, 3, 0
Parallel, serial, mouse ports	1, 2, 0	1, 2, 1	1, 2, 0	1, 2, 0	1, 2, 0
Display circuitry location	PCI card	PCI card	ISA card	ISA card	PCI card
Video chip set manufacturer	ATI	Matrox	ATI	Matrox	Tseng
Video RAM	2Mb–4Mb	2Mb	1Mb–2Mb	2Mb	1Mb–2Mb

●—Yes　○—No　N/A—Not applicable　INA—Information not available

Table Continues →

90-MHz Pentium PCs

	NETiS N590 Pentium System	Novacor Nova Pentium 90	Pactron Quake 9NSX90	Polywell Poly 586-90VLB	Royal Media Master IV
List price (tested configuration)	$$$	$$$	$$$	$$$	$$$
Hard-disk capacity and interface	540Mb SCSI-2	340Mb IDE	540Mb IDE	540Mb IDE	515Mb SCSI-2
Dealers/Direct-distribution channel	○/●	●/●	●/●	○/●	○/●
Case style	Desktop	Tower	Tower	Mini-tower	Tower
Power supply (and number of connectors)	250W (5)	250W (6)	300W (6)	230W (7)	250W (7)
DOS, Microsoft Windows version	DOS 6.21, Windows 3.11	DOS 6.2, Windows 3.1	DOS 6.2, Windows 3.1	DOS 6.21, Windows 3.11	DOS 6.2, Windows for Workgroups 3.11
Warranty	1 year	1 year	2 years	2 years parts, 5 years labor	1 year parts, lifetime labor
On-site service charge	$150.00 (1 year)	N/A	$150.00 (1 year)	$75.00 (1 year)	$50.00 (1 year)
PROCESSOR AND MEMORY					
Bus architecture (primary)	ISA	ISA	ISA	ISA	ISA
Bus architecture (secondary)	PCI and VL-Bus	PCI	PCI and VL-Bus	VL-Bus	PCI
Motherboard manufacturer	Super Micro	Intel/Digicom	Super Micro	TM Corp.	Super Micro
Chip set manufacturer	OPTi	Intel/Digicom	OPTi	OPTi	Intel
Processor upgrade path	ZIF	ZIF	Standard socket	ZIF	ZIF
BIOS version (or date)	AMI (5/2/94)	AMI 1.00.03.AXIZ	AMI (12/15/93)	AMI (3/1/94)	Award (5/11/94)
Flash BIOS/16550 UART support	●/●	●/●	●/●	●/●	●/○
Installable system RAM	2Mb–128Mb	2Mb–128Mb	2Mb–128Mb	8Mb–128Mb	4Mb–128Mb
External RAM cache	128K–512K	0–256K	256K–512K	256K–512K	256K–512K
Cache architecture	Direct-mapped	Four-way set-associative	Two-way set-associative	Direct-mapped	Direct-mapped
Cache write design	Write-back	Write-back	Write-through	Write-back	Write-back
COMPONENTS					
Available hard-disk sizes	200Mb–2Gb	340Mb–1.2Gb	120Mb–4Gb	420Mb–9Gb	515Mb–2Gb
Disk controller location	PCI card	Motherboard (PCI)	VL-Bus card	VL-Bus card	PCI card
Accessible drive bays (5.25", 3.5")	3, 2	4, 0	5, 0	3, 2	6, 0
Internal drive bays (5.25", 3.5")	0, 2	2, 3	6, 0	0, 3	0, 5
Floppy disk drives	1.2Mb, 1.44Mb	1.2Mb, 1.44Mb	1.44Mb	1.44Mb	1.44Mb
CD-ROM drive	Toshiba 3401B	Panasonic CR-562-B	Sony CDU-33A	Philips 562	NEC CDR510
ISA, EISA, MCA slots	3, 0, 0	5, 0, 0	5, 0, 0	5, 0, 0	4, 0, 0
VL-Bus, PCI, proprietary local-bus slots	2, 4, 0	0, 6, 0	2, 4, 0	3, 0, 0	0, 4, 0
Parallel, serial, mouse ports	1, 2, 0	1, 2, 0	1, 2, 1	1, 2, 0	1, 2, 0
Display circuitry location	PCI card	Motherboard (PCI)	PCI card	VL-Bus card	PCI card
Video chip set manufacturer	ATI	Tseng	Weitek	S3	ATI
Video RAM	1Mb–2Mb	1Mb–2Mb	1Mb–2Mb	1Mb–4Mb	2Mb–4Mb

●—Yes   ○—No   N/A—Not applicable   INA—Information not available

90-MHz Pentium PCs

	Sidus SCI9P590PDT	Solmicro Arena PVi90	Sys Performance Pentium 90 Full Tower	Tagram ThunderboltP90	Tagram Thunderbolt PCI 90
List price (tested configuration)	$$$	$$$	$$$	$$$	$$$
Hard-disk capacity and interface	810Mb IDE	540Mb IDE	976Mb IDE	527Mb IDE	528Mb IDE
Dealers/Direct-distribution channel	●/●	○/●	●/●	●/●	●/●
Case style	Desktop	Tower	Tower	Desktop	Desktop
Power supply (and number of connectors)	200W (5)	250W (6)	300W (10)	250W (5)	250W (5)
DOS, Microsoft Windows version	DOS 6.21, Windows for Workgroups 3.11	DOS 6.2, Windows 3.11	DOS 6.21, Windows for Workgroups 3.11	DOS 6.21, Windows for Workgroups 3.11	DOS 6.21, Windows for Workgroups 3.11
Warranty	1 year	1 year	1 year	3 years	3 years
On-site service charge	Varies	$79.00 (1 year)	N/A	$30.00 (1 year)	$30.00 (1 year)
PROCESSOR AND MEMORY					
Bus architecture (primary)	ISA	ISA	ISA	ISA	ISA
Bus architecture (secondary)	PCI	PCI and VL-Bus	PCI	VL-Bus	PCI and VL-Bus
Motherboard manufacturer	Micronics	Super Micro	Giga-Byte Technology Co.	BCM Advanced Research	BCM Advanced Research
Chip set manufacturer	Intel	OPTi	Intel	Intel	OPTi
Processor upgrade path	ZIF	ZIF	ZIF	ZIF	ZIF
BIOS version (or date)	Phoenix 4.03 M54PI-PXX	AMI (12/15/93)	Award (5/10/94)	AMI (11/11/94)	AMI (11/11/92)
Flash BIOS/16550 UART support	●/●	●/●	●/○	○/○	●/●
Installable system RAM	4Mb–192Mb	4Mb–128Mb	2Mb–512Mb	1Mb–128Mb	4Mb–128Mb
External RAM cache	0–512K	128K–512K	256K–512K	128K–1Mb	256K–1Mb
Cache architecture	Direct-mapped	Direct-mapped	Direct-mapped	Two-way set-associative	Direct-mapped
Cache write design	Write-back	Write-back	Write-back	Write-back	Write-back
COMPONENTS					
Available hard-disk sizes	170Mb–1.2Gb	170Mb–1Gb	540Mb–4Gb	210Mb–2Gb	210Mb–2Gb
Disk controller location	Motherboard (PCI)	VL-Bus card	PCI card	VL-Bus card	Motherboard (PCI)
Accessible drive bays (5.25", 3.5")	2, 1	4, 0	4, 1	2, 2	2, 2
Internal drive bays (5.25", 3.5")	1, 2	2, 2	1, 3	3, 3	0, 3
Floppy disk drives	1.44Mb	1.44Mb	Dual 1.2Mb/1.44Mb	1.44Mb	1.44Mb
CD-ROM drive	Sony CDU-33A	Chinon CDS-535	Toshiba M-3401B	Panasonic CR-562	Panasonic CR-562
ISA, EISA, MCA slots	5, 0, 0	3, 0, 0	4, 0, 0	5, 0, 0	3, 0, 0
VL-Bus, PCI, proprietary local-bus slots	0, 2, 0	2, 4, 0	0, 4, 0	3, 0, 0	2, 3, 0
Parallel, serial, mouse ports	1, 2, 0	1, 2, 0	1, 2, 0	1, 1, 0	1, 2, 0
Display circuitry location	PCI card	PCI card	PCI card	VL-Bus card	PCI card
Video chip set manufacturer	Matrox	ATI	ATI	Tseng	Tseng
Video RAM	2Mb–4Mb	2Mb	2Mb–4Mb	1Mb–2Mb	1Mb–2Mb

●—Yes ○—No N/A—Not applicable INA—Information not available

Table Continues →

■ 90-MHz Pentium PCs

	Tangent PCI-590	Tri-CAD Vigor Pentium-90	Xinetron Green Pentium 90MHz	Zenon Z-Titan Pentium 90MHz	ZEOS Pantera 90
List price (tested configuration)	$$$	$$$$	$$$$	$$$	$$$
Hard-disk capacity and interface	540Mb IDE	Two 527Mb IDE	1.2Gb SCSI-2	540Mb IDE	528Mb IDE
Dealers/Direct-distribution channel	○/●	●/●	○/●	○/●	○/●
Case style	Mini-tower	Mini-tower	Tower	Mini-tower	Tower
Power supply (and number of connectors)	200W (6)	200W (5)	250W (8)	230W (6)	200W (8)
DOS, Microsoft Windows version	DOS 6.2, Windows for Workgroups 3.11	DOS 6.21, Windows 3.11	DOS 6.2, Windows 3.11	DOS 6.2, Windows for Workgroups 3.11	DOS 6.2, Windows for Workgroups 3.11
Warranty	1 year	2 years parts, lifetime labor	2 years parts, 3 years labor	1 year parts, lifetime labor	1 year
On-site service charge	Included (1 year)	Included (1 year)	$90.00 (1 year)	Included (1 year)	$59.00 (1 year)
PROCESSOR AND MEMORY					
Bus architecture (primary)	ISA	ISA	ISA	ISA	ISA
Bus architecture (secondary)	PCI	PCI	PCI and VL-Bus	PCI	PCI
Motherboard manufacturer	Intel	Intel	Super Micro	Intel	ZEOS
Chip set manufacturer	Intel	Intel	OPTi	Intel	Intel
Processor upgrade path	ZIF	ZIF	ZIF	ZIF	ZIF
BIOS version (or date)	AMI (3/23/94)	AMI 1.00.03.AX12	AMI (2/1/94)	AMI (3/23/94)	Phoenix 4.03
Flash BIOS/16550 UART support	●/●	●/●	●/●	●/●	●/●
Installable system RAM	8Mb–128Mb	8Mb–128Mb	4Mb–128Mb	4Mb–128Mb	4Mb–192Mb
External RAM cache	256K	256K	256K–512K	256K	0–512K
Cache architecture	Direct-mapped	Direct-mapped	Direct-mapped	Direct-mapped	Direct-mapped
Cache write design	Write-through	Write-back	Write-back	Write-back	Write-back
COMPONENTS					
Available hard-disk sizes	260Mb–3.5Gb	340Mb–6.8Gb	170Mb–8Gb	213Mb–1Gb	214Mb–2Gb
Disk controller location	Motherboard (PCI)	PCI card	PCI card	Motherboard	Motherboard (PCI)
Accessible drive bays (5.25", 3.5")	3, 2	3, 2	4, 0	3, 2	4, 0
Internal drive bays (5.25", 3.5")	2, 2	0, 2	3, 0	0, 3	2, 4
Floppy disk drives	1.44Mb	1.44Mb	1.44Mb	1.44Mb	1.44Mb
CD-ROM drive	Sony CDU-33A-01	Sony CDU-33A	Toshiba 3401B	Mitsumi CRMCFX100102	Mitsumi CRMCFX0011D
ISA, EISA, MCA slots	4, 0, 0	5, 0, 0	3, 0, 0	5, 0, 0	5, 0, 0
VL-Bus, PCI, proprietary local-bus slots	0, 3, 0	0, 3, 0	2, 4, 0	0, 3, 0	0, 3, 0
Parallel, serial, mouse ports	1, 2, 0	1, 2, 0	1, 2, 0	2, 1, 1	1, 2, 0
Display circuitry location	PCI card	PCI card	PCI card	PCI card	PCI card
Video chip set manufacturer	S3	ATI	ATI	ATI	S3
Video RAM	2Mb–4Mb	2Mb	1Mb–2Mb	2Mb–4Mb	2Mb–4Mb

●—Yes   ○—No   N/A—Not applicable   INA—Information not available

End ■

COMPARISON CHART

MONITORS

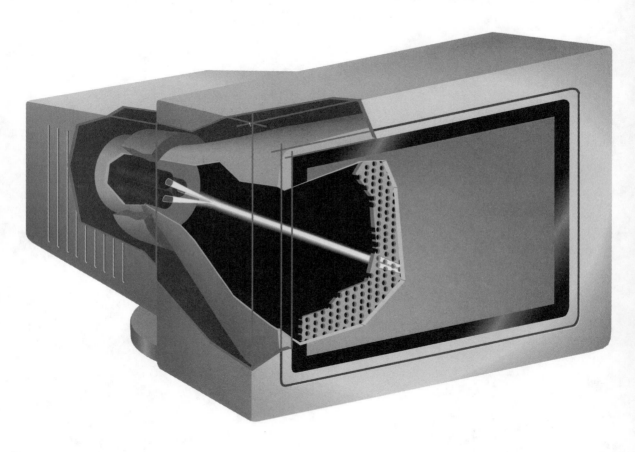

B.1 14-Inch Monitors

(Products listed in alphabetical order by company name)	Aamazing CM8428MX	ADI MicroScan 3E	ADI MicroScan 3E+	AOC CMLB-337	Arche 214MH VGA Monitor
Price	$	$	$	$	$
PHYSICAL SPECIFICATIONS					
Dimensions (HWD, in inches)	14 × 14.5 × 15.5	15 × 15 × 14	15 × 15 × 14	14.1 × 14 × 15	15 × 14 × 14
Weight (pounds)	27.6	28	28	27.2	25.4
Length of power cable (inches)	72	72	72	60	72
Adapter cable included	Captive to miniDB-15	Captive to miniDB-15	Captive to miniDB-15	Captive to DB-15	MiniDB-15 to miniDB-15
SIGNAL COMPATIBILITY					
1,280 × 1,024	○	●	●	○	○
1,024 × 768 (noninterlaced)	●	●	●	●	●
1,024 × 768 (interlaced)	●	●	●	●	●
Super VGA (800 × 600)	●	●	●	●	●
VGA (640 × 480)	●	●	●	●	●
MCGA/Hercules	●/○	●/○	●/○	○/○	○/○
Mac II/Apple II GS	○/○	○/○	○/○	●/●	○/○
OPERATIONAL FEATURES					
Fixed or variable frequency	Variable	Variable	Variable	Variable	Fixed
Maximum noninterlaced resolution (pixels)	1,024 × 768	1,024 × 768	1,024 × 768	1,024 × 768	1,024 × 768
Video bandwidth (MHz)	65	65	75	80	65
Vertical scanning frequency (Hz)	50–90	50–100	50–100	50–90	45–100
Horizontal scanning frequency (kHz)	32–48	30–50	30–58	30–60	32–49
Maximum vertical refresh rates (Hz)					
1,280 × 1,024	N/A	87	87	N/A	N/A
1,024 × 768 noninterlaced	60	60	72	72	60
Super VGA (800 × 600)	72	72	72	72	72
VGA (640 × 480)	72	72	72	72	72
Phosphor persistence	Medium-short	Medium-short	Medium-short	Medium-short	Medium-short
Dot pitch or aperture grill pitch (mm)	0.28	0.28	0.28	0.28	0.28
Analog or digital controls	Analog	Digital	Digital	Analog	Analog
Power consumption (watts)	90	85	85	80	90
Microprocessor included	○	●	●	○	○
Number of simultaneously stored settings	N/A	9	10	N/A	N/A
Number of user-definable settings	N/A	9	10	N/A	N/A
CONTROLS					
Brightness	●	●	●	●	●
Contrast	●	●	●	●	●
Color matching	○	○	○	○	○
Horizontal position	●	●	●	●	●
Vertical position	●	●	●	●	●
Horizontal size	●	●	●	●	○
Vertical size	●	●	●	●	●
Pincushioning	○	●	●	○	○
Barrel distortion	○	●	●	○	○
Degaussing	○	○	○	○	○
120-/240-volt switching	○	○	○	○	● (auto-sensing)
VLF/ELF radiation control	○/○	○/○	○/○	●/●	○/○

●—Yes ○—No N/A—Not applicable INA—Information not available

Table Continues →

ZIFF-DAVIS PRESS

■ 14-Inch Monitors

	Compaq 1024 Color Monitor	CTX CMS-1461	Darius HRN-1424	Dell UltraScan 14C	Dell UltraScan 14LR
Price	$	$	$	$	$
PHYSICAL SPECIFICATIONS					
Dimensions (HWD, in inches)	15 × 15 × 14	16 × 14.3 × 15	14 × 13.5 × 12.3	15 × 14 × 14.5	13.9 × 13.7 × 15.2
Weight (pounds)	28	22	24.8	27.3	26
Length of power cable (inches)	60	60	72	72	60
Adapter cable included	Captive to miniDB-15	Captive to DB-15	Captive to miniDB-15	Captive to miniDB-15	Captive to DB-15
SIGNAL COMPATIBILITY					
1,280 × 1,024	○	●	○	○	○
1,024 × 768 (noninterlaced)	●	●	●	●	●
1,024 × 768 (interlaced)	●	●	●	●	●
Super VGA (800 × 600)	●	●	●	●	●
VGA (640 × 480)	●	●	●	●	●
MCGA/Hercules	●/○	○/○	●/○	●/○	○/○
Mac II/Apple II GS	○/○	○/○	○/○	○/○	●/○
OPERATIONAL FEATURES					
Fixed or variable frequency	Variable	Variable	Variable	Variable	Variable
Maximum noninterlaced resolution (pixels)	1,024 × 768	1,024 × 768	1,024 × 768	1,024 × 768	1,024 × 768
Video bandwidth (MHz)	75	85	50	80	70
Vertical scanning frequency (Hz)	50–100	50–90	47–100	50–90	50–90
Horizontal scanning frequency (kHz)	30–58	30–60	31–60	30–60	30–58
Maximum vertical refresh rates (Hz)					
1,280 × 1,024	N/A	87	N/A	N/A	N/A
1,024 × 768 noninterlaced	72	70	70	72	72
Super VGA (800 × 600)	72	72	72	72	72
VGA (640 × 480)	75	72	72	72	73
Phosphor persistence	Medium-short	Medium-short	Medium-short	Medium-short	Medium-short
Dot pitch or aperture grill pitch (mm)	0.28	0.28	0.28	0.28	0.28
Analog or digital controls	Digital	Analog	Analog	Analog	Digital
Power consumption (watts)	85	80	75	110	90
Microprocessor included	●	○	○	○	●
Number of simultaneously stored settings	10	N/A	N/A	N/A	12
Number of user-definable settings	10	N/A	N/A	N/A	6
CONTROLS					
Brightness	●	●	●	●	●
Contrast	●	●	●	●	●
Color matching	○	○	○	○	○
Horizontal position	●	●	●	●	●
Vertical position	●	●	●	●	●
Horizontal size	●	●	●	●	●
Vertical size	●	●	●	●	●
Pincushioning	●	○	○	○	●
Barrel distortion	●	○	○	○	●
Degaussing	○	○	○	○	○
120-/240-volt switching	○	● (auto sensing)	○	○	○
VLF/ELF radiation control	○/○	Optional	○/○	○/○	●/●

●—Yes ○—No N/A—Not applicable INA—Information not available

14-Inch Monitors ■

	FORA Addonics C141	FORA Addonics C143	IBM PS/Value-Point 6312 Color Display	IBM PS/Value-Point 6314 Color Display	IOcomm ThinkSync 4E
Price	$	$	$	$	$
PHYSICAL SPECIFICATIONS					
Dimensions (HWD, in inches)	15 × 14 × 14.5	13.4 × 14 × 15	11 × 14 × 15	15 × 14 × 16	14.3 × 14.5 × 14.8
Weight (pounds)	27.3	24.2	24	33	26.2
Length of power cable (inches)	72	60	73	73	72
Adapter cable included	Captive to miniDB-15	Captive to miniDB-15	Captive to miniDB-15	MiniDB-15 to miniDB-15	Captive to miniDB-15
SIGNAL COMPATIBILITY					
1,280 × 1,024	○	○	○	○	●
1,024 × 768 (noninterlaced)	●	●	●	●	●
1,024 × 768 (interlaced)	●	●	●	●	●
Super VGA (800 × 600)	●	●	●	●	●
VGA (640 × 480)	●	●	●	●	●
MCGA/Hercules	●/○	○/○	●/○	●/○	●/○
Mac II/Apple II GS	○/○	○/○	○/○	○/○	○/○
OPERATIONAL FEATURES					
Fixed or variable frequency	Variable	Fixed	Variable	Variable	Variable
Maximum noninterlaced resolution (pixels)	1,024 × 768	1,024 × 768	1,024 × 768	1,024 × 768	1,024 × 768
Video bandwidth (MHz)	80	65	75	85	65
Vertical scanning frequency (Hz)	50–90	47–100	47–100	50–120	50–90
Horizontal scanning frequency (kHz)	30–60	32–48	31–50	30–60	32–48
Maximum vertical refresh rates (Hz)					
1,280 × 1,024	N/A	N/A	N/A	N/A	88
1,024 × 768 noninterlaced	72	60	60	72	60
Super VGA (800 × 600)	72	72	72	72	72
VGA (640 × 480)	72	72	75	75	72
Phosphor persistence	Medium-short	Medium-short	Short	Short	Medium-short
Dot pitch or aperture grill pitch (mm)	0.28	0.28	0.28	0.28	0.28
Analog or digital controls	Analog	Analog	Analog	Digital	Analog
Power consumption (watts)	110	100	85	80	89
Microprocessor included	○	○	○	●	○
Number of simultaneously stored settings	N/A	N/A	N/A	13	N/A
Number of user-definable settings	N/A	N/A	N/A	13	N/A
CONTROLS					
Brightness	●	●	●	●	●
Contrast	●	●	●	●	●
Color matching	○	○	○	●	○
Horizontal position	●	●	●	●	●
Vertical position	●	●	●	●	●
Horizontal size	●	●	●	●	○
Vertical size	●	●	●	●	●
Pincushioning	○	○	○	●	●
Barrel distortion	○	○	○	●	○
Degaussing	○	○	○	○	○
120-/240-volt switching	○	●	○	○	● (auto-sensing)
VLF/ELF radiation control	○/○	○/○	●/○	●/○	○/○

●—Yes   ○—No   N/A—Not applicable   INA—Information not available   **Table Continues →**

14-Inch Monitors

	MAG LX1460	MAG MX14S	Mitsuba 710VX	Mitsubishi Diamond Pro 14	Neotec NT-1456
Price	$	$	$	$	$
PHYSICAL SPECIFICATIONS					
Dimensions (HWD, in inches)	14 × 14 × 15	14.3 × 14 × 16	14 × 14 × 14	13.9 × 13.7 × 15.2	14.3 × 14.3 × 16
Weight (pounds)	26.5	34.0	27.3	26.5	27.5
Length of power cable (inches)	60	60	70	60	72
Adapter cable included	Captive to miniDB-15	Captive to DB-15	Captive to miniDB-15	Captive to miniDB-15	Captive to DB-15
SIGNAL COMPATIBILITY					
1,280 × 1,024	●	●	○	○	○
1,024 × 768 (noninterlaced)	●	●	●	●	●
1,024 × 768 (interlaced)	●	●	●	●	●
Super VGA (800 × 600)	●	●	●	●	●
VGA (640 × 480)	●	●	●	●	●
MCGA/Hercules	●/○	○/○	○/○	○/○	●/○
Mac II/Apple II GS	●/○	●/○	○/○	●/○	○/○
OPERATIONAL FEATURES					
Fixed or variable frequency	Variable	Variable	Variable	Variable	Variable
Maximum noninterlaced resolution (pixels)	1,024 × 768	1,280 × 1,024	1,024 × 768	1,024 × 768	1,280 × 960
Video bandwidth (MHz)	80	100	65	70	75
Vertical scanning frequency (Hz)	50–100	50–120	56–87	50–90	50–120
Horizontal scanning frequency (kHz)	30–60	30–64	32–48	30–58	30–56
Maximum vertical refresh rates (Hz)					
1,280 × 1,024	87	60	N/A	N/A	N/A
1,024 × 768 noninterlaced	72	76	60	72	70
Super VGA (800 × 600)	85	76	72	72	72
VGA (640 × 480)	85	76	72	73	72
Phosphor persistence	Medium-short	Medium-short	Medium-short	Medium-short	Medium-short
Dot pitch or aperture grill pitch (mm)	0.28	0.25	0.28	0.28	0.28
Analog or digital controls	Analog	Digital	Analog	Digital	Analog
Power consumption (watts)	110	110	90	90	80
Microprocessor included	○	●	○	●	○
Number of simultaneously stored settings	N/A	17	N/A	12	N/A
Number of user-definable settings	N/A	8	N/A	6	N/A
CONTROLS					
Brightness	●	●	●	●	●
Contrast	●	●	●	●	●
Color matching	○	○	○	○	○
Horizontal position	●	●	●	●	●
Vertical position	●	●	●	●	●
Horizontal size	●	●	○	●	●
Vertical size	●	●	●	●	●
Pincushioning	●	○	○	●	○
Barrel distortion	○	○	○	●	○
Degaussing	●	○	○	○	○
120-/240-volt switching	●	○	○	○	○
VLF/ELF radiation control	○/○	●/●	○/○	●/●	○/○

●—Yes ○—No N/A—Not applicable INA—Information not available

14-Inch Monitors

	Optiquest 1000S	Optiquest 1500D	Packard Bell PB8548SVGL	Philips Magnavox MagnaScan/14 Model CM9214	Qume QM857
Price	$	$	$	$	$
PHYSICAL SPECIFICATIONS					
Dimensions (HWD, in inches)	14 × 14 × 14	15 × 15 × 14	12.5 × 14.5 × 15.75	13.8 × 14 × 15.5	13.5 × 14 × 15
Weight (pounds)	24.2	28	35	35	35
Length of power cable (inches)	72	72	72	78	60
Adapter cable included	Captive to miniDB-15	Captive to miniDB-15	Captive to miniDB-15	Captive to DB-15	Captive to DB-15
SIGNAL COMPATIBILITY					
1,280 × 1,024	○	●	○	○	○
1,024 × 768 (noninterlaced)	●	●	●	●	●
1,024 × 768 (interlaced)	●	●	●	●	●
Super VGA (800 × 600)	●	●	●	●	●
VGA (640 × 480)	●	●	●	●	●
MCGA/Hercules	○/○	●/○	○/○	○/○	○/○
Mac II/Apple II GS	○/○	○/○	○/○	●/○	●/○
OPERATIONAL FEATURES					
Fixed or variable frequency	Fixed	Variable	Fixed	Variable	Variable
Maximum noninterlaced resolution (pixels)	1,024 × 768	1,024 × 768	1,024 × 768	1,024 × 768	1,024 × 768
Video bandwidth (MHz)	65	75	65	75	65
Vertical scanning frequency (Hz)	47–100	50–100	50–90	50–100	50–90
Horizontal scanning frequency (kHz)	32–48	30–58	32–48	30–58	30–60
Maximum vertical refresh rates (Hz)					
1,280 × 1,024	N/A	87	N/A	N/A	N/A
1,024 × 768 noninterlaced	60	72	60	70	72
Super VGA (800 × 600)	72	72	72	72	72
VGA (640 × 480)	72	72	72	72	72
Phosphor persistence	Medium-short	Medium-short	Medium-short	Medium-short	Medium-short
Dot pitch or aperture grill pitch (mm)	0.28	0.28	0.28	0.28	0.28
Analog or digital controls	Analog	Digital	Analog	Analog	Analog
Power consumption (watts)	100	85	85	85	80
Microprocessor included	○	●	○	○	○
Number of simultaneously stored settings	N/A	10	N/A	N/A	N/A
Number of user-definable settings	N/A	10	N/A	N/A	N/A
CONTROLS					
Brightness	●	●	●	●	●
Contrast	●	●	●	●	●
Color matching	○	○	○	○	○
Horizontal position	●	●	●	●	●
Vertical position	●	●	●	●	●
Horizontal size	●	●	●	●	●
Vertical size	●	●	●	●	●
Pincushioning	○	●	○	○	○
Barrel distortion	○	●	○	○	○
Degaussing	○	○	○	○	○
120-/240-volt switching	●	○	●	○	○
VLF/ELF radiation control	○/○	○/○	●/○	○/○	Optional

●—Yes　○—No　N/A—Not applicable　INA—Information not available

Table Continues →

■ 14-Inch Monitors

	Relisys RE-1458	Sampo AlphaScan Plus	Samtron SC-428TX	Seiko CM1450	Sony CPD-1304S
Price	$	$	$	$	$
PHYSICAL SPECIFICATIONS					
Dimensions (HWD, in inches)	13.8 × 15 × 15.3	15 × 14 × 14.5	14 × 13.5 × 15	13.5 × 13.8 × 14	14 × 13.8 × 16.3
Weight (pounds)	35	27.3	35	35	35
Length of power cable (inches)	72	72	72	72	60
Adapter cable included	Captive to DB-15	Captive to miniDB-15	Captive to miniDB-15	Captive to miniDB-15	Captive to DB-15
SIGNAL COMPATIBILITY					
1,280 × 1,024	○	○	○	○	○
1,024 × 768 (noninterlaced)	●	●	●	●	●
1,024 × 768 (interlaced)	●	●	●	●	●
Super VGA (800 × 600)	●	●	●	●	●
VGA (640 × 480)	●	●	●	●	●
MCGA/Hercules	○/○	●/○	●/○	●/○	○/○
Mac II/Apple II GS	○/○	○/○	○/○	○/○	●/○
OPERATIONAL FEATURES					
Fixed or variable frequency	Variable	Variable	Fixed	Variable	Variable
Maximum noninterlaced resolution (pixels)	1,024 × 768	1,024 × 768	1,024 × 768	1,024 × 768	1,024 × 768
Video bandwidth (MHz)	75	80	65	60	60
Vertical scanning frequency (Hz)	50–120	50–90	50–90	50–90	55–110
Horizontal scanning frequency (kHz)	30–58	30–60	32–48	31–50	28–57
Maximum vertical refresh rates (Hz)					
1,280 × 1,024	N/A	N/A	N/A	N/A	N/A
1,024 × 768 noninterlaced	70	72	60	60	70
Super VGA (800 × 600)	72	72	72	72	72
VGA (640 × 480)	72	72	72	72	72
Phosphor persistence	Medium-short	Medium-short	Medium-short	Medium-short	Medium-short
Dot pitch or aperture grill pitch (mm)	0.28	0.28	0.28	0.25	0.25
Analog or digital controls	Analog	Analog	Analog	Analog	Analog
Power consumption (watts)	110	110	70	150	100
Microprocessor included	○	○	○	○	○
Number of simultaneously stored settings	N/A	N/A	N/A	N/A	N/A
Number of user-definable settings	N/A	N/A	N/A	N/A	N/A
CONTROLS					
Brightness	●	●	●	●	●
Contrast	●	●	●	●	●
Color matching	○	○	○	○	○
Horizontal position	●	●	●	●	●
Vertical position	●	●	●	●	●
Horizontal size	●	●	●	●	●
Vertical size	●	●	●	●	●
Pincushioning	○	○	○	○	○
Barrel distortion	○	○	○	○	○
Degaussing	○	○	○	○	○
120-/240-volt switching	● (auto-sensing)	○	○	○	● (auto-sensing)
VLF/ELF radiation control	○/●	○/○	●/●	○/○	●/●

●—Yes   ○—No   N/A—Not applicable   INA—Information not available

14-Inch Monitors ■

	Sunshine CM8+	TVM MediaScan 4A+	ViewSonic 5E	ViewSonic 6	WEN JK1466 Color Monitor
Price	$	$	$	$	$
PHYSICAL SPECIFICATIONS					
Dimensions (HWD, in inches)	13.8 × 14.3 × 15.5	15 × 15 × 15	14 × 14 × 15	15 × 14 × 15	14.5 × 14.5 × 14
Weight (pounds)	35	35	30.8	24.2	26.7
Length of power cable (inches)	72	60	54	60	72
Adapter cable included	Captive to miniDB-15	Captive to miniDB-15	Captive to miniDB-15	Captive to miniDB-15	Captive to miniDB-15
SIGNAL COMPATIBILITY					
1,280 × 1,024	○	○	○	○	○
1,024 × 768 (noninterlaced)	●	●	●	●	●
1,024 × 768 (interlaced)	●	●	●	●	●
Super VGA (800 × 600)	●	●	●	●	●
VGA (640 × 480)	●	●	●	●	●
MCGA/Hercules	○/○	●/○	●/○	●/○	●/●
Mac II/Apple II GS	○/○	○/○	○/○	○/○	●/●
OPERATIONAL FEATURES					
Fixed or variable frequency	Variable	Fixed	Variable	Variable	Variable
Maximum noninterlaced resolution (pixels)	1,024 × 768	1,024 × 768	1,024 × 768	1,024 × 768	1,024 × 768
Video bandwidth (MHz)	64	65	80	65	70
Vertical scanning frequency (Hz)	50–90	47–100	50–90	50–90	48–90
Horizontal scanning frequency (kHz)	30–48	32–48	31–60	30–50	30–59
Maximum vertical refresh rates (Hz)					
1,280 × 1,024	N/A	N/A	N/A	N/A	N/A
1,024 × 768 noninterlaced	60	60	72	60	72
Super VGA (800 × 600)	72	72	72	72	72
VGA (640 × 480)	70	72	72	72	72
Phosphor persistence	Medium-short	Medium-short	Medium-short	Medium-short	Medium-short
Dot pitch or aperture grill pitch (mm)	0.28	0.28	0.28	0.28	0.28
Analog or digital controls	Analog	Analog	Analog	Analog	Analog
Power consumption (watts)	75	100	100	85	80
Microprocessor included	○	○	○	○	○
Number of simultaneously stored settings	N/A	N/A	N/A	N/A	N/A
Number of user-definable settings	N/A	N/A	N/A	N/A	N/A
CONTROLS					
Brightness	●	●	●	●	●
Contrast	●	●	●	●	●
Color matching	○	○	○	○	○
Horizontal position	●	●	●	●	●
Vertical position	●	●	●	○	●
Horizontal size	○	●	●	●	○
Vertical size	●	●	●	●	●
Pincushioning	○	○	○	○	○
Barrel distortion	○	○	○	○	○
Degaussing	○	○	○	○	○
120-/240-volt switching	○	●	●	○	●
VLF/ELF radiation control	Optional	○/○	○/○	○/○	Optional

●—Yes   ○—No   N/A—Not applicable   INA—Information not available   **End ■**

■ B.2   15-Inch Monitors

(Products listed in alphabetical order by company name)	Aamazing CM1528FS	AcerView 56L	ADI MicroScan 4A	AOC CM-536	Compaq QVision 150
Price	$	$	$	$	$
PHYSICAL SPECIFICATIONS					
Dimensions (HWD, in inches)	14.3 × 14.3 × 15	14 × 14 × 15	15 × 15 × 15	14.5 × 14.5 × 15	16 × 16 × 17
Weight (pounds)	27.1	35	30	31.9	45
Length of power cable (inches)	72	72	72	60	80
Adapter cable included	MiniDB-15 to miniDB-15	Captive to miniDB-15	Captive to miniDB-15	Captive to DB-15	BNC-5 to miniDB-15
SIGNAL COMPATIBILITY					
1,280 × 1,024	●	○	●	●	○
1,024 × 768 (noninterlaced)	●	●	●	●	●
1,024 × 768 (interlaced)	●	●	●	●	○
Super VGA (800 × 600)	●	●	●	●	●
VGA (640 × 480)	●	●	●	●	●
MCGA/Hercules	●/○	●/○	●/○	○/○	●/●
Mac II/Apple II GS	○/○	●/○	○/○	●/●	●/●
OPERATIONAL FEATURES					
Fixed or variable frequency	Variable	Variable	Variable	Variable	Variable
Maximum noninterlaced resolution (pixels)	1,280 × 1,024	1,024 × 768	1,024 × 768	1,280 × 1,024	1,024 × 768
Video bandwidth (MHz)	85	80	75	100	75
Vertical scanning frequency (Hz)	47–104	50–90	50–100	50–90	50–100
Horizontal scanning frequency (kHz)	28–64	31–60	30–58	30–68	32–58
Maximum vertical refresh rates (Hz)					
1,280 × 1,024	72	N/A	87	60	N/A
1,024 × 768 noninterlaced	74	72	72	72	72
Super VGA (800 × 600)	74	72	72	72	72
VGA (640 × 480)	74	84	72	72	75
Phosphor persistence	Medium-short	Medium	Medium-short	Medium-short	Medium-short
Dot pitch or aperture grill pitch (mm)	0.28	0.28	0.28	0.28	0.26
Analog or digital controls	Analog	Digital	Digital	Digital	Digital
Power consumption (watts)	132	110	90	110	175
Microprocessor included	○	●	●	●	●
Number of simultaneously stored settings	N/A	32	10	36	14
Number of user-definable settings	N/A	32	10	36	6
CONTROLS					
Brightness	●	●	●	●	●
Contrast	●	●	●	●	●
Color matching	○	○	○	○	○
Horizontal position	●	●	●	●	●
Vertical position	●	●	●	●	●
Horizontal size	●	●	●	●	●
Vertical size	●	●	●	●	●
Pincushioning	○	●	●	○	○
Barrel distortion	○	●	●	○	○
Degaussing	○	○	○	○	○
120-/240-volt switching	○	○	○	● (auto-sensing)	○
VLF/ELF radiation control	○/○	●/●	○/○	Optional	●/●

●—Yes   ○—No   N/A—Not applicable   INA—Information not available

15-Inch Monitors

	Dell UltraScan 15FS	Dell UltraScan 15LR	FORA Addonics C152/LR	Hitachi/Nissei SuperScan 15	IBM PS/Value-Point 6319 Color Display
Price	$	$	$	$	$
PHYSICAL SPECIFICATIONS					
Dimensions (HWD, in inches)	15 × 14 × 15	15.5 × 14.5 × 16.5	14 × 14 × 15	15 × 14 × 16	16 × 15 × 16
Weight (pounds)	35	40.2	35	37.8	34
Length of power cable (inches)	72	72	60	72	73
Adapter cable included	Captive to miniDB-15	Captive to miniDB-15	Captive to miniDB-15	Captive to DB-15	MiniDB-15 to miniDB-15
SIGNAL COMPATIBILITY					
1,280 × 1,024	○	○	○	○	○
1,024 × 768 (noninterlaced)	●	●	●	●	●
1,024 × 768 (interlaced)	●	●	●	●	●
Super VGA (800 × 600)	●	●	●	●	●
VGA (640 × 480)	●	●	●	●	●
MCGA/Hercules	●/○	●/○	●/○	○/○	●/○
Mac II/Apple II GS	○/○	○/○	●/○	●/○	○/○
OPERATIONAL FEATURES					
Fixed or variable frequency	Variable	Variable	Variable	Variable	Variable
Maximum noninterlaced resolution (pixels)	1,024 × 768	1,024 × 768	1,024 × 768	1,024 × 768	1,024 × 768
Video bandwidth (MHz)	80	75	80	75	85
Vertical scanning frequency (Hz)	50–90	55–90	50–90	50–100	50–120
Horizontal scanning frequency (kHz)	30–60	32–57	31–60	30–58	30–60
Maximum vertical refresh rates (Hz)					
1,280 × 1,024	N/A	N/A	N/A	N/A	N/A
1,024 × 768 noninterlaced	72	70	72	72	72
Super VGA (800 × 600)	72	72	72	72	72
VGA (640 × 480)	72	72	84	72	75
Phosphor persistence	Medium-short	Medium-short	Medium	Medium-short	Short
Dot pitch or aperture grill pitch (mm)	0.28	0.28	0.28	0.28	0.28
Analog or digital controls	Analog	Analog	Digital	Analog	Digital
Power consumption (watts)	120	120	110	110	80
Microprocessor included	○	○	●	○	●
Number of simultaneously stored settings	N/A	N/A	32	N/A	13
Number of user-definable settings	N/A	N/A	32	N/A	13
CONTROLS					
Brightness	●	●	●	●	●
Contrast	●	●	●	●	●
Color matching	○	○	○	○	●
Horizontal position	●	●	●	●	●
Vertical position	●	●	●	●	●
Horizontal size	●	●	●	●	●
Vertical size	●	●	●	●	●
Pincushioning	○	●	●	○	●
Barrel distortion	○	○	●	○	●
Degaussing	○	●	○	○	○
120-/240-volt switching	○	○	○	○	○
VLF/ELF radiation control	○/○	●/●	●/●	●/●	●/○

●—Yes   ○—No   N/A—Not applicable   INA—Information not available

Table Continues →

ZIFF-DAVIS PRESS

■ 15-Inch Monitors

	IOcomm ThinkSync 5	MAG MX15F	Nanao Flexscan F340iW	NEC MultiSync 3FGX	NEC MultiSync 4FG
Price	$	$	$	$	$
PHYSICAL SPECIFICATIONS					
Dimensions (HWD, in inches)	14.3 × 14.5 × 15	14 × 14 × 16.5	14.9 × 14.4 × 16.2	15.6 × 14.6 × 16.3	15.6 × 14.6 × 16.3
Weight (pounds)	31	35.9	35.2	36.5	39.2
Length of power cable (inches)	72	60	80	72	72
Adapter cable included	MiniDB-15 to miniDB-15	Captive to DB-15	Captive to miniDB-15	Captive to DB-15	Captive to DB-15
SIGNAL COMPATIBILITY					
1,280 × 1,024	●	●	○	○	○
1,024 × 768 (noninterlaced)	●	●	●	●	●
1,024 × 768 (interlaced)	●	●	●	●	●
Super VGA (800 × 600)	●	●	●	●	●
VGA (640 × 480)	●	●	●	●	●
MCGA/Hercules	●/○	○/○	●/○	●/○	●/○
Mac II/Apple II GS	○/○	●/○	●/●	●/○	●/○
OPERATIONAL FEATURES					
Fixed or variable frequency	Variable	Variable	Variable	Variable	Variable
Maximum noninterlaced resolution (pixels)	1,280 × 1,024	1,280 × 1,024	1,024 × 768	1,024 × 768	1,024 × 768
Video bandwidth (MHz)	100	100	75	65	75
Vertical scanning frequency (Hz)	40–100	50–120	55–90	55–90	55–90
Horizontal scanning frequency (kHz)	30–65	30–68	27–61	32–49	27–57
Maximum vertical refresh rates (Hz)					
1,280 × 1,024	60	60	N/A	N/A	N/A
1,024 × 768 noninterlaced	76	76	76	60	70
Super VGA (800 × 600)	76	76	90	72	80
VGA (640 × 480)	72	76	90	72	90
Phosphor persistence	Medium-short	Medium-short	Medium-short	Medium-short	Medium-short
Dot pitch or aperture grill pitch (mm)	0.28	0.28	0.28	0.28	0.28
Analog or digital controls	Analog	Digital	Digital	Analog	Digital
Power consumption (watts)	110	110	100	100	105
Microprocessor included	○	●	●	○	●
Number of simultaneously stored settings	N/A	17	28	N/A	19
Number of user-definable settings	N/A	8	28	N/A	4
CONTROLS					
Brightness	●	●	●	●	●
Contrast	●	●	●	●	●
Color matching	○	○	●	○	●
Horizontal position	●	●	●	●	●
Vertical position	●	●	●	●	●
Horizontal size	●	●	●	●	●
Vertical size	●	●	●	●	●
Pincushioning	●	○	●	●	●
Barrel distortion	○	○	●	●	●
Degaussing	○	○	●	●	●
120-/240-volt switching	● (auto-sensing)	○	○	○	○
VLF/ELF radiation control	○/○	●/●	●/●	●/●	●/●

●—Yes ○—No N/A—Not applicable INA—Information not available

15-Inch Monitors

	Optiquest 2000D	Optiquest 2000DX	Relisys RE-1558	Sampo AlphaScan 15	Sunshine CM15C
Price	$	$	$	$	$
PHYSICAL SPECIFICATIONS					
Dimensions (HWD, in inches)	15 × 15 × 15	14 × 14 × 15	15.8 × 15 × 16.3	15 × 14 × 15	14.5 × 14.8 × 15.5
Weight (pounds)	30	35	35	35	35
Length of power cable (inches)	72	72	72	72	72
Adapter cable included	Captive to miniDB-15	Captive to miniDB-15	Captive to DB-15	Captive to miniDB-15	Captive to miniDB-15
SIGNAL COMPATIBILITY					
1,280 × 1,024	●	○	○	●	●
1,024 × 768 (noninterlaced)	●	●	●	●	●
1,024 × 768 (interlaced)	●	●	●	●	●
Super VGA (800 × 600)	●	●	●	●	●
VGA (640 × 480)	●	●	●	●	●
MCGA/Hercules	●/○	●/○	○/○	●/○	○/○
Mac II/Apple II GS	○/○	●/○	○/○	○/○	○/○
OPERATIONAL FEATURES					
Fixed or variable frequency	Variable	Variable	Variable	Variable	Variable
Maximum noninterlaced resolution (pixels)	1,024 × 768	1,024 × 768	1,024 × 768	1,280 × 1,024	1,280 × 1,024
Video bandwidth (MHz)	75	80	75	80	85
Vertical scanning frequency (Hz)	50–100	50–90	50–120	50–90	40–90
Horizontal scanning frequency (kHz)	30–58	31–60	30–58	30–64	30–64
Maximum vertical refresh rates (Hz)					
1,280 × 1,024	87	N/A	N/A	60	60
1,024 × 768 noninterlaced	72	72	70	72	76
Super VGA (800 × 600)	72	72	72	72	72
VGA (640 × 480)	72	84	72	72	70
Phosphor persistence	Medium-short	Medium	Medium-short	Medium-short	Medium-short
Dot pitch or aperture grill pitch (mm)	0.28	0.28	0.28	0.28	0.28
Analog or digital controls	Digital	Digital	Analog	Analog	Analog
Power consumption (watts)	90	110	110	120	100
Microprocessor included	●	●	○	○	○
Number of simultaneously stored settings	10	32	N/A	N/A	N/A
Number of user-definable settings	10	32	N/A	N/A	N/A
CONTROLS					
Brightness	●	●	●	●	●
Contrast	●	●	●	●	●
Color matching	○	○	○	○	○
Horizontal position	●	●	●	●	●
Vertical position	●	●	●	●	●
Horizontal size	●	●	●	●	●
Vertical size	●	●	●	●	●
Pincushioning	●	●	○	○	○
Barrel distortion	●	●	○	○	○
Degaussing	○	○	○	○	●
120-/240-volt switching	○	○	● (auto-sensing)	○	○
VLF/ELF radiation control	○/○	●/●	○/●	○/○	Optional

●—Yes ○—No N/A—Not applicable INA—Information not available

Table Continues →

15-Inch Monitors

	Taxan MultiVision 550	TVM LowRadiation 5A+	ViewSonic 6FS
Price	$	$	$
PHYSICAL SPECIFICATIONS			
Dimensions (HWD, in inches)	15 × 14 × 15	15.3 × 14.5 × 16	14 × 14 × 15
Weight (pounds)	35	35	35
Length of power cable (inches)	72	72	60
Adapter cable included	Captive to miniDB-15	Captive to miniDB-15	Captive to miniDB-15
SIGNAL COMPATIBILITY			
1,280 × 1,024	○	●	●
1,024 × 768 (noninterlaced)	●	●	●
1,024 × 768 (interlaced)	●	●	●
Super VGA (800 × 600)	●	●	●
VGA (640 × 480)	●	●	●
MCGA/Hercules	●/○	●/○	●/○
Mac II/Apple II GS	○/○	○/○	○/○
OPERATIONAL FEATURES			
Fixed or variable frequency	Variable	Variable	Variable
Maximum noninterlaced resolution (pixels)	1,024 × 768	1,024 × 768	1,024 × 768
Video bandwidth (MHz)	80	65	80
Vertical scanning frequency (Hz)	50–90	40–100	50–90
Horizontal scanning frequency (kHz)	30–60	30–57	31–60
Maximum vertical refresh rates (Hz)			
1,280 × 1,024	N/A	88	87
1,024 × 768 noninterlaced	70	72	72
Super VGA (800 × 600)	72	72	72
VGA (640 × 480)	72	72	84
Phosphor persistence	Medium-short	Medium-short	Medium
Dot pitch or aperture grill pitch (mm)	0.28	0.28	0.28
Analog or digital controls	Analog	Digital	Digital
Power consumption (watts)	110	90	110
Microprocessor included	○	●	●
Number of simultaneously stored settings	N/A	15	32
Number of user-definable settings	N/A	15	32
CONTROLS			
Brightness	●	●	●
Contrast	●	●	●
Color matching	○	○	○
Horizontal position	●	●	●
Vertical position	●	●	●
Horizontal size	●	●	●
Vertical size	●	●	●
Pincushioning	○	○	●
Barrel distortion	○	○	●
Degaussing	○	○	○
120-/240-volt switching	○	○	○
VLF/ELF radiation control	○/○	●/○	●/●

●—Yes ○—No N/A—Not applicable INA—Information not available

End ■

B.3   16-Inch Monitors

(Products listed in alphabetical order by company name)	Dell Graphics Performance Display 16C	HP D1188A	Idek MF-5117	IOcomm ThinkSync 17 CM–7126	Mitsubishi Diamond Scan 16L
Price	$	$$$	$$	$$	$$
PHYSICAL SPECIFICATIONS					
Tilt/swivel base	●	○	●	●	●
Case dimensions (HWD, in inches)	16 × 15.8 × 17.8	14 × 15.8 × 17.9	16.3 × 15.8 × 16.3	15.3 × 16 × 16.5	14 × 15.8 × 17.9
Weight (pounds)	42	43	43	50	42
Type of connector(s) on monitor	DB-9, BNC-5	BNC-5	DB-15	BNC-5	BNC-5
COMPATABILITY					
1,280 × 1,024	○	●	○	●	●
1,024 × 768 (noninterlaced)	●	●	●	●	●
1,024 × 768 (interlaced)	●	●	●	●	●
Super VGA (800 × 600)	●	●	●	●	●
VGA (640 × 480)	●	●	●	●	●
MCGA	●	○	●	●	○
EGA	●	○	●	○	○
OPERATIONAL FEATURES					
Maximum resolution (pixels)	1,280 × 800	1,280 × 1,024	1,024 × 768	1,280 × 1,024	1,280 × 1,024
Video bandwidth (MHz)	50 (analog), 30 (digital/TLL)	100 (analog)	65 (analog)	136 (analog)	100 (analog)
Vertical scanning frequency range (Hz)	50–80	50–90	50–90	50–90	50–90
Horizontal scanning frequency range (kHz)	20–50	30–64	21.9–50	30–75	30–64
Can maintain image size across resolution modes	●	●	●	●	●
Phosphor persistence	Short	Medium	Short	Medium-short	Medium
Dot pitch (mm)	0.31	0.28	0.28	0.26	0.31
Inputs:					
Analog D-sub connector	9-pin mini	None	15-pin standard	None	None
Analog BNC coaxial connector (sync on green, composite sync, and separate sync)	●	●	●	●	●
Digital/TTL	●	○	●	○	○
CONTROLS					
Brightness	● (analog)	● (analog)	● (analog)	● (analog)	● (analog)
Contrast	● (analog)	● (analog)	● (analog)	● (analog)	● (analog)
Color	● (analog)	○	○	○	○
Horizontal position	● (analog)	● (analog)	● (analog)	● (digital)	● (analog)
Vertical position	● (analog)	● (analog)	● (analog)	● (digital)	● (analog)
Horizontal size	● (analog)	● (analog)	● (analog)	● (digital)	● (analog)
Vertical size	● (analog)	● (analog)	● (analog)	● (digital)	● (analog)
Pincushioning	● (analog)	○	● (digital)	● (digital)	● (digital)
Convergence	● (analog)	○	○	○	○
Degaussing	○	●	○	○	●
8/16/64-color switch	●	○	●	○	○
Text color switch	●	○	○	○	○
120/240-volt switch	○	●	●	○	●

●—Yes   ○—No   N/A—Not applicable   INA—Information not available

Table Continues →

■ 16-Inch Monitors

	Mitsubishi HL6615(TK)	Nanao FlexScan 9070U	Nanao FlexScan 9080i	NEC MultiSync 4D	Philips FC17AS
Price	$$	$$	$$	$$	$$$
PHYSICAL SPECIFICATIONS					
Tilt/swivel base	●	●	●	●	●
Case dimensions (HWD, in inches)	14 × 15.8 × 17.9	15.9 × 15.8 × 17.7	15.9 × 15.8 × 17.7	15.4 × 15.2 × 18.7	15.6 × 16.1 × 18.1
Weight (pounds)	44	42	42	50	51
Type of connector(s) on monitor	BNC-5	DB-9, BNC-5	DB-9	DB-15	BNC-5
COMPATABILITY					
1,280 × 1,024	●	○	●	○	●
1,024 × 768 (noninterlaced)	●	●	●	●	●
1,024 × 768 (interlaced)	●	●	●	●	●
Super VGA (800 × 600)	●	●	●	●	●
VGA (640 × 480)	●	●	●	●	●
MCGA	○	●	●	●	○
EGA	○	●	○	●	○
OPERATIONAL FEATURES					
Maximum resolution (pixels)	1,280 × 1,024	1,280 × 800	1,280 × 1,024	1,024 × 768	1,280 × 1,024
Video bandwidth (MHz)	110 (analog)	50 (analog), 30 (digital/TLL)	60 (analog)	75 (analog)	110 (analog)
Vertical scanning frequency range (Hz)	50–120	50–90	50–90	50–90	50–140
Horizontal scanning frequency range (kHz)	30–64	20–50	30–64	30–57	30–66
Can maintain image size across resolution modes	●	●	●	●	○
Phosphor persistence	Medium	Short	Short	Short	Medium-short
Dot pitch (mm)	0.31	0.28	0.28	0.28	0.26
Inputs:					
Analog D-sub connector	None	9-pin	9-pin	15-pin mini or 15-pin standard	None
Analog BNC coaxial connector (sync on green, composite sync, and separate sync)	●	●	●	●	●
Digital/TTL	○	●	○	○	○
CONTROLS					
Brightness	● (analog)	● (analog)	● (analog)	● (analog)	● (analog)
Contrast	● (analog)	● (analog)	● (analog)	● (analog)	● (analog)
Color	○	○	○	○	○
Horizontal position	● (analog)	● (analog)	● (digital)	● (digital)	● (analog)
Vertical position	● (analog)	● (analog)	● (digital)	● (digital)	● (analog)
Horizontal size	● (analog)	● (analog)	● (digital)	● (digital)	● (analog)
Vertical size	● (analog)	● (analog)	● (digital)	● (digital)	● (analog)
Pincushioning	● (digital)	● (analog)	● (digital)	○	○
Convergence	○	● (analog)	● (analog)	○	○
Degaussing	●	○	○	●	●
8/16/64-color switch	○	●	○	○	○
Text color switch	○	●	●	○	○
120/240-volt switch	●	○	○	○	●

●—Yes ○—No N/A—Not applicable INA—Information not available

End ■

B.4   17-Inch Monitors

(Products listed in alphabetical order by company name)	AcerView 76i	Addonics 172 GLR	ADI MicroScan 5EP	Altima V-Scan 80	Amdek AM/817E
List price	None quoted	$	None quoted	None quoted	$
Estimated street price	$	$	$	$	None quoted
Tube manufacturer	Matsushita	Matsushita	Hitachi	Hitachi	Hitachi
Type of tube	Flat-square	Flat-square	Flat-square	Flat-square	Flat-square
Dot pitch or aperture-grill pitch (mm)	0.27	0.28	0.28	0.26	0.26
Antiglare treatment	AGRAS coating	AGRAS coating	Bonded panel	Silica coating	Silica coating
Active screen size (diagonal, in inches)	16.1	16.1	15.5	15.9	16.6
Image can be extended to screen edges	●	●	●	●	●
Dimensions (HWD, in inches)	16.9 x 16.3 x 16.8	17.1 x 16.3 x 16.8	15.8 x 16.1 x 17.5	16.1 x 16.1 x 18	16 x 16.5 x 18.3
Weight	42 lbs. 8 oz.	42 lbs. 10 oz.	40 lbs. 6 oz.	49 lbs. 8 oz.	46 lbs. 6 oz.
Type of adapter:					
Captive to 15-pin/15-pin to 15-pin	○/●	○/●	○/●	○/●	○/○
BNC-3 to 15-pin/BNC-5 to 15-pin	○/○	○/○	○/○	○/●	○/●
FCC certification	Class B	Class B	Class B	Class B	Class B
Energy Star–certified/VESA DPMS–compliant	●/●	●/●	●/●	○/○	●/●
TCO compliance claimed	○	○	○	○	○
Color-matching software	INA	INA	INA	INA	INA
OPERATIONAL FEATURES					
Vertical scanning frequency (Hz)	50–90	50–90	50–100	50–90	47–105
Horizontal scanning frequency (kHz)	30–64	31–64	30–64	30–94	24–82
Maximum noninterlaced resolution	1,280 x 1,024	1,280 x 1,024	1,280 x 1,024	1,600 x 1,280	1,600 x 1,200
Maximum interlaced resolution	1,280 x 1,024	1,024 x 768	1,600 x 1,280	1,600 x 1,280	1,280 x 1,024
Maximum noninterlaced refresh rates (Hz):					
1,280 x 1,024; 1,024 x 768	60, 72	60, 72	60, 76	72, 90	76, 76
800 x 600; 640 x 480	72, 60	72, 75	90, 100	90, 90	72, 72
Claimed power consumption (watts):					
Maximum, Standby mode	140, 15	130, 15	105, 15	135, N/A	150, N/A
Suspend, Off mode	15, 5	15, 5	15, 4	N/A, N/A	15, N/A
CONTROLS					
Manual controls	Digital	Digital	Analog/digital	Analog/digital	Analog/digital
On-screen menu controls	In on-board ROM	None	None	None	None
Changes in manual controls automatically reflected in on-screen controls and vice versa	●	N/A	N/A	N/A	N/A
Manual degaussing/ Degaussing on power-up	●/●	●/○	●/●	●/●	●/●
Color matching/Pincushioning	●/●	○/●	●/●	●/●	●/●
Trapezoidal adjustment/ Orthogonality	●/○	●/○	●/○	○/○	○/○
Tilt or rotation/Convergence	○/○	○/○	●/○	○/○	●/○
CUSTOMER SERVICE					
Technical support number	800-445-6495	408-943-0100	800-228-0530	510-356-5600	800-800-9973
Technical support hours (eastern time)	24 hours, 7 days	11:30–8:30 M–F	11:30–8:30 M–F	10:00–7:00 M–F	10:00–8:00 M–F
BBS	○	●	○	○	●
Warranty	1 year	2 years	2 years	2 years	1 year

●—Yes   ○— No   N/A—Not applicable   INA—Information not available

Table Continues →

■ 17-Inch Monitors

	Apple Multiple Scan 17 Display	ASTVision 7L	Compaq QVision 172	CTX 1765GM	CTX 1785GM
List price	$	$	None quoted	$	$
Estimated street price	None quoted	$	$	$	$
Tube manufacturer	Sony	Hitachi	Sony	Matsushita	Hitachi
Type of tube	Trinitron	Flat-square	Trinitron	Flat-square	Flat-square
Dot pitch or aperture-grill pitch (mm)	0.26	0.28	0.26	0.27	0.26
Antiglare treatment	ARAS coating	ARAS coating	ARAS coating	AGRAS coating	AGRAS coating
Active screen size (diagonal, in inches)	16	16.2	15.7	16	16
Image can be extended to screen edges	●	●	●	●	●
Dimensions (HWD, in inches)	16.7 x 15.9 x 17.8	15.5 x 16.4 x 16.8	16.4 x 16.6 x 18.3	17 x 16.5 x 18.5	17.1 x 16.5 x 18.6
Weight	50 lbs.	46 lbs. 14 oz.	48 lbs. 2 oz.	46 lbs. 5 oz.	47 lbs. 2 oz.
Type of adapter:					
Captive to 15-pin/15-pin to 15-pin	○/●	○/●	●/○	●/○	○/●
BNC-3 to 15-pin/BNC-5 to 15-pin	○/○	○/●	○/○	○/○	○/●
FCC certification	Class B	Class B	Class B	Class B	Class B
Energy Star–certified/VESA DPMS–compliant	●/●	●/●	●/○	●/●	●/●
TCO compliance claimed	○	○	○	○	○
Color-matching software	INA	INA	INA	INA	INA
OPERATIONAL FEATURES					
Vertical scanning frequency (Hz)	50–120	50–90	50–110	50–100	50–100
Horizontal scanning frequency (kHz)	30–64	30–64	31.5–82	30–65	30–85
Maximum noninterlaced resolution	1,280 x 1,024	1,280 x 1,024	1,280 x 1,024	1,280 x 1,024	1,600 x 1,280
Maximum interlaced resolution	N/A	1,280 x 1,024	1,024 x 768	1,280 x 1,024	1,600 x 1,280
Maximum noninterlaced refresh rates (Hz):					
1,280 x 1,024; 1,024 x 768	60, 72	60, 75	76, 76	60, 75	75, 75
800 x 600; 640 x 480	75, 75	75, 75	75, 75	75, 75	75, 75
Claimed power consumption (watts):					
Maximum, Standby mode	150, 15	126, 95	150, 30	130, 75	130, 75
Suspend, Off mode	15, 11	6, 6	30, 7	9, 5	9, 5
CONTROLS					
Manual controls	Digital	Digital	Digital	Analog/digital	Analog/digital
On-screen menu controls	Software	None	None	None	None
Changes in manual controls automatically reflected in on-screen controls and vice versa	●	N/A	N/A	N/A	N/A
Manual degaussing/Degaussing on power-up	○/●	●/●	●/●	●/●	●/●
Color matching/Pincushioning	●/●	●/○	●/●	●/●	●/●
Trapezoidal adjustment/Orthogonality	○/○	○/○	●/○	●/○	●/○
Tilt or rotation/Convergence	●/●	○/○	●/●	●/○	●/○
CUSTOMER SERVICE					
Technical support number	800-767-2775	800-876-4278	800-652-6672	800-888-2012	800-888-2012
Technical support hours (eastern time)	9:00–9:00 M–F	24 hours, 7 days	24 hours, 7 days	11:30–8:00 M–F	11:30–8:00 M–F
BBS	○	●	●	●	●
Warranty	1 year	1 year	1 year	2 years	2 years

●—Yes ○—No N/A—Not applicable INA—Information not available

17-Inch Monitors ■

	ETC ViewMagic CA-1765SPL	Goldstar Model 1725	Hyundai HL-7682A	IBM 17P	Iiyama VisionMaster 17 Model MF-8617A
List price	$	$	$$	$	$
Estimated street price	$	$	$	None quoted	$
Tube manufacturer	Hitachi	Hitachi	Hitachi	Sony	Hitachi
Type of tube	Flat-square	Flat-square	Flat-square	Trinitron	Flat-square
Dot pitch or aperture-grill pitch (mm)	0.26	0.28	0.26	0.26	0.26
Antiglare treatment	Etch treatment	Etch treatment	Etch treatment	Silica coating	Silica coating
Active screen size (diagonal, in inches)	16.1	16	16	15.4	15.8
Image can be extended to screen edges	●	●	●	●	INA
Dimensions (HWD, in inches)	15.7 x 16.5 x 17.4	17.1 x 16.5 x 18.5	16.5 x 18 x 20	17.1 x 16.1 x 18.3	16.5 x 16.3 x 19.3
Weight	40 lbs. 3 oz.	44 lbs. 10 oz.	47 lbs.	49 lbs. 14 oz.	48 lbs. 1 oz.
Type of adapter:					
Captive to 15-pin/15-pin to 15-pin	○/●	○/●	○/●	○/●	○/●
BNC-3 to 15-pin/BNC-5 to 15-pin	○/○	○/○	○/●	○/●	○/○
FCC certification	Class B	Class B	Class A	Class B	INA
Energy Star–certified/VESA DPMS–compliant	●/●	●/●	●/●	●/●	●/●
TCO compliance claimed	○	○	○	● (European model only)	○
Color-matching software	INA	INA	INA	INA	Sonnetech's Colorific (optional)
OPERATIONAL FEATURES					
Vertical scanning frequency (Hz)	50–120	50–120	45–100	50–110	50–120
Horizontal scanning frequency (kHz)	30–65	30–65	30–82	30–82	27–86
Maximum noninterlaced resolution	1,280 x 1,024	1,280 x 1,024	1,280 x 1,024	1,360 x 1,024	1,600 x 1,280
Maximum interlaced resolution	1,280 x 1,024	1,280 x 1,024	1,024 x 768	1,600 x 1,280	INA
Maximum noninterlaced refresh rates (Hz):					
1,280 x 1,024; 1,024 x 768	60, 72	60, 76	70, 70	77, 100	80, 105
800 x 600; 640 x 480	72, 75	72, 72	72, 67	110, 110	120, 120
Claimed power consumption (watts):					
Maximum, Standby mode	85, 17	100, 15	130, 8	110, 80	140, 15
Suspend, Off mode	17, 16*	15, 8	8, 5	30, 8	7, 3
CONTROLS					
Manual controls	Digital	Analog/digital	Digital	Digital	INA
On-screen menu controls	In on-board ROM	None	None	None	INA
Changes in manual controls automatically reflected in on-screen controls and vice versa	○	N/A	N/A	N/A	INA
Manual degaussing/ Degaussing on power-up	●/●	●/●	●/●	●/●	●/●
Color matching/Pincushioning	●/●	○/●	●/●	●/●	●/●
Trapezoidal adjustment/ Orthogonality	●/○	●/○	●/○	●/○	●/○
Tilt or rotation/Convergence	●/○	○/○	●/○	○/●	●/○
CUSTOMER SERVICE					
Technical support number	510-226-6250	800-222-6457	800-289-4986	800-426-7378	800-394-4335
Technical support hours (eastern time)	11:30–8:30 M–F	9:00–6:00 M–F	11:00–8:00 M–F	24 hours, 7 days	8:30–5:00 M–F
BBS	○	○	○	○	○
Warranty	2 years	2 years	2 years	3 years	3 years

●—Yes ○—No N/A—Not applicable INA—Information not available

Table Continues →

■ 17-Inch Monitors

	IDEK/Iiyama VisionMaster MF-8617	Ikegami CT-17A	MAG MXP17F	MAG DX17F	MiTAC Performance Series L1782
List price	$	$$	$	$	$
Estimated street price	$	$	$	None quoted	$
Tube manufacturer	Hitachi	Sony	Toshiba	Hitachi	Hitachi
Type of tube	Flat-square	Trinitron	Flat-square	Flat-square	Flat-square
Dot pitch or aperture-grill pitch (mm)	0.26	0.26	0.26	0.26	0.26
Antiglare treatment	Bonded panel	Bonded panel	AGRAS coating	Etch treatment	ARAG coating
Active screen size (diagonal, in inches)	15.8	15.9	16	16	15.8
Image can be extended to screen edges	●	●	●	○	●
Dimensions (HWD, in inches)	16.8 x 16.4 x 18	16.5 x 16.4 x 18.3	16.8 x 17.3 x 18.8	16.5 x 16.1 x 17.3	17 x 16.6 x 17.3
Weight	47 lbs. 10 oz.	61 lbs. 14 oz.	52 lbs. 2 oz.	41 lbs. 14 oz.	43 lbs. 5 oz.
Type of adapter:					
Captive to 15-pin/15-pin to 15-pin	○/●	○/●	●/○	○/●	○/●
BNC-3 to 15-pin/BNC-5 to 15-pin	●/●	○/●	●/●	○/○	○/○
FCC certification	Class B	Class A	Class B	Class B	Class B
Energy Star–certified/VESA DPMS–compliant	●/●	○/○	●/●	●/●	○/○
TCO compliance claimed	○	○	Optional ($99)	○	○
Color-matching software	Sonnetech's Colorific (optional)	INA	INA	INA	INA
OPERATIONAL FEATURES					
Vertical scanning frequency (Hz)	50–120	50–150	50–120	50–100	47–120
Horizontal scanning frequency (kHz)	24–86	30–81	30–82	30–64	29–82
Maximum noninterlaced resolution	1,600 x 1,280	1,600 x 1,280	1,600 x 1,280	1,280 x 1,024	1,600 x 1,280
Maximum interlaced resolution	N/A	N/A	1,600 x 1,280	1,280 x 1,024	1,600 x 1,280
Maximum noninterlaced refresh rates (Hz):					
1,280 x 1,024; 1,024 x 768	80, 80	76, 76	76, 85	60, 76	60, 76
800 x 600; 640 x 480	80, 80	76, 76	120, 120	85, 100	76, 76
Claimed power consumption (watts):					
Maximum, Standby mode	130, 15	135, N/A	130, 30	120, 20	N/A, N/A
Suspend, Off mode	8, 6	N/A, N/A	30, 10	20, 10	N/A, N/A
CONTROLS					
Manual controls	Digital	Digital	Analog/digital	Analog/digital	Analog/digital
On-screen menu controls	None (displayed on LCD panel instead)	None	None (displayed on LCD panel instead)	None	In on-board ROM
Changes in manual controls automatically reflected in on-screen controls and vice versa	N/A	N/A	N/A	N/A	●
Manual degaussing/ Degaussing on power-up	●/●	●/●	●/●	●/●	●/●
Color matching/Pincushioning	●/●	●/●	●/●	○/●	●/●
Trapezoidal adjustment/ Orthogonality	●/○	○/○	●/○	○/○	●/○
Tilt or rotation/Convergence	●/○	○/●	●/○	●/○	○/○
CUSTOMER SERVICE					
Technical support number	800-394-4335	201-368-9171	800-827-3998	800-827-3998	800-756-2888
Technical support hours (eastern time)	8:30–5:00 M–F	9:00–5:00 M–F	11:00–8:00 M–F	11:00–8:00 M–F	9:30–8:30 M–F
BBS	○	○	○	○	○
Warranty	3 years	2 years	1 year; 2 years CRT	1 year; 2 years CRT	3 years

●—Yes   ○—No   N/A—Not applicable   INA—Information not available

17-Inch Monitors ■

	Mitsubishi Diamond Pro 17TX	Mitsubishi Diamond Scan 17FS	Nanao FlexScan F2●17	Nanao FlexScan F2●17EX	Nanao FlexScan F550iW
List price	None quoted	$	None quoted	None quoted	$
Estimated street price	$	$	$	$	$
Tube manufacturer	Mitsubishi	Mitsubishi	Mitsubishi	Hitachi	Mitsubishi
Type of tube	Diamondtron	Flat-square	Flat-square	Flat-square	Flat-square
Dot pitch or aperture-grill pitch (mm)	0.25	0.28	0.28	0.26	0.28
Antiglare treatment	ARAS coating	ARAS coating	AGRAS coating	AGRAS coating	ARAS coating
Active screen size (diagonal, in inches)	16.0	15.7	16.0	16.0	15.6
Image can be extended to screen edges	INA	●	INA	INA	●
Dimensions (HWD, in inches)	15.8 x 16.2 x 16.8	15.8 x 16.3 x 17.2	16.2 x 16.1 x 17.5	16.2 x 16.1 x 17.5	16.4 x 16.1 x 17.5
Weight	50 lbs.	37 lbs. 14 oz.	43 lbs. 10 oz.	44 lbs. 8 oz.	49 lbs. 6 oz.
Type of adapter:					
Captive to 15-pin/15-pin to 15-pin	○/●	○/●	○/●	○/●	○/●
BNC-3 to 15-pin/BNC-5 to 15-pin	○/●	○/○	●/●	●/●	○/●
FCC certification	INA	Class B	INA	INA	Class B
Energy Star–certified/VESA DPMS–compliant	INA	●/●	●/●	●/●	●/●
TCO compliance claimed	●	●	○	●	●
Color-matching software	Sonnetech's Colorific	Sonnetech's Colorific (optional)	Sonnetech's Colorific	Sonnetech's Colorific	Sonnetech's Colorific
OPERATIONAL FEATURES					
Vertical scanning frequency (Hz)	50–152	50–130	55–120	55–160	55–90
Horizontal scanning frequency (kHz)	30–86	30–78	30–69	30–86	27–65
Maximum noninterlaced resolution	1,600 x 1,280	1,280 x 1,024	1,280 x 1,024	1,600 x 1,280	1,280 x 1,024
Maximum interlaced resolution	INA	1,280 x 1,024	INA	INA	1,280 x 1,024
Maximum noninterlaced refresh rates (Hz):					
1,280 x 1,024; 1,024 x 768	75, 100	74, 74	66, 87	82, 110	60, 80
800 x 600; 640 x 480	120, 152	76, 76	110, 120	140, 160	90, 90
Claimed power consumption (watts):					
Maximum, Standby mode	120, 95	120, 96	90, 10	95, 10	120, 10–12
Suspend, Off mode	30, 8	30, 5	N/A, 5	N/A, 5	8–10, 2–4
CONTROLS					
Manual controls	INA	Digital	INA	INA	Digital
On-screen menu controls	INA	Optional software	INA	INA	None
Changes in manual controls automatically reflected in on-screen controls and vice versa	INA	● (with software)	INA	INA	N/A
Manual degaussing/ Degaussing on power-up	●/●	●/●	●/●	●/●	●/●
Color matching/Pincushioning	●/●	●/●	●/●	●/●	●/●
Trapezoidal adjustment/ Orthogonality	●/●	●/○	●/○	●/○	●/○
Tilt or rotation/Convergence	●/●	○/○	●/●	●/●	○/●
CUSTOMER SERVICE					
Technical support number	800-344-6352	800-344-6352	800-800-5202	800-800-5202	800-800-5202
Technical support hours (eastern time)	11:00–7:30 M–F	11:00–7:30 M–F	8:30–5:00 M–F	8:30–5:00 M–F	8:30–5:00 M–F
BBS	●	○	●	●	●
Warranty	3 years	3 years	3 years	3 years	3 years

●—Yes   ○—No   N/A—Not applicable   INA—Information not available

Table Continues →

■ 17-Inch Monitors

	Nanao FlexScan F560iW	Nanao FlexScan T2●17TS	Nanao FlexScan T2●17	NEC MultiSync 5FGe	NEC MultiSync 5FGp
List price	$	None quoted	None quoted	$	$
Estimated street price	$	$	$	$	$
Tube manufacturer	Mitsubishi	Mitsubishi	Sony	NEC	NEC
Type of tube	Flat-square	Diamondtron	Trinitron	Flat-square	Flat-square
Dot pitch or aperture-grill pitch (mm)	0.26	0.25	0.25	0.28	0.28
Antiglare treatment	ARAS coating	AGRAS coating	AGRAS coating	Optional OCLI panel ($100)	Proprietary OptiClear surface
Active screen size (diagonal, in inches)	15.8	16.0	16.0	15.6	15.5
Image can be extended to screen edges	●	INA	INA	●	●
Dimensions (HWD, in inches)	16.4 x 16.1 x 17.5	16.0 x 16.3 x 17.5	16.0 x 16.3 x 18.6	17.8 x 16.4 x 19.8	17.8 x 16.4 x 19.6
Weight	50 lbs. 6 oz.	48 lbs. 3 oz.	53 lbs. 14 oz.	53 lbs. 5 oz.	56 lbs. 6 oz.
Type of adapter:					
Captive to 15-pin/15-pin to 15-pin	○/●	○/●	○/●	●/○	●/●
BNC-3 to 15-pin/BNC-5 to 15-pin	○/●	●/●	●/●	○/○	●/●
FCC certification	Class B	INA	INA	Class B	Class A
Energy Star–certified/VESA DPMS–compliant	●/●	●/●	●/●	○/●	●/●
TCO compliance claimed	○	●	●	○	○
Color-matching software	Sonnetech's Colorific	Sonnetech's Colorific	Sonnetech's Colorific	Sonnetech's Colorific (optional)	Sonnetech's Colorific (optional)
OPERATIONAL FEATURES					
Vertical scanning frequency (Hz)	55–90	55–160	55–160	55–90	55–90
Horizontal scanning frequency (kHz)	30–82	30–86	30–85	31–62	27–79
Maximum noninterlaced resolution	1,280 x 1,024	1,600 x 1,280	1,600 x 1,280	1,024 x 768	1,280 x 1,024
Maximum interlaced resolution	1,280 x 1,024	INA	INA	1,024 x 768	1,280 x 1,024
Maximum noninterlaced refresh rates (Hz):					
1,280 x 1,024; 1,024 x 768	76, 90	82, 110	80, 108	N/A, 76	74, 76
800 x 600; 640 x 480	90, 90	140, 160	138, 160	76, 76	76, 76
Claimed power consumption (watts):					
Maximum, Standby mode	120, 10–12	115, 10	140, 15	100, 93	155, 144
Suspend, Off mode	8–10, 2–4	N/A, 5	N/A, 8	20, 20	31, 31
CONTROLS					
Manual controls	Digital	INA	INA	Digital	Analog/digital
On-screen menu controls	None	INA	INA	None	None
Changes in manual controls automatically reflected in on-screen controls and vice versa	N/A	INA	INA	N/A	N/A
Manual degaussing/ Degaussing on power-up	●/●	●/●	●/●	●/●	●/●
Color matching/Pincushioning	●/●	●/●	●/●	○/●	●/●
Trapezoidal adjustment/ Orthogonality	●/○	●/○	●/○	○/○	○/○
Tilt or rotation/Convergence	○/○	●/●	●/●	●/○	○/○
CUSTOMER SERVICE					
Technical support number	800-800-5202	800-800-5202	800-800-5202	800-388-8888	800-388-8888
Technical support hours (eastern time)	8:30–5:00 M–F	8:30–5:00 M–F	8:30–5:00 M–F	8:30–8:30 M–F	8:30–8:30 M–F
BBS	●	●	●	●	●
Warranty	3 years; 1 year CRT	3 years	3 years	3 years; 1 year CRT	3 years

●—Yes ○—No N/A—Not applicable INA—Information not available

17-Inch Monitors

	NEC MultiSync XV17	NEC MultiSync XE17	NEC MultiSync XP17	Nissei Sangyo/ Hitachi SuperScan Elite 17	Nokia Multigraph 447X
List price	None quoted	None quoted	None quoted	None quoted	$
Estimated street price	$	$	$	$	$
Tube manufacturer	NEC	NEC	NEC	Hitachi	Sony
Type of tube	Flat-square	Flat-square	Flat-square	Flat-square	Trinitron
Dot pitch or aperture-grill pitch (mm)	0.28	0.28	0.28	0.26	0.26
Antiglare treatment	None	ARAS coating	ARAS coating	ARAS coating	Silica coating
Active screen size (diagonal, in inches)	15.6	15.6	15.6	15.9	15.4
Image can be extended to screen edges	INA	INA	INA	●	●
Dimensions (HWD, in inches)	16.3 x 16.1 x 17.5	16.8 x 16.5 x 18.9	16.4 x 16.4 x 19.5	16.9 x 16 x 18.3	16.4 x 16.8 x 18.1
Weight	46 lbs. 6 oz.	48 lbs. 14 oz.	52 lbs. 5 oz.	47 lbs. 11 oz.	45 lbs. 13 oz.
Type of adapter:					
Captive to 15-pin/15-pin to 15-pin	●/○	●/○	●/○	○/●	○/●
BNC-3 to 15-pin/BNC-5 to 15-pin	○/○	○/○	○/●	○/●	●/●
FCC certification	INA	INA	INA	Class B	Class B
Energy Starcertified/VESA DPMS—compliant	●/●	●/●	●/●	●/●	●/●
TCO compliance claimed	Optional ($69)	Optional ($69)	Optional ($69)	○	Optional ($199)
Color-matching software	Sonnetech's Colorific (optional)	Sonnetech's Colorific	Sonnetech's Colorific	INA	Sonnetech's Colorific (optional)
OPERATIONAL FEATURES					
Vertical scanning frequency (Hz)	55-100	55-120	55-160	55–120	50–110
Horizontal scanning frequency (kHz)	31–65	31–65	31–82	30–82	30–82
Maximum noninterlaced resolution	1,280 x 1,024	1,280 x 1,024	1,280 x 1,024	1,600 x 1,200	1,600 x 1,280
Maximum interlaced resolution	INA	INA	INA	1,600 x 1,200	N/A
Maximum noninterlaced refresh rates (Hz):					
1,280 x 1,024; 1,024 x 768	60, 76	60, 76	76, 76	77, 102	76, 95
800 x 600; 640 x 480	76, 75	76, 75	76, 75	120, 120	110, 110
Claimed power consumption (watts):					
Maximum, Standby mode	130, 13	105, 11	147, 15	125, 25	120, 8
Suspend, Off mode	8, 0	8, 0	8, 0	25, 8	N/A, 6
CONTROLS					
Manual controls	INA	INA	INA	Digital	None
On-screen menu controls	INA	INA	INA	Software	In on-board ROM
Changes in manual controls automatically reflected in on-screen controls and vice versa	INA	INA	INA	●	○
Manual degaussing/ Degaussing on power-up	●/●	●/●	●/●	●/○	●/●
Color matching/Pincushioning	●/●	●/●	●/●	●/●	●/●
Trapezoidal adjustment/ Orthogonality	●/○	●/○	●/○	●/○	●/●
Tilt or rotation/Convergence	●/○	●/○	●/○	○/○	●/●
CUSTOMER SERVICE					
Technical support number	800-388-8888	800-388-8888	800-388-8888	617-461-8300	800-483-7952
Technical support hours (eastern time)	8:00–8:00 M–F	8:00–8:00 M–F	8:00–8:00 M–F	9:00–5:00 M–F	9:00–7:00 M–F
BBS	●	●	●	○	○
Warranty	3 years	3 years	3 years	3 years	3 years (2 yrs. CRT)

●—Yes ○—No N/A—Not applicable INA—Information not available

Table Continues →

■ 17-Inch Monitors

	Nokia Valuegraph 447L	Optiquest 4000TC	Orchestra MultiSystems The Tuba	Packard Bell PB8517SVGM	Panasonic PanaSync C1791E
List price	$	$	$	None quoted	$
Estimated street price	$	$	$	$	$
Tube manufacturer	Hitachi	Sony	Hitachi	Mitsubishi	Mitsubishi
Type of tube	Flat-square	Trinitron	Flat-square	Flat-square	Flat-square
Dot pitch or aperture-grill pitch (mm)	0.28	0.25	0.26	0.28	0.28
Antiglare treatment	AGRAS coating	ARAS coating	Etch treatment	AGRAS coating	AGRAS coating
Active screen size (diagonal, in inches)	15.5	15.8	15.8	15.8	15.8
Image can be extended to screen edges	INA	●	●	●	●
Dimensions (HWD, in inches)	16.5 x 16.4 x 19.5	16.3 x 16.1 x 19.1	16.9 x 16.2 x 17.5	16.3 x 16.1 x 17.3	16.3 x 16.1 x 17.3
Weight	41 lbs. 2 oz.	52 lbs. 13 oz.	43 lbs. 2 oz.	37 lbs. 8 oz.	37 lbs. 3 oz.
Type of adapter:					
Captive to 15-pin/15-pin to 15-pin	●/○	●/○	●/●	○/●	○/●
BNC-3 to 15-pin/BNC-5 to 15-pin	○/○	○/○	●/●	○/○	○/○
FCC certification	INA	Class B	Class B	Class B	Class B
Energy Star–certified/VESA DPMS–compliant	INA	●/	○/○	●/●	●/●
TCO compliance claimed	○	○	○	○	●/○
Color-matching software	Sonnetech's Colorific (optional)	Sonnetech's Colorific (optional)	INA	INA	INA
OPERATIONAL FEATURES					
Vertical scanning frequency (Hz)	48–100	50–90	50–90	50–160	50–160
Horizontal scanning frequency (kHz)	30–64	24–64	31–82	30–64	30–64
Maximum noninterlaced resolution	1,280 x 1,024	1,280 x 1,024	1,600 x 1,280	1,280 x 1,024	1,280 x 1,024
Maximum interlaced resolution	INA	1,600 x 1,280	1,280 x 1,024	1,280 x 1,024	1,280 x 1,024
Maximum noninterlaced refresh rates (Hz):					
1,280 x 1,024; 1,024 x 768	60, 76	60, 76	74, 76	60, 72	60, 72
800 x 600; 640 x 480	90, 90	90, 90	72, 72	75, 75	72, 72
Claimed power consumption (watts):					
Maximum, Standby mode	120, 8	150, 25	N/A, N/A	130, 75	130, 30
Suspend, Off mode	3, 0	25, 5	N/A, N/A	15, 8	30, 8
CONTROLS					
Manual controls	INA	Analog/digital	Digital	Digital	Digital
On-screen menu controls	INA	None	None	In on-board ROM	In on-board ROM
Changes in manual controls automatically reflected in on-screen controls and vice versa	INA	N/A	N/A	○	○
Manual degaussing/ Degaussing on power-up	●/●	●/●	●/●	●/○	●/●
Color matching/Pincushioning	○/●	●/●	○/○	●/●	●/●
Trapezoidal adjustment/ Orthogonality	●/○	○/○	○/○	●/●	●/●
Tilt or rotation/Convergence	○/○	○/○	○/○	○/○	○/○
CUSTOMER SERVICE					
Technical support number	800-483-7952	800-843-6784	800-237-9988	800-733-4411	800-726-2797
Technical support hours (eastern time)	9:00–7:00 M–F	11:00–8:00 M–F	10:00–9:00 M–F	24 hours, 7 days	9:00–5:00 M–F
BBS	○	○	○	●	●
Warranty	3 years (2 years on CRT)	2 years parts, 1 year labor	3 years	1 year	1 year

●—Yes ○—No N/A—Not applicable INA—Information not available

17-Inch Monitors

	Philips Brilliance 1720	Radius PrecisionColor Display/17	Samsung SyncMaster 17GL	Samsung SyncMaster 17GLs	Sceptre CL-617GL+
List price	$	$	$	$	$
Estimated street price	$	$	$	$	$
Tube manufacturer	Matsushita	Sony	Hitachi	Hitachi	Hitachi
Type of tube	Flat-square	Trinitron	Flat-square	Flat-square	Flat-square
Dot pitch or aperture-grill pitch (mm)	0.27	0.26	0.28	0.26	0.26
Antiglare treatment	AGRAS coating	Silica coating	Etch treatment	ARAS coating	Silica coating
Active screen size (diagonal, in inches)	16.1	15.9	15.6	15.6	15.9
Image can be extended to screen edges	●	●	●	●	●
Dimensions (HWD, in inches)	16.4 x 16.4 x 17.3	16.1 x 16 x 17.8	17 x 16.6 x 17	17 x 16.6 x 17	15.4 x 16.2 x 17.4
Weight	44 lbs. 3 oz.	48 lbs. 3 oz.	46 lbs. 10 oz.	46 lbs. 14 oz.	41 lbs. 3 oz.
Type of adapter:					
Captive to 15-pin/15-pin to 15-pin	○/●	○/○	○/●	○/●	●/○
BNC-3 to 15-pin/BNC-5 to 15-pin	○/●	○/●	○/○	○/●	○/○
FCC certification	Class B	Class B	Class B	Class B	Class B
Energy Star–certified/VESA DPMS–compliant	●/●	●/●	●/●	●/●	●/●
TCO compliance claimed	○	○	○	○	Optional ($30)
Color-matching software	INA	INA	INA	INA	INA
OPERATIONAL FEATURES					
Vertical scanning frequency (Hz)	50–120	50–150	50–100	50–120	50–90
Horizontal scanning frequency (kHz)	30–82	29–82	30–65	30–82	30–66
Maximum noninterlaced resolution	1,600 x 1,280	1,600 x 1,280	1,280 x 1,024	1,280 x 1,024	1,280 x 1,024
Maximum interlaced resolution	1,600 x 1,280	1,600 x 1,280	1,024 x 768	1,024 x 768	N/A
Maximum noninterlaced refresh rates (Hz):					
1,280 x 1,024; 1,024 x 768	76, 100	75, 75	60, 76	76, 76	60, 75
800 x 600; 640 x 480	100, 100	72, 75	76, 76	76, 76	75, 75
Claimed power consumption (watts):					
Maximum, Standby mode	110, 10	140, 15	83, 54	86, 57	110, 100
Suspend, Off mode	10, 5	15, 10	22, 6	20, 7	15, 5
CONTROLS					
Manual controls	Analog/digital	Digital	Analog/digital	Analog/digital	Analog/digital
On-screen menu controls	None	None	None	In on-board ROM	None
Changes in manual controls automatically reflected in on-screen controls and vice versa	N/A	N/A	N/A	●	N/A
Manual degaussing/ Degaussing on power-up	●/●	○/●	●/●	●/●	●/●
Color matching/Pincushioning	○/●	●/●	○/●	●/●	○/●
Trapezoidal adjustment/ Orthogonality	●/○	○/○	●/○	●/○	○/○
Tilt or rotation/Convergence	○/○	●/●	○/○	○/●	○/○
CUSTOMER SERVICE					
Technical support number	800-835-3506	408-434-1012	800-726-7864	800-726-7864	800-788-2878
Technical support hours (eastern time)	8:00 A.M.–9:00 P.M. M–F	9:00–9:00 M–F	9:00–6:00 M–F	9:00–6:00 M–F	8:30–5:30 M–F
BBS	○	●	●	●	●
Warranty	3 years	1 year	2 years	2 years	3 years

●—Yes ○—No N/A—Not applicable INA—Information not available

Table Continues →

■ 17-Inch Monitors

	SDIS ErgoView 170	Sony MultiScan 17se	SuperMac SuperMatch 17 XL	Tatung Omniscan CM17MKR	ViewSonic 17
List price	$$	$	$	$	$
Estimated street price	$	None quoted	$	$	$
Tube manufacturer	Matsushita	Sony	Matsushita	Hitachi	Matsushita
Type of tube	Flat-square	Trinitron	Flat-square	Flat-square	Flat-square
Dot pitch or aperture-grill pitch (mm)	0.27	0.26	0.28	0.28	0.27
Antiglare treatment	AGRAS coating	Silica coating	AGRAS coating	ARAG coating	ARAG coating
Active screen size (diagonal, in inches)	16.4	16	16.1	15.9	15.8
Image can be extended to screen edges	●	●	●	●	●
Dimensions (HWD, in inches)	16.5 x 16.6 x 17.4	16.1 x 16 x 17.9	16.5 x 16.3 x 16.8	16.9 x 16.3 x 19	16.6 x 16.1 x 17.1
Weight	44 lbs. 8 oz.	48 lbs. 11 oz.	42 lbs. 5 oz.	49 lbs. 6 oz.	39 lbs. 10 oz.
Type of adapter:					
Captive to 15-pin/15-pin to 15-pin	○/●	○/○	○/○	○/●	○/●
BNC-3 to 15-pin/BNC-5 to 15-pin	○/●	○/●	○/○	○/Optional	○/●
FCC certification	Class B	Class B	Class B	Class A	Class B
Energy Star–certified/VESA DPMS–compliant	○/○	●/●	●/●	●/●	●/●
TCO compliance claimed	○	○	○	○	○
Color-matching software	INA	INA	INA	INA	Sonnetech's Colorific (optional)
OPERATIONAL FEATURES					
Vertical scanning frequency (Hz)	50–120	50–150	50–90	50–120	50–160
Horizontal scanning frequency (kHz)	30–82	32–82	31–64	30–82	30–82
Maximum noninterlaced resolution	1,600 x 1,280	1,600 x 1,280	1,280 x 1,024	1,600 x 1,280	1,600 x 1,280
Maximum interlaced resolution	N/A	N/A	N/A	1,600 x 1,280	1,600 x 1,280
Maximum noninterlaced refresh rates (Hz):					
1,280 x 1,024; 1,024 x 768	76, 100	77, 100	60, 75	75, 75	76, 100
800 x 600; 640 x 480	120, 120	100, 100	75, 84	75, 75	120, 150
Claimed power consumption (watts):					
Maximum, Standby mode	125, N/A	140, N/A	125, 9	130, 104	140, 112
Suspend, Off mode	N/A, N/A	14, 10	9, 2	5, 5	30, 8
CONTROLS					
Manual controls	Analog/digital	Digital	Digital	Analog/digital	Digital
On-screen menu controls	None	None	None	None	In on-board ROM
Changes in manual controls automatically reflected in on-screen controls and vice versa	N/A	N/A	N/A	N/A	●
Manual degaussing/ Degaussing on power-up	●/●	○/●	●/●	●/●	●/●
Color matching/Pincushioning	○/●	●/●	○/●	○/●	●/●
Trapezoidal adjustment/ Orthogonality	●/●	○/○	●/○	○/○	●/○
Tilt or rotation/Convergence	●/○	●/●	○/○	○/○	●/○
CUSTOMER SERVICE					
Technical support number	510-770-2900	408-894-0225	800-541-7680	310-637-2105	800-888-8583
Technical support hours (eastern time)	10:00–8:00 M–F	11:00–8:00 M–F	6:00–5:00 MWF, 6:00–4:00 Th	10:30–8:30 M–F	10:00–9:00 M–F
BBS	●	●	●	●	●
Warranty	1 year	1 year; 2 years CRT	1 year	2 years	3 years parts, 1 year labor

●—Yes   ○—No   N/A—Not applicable   INA—Information not available

17-Inch Monitors ■

	ViewSonic 17G	ViewSonic 17GA	ViewSonic 17GS	ViewSonic 17PS	Wen JK1775 Digital Control Color Monitor
List price	$	$	$	$	$
Estimated street price	$	$	$	$	$
Tube manufacturer	Mitsubishi	Matsushita	Matsushita	Matsushita	Hitachi
Type of tube	Flat-square	Flat-square	Flat-square	Flat-square	Flat-square
Dot pitch or aperture-grill pitch (mm)	0.28	0.27	0.27	0.25	0.26
Antiglare treatment	ARAG coating	ARAG coating	ARAG coating	ARAG coating	ARAS coating
Active screen size (diagonal, in inches)	15.8	16.0	15.7	15.7	15.9
Image can be extended to screen edges	●	INA	INA	INA	●
Dimensions (HWD, in inches)	16.6 x 16.1 x 17.3	16.1 x 17.1 x 17.5	16.4 x 16.1 x 17.1	16.3 x 16.1 x 17.1	16.1 x 15.9 x 17.5
Weight	31 lbs. 10 oz.	40 lbs.	37 lbs. 12 oz.	38 lbs. 5 oz.	51 lbs.
Type of adapter:					
Captive to 15-pin/15-pin to 15-pin	○/●	○/●	○/●	○/●	○/●
BNC-3 to 15-pin/BNC-5 to 15-pin	○/○	○/○	○/○	○/●	○/Optional
FCC certification	Class B	INA	INA	INA	Class B
Energy Star–certified/VESA DPMS–compliant	●/●	●/●	●/●	●/●	●/●
TCO compliance claimed	○	○	●	●	○
Color-matching software	Sonnetech's Colorific (optional)	Sonnetech's Colorific (optional)	Sonnetech's Colorific (optional)	Sonnetech's Colorific (optional)	INA
OPERATIONAL FEATURES					
Vertical scanning frequency (Hz)	50–160	50–160	50–160	50–160	50–90
Horizontal scanning frequency (kHz)	30–64	30–69	30–69	30–82	30–81
Maximum noninterlaced resolution	1,280 x 1,024	1,280 x 1,024	1,280 x 1,024	1,280 x 1,024	1,280 x 1,024
Maximum interlaced resolution	1,280 x 1,024	INA	INA	INA	N/A
Maximum noninterlaced refresh rates (Hz):					
1,280 x 1,024; 1,024 x 768	60, 76	65, 86	65, 86	77, 101	72, 75
800 x 600; 640 x 480	90, 115	108, 134	108, 134	128, 152	75, 75
Claimed power consumption (watts):					
Maximum, Standby mode	130, 104	150, 120	110, 90	120, 100	130, 30
Suspend, Off mode	30, 8	30, 8	30, 8	30, 8	15, 2
CONTROLS					
Manual controls	Analog/digital	INA	INA	INA	Analog/digital
On-screen menu controls	In on-board ROM	INA	INA	INA	None
Changes in manual controls automatically reflected in on-screen controls and vice versa	○	INA	INA	INA	N/A
Manual degaussing/ Degaussing on power-up	●/●	●/●	●/●	●/●	●/●
Color matching/Pincushioning	●/●	●/●	●/●	●/●	○/○
Trapezoidal adjustment/ Orthogonality	●/○	●/○	●/○	●/○	○/○
Tilt or rotation/Convergence	○/○	●/○	●/○	●/○	○/○
CUSTOMER SERVICE					
Technical support number	800-888-8583	800-888-8583	800-888-8583	800-888-8583	914-347-7515
Technical support hours (eastern time)	10:00–9:00 M–F	10:00–9:00 M–F	10:00–9:00 M–F	10:00–9:00 M–F	10:00–5:00 M–F
BBS	●	●	●	●	○
Warranty	2 years parts, 1 year labor	3 years parts, 1 year labor	3 years parts, 1 year labor	3 years parts, 1 year labor	1 year

●—Yes   ○—No   N/A—Not applicable   INA—Information not available

End ■

COMPARISON CHART

VIDEO CARDS

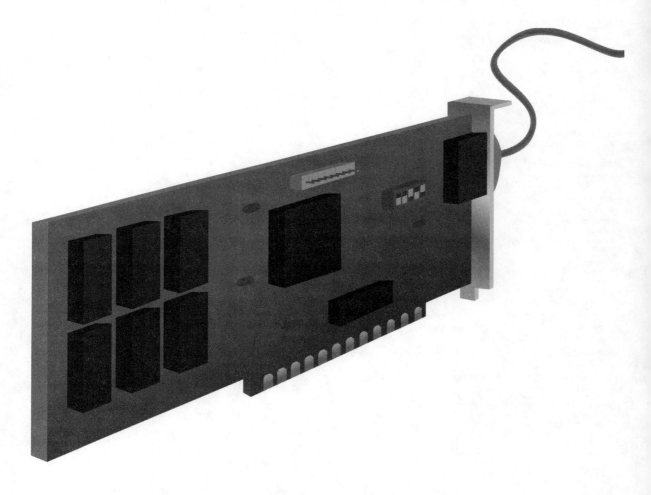

C.1   VGA Boards

(Products listed in alphabetical order by company name)	Allstar Microsystems Peacock Plus EVGA	AST Research AST-VGA Plus	ATI Technologies VGA Wonder	Communication Inter-Globe Toucan VGA 1024	Genoa Systems SuperVGA Model 5400
Price (tested configuration)	$	$	$	$	$
Video memory	512K	512K	512K	512K	512K
Base price	$	$	$	$	$
Video memory	256K	256K	256K	256K	512K
Video BIOS	8-bit, 16-bit	8-bit, 16-bit	8-bit, 16-bit	8-bit, 16-bit	8-bit, 16-bit
Video RAM	8-bit, 16-bit	8-bit, 16-bit	8-bit, 16-bit	8-bit, 16-bit	8-bit
VIDEO STANDARDS					
CGA	●	●	●	●	●
EGA	●	●	●	●	●
VGA	●	●	●	●	●
Super VGA	●	●	●	●	●
1,024 × 768	●	○	●	●	●
CONNECTORS					
9-pin	●	○	●	●	●
15-pin	●	●	●	●	●
VGA	○	○	●	●	●
Mouse	○	○	●	●	○
OUTPUT					
TTL	●	○	●	●	●
Analog	●	●	●	●	●
MAXIMUM RESOLUTION					
Graphics (pixels)	1,024 × 768	800 × 600	1,024 × 768	1,024 × 768	1,024 × 768
Text (columns × rows)	132 × 44	132 × 43	132 × 60	132 × 44	132 × 60
Maximum number of colors in highest-resolution mode	256 (800 × 600)	256 (640 × 480)	256 (800 × 600)	256 (800 × 600)	256 (800 × 600)
Total number of colors	262,144	262,144	262,144	262,144	262,144
SOFTWARE DRIVERS					
Utilities	BIOS to RAM, font editor and shader, mode switching, monitor selection, nonstandard text modes, zoom	BIOS to RAM, diagnostics, mode switching	BIOS to RAM, diagnostics, mode switching, mouse driver, system information	BIOS to RAM, diagnostics, font loader, mode switching	ANSI.SYS emulator, BIOS to RAM, mode switching, smooth scroll

Table Continues →

■ VGA Boards

	HP Video Graphics Adapter	Intelligent VGA Model 650	Orchid Technology ProDesigner Plus VGA	Paradise Systems VGA Professional	Renaissance RVGA II
Price (tested configuration)	$	$	$	$	$
Video memory	512K	256K	512K	512K	256K
Base price	$	$	$	$	$
Video memory	256K	256K	512K	512K	256K
Video BIOS	8-bit, 16-bit	8-bit, 16-bit	8-bit, 16-bit	8-bit, 16-bit	8-bit, 16-bit
Video RAM	8-bit	8-bit, 16-bit	8-bit, 16-bit	8-bit, 16-bit	8-bit
VIDEO STANDARDS					
CGA	●	●	●	●	●
EGA	●	●	●	●	●
VGA	●	●	●	●	●
Super VGA	●	●	●	●	●
1,024 × 768	○	○	●	○	○
CONNECTORS					
9-pin	○	○	○	○	●
15-pin	●	●	●	●	●
VGA	●	●	●	●	●
Mouse	○	○	○	○	○
OUTPUT					
TTL	○	○	○	○	●
Analog	●	●	●	●	●
MAXIMUM RESOLUTION					
Graphics (pixels)	800 × 600	800 × 600	1,024 × 768	800 × 600	800 × 600
Text (columns × rows)	132 × 43	132 × 43	132 × 44	132 × 43	132 × 60
Maximum number of colors in highest-resolution mode	256 (640 × 480)	256 (640 × 400)	256 (800 × 600)	256 (640 × 480)	256 (320 × 200)
Total number of colors	262,144	262,144	262,144	262,144	262,144
SOFTWARE DRIVERS					
Utilities	Font loader, video mode set program	BIOS to RAM, 8/16-bit confirm operation test, mode switching, screen saver	ANSI.SYS emulator, BIOS to RAM, font editor, font loader, hotkey/hot zoom, mode switching	BIOS to RAM, 8/16-bit confirm operation test, mode switching, screen saver	BIOS to RAM, HGC emulator, mode switching

●—Yes   ○—No   N/A—Not applicable

VGA Boards ■

	SOTA VGA/16	STB Systems VGA EM-16	Tatung VGA	Tecmar VGA/AD	Video Seven V-RAM VGA
Price (tested configuration)	$	$	$	$	$
Video memory	512K	512K	256K	512K	512K
Base price	$	$	$	$	$
Video memory	256K	256K	256K	512K	256K
Video BIOS	8-bit, 16-bit	8-bit	8-bit, 16-bit	8-bit	8-bit, 16-bit
Video RAM	8-bit, 16-bit	8-bit, 16-bit	8-bit, 16-bit	8-bit, 16-bit	8-bit, 16-bit
VIDEO STANDARDS					
CGA	●	●	●	●	●
EGA	●	●	●	●	●
VGA	●	●	●	●	●
Super VGA	●	●	●	●	●
1,024 × 768	●	●	○	●	●
CONNECTORS					
9-pin	●	●	○	●	○
15-pin	●	●	●	●	●
VGA	●	●	○	●	●
Mouse	●	○	○	○	○
OUTPUT					
TTL	●	●	○	●	○
Analog	●	●	●	●	●
MAXIMUM RESOLUTION					
Graphics (pixels)	1,024 × 768	1,024 × 768	800 × 600	1,024 × 768	1,024 × 768
Text (columns × rows)	132 × 43	132 × 44	132 × 43	132 × 60	132 × 43
Maximum number of colors in highest-resolution mode	256 (800 × 600)	256 (800 × 600)	256 (640 × 400)	256 (800 × 600)	256 (800 × 600)
Total number of colors	262,144	262,144	262,144	262,144	262,144
SOFTWARE DRIVERS					
Utilities	ANSI.SYS emulator, diagnostics, memory upgrade, mode switching	BIOS to RAM, demo program, hotkey/hot zoom, mode switching	BIOS to RAM, CGA and HGC emulator, mode switching, screen saver	ANSI.SYS, BIOS to RAM, diagnostics, keyboard access, mode switching, screen saver	Directory utility, mode forcing, screen cleaning, text mode selection

●—Yes   ○—No   N/A—Not applicable

E n d ■

■ C.2   1,024 x 768 Graphics Adapters

(Products listed in alphabetical order by company name)	Artist XJ10	Cardinal VGA600	Compaq Computer Advanced Graphics 1024	Dell GPX-1024/256	Enertronics Research Aurora 1024N
Price	$$$	$	$$	$	$
BUS TYPE					
ISA 8-bit	●	●	●	●	●
ISA 16-bit	●	●	●	●	●
MCA	○	○	○	○	○
EISA	○	○	○	○	○
PHYSICAL CHARACTERISTICS					
Board size (inches):					
Length	13.25	8	13.5	13.5	13.25
Height	4.5	4.25	4.5	4.5	4.5
Thickness	0.75	0.5	0.5	0.75	0.5
HIGH-RESOLUTION CHARACTERISTICS					
High-resolution graphics coprocessor	Hitachi	None	Texas Instruments	Texas Instruments	Texas Instruments
High-resolution memory	1Mb	N/A	1Mb	1Mb	1Mb
VGA CHARACTERISTICS					
VGA and high resolution on the same card	○	●	○	○	○
Accepts VGA daughtercard	●	N/A	○	●	○
Accepts VGA pass-through	●	N/A	●	●	●
Pass-through cable included	○	N/A	●	●	●
VGA BIOS ROM manufacturer	Cirrus Logic/Award	Cardinal	Compaq	Renaissance	Cirrus Logic/Award
VGA graphics processor	Cirrus Logic	C&T	Paradise	Renaissance	Cirrus Logic
VGA memory	256K	512K	256K	256K	256K
MAXIMUM RESOLUTION					
Graphics (pixels):					
Maximum addressable pixels	1,024 × 768	1,024 × 768	1,024 × 768	1,024 × 768	1,024 × 768
Maximum visible pixels	1,024 × 768	1,024 × 768	1,024 × 768	1,024 × 768	1,024 × 768
Text (columns × rows)	N/A	132 × 50	N/A	132 × 40	146 × 51
Colors in 1,024 × 768 mode:					
Palette	16,777,220	262,144	16,777,220	16,777,220	262,144
Maximum simultaneously displayable	256	16	16	16	256
VIDEO STANDARDS					
CGA	●	●	○	○	●
MDA	●	●	○	○	●
Hercules	●	●	○	○	●
EGA	●	●	○	○	●
VGA	●	●	●	●	●
Super VGA (800 × 600)	●	●	○	●	○
1,024 × 768	●	●	●	●	●
8514/A	○	○	○	●	●
OUTPUT					
TTL	○	●	○	○	●
Analog	●	●	●	●	●
CONNECTORS					
9-pin	○	●	○	○	○
9-pin to BNC	●	○	○	○	○
15-pin	○	●	●	●	●

●—Yes   ○—No   N/A—Not applicable

1,024 x 768 Graphics Adapters ■

	Genoa Systems Super VGA 6400	Headland Technology Video Seven VRAM VGA	Matrox PG-1024V	NEC MultiSync Graphics Engine	Number Nine Computer Corp. Pepper Pro 1024
Price	$	$	$$	$$	$$
BUS TYPE					
ISA 8-bit	●	●	○	○	●
ISA 16-bit	●	●	●	●	●
MCA	○	○	○	●	●
EISA	○	○	○	○	○
PHYSICAL CHARACTERISTICS					
Board size (inches):					
Length	8	13.5	13.25	13.25	13.25
Height	4.25	3	4.5	4.5	4
Thickness	0.5	0.5	0.75	0.5	0.5
HIGH-RESOLUTION CHARACTERISTICS					
High-resolution graphics coprocessor	None	None	Texas Instruments	Texas Instruments	Texas Instruments
High-resolution memory	N/A	N/A	512K	1Mb	1Mb
VGA CHARACTERISTICS					
VGA and high resolution on the same card	●	●	○	●	○
Accepts VGA daughtercard	N/A	N/A	○	N/A	○
Accepts VGA pass-through	N/A	N/A	●	N/A	●
Pass-through cable included	N/A	N/A	●	N/A	●
VGA BIOS ROM manufacturer	Genoa	Video Seven	N/A	C&T	N/A
VGA graphics processor	Genoa	Video Seven	N/A	C&T	N/A
VGA memory	512K	512K	N/A	256K	N/A
MAXIMUM RESOLUTION					
Graphics (pixels):					
Maximum addressable pixels	1,024 × 768	1,024 × 768	1,024 × 1,024	1,024 × 768	4,096 × 2,048
Maximum visible pixels	1,024 × 768	1,024 × 768	1,024 × 768	1,024 × 768	1,024 × 768
Text (columns × rows)	132 × 60	132 × 43	N/A	132 × 60	150 × 50
Colors in 1,024 × 768 mode:					
Palette	262,144	262,144	4,096	16,777,220	16,777,220
Maximum simultaneously displayable	16	16	16	256	256
VIDEO STANDARDS					
CGA	●	●	●	●	○
MDA	●	●	○	●	○
Hercules	●	●	○	●	○
EGA	●	●	○	●	○
VGA	●	●	○	●	●
Super VGA (800 × 600)	●	●	○	●	○
1,024 × 768	●	●	●	●	●
8514/A	●	○	○	●	○
OUTPUT					
TTL	○	○	○	○	○
Analog	●	●	●	●	●
CONNECTORS					
9-pin	○	○	○	○	○
9-pin to BNC	○	○	●	○	○
15-pin	●	●	○	●	●

●—Yes ○—No N/A—Not applicable   **Table Continues →**

■ 1,024 x 768 Graphics Adapters

	Orchid Technology ProDesigner Plus	PCG Photon Performa	Renaissance GRX Rendition II	Samsung SVGA16	STB VGA EM-16
Price	$	$	$$	$	$
BUS TYPE					
ISA 8-bit	●	●	●	●	●
ISA 16-bit	●	●	●	●	●
MCA	○	○	○	○	○
EISA	○	●	○	○	○
PHYSICAL CHARACTERISTICS					
Board size (inches):					
Length	13.25	8	13.25	9.75	8.5
Height	3	4.5	4.5	4	4
Thickness	0.5	0.5	0.75	0.5	0.5
HIGH-RESOLUTION CHARACTERISTICS					
High-resolution graphics coprocessor	None	PCG	Texas Instruments	None	None
High-resolution memory	N/A	512K	1Mb	N/A	N/A
VGA CHARACTERISTICS					
VGA and high resolution on the same card	●	●	○	●	●
Accepts VGA daughtercard	N/A	N/A	●	N/A	N/A
Accepts VGA pass-through	N/A	N/A	●	N/A	N/A
Pass-through cable included	N/A	N/A	●	N/A	N/A
VGA BIOS ROM manufacturer	Tseng	PCG	Renaissance	Tseng	STB/Award
VGA graphics processor	Tseng	PCG	Renaissance	Tseng	Tseng
VGA memory	512K	1Mb	256K	256K	512K
MAXIMUM RESOLUTION					
Graphics (pixels):					
Maximum addressable pixels	1,024 × 768	1,024 × 768	1,024 × 768	1,024 × 768	1,024 × 768
Maximum visible pixels	1,024 × 768	1,024 × 768	1,024 × 768	1,024 × 768	1,024 × 768
Text (columns × rows)	132 × 44	132 × 25	128 × 64	132 × 44	133 × 44
Colors in 1,024 × 768 mode:					
Palette	262,144	262,144	16,777,220	262,144	262,144
Maximum simultaneously displayable	16	16	256	16	16
VIDEO STANDARDS					
CGA	●	●	○	●	●
MDA	●	●	○	●	●
Hercules	●	●	○	●	●
EGA	●	●	○	●	●
VGA	●	●	●	●	●
Super VGA (800 × 600)	●	●	●	●	●
1,024 × 768	●	●	●	●	●
8514/A	○	○	●	○	○
OUTPUT					
TTL	○	●	○	●	●
Analog	●	●	●	●	●
CONNECTORS					
9-pin	○	●	○	●	●
9-pin to BNC	○	○	○	○	○
15-pin	●	●	●	●	●

●—Yes ○—No N/A—Not applicable

1,024 x 768 Graphics Adapters

	Tecmar VGA/AD	Trident 8916	Vermont Microsystems Cobra Plus/HS
Price	$	$	$$$
BUS TYPE			
ISA 8-bit	●	●	●
ISA 16-bit	●	●	●
MCA	○	○	○
EISA	○	○	○
PHYSICAL CHARACTERISTICS			
Board size (inches):			
Length	11	8.5	13.5
Height	4	4.25	4.5
Thickness	0.5	0.75	0.5
HIGH-RESOLUTION CHARACTERISTICS			
High-resolution graphics coprocessor	None	None	Texas Instruments
High-resolution memory	N/A	N/A	1.5Mb
VGA CHARACTERISTICS			
VGA and high resolution on the same card	●	●	○
Accepts VGA daughtercard	N/A	N/A	○
Accepts VGA pass-through	N/A	N/A	●
Pass-through cable included	N/A	N/A	●
VGA BIOS ROM manufacturer	Tecmar	Trident	Video Seven
VGA graphics processor	Tseng	Trident	Video Seven
VGA memory	512K	1Mb	512K
MAXIMUM RESOLUTION			
Graphics (pixels):			
Maximum addressable pixels	1,440 × 720	1,024 × 768	1,024 × 768
Maximum visible pixels	1,440 × 720	1,024 × 768	1,024 × 768
Text (columns × rows)	132 × 60	132 × 60	N/A
Colors in 1,024 × 768 mode:			
Palette	262,144	16,777,220	16,777,220
Maximum simultaneously displayable	16	256	256
VIDEO STANDARDS			
CGA	●	●	○
MDA	●	●	○
Hercules	●	●	○
EGA	●	●	○
VGA	●	●	●
Super VGA (800 × 600)	●	●	○
1,024 × 768	●	●	●
8514/A	○	○	●
OUTPUT			
TTL	●	●	○
Analog	●	●	●
CONNECTORS			
9-pin	●	●	○
9-pin to BNC	○	○	●
15-pin	●	●	○

●—Yes ○—No N/A—Not applicable

End ■

■ C.3   24-Bit Graphics Adapters

(Products listed in alphabetical order by company name)	BleuMont Truc	Everex Viewpoint TC	Matrox Impression/AT-S True-Color Graphics Controller	Opta Mona Lisa 24-Bit Color Display Board	RasterOps ColorBoard 1024MC Display Adapter	TrueVision 1024-32
Price	$$$	$	$$$	$$	$$$	$$$
Interfaces available:						
ISA (16-bit)	●	●	●	●	○	●
MCA	○	○	○	○	●	○
PERFORMANCE CHARACTERISTICS						
Graphics coprocessor	8514/A	None	TI 34020	TI 34020	None	TI 34020
Memory:						
DRAM (standard/maximum)	N/A	1Mb/1Mb	1Mb/1Mb	2Mb/4Mb	N/A	1Mb/16Mb
VRAM (standard/maximum)	3Mb/3Mb	N/A	3Mb/3Mb	2Mb/4Mb	3Mb/3Mb	3Mb/3Mb
VGA type	Pass-through	On-board	Pass-through	On-board	Pass-through	On-board
On-board VGA BIOS	N/A	Everex 1.01	N/A	Tseng ET 4000 AX	N/A	Tseng/TrueVision 1.4
On-board VGA chip set	N/A	Tseng	N/A	Tseng	N/A	Tseng
VGA memory	N/A	1Mb	N/A	512K	N/A	512K
VESA-compliant	N/A	●	N/A	○	N/A	●
Maximum resolution addressable (pixels)	1,024 × 1,024	1,664 × 1,280	1,152 × 882	1,152 × 900	1,024 × 1,024	1,024 × 768
Maximum resolution displayable (pixels)	1,024 × 768	1,280 × 1,024	1,152 × 882	1,152 × 900	1,024 × 768	1,024 × 768
Maximum columns and rows in text mode	132 × 44	132 × 44	N/A	132 × 44	N/A	132 × 50
COLORS						
Maximum colors at:						
640 × 480 resolution	16.8 million	16.8 million	N/A	16.8 million	N/A	16.8 million
800 × 600 resolution	16.8 million	256	N/A	16.8 million	N/A	16.8 million
1,024 × 768 resolution	16.8 million	256	16.8 million	16.8 million	16.8 million	16.8 million
RAM DAC manufacturer	Brooktree	Brooktree	Brooktree	Brooktree	Brooktree	Brooktree
OUTPUT CHARACTERISTICS						
Maximum vertical refresh rates (in hertz):						
1,024 × 768 (noninterlaced)	70	60	60	72	75	76
1,024 × 768 (interlaced)	N/A	79	N/A	72	N/A	87
Digital/TTL output	○	○	○	○	○	○
Analog output	●	●	●	●	●	●
Connectors	15-pin mini D-sub	15-pin mini D-sub	None	15-pin mini D-sub	None	15-pin mini D-sub
Adapter cable included	○	○	●	○	●	●
CUSTOMER SUPPORT						
Hardware warranty	1 year	2 years	1 year	1 year	3 years	1 year
Free technical support	●	●	●	●	●	●
Toll-free number	○	○	●	●	●	○
BBS	○	●	●	●	●	●
Fax	○	○	●	●	○	○

●—Yes   ○—No   N/A—Not applicable

C.4   High-Resolution Graphics Adapters ■

(Products listed in alphabetical order by company name)	Acronics Systems Inc.	Acronics Systems Inc.	Actix Systems Inc.	Actix Systems Inc.	Actix Systems Inc.
	ASI2000 Orion VLB 64	**ASI2020 Taurus PCI 64**	**Graphics-Engine 64 VLB**	**Graphics-Engine 64 PCI**	**Graphics-Engine Ultra 64 PCI**
List price (tested configuration)	$	$	$	$	$
Graphics accelerator chip	Cirrus Logic CL-GD5434	Cirrus Logic CL-GD5434	S3 Vision864	S3 Vision864	S3 Vision964
Includes video acceleration	○	○	○	○	○
Separate video-playback acceleration chip	○	○	○	○	○
Video-playback chip manufacturer	N/A	N/A	N/A	N/A	N/A
VGA BIOS manufacturer	Cirrus Logic	Cirrus Logic	Phoenix	Phoenix	Phoenix
VGA pass-through connector	●	●	●	●	●
Hardware cursor	●	●	●	●	●
Display memory	2Mb 70-ns DRAM	2Mb 70-ns DRAM	2Mb 70-ns DRAM	2Mb 70-ns DRAM	2Mb 60-ns VRAM
Maximum installable memory	2Mb	4Mb	4Mb	4Mb	4Mb
RAMDAC	On chip	On chip	ATT21C498	ATT21C498	TVP 3025
Uses DIP switches	○	○	○	○	○
Uses jumpers	○	○	○	○	○
Settings are configurable in an on-board EEPROM	○	○	○	○	○
DISPLAY CHARACTERISTICS					
Maximum noninterlaced graphics resolution (dpi)	1,280 x 1,024	1,280 x 1,024	1,600 x 1,200	1,600 x 1,200	1,600 x 1,200
Maximum number of colors at:					
1,600-by-1,200 resolution	N/A	N/A	256	256	256
1,280-by-1,024 resolution	256	256	256	256	256
1,024-by-768 resolution	65,000	65,000	65,000	65,000	65,000
800-by-600 resolution	16.7 million	16.7 million	16.7 million	16.7 million	16.7 million
SOFTWARE FEATURES					
Drivers included:					
AutoCAD	●	●	●	●	●
Other CAD drivers	MicroStation, 3DStudio	MicroStation, 3DStudio	Generic CADD, Versa CAD	Generic CADD, Versa CAD	Generic CADD, Versa CAD
Corel Ventura	●	●	●	●	●
OS/2 2.1	●	●	●	●	●
Windows NT	●	●	●	●	●
Proprietary resolution-switching dialog box	●	●	●	●	●
User can change resolution without rebooting Windows	○	○	○	○	○
Zoom	○	○	○	○	○
Virtual display	○	○	○	○	○
Refresh-rate selection utility	●	●	●	●	●

●—Yes ○—No N/A—Not applicable   INA—Information not available

Table Continues →

High-Resolution Graphics Adapters

	American Megatrends Inc. **Fast View VLB**	American Megatrends Inc. **Fast View PCI**	Appian Technology Inc. **Renegade 1280 VLB**	ATI Technologies Inc. **Graphics XPression 2MB VLB**	ATI Technologies Inc. **Graphics XPression 2MB PCI**
List price (tested configuration)	$	$	$	$	$
Graphics accelerator chip	Weitek Power 9000	Weitek Power 9000	Appian AGC98032	ATI mach64	ATI mach64
Includes video acceleration	○	○	○	●	●
Separate video-playback acceleration chip	○	○	●	○	○
Video-playback chip manufacturer	N/A	N/A	Cirrus Logic	N/A	N/A
VGA BIOS manufacturer	Weitek	Weitek	Cirrus Logic	ATI	ATI
VGA pass-through connector	●	●	○	●	●
Hardware cursor	●	●	●	●	●
Display memory	2Mb 70-ns VRAM	2Mb 60-ns VRAM	2Mb 80-ns VRAM	2Mb 60-ns DRAM	2Mb 60-ns DRAM
Maximum installable memory	2Mb	2Mb	2Mb	2Mb	2Mb
RAMDAC	BT485	BT485	TVP 3010	STG 1702J-13Z	STG 1702J-13Z
Uses DIP switches	○	○	○	○	○
Uses jumpers	●	○	●	○	○
Settings are configurable in an on-board EEPROM	○	○	○	●	●
DISPLAY CHARACTERISTICS					
Maximum noninterlaced graphics resolution (dpi)	1,280 x 1,024	1,280 x 1,024	1,024 x 768	1,280 x 1,024	1,280 x 1,024
Maximum number of colors at:					
1,600-by-1,200 resolution	N/A	N/A	N/A	N/A	N/A
1,280-by-1,024 resolution	256	256	256	256	256
1,024-by-768 resolution	65,000	65,000	65,000	65,000	65,000
800-by-600 resolution	16.7 million	16.7 million	65,000	16.7 million	16.7 million
SOFTWARE FEATURES					
Drivers included:					
AutoCAD	●	○	●	●	●
Other CAD drivers	MicroStation	MicroStation	MicroStation, 3DStudio	MicroStation, 3DStudio	MicroStation, 3DStudio
Corel Ventura	●	●	○	●	●
OS/2 2.1	●	●	○	●	●
Windows NT	●	●	●	●	●
Proprietary resolution-switching dialog box	○	○	●	●	●
User can change resolution without rebooting Windows	○	○	○	●	●
Zoom	○	○	○	●	●
Virtual display	○	○	●	●	●
Refresh-rate selection utility	●	●	●	●	●

●—Yes ○—No N/A—Not applicable INA—Information not available

High-Resolution Graphics Adapters ■

	ATI Technologies Inc.	ATI Technologies Inc.	ATI Technologies Inc.	ATI Technologies Inc.	Boca Research Inc.
	Winturbo VLB	**Winturbo PCI**	**Graphics Pro Turbo VLB**	**Graphics Pro Turbo PCI**	**Boca Voyager VLB**
List price (tested configuration)	$	$	$	$	$
Graphics accelerator chip	ATI mach64	ATI mach64	ATI mach64	ATI mach64	C&T 64300, Wingine DGX
Includes video acceleration	●	●	INA	INA	●
Separate video-playback acceleration chip	○	○	INA	INA	○
Video-playback chip manufacturer	N/A	N/A	INA	INA	N/A
VGA BIOS manufacturer	ATI	ATI	ATI	ATI	C&T
VGA pass-through connector	●	●	●	●	●
Hardware cursor	●	●	●	●	●
Display memory	2MB 60-ns VRAM	2Mb 60-ns VRAM	2Mb VRAM	2Mb VRAM	2Mb 70-ns DRAM
Maximum installable memory	2Mb	2Mb	4Mb VRAM	4Mb VRAM	2Mb
RAMDAC	68860 SpectraDAC	68860 SpectraDAC	ATI 68860	ATI 68860	On chip
Uses DIP switches	○	○	INA	INA	○
Uses jumpers	○	○	INA	INA	○
Settings are configurable in an on-board EEPROM	●	●	INA	INA	○
DISPLAY CHARACTERISTICS					
Maximum noninterlaced graphics resolution (dpi)	1,280 x 1,024	1,280 x 1,024	1,280 x 1,024	1,280 x 1,024	1,024 x 768
Maximum number of colors at:					
1,600-by-1,200 resolution	N/A	N/A	N/A	N/A	N/A
1,280-by-1,024 resolution	256	256	16.7 million	16.7 million	N/A
1,024-by-768 resolution	65,000	65,000	16.7 million	16.7 million	256
800-by-600 resolution	16.7 million	16.7 million	16.7 million	16.7 million	65,000
SOFTWARE FEATURES					
Drivers included:					
AutoCAD	●	●	●	●	●
Other CAD drivers	MicroStation, 3DStudio	MicroStation, 3DStudio	INA	INA	None
Corel Ventura	●	●	INA	INA	●
OS/2 2.1	●	●	●	●	Optional
Windows NT	●	●	INA	INA	●
Proprietary resolution-switching dialog box	●	●	INA	INA	○
User can change resolution without rebooting Windows	●	●	INA	INA	○
Zoom	●	●	●	●	○
Virtual display	●	●	●	●	○
Refresh-rate selection utility	●	●	●	●	●

●—Yes ○—No N/A—Not applicable INA—Information not available

Table Continues →

High-Resolution Graphics Adapters

	Brilliant Computer Products	Brilliant Computer Products	Cardexpert Technology Inc.	Cardexpert Technology Inc.	Diamond Multimedia Systems Inc.
	Cloud9 VLB	Cloud9 Thunder64 PCI	Cardex Challenger32 VLB	Cardex Challenger Pro PCI	SpeedStar 64 PCI
List price (tested configuration)	$	$	$	$	$
Graphics accelerator chip	NCR 77C32BLT	S3 Vision864	Tseng Labs ET4000/W32p	Tseng Labs ET4000/W32p	Cirrus Logic CL-GD5434
Includes video acceleration	○	○	○	○	○
Separate video-playback acceleration chip	○	○	○	○	○
Video-playback chip manufacturer	N/A	N/A	N/A	N/A	N/A
VGA BIOS manufacturer	NCR	Phoenix, S3	Tseng Labs	Tseng Labs	Diamond
VGA pass-through connector	●	●	●	●	●
Hardware cursor	●	●	●	●	●
Display memory	2Mb 45-ns DRAM	2Mb 60-ns DRAM	2Mb 45-ns DRAM	2Mb 45-ns DRAM	2Mb 60-ns DRAM
Maximum installable memory	2Mb	2Mb	2Mb	2Mb	2Mb
RAMDAC	ChronDAC CH8391v	SDAC	STG 1702J-13Z	STG 1702J-13Z	On chip
Uses DIP switches	○	○	○	○	○
Uses jumpers	●	●	●	●	●
Settings are configurable in an on-board EEPROM	○	○	○	○	○
DISPLAY CHARACTERISTICS					
Maximum noninterlaced graphics resolution (dpi)	1,280 x 1,024	1,280 x 1,024	1,280 x1,024	1,280 x 1,024	1,280 x 1,024
Maximum number of colors at:					
1,600-by-1,200 resolution	N/A	N/A	N/A	N/A	N/A
1,280-by-1,024 resolution	256	256	256	256	256
1,024-by-768 resolution	65,000	65,000	65,000	65,000	65,000
800-by-600 resolution	16.7 million	16.7 million	16.7 million	16.7 million	16.7 million
SOFTWARE FEATURES					
Drivers included:					
AutoCAD	●	●	●	●	●
Other CAD drivers	None	MicroStation	None	None	None
Corel Ventura	○	○	●	●	○
OS/2 2.1	Optional	Optional	●	●	●
Windows NT	●	●	●	●	●
Proprietary resolution-switching dialog box	●	○	●	●	●
User can change resolution without rebooting Windows	○	○	○	○	○
Zoom	○	○	○	○	○
Virtual display	○	○	○	○	○
Refresh-rate selection utility	●	●	●	●	●

●—Yes ○—No N/A—Not applicable INA—Information not available

High-Resolution Graphics Adapters ▪

	Diamond Multimedia Systems Inc. **Stealth 32 VLB**	Diamond Multimedia Systems Inc. **Stealth 32 PCI**	Diamond Multimedia Systems Inc. **Stealth 64 DRAM VLB**	Diamond Multimedia Systems Inc. **Stealth 64 DRAM PCI**	Diamond Multimedia Systems Inc. **Stealth 64 VRAM VLB**
List price (tested configuration)	$	$	$	$	$
Graphics accelerator chip	Tseng Labs ET4000/W32p	Tseng Labs ET4000/W32p	S3 Vision 864	S3 Vision 864	S3 Vision964
Includes video acceleration	○	○	○	○	○
Separate video-playback acceleration chip	○	○	○	○	○
Video-playback chip manufacturer	N/A	N/A	N/A	N/A	N/A
VGA BIOS manufacturer	Diamond	Diamond	Diamond	Diamond	Diamond
VGA pass-through connector	●	●	●	●	●
Hardware cursor	●	●	●	●	●
Display memory	2Mb 60 -ns DRAM	2Mb 60 -ns DRAM	2Mb 60-ns DRAM	2Mb 70 -ns DRAM	2Mb 60-ns VRAM
Maximum installable memory	2Mb	2Mb	2Mb	2Mb	4Mb
RAMDAC	STG 1702J-13Z	STG 1702J-13Z	SDAC	SDAC	BT485
Uses DIP switches	○	○	○	○	○
Uses jumpers	○	○	○	○	○
Settings are configurable in an on-board EEPROM	○	○	○	○	○
DISPLAY CHARACTERISTICS					
Maximum noninterlaced graphics resolution (dpi)	1,280 x 1,024	1,280 x 1,024	1,280 x 1,024	1,280 x 1,024	1,280 x 1,024
Maximum number of colors at:					
1,600-by-1,200 resolution	N/A	N/A	N/A	N/A	N/A
1,280-by-1,024 resolution	256	256	256	256	256
1,024-by-768 resolution	65,000	65,000	65,000	65,000	65,000
800-by-600 resolution	16.7 million	16.7 million	16.7 million	16.7 million	16.7 million
SOFTWARE FEATURES					
Drivers included:					
AutoCAD	●	●	●	●	●
Other CAD drivers	None	None	MicroStation	MicroStation	MicroStation
Corel Ventura	●	●	○	○	○
OS/2 2.1	●	●	●	●	●
Windows NT	●	●	●	●	●
Proprietary resolution-switching dialog box	●	●	●	●	●
User can change resolution without rebooting Windows	○	○	●	●	●
Zoom	●	●	●	●	●
Virtual display	●	●	●	●	●
Refresh-rate selection utility	●	●	●	●	●

●—Yes ○—No N/A—Not applicable   INA—Information not available

Table Continues →

High-Resolution Graphics Adapters

	Diamond Multimedia Systems Inc. Stealth 64 VRAM PCI	Diamond Multimedia Systems Inc. Viper Pro	Diamond Multimedia Systems Inc. Viper SE VLB	Diamond Multimedia Systems Inc. Viper SE PCI	ELSA Inc. Winner 1000PRO VLB
List price (tested configuration)	$	$	$	$	$
Graphics accelerator chip	S3 Vision 964	Weitek P9100	Weitek Power 9100	Weitek Power 9100	S3 Vision864
Includes video acceleration	○	INA	○	○	○
Separate video-playback acceleration chip	○	INA	○	○	○
Video-playback chip manufacturer	N/A	INA	N/A	N/A	N/A
VGA BIOS manufacturer	Diamond	Diamond	Diamond	Diamond	ELSA
VGA pass-through connector	●	○	●	●	●
Hardware cursor	●	●	●	●	●
Display memory	2Mb 60-ns VRAM	4Mb VRAM	2Mb 70-ns VRAM	2Mb 70-ns VRAM	2Mb 70-ns DRAM
Maximum installable memory	4Mb	4Mb VRAM	4Mb	4Mb	2Mb
RAMDAC	BT485	RGB525	RGB525	RGB525	ATT21C498
Uses DIP switches	○	INA	○	○	●
Uses jumpers	○	INA	●	○	○
Settings are configurable in an on-board EEPROM	○	INA	○	○	●
DISPLAY CHARACTERISTICS					
Maximum noninterlaced graphics resolution (dpi)	1,280 x 1,024	1,600 x 1,200	1,600 x 1,200	1,600 x 1,200	1,280 x 1,024
Maximum number of colors at:					
1,600-by-1,200 resolution	N/A	INA	256	256	N/A
1,280-by-1,024 resolution	256	16.7 million	256	256	256
1,024-by-768 resolution	65,000	16.7 million	65,000	65,000	256
800-by-600 resolution	16.7 million	16.7 million	16.7 million	16.7 million	16.7 million
SOFTWARE FEATURES					
Drivers included:					
AutoCAD	●	●	●	●	●
Other CAD drivers	MicroStation	INA	MicroStation, 3DStudio	MicroStation, 3DStudio	None
Corel Ventura	○	INA	○	○	○
OS/2 2.1	●	Optional	●	●	●
Windows NT	●	INA	●	●	●
Proprietary resolution-switching dialog box	●	INA	●	●	●
User can change resolution without rebooting Windows	●	INA	●	●	○
Zoom	●	○	○	○	○
Virtual display	●	○	○	○	●
Refresh-rate selection utility	●	●	●	●	●

●—Yes ○—No N/A—Not applicable INA—Information not available

High-Resolution Graphics Adapters

	ELSA Inc. Winner 1000PRO PCI	ELSA Inc. Winner 2000PRO-PCI	Genoa Systems Corp. Hornet VLB	Genoa Systems Corp. Phantom 64 VLB	Hercules Computer Technology Inc. Dynamite Power VLB
List price (tested configuration)	$	$	$	$	$
Graphics accelerator chip	S3 Vision864	S3 Vision964	NCR 77C32BLT	S3 Vision864	Tseng ET4000/W32p
Includes video acceleration	○	INA	○	○	○
Separate video-playback acceleration chip	○	INA	○	○	○
Video-playback chip manufacturer	N/A	INA	N/A	N/A	N/A
VGA BIOS manufacturer	ELSA	ELSA	NCR	Phoenix	Tseng Labs
VGA pass-through connector	●	●	●	●	●
Hardware cursor	●	●	●	●	●
Display memory	2Mb 70-ns DRAM	4Mb VRAM	2Mb 70-ns DRAM	2Mb 70-ns DRAM	2 Mb 60-ns DRAM
Maximum installable memory	2Mb	4Mb VRAM	2Mb	2Mb	2Mb
RAMDAC	ATT21C498	TI 3020	MU9C9910V	SDAC	STG 1702J-13Z
Uses DIP switches	○	INA	○	○	○
Uses jumpers	○	INA	○	○	●
Settings are configurable in an on-board EEPROM	●	INA	○	○	○
DISPLAY CHARACTERISTICS					
Maximum noninterlaced graphics resolution (dpi)	1,280 x 1,024	1,600 x 1,200	1,280 x 1,024	1,600 x 1,200	1,280 x 1,024
Maximum number of colors at:					
1,600-by-1,200 resolution	N/A	INA	N/A	256	N/A
1,280-by-1,024 resolution	256	65,536	256	256	256
1,024-by-768 resolution	256	16.7 million	256	65,000	65,000
800-by-600 resolution	16.7 million	16.7 million	16.7 million	16.7 million	16.7 million
SOFTWARE FEATURES					
Drivers included:					
AutoCAD	●	●	●	●	●
Other CAD drivers	None	INA	None	Generic CADD	3DStudio
Corel Ventura	○	INA	○	○	○
OS/2 2.1	●	●	●	●	●
Windows NT	●	INA	●	●	●
Proprietary resolution-switching dialog box	●	INA	●	●	●
User can change resolution without rebooting Windows	●	INA	●	●	●
Zoom	○	○	○	○	○
Virtual display	●	●	●	●	○
Refresh-rate selection utility	●	●	●	●	●

●—Yes ○—No N/A—Not applicable INA—Information not available

Table Continues →

High-Resolution Graphics Adapters

	Matrox Graphics Inc MGA Impression	Matrox Graphics Inc MGA Impression	Matrox Graphics Inc MGA Impression Plus PCI	Matrox Graphics Inc MGA Ultima Plus VLB	Matrox Graphics Inc MGA Ultima Plus PCI
List price (tested configuration)	$	$	$	$	$
Graphics accelerator chip	MGA 64	MGA 64	Matrox MGA	MGA 64	MGA 64
Includes video acceleration	INA	INA	○	INA	INA
Separate video-playback acceleration chip	INA	INA	○	INA	INA
Video-playback chip manufacturer	INA	INA	N/A	INA	INA
VGA BIOS manufacturer	LSI Logic	LSI Logic	LSI Logic	LSI Logic	LSI Logic
VGA pass-through connector	●	●	●	●	●
Hardware cursor	●	●	●	●	●
Display memory	3Mb VRAM	3Mb VRAM, 2Mb DRAM	2 Mb 60-ns VRAM	4Mb VRAM	4Mb VRAM
Maximum installable memory	3Mb VRAM, 2Mb DRAM	3Mb VRAM, 2Mb DRAM	4Mb	4Mb VRAM	4Mb VRAM
RAMDAC	BT485	BT485	TVP 3026	TI 3020	TI 3020
Uses DIP switches	INA	INA	○	INA	INA
Uses jumpers	INA	INA	○	INA	INA
Settings are configurable in an on-board EEPROM	INA	INA	●	INA	INA
DISPLAY CHARACTERISTICS					
Maximum noninterlaced graphics resolution (dpi)	1,600 x 1,200	1,600 x 1,200	1,600 x 1,200	1,600 x 1,200	1,600 x 1,200
Maximum number of colors at:					
1,600-by-1,200 resolution	INA	INA	256	INA	INA
1,280-by-1,024 resolution	N/A	N/A	256	65,536	65,536
1,024-by-768 resolution	16.7 million	16.7 million	65,000	16.7 million	16.7 million
800-by-600 resolution	16.7 million	16.7 million	16.7 million	16.7 million	16.7 million
SOFTWARE FEATURES					
Drivers included:					
AutoCAD	●	●	●	●	●
Other CAD drivers	INA	INA	MicroStation	INA	INA
Corel Ventura	INA	INA	○	INA	INA
OS/2 2.1	Optional	Optional	Optional	Optional	Optional
Windows NT	INA	INA	●	INA	INA
Proprietary resolution-switching dialog box	INA	INA	●	INA	INA
User can change resolution without rebooting Windows	INA	INA	●	INA	INA
Zoom	●	●	●	●	●
Virtual display	●	●	●	●	●
Refresh-rate selection utility	●	●	●	●	●

●—Yes ○—No N/A—Not applicable INA—Information not available

High-Resolution Graphics Adapters ■

	Matrox Graphics Inc	Media Vision	Micro-Labs Inc.	Micro-Labs Inc.	miro Computer Products Inc.
	MGA Ultima Plus 200	Pro Graphics 1024	Ultimate TrueColor/XLp/VLB	Ultimate TrueColor/XLp/PCI	miroCrystal 20SD VLB
List price (tested configuration)	$	$	$	$	$
Graphics accelerator chip	MGA 64	MVV452	Tseng ET4000/W32p	Tseng ET4000/W32p	S3 Vision864
Includes video acceleration	INA	INA	○	○	○
Separate video-playback acceleration chip	INA	INA	○	○	○
Video-playback chip manufacturer	INA	INA	N/A	N/A	N/A
VGA BIOS manufacturer	LSI Logic	Cirrus	Tseng Labs	Tseng Labs	S3, miro
VGA pass-through connector	●	○	●	●	●
Hardware cursor	●	●	●	●	●
Display memory	4Mb VRAM	2.25Mb VRAM	2Mb 45-ns DRAM	2Mb 45-ns DRAM	2Mb 70-ns DRAM
Maximum installable memory	4Mb VRAM	2.25Mb VRAM	2Mb	2Mb	2Mb
RAMDAC	TI 3020	MVV462	STG 1702J-13Z	STG 1702J-13Z	SDAC
Uses DIP switches	INA	INA	○	○	○
Uses jumpers	INA	INA	●	●	○
Settings are configurable in an on-board EEPROM	INA	INA	○	○	○
DISPLAY CHARACTERISTICS					
Maximum noninterlaced graphics resolution (dpi)	1,600 x 1,200	1,024 x 768	1,280 x 1,024	1,280 x 1,024	1,408 x 1,024
Maximum number of colors at:					
1,600-by-1,200 resolution	INA	N/A	N/A	N/A	N/A
1,280-by-1,024 resolution	65,536	N/A	256	256	256
1,024-by-768 resolution	16.7 million	16.7 million	65,000	65,000	65,000
800-by-600 resolution	16.7 million	16.7 million	16.7 million	16.7 million	16.7 million
SOFTWARE FEATURES					
Drivers included:					
AutoCAD	●	●	●	●	●
Other CAD drivers	INA	INA	MicroStation, 3DStudio	MicroStation, 3DStudio	MicroStation
Corel Ventura	INA	INA	●	●	○
OS/2 2.1	Optional	○	●	●	●
Windows NT	INA	INA	●	●	○
Proprietary resolution-switching dialog box	INA	INA	○	○	●
User can change resolution without rebooting Windows	INA	INA	○	○	● (except in 640-by-480 and 800-by-600 modes)
Zoom	●	○	○	○	●
Virtual display	●	○	○	○	●
Refresh-rate selection utility	●	●	●	●	●

●—Yes ○—No N/A—Not applicable INA—Information not available

Table Continues →

High-Resolution Graphics Adapters

	miro Computer Products Inc.	miro Computer Products Inc.	miro Computer Products Inc.	miro Computer Products Inc.	miro Computer Products Inc.
	miroCrystal 20SD PCI	miroCrystal 20SV VLB	miroCrystal 20SV PCI	miroCrystal 32S VLB	miroCrystal 32S PCI
List price (tested configuration)	$	$	$	$	$
Graphics accelerator chip	S3 Vision864	S3 Vision964	S3 Vision964	S3 Vision964	S3 Vision964
Includes video acceleration	○	○	○	INA	INA
Separate video-playback acceleration chip	○	○	○	INA	INA
Video-playback chip manufacturer	N/A	N/A	N/A	INA	INA
VGA BIOS manufacturer	S3, miro	S3, miro	S3, miro	S3, miro	S3, miro
VGA pass-through connector	●	●	●	○	○
Hardware cursor	●	●	●	●	●
Display memory	2Mb 70-ns DRAM	2Mb 70-ns VRAM	2Mb 70-ns VRAM	4Mb VRAM	4Mb VRAM
Maximum installable memory	2Mb	2Mb	2Mb	4Mb VRAM	4Mb VRAM
RAMDAC	SDAC	BT485	BT485	BT485	BT485
Uses DIP switches	○	○	○	INA	INA
Uses jumpers	○	○	○	INA	INA
Settings are configurable in an on-board EEPROM	○	○	○	INA	INA
DISPLAY CHARACTERISTICS					
Maximum noninterlaced graphics resolution (dpi)	1,408 x 1,024	1,408 x 1,024	1,408 x 1,024	1,408 x 1,024	1,408 x 1,024
Maximum number of colors at:					
1,600-by-1,200 resolution	N/A	N/A	N/A	N/A	N/A
1,280-by-1,024 resolution	256	256	256	65,536	65,536
1,024-by-768 resolution	65,000	65,000	65,000	16.7 million	16.7 million
800-by-600 resolution	16.7 million	16.7 million	16.7 million	16.7 million	16.7 million
SOFTWARE FEATURES					
Drivers included:					
AutoCAD	●	●	●	●	●
Other CAD drivers	MicroStation	MicroStation	MicroStation	INA	INA
Corel Ventura	○	○	○	INA	INA
OS/2 2.1	●	●	●	Optional	Optional
Windows NT	●	●	●	INA	INA
Proprietary resolution-switching dialog box	●	●	●	INA	INA
User can change resolution without rebooting Windows	● (except in 640-by-480 and 800-by-600 modes)	● (except in 640-by-480 and 800-by-600 modes)	● (except in 640-by-480 and 800-by-600 modes)	INA	INA
Zoom	●	●	●	●	●
Virtual display	●	●	●	●	●
Refresh-rate selection utility	●	●	●	●	●

●—Yes ○—No N/A—Not applicable INA—Information not available

High-Resolution Graphics Adapters

	MiTAC USA	Number Nine Computer Corp.	Number Nine Computer Corp.	Number Nine Computer Corp.	Number Nine Computer Corp.
	MiTAC W32P PCI	**#9GXE64 VLB**	**#9GXE64 PCI**	**#9GXE64-Pro VLB**	**#9GXE64-ProPCI**
List price (tested configuration)	$	$	$	$	$
Graphics accelerator chip	Tseng ET4000/W32p	S3 Vision864	S3 Vision864	S3 Vision964	S3 Vision964
Includes video acceleration	○	○	○	○	○
Separate video-playback acceleration chip	○	○	○	○	○
Video-playback chip manufacturer	N/A	N/A	N/A	N/A	N/A
VGA BIOS manufacturer	Tseng Labs	Number Nine	Number Nine	Number Nine	Number Nine
VGA pass-through connector	●	●	●	●	●
Hardware cursor	●	●	●	●	●
Display memory	2 Mb 70-ns DRAM	2Mb 70-ns DRAM	2Mb 70-ns DRAM	2 Mb 70-ns VRAM	2Mb 70-ns VRAM
Maximum installable memory	2Mb	2Mb	2Mb	4Mb	4Mb
RAMDAC	CH8398	ATT21C498	ATT21C498	TVP 3025	TVP 3025
Uses DIP switches	○	○	○	○	○
Uses jumpers	○	○	○	○	○
Settings are configurable in an on-board EEPROM	○	○	○	○	○
DISPLAY CHARACTERISTICS					
Maximum noninterlaced graphics resolution (dpi)	1,280 x 1,024	1,280 x 1,024	1,280 x 1,024	1,280 x 1,024	1,280 x 1,024
Maximum number of colors at:					
1,600-by-1,200 resolution	N/A	N/A	N/A	N/A	N/A
1,280-by-1,024 resolution	256	256	256	256	256
1,024-by-768 resolution	65,000	65,000	65,000	65,000	65,000
800-by-600 resolution	16.7 million	16.7 million	16.7 million	16.7 million	16.7 million
SOFTWARE FEATURES					
Drivers included:					
AutoCAD	●	●	●	●	●
Other CAD drivers	None	MicroStation, 3DStudio	MicroStation, 3DStudio	MicroStation, 3DStudio	MicroStation, 3DStudio
Corel Ventura	●	○	○	●	●
OS/2 2.1	●	Optional	Optional	Optional	Optional
Windows NT	●	●	●	●	●
Proprietary resolution-switching dialog box	●	●	●	●	●
User can change resolution without rebooting Windows	○	○	○	○	○
Zoom	○	●	●	●	●
Virtual display	○	●	●	●	●
Refresh-rate selection utility	●	●	●	●	●

●—Yes ○—No N/A—Not applicable INA—Information not available

Table Continues →

High-Resolution Graphics Adapters

	Orchid Technology	Personal Computer Graphics Corp.	RasterOps Corp.	Spider Graphics Inc.	Spider Graphics Inc.
	Kelvin 64 VLB	Photon Torpedo 864 PCI	Truevision Color-Impact 100 VLB	Spider 256 Cache VLB	Spider 64 PCI
List price (tested configuration)	$	$	$	$	$
Graphics accelerator chip	Cirrus Logic CL-GD5434	S3 Vision864	Cirrus Logic CL-GD5434	C&T 64300, Wing-ine DGX	Cirrus Logic CL-GD5434
Includes video acceleration	○	○	○	○	○
Separate video-playback acceleration chip	○	○	○	○	○
Video-playback chip manufacturer	N/A	N/A	N/A	N/A	N/A
VGA BIOS manufacturer	Cirrus Logic	PCG	Quantel	Spider	Spider
VGA pass-through connector	●	●	●	●	●
Hardware cursor	●	●	●	●	●
Display memory	2Mb 70-ns DRAM	2Mb 60-ns DRAM	2Mb 70-ns DRAM	2Mb 70-ns DRAM	4Mb 80-ns DRAM
Maximum installable memory	2Mb	4Mb	2Mb	2Mb	4Mb
RAMDAC	On chip	On chip	On chip	On chip	On chip
Uses DIP switches	○	●	○	○	○
Uses jumpers	○	●	●	○	○
Settings are configurable in an on-board EEPROM	○	●	○	●	○
DISPLAY CHARACTERISTICS					
Maximum noninterlaced graphics resolution (dpi)	1,280 x 1,024	1,600 x 1,200	1,280 x 1,024	1,024 x 768	1,280 x 1,024
Maximum number of colors at:					
1,600-by-1,200 resolution	N/A	256	N/A	N/A	N/A
1,280-by-1,024 resolution	256	256	256	N/A	65,000
1,024-by-768 resolution	65,000	65,000	65,000	256	65,000
800-by-600 resolution	16.7 million	16.7 million	16.7 million	65,000	16.7 million
SOFTWARE FEATURES					
Drivers included:					
AutoCAD	●	●	●	●	●
Other CAD drivers	3DStudio	Generic CADD, MicroStation	3DStudio	3DStudio	3DStudio
Corel Ventura	○	●	●	○	○
OS/2 2.1	●	●	●	●	●
Windows NT	●	●	●	●	●
Proprietary resolution-switching dialog box	●	○	●	●	●
User can change resolution without rebooting Windows	○	○	●	●	●
Zoom	●	○	○	○	○
Virtual display	●	○	○	●	●
Refresh-rate selection utility	●	●	●	●	●

●—Yes ○—No N/A—Not applicable INA—Information not available

High-Resolution Graphics Adapters ■

	Spider Graphics Inc.	Spider Graphics Inc.	STB Systems Inc.	STB Systems Inc.	STB Systems Inc.
	Tarantula 64 VLB	**Tarantula 64 PCI**	**Pegasus VL**	**PowerGraph 64 PCI**	**PowerGraph Pro PCI**
List price (tested configuration)	$	$	$	$	$
Graphics accelerator chip	S3 Vision964	S3 Vision964	S3 928	S3 Trio64	S3 Vision864
Includes video acceleration	○	○	INA	○	○
Separate video-playback acceleration chip	○	○	INA	○	○
Video-playback chip manufacturer	N/A	N/A	INA	N/A	N/A
VGA BIOS manufacturer	Spider	Spider	STB	STB	STB
VGA pass-through connector	●	●	●	●	●
Hardware cursor	●	●	●	●	●
Display memory	2Mb 70-ns VRAM	2Mb 70-ns VRAM	4Mb VRAM	2Mb 45-ns DRAM	2 Mb 45-ns DRAM
Maximum installable memory	4Mb	4Mb	4Mb VRAM	2Mb	2 Mb
RAMDAC	BT485	BT485	BT485	On chip	SDAC
Uses DIP switches	○	○	INA	○	○
Uses jumpers	●	●	INA	○	○
Settings are configurable in an on-board EEPROM	○	○	INA	●	●
DISPLAY CHARACTERISTICS					
Maximum noninterlaced graphics resolution (dpi)	1,600 x 1,200	1,600 x 1,200	1,600 x 1,200	1,280 x 1,024	1,280 x 1,024
Maximum number of colors at:					
1,600-by-1,200 resolution	65,000	65,000	INA	N/A	N/A
1,280-by-1,024 resolution	65,000	65,000	64,000	256	256
1,024-by-768 resolution	65,000	65,000	16.7 million	65,000	65,000
800-by-600 resolution	16.7 million	16.7 million	16.7 million	16.7 million	16.7 million
SOFTWARE FEATURES					
Drivers included:					
AutoCAD	●	●	●	●	●
Other CAD drivers	3DStudio	3DStudio	INA	MicroStation	MicroStation
Corel Ventura	○	○	INA	●	●
OS/2 2.1	●	●	●	●	●
Windows NT	●	●	INA	●	●
Proprietary resolution-switching dialog box	●	●	INA	●	●
User can change resolution without rebooting Windows	●	●	INA	●	●
Zoom	○	○	○	●	●
Virtual display	●	●	○	●	●
Refresh-rate selection utility	●	●	●	●	●

●—Yes ○—No N/A—Not applicable INA—Information not available   **Table Continues →**

■ High-Resolution Graphics Adapters

	SuperMac	SuperMac	VidTech Microsystems Inc.	Western Digital Corp.
	Spectrum/24 ISA	Spectrum/24 VLB	FastMax P20 PCI	Paradise Bahamas 64 PCI
List price (tested configuration)	$	$	$	$
Graphics accelerator chip	SuperMac SQD	SuperMac SQD	S3 Vision864	S3 Vision864
Includes video acceleration	INA	INA	○	○
Separate video-playback acceleration chip	INA	INA	○	○
Video-playback chip manufacturer	INA	INA	N/A	N/A
VGA BIOS manufacturer	Cirrus	Cirrus	S3	S3
VGA pass-through connector	●	●	●	●
Hardware cursor	○	○	●	●
Display memory	3Mb VRAM	3Mb VRAM	2Mb 70-ns DRAM	2Mb 60-ns DRAM
Maximum installable memory	3Mb VRAM	3Mb VRAM	2Mb	2Mb
RAMDAC	Analog Devices 471	Analog Devices 471	SDAC	SDAC
Uses DIP switches	INA	INA	○	○
Uses jumpers	INA	INA	○	○
Settings are configurable in an on-board EEPROM	INA	INA	○	○
DISPLAY CHARACTERISTICS				
Maximum noninterlaced graphics resolution (dpi)	1,152 x 910	1,152 x 910	1,600 x 1,200	1,600 x 1,200
Maximum number of colors at:				
1,600-by-1,200 resolution	N/A	N/A	256	256
1,280-by-1,024 resolution	N/A	N/A	256	256
1,024-by-768 resolution	16.7 million	16.7 million	65,000	65,000
800-by-600 resolution	16.7 million	16.7 million	16.7 million	16.7 million
SOFTWARE FEATURES				
Drivers included:				
AutoCAD	○	○	●	●
Other CAD drivers	N/A	N/A	MicroStation, 3DStudio	MicroStation
Corel Ventura	INA	INA	○	○
OS/2 2.1	○	○	●	●
Windows NT	INA	INA	●	●
Proprietary resolution-switching dialog box	INA	INA	●	○
User can change resolution without rebooting Windows	INA	INA	●	○
Zoom	○	○	●	○
Virtual display	○	○	○	○
Refresh-rate selection utility	●	●	●	●

●—Yes ○—No N/A—Not applicable INA—Information not available

End ■

COMPARISON CHART

PRINTERS

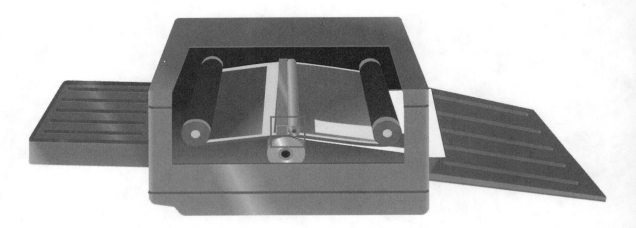

D.1 Dot-Matrix Printers

(Products listed in alphabetical order by company name)	AMT Accel-212	AMT Accel-214	AMT Accel-242	AMT Accel-244	AMT Accel-292
Price (tested configuration)	$	$	$	$	$
PHYSICAL CHARACTERISTICS					
Dimensions (HWD, in inches)	INA	INA	INA	INA	INA
Weight (pounds)	INA	INA	INA	INA	INA
Carriage size	Narrow	Wide	Narrow	Wide	Narrow
Number of pins	9	9	24	24	Dual-head 9-pin
Maximum resolution (horizontal by vertical dots per inch)	240 x 216	240 x 216	360 x 360	360 x 360	240 x 216
Color capability	○	○	○	○	○
Memory	8K	8K	8K	8K	8K
Parallel interface	●	●	●	●	●
Serial interface	●	●	●	●	●
PAPER HANDLING					
Paper parking	●	●	●	●	●
Paper feeds:					
Pressure	●	●	●	●	●
Tractor	●	●	●	●	●
Internal	●	●	●	●	●
External	●	●	●	●	●
Push	●	●	●	●	●
Pull	●	●	●	●	●
Paper paths:					
Rear U path	●	●	●	●	●
Bottom vertical	●	●	●	●	●
Front L path	○	○	○	○	○
Rear L path	○	○	○	○	○
Rated maximum paper weight (pounds)	24	24	24	24	24
FONTS AND FEATURES					
Emulations	●	●	●	●	●
Typefaces:					
Courier	○	○	●	●	○
Gothic	○	○	○	○	○
Orator	○	○	●	●	○
Prestige/Elite	○	○	●	●	●
Sans serif	●	●	●	●	●
Script	○	○	●	●	○
Times Roman	●	●	●	●	●
Standard mode, quiet mode (dB)	55, N/A	55, N/A	55, 53	55, 53	57, N/A

●—Yes ○—No N/A—Not applicable INA—Information not available

Table Continues →

■ Dot-Matrix Printers

	AMT Accel-294	AMT Accel-535dsi	Alps DMX 180	ALPS DMX800	Axonix MilWrite
Price (tested configuration)	$	$$$	$	$$	$
PHYSICAL CHARACTERISTICS					
Dimensions (HWD, in inches)	INA	12 x 24 x 19	5 x 15 x 9	7 x 24 x 17	INA
Weight (pounds)	INA	57	7	44	INA
Carriage size	Wide	Wide	Narrow	Wide	Narrow
Number of pins	Dual-head 9-pin	24	24	18	9
Maximum resolution (horizontal by vertical dots per inch)	240 x 216	INA	INA	240 x 216	240 x 216
Color capability	○	INA	INA	●	○
Memory	8K	INA	INA	128K	8K
Parallel interface	●	●	●	●	●
Serial interface	●	●	○	●	Optional
PAPER HANDLING					
Paper parking	●	INA	INA	●	●
Paper feeds:					
Pressure	●	INA	INA	●	●
Tractor	●	INA	INA	●	●
Internal	●	INA	INA	●	●
External	●	INA	INA	Optional	○
Push	●	INA	INA	●	●
Pull	●	INA	INA	Optional	○
Paper paths:					
Rear U path	●	○	●	●	●
Bottom vertical	●	●	○	●	○
Front L path	○	○	●	○	○
Rear L path	○	●	●	●	●
Rated maximum paper weight (pounds)	24	24	20	22	21
FONTS AND FEATURES					
Emulations	●	●	●	●	○
Typefaces:					
Courier	○	INA	INA	●	●
Gothic	○	INA	INA	●	●
Orator	○	INA	INA	○	○
Prestige/Elite	○	INA	INA	●	●
Sans serif	●	INA	INA	●	●
Script	○	INA	INA	○	●
Times Roman	●	INA	INA	●	○
Standard mode, quiet mode (dB)	57, N/A	55, N/A	N/A, N/A	57, 55	55, 50

●—Yes   ○—No   N/A—Not applicable   INA—Information not available

Dot-Matrix Printers ■

	Brother M-1309	Brother M-1324	Brother M-4309A	CIE CI-250 LXP	CIE CI-500
Price (tested configuration)	$	$	$$	$$	$$$$
PHYSICAL CHARACTERISTICS					
Dimensions (HWD, in inches)	5 x 18 x 13	5 x 18 x 13	INA	7 x 24 x 23	13 x 28 x 20
Weight (pounds)	11	11	INA	33	110 (with stand)
Carriage size	Narrow	Narrow	Wide	Wide	Wide
Number of pins	18	24	18	18	34
Maximum resolution (horizontal by vertical dots per inch)	240 x 216	360 x 360	240 x 216	240 x 216	205 x 288
Color capability	○	○	●	○	○
Memory	8K	8K	96K	8K	8K
Parallel interface	●	●	●	●	●
Serial interface	○	●	●	●	●
PAPER HANDLING					
Paper parking	●	●	●	●	●
Paper feeds:					
Pressure	●	●	●	●	○
Tractor	●	●	●	●	●
Internal	●	●	●	●	●
External	●	●	Optional	○	○
Push	●	●	●	●	●
Pull	●	●	Optional	●	●
Paper paths:					
Rear U path	●	●	●	●	○
Bottom vertical	●	○	●	●	●
Front L path	○	○	○	○	○
Rear L path	●	●	●	●	○
Rated maximum paper weight (pounds)	24	24	27	24	100
FONTS AND FEATURES					
Emulations	●	●	●	●	●
Typefaces:					
Courier	●	●	●	●	●
Gothic	●	●	●	○	○
Orator	○	○	●	○	○
Prestige/Elite	●	●	●	○	○
Sans serif	○	●	●	●	●
Script	○	●	○	○	○
Times Roman	○	●	●	○	○
Standard mode, quiet mode (dB)	INA	INA	57, 55	INA	INA

●—Yes　○—No　N/A—Not applicable　INA—Information not available

Table Continues →

■ Dot-Matrix Printers

	C. Itoh ProWriter C-410	C. Itoh ProWriter C-415	C. Itoh ProWriter C-420	C. Itoh ProWriter C-425	C. Itoh ProWriter C-610II Document Printer
Price (tested configuration)	$	$	$	$	$
PHYSICAL CHARACTERISTICS					
Dimensions (HWD, in inches)	5 x 17 x 12	5 x 22 x 12	5 x 17 x 12	5 x 22 x 12	INA
Weight (pounds)	14	18	14	18	INA
Carriage size	Narrow	Wide	Narrow	Wide	Narrow
Number of pins	9	9	24	24	24
Maximum resolution (horizontal by vertical dots per inch)	INA	INA	INA	INA	360 x 360
Color capability	INA	INA	INA	INA	○
Memory	INA	INA	INA	INA	26K
Parallel interface	●	●	●	●	●
Serial interface	Optional	Optional	Optional	Optional	●
PAPER HANDLING					
Paper parking	INA	INA	INA	INA	●
Paper feeds:					
Pressure	INA	INA	INA	INA	●
Tractor	INA	INA	INA	INA	●
Internal	INA	INA	INA	INA	●
External	INA	INA	INA	INA	○
Push	INA	INA	INA	INA	●
Pull	INA	INA	INA	INA	○
Paper paths:					
Rear U path	○	○	○	○	INA
Bottom vertical	●	●	●	●	INA
Front L path	○	○	○	○	INA
Rear L path	●	●	●	●	INA
Rated maximum paper weight (pounds)	21	21	21	21	35
FONTS AND FEATURES					
Emulations	●	●	●	●	●
Typefaces:					
Courier	INA	INA	INA	INA	●
Gothic	INA	INA	INA	INA	○
Orator	INA	INA	INA	INA	○
Prestige/Elite	INA	INA	INA	INA	○
Sans serif	INA	INA	INA	INA	●
Script	INA	INA	INA	INA	○
Times Roman	INA	INA	INA	INA	●
Standard mode, quiet mode (dB)	55, 53	55, 53	55, 53	55, 53	58, 55

●—Yes　○—No　N/A—Not applicable　INA—Information not available

Dot-Matrix Printers

	C. Itoh ProWriter C-615II Document Printer	C. Itoh ProWriter C-615III Multifunction Printer	Citizen GSX-130	Citizen GSX-140 Plus	Citizen GSX-145
Price (tested configuration)	$	$$	$	$	$
PHYSICAL CHARACTERISTICS					
Dimensions (HWD, in inches)	INA	8 x 18 x 14	5 x 16 x 13	5 x 16 x 13	6 x 23 x 13
Weight (pounds)	INA	27	12	12	17
Carriage size	Wide	Narrow	Narrow	Narrow	Wide
Number of pins	24	24	24	24	24
Maximum resolution (horizontal by vertical dots per inch)	360 x 360	INA	360 x 360	360 x 360	360 x 360
Color capability	○	INA	●	●	●
Memory	26K	INA	8K	8K	8K
Parallel interface	●	●	○	○	○
Serial interface	●	●	○	○	○
PAPER HANDLING					
Paper parking	●	INA	●	●	●
Paper feeds:					
Pressure	●	INA	●	●	●
Tractor	●	INA	●	●	●
Internal	●	INA	●	●	●
External	○	INA	●	●	●
Push	●	INA	●	●	●
Pull	○	INA	●	●	●
Paper paths:					
Rear U path	INA	●	●	●	●
Bottom vertical	INA	○	●	●	●
Front L path	INA	○	○	○	○
Rear L path	INA	○	○	○	○
Rated maximum paper weight (pounds)	35	N/A	27	27	27
FONTS AND FEATURES					
Emulations	●	●	●	●	●
Typefaces:					
Courier	●	INA	●	●	●
Gothic	○	INA	○	○	○
Orator	○	INA	○	●	○
Prestige/Elite	○	INA	●	●	●
Sans serif	●	INA	●	●	●
Script	○	INA	○	●	○
Times Roman	●	INA	●	●	●
Standard mode, quiet mode (dB)	58, 55	65, 55	INA	INA	INA

●—Yes ○—No N/A—Not applicable INA—Information not available

Table Continues →

■ Dot-Matrix Printers

	Citizen GSX-220	Citizen GSX-240	Citizen PN48	Citizen 200GX Fifteen	Dataproducts LX 455
Price (tested configuration)	$	$	$	$	$$$$
PHYSICAL CHARACTERISTICS					
Dimensions (HWD, in inches)	7 x 15 x 8	5 x 17 x 13	2 x 12 x 4	5 x 23 x 13	INA
Weight (pounds)	9	11	3 (with battery)	17	INA
Carriage size	Narrow	Narrow	Narrow	Wide	Wide
Number of pins	24	24	48	9	33
Maximum resolution (horizontal by vertical dots per inch)	INA	360 x 360	360 x 360	240 x 216	120 x 144
Color capability	INA	Optional	○	●	○
Memory	INA	8K	4K	8K	12K
Parallel interface	●	●	○	○	●
Serial interface	○	Optional	○	○	●
PAPER HANDLING					
Paper parking	INA	●	○	●	○
Paper feeds:					
Pressure	INA	●	●	●	○
Tractor	INA	●	○	●	●
Internal	INA	●	N/A	●	●
External	INA	●	N/A	●	○
Push	INA	●	N/A	●	●
Pull	INA	●	N/A	●	●
Paper paths:					
Rear U path	○	○	○	●	○
Bottom vertical	○	●	●	●	●
Front L path	○	○	○	○	○
Rear L path	●	○	●	○	○
Rated maximum paper weight (pounds)	27	26	28	27	120
FONTS AND FEATURES					
Emulations	●	●	●	●	●
Typefaces:					
Courier	INA	●	●	●	●
Gothic	INA	○	○	○	●
Orator	INA	○	○	○	○
Prestige/Elite	INA	●	○	○	○
Sans serif	INA	●	○	●	●
Script	INA	○	○	○	○
Times Roman	INA	●	●	●	○
Standard mode, quiet mode (dB)	48, N/A	47, 43	INA	INA	55, N/A

●—Yes ○—No N/A—Not applicable INA—Information not available

Dot-Matrix Printers

	Datasouth Performax	Datasouth XL-300	DEC LA 75 Plus Companion Printer	DEC LA 424 MultiPrinter	DECWriter 65
Price (tested configuration)	$$$	$$	$	$	$
PHYSICAL CHARACTERISTICS					
Dimensions (HWD, in inches)	9 x 26 x 18	8 x 25 x 16	5 x 17 x 15	7 x 24 x 12	7 x 15 x 10
Weight (pounds)	47	35	11	32	8
Carriage size	Wide	Wide	Narrow	Wide	Narrow
Number of pins	18	9	24	24	24
Maximum resolution (horizontal by vertical dots per inch)	360 x 288	240 x 360	360 x 180	360 x 180	INA
Color capability	○	○	●	●	INA
Memory	128K	3K	8K	8K	INA
Parallel interface	●	●	●	●	●
Serial interface	●	●	●	●	○
PAPER HANDLING					
Paper parking	●	○	●	●	INA
Paper feeds:					
Pressure	○	○	●	●	INA
Tractor	●	●	●	●	INA
Internal	●	●	●	●	INA
External	○	○	○	○	INA
Push	●	○	●	●	INA
Pull	●	●	●	○	INA
Paper paths:					
Rear U path	○	○	●	●	●
Bottom vertical	●	●	●	●	○
Front L path	●	●	○	○	●
Rear L path	○	○	○	○	○
Rated maximum paper weight (pounds)	24	35	24	24	24
FONTS AND FEATURES					
Emulations	●	●	○	○	●
Typefaces:					
Courier	●	●	●	●	INA
Gothic	○	○	○	○	INA
Orator	○	○	○	○	INA
Prestige/Elite	●	●	○	○	INA
Sans serif	○	○	○	○	INA
Script	○	○	○	○	INA
Times Roman	○	○	○	○	INA
Standard mode, quiet mode (dB)	INA	INA	53, 51	56, 53	48, N/A

●—Yes   ○—No   N/A—Not applicable   INA—Information not available

Table Continues →

■ Dot-Matrix Printers

	Digital LA600 MultiPrinter	Epson ActionPrinter 3250	Epson ActionPrinter 3260	Epson ActionPrinter 5000+	Epson DFX 5000+
Price (tested configuration)	$$$	$	$	$	$$
PHYSICAL CHARACTERISTICS					
Dimensions (HWD, in inches)	11 x 25 x 16	5 x 15 x 10	5 x 10 x 15	6 x 17 x 15	15 x 28 x 15
Weight (pounds)	50	12	10	15	64
Carriage size	Wide	Narrow	Narrow	Narrow	Wide
Number of pins	24	24	24	24	9
Maximum resolution (horizontal by vertical dots per inch)	INA	360 x 360	INA	INA	INA
Color capability	INA	○	INA	INA	INA
Memory	INA	11K	INA	INA	INA
Parallel interface	●	●	●	●	●
Serial interface	●	○	○	Optional	●
PAPER HANDLING					
Paper parking	INA	●	INA	INA	INA
Paper feeds:					
Pressure	INA	●	INA	INA	INA
Tractor	INA	●	INA	INA	INA
Internal	INA	Optional	INA	INA	INA
External	INA	○	INA	INA	INA
Push	INA	Optional	INA	INA	INA
Pull	INA	○	INA	INA	INA
Paper paths:					
Rear U path	●	○	○	●	○
Bottom vertical	●	●	○	●	○
Front L path	●	●	●	●	●
Rear L path	○	●	●	●	●
Rated maximum paper weight (pounds)	24	24	24	24	24
FONTS AND FEATURES					
Emulations	●	○	●	●	●
Typefaces:					
Courier	INA	●	INA	INA	INA
Gothic	INA	○	INA	INA	INA
Orator	INA	○	INA	INA	INA
Prestige/Elite	INA	●	INA	INA	INA
Sans serif	INA	●	INA	INA	INA
Script	INA	●	INA	INA	INA
Times Roman	INA	●	INA	INA	INA
Standard mode, quiet mode (dB)	53, N/A	50, N/A	47, N/A	47, N/A	55, N/A

●—Yes ○—No N/A—Not applicable INA—Information not available

Dot-Matrix Printers

	Epson LQ-200	Epson LQ-570	Epson LQ-870	Epson LQ-1170	Epson LX-300
Price (tested configuration)	$	$	$	$	$
PHYSICAL CHARACTERISTICS					
Dimensions (HWD, in inches)	6 x 15 x 13	6 x 17 x 15	7 x 18 x 15	7 x 25 x 15	5 x 11 x 15
Weight (pounds)	15	15	20	27	9
Carriage size	Narrow	Narrow	Narrow	Wide	Narrow
Number of pins	24	24	24	24	9
Maximum resolution (horizontal by vertical dots per inch)	360 x 360	360 x 360	360 x 360	360 x 360	INA
Color capability	○	○	○	○	INA
Memory	8K	8K	8K	8K	INA
Parallel interface	●	●	●	●	●
Serial interface	○	●	○	○	●
PAPER HANDLING					
Paper parking	○	●	●	●	INA
Paper feeds:					
Pressure	●	●	●	●	INA
Tractor	●	●	●	●	INA
Internal	○	●	●	●	INA
External	●	○	○	○	INA
Push	○	●	●	●	INA
Pull	●	○	○	○	INA
Paper paths:					
Rear U path	●	●	●	●	●
Bottom vertical	●	●	●	●	○
Front L path	○	●	●	●	○
Rear L path	○	●	●	●	○
Rated maximum paper weight (pounds)	22	22	22	22	24
FONTS AND FEATURES					
Emulations	●	●	●	●	●
Typefaces:					
Courier	●	●	●	●	INA
Gothic	○	○	○	○	INA
Orator	●	●	●	●	INA
Prestige/Elite	●	●	●	●	INA
Sans serif	●	●	●	●	INA
Script	●	●	●	●	INA
Times Roman	●	●	●	●	INA
Standard mode, quiet mode (dB)	INA	INA	INA	INA	48, N/A

●—Yes　○—No　N/A—Not applicable　INA—Information not available

Table Continues →

■ Dot-Matrix Printers

	Fujitsu DL1150	Fujitsu DL1200 PC PrintPartner	Fujitsu DL1250	Fujitsu DL3600	Fujitsu DL3800
Price (tested configuration)	$	$	$	$	$
PHYSICAL CHARACTERISTICS					
Dimensions (HWD, in inches)	8 x 18 x 10	INA	8 x 21 x 10	9 x 23 x 14	8 x 22 x 13
Weight (pounds)	13	INA	14	27	19
Carriage size	Narrow	Wide	Wide	Wide	Wide
Number of pins	24	24	24	24	24
Maximum resolution (horizontal by vertical dots per inch)	INA	360 x 360	INA	360 x 360	INA
Color capability	INA	Optional	INA	●	INA
Memory	INA	32K	INA	24K	INA
Parallel interface	●	●	●	●	●
Serial interface	●	Optional	●	○	●
PAPER HANDLING					
Paper parking	INA	●	INA	●	INA
Paper feeds:					
Pressure	INA	●	INA	●	INA
Tractor	INA	●	INA	●	INA
Internal	INA	●	INA	●	INA
External	INA	○	INA	○	INA
Push	INA	●	INA	●	INA
Pull	INA	●	INA	○	INA
Paper paths:					
Rear U path	○	○	○	●	○
Bottom vertical	○	○	○	○	○
Front L path	○	○	○	○	○
Rear L path	●	●	●	●	●
Rated maximum paper weight (pounds)	22	22	22	22	22
FONTS AND FEATURES					
Emulations	●	●	●	●	●
Typefaces:					
Courier	INA	●	INA	●	INA
Gothic	INA	○	INA	○	INA
Orator	INA	○	INA	○	INA
Prestige/Elite	INA	●	INA	●	INA
Sans serif	INA	○	INA	○	INA
Script	INA	○	INA	○	INA
Times Roman	INA	○	INA	○	INA
Standard mode, quiet mode (dB)	52, N/A	52, N/A	52, N/A	INA	49, N/A

●—Yes ○—No N/A—Not applicable INA—Information not available

Dot-Matrix Printers

	Fujitsu DL5800 Power PrintPartner	Fujitsu DL6400	Genicom 3840E	Genicom 3840EM	Genicom 3940IP
Price (tested configuration)	$$	$$	$$$	$$$	$$$
PHYSICAL CHARACTERISTICS					
Dimensions (HWD, in inches)	INA	13 x 27 x 14	12 x 27 x 14	12 x 27 x 14	12 x 27 x 16
Weight (pounds)	INA	55	52	52	54
Carriage size	Wide	Wide	Wide	Wide	Wide
Number of pins	24	24	18	18	18
Maximum resolution (horizontal by vertical dots per inch)	360 x 360	INA	400 x 144	INA	INA
Color capability	○	INA	○	INA	INA
Memory	32K	INA	64K	INA	INA
Parallel interface	●	●	●	●	●
Serial interface	●	●	●	●	○
PAPER HANDLING					
Paper parking	●	INA	●	INA	INA
Paper feeds:					
Pressure	●	INA	○	INA	INA
Tractor	●	INA	●	INA	INA
Internal	●	INA	●	INA	INA
External	Optional	INA	○	INA	INA
Push	●	INA	●	INA	INA
Pull	Optional	INA	○	INA	INA
Paper paths:					
Rear U path	●	○	○	●	○
Bottom vertical	●	○	●	●	●
Front L path	○	○	●	●	●
Rear L path	○	●	●	●	●
Rated maximum paper weight (pounds)	22	22	110	25	100
FONTS AND FEATURES					
Emulations	○	●	●	●	●
Typefaces:					
Courier	●	INA	●	INA	INA
Gothic	○	INA	●	INA	INA
Orator	○	INA	●	INA	INA
Prestige/Elite	●	INA	○	INA	INA
Sans serif	○	INA	○	INA	INA
Script	○	INA	○	INA	INA
Times Roman	○	INA	○	INA	INA
Standard mode, quiet mode (dB)	55, N/A	55, N/A	INA	55, N/A	55, N/A

●—Yes   ○—No   N/A—Not applicable   INA—Information not available

Table Continues →

▮ Dot-Matrix Printers

	Genicom 4440 XT	Genicom 4840	IBM Personal Printer Series II 2380	IBM Personal Printer Series II 2381	IBM Personal Printer Series II 2390
Price (tested configuration)	$$$$$	$$$$$	$	$	$
PHYSICAL CHARACTERISTICS					
Dimensions (HWD, in inches)	INA	42 x 27 x 25	10 x 19 x 15	10 x 25 x 15	10 x 19 x 15
Weight (pounds)	INA	170	15	19	15
Carriage size	Wide	Wide	Narrow	Wide	Narrow
Number of pins	66	66	9	9	24
Maximum resolution (horizontal by vertical dots per inch)	140 x 144	INA	240 x 144	240 x 144	360 x 360
Color capability	○	INA	○	○	○
Memory	2K	INA	11K	11K	32K
Parallel interface	●	●	●	●	●
Serial interface	●	●	○	○	○
PAPER HANDLING					
Paper parking	○	INA	●	●	●
Paper feeds:					
Pressure	○	INA	●	●	●
Tractor	●	INA	●	●	●
Internal	●	INA	●	●	●
External	○	INA	○	○	○
Push	●	INA	●	●	●
Pull	●	INA	●	●	●
Paper paths:					
Rear U path	○	○	○	○	○
Bottom vertical	●	●	●	●	●
Front L path	○	○	●	●	●
Rear L path	○	○	○	○	○
Rated maximum paper weight (pounds)	100	100	24	24	24
FONTS AND FEATURES					
Emulations	●	●	●	●	●
Typefaces:					
Courier	●	INA	●	●	●
Gothic	●	INA	●	●	●
Orator	○	INA	○	○	●
Prestige/Elite	○	INA	○	○	●
Sans serif	○	INA	○	○	○
Script	○	INA	○	○	●
Times Roman	○	INA	○	○	○
Standard mode, quiet mode (dB)	55, N/A	54, N/A	INA	INA	INA

●—Yes   ○—No   N/A—Not applicable   INA—Information not available

Dot-Matrix Printers

	IBM Personal Printer Series II 2391	IBM Proprinter 24P	IBM 4226 Printer	Mannesmann Tally MT82	Mannesmann Tally MT150/9
Price (tested configuration)	$	$	$$	$	$
PHYSICAL CHARACTERISTICS					
Dimensions (HWD, in inches)	10 x 25 x 15	5 x 16 x 14	12 x 25 x 11	10 x 16 x 12	6 x 18 x 13
Weight (pounds)	19	18	46	13	21
Carriage size	Wide	Narrow	Wide	Narrow	Narrow
Number of pins	24	24	9	24	9
Maximum resolution (horizontal by vertical dots per inch)	360 x 360	360 x 360	240 x 144	360 x 180	240 x 216
Color capability	○	○	○	○	○
Memory	32K	32K	22K	11K	10K
Parallel interface	●	●	●	●	●
Serial interface	○	○	●	○	Optional
PAPER HANDLING					
Paper parking	●	●	○	●	●
Paper feeds:					
Pressure	●	●	○	●	●
Tractor	●	●	●	●	●
Internal	●	●	●	●	●
External	○	○	○	○	○
Push	●	●	●	●	●
Pull	●	○	○	○	Optional
Paper paths:					
Rear U path	○	●	○	○	●
Bottom vertical	●	○	○	○	●
Front L path	●	○	○	○	●
Rear L path	○	○	○	●	○
Rated maximum paper weight (pounds)	24	24	24	24	24
FONTS AND FEATURES					
Emulations	●	●	●	●	●
Typefaces:					
Courier	●	●	●	○	●
Gothic	●	●	●	○	○
Orator	●	●	○	○	○
Prestige/Elite	●	●	○	○	○
Sans serif	○	○	○	●	●
Script	●	●	○	○	○
Times Roman	○	○	○	●	○
Standard mode, quiet mode (dB)	INA	INA	INA	INA	53, N/A

●—Yes ○—No N/A—Not applicable INA—Information not available

Table Continues →

■ Dot-Matrix Printers

	Mannesmann Tally MT150/24	Mannesmann Tally MT151/9	Mannesmann Tally MT151/24	Mannesmann Tally MT661	Mannesmann Tally T6082
Price (tested configuration)	$	$	$	$$$$$	$$$$$
PHYSICAL CHARACTERISTICS					
Dimensions (HWD, in inches)	6 x 18 x 13	INA	INA	45 x 32 x 22	42 x 32 x 28
Weight (pounds)	21	INA	INA	77	260
Carriage size	Narrow	Wide	Wide	Wide	Wide
Number of pins	24	9	24	66	66
Maximum resolution (horizontal by vertical dots per inch)	360 x 360	240 x 216	360 x 360	240 x 240	INA
Color capability	○	○	○	○	INA
Memory	24K	10K	24K	8K	INA
Parallel interface	●	●	●	●	●
Serial interface	Optional	Optional	Optional	●	●
PAPER HANDLING					
Paper parking	●	●	●	○	INA
Paper feeds:					
Pressure	●	●	●	○	INA
Tractor	●	●	●	●	INA
Internal	●	●	●	●	INA
External	○	○	○	○	INA
Push	●	●	●	●	INA
Pull	Optional	Optional	Optional	●	INA
Paper paths:					
Rear U path	●	●	●	○	○
Bottom vertical	●	●	●	●	○
Front L path	○	○	○	○	○
Rear L path	○	○	○	○	○
Rated maximum paper weight (pounds)	24	24	24	100	100
FONTS AND FEATURES					
Emulations	●	●	●	●	●
Typefaces:					
Courier	●	●	●	●	INA
Gothic	○	○	○	●	INA
Orator	○	○	○	○	INA
Prestige/Elite	●	○	●	○	INA
Sans serif	●	●	●	○	INA
Script	●	○	●	○	INA
Times Roman	●	○	●	○	INA
Standard mode, quiet mode (dB)	53, N/A	53, N/A	53, N/A	INA	50, N/A

●—Yes ○—No N/A—Not applicable INA—Information not available

Dot-Matrix Printers ■

	NEC Pinwriter P3200	NEC Pinwriter P3300	NEC Pinwriter P9300	Okidata Microline 184 Turbo	Okidata Pacemark 3410
Price (tested configuration)	$	$	$	$	$$
PHYSICAL CHARACTERISTICS					
Dimensions (HWD, in inches)	6 x 17 x 14	6 x 23 x 14	8 x 24 x 15	3 x 14 x 11	15 x 25 x 19
Weight (pounds)	19	25	33	10	63
Carriage size	Narrow	Wide	Wide	Narrow	Wide
Number of pins	24	24	24	9	9
Maximum resolution (horizontal by vertical dots per inch)	360 x 360	360 x 360	360 x 360	240 x 216	240 x 216
Color capability	○	○	○	○	○
Memory	8K	8K	80K	2K	64K
Parallel interface	●	●	●	●	●
Serial interface	○	○	○	Optional	●
PAPER HANDLING					
Paper parking	●	●	●	○	●
Paper feeds:					
Pressure	●	●	●	●	●
Tractor	●	●	●	●	●
Internal	●	●	●	●	●
External	○	○	○	Optional	Optional
Push	●	●	●	●	●
Pull	○	○	○	Optional	Optional
Paper paths:					
Rear U path	●	●	●	●	○
Bottom vertical	○	○	●	●	●
Front L path	○	○	○	○	○
Rear L path	○	○	○	○	○
Rated maximum paper weight (pounds)	24	24	24	24	24
FONTS AND FEATURES					
Emulations	●	●	●	○	○
Typefaces:					
Courier	●	●	●	○	●
Gothic	●	●	●	○	●
Orator	○	○	○	○	○
Prestige/Elite	●	●	●	○	○
Sans serif	●	●	●	○	○
Script	○	○	○	○	○
Times Roman	●	●	●	○	○
Standard mode, quiet mode (dB)	INA	INA	INA	55, N/A	58, N/A

●—Yes   ○—No   N/A—Not applicable   INA—Information not available   **Table Continues** →

◼ Dot-Matrix Printers

	OTC Euroline 400	OTC Euroline 600	OTC DuraLine	Panasonic KX-P1123	Panasonic KX-P1124i
Price (tested configuration)	$$$$	$$$$$	$$$	$	$
PHYSICAL CHARACTERISTICS					
Dimensions (HWD, in inches)	INA	INA	6 x 27 x 17	5 x 16 x 13	6 x 17 x 14
Weight (pounds)	INA	INA	110	16	19
Carriage size	Wide	Wide	Wide	Narrow	Narrow
Number of pins	Dual-head 21-pin	Triple-head 21-pin	27	24	24
Maximum resolution (horizontal by vertical dots per inch)	240 x 216	240 x 216	240 x 216	360 x 360	360 x 360
Color capability	○	○	○	○	○
Memory	7.8K	7.8K	2K	10K	12K
Parallel interface	●	●	●	●	●
Serial interface	●	●	●	○	○
PAPER HANDLING					
Paper parking	○	○	○	●	●
Paper feeds:					
Pressure	○	○	○	●	●
Tractor	●	●	●	●	●
Internal	●	●	●	●	●
External	○	○	○	○	○
Push	○	○	○	●	●
Pull	●	●	○	●	●
Paper paths:					
Rear U path	○	●	○	●	●
Bottom vertical	●	●	●	●	●
Front L path	○	○	●	●	●
Rear L path	○	○	○	○	○
Rated maximum paper weight (pounds)	120	120	104	24	24
FONTS AND FEATURES					
Emulations	●	●	●	●	●
Typefaces:					
Courier	○	○	○	●	●
Gothic	○	○	○	○	○
Orator	○	○	○	●	●
Prestige/Elite	○	○	○	●	●
Sans serif	○	○	○	●	●
Script	○	○	○	●	●
Times Roman	○	○	○	○	●
Standard mode, quiet mode (dB)	53, 48	53, 48	INA	INA	INA

●—Yes   ○—No   N/A—Not applicable   INA—Information not available

Dot-Matrix Printers

	Panasonic KX-P1150	Panasonic KX-P2123	Panasonic KX-P2124	Panasonic KX-P2135	Panasonic KX-P2180
Price (tested configuration)	$	$	$	$	$
PHYSICAL CHARACTERISTICS					
Dimensions (HWD, in inches)	5 x 17 x 12	6 x 18 x 14	6 x 19 x 15	6 x 17 x 12	6 x 18 x 14
Weight (pounds)	11	19	19	11	19
Carriage size	Narrow	Narrow	Narrow	Narrow	Narrow
Number of pins	9	24	24	24	9
Maximum resolution (horizontal by vertical dots per inch)	INA	360 x 360	360 x 360	INA	240 x 216
Color capability	INA	Optional	Optional	INA	Optional
Memory	INA	14K	20K	INA	4K
Parallel interface	●	●	●	●	●
Serial interface	○	Optional	Optional	○	Optional
PAPER HANDLING					
Paper parking	INA	●	●	INA	●
Paper feeds:					
Pressure	INA	●	●	INA	●
Tractor	INA	●	●	INA	●
Internal	INA	●	●	INA	●
External	INA	○	○	INA	○
Push	INA	●	●	INA	●
Pull	INA	●	●	INA	●
Paper paths:					
Rear U path	●	●	●	●	●
Bottom vertical	○	●	●	○	●
Front L path	○	○	○	○	○
Rear L path	○	○	○	○	○
Rated maximum paper weight (pounds)	24	24	24	24	24
FONTS AND FEATURES					
Emulations	●	●	●	●	●
Typefaces:					
Courier	INA	●	●	INA	●
Gothic	INA	○	○	INA	○
Orator	INA	○	●	INA	○
Prestige/Elite	INA	●	●	INA	●
Sans serif	INA	●	●	INA	●
Script	INA	●	●	INA	●
Times Roman	INA	●	●	INA	●
Standard mode, quiet mode (dB)	55, N/A	47, 44	47, 44	47, 44	48, 45

●—Yes ○—No N/A—Not applicable INA—Information not available

Table Continues →

■ Dot-Matrix Printers

	Panasonic KX-P2624	Printronix P3240	Samsung SP-0912	Samsung SP-2412	Samsung SP-2417
Price (tested configuration)	$	$$$$$	$	$	$
PHYSICAL CHARACTERISTICS					
Dimensions (HWD, in inches)	7 x 23 x 16	42 x 27 x 29	4 x 16 x 14	12 x 16 x 14	5 x 16 x 14
Weight (pounds)	34	210	19	18	10
Carriage size	Wide	Wide	Narrow	Narrow	Narrow
Number of pins	24	34	9	24	24
Maximum resolution (horizontal by vertical dots per inch)	360 x 360	180 x 96	INA	INA	INA
Color capability	○	○	INA	INA	INA
Memory	26K	2K	INA	INA	INA
Parallel interface	●	●	●	●	●
Serial interface	○	●	●	Optional	●
PAPER HANDLING					
Paper parking	●	○	INA	INA	INA
Paper feeds:					
Pressure	●	○	INA	INA	INA
Tractor	●	●	INA	INA	INA
Internal	●	●	INA	INA	INA
External	○	○	INA	INA	INA
Push	●	○	INA	INA	INA
Pull	●	●	INA	INA	INA
Paper paths:					
Rear U path	●	○	●	○	●
Bottom vertical	●	●	●	●	○
Front L path	●	○	○	○	●
Rear L path	○	○	●	○	●
Rated maximum paper weight (pounds)	24	100	36	36	35
FONTS AND FEATURES					
Emulations	●	●	●	●	●
Typefaces:					
Courier	●	○	INA	INA	INA
Gothic	○	○	INA	INA	INA
Orator	●	○	INA	INA	INA
Prestige/Elite	●	○	INA	INA	INA
Sans serif	●	●	INA	INA	INA
Script	●	○	INA	INA	INA
Times Roman	●	○	INA	INA	INA
Standard mode, quiet mode (dB)	INA	INA	58, N/A	60, 55	46, N/A

●—Yes ○—No N/A—Not applicable INA—Information not available

Dot-Matrix Printers

	Seikosha BP 5780	Seikosha LT 20	Seikosha SP-2400	Seikosha SP-2415	Star Micronics NX-1001 Multi-Font
Price (tested configuration)	$$	$	$	$	$
PHYSICAL CHARACTERISTICS					
Dimensions (HWD, in inches)	10 x 24 x 12	2 x 15 x 11	4 x 15 x 11	5 x 21 x 11	5 x 17 x 16
Weight (pounds)	44	8	7	9	11
Carriage size	Wide	Narrow	Narrow	Wide	Narrow
Number of pins	18	24	9	9	9
Maximum resolution (horizontal by vertical dots per inch)	240 x 216	360 x 180	240 x 216	240 x 216	216 x 240
Color capability	○	○	○	○	○
Memory	20K	1K	1K	17K	4K
Parallel interface	●	●	●	●	●
Serial interface	●	○	○	●	○
PAPER HANDLING					
Paper parking	●	○	●	●	●
Paper feeds:					
Pressure	●	●	●	●	●
Tractor	●	○	●	●	●
Internal	●	N/A	●	●	●
External	○	N/A	○	○	○
Push	●	N/A	●	●	●
Pull	○	N/A	○	○	○
Paper paths:					
Rear U path	○	○	●	●	○
Bottom vertical	○	○	○	○	○
Front L path	○	○	○	○	○
Rear L path	●	○	○	○	●
Rated maximum paper weight (pounds)	24	21	21	21	24
FONTS AND FEATURES					
Emulations	●	●	○	○	●
Typefaces:					
Courier	○	○	●	●	●
Gothic	○	○	●	●	○
Orator	○	○	○	○	●
Prestige/Elite	○	○	●	●	○
Sans serif	●	●	●	●	●
Script	○	○	●	●	○
Times Roman	●	●	○	○	○
Standard mode, quiet mode (dB)	INA	INA	56, 55	57, 55	INA

●—Yes ○—No N/A—Not applicable INA—Information not available

Table Continues →

■ Dot-Matrix Printers

	Star Micronics NX-1020 Rainbow	Star Micronics NX-2420 Multi-Font	Star Micronics NX-2420 Rainbow	Star Micronics NX-2450 Rainbow	Star Micronics NX-2480
Price (tested configuration)	$	$	$	$	$
PHYSICAL CHARACTERISTICS					
Dimensions (HWD, in inches)	6 x 19 x 17	7 x 19 x 14	7 x 19 x 14	7 x 15 x 19	7 x 19 x 15
Weight (pounds)	14	15	15	14	16
Carriage size	Narrow	Narrow	Narrow	Narrow	Narrow
Number of pins	9	24	24	24	24
Maximum resolution (horizontal by vertical dots per inch)	216 x 240	360 x 360	360 x 360	INA	INA
Color capability	●	○	●	INA	INA
Memory	16K	7K	30K	INA	INA
Parallel interface	●	●	●	●	●
Serial interface	○	○	○	Optional	Optional
PAPER HANDLING					
Paper parking	●	●	●	INA	INA
Paper feeds:					
Pressure	●	●	●	INA	INA
Tractor	●	●	●	INA	INA
Internal	●	●	●	INA	INA
External	○	○	○	INA	INA
Push	●	●	●	INA	INA
Pull	●	●	●	INA	INA
Paper paths:					
Rear U path	○	○	○	●	●
Bottom vertical	●	●	●	○	●
Front L path	○	○	○	○	○
Rear L path	●	●	●	●	○
Rated maximum paper weight (pounds)	24	24	24	24	24
FONTS AND FEATURES					
Emulations	●	●	●	●	●
Typefaces:					
Courier	●	●	●	INA	INA
Gothic	○	○	○	INA	INA
Orator	●	○	○	INA	INA
Prestige/Elite	○	●	●	INA	INA
Sans serif	●	●	●	INA	INA
Script	●	●	●	INA	INA
Times Roman	○	●	●	INA	INA
Standard mode, quiet mode (dB)	INA	INA	INA	51, 48	46, 45

●—Yes   ○—No   N/A—Not applicable   INA—Information not available

Dot-Matrix Printers

	Star Micronics NX-2430 Multi-Font	Star Micronics XB-2420 Multi-Font	Star Micronics XB-2425 Multi-Font	Star Micronics XR-1020 Multi-Font	Star Micronics XR-1520 Multi-Font
Price (tested configuration)	$	$	$	$	$
PHYSICAL CHARACTERISTICS					
Dimensions (HWD, in inches)	6 x 17 x 13	7 x 19 x 20	7 x 25 x 20	7 x 19 x 20	7 x 25 x 20
Weight (pounds)	14	22	27	21	26
Carriage size	Narrow	Narrow	Wide	Narrow	Wide
Number of pins	24	24	24	9	9
Maximum resolution (horizontal by vertical dots per inch)	360 x 360	360 x 360	360 x 360	216 x 240	216 x 240
Color capability	○	●	●	●	●
Memory	16K	29K	76K	32K	32K
Parallel interface	●	●	●	●	●
Serial interface	Optional	○	○	○	○
PAPER HANDLING					
Paper parking	●	●	●	●	●
Paper feeds:					
Pressure	●	●	●	●	●
Tractor	●	●	●	●	●
Internal	●	●	●	●	●
External	Optional	○	○	○	○
Push	●	●	●	●	●
Pull	Optional	○	○	○	○
Paper paths:					
Rear U path	●	○	○	○	○
Bottom vertical	●	●	●	●	●
Front L path	○	○	○	○	○
Rear L path	○	●	●	●	●
Rated maximum paper weight (pounds)	24	24	24	24	24
FONTS AND FEATURES					
Emulations	●	●	●	●	●
Typefaces:					
Courier	●	●	●	●	●
Gothic	○	○	○	○	○
Orator	○	●	●	●	●
Prestige/Elite	●	●	●	●	●
Sans serif	●	●	●	●	●
Script	●	●	●	●	●
Times Roman	●	●	●	●	●
Standard mode, quiet mode (dB)	54, 51	INA	INA	INA	INA

●—Yes ○—No N/A—Not applicable INA—Information not available

Table Continues →

Dot-Matrix Printers

	Tandy DMP 135	Tandy DMP 136	Tandy DMP 202	Tandy DMP 310 Slimline Printer	Unisys AP 1371
Price (tested configuration)	$	$	$	$	$$$
PHYSICAL CHARACTERISTICS					
Dimensions (HWD, in inches)	5 x 15 x 14	6 x 17 x 14	5 x 16 x 14	2 x 11 x 15	INA
Weight (pounds)	8	11	9	6	INA
Carriage size	Narrow	Narrow	Narrow	Narrow	Wide
Number of pins	9	9	24	24	18
Maximum resolution (horizontal by vertical dots per inch)	240 x 215	240 x 215	360 x 180	360 x 180	240 x 144
Color capability	○	●	○	○	●
Memory	1K	24K	12K	11K	32K
Parallel interface	●	●	●	●	●
Serial interface	○	○	○	○	●
PAPER HANDLING					
Paper parking	●	●	●	○	●
Paper feeds:					
Pressure	●	●	●	●	●
Tractor	●	●	●	○	●
Internal	●	●	●	○	Optional
External	○	○	○	○	Optional
Push	●	●	●	○	Optional
Pull	○	●	○	○	○
Paper paths:					
Rear U path	●	●	●	INA	●
Bottom vertical	○	●	○	INA	●
Front L path	○	○	○	INA	●
Rear L path	○	○	○	INA	●
Rated maximum paper weight (pounds)	20	27	20	21	32
FONTS AND FEATURES					
Emulations	●	●	●	○	●
Typefaces:					
Courier	●	●	●	●	●
Gothic	●	●	○	○	○
Orator	○	○	○	○	○
Prestige/Elite	●	○	○	○	○
Sans serif	●	●	○	○	●
Script	○	○	○	○	○
Times Roman	○	●	○	○	○
Standard mode, quiet mode (dB)	INA	INA	INA	57, 55	Less than 55, 51

●—Yes　○—No　N/A—Not applicable　INA—Information not available

End ■

D.2 Ink Jet Printers

(Products listed in alphabetical order by company name)	CalComp Tech Jet Personal	Canon BJ-20 Bubble Jet Printer	Canon BJ-100 Bubble Jet	Canon BJ-200e Bubble Jet	Canon BJ-300 Bubble Jet Printer
Price (tested configuration)	$	$	$	$	$
PHYSICAL CHARACTERISTICS					
Dimensions (HWD, in inches)	8 × 7 × 8	INA	7 × 14 × 8	7 × 14 × 8	13 x 19 x 13
Weight (pounds)	8	INA	7	7	15
Carriage size	INA	Narrow	INA	INA	Narrow
Number of jets	54	64	64	64	64
Maximum resolution (horizontal by vertical dots per inch)	360 × 360	360 × 360	360 × 360	360 × 360	360 × 360
Color capability	○	○	○	○	○
Memory	INA	37K	INA	INA	30K
Parallel interface	●	●	●	●	●
Serial interface	○	○	○	○	○
PAPER HANDLING					
Rated maximum paper weight (pounds)	24	28	28	28	34
Paper parking	INA	N/A	INA	INA	●
Paper feeds:					
Pressure	●	●	○	●	●
Tractor	○	○	○	○	●
Paper paths:					
Top U path	○	○	○	○	○
Rear U path	●	○	○	○	○
Bottom vertical	○	●	○	○	○
Front L path	○	○	○	○	●
Rear L path	○	○	●	●	●
Media supported:					
Card stock	○	●	●	●	INA
Transparencies	●	●	●	●	INA
Envelopes	●	●	●	●	INA
Landscape printing	●	○	●	●	INA
FONTS AND FEATURES					
Emulations	●	●	●	●	●
Includes scalable fonts	●	○	○	●	INA
Printer-specific Microsoft Windows 3.1 driver	●	○	●	●	INA

●—Yes ○—No N/A—Not applicable INA—Information not available

Table Continues →

■ Ink Jet Printers

	Canon BJ-330 Bubble Jet Printer	Canon BJ-600 Bubble Jet	Canon BJC-800 Bubble Jet Printer	Canon BJ-4000 Bubble Jet	Citizen Projet II
Price (tested configuration)	$	$	$$$	$	$
PHYSICAL CHARACTERISTICS					
Dimensions (HWD, in inches)	14 x 24 x 13	7 × 14 × 8	INA	7 × 14 × 8	6 × 15 × 14
Weight (pounds)	19	10	INA	8	9
Carriage size	Wide	INA	Wide	INA	INA
Number of jets	64	256	64	126	50
Maximum resolution (horizontal by vertical dots per inch)	360 x 360	360 x 360	360 x 360	360 x 360	300 × 300
Color capability	○	●	●	●	○
Memory	30K	INA	7K	INA	INA
Parallel interface	●	●	●	●	●
Serial interface	○	○	○	○	○
PAPER HANDLING					
Rated maximum paper weight (pounds)	34	28	24	28	27
Paper parking	●	INA	N/A	INA	INA
Paper feeds:					
Pressure	●	●	●	●	○
Tractor	●	○	○	○	○
Paper paths:					
Top U path	○	○	○	○	○
Rear U path	○	○	○	○	○
Bottom vertical	○	○	○	○	○
Front L path	●	○	●	○	○
Rear L path	●	●	○	●	●
Media supported:					
Card stock	INA	●	○	●	●
Transparencies	INA	●	●	●	●
Envelopes	INA	●	●	●	●
Landscape printing	INA	●	○	●	●
FONTS AND FEATURES					
Emulations	●	●	N/A	●	●
Includes scalable fonts	INA	●	○	●	○
Printer-specific Microsoft Windows 3.1 driver	INA	●	●	●	●

●—Yes   ○—No   N/A—Not applicable   INA—Information not available

Ink Jet Printers ■

	C. Itoh ProWriter Speed Jet CJ-300 Lite	C. Itoh ProWriter Speed Jet CJ-300	DEC Colorwriter 520ic	DECmultiJET 2000	Eastman Kodak Diconix Color 4 Printer
Price (tested configuration)	$	$	$	$	$$
PHYSICAL CHARACTERISTICS					
Dimensions (HWD, in inches)	6 × 16 × 13	6 × 16 × 13	7 × 15 × 16	INA	4 x 20 x 18
Weight (pounds)	12	12	11	INA	13
Carriage size	INA	INA	INA	Narrow	Narrow
Number of jets	128	128	50	50	12
Maximum resolution (horizontal by vertical dots per inch)	300 × 300	300 × 300	300 × 300	300 × 300	192 × 192
Color capability	○	○	●	○	●
Memory	INA	INA	INA	8K	64K
Parallel interface	●	●	●	●	●
Serial interface	○	Optional	●	○	○
PAPER HANDLING					
Rated maximum paper weight (pounds)	24	24	24	36	24
Paper parking	INA	INA	INA	●	○
Paper feeds:					
Pressure	●	●	●	●	●
Tractor	○	○	●	Optional	●
Paper paths:					
Top U path	○	○	○	○	○
Rear U path	○	○	●	○	●
Bottom vertical	○	○	○	○	○
Front L path	●	●	●	○	○
Rear L path	○	○	○	●	●
Media supported:					
Card stock	●	●	●	●	INA
Transparencies	●	●	●	●	INA
Envelopes	●	●	●	●	INA
Landscape printing	●	●	●	●	INA
FONTS AND FEATURES					
Emulations	●	●	●	○	●
Includes scalable fonts	○	○	●	○	INA
Printer-specific Microsoft Windows 3.1 driver	●	●	●	●	INA

●—Yes ○—No N/A—Not applicable INA—Information not available

Table Continues →

■ Ink Jet Printers

	Epson Stylus 400	Epson Stylus 800+	Epson Stylus 1000	Epson Stylus Color	HP DeskJet 320
Price (tested configuration)	$	$	$	$	$
PHYSICAL CHARACTERISTICS					
Dimensions (HWD, in inches)	6 × 17 × 10	6 × 17 × 10	6 × 26 × 20	8 × 19 × 21	3 × 12 × 6
Weight (pounds)	11	11	19	16	5
Carriage size	INA	INA	INA	INA	INA
Number of jets	48	48	48	64 (black) 48 (color)	54 (black) 48 (color)
Maximum resolution (horizontal by vertical dots per inch)	360 × 360	360 × 360	360 × 360	720 × 720	600 x 300
Color capability	○	○	○	●	●
Memory	INA	INA	INA	INA	INA
Parallel interface	●	●	●	●	●
Serial interface	○	○	○	●	Optional
PAPER HANDLING					
Rated maximum paper weight (pounds)	24	24	24	24	24
Paper parking	INA	INA	INA	INA	INA
Paper feeds:					
Pressure	●	●	●	●	○
Tractor	○	○	●	○	○
Paper paths:					
Top U path	○	●	○	○	○
Rear U path	○	○	○	○	○
Bottom vertical	○	○	○	○	●
Front L path	●	●	●	●	○
Rear L path	○	○	○	○	○
Media supported:					
Card stock	○	○	●	○	●
Transparencies	●	●	●	●	●
Envelopes	●	●	●	●	●
Landscape printing	●	●	●	●	●
FONTS AND FEATURES					
Emulations	●	●	●	●	●
Includes scalable fonts	●	●	●	●	●
Printer-specific Microsoft Windows 3.1 driver	●	●	●	●	●

●—Yes   ○—No   N/A—Not applicable   INA—Information not available

Ink Jet Printers ▮

	HP DeskJet 500C	HP DeskJet 540	HP DeskJet 550C	HP DeskJet 560C	HP DeskJet 1200C-PS
Price (tested configuration)	$	$	$	$	$$$
PHYSICAL CHARACTERISTICS					
Dimensions (HWD, in inches)	8 x 17 x 15	8 x 17 x 16	8 x 18 x 15	11 x 19 x 17	11 x 19 x 17
Weight (pounds)	14	12	15	15	29
Carriage size	Narrow	INA	Narrow	INA	INA
Number of jets	50 (black) 48 (color)	54 (black) 48 (color)	50 (black) 48 (color)	54 (black) 48 (color)	108 (black) 416 (color)
Maximum resolution (horizontal by vertical dots per inch)	300 x 300	600 x 300	300 x 300	600 x 300	600 x 300
Color capability	●	●	●	●	●
Memory	48K	INA	80K	INA	INA
Parallel interface	●	●	●	●	●
Serial interface	○	Optional	○	Optional	Optional
PAPER HANDLING					
Rated maximum paper weight (pounds)	24	36	36	36	36
Paper parking	N/A	INA	N/A	INA	INA
Paper feeds:					
Pressure	●	○	●	●	●
Tractor	○	○	○	○	○
Paper paths:					
Top U path	INA	●	INA	○	○
Rear U path	INA	○	INA	○	○
Bottom vertical	INA	○	INA	○	○
Front L path	INA	○	INA	●	●
Rear L path	INA	○	INA	○	○
Media supported:					
Card stock	○	●	○	●	●
Transparencies	●	●	●	●	●
Envelopes	●	●	●	●	●
Landscape printing	●	●	●	●	●
FONTS AND FEATURES					
Emulations	N/A	●	N/A	●	●
Includes scalable fonts	○	●	○	●	●
Printer-specific Microsoft Windows 3.1 driver	●	●	●	●	●

●—Yes ○—No N/A—Not applicable INA—Information not available

Table Continues →

Ink Jet Printers

	HP PaintJet XL300	IBM ExecJet Printer	Olivetti JP 450	Royal CJP 450	Star Micronics StarJet SJ-48
Price (tested configuration)	$$$	$	$	$	$
PHYSICAL CHARACTERISTICS					
Dimensions (HWD, in inches)	10 x 30 x 20	14 x 24 x 13	7 x 15 x 18	INA	7 x 12 x 8
Weight (pounds)	45	19	11	INA	4
Carriage size	Wide	Wide	INA	Narrow	Narrow
Number of jets	50	64	50 (black) 51 (color)	50	64
Maximum resolution (horizontal by vertical dots per inch)	300 x 300	360 x 360	300 x 300	300 x 300	360 x 360
Color capability	●	○	●	○	○
Memory	2Mb	30K	INA	10.5K	28K
Parallel interface	●	●	●	●	●
Serial interface	○	○	Optional	○	●
PAPER HANDLING					
Rated maximum paper weight (pounds)	24	34	35	24	28
Paper parking	N/A	●	INA	N/A	○
Paper feeds:					
Pressure	●	●	●	●	●
Tractor	○	●	Optional	○	○
Paper paths:					
Top U path	INA	○	●	INA	○
Rear U path	INA	○	○	INA	○
Bottom vertical	INA	○	○	INA	●
Front L path	INA	●	●	INA	○
Rear L path	INA	●	○	INA	○
Media supported:					
Card stock	●	INA	●	●	INA
Transparencies	●	INA	●	●	INA
Envelopes	○	INA	●	●	INA
Landscape printing	●	INA	●	●	INA
FONTS AND FEATURES					
Emulations	N/A	●	●	○	●
Includes scalable fonts	●	INA	●	○	INA
Printer-specific Microsoft Windows 3.1 driver	●	INA	●	●	INA

●—Yes   ○—No   N/A—Not applicable   INA—Information not available

Ink Jet Printers ▪

TI microMarc Color

Price (tested configuration)	$

PHYSICAL CHARACTERISTICS

Dimensions (HWD, in inches)	7 x 15 x 18
Weight (pounds)	11
Carriage size	INA
Number of jets	50 (black) 51 (color)
Maximum resolution (horizontal by vertical dots per inch)	300 x 300
Color capability	●
Memory	INA
Parallel interface	●
Serial interface	○

PAPER HANDLING

Rated maximum paper weight (pounds)	24
Paper parking	INA
Paper feeds:	
Pressure	●
Tractor	●
Paper paths:	
Top U path	○
Rear U path	●
Bottom vertical	○
Front L path	●
Rear L path	○
Media supported:	
Card stock	○
Transparencies	●
Envelopes	●
Landscape printing	●

FONTS AND FEATURES

Emulations	●
Includes scalable fonts	○
Printer-specific Microsoft Windows 3.1 driver	●

●—Yes ○—No N/A—Not applicable INA—Information not available   **End ▪**

■ D.3 Desktop Laser Printers

(Products listed in alphabetical order by company name)	Apple LaserWriter IIf	Apple LaserWriter IIg	Apple LaserWriter Select	Apple Personal LaserWriter NTR	Bézier BP4040
Price (tested configuration)	$$$	$$$$	$$	$$	$$
PHYSICAL CHARACTERISTICS					
Dimensions (HWD, in inches)	INA	INA	8 × 15 × 8	8 × 15 × 18	8 × 28 × 14
Weight (pounds)	INA	INA	26	30	26
ENGINE					
Model	Canon SX	Canon SX	Fuji Xerox P1	Canon LX	Canon LX
Rated speed (pages per minute)	8	8	10	4	4
Memory	32Mb	32Mb	7Mb	4Mb	2Mb
Maximum resolution (horizontal by vertical dots per inch)	300 × 300	300 × 300	600 × 600	300 × 300	300 × 300
INTERFACES					
Parallel	○	○	●	●	●
Serial	●	●	●	●	●
LocalTalk	INA	INA	●	INA	INA
SCSI	● (hard disk only)	● (hard disk only)	○	○	INA
AppleTalk	●	●	INA	●	●
Ethernet	○	●	○	○	INA
Automatic interface switching	●	●	●	●	●
Simultaneously active ports	○	○	●	○	●
PAPER HANDLING					
Number of paper cassettes	INA	INA	INA	INA	1
Cassette capacity (sheets)	200	200	250	70	70
Duplexing	○	○	○	○	○
FONTS AND FEATURES					
HP PCL support	PCL 4	PCL 4	PCL 5	PCL 4	PCL 4
Supports scalable fonts	INA	INA	INA	INA	○
Accepts HP-compatible font cartridges	○	○	INA	○	○
PostScript language support	Adobe PostScript Level 2	Adobe PostScript Level 2	Adobe PostScript Level 2	Adobe PostScript Level 2	Microsoft TrueImage
Supports Type 1 fonts	●	●	●	●	●
Other emulations	INA	INA	○	INA	INA
Supports resolution enhancement	●	●	●	○	INA
Supports automatic emulation switching	○	○	●	○	○
Accepts proprietary font cards	INA	INA	INA	INA	○
Printer-specific Microsoft Windows 3.1 driver available	○	○	INA	○	INA
GDI support	INA	INA	○	INA	INA
TrueType rasterizer in firmware	INA	INA	●	INA	INA

●—Yes ○—No N/A—Not applicable INA—Information not available

Desktop Laser Printers

	Brother HL-4PS	Brother HL-4Ve	Brother HL-8V	Brother HL-10V	Brother HL-630
Price (tested configuration)	$$$	$$	$$$	$$	$
PHYSICAL CHARACTERISTICS					
Dimensions (HWD, in inches)	8 × 16 × 14	INA	9 × 18 × 25	11 × 16 × 15	7 × 14 × 14
Weight (pounds)	27	INA	44	37	17
ENGINE					
Model	Canon LX	Canon LX	Canon SX	Brother HL-10V	Brother HL-630
Rated speed (pages per minute)	4	4	8	10	6
Memory	2Mb	5Mb	1Mb	5Mb	5Mb
Maximum resolution (horizontal by vertical dots per inch)	300 × 300	300 × 300	300 × 300	300 × 300	N/A
INTERFACES					
Parallel	●	●	●	●	●
Serial	●	●	●	●	Optional
LocalTalk	INA	INA	INA	INA	○
SCSI	INA	○	INA	○	○
AppleTalk	●	○	○	Optional	INA
Ethernet	INA	○	INA	○	○
Automatic interface switching	○	○	●	○	●
Simultaneously active ports	○	○	○	○	●
PAPER HANDLING					
Number of paper cassettes	1	INA	1	INA	INA
Cassette capacity (sheets)	50	70	200	250	200
Duplexing	○	○	○	○	○
FONTS AND FEATURES					
HP PCL support	PCL 4	PCL 5	PCL 5	PCL 5	PCL 4
Supports scalable fonts	●	INA	●	INA	INA
Accepts HP-compatible font cartridges	○	○	●	●	INA
PostScript language support	Brother BR-Script	BR-Script (optional)	None	BR-Script (optional)	N/A
Supports Type 1 fonts	●	●	○	●	○
Other emulations	INA	INA	INA	INA	●
Supports resolution enhancement	INA	●	INA	●	○
Supports automatic emulation switching	○	●	○	●	●
Accepts proprietary font cards	●	INA	●	INA	INA
Printer-specific Microsoft Windows 3.1 driver available	INA	○	INA	○	INA
GDI support	INA	INA	INA	INA	●
TrueType rasterizer in firmware	INA	INA	INA	INA	○

●—Yes ○—No N/A—Not applicable INA—Information not available

Table Continues →

Desktop Laser Printers

	Canon LBP-430	Canon LBP-860	C. Itoh CI-44 Little Laser	C. Itoh ProWriter CI-8Xtra	C. Itoh ProWriter CI-8Xtra+
Price (tested configuration)	$	$$	$	$$	$$
PHYSICAL CHARACTERISTICS					
Dimensions (HWD, in inches)	6 × 15 × 15	12 × 17 × 16	7 × 14 × 11	9 × 16 × 16	9 × 16 × 16
Weight (pounds)	18	37	11	31	31
ENGINE					
Model	Canon LBP-PX	Canon LBP-Ex	TEC LB-1000	TEC 1323	TEC 1323
Rated speed (pages per minute)	4	8	4	8	8
Memory	1Mb	2Mb	0Mb	4Mb	4Mb
Maximum resolution (horizontal by vertical dots per inch)	N/A	600 × 600	300 × 300	N/A	600 × 600
INTERFACES					
Parallel	●	●	●	○	●
Serial	○	●	○	Optional	Optional
LocalTalk	○	●	○	○	○
SCSI	○	○	○	○	○
AppleTalk	INA	INA	INA	INA	INA
Ethernet	○	○	○	○	○
Automatic interface switching	○	●	○	●	●
Simultaneously active ports	○	●	○	●	●
PAPER HANDLING					
Number of paper cassettes	INA	INA	INA	INA	INA
Cassette capacity (sheets)	100	250	100	250	250
Duplexing	○	○	○	○	○
FONTS AND FEATURES					
HP PCL support	PCL 5	PCL 5e	PCL 4 (Optional)	PCL 5	PCL 5
Supports scalable fonts	INA	INA	INA	INA	INA
Accepts HP-compatible font cartridges	INA	INA	INA	INA	INA
PostScript language support	N/A	Adobe Level 2 (optional)	Level 1 clone	N/A	Level 2 clone
Supports Type 1 fonts	○	○	○	○	●
Other emulations	○	○	○	○	○
Supports resolution enhancement	●	○	Optional	●	●
Supports automatic emulation switching	○	●	○	●	●
Accepts proprietary font cards	INA	INA	INA	INA	INA
Printer-specific Microsoft Windows 3.1 driver available	INA	INA	INA	INA	INA
GDI support	○	○	●	●	●
TrueType rasterizer in firmware	○	●	○	○	○

●—Yes ○—No N/A—Not applicable INA—Information not available

Desktop Laser Printers

	C. Itoh ProWriter CI-8XA	C. Itoh ProWriter CI-4	C. Itoh ProWriter Desktop Laser Printer CI-8	C. Itoh ProWriter Desktop Laser Printer CI-8E	Dataproducts LZR 960
Price (tested configuration)	$$	$	$$	$$	$$$
PHYSICAL CHARACTERISTICS					
Dimensions (HWD, in inches)	9 × 17 × 16	8 × 14 × 23	INA	INA	11 × 13 × 14
Weight (pounds)	31	29	INA	INA	34
ENGINE					
Model	TEC 1323	TEC 1321C	TEC 1323D	TEC 1323CE	Sharp JX-95
Rated speed (pages per minute)	8	4	8	8	9
Memory	4Mb	512K	5Mb	5Mb	2Mb
Maximum resolution (horizontal by vertical dots per inch)	600 × 600	300 × 300	300 × 300	300 × 300	300 × 300
INTERFACES					
Parallel	●	●	●	●	●
Serial	○	●	●	●	●
LocalTalk	●	INA	INA	INA	INA
SCSI	○	INA	○	○	INA
AppleTalk	INA	○	Optional	○	●
Ethernet	○	INA	○	○	INA
Automatic interface switching	●	○	○	○	●
Simultaneously active ports	●	○	○	○	●
PAPER HANDLING					
Number of paper cassettes	INA	1	INA	INA	1
Cassette capacity (sheets)	250	100	250	250	250
Duplexing	○	○	○	○	○
FONTS AND FEATURES					
HP PCL support	PCL 5	PCL 4	PCL 5	PCL 5	PCL 4
Supports scalable fonts	INA	○	INA	INA	○
Accepts HP-compatible font cartridges	INA	●	●	●	○
PostScript language support	Level 2 clone	None	Destiny PDL (optional)	Destiny PDL (optional)	Adobe Level 2
Supports Type 1 fonts	●	○	●	●	●
Other emulations	○	INA	INA	INA	INA
Supports resolution enhancement	●	INA	●	●	INA
Supports automatic emulation switching	●	○	○	○	○
Accepts proprietary font cards	INA	○	INA	INA	●
Printer-specific Microsoft Windows 3.1 driver available	INA	INA	○	○	INA
GDI support	●	INA	INA	INA	INA
TrueType rasterizer in firmware	●	INA	INA	INA	INA

●—Yes   ○—No   N/A—Not applicable   INA—Information not available

Table Continues →

■ Desktop Laser Printers

	DEClaser 1800	DEClaser 5100	Eastman Kodak Ektaplus 7008	Epson ActionLaser 1600	Epson ActionLaser II
Price (tested configuration)	$	$$	$	$	$
PHYSICAL CHARACTERISTICS					
Dimensions (HWD, in inches)	9 × 14 × 18	12 × 16 × 16	9 × 15 × 16	9 × 15 × 18	INA
Weight (pounds)	19	37	38	22	INA
ENGINE					
Model	Minolta SP6X	Canon LBP-EX	TEC 1306C	Minolta SP-6XH	Ricoh LP-1200
Rated speed (pages per minute)	6	8	8	6	6
Memory	1Mb	6Mb	1.5Mb	2Mb	5.5Mb
Maximum resolution (horizontal by vertical dots per inch)	300 × 300	600 × 600	300 × 300	600 × 600	300 × 300
INTERFACES					
Parallel	●	●	●	●	●
Serial	●	●	●	●	●
LocalTalk	○	●	INA	Optional	INA
SCSI	○	○	○	○	○
AppleTalk	INA	INA	○	INA	○
Ethernet	○	Optional	○	Optional	○
Automatic interface switching	●	●	○	●	●
Simultaneously active ports	●	●	○	●	●
PAPER HANDLING					
Number of paper cassettes	INA	INA	1	INA	INA
Cassette capacity (sheets)	150	250	200	150	100
Duplexing	○	○	○	○	○
FONTS AND FEATURES					
HP PCL support	PCL 5	PCL 5e	PCL 4	PCL 5e	PCL4
Supports scalable fonts	INA	INA	○	INA	INA
Accepts HP-compatible font cartridges	INA	INA	○	INA	●
PostScript language support	N/A	Adobe Level 2	None	Level 2 clone (optional)	Adobe PostScript (optional)
Supports Type 1 fonts	○	●	○	●	●
Other emulations	●	●	INA	●	INA
Supports resolution enhancement	●	●	INA	●	○
Supports automatic emulation switching	●	●	○	●	○
Accepts proprietary font cards	INA	INA	●	INA	INA
Printer-specific Microsoft Windows 3.1 driver available	INA	INA	INA	INA	○
GDI support	○	○	INA	○	INA
TrueType rasterizer in firmware	○	●	INA	●	INA

●—Yes ○—No N/A—Not applicable INA—Information not available

Desktop Laser Printers

	Epson EPL-7000	Epson EPL-7500	Epson EPL-8000	Fujitsu Print Partner 10	GCC BLP II
Price (tested configuration)	$	$$$	$$	$$	$$
PHYSICAL CHARACTERISTICS					
Dimensions (HWD, in inches)	8 × 20 × 25	8 × 20 × 25	11 × 19 × 15	INA	5 × 17 × 23
Weight (pounds)	40	40	40	INA	23
ENGINE					
Model	Minolta SP101	Minolta SP101	Minolta NC-10	Minolta SP10	Oki Electric OL-400
Rated speed (pages per minute)	6	6	10	10	4
Memory	512K	2Mb	7.5Mb	9Mb	2Mb
Maximum resolution (horizontal by vertical dots per inch)	300 × 300	300 × 300	300 × 300	300 × 300	300 × 300
INTERFACES					
Parallel	●	●	●	●	○
Serial	●	●	●	●	○
LocalTalk	INA	INA	INA	INA	INA
SCSI	INA	INA	○	○	●
AppleTalk	○	●	○	Optional	●
Ethernet	INA	INA	○	○	○
Automatic interface switching	●	○	●	●	N/A
Simultaneously active ports	●	○	●	●	N/A
PAPER HANDLING					
Number of paper cassettes	1	1	INA	INA	1
Cassette capacity (sheets)	250	250	250	250	200
Duplexing	○	○	○	○	○
FONTS AND FEATURES					
HP PCL support	PCL 4	PCL 4	PCL 5	PCL 5	None
Supports scalable fonts	○	○	INA	INA	N/A
Accepts HP-compatible font cartridges	●	○	●	●	N/A
PostScript language support	None	Adobe Level 1	Adobe Postscript (optional)	Microsoft TrueImage (optional)	Adobe Level 1
Supports Type 1 fonts	○	●	●	●	●
Other emulations	INA	INA	INA	INA	INA
Supports resolution enhancement	INA	INA	●	●	INA
Supports automatic emulation switching	○	○	●	● (via software)	○
Accepts proprietary font cards	○	○	INA	INA	●
Printer-specific Microsoft Windows 3.1 driver available	INA	INA	○	○	INA
GDI support	INA	INA	INA	INA	INA
TrueType rasterizer in firmware	INA	INA	INA	INA	INA

●—Yes ○—No N/A—Not applicable INA—Information not available

Table Continues →

■ Desktop Laser Printers

	GCC BLP IIS	HP LaserJet 4	HP LaserJet 4 Plus	HP LaserJet 4L	HP LaserJet 4M
Price (tested configuration)	$$$	$$	$$	$	$$$
PHYSICAL CHARACTERISTICS					
Dimensions (HWD, in inches)	5 × 17 × 23	INA	12 × 17 × 16	7 × 15 × 14	INA
Weight (pounds)	23	INA	37	16	INA
ENGINE					
Model	Oki Electric OL-800	Canon P-270	Canon EX	Canon PX	Canon P-270
Rated speed (pages per minute)	8	8	12	4	8
Memory	2Mb	34Mb	2Mb	1Mb	26Mb
Maximum resolution (horizontal by vertical dots per inch)	300 × 300	600 × 600	600 × 600	N/A	600 × 600
INTERFACES					
Parallel	○	●	●	●	●
Serial	○	●	●	○	●
LocalTalk	INA	INA	Optional	○	INA
SCSI	●	○	○	INA	○
AppleTalk	●	Optional	INA	INA	●
Ethernet	○	Optional	Optional	Optional	Optional
Automatic interface switching	N/A	●	●	○	●
Simultaneously active ports	N/A	●	●	○	●
PAPER HANDLING					
Number of paper cassettes	1	INA	INA	INA	INA
Cassette capacity (sheets)	200	250, 100	250	100	250, 100
Duplexing	○	○	Optional	○	○
FONTS AND FEATURES					
HP PCL support	None	Enhanced PCL 5	PCL 5e	PLC 5	Enhanced PCL 5
Supports scalable fonts	N/A	INA	INA	INA	INA
Accepts HP-compatible font cartridges	N/A	●	INA	INA	●
PostScript language support	Adobe Level 1	Adobe PostScript Level 2 (optional)	Adobe Level 2	N/A	Adobe PostScript Level 2
Supports Type 1 fonts	●	●	●	○	●
Other emulations	INA	INA	●	●	INA
Supports resolution enhancement	INA	●	●	●	●
Supports automatic emulation switching	○	●	●	○	●
Accepts proprietary font cards	●	INA	INA	INA	INA
Printer-specific Microsoft Windows 3.1 driver available	INA	● (included)	INA	INA	● (included)
GDI support	INA	INA	○	○	INA
TrueType rasterizer in firmware	INA	INA	Optional	○	INA

●—Yes ○—No N/A—Not applicable INA—Information not available

Desktop Laser Printers

	HP LaserJet 4M Plus	HP LaserJet 4P	HP LaserJet IIP Plus	HP LaserJet IIIP	HP Color LaserJet
Price (tested configuration)	$$$	$	$	$$	$$$$$
PHYSICAL CHARACTERISTICS					
Dimensions (HWD, in inches)	12 × 17 × 16	7 × 15 × 15	INA	8 × 14 × 25	15 × 24 × 19
Weight (pounds)	37	20	INA	22	103
ENGINE					
Model	Canon EX	Canon PXII	Canon LX	Canon LX	Proprietary (Konica)
Rated speed (pages per minute)	12	4	4	4	10
Memory	6Mb	6Mb	4.5Mb	1Mb	8Mb
Maximum resolution (horizontal by vertical dots per inch)	600 × 600	600 × 600	300 × 300	300 × 300	300 × 300
INTERFACES					
Parallel	●	●	●	●	●
Serial	●	●	○	●	Optional
LocalTalk	●	○	INA	INA	Optional
SCSI	○	○	○	INA	○
AppleTalk	INA	INA	○	○	INA
Ethernet	●	Optional	○	INA	Optional
Automatic interface switching	●	●	N/A	○	●
Simultaneously active ports	●	●	N/A	○	●
PAPER HANDLING					
Number of paper cassettes	INA	INA	INA	1	INA
Cassette capacity (sheets)	250	250	70	70	250
Duplexing	Optional	○	○	○	○
FONTS AND FEATURES					
HP PCL support	PCL 5e	PCL 5e	PCL 4	PCL 5	Enhanced PCL 5
Supports scalable fonts	INA	INA	INA	●	INA
Accepts HP-compatible font cartridges	INA	INA	●	●	INA
PostScript language support	Adobe PostScript Level 2	Adobe PostScript Level 2	Adobe PostScript (optional)	None	Adobe PostScript Level 2 (optional)
Supports Type 1 fonts	●	●	●	○	●
Other emulations	●	●	INA	INA	○
Supports resolution enhancement	●	●	○	INA	●
Supports automatic emulation switching	●	●	○	○	Optional
Accepts proprietary font cards	INA	INA	INA	●	INA
Printer-specific Microsoft Windows 3.1 driver available	INA	INA	● (in Windows 3.1 and via BBS)	INA	INA
GDI support	○	○	INA	INA	○
TrueType rasterizer in firmware	○	●	INA	INA	●

●—Yes   ○—No   N/A—Not applicable   INA—Information not available

Table Continues →

■ Desktop Laser Printers

	IBM LaserPrinter 5e	IBM LaserPrinter 6	IBM LaserPrinter 6P	IBM LaserPrinter 10	IBM LaserPrinter 10P
Price (tested configuration)	$$	$$	$$	$$	$$$
PHYSICAL CHARACTERISTICS					
Dimensions (HWD, in inches)	12 × 14 × 21	12 × 14 × 21	INA	12 × 14 × 21	INA
Weight (pounds)	33	33	INA	33	INA
ENGINE					
Model	IBM/Lexmark 4029 Model 10	IBM/Lexmark 4029 Model 20	IBM/Lexmark 4029	IBM/Lexmark 4029 Model 30	IBM/Lexmark 4029
Rated speed (pages per minute)	5	6	6	10	10
Memory	1Mb	1Mb	9Mb	1Mb	9Mb
Maximum resolution (horizontal by vertical dots per inch)	300 × 300	300 × 300	300 × 300	300 × 300	600 × 600
INTERFACES					
Parallel	●	INA	●	INA	●
Serial	●	●	●	●	●
LocalTalk	INA	INA	INA	INA	INA
SCSI	INA	INA	○	INA	○
AppleTalk	○	●	Optional	●	Optional
Ethernet	INA	INA	Optional	INA	Optional
Automatic interface switching	○	○	○	●	○
Simultaneously active ports	○	○	○	○	○
PAPER HANDLING					
Number of paper cassettes	1	1	INA	1	INA
Cassette capacity (sheets)	200	200	200	200	200
Duplexing	○	○	○	○	○
FONTS AND FEATURES					
HP PCL support	PCL 4	PCL 4	PCL 4	PCL 4	PCL 4
Supports scalable fonts	○	○	INA	○	INA
Accepts HP-compatible font cartridges	○	○	○	○	○
PostScript language support	None	None	Adobe PostScript	None	Adobe PostScript
Supports Type 1 fonts	●	●	●	●	●
Other emulations	INA	INA	INA	INA	INA
Supports resolution enhancement	INA	INA	●	INA	●
Supports automatic emulation switching	○	○	● (via software)	○	● (via software)
Accepts proprietary font cards	●	●	INA	●	INA
Printer-specific Microsoft Windows 3.1 driver available	INA	INA	● (included)	INA	● (included)
GDI support	INA	INA	INA	INA	INA
TrueType rasterizer in firmware	INA	INA	INA	INA	INA

●—Yes   ○—No   N/A—Not applicable   INA—Information not available

Desktop Laser Printers

	Kyocera Ecosys a-Si Printer FS-1500A	LaserMaster TrueTech 800/4	LaserMaster TrueTech 1000	LaserMaster Unity 1000	LaserMaster Unity 1200xl
Price (tested configuration)	$$	$$$	$$$$$	$$$$$	$$$$$
PHYSICAL CHARACTERISTICS					
Dimensions (HWD, in inches)	9 × 14 × 14	9 × 28 × 14	9 × 18 × 26	INA	8 × 19 × 18
Weight (pounds)	30	24	38	INA	51
ENGINE					
Model	Ecosys	Canon LX	Canon SX	Canon SX	Toshiba TN-7270
Rated speed (pages per minute)	10	4	8	8	8
Memory	5Mb	6Mb	9Mb	48Mb	48Mb
Maximum resolution (horizontal by vertical dots per inch)	300 × 300	800 × 800	1,000 × 1,000	1,000 × 1,000	1,200 × 1,200
INTERFACES					
Parallel	●	INA	○	●	●
Serial	●	○	○	●	●
LocalTalk	INA	INA	INA	INA	INA
SCSI	○	INA	INA	○	○
AppleTalk	Optional	○	○	●	●
Ethernet	Optional	INA	INA	Optional	Optional
Automatic interface switching	●	●	N/A	●	●
Simultaneously active ports	●	N/A	N/A	●	●
PAPER HANDLING					
Number of paper cassettes	INA	2	1	INA	INA
Cassette capacity (sheets)	250	50, 250	250	200	150
Duplexing	Optional	○	○	○	○
FONTS AND FEATURES					
HP PCL support	PCL 5	None	None	PCL 4	PCL 4
Supports scalable fonts	INA	N/A	N/A	INA	INA
Accepts HP-compatible font cartridges	●	N/A	N/A	○	●
PostScript language support	Kyocera PDL (optional)	Microsoft TrueImage	Microsoft TrueImage	LaserMaster Enhanced TrueImage	LaserMaster Enhanced TrueImage
Supports Type 1 fonts	●	●	●	●	●
Other emulations	INA	INA	INA	INA	INA
Supports resolution enhancement	●	INA	INA	●	●
Supports automatic emulation switching	○	●	○	●	●
Accepts proprietary font cards	INA	○	○	INA	INA
Printer-specific Microsoft Windows 3.1 driver available	●	INA	INA	● (included)	● (included)
GDI support	INA	INA	INA	INA	INA
TrueType rasterizer in firmware	INA	INA	INA	INA	INA

●—Yes ○—No N/A—Not applicable INA—Information not available

Table Continues →

Desktop Laser Printers

	LaserMaster WinPrinter 800	Lexmark IBM Laser Printer 40375E	Lexmark Winwriter 600	Lexmark IBM Laser Printer 4039 12R Plus	Lexmark IBM Laser Printer 4039 12L Plus
Price (tested configuration)	$$	$	$	$$	$$
PHYSICAL CHARACTERISTICS					
Dimensions (HWD, in inches)	8 × 14 × 16	10 × 15 × 18	12 × 20 × 21	12 × 15 × 21	16 × 15 × 21
Weight (pounds)	24	30	35	40	46
ENGINE					
Model	Canon LX	Lexmark 4037	Lexmark 4029	Lexmark 4039	Lexmark 4039
Rated speed (pages per minute)	4	5	8	12	12
Memory	None	512Kb	2Mb	2Mb	4Mb
Maximum resolution (horizontal by vertical dots per inch)	800 × 800 (600 × 600 with 5Mb RAM)	300 × 300	300 × 300	600 × 600	600 × 600
INTERFACES					
Parallel	○	●	●	●	●
Serial	○	Optional	●	●	●
LocalTalk	INA	○	○	Optional	Optional
SCSI	○	○	○	○	○
AppleTalk	○	INA	INA	INA	INA
Ethernet	○	○	N/A	Optional	Optional
Automatic interface switching	N/A	○	●	●	●
Simultaneously active ports	N/A	●	○	●	●
PAPER HANDLING					
Number of paper cassettes	INA	INA	INA	INA	INA
Cassette capacity (sheets)	50	150	200	200	500
Duplexing	○	○	○	Optional	Optional
FONTS AND FEATURES					
HP PCL support	PCL 4	PCL 4	PCL 4	PCL 5e	PCL 5e
Supports scalable fonts	INA	INA	INA	INA	INA
Accepts HP-compatible font cartridges	●	INA	INA	INA	INA
PostScript language support	LaserMaster Enhanced TrueImage	N/A	N/A	Level 2 clone	Level 2 clone
Supports Type 1 fonts	●	○	○	●	●
Other emulations	INA	●	○	○	○
Supports resolution enhancement	●	●	●	●	●
Supports automatic emulation switching	●	●	●	●	●
Accepts proprietary font cards	INA	INA	INA	INA	INA
Printer-specific Microsoft Windows 3.1 driver available	● (included)	INA	INA	INA	INA
GDI support	INA	○	●	●	●
TrueType rasterizer in firmware	INA	●	●	●	●

●—Yes ○—No N/A—Not applicable INA—Information not available

ZIFF-DAVIS PRESS

Desktop Laser Printers ■

	Mannesmann Tally MT735	Mannesmann Tally MT908	Mannesmann Tally MT911 PS	Mannesmann Tally T9008	Microtek TrueLaser
Price (tested configuration)	$	$$	$$$	$$	$$$
PHYSICAL CHARACTERISTICS					
Dimensions (HWD, in inches)	2 × 11 × 9	9 × 16 × 16	9 × 18 × 24	11 × 16 × 15	9 × 25 × 16
Weight (pounds)	8	31	42	38	35
ENGINE					
Model	Mannesmann Tally 735	TEC 1323D	Konica LP3110	TEC LB 3500	TEC INF 1305-Z
Rated speed (pages per minute)	6	8	10	8	6
Memory	1Mb	5Mb	2.5Mb	2Mb	2Mb
Maximum resolution (horizontal by vertical dots per inch)	300 × 300	300 × 300	300 × 300	600 × 600	300 × 300
INTERFACES					
Parallel	●	●	●	●	●
Serial	○	●	●	●	●
LocalTalk	INA	INA	INA	Optional	INA
SCSI	INA	○	INA	○	○
AppleTalk	○	Optional	○	INA	●
Ethernet	INA	○	INA	Optional	○
Automatic interface switching	N/A	○	○	●	●
Simultaneously active ports	N/A	○	○	●	●
PAPER HANDLING					
Number of paper cassettes	1	INA	2	INA	1
Cassette capacity (sheets)	80	250	200, 200	250	150
Duplexing	○	○	○	○	○
FONTS AND FEATURES					
HP PCL support	PCL 4	PCL 5	PCL 4	PCL 5e	PCL 4
Supports scalable fonts	○	INA	○	INA	○
Accepts HP-compatible font cartridges	○	●	○	INA	○
PostScript language support	None	Destiny PDL (optional)	Microsoft Interpreter	Level 2 clone (optional)	Microsoft TrueImage
Supports Type 1 fonts	○	●	●	●	●
Other emulations	INA	INA	INA	INA	INA
Supports resolution enhancement	INA	●	INA	●	INA
Supports automatic emulation switching	○	○	○	●	○
Accepts proprietary font cards	○	INA	●	INA	●
Printer-specific Microsoft Windows 3.1 driver available	INA	○	INA	INA	INA
GDI support	INA	INA	INA	○	INA
TrueType rasterizer in firmware	INA	INA	INA	●	INA

●—Yes   ○—No   N/A—Not applicable   INA—Information not available

Table Continues →

Desktop Laser Printers

	NEC Silentwriter Model 95	NEC Silentwriter2 990	NewGen TurboPS/300p	NewGen TurboPS/400p	NewGen TurboPS/630En
Price (tested configuration)	$$	$$$$	$$	$$$	$$$
PHYSICAL CHARACTERISTICS					
Dimensions (HWD, in inches)	INA	11 × 25 × 17	8 × 16 × 14	8 × 16 × 14	9 × 18 × 26
Weight (pounds)	INA	49	24	24	44
ENGINE					
Model	Minolta	Canon LBBP-UX	Canon LX	Canon LX	Canon SX
Rated speed (pages per minute)	6	8	4	4	8
Memory	5Mb	2Mb	16Mb	16Mb	32Mb
Maximum resolution (horizontal by vertical dots per inch)	300 × 300	300 × 300	300 × 300	400 × 400	600 × 300
INTERFACES					
Parallel	●	●	●	●	●
Serial	●	●	●	●	●
LocalTalk	INA	INA	INA	INA	INA
SCSI	○	INA	Optional (hard disk only)	Optional (hard disk only)	● (hard disk only)
AppleTalk	●	●	●	●	●
Ethernet	Optional	INA	○	○	●
Automatic interface switching	●	○	●	●	●
Simultaneously active ports	●	○	●	●	●
PAPER HANDLING					
Number of paper cassettes	INA	1	INA	INA	INA
Cassette capacity (sheets)	250	200	70	70	200
Duplexing	○	○	○	○	○
FONTS AND FEATURES					
HP PCL support	PCL 5	PCL 4	PCL 4	PCL 4	PCL 4
Supports scalable fonts	INA	●	INA	INA	INA
Accepts HP-compatible font cartridges	●	○	○	○	○
PostScript language support	Adobe PostScript Level 2	Adobe Level 1	NewGen PDL	NewGen PDL	NewGen PDL
Supports Type 1 fonts	●	●	●	●	●
Other emulations	INA	INA	INA	INA	INA
Supports resolution enhancement	●	INA	○	●	○
Supports automatic emulation switching	● (via software)	●	●	●	●
Accepts proprietary font cards	INA	○	INA	INA	INA
Printer-specific Microsoft Windows 3.1 driver available	● (included)	INA	● (included)	● (included)	● (included)
GDI support	INA	INA	INA	INA	INA
TrueType rasterizer in firmware	INA	INA	INA	INA	INA

●—Yes ○—No N/A—Not applicable INA—Information not available

Desktop Laser Printers ◼

	NewGen TurboPS/660	NewGen TurboPS/840e	NewGen TurboPS/880	Okidata OL400e	Okidata OL410e
Price (tested configuration)	$$$	$$$	$$$$	$	$
PHYSICAL CHARACTERISTICS					
Dimensions (HWD, in inches)	9 × 18 × 26	13 × 23 × 22	9 × 18 × 26	6 × 13 × 14	6 × 13 × 14
Weight (pounds)	44	56	44	17	17
ENGINE					
Model	Canon SX	Canon SX	Canon SX	OKI OL400e	OKI OL400e
Rated speed (pages per minute)	8	8	8	4	4
Memory	32Mb	32Mb	32Mb	512Kb	2Mb
Maximum resolution (horizontal by vertical dots per inch)	600 × 600	800 × 400	800 × 800	N/A	N/A
INTERFACES					
Parallel	●	●	●	●	●
Serial	●	●	●	●	●
LocalTalk	INA	INA	INA	○	○
SCSI	● (hard disk only)	● (hard disk only)	● (hard disk only)	○	○
AppleTalk	●	●	●	INA	INA
Ethernet	Optional	Optional	●	○	○
Automatic interface switching	●	●	●	●	●
Simultaneously active ports	●	●	●	●	●
PAPER HANDLING					
Number of paper cassettes	INA	INA	INA	INA	INA
Cassette capacity (sheets)	200	200	200	100	100
Duplexing	○	○	○	○	○
FONTS AND FEATURES					
HP PCL support	PCL 4	PCL 4	PCL 4	PCL 4.5	PCL 5
Supports scalable fonts	INA	INA	INA	INA	INA
Accepts HP-compatible font cartridges	○	○	○	INA	INA
PostScript language support	NewGen PDL	NewGen PDL	NewGen PDL	N/A	N/A
Supports Type 1 fonts	●	●	●	●	●
Other emulations	INA	INA	INA	○	○
Supports resolution enhancement	●	●	●	○	●
Supports automatic emulation switching	●	●	●	○	○
Accepts proprietary font cards	INA	INA	INA	INA	INA
Printer-specific Microsoft Windows 3.1 driver available	● (included)	● (included)	● (included)	INA	INA
GDI support	INA	INA	INA	○	○
TrueType rasterizer in firmware	INA	INA	INA	○	○

●—Yes ○—No N/A—Not applicable INA—Information not available

Table Continues →

■ Desktop Laser Printers

	Okidata OL810 LED Page Printer	Okidata OL830	Panasonic SideWriter KX-R4400	Panasonic KX-P4410	Panasonic KX-P4430
Price (tested configuration)	$$	$$	$	$	$$
PHYSICAL CHARACTERISTICS					
Dimensions (HWD, in inches)	8 × 18 × 18	6 × 18 × 18	12 × 5 × 5	9 × 15 × 16	9 × 15 × 16
Weight (pounds)	24	37	15	31	31
ENGINE					
Model	Oki Electric OL-800	Oki Electric OL-800	Matsushita 4400	Panasonic 4400	Panasonic 4400
Rated speed (pages per minute)	8	8	4	5	5
Memory	5Mb	2Mb	1Mb	4.5Mb	5Mb
Maximum resolution (horizontal by vertical dots per inch)	300 × 300	300 × 300	300 × 300	300 × 300	300 × 300
INTERFACES					
Parallel	●	●	●	●	●
Serial	Optional	○	Optional	○	●
LocalTalk	INA	INA	Optional	INA	INA
SCSI	○	INA	○	○	○
AppleTalk	Optional	○	INA	○	○
Ethernet	○	INA	○	○	○
Automatic interface switching	●	N/A	○	N/A	●
Simultaneously active ports	●	N/A	○	N/A	○
PAPER HANDLING					
Number of paper cassettes	INA	1	INA	INA	INA
Cassette capacity (sheets)	200	200	100	200	200
Duplexing	○	○	○	○	○
FONTS AND FEATURES					
HP PCL support	PCL 5	PCL 4	PCL 4	PCL 4	PCL 5
Supports scalable fonts	INA	N/A	INA	INA	INA
Accepts HP-compatible font cartridges	○	○	INA	●	●
PostScript language support	Adobe PostScript (optional)	Adobe Level 1	Adobe PostScript Level 2 (optional)	None	None
Supports Type 1 fonts	INA	●	N/A	○	○
Other emulations	INA	INA	○	INA	INA
Supports resolution enhancement	●	INA	○	○	●
Supports automatic emulation switching	○	●	○	○	○
Accepts proprietary font cards	INA	●	INA	INA	INA
Printer-specific Microsoft Windows 3.1 driver available	● (included)	INA	INA	●	●
GDI support	INA	INA	○	INA	INA
TrueType rasterizer in firmware	INA	INA	○	INA	INA

●—Yes ○—No N/A—Not applicable INA—Information not available

Desktop Laser Printers ▧

	Panasonic KX-P4455 Laser Partner	QMS PS-815	QMS PS-815 MR	QMS PS-825	QMS 1060 Print System
Price (tested configuration)	$$$	$$$$	$$$$	$$$$	$$$
PHYSICAL CHARACTERISTICS					
Dimensions (HWD, in inches)	15 × 28 × 17	9 × 18 × 25	9 × 18 × 25	12 × 18 × 25	14 × 16 × 19
Weight (pounds)	60	44	44	55	38
ENGINE					
Model	Matsushita KX-P4455	Canon SX	Canon SX	Canon SX	INA
Rated speed (pages per minute)	11	8	8	8	10
Memory	2Mb	2Mb	6Mb	2Mb	8Mb
Maximum resolution (horizontal by vertical dots per inch)	300 × 300	300 × 300	600 × 600	300 × 300	600 × 600
INTERFACES					
Parallel	●	●	●	●	●
Serial	●	●	●	●	●
LocalTalk	INA	INA	INA	INA	●
SCSI	○	INA	INA	INA	Optional
AppleTalk	●	●	●	●	INA
Ethernet	○	INA	INA	INA	Optional
Automatic interface switching	○	●	●	●	●
Simultaneously active ports	○	●	●	●	●
PAPER HANDLING					
Number of paper cassettes	2	1	1	2	INA
Cassette capacity (sheets)	250, 250	200	200	200, 200	500
Duplexing	○	○	○	○	○
FONTS AND FEATURES					
HP PCL support	PCL 4	PCL 4	PCL 4	PCL 4	PCL 5
Supports scalable fonts	N/A	○	○	○	INA
Accepts HP-compatible font cartridges	○	●	●	●	INA
PostScript language support	Adobe Level 1	Adobe Level 1	Adobe Level 1	Adobe Level 1	Level 2 clone
Supports Type 1 fonts	●	●	●	●	●
Other emulations	INA	INA	INA	INA	●
Supports resolution enhancement	INA	INA	INA	INA	○
Supports automatic emulation switching	○	●	●	●	●
Accepts proprietary font cards	●	●	●	●	INA
Printer-specific Microsoft Windows 3.1 driver available	INA	INA	INA	INA	INA
GDI support	INA	INA	INA	INA	○
TrueType rasterizer in firmware	INA	INA	INA	INA	●

●—Yes   ○—No   N/A—Not applicable   INA—Information not available

Table Continues →

■ Desktop Laser Printers

	QMS Magicolor	Samsung Finalé 8000	Sharp JX-9400H	Sharp JX-9460PS	Sharp JX-9500H
Price (tested configuration)	$$$$$	$$	$	$	$$
PHYSICAL CHARACTERISTICS					
Dimensions (HWD, in inches)	15 × 21 × 22	INA	11 × 13 × 14	11 × 13 × 14	11 × 13 × 14
Weight (pounds)	86	INA	27	27	33
ENGINE					
Model	Hitachi proprietary	Samsung F8000	Sharp JX-9400	Sharp 9460	Sharp JX-95
Rated speed (pages per minute)	8	8	8	6	9
Memory	12Mb	18Mb	1.5Mb	2Mb	512K
Maximum resolution (horizontal by vertical dots per inch)	600 × 600	300 × 300 (600 × 600 with optional Image-Resolution Kit)	300 × 300	600 × 600	300 × 300
INTERFACES					
Parallel	●	●	●	●	●
Serial	●	●	Optional	Optional	●
LocalTalk	●	INA	○	Optional	INA
SCSI	●	○	○	○	INA
AppleTalk	INA	Optional	INA	INA	○
Ethernet	Optional	Optional	○	○	INA
Automatic interface switching	●	●	○	●	○
Simultaneously active ports	●	●	○	●	○
PAPER HANDLING					
Number of paper cassettes	INA	INA	INA	INA	1
Cassette capacity (sheets)	250	250, 250	250	250	250
Duplexing	○	○	○	○	○
FONTS AND FEATURES					
HP PCL support	PCL 5c	PCL 5	PCL 4	PCL 5	PCL 4
Supports scalable fonts	INA	INA	INA	INA	○
Accepts HP-compatible font cartridges	INA	●	INA	INA	○
PostScript language support	Level 2 clone	Samsung PDL	N/A	Level 1 clone	None
Supports Type 1 fonts	●	●	N/A	●	○
Other emulations	●	INA	●	●	INA
Supports resolution enhancement	○	Optional	○	●	INA
Supports automatic emulation switching	●	● (via software)	○	Optional	○
Accepts proprietary font cards	INA	INA	INA	INA	●
Printer-specific Microsoft Windows 3.1 driver available	INA	●	INA	INA	INA
GDI support	○	INA	○	○	INA
TrueType rasterizer in firmware	●	INA	○	○	INA

●—Yes ○—No N/A—Not applicable INA—Information not available

Desktop Laser Printers ■

	Sharp JX-9500PS	Sharp JX-9660PS	Star Micronics LaserPrinter 4	Star Micronics LaserPrinter 4 StarScript	Tandy LP 950
Price (tested configuration)	$$$	$$	$	$$	$$
PHYSICAL CHARACTERISTICS					
Dimensions (HWD, in inches)	11 × 13 × 14	13 × 13 × 14	9 × 25 × 14	9 × 25 × 14	11 × 13 × 15
Weight (pounds)	33	32	25	25	33
ENGINE					
Model	Sharp JX-95	Sharp JX-9660	Canon LX	Canon LX	Sharp JX-95
Rated speed (pages per minute)	6	8	4	4	6
Memory	2.5Mb	2Mb	1Mb	2Mb	512K
Maximum resolution (horizontal by vertical dots per inch)	300 × 300	600 × 600	300 × 300	300 × 300	300 × 300
INTERFACES					
Parallel	●	●	●	●	●
Serial	○	●	●	●	●
LocalTalk	INA	●	INA	INA	INA
SCSI	INA	○	INA	INA	INA
AppleTalk	○	INA	○	●	○
Ethernet	INA	○	INA	INA	
Automatic interface switching	N/A	●	○	○	●
Simultaneously active ports	N/A	●	○	○	○
PAPER HANDLING					
Number of paper cassettes	1	INA	1	1	1
Cassette capacity (sheets)	250	250	50	50	250
Duplexing	○	○	○	○	○
FONTS AND FEATURES					
HP PCL support	PCL 4	PCL 5	PCL 4	PCL 4	PCL 4
Supports scalable fonts	○	INA	○	○	○
Accepts HP-compatible font cartridges	○	INA	●	●	●
PostScript language support	Adobe Level 1	Level 1 clone	None	Star Micronics StarScript	None
Supports Type 1 fonts	●	●	○	●	○
Other emulations	INA	●	INA	INA	INA
Supports resolution enhancement	INA	●	INA	INA	INA
Supports automatic emulation switching	○	Optional	○	○	○
Accepts proprietary font cards	●	INA	○	●	●
Printer-specific Microsoft Windows 3.1 driver available	INA	INA	INA	INA	INA
GDI support	INA	○	INA	INA	INA
TrueType rasterizer in firmware	INA	○	INA	INA	INA

●—Yes ○—No N/A—Not applicable INA—Information not available

T a b l e C o n t i n u e s →

■ Desktop Laser Printers

	TI microLaser 600	TI microLaser Pro 600 PS23	TI microLaser Power Pro	TI microLaser Turbo	TI microWriter PS23
Price (tested configuration)	$	$$	$$	$$	$
PHYSICAL CHARACTERISTICS					
Dimensions (HWD, in inches)	10 × 14 × 15	13 × 13 × 14	13 × 13 × 14	11 × 13 × 14	10 × 14 × 15
Weight (pounds)	33	32	32	33	33
ENGINE					
Model	Samsung SL 1050	Sharp JX-9600	Sharp JX-9612	Sharp JX-9500	Samsung SL1050
Rated speed (pages per minute)	5	8	12	9	5
Memory	2Mb	6Mb	6Mb	10.5Mb	2Mb
Maximum resolution (horizontal by vertical dots per inch)	600 × 600	600 × 600	600 × 600	300 × 300	300 × 300
INTERFACES					
Parallel	●	●	●	●	●
Serial	Optional	Optional	Optional	Optional	Optional
LocalTalk	●	●	●	INA	○
SCSI	Optional	Optional	Optional	Optional (hard disk only)	○
AppleTalk	INA	INA	INA	Optional	INA
Ethernet	○	Optional	Optional	Optional	○
Automatic interface switching	●	●	●	●	○
Simultaneously active ports	●	●	●	●	○
PAPER HANDLING					
Number of paper cassettes	INA	INA	INA	INA	INA
Cassette capacity (sheets)	250	250	250	250	250
Duplexing	○	○	○	○	○
FONTS AND FEATURES					
HP PCL support	PCL 5	PCL 5	PCL 5	PCL 4	PCL 4
Supports scalable fonts	INA	INA	INA	INA	INA
Accepts HP-compatible font cartridges	INA	INA	INA	●	INA
PostScript language support	Adobe PostScript Level 2	Adobe PostScript Level 2	Adobe PostScript Level 2	Adobe PostScript Level 2	Adobe level 1
Supports Type 1 fonts	●	●	●	●	●
Other emulations	○	○	○	INA	●
Supports resolution enhancement	○	○	○	○	○
Supports automatic emulation switching	●	●	●	●	●
Accepts proprietary font cards	INA	INA	INA	INA	INA
Printer-specific Microsoft Windows 3.1 driver available	INA	INA	INA	○	INA
GDI support	○	○	○	INA	○
TrueType rasterizer in firmware	●	○	●	INA	○

●—Yes ○—No N/A—Not applicable INA—Information not available

Desktop Laser Printers

	Toshiba PageLaser GX200	Unisys AP312 Plus	Xante Accel-a-Writer 8000	Xerox 4505ps	Xerox 4510ps
Price (tested configuration)	$$	$$	$$$	$$	$$
PHYSICAL CHARACTERISTICS					
Dimensions (HWD, in inches)	INA	12 × 15 × 21	9 × 18 × 19	10 × 14 × 16	10 × 14 × 16
Weight (pounds)	INA	40	42	31	31
ENGINE					
Model	TEC LB-1323	Lexmark 4039	Canon SX	Fuji Xerox XP-5	Fuji Xerox XP-10
Rated speed (pages per minute)	8	12	8	5	10
Memory	5Mb	2Mb	16Mb	6Mb	6Mb
Maximum resolution (horizontal by vertical dots per inch)	300 × 300	600 × 600	600 × 600	600 × 600	600 × 600
INTERFACES					
Parallel	●	●	●	●	●
Serial	●	●	●	●	●
LocalTalk	INA	○	INA	Optional	Optional
SCSI	○	○	● (hard disk only)	○	○
AppleTalk	○	INA	●	INA	INA
Ethernet	Optional	Optional	○	Optional	Optional
Automatic interface switching	○	●	○	●	●
Simultaneously active ports	○	●	●	●	●
PAPER HANDLING					
Number of paper cassettes	INA	INA	INA	INA	INA
Cassette capacity (sheets)	250	200	200	250	250
Duplexing	○	Optional	○	○	○
FONTS AND FEATURES					
HP PCL support	PCL 5	PCL 5e	PCL 4	PCL 5e	PCL 5e
Supports scalable fonts	INA	INA	INA	INA	INA
Accepts HP-compatible font cartridges	●	INA	○	INA	INA
PostScript language support	Toshiba PDL (optional)	Level 2 clone	Phoenix	Adobe PostScript Level 2	Adobe PostScript Level 2
Supports Type 1 fonts	●	●	●	●	●
Other emulations	INA	○	INA	○	○
Supports resolution enhancement	●	●	●	●	●
Supports automatic emulation switching	○	●	○	●	●
Accepts proprietary font cards	INA	INA	INA	INA	INA
Printer-specific Microsoft Windows 3.1 driver available	○	INA	○	INA	INA
GDI support	INA	○	INA	○	○
TrueType rasterizer in firmware	INA	●	INA	●	●

●—Yes ○—No N/A—Not applicable INA—Information not available

Table Continues →

Desktop Laser Printers

	Xerox 4900 Color Laser Printer
Price (tested configuration)	$$$$$
PHYSICAL CHARACTERISTICS	
Dimensions (HWD, in inches)	15 × 24 × 22
Weight (pounds)	108
ENGINE	
Model	Hitachi color engine
Rated speed (pages per minute)	12
Memory	6Mb
Maximum resolution (horizontal by vertical dots per inch)	1,200 × 300
INTERFACES	
Parallel	●
Serial	●
LocalTalk	●
SCSI	○
AppleTalk	INA
Ethernet	Optional
Automatic interface switching	●
Simultaneously active ports	●
PAPER HANDLING	
Number of paper cassettes	INA
Cassette capacity (sheets)	250
Duplexing	○
FONTS AND FEATURES	
HP PCL support	PCL 5
Supports scalable fonts	INA
Accepts HP-compatible font cartridges	INA
PostScript language support	Adobe PostScript Level 2
Supports Type 1 fonts	●
Other emulations	○
Supports resolution enhancement	●
Supports automatic emulation switching	●
Accepts proprietary font cards	INA
Printer-specific Microsoft Windows 3.1 driver available	INA
GDI support	○
TrueType rasterizer in firmware	●

●—Yes   ○—No   N/A—Not applicable   INA—Information not available

End ■

D.4 Shared Laser Printers

(Products listed in alphabetical order by company name)	AMT TracJet Laser Printer	Advanced Matrix AMT TracJet III	ALPS LSX1600	Compaq PageMarq 15	Compaq PageMarq 20
Price (tested configuration)	$$$$	$$$$$	$$$	$$$	$$$$
PHYSICAL CHARACTERISTICS					
Dimensions (HWD, in inches)	INA	7 × 18 × 21	11 × 18 × 20	17 × 20 × 17	19 × 20 × 17
ENGINE					
Model	Pentax PL-F0301	Pentax PL-0301	MKE Matsushita V50	Fuji Xerox	Fuji Xerox
Rated speed (pages per minute)	16	16	16	15	20
Single-cartridge toner/developer/drum	○	INA	○	●	●
Toner capacity (copies)	4,000	8,000	10,000	12,000	12,000
Memory (as tested)	8Mb	4Mb	7Mb	18Mb	20Mb
Maximum resolution (horizontal by vertical dots per inch)	300 × 300	300 × 300	300 × 300	800 × 400	800 × 400
Controller with RISC processor	○	●	○	●	●
INTERFACES					
Parallel	●	●	●	●	●
Serial	●	●	●	●	●
AppleTalk	○	INA	○	Optional	Optional
SCSI port	○	○	○	○	○
LocalTalk	INA	○	INA	INA	INA
Ethernet	○	○	○	Optional	Optional
Token-Ring	○	○	○	Optional	Optional
Automatic interface switching	○	●	○	●	●
Simultaneously active ports	○	●	○	●	●
PAPER HANDLING					
Standard cassette capacity (sheets)	N/A	N/A	500, 250	500, 250	500, 500, 500
Letter-size paper (8.5 × 11inches)	INA	INA	●	●	●
Legal-size paper (8.5 × 14 inches)	INA	INA	●	●	●
Duplexing	○	○	●	○	○
Rated maximum paper weight (pounds)	20	24	35	32	32
FONTS AND FEATURES					
HP PCL support	PCL 4	PCL 5	PCL 4	PCL 5	PCL 5
Accepts HP-compatible font cartridges	●	INA	●	○	○
PostScript language support	None	Level 2 clone (optional)	ALPScript PDL (optional)	Adobe PostScript Level 2	Adobe PostScript Level 2
Supports Type 1 fonts	N/A	●	●	●	●
Supports resolution enhancement	○	○	○	●	●
Supports automatic emulation switching	○	●	○	●	●
Printer-specific Microsoft Windows 3.1 driver	○	INA	● (in Windows 3.1)	● (included)	● (included)

●—Yes   ○—No   N/A—Not applicable   INA—Information not available

Table Continues →

■ Shared Laser Printers

	Dataproducts LZR 1555	Dataproducts LZR 1560	Dataproducts LZR 2080	DEClaser 3250	Digital PrintServer 17/600
Price (tested configuration)	$$$	$$$	$$$$	$$$$	$$$$
PHYSICAL CHARACTERISTICS					
Dimensions (HWD, in inches)	13 × 22 × 22	13 × 20 × 22	13 × 20 × 21	INA	19 × 18 × 22
ENGINE					
Model	Fuji Xerox XP-15	Fuji Xerox XP-15	Fuji Xerox XP-20	Fuji Xerox 4213	Canon LPS 17-A2
Rated speed (pages per minute)	15	15	20	13	17
Single-cartridge toner/ developer/drum	●	●	INA	○	INA
Toner capacity (copies)	12,000	12,000	11,000	6,000	8,000
Memory (as tested)	16Mb	16Mb	8Mb	10.5Mb	16Mb
Maximum resolution (horizontal by vertical dots per inch)	400 × 400	400 × 400	400 × 400	300 × 300	300 × 300
Controller with RISC processor	○	●	●	○	CISC
INTERFACES					
Parallel	●	●	○	●	○
Serial	●	●	●	●	○
AppleTalk	○	●	INA	○	INA
SCSI port	○	● (for hard disk storage only)	●	○	○
LocalTalk	INA	INA	●	INA	○
Ethernet	○	○	●	Optional	●
Token-Ring	○	○	○	○	○
Automatic interface switching	○	○	○	○	○
Simultaneously active ports	●	●	●	○	○
PAPER HANDLING					
Standard cassette capacity (sheets)	250, 250	250, 250	250, 250	250, 250	500, 500
Letter-size paper (8.5 × 11inches)	●	●	INA	INA	INA
Legal-size paper (8.5 × 14 inches)	●	●	INA	INA	INA
Duplexing	○	○	○	●	Optional
Rated maximum paper weight (pounds)	32	32	24	32	24
FONTS AND FEATURES					
HP PCL support	PCL 5	PCL 4	PCL 4	PCL 4	PCL 5
Accepts HP-compatible font cartridges	●	○	INA	○	INA
PostScript language support	None	Adobe PostScript Level 2	Adobe Level 2	Xerox PDL	Adobe Level 2
Supports Type 1 fonts	N/A	●	●	●	●
Supports resolution enhancement	○	○	●	○	●
Supports automatic emulation switching	○	○	○	● (via software)	●
Printer-specific Microsoft Windows 3.1 driver	● (included)	● (included)	INA	● (available on request)	INA

●—Yes   ○—No   N/A—Not applicable   INA—Information not available

Shared Laser Printers ■

	Eastman Kodak Ektaplus 7016 PS	Genicom Model 7170	HP LaserJet IIISi	HP LaserJet 4V	HP LaserJet 4MV
Price (tested configuration)	$$$$	$$$$	$$$$	$$$	$$$
PHYSICAL CHARACTERISTICS					
Dimensions (HWD, in inches)	16 × 28 × 21	13 × 19 × 18	17 × 22 × 24	13 × 18 × 21	13 × 18 × 21
ENGINE					
Model	Kodak LED QEXP-QT99	Toshiba G750	Canon	Canon BX-2	Canon BX-2
Rated speed (pages per minute)	16	17	17	16	16
Single-cartridge toner/developer/drum	○	●	●	INA	INA
Toner capacity (copies)	4,000	13,000	8,000	8,100	8,100
Memory (as tested)	2Mb	9Mb	1Mb	4Mb	12Mb
Maximum resolution (horizontal by vertical dots per inch)	300 × 300	300 × 300	300 × 300	600 × 600	600 × 600
Controller with RISC processor	○	○	●	●	●
INTERFACES					
Parallel	●	●	●	●	●
Serial	●	●	●	●	●
AppleTalk	○	Optional	●	INA	INA
SCSI port	○	○	○	○	○
LocalTalk	INA	INA	INA	Optional	Optional
Ethernet	○	Optional	○	Optional	●
Token-Ring	○	Optional	○	Optional	●
Automatic interface switching	○	○	●	●	●
Simultaneously active ports	●	○	○	●	●
PAPER HANDLING					
Standard cassette capacity (sheets)	500	250, 250	1,000	250, 100	250, 100
Letter-size paper (8.5 × 11inches)	●	●	●	INA	INA
Legal-size paper (8.5 × 14 inches)	○	●	●	INA	INA
Duplexing	○	Optional	○	○	○
Rated maximum paper weight (pounds)	24	36	28	28	28
FONTS AND FEATURES					
HP PCL support	PCL 4	PCL 5	PCL 4, PCL 5	Enhanced PCL 5	Enhanced PCL 5
Accepts HP-compatible font cartridges	○	●	●	INA	INA
PostScript language support	Adobe Level 1	GeniScript PDL (optional)	None	Adobe Level 2 (optional)	Adobe Level 2
Supports Type 1 fonts	●	●	○	●	●
Supports resolution enhancement	INA	●	INA	●	●
Supports automatic emulation switching	○	●	○	●	●
Printer-specific Microsoft Windows 3.1 driver	INA	● (included)	INA	INA	INA

●—Yes ○—No N/A—Not applicable INA—Information not available

Table Continues →

Shared Laser Printers

	HP LaserJet 4Si MX	IBM LaserPrinter 10L	Kentek K30D	Kyocera F-5000A	LaserMaster TrueTech 1200
Price (tested configuration)	$$$$	$$$	$$$$$	$$$$$	$$$$$
PHYSICAL CHARACTERISTICS					
Dimensions (HWD, in inches)	17 × 22 × 30	17 × 14 × 21	INA	13 × 42 × 19	14 × 37 × 21
ENGINE					
Model	Canon LBP-NX	IBM proprietary	Kentek K30D	Kyocera LBP27	Hitachi Laserbeam 2000
Rated speed (pages per minute)	17	10	30	12	20
Single-cartridge toner/developer/drum	INA	●	○	○	○
Toner capacity (copies)	10,250	15,000	13,000	5,000	3,000
Memory (as tested)	10Mb	1Mb	22Mb	3Mb	17Mb
Maximum resolution (horizontal by vertical dots per inch)	600 × 600	300 × 300	300 × 300	300 × 300	1,200 × 800
Controller with RISC processor	●	○	●	○	●
INTERFACES					
Parallel	●	●	●	●	○
Serial	○	●	●	●	○
AppleTalk	INA	○	○	○	○
SCSI port	○	○	○	○	○
LocalTalk	●	INA	INA	INA	INA
Ethernet	●	○	Optional	○	○
Token-Ring	Optional	○	○	○	○
Automatic interface switching	●	○	○	●	N/A
Simultaneously active ports	●	○	○	○	N/A
PAPER HANDLING					
Standard cassette capacity (sheets)	500, 500	700	550, 250	250	250
Letter-size paper (8.5 × 11inches)	INA	●	INA	●	●
Legal-size paper (8.5 × 14 inches)	INA	●	INA	●	●
Duplexing	Optional	○	●	○	○
Rated maximum paper weight (pounds)	28	175	24	24	24
FONTS AND FEATURES					
HP PCL support	Enhanced PCL 5	PCL 4	PCL 5	PCL 4	PCL 4
Accepts HP-compatible font cartridges	INA	○	○	○	○
PostScript language support	Adobe Level 2	None	PhoenixPage PDL (optional)	None	Microsoft TrueImage
Supports Type 1 fonts	●	○	●	○	●
Supports resolution enhancement	●	INA	○	INA	INA
Supports automatic emulation switching	●	○	○	○	●
Printer-specific Microsoft Windows 3.1 driver	INA	INA	○	INA	INA

●—Yes   ○—No   N/A—Not applicable   INA—Information not available

Shared Laser Printers

	Lexmark IBM LaserPrinter 4039 16L Plus	NewGen TurboPS/ 1200T	OTC LaserMatrix 1000 Model 5	Printronix L1016 Continuous Form Laser Printer	QMS 1660 Print System
Price (tested configuration)	$$$	$$$$$	$$$$	$$$$$	$$$$
PHYSICAL CHARACTERISTICS					
Dimensions (HWD, in inches)	16 × 15 × 21	19 × 23 × 26	INA	INA	12 × 18 × 23
ENGINE					
Model	Lexmark 4039	Copal SLB-6000	Asahi Optical FL1	Pentax PL-F0301	Canon LBP-BX
Rated speed (pages per minute)	16	12	16	16	16
Single-cartridge toner/ developer/drum	INA	○	○	○	INA
Toner capacity (copies)	10,000	5,000	4,000	8,000	7,500
Memory (as tested)	4Mb	48Mb	9Mb	24Mb	12Mb
Maximum resolution (horizontal by vertical dots per inch)	600 × 600	1,200 × 600	300 × 300	300 × 300	300 × 300
Controller with RISC processor	●	●	●	○	●
INTERFACES					
Parallel	●	●	●	●	●
Serial	●	●	●	●	●
AppleTalk	INA	●	○	○	INA
SCSI port	○	● (for hard disk storage only)	○	○	Optional
LocalTalk	Optional	INA	INA	INA	●
Ethernet	Optional	●	○	○	Optional
Token-Ring	Optional	○	○	○	Optional
Automatic interface switching	●	●	●	○	●
Simultaneously active ports	●	●	●	○	●
PAPER HANDLING					
Standard cassette capacity (sheets)	500	250, 250	N/A	N/A	250, 100
Letter-size paper (8.5 × 11 inches)	INA	●	INA	INA	INA
Legal-size paper (8.5 × 14 inches)	INA	●	INA	INA	INA
Duplexing	Optional	○	○	○	○
Rated maximum paper weight (pounds)	24	34	40	24	34
FONTS AND FEATURES					
HP PCL support	PCL 5e	PCL 4	PCL 5	None	PCL 5
Accepts HP-compatible font cartridges	INA	○	●	N/A	INA
PostScript language support	Level 2 clone	NewGen PostScript PDL	None	PhoenixPage PDL (optional)	Level 2 clone
Supports Type 1 fonts	●	●	N/A	●	●
Supports resolution enhancement	●	●	○	○	○
Supports automatic emulation switching	●	●	○	○	●
Printer-specific Microsoft Windows 3.1 driver	INA	● (included)	○	○	INA

●—Yes   ○—No   N/A—Not applicable   INA—Information not available

Table Continues →

■ Shared Laser Printers

	QMS 1725 SLS Print System	QMS 3225 Print System	QMS-PS 1700	Sharp JX-9700	Synergystex CF1000 Continuous Form Laser Printer
Price (tested configuration)	$$$$	$$$$$	$$$$$	$$$	$$$$
PHYSICAL CHARACTERISTICS					
Dimensions (HWD, in inches)	19 × 22 × 22	30 × 37 × 26	INA	11 × 16 × 17	INA
ENGINE					
Model	Canon NX	Ricoh M32	Canon NX	Sharp JX-97	Pentax PL-F0301
Rated speed (pages per minute)	17	32	17	16	16
Single-cartridge toner/ developer/drum	INA	INA	●	○	○
Toner capacity (copies)	8,000	20,000	8,000	5,000	4,000
Memory (as tested)	13Mb	16Mb	32Mb	1Mb	8Mb
Maximum resolution (horizontal by vertical dots per inch)	300 × 300	400 × 400	600 × 600	300 × 300	300 × 300
Controller with RISC processor	●	●	●	○	○
INTERFACES					
Parallel	●	●	●	●	●
Serial	●	●	●	●	●
AppleTalk	INA	INA	●	○	○
SCSI port	●	●	● (for hard disk storage only)	○	○
LocalTalk	●	●	INA	INA	INA
Ethernet	Optional	Optional	Optional	○	○
Token-Ring	Optional	Optional	Optional	○	○
Automatic interface switching	●	●	●	○	○
Simultaneously active ports	●	●	●	○	○
PAPER HANDLING					
Standard cassette capacity (sheets)	500, 500	250, 250	500, 500	250	N/A
Letter-size paper (8.5 × 11inches)	INA	INA	INA	●	INA
Legal-size paper (8.5 × 14 inches)	INA	INA	INA	●	INA
Duplexing	Optional	Optional	Optional	○	○
Rated maximum paper weight (pounds)	36	24	36	34	24
FONTS AND FEATURES					
HP PCL support	PCL 5	PCL 5	PCL 4	PCL 4	PCL 4
Accepts HP-compatible font cartridges	INA	INA	○	○	●
PostScript language support	Level 2 clone	Level 2 clone	Adobe PostScript Level 1	None	None
Supports Type 1 fonts	●	●	●	○	N/A
Supports resolution enhancement	○	○	○	INA	○
Supports automatic emulation switching	●	●	●	○	○
Printer-specific Microsoft Windows 3.1 driver	INA	INA	● (included)	INA	○

●—Yes   ○—No   N/A—Not applicable   INA—Information not available

Shared Laser Printers ■

	TI microLaser XL PS35	TI microLaser XL Turbo	Toshiba PageLaser GX400	Xante Accel-a-Writer	Xerox 4520mp
Price (tested configuration)	$$$	$$$	$$$$	$$$$	$$$$
PHYSICAL CHARACTERISTICS					
Dimensions (HWD, in inches)	11 × 16 × 17	11 × 17 × 16	INA	12 × 18 × 20	21 × 20 × 16
ENGINE					
Model	Sharp JX-97	Sharp JX-9700	Toshiba G750	Canon BX-2	Fuji Xerox XP-20
Rated speed (pages per minute)	16	16	17	16	20
Single-cartridge toner/ developer/drum	○	○	●	INA	INA
Toner capacity (copies)	6,000	6,000	13,000	7,500	14,000
Memory (as tested)	1.5Mb	10.5Mb	9Mb	12Mb	8Mb
Maximum resolution (horizontal by vertical dots per inch)	300 × 300	300 × 300	300 × 300	600 × 600	800 × 800
Controller with RISC processor	○	●	○	●	●
INTERFACES					
Parallel	●	●	●	●	●
Serial	○	Optional	●	●	●
AppleTalk	○	Optional	Optional	INA	INA
SCSI port	○	Optional (for hard disk storage only)	○	●	○
LocalTalk	INA	INA	INA	●	Optional
Ethernet	○	Optional	Optional	Optional	●
Token-Ring	○	○	Optional	○	Optional
Automatic interface switching	○	●	○	●	●
Simultaneously active ports	○	●	○	●	●
PAPER HANDLING					
Standard cassette capacity (sheets)	250	250	250, 250	250, 250	250, 250
Letter-size paper (8.5 × 11inches)	●	●	●	INA	INA
Legal-size paper (8.5 × 14 inches)	●	●	INA	INA	INA
Duplexing	○	○	Optional	○	○
Rated maximum paper weight (pounds)	24	34	36	34	36
FONTS AND FEATURES					
HP PCL support	PCL 4	PCL 4	PCL 5	PCL 5	PCL 5e
Accepts HP-compatible font cartridges	○	○	●	INA	INA
PostScript language support	Adobe Level 1	Adobe PostScript Level 2	Toshiba PDL (optional)	Adobe Level 2	Adobe Level 2
Supports Type 1 fonts	●	●	●	●	●
Supports resolution enhancement	INA	○	●	●	●
Supports automatic emulation switching	○	●	●	●	●
Printer-specific Microsoft Windows 3.1 driver	INA	● (included)	● (included)	INA	INA

●—Yes ○—No N/A—Not applicable INA—Information not available   **Table Continues** →

■ Shared Laser Printers

	Xerox 4420mp
Price (tested configuration)	$$$$$
PHYSICAL CHARACTERISTICS	
Dimensions (HWD, in inches)	42 × 39 × 22
ENGINE	
Model	Fuji Xerox P500
Rated speed (pages per minute)	20
Single-cartridge toner/developer/drum	INA
Toner capacity (copies)	15,000
Memory (as tested)	8Mb
Maximum resolution (horizontal by vertical dots per inch)	300 × 300
Controller with RISC processor	●
INTERFACES	
Parallel	●
Serial	●
AppleTalk	INA
SCSI port	○
LocalTalk	Optional
Ethernet	Optional
Token-Ring	Optional
Automatic interface switching	●
Simultaneously active ports	●
PAPER HANDLING	
Standard cassette capacity (sheets)	250, 250
Letter-size paper (8.5 × 11inches)	INA
Legal-size paper (8.5 × 14 inches)	INA
Duplexing	●
Rated maximum paper weight (pounds)	110
FONTS AND FEATURES	
HP PCL support	PCL 5e
Accepts HP-compatible font cartridges	INA
PostScript language support	Adobe Level 2
Supports Type 1 fonts	●
Supports resolution enhancement	●
Supports automatic emulation switching	●
Printer-specific Microsoft Windows 3.1 driver	INA

●—Yes   ○—No   N/A—Not applicable   INA—Information not available

End ■

D.5 Color PostScript Printers

(Products listed in alphabetical order by company name)	Brother HS-1PS Level 2 Color	Brother HT-500PS	CalComp ColorMaster Plus 6613PS	DEColorwriter 1000	Eastman Kodak ColorEase PS Printer
Price (tested configuration)	$$$$$	$$$$	$$$$$	$$$	$$$$$
PHYSICAL CHARACTERISTICS					
Dimensions (HWD, in inches)	17 × 23 × 19	11 × 17 × 17	INA	11 × 13 × 18	12 × 17 × 21
Weight (pounds)	110	65	INA	40	60
ENGINE					
Engine type	Solid ink	Thermal wax transfer	Thermal wax transfer	Thermal wax transfer	Thermal dye transfer
Model	Brother HS-1	Mitsubishi G370	CalComp 6613	Tektronix/Sharp Model 4681	Proprietary (Eastman Kodak)
Memory (tested configuration)	12Mb	21Mb	34Mb	8Mb	16Mb
Maximum resolution (horizontal by vertical dots per inch)	300 × 300	300 × 300	300 × 300	600 × 300	300 × 300
Controller	Brother HS-1 PS-2	Brother HT-500PS	CalComp 6613	INA	Proprietary (Sun-designed)
Controller with RISC processor	25-MHz IDT R305	None	16-MHz i960KB	16-MHz AMD AM29000	40-MHz Sun SPARC
INTERFACES					
Parallel	●	●	●	●	●
Serial	●	●	●	●	●
AppleTalk	●	●	●	●	●
SCSI port	INA	● (for hard disk)	● (for hard disk)	INA	INA
Automatic interface switching	●	●	●	●	●
Simultaneously active ports	●	○	●	●	●
PAPER HANDLING					
Accepts plain paper	●	○	○	●	○
Paper capacity (sheets)	INA	INA	INA	INA	INA
Letter-size paper (8.5 × 11 inches)	●	●	●	●	●
Size of printable area (inches)	8.2 × 10.3	8.1 × 9	8.1 × 10.6	8 × 8.9	8.1 × 10.6
Legal-size paper (8.5 × 14 inches)	●	●	●	○	○
Size of printable area (inches)	8.2 × 13.3	8.1 × 12	8.1 × 10.6	N/A	N/A
B-size paper (11 × 17 inches)	●	○	●	○	○
Size of printable area (inches)	11.8 × 19.3	N/A	10.6 × 16.6	N/A	N/A
Duplexing	INA	○	●	INA	INA
Rated maximum paper weight (pounds)	INA	INA	INA	INA	INA
FONTS AND FEATURES					
PostScript language support	Level 2 clone	INA	INA	Adobe Level 2	Adobe Level 2
Supports Type 1 fonts	●	●	●	●	●
Printer-specific Microsoft Windows 3.1 driver	INA	● (on request)	● (included)	INA	INA
Automatic emulation switching	INA	●	●	INA	INA
Pantone certified	○	●	●	●	○
Color separations	●	●	●	○	○
CONTROLS					
Control panels	INA	●	●	INA	INA
LCD	INA	●	●	INA	INA
Number of characters	INA	32	32	INA	INA
Control panel buttons:					
Color separation	INA	●	●	INA	INA
Paper size	INA	●	●	INA	INA
Image size	INA	○	●	INA	INA
Ribbon type	INA	○	●	INA	INA

●—Yes ○—No N/A—Not applicable INA—Information not available

Table Continues →

■ Color PostScript Printers

	Fargo PrimeraPro Color Printer	Mitsubishi DiamondColor Print 300PS	Mitsubishi CHC-S446i ColorStream/DS	Mitsubishi Shinbo Color Stream DS/ Plus CHC-574bi	NEC Colormate PS Model 40
Price (tested configuration)	$$	$$$$$	$$$$$	$$$$$	$$$$$
PHYSICAL CHARACTERISTICS					
Dimensions (HWD, in inches)	6 × 14 × 10	INA	INA	13 × 20 × 18	17 × 16 × 18
Weight (pounds)	16	INA	INA	104	55
ENGINE					
Engine type	Thermal dye/thermal wax transfer	Dye sublimation	Dye sublimation	Thermal dye transfer	Thermal wax transfer
Model	Proprietary (Fargo)	Mitsubishi S3600-30U	Shinko CHC-S446i	Shinbo CHC-5745	NEC Colormate
Memory (tested configuration)	32K	32Mb (printer), 38Mb (controller)	38Mb	54Mb	4Mb
Maximum resolution (horizontal by vertical dots per inch)	600 × 300	300 × 300	300 × 300	300 × 300	300 × 300
Controller	N/A	Quintar Q-Script 2000	Mitsubishi i-PCB	Proprietary (Quintar-designed)	INA
Controller with RISC processor	N/A	20-MHz AMD 29000	25-MHz AMD 29050	25-MHz AMD Am 29050	None
INTERFACES					
Parallel	●	●	●	●	●
Serial	○	●	●	●	●
AppleTalk	●	●	●	●	●
SCSI port	INA	○	●	INA	●
Automatic interface switching	○	●	●	●	○
Simultaneously active ports	○	○	●	●	○
PAPER HANDLING					
Accepts plain paper	●	○	○	○	○
Paper capacity (sheets)	INA	INA	INA	INA	100
Letter-size paper (8.5 × 11 inches)	●	●	●	●	●
Size of printable area (inches)	8.5 × 9.3	8.1 × 9	8.2 × 9.3	8.2 × 8.9	8.1 × 9
Legal-size paper (8.5 × 14 inches)	●	●	●	○	○
Size of printable area (inches)	N/A	8.1 × 11	8.5 × 12.3 (on super A–size paper)	N/A	N/A
B-size paper (11 × 17 inches)	○	○	○	●	○
Size of printable area (inches)	N/A	N/A	N/A	11.7 × 17.1	N/A
Duplexing	INA	○	○	INA	○
Rated maximum paper weight (pounds)	INA	INA	INA	INA	24
FONTS AND FEATURES					
PostScript language support	Adobe Level 2 (optional)	INA	INA	Level 2 clone	Adobe
Supports Type 1 fonts	●	●	●	●	●
Printer-specific Microsoft Windows 3.1 driver	INA	● (included)	● (included)	INA	INA
Automatic emulation switching	INA	○	●	INA	INA
Pantone certified	○	○	○	○	INA
Color separations	○	○	●	●	INA
CONTROLS					
Control panels	INA	● (on printer and controller)	●	INA	INA
LCD	INA	● (on printer and controller)	●	INA	INA
Number of characters	INA	64 (on printer), 16 (on controller)	16	INA	INA
Control panel buttons:					
Color separation	INA	○	○	INA	INA
Paper size	INA	○	○	INA	INA
Image size	INA	○	○	INA	INA
Ribbon type	INA	○	○	INA	INA

●—Yes   ○—No   N/A—Not applicable   INA—Information not available

Color PostScript Printers

	Océ Graphics G5241-PS	QMS ColorScript 100 Model 10p	QMS ColorScript 100 Model 30si	Seiko ColorPoint PSX Model 4	Seiko ColorPoint PSX Model 14
Price (tested configuration)	$$$$$	$$$$$	$$$$$	$$$$$	$$$$$
PHYSICAL CHARACTERISTICS					
Dimensions (HWD, in inches)	10 × 16 × 24	12 × 17 × 22	INA	8 × 14 × 25	8 × 18 × 31
Weight (pounds)	42	65	INA	41	47
ENGINE					
Engine type	Thermal wax transfer	Thermal wax transfer	Thermal wax transfer	Thermal wax transfer	Thermal wax transfer
Model	Shinko 445	Mitsubishi G370	Mitsubishi G650	Seiko CH5504-DX10	Seiko CH5514-RX18
Memory (tested configuration)	8Mb	4Mb	12Mb (included)	10Mb	18Mb
Maximum resolution (horizontal by vertical dots per inch)	300 × 300	300 × 300	300 × 300	300 × 300	300 × 300
Controller	INA	INA	QMS 30si	INA	INA
Controller with RISC processor	None	None	None	Intel 80960	intel 80960
INTERFACES					
Parallel	●	●	●	●	●
Serial	●	●	●	●	●
AppleTalk	●	●	●	●	●
SCSI port	●	●	● (for hard disk)	○	○
Automatic interface switching	○	○	○	●	●
Simultaneously active ports	○	○	○	●	●
PAPER HANDLING					
Accepts plain paper	○	○	○	○	○
Paper capacity (sheets)	100	100	INA	145	80
Letter-size paper (8.5 × 11 inches)	●	●	●	●	●
Size of printable area (inches)	8.2 × 9.3	8.1 × 9	8.1 × 8.9	8.2 × 10.7	8.2 × 10.7
Legal-size paper (8.5 × 14 inches)	○	○	○	○	○
Size of printable area (inches)	N/A	N/A	N/A	N/A	N/A
B-size paper (11 × 17 inches)	○	○	●	○	●
Size of printable area (inches)	N/A	N/A	10.6 × 14.9	N/A	10.8 × 16
Duplexing	○	○	○	○	○
Rated maximum paper weight (pounds)	24	INA	INA	22	22
FONTS AND FEATURES					
PostScript language support	Adobe	Adobe	INA	PhoenixPage	PhoenixPage
Supports Type 1 fonts	●	●	●	●	●
Printer-specific Microsoft Windows 3.1 driver	INA	INA	● (via BBS and in Windows 3.1)	INA	INA
Automatic emulation switching	INA	INA	● (via software)	INA	INA
Pantone certified	INA	INA	●	INA	INA
Color separations	INA	INA	●	INA	INA
CONTROLS					
Control panels	INA	INA	●	INA	INA
LCD	INA	INA	○	INA	INA
Number of characters	INA	INA	N/A	INA	INA
Control panel buttons:					
Color separation	INA	INA	○	INA	INA
Paper size	INA	INA	○	INA	INA
Image size	INA	INA	●	INA	INA
Ribbon type	INA	INA	○	INA	INA

●—Yes ○—No N/A—Not applicable INA—Information not available

Table Continues →

■ Color PostScript Printers

	Seiko Professional ColorPoint2 PSF Model 14	Tektronix Phaser 220e	Tektronix Phaser 220i	Tektronix Phaser 300i	Tektronix Phaser 440
Price (tested configuration)	$$$$$	$$$$	$$$$$	$$$$$	$$$$$
PHYSICAL CHARACTERISTICS					
Dimensions (HWD, in inches)	14 × 19 × 22	11 × 18 × 13	11 × 18 × 13	14 × 27 × 25	11 × 18 × 13
Weight (pounds)	77	40	40	90	46
ENGINE					
Engine type	Thermal dye/thermal wax transfer	Thermal wax transfer	Thermal wax transfer	Solid ink	Thermal dye transfer
Model	Proprietary (Seiko Instruments)	Tektronix/Sharp Model 4681	Tektronix/Sharp Model 4681	Tektronix/Sharp Model 4699	Tektronix/Sharp Model 4685
Memory (tested configuration)	24Mb	8Mb	10Mb	10Mb	16Mb
Maximum resolution (horizontal by vertical dots per inch)	300 × 300	600 × 300	600 × 300	300 × 300	300 × 300
Controller	Proprietary (Seiko Instruments)	Tektronix PXe series	Tektronix PXi series	Tektronix PXi series	Tektronix PXi series
Controller with RISC processor	33-MHz Intel 80960 CF Superscalar	24-MHz AMD Am 29000	24-MHz AMD Am 29000	24-MHz AMD Am 29000	24-MHz AMD Am 29000
INTERFACES					
Parallel	●	●	●	●	●
Serial	●	●	●	●	●
AppleTalk	●	●	●	●	●
SCSI port	INA	INA	INA	INA	INA
Automatic interface switching	●	●	●	●	●
Simultaneously active ports	●	●	●	●	●
PAPER HANDLING					
Accepts plain paper	○	●	●	●	○
Paper capacity (sheets)	INA	INA	INA	INA	INA
Letter-size paper (8.5 × 11 inches)	●	●	●	●	●
Size of printable area (inches)	8.3 × 8.9	8.1 × 10	8.1 × 10	8 × 10.5	8.3 × 10.4
Legal-size paper (8.5 × 14 inches)	●	●	●	●	●
Size of printable area (inches)	8.3 × 10.7	8.1 × 10.6	8.1 × 10.6	8 × 13.5	9.6 × 13.3
B-size paper (11 × 17 inches)	●	○	○	○	○
Size of printable area (inches)	11 × 17	N/A	N/A	N/A	N/A
Duplexing	INA	INA	INA	INA	INA
Rated maximum paper weight (pounds)	INA	INA	INA	INA	INA
FONTS AND FEATURES					
PostScript language support	Adobe Level 2	Adobe Level 2	Adobe Level 2	Adobe Level 2	Adobe Level 2
Supports Type 1 fonts	●	●	●	●	●
Printer-specific Microsoft Windows 3.1 driver	INA	INA	INA	INA	INA
Automatic emulation switching	INA	INA	INA	INA	INA
Pantone certified	○	●	●	●	●
Color separations	●	○	○	○	○
CONTROLS					
Control panels	INA	INA	INA	INA	INA
LCD	INA	INA	INA	INA	INA
Number of characters	INA	INA	INA	INA	INA
Control panel buttons:					
Color separation	INA	INA	INA	INA	INA
Paper size	INA	INA	INA	INA	INA
Image size	INA	INA	INA	INA	INA
Ribbon type	INA	INA	INA	INA	INA

●—Yes ○—No N/A—Not applicable INA—Information not available

Color PostScript Printers ■

	Tektronix Phaser 480	Tektronix Phaser II PXe	Tektronix Phaser II PXi	Tektronix Phaser IIsd	Tektronix Phaser III PXi
Price (tested configuration)	$$$$$	$$$$	$$$$$	$$$$$	$$$$$
PHYSICAL CHARACTERISTICS					
Dimensions (HWD, in inches)	13 × 22 × 21	INA	15 × 17 × 27	INA	14 × 25 × 27
Weight (pounds)	93	INA	73	INA	90
ENGINE					
Engine type	Thermal dye transfer	Thermal wax transfer	Thermal wax transfer	Dye sublimation	Solid ink
Model	Tektronix/Mitsubishi Model 4688	Sharp/Tek 4694	Sharp 4694	Sharp/Tek 4684	Tektronix 4698
Memory (tested configuration)	32Mb	8Mb	6Mb	64Mb	18Mb
Maximum resolution (horizontal by vertical dots per inch)	300 × 300	300 × 300	300 × 300	300 × 300	300 × 300
Controller	Tektronix PXi series	Tektronix 4694PXe	INA	Tektronix 4684SD	Tektronix 4698 PXi
Controller with RISC processor	24-MHz AMD Am 29000	16-MHz AMD 29000	AMD 29000	24-MHz AMD 29000	24-MHz AMD 29000
INTERFACES					
Parallel	●	●	●	●	●
Serial	●	●	●	●	●
AppleTalk	●	●	●	●	●
SCSI port	INA	○	●	● (for hard disk)	● (for hard disk)
Automatic interface switching	●	●	●	●	●
Simultaneously active ports	●	●	●	●	●
PAPER HANDLING					
Accepts plain paper	○	○	○	○	●
Paper capacity (sheets)	INA	INA	100	INA	200
Letter-size paper (8.5 × 11 inches)	●	●	●	●	●
Size of printable area (inches)	8.2 × 10	8.1 × 8.8	8.1 × 8.8	8.1 × 8.8	8.1 × 10.5
Legal-size paper (8.5 × 14 inches)	○	●	●	●	●
Size of printable area (inches)	N/A	8.1 × 10.8	8.1 × 11.6	8.1 × 10.8	8.1 × 13.5
B-size paper (11 × 17 inches)	●	○	○	○	●
Size of printable area (inches)	11.9 × 17.2	N/A	N/A	N/A	10.6 × 16.5
Duplexing	INA	○	○	○	○
Rated maximum paper weight (pounds)	INA	INA	20	INA	INA
FONTS AND FEATURES					
PostScript language support	Adobe Level 2	INA	Adobe Level 2	INA	INA
Supports Type 1 fonts	●	●	●	●	●
Printer-specific Microsoft Windows 3.1 driver	INA	● (included and in Windows 3.1)	INA	● (included and in Windows 3.1)	● (in Windows 3.1)
Automatic emulation switching	INA	● (via software)	INA	○	● (via software)
Pantone certified	●	●	INA	●	●
Color separations	○	○	INA	○	○
CONTROLS					
Control panels	INA	○	INA	○	●
LCD	INA	N/A	INA	N/A	●
Number of characters	INA	N/A	INA	N/A	48
Control panel buttons:					
Color separation	INA	N/A	INA	N/A	○
Paper size	INA	N/A	INA	N/A	○
Image size	INA	N/A	INA	N/A	○
Ribbon type	INA	N/A	INA	N/A	○

●—Yes   ○—No   N/A—Not applicable   INA—Information not available

End ■

COMPARISON CHART

TAPE BACKUPS

Tape Backups ■

(Products listed in alphabetical order by company name)	Alloy Retriever/250ce	Colorado Memory Systems Jumbo 250 External	Colorado Jumbo 700	Colorado Trakker 700	COREtape Light
Price	$	$	$	$	$
Device type	External	External	Internal	External	External
Dimensions (HWD, in inches)	2 x 6 x 9.5	2.5 x 4.5 x 9	INA	INA	3 x 4.5 x 7
Standard-configuration controller	●	●	○	●	○
Accelerated	○	N/A	N/A	INA	N/A
ISA 8-bit	●	N/A	N/A	INA	N/A
OPTIONS					
Accelerated controller	○	●	Optional	N/A	○
Other available controllers or interfaces	EISA, MCA	None	INA	INA	MCA
PERFORMANCE AND COMPATIBILITY					
Formatted/compressed capacity	INA	INA	340Mb, 680Mb	340Mb, 680Mb	INA
Rated maximum transfer speed (megabytes per minute)	INA	INA	9.3	8	INA
PHYSICAL CHARACTERISTICS					
Media: QIC-wide format/extended length minicassettes	INA	INA	○/○	○/○	INA
Media speed (inches per second):					
Standard configuration	34	34	INA	INA	73
With optional accelerated controller	N/A	68	INA	INA	N/A
Power source	Host	Host	INA	INA	Host
SOFTWARE CHARACTERISTICS					
Software (tested configuration)	*ResQ120*, Version 2.0	*Jumbo Tape*, Version 2.50	*Colorado Backup for Windows Lite*, Version 2.02	*Colorado Backup for Windows Lite*, Version 2.02	*COREfast*, Version 2.0
Background operation	○	○	●	●	●
Compatible third-party software	*Central Point Backup*	*Central Point Backup, Norton Backup*	INA	INA	*Central Point Backup, PC Tools, Sytos*
BACKUP AND RESTORE CHARACTERISTICS					
Backup and restore types permitted:					
Image	○	○	○	○	●
Modified image	○	●	○	○	○
File-by-file	●	●	Optional	Optional	●
Backup and restore range types:					
Entire disk	●	●	INA	INA	○
Multiple disks or partitions	●	●	INA	INA	○
Copies hidden and system files during backups:					
Image	N/A	N/A	●	●	●
File-by-file	User option	●	●	●	User option
Allows scheduled backups	INA	INA	○	○	INA
NETWORK CHARACTERISTICS					
Networks supported	NetWare, PC LAN, 3+Open	NetWare, 3+Open	NetWare, LANtastic, WfWG	NetWare, LANtastic, WfWG	NetWare, 3+Open
Backup system resides on workstation/server	●/●	●/○	INA	INA	●/○
Workstation automatically logs off network after unattended backup	○	○	INA	INA	●
Tape system supports multiple volumes on single tape	●	●	INA	INA	●

●—Yes   ○—No   N/A—Not applicable

Table Continues →

■ Tape Backups

	Conner TapeStar 850 (internal)	Conner TapeStar 850 (external)	Everex Excel 120F	Exabyte EXB-1500	Iomega Tape 510
Price	$	$	$	$	$
Device type	Internal	External	External	Internal	Internal
Dimensions (HWD, in inches)	INA	INA	2.5 x 6 x 10.5	INA	INA
Standard-configuration controller	○	●	○	○	○
Accelerated	N/A	INA	N/A	N/A	N/A
ISA 8-bit	N/A	INA	N/A	N/A	N/A
OPTIONS					
Accelerated controller	Optional	N/A	○	Optional	Optional
Other available controllers or interfaces	INA	INA	EISA, MCA	INA	INA
PERFORMANCE AND COMPATIBILITY					
Formatted/compressed capacity	425Mb, 850Mb	425Mb, 850Mb	INA	680Mb, 136Gb	340Mb, 680Mb
Rated maximum transfer speed (megabytes per minute)	9.5	9.5	INA	9	9.5
PHYSICAL CHARACTERISTICS					
Media: QIC-wide format/extended length minicassettes	●/●	●/●	INA	○/●	○/●
Media speed (inches per second):					
Standard configuration	INA	INA	50	INA	INA
With optional accelerated controller	INA	INA	N/A	INA	INA
Power source	INA	INA	Direct AC plug	INA	INA
SOFTWARE CHARACTERISTICS					
Software (tested configuration)	*Conner Backup Exec,* Version 2.0	*Conner Backup Exec,* Version 2.0	*FTape,* Version 3.0	*Arcada Backup*	*Iomega Backup Plus,* Version 4.0
Background operation	●	●	○	●	●
Compatible third-party software	INA	INA	None	INA	INA
BACKUP AND RESTORE CHARACTERISTICS					
Backup and restore types permitted:					
Image	●	●	●	●	●
Modified image	●	●	●	●	●
File-by-file	●	●	●	●	●
Backup and restore range types:					
Entire disk	INA	INA	●	INA	INA
Multiple disks or partitions	INA	INA	●	INA	INA
Copies hidden and system files during backups:					
Image	●	●	●	●	●
File-by-file	●	●	User option	●	●
Allows scheduled backups	●	●	INA	●	●
NETWORK CHARACTERISTICS					
Networks supported	*NetWare, LANtastic, WfWG*	*NetWare, LANtastic, WfWG*	*NetWare*	*NetWare, LANtastic, WfWG*	*NetWare, LANtastic, WfWG*
Backup system resides on workstation/server	INA	INA	●/○	INA	INA
Workstation automatically logs off network after unattended backup	INA	INA	●	INA	INA
Tape system supports multiple volumes on single tape	INA	INA	●	INA	INA

●—Yes ○—No N/A—Not applicable

Tape Backups ■

	Irwin AccuTrak Plus A250E	Maynard ArchiveXL 5580e Tape Backup	Micro Solutions Backpack Tape Drive	Mountain FileSafe External 8000Plus	Summit Express SE250 Tape Backup
Price	$	$	$	$	$
Device type	External	External	External	External	Internal
Dimensions (HWD, in inches)	2.5 x 5 x 7.5	2.5 x 5 x 9	2.5 x 4 x 8	2.3 x 5 x 11	2 x 4 x 6.5
Standard-configuration controller	●	○	○	○	○
Accelerated	●	N/A	N/A	N/A	N/A
ISA 8-bit	●	N/A	N/A	N/A	N/A
OPTIONS					
Accelerated controller	●	○	○	●	●
Other available controllers or interfaces	MCA	MCA	EISA, MCA	ISA 16-bit, MCA	ISA 16-bit, MCA
PERFORMANCE AND COMPATIBILITY					
Formatted/compressed capacity	INA	INA	INA	INA	INA
Rated maximum transfer speed (megabytes per minute)	INA	INA	INA	INA	INA
PHYSICAL CHARACTERISTICS					
Media: QIC-wide format/extended length minicassettes	INA	INA	INA	INA	INA
Media speed (inches per second):					
Standard configuration	86	50	25	68	34
With optional accelerated controller	86	N/A	N/A	68	68
Power source	Host	Host	External transformer	Direct AC plug	Host
SOFTWARE CHARACTERISTICS					
Software (tested configuration)	*EzTape*, Version 2.22	*QICstream*, Version 2.0XL	*BPBackup*, Version 1.30.03	*FileSafe*, Version 2.35	*Central Point Backup*, Version 7.1
Background operation	● (Microsoft Windows version)	●	●	●	●
Compatible third-party software	*Central Point Backup, PC Tools*	*Central Point Backup, PC Tools*	None	*Central Point Backup, PC Tools*	None
BACKUP AND RESTORE CHARACTERISTICS					
Backup and restore types permitted:					
Image	○	○	○	●	○
Modified image	○	○	○	○	○
File-by-file	●	●	●	●	●
Backup and restore range types:					
Entire disk	●	●	○	●	●
Multiple disks or partitions	●	○	○	●	●
Copies hidden and system files during backups:					
Image	N/A	N/A	N/A	●	N/A
File-by-file	User option	User option	User option	●	User option
Allows scheduled backups	INA	INA	INA	INA	INA
NETWORK CHARACTERISTICS					
Networks supported	Microsoft LAN Manager, NetWare, PC LAN, 3+Open	NetWare, 3+Open	NetWare, 3+Open	LANtastic, NetWare	NetWare
Backup system resides on workstation/server	●/○	●/○	●/○	●/○	●/○
Workstation automatically logs off network after unattended backup	○	○	○	○	○
Tape system supports multiple volumes on single tape	●	●	●	●	●

●—Yes ○—No N/A—Not applicable

Table Continues →

■ Tape Backups

	Tallgrass FS250e	Tallgrass FS300e	Tecmar MiniVault 250	Wangtek E3080PK
Price	$	$	$	$
Device type	External	External	External	External
Dimensions (HWD, in inches)	4.5 x 4 x 8.5	4.5 x 4 x 8.5	3.5 x 5.5 x 8	3.5 x 5.5 x 8
Standard-configuration controller	○	●	○	○
Accelerated	N/A	●	N/A	N/A
ISA 8-bit	N/A	●	N/A	N/A
OPTIONS				
Accelerated controller	○	●	●	●
Other available controllers or interfaces	EISA, MCA	EISA, MCA	MCA	EISA
PERFORMANCE AND COMPATIBILITY				
Formatted/compressed capacity	INA	INA	INA	INA
Rated maximum transfer speed (megabytes per minute)	INA	INA	INA	INA
PHYSICAL CHARACTERISTICS				
Media: QIC-wide format/extended length minicassettes	INA	INA	INA	INA
Media speed (inches per second):				
Standard configuration	34	68	34	34
With optional accelerated controller	N/A	N/A	68	68
Power source	Direct AC plug	Direct AC plug	Host	Host
SOFTWARE CHARACTERISTICS				
Software (tested configuration)	*FileSECURE*, Version 1.52	*FileSECURE*, Version 1.52	*MiniVault*, Version 1.3	*Central Point Backup*, Version 7.1
Background operation	○	○	○	●
Compatible third-party software	*Central Point Backup*	*Central Point Backup*	*Central Point Backup*	*Sytos*
BACKUP AND RESTORE CHARACTERISTICS				
Backup and restore types permitted:				
Image	○	○	●	○
Modified image	○	○	●	○
File-by-file	●	●	●	●
Backup and restore range types:				
Entire disk	●	●	○	●
Multiple disks or partitions	●	●	○	●
Copies hidden and system files during backups:				
Image	N/A	N/A	●	N/A
File-by-file	●	●	User option	User option
Allows scheduled backups	INA	INA	INA	INA
NETWORK CHARACTERISTICS				
Networks supported	Any NetBIOS network, *NetWare*	Any NetBIOS network, *NetWare*	*LANtastic*, *NetWare*, *PC-Net*, *3+Open*	*NetWare*
Backup system resides on workstation/server	●/○	●/○	●/○	●/○
Workstation automatically logs off network after unattended backup	●	●	●	○
Tape system supports multiple volumes on single tape	●	●	●	●

●—Yes ○—No N/A—Not applicable

End ■

COMPARISON CHART

CD-ROM DRIVES

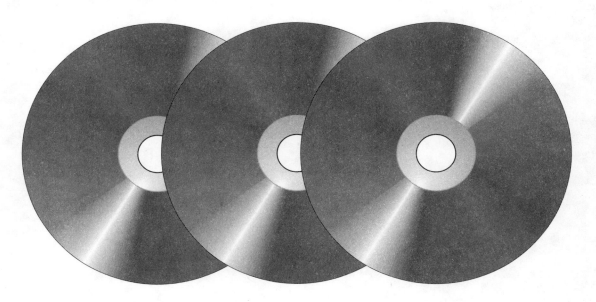

F.1   CD-ROM Drives

(Products listed in review order)	ALR Express CDE-1200	Aztech CDA268-03i	AppleCD 300e Plus	APS MobilStor CD	CD Porta-Drive T3501
Price					
Internal drive	$	$	$	N/A	$
External drive	N/A	N/A	$	$	$
Interface card	Optional	●	○	N/A	○
GENERAL FEATURES					
Speed	2x	2x	2x	2x	4x
Data transfer rate (kilobytes per second)	307	300	342	300	600
Buffer size	128K	128K	256K	250K	256K
Average access time (milliseconds)	350	350	290	320	150
Types of connections	ATAPI IDE	ATAPI IDE	SCSI	Parallel	SCSI, SCSI/parallel
Mechanism manufacturer	Philips	Philips	Matsushita	Sony	Toshiba
Mechanism model	CDM12.4	CDM12.4	CR-503-B	CDU-55D	3501
Dimensions of external version (HWD, in inches)	N/A	N/A	2.3 x 6.2 x 13.1	2 x 7 x 11	2 x 6 x 9
Weight of external version (pounds)	N/A	N/A	5.7	4.4	3
Requires caddies	○	○	○	○	●
Power indicator/Busy indicator	●/●	○/●	●/●	●/●	●/●
Manual eject/Software eject	○/●	●/●	●/●	●/●	●/●
Headphone jack/Volume knob	●/●	●/●	●/●	●/●	●/●
RCA jacks/Red Book audio connector	N/A /●	N/A /●	●/○	●/N/A	●/●
CUSTOMER SUPPORT					
Toll-free technical support	●	●	●	●	○
Telephone support hours (eastern time)	9:00–9:00 M–F, 9:00–4:00 Sat.	11:00–8:00 M–F	9:00–8:00 M–F	9:00–9:00 M–F, 10:00–6:00 Sat.	12:00–7:30 M–F
24-hour BBS	●	●	●	●	●
Warranty coverage	1 year	1 year	1 year	1 year	1 year

●—Yes ○—No N/A—Not applicable INA—Information not available

Table Continues →

ZIFF-DAVIS PRESS

■ CD-ROM Drives

	CD Porta-Drive T4100	Chinon CDS-535	CD Shuttle PSM	Creative Labs OmniCD	Creative Labs Omni4x
Price					
Internal drive	N/A	$	N/A	N/A	$
External drive	$	$	$	$	N/A
Interface card	N/A	●	N/A	●	○
GENERAL FEATURES					
Speed	2x	2x	4x	2x	4x
Data transfer rate (kilobytes per second)	300	300	600	300	600
Buffer size	64K	256K	256K	64K	256K
Average access time (milliseconds)	250	220	150	350	240
Types of connections	SCSI, SCSI/parallel	SCSI	SCSI, SCSI/parallel	Proprietary	SCSI
Mechanism manufacturer	Toshiba	Chinon	Toshiba	Panasonic	NEC
Mechanism model	4100	CDS-535	3501E	CR563	CDR-511
Dimensions of external version (HWD, in inches)	1 x 6 x 8	2.2 x 6 x 9.8	2.3 x 6.5 x 13.5	2.3 x 8 x 11.3	N/A
Weight of external version (pounds)	1	5.5	7	4.8	N/A
Requires caddies	○	●	●	○	●
Power indicator/Busy indicator	○/●	●/●	●/●	●/●	●/●
Manual eject/Software eject	○/○	●/●	●/○	●/●	●/●
Headphone jack/Volume knob	●/●	●/●	●/●	●/●	●/●
RCA jacks/Red Book audio connector	●/N/A	○/●	●/N/A	●/N/A	N/A/●
CUSTOMER SUPPORT					
Toll-free technical support	○	●	●	○	○
Telephone support hours (eastern time)	12:00–7:30 M–F	11:30–8:00 M–F	9:00–5:30 M–F	9:00 A.M.–1:00 A.M., 7 days	9:00 A.M.– 1:00 A.M., 7 days
24-hour BBS	○	●	●	●	●
Warranty coverage	1 year	1 year	1 year	1 year	1 year

●—Yes   ○—No   N/A—Not applicable   INA—Information not available

CD-ROM Drives ■

	Dynatek CDS654	Fidelity TransCD	Mitsumi FX400	Mitsumi FXN01DE	Goldstar GCD-R320B
Price					
Internal drive	$	N/A	$	$	$
External drive	$	$	N/A	N/A	N/A
Interface card	Optional	N/A	N/A	N/A	○
GENERAL FEATURES					
Speed	4x	2x	4x	2x	2x
Data transfer rate (kilobytes per second)	600	300	600	300	300
Buffer size	256K	32K	128K	128K	64K
Average access time (milliseconds)	150	250	250	318	250
Types of connections	SCSI	Parallel	ATAPI IDE	ATAPI IDE	SCSI
Mechanism manufacturer	Toshiba	Fidelity	Mitsumi	Mitsumi	Goldstar
Mechanism model	XM3501 B	TCD2X-P	FX400	FXN01DE	GCD-R320B
Dimensions of external version (HWD, in inches)	2.5 x 8.5 x 10.9	2 x 6 x 11.5	N/A	N/A	N/A
Weight of external version (pounds)	3	5	N/A	N/A	N/A
Requires caddies	●	○	○	○	○
Power indicator/Busy indicator	●/●	●/●	○/●	○/●	○/●
Manual eject/Software eject	●/●	●/○	●/●	●/●	●/●
Headphone jack/Volume knob	●/●	●/●	●/●	○/●	●/●
RCA jacks/Red Book audio connector	●/●	●/N/A	N/A/●	N/A/●	N/A/●
CUSTOMER SUPPORT					
Toll-free technical support	●	○	●	●	●
Telephone support hours (eastern time)	4:00 A.M.– 8:00 P.M. M–F	9:00–5:30 M–F	7:00 A.M.–1:00 A.M. M–F, 10:00–2:00 Sat..	24 hours, 7 days	10:00–5:00 M–F
24-hour BBS	●	●	●	●	○
Warranty coverage	2 years	1 year	1 year	2 year	1 year

●—Yes ○—No N/A—Not applicable INA—Information not available

Table Continues →

CD-ROM Drives

	Liberty 115CDT4xP	ReNO Portable CD-ROM Player	Mountain CD7	NEC CDR-260R	NEC MultiSpin 3Xp Plus
Price					
Internal drive	N/A	N/A	N/A	$	N/A
External drive	$	$	$	N/A	$
Interface card	Optional	Optional	N/A	N/A	●
GENERAL FEATURES					
Speed	4x	2x	2x	2x	3x
Data transfer rate (kilobytes per second)	600	306	300	300	500
Buffer size	256K	64K	64K	256K	256K
Average access time (milliseconds)	150	180	380	320	240
Types of connections	SCSI, SCSI/Parallel	SCSI	SCSI	ATAPI IDE	SCSI
Mechanism manufacturer	Toshiba	Matsushita	Nakamichi	NEC	NEC
Mechanism model	XM3501	Proprietary	2X CD drive	CDR-260R	NEC 3X
Dimensions of external version (HWD, in inches)	1.9 x 6.8 x 9	1 x 6.3 x 10.3	3.7 x 7.8 x 12.6	N/A	2.2 x 6.1 x 10.1
Weight of external version (pounds)	4.2	1.2	4.1	N/A	4.6
Requires caddies	●	○	○	○	●
Power indicator/Busy indicator	●/●	●/●	●/●	○ ●	●/●
Manual eject/Software eject	●/●	●/○	●/●	●/○	●/○
Headphone jack/Volume knob	●/●	●/●	●/●	●/●	●/●
RCA jacks/Red Book audio connector	●/N/A	●/N/A	●/N/A	N/A/●	●/N/A
CUSTOMER SUPPORT					
Toll-free technical support	○	●	○	●	●
Telephone support hours (eastern time)	5:00 A.M.–2:00 P.M. M–F	9:00 A.M.–11:00 P.M. M–F; 11:00–7:00 Sat., Sun.	10:00–10:00 M–F	24 hours, 7 days	8:00 A.M.–8:30 P.M. M–F
24-hour BBS	●	●	●	●	●
Warranty coverage	1 year	1 year	1 year	1 year	2 years

●—Yes   ○—No   N/A—Not applicable   INA—Information not available

CD-ROM Drives ■

	NEC MultiSpin 4X	Panasonic LK-MC579BP	Panasonic LK-MC509S	Philips CDD300	Pioneer DRM-604X
Price					
Internal drive	$	$	N/A	$	N/A
External drive	$	N/A	$	N/A	$
Interface card	●	●	○	●	Optional
GENERAL FEATURES					
Speed	4x	2x	2x	2x	4x
Data transfer rate (kilobytes per second)	600	300	300	307	614
Buffer size	256K	256K	256K	256K	128K
Average access time (milliseconds)	220	280	280	290	300
Types of connections	SCSI	ATAPI IDE	SCSI	ATAPI IDE	SCSI
Mechanism manufacturer	NEC	Matsushita	Matsushita	Philips	Pioneer
Mechanism model	NEC 4X	CR57X	CR50X	CDM12.4	DRM-604X
Dimensions of external version (HWD, in inches)	3 x 6.9 x 13	N/A	2.3 x 6.2 x 12.4	N/A	4.1 x 8.3 x 14.6
Weight of external version (pounds)	6.4	N/A	5.7	N/A	9.1
Requires caddies	●	○	○	○	●
Power indicator/Busy indicator	●/●	●/●	●/●	○ ●	●/●
Manual eject/Software eject	●/○	●/●	●/●	●/●	●/●
Headphone jack/Volume knob	●/●	●/●	●/●	●/●	●/●
RCA jacks/Red Book audio connector	●/●	N/A/●	●/N/A	N/A/●	●/N/A
CUSTOMER SUPPORT					
Toll-free technical support	●	●	●	●	●
Telephone support hours (eastern time)	8:00 A.M.–8:30 P.M. M–F	24 hours, 7 days	24 hours, 7 days	24 hours, 7 days	9:00–7:00 M–F
24-hour BBS	●	●	●	●	●
Warranty coverage	2 years	2 years	2 years	2 years	1 year

●—Yes ○—No N/A—Not applicable INA—Information not available

Table Continues →

CD-ROM Drives

	Plextor 4PLeX PX-43CH	Sony CDU-55E	Sony CDU-55S	Toshiba XM-3501	Toshiba XM-4100A
Price					
Internal drive	$	$	$	$	N/A
External drive	$	N/A	$	$	$
Interface card	Optional	Optional	Optional	Optional	Optional
GENERAL FEATURES					
Speed	4x	2x	2.4x	4x	2x
Data transfer rate (kilobytes per second)	600	300	360	600	300
Buffer size	1Mb	256K	256K	256K	64K
Average access time (milliseconds)	220	250	220	120	320
Types of connections	SCSI	ATAPI IDE	SCSI	SCSI	SCSI, SCSI/parallel (optional)
Mechanism manufacturer	Plextor	Sony	Sony	Toshiba	Toshiba
Mechanism model	PX-43CH	CDU-55E	CDU-55S	XM-3501	XM-4100
Dimensions of external version (HWD, in inches)	7 x 2.4 x 12	N/A	2 x 7 x 12.9	2.7 x 8.7 x 9.8	1.3 x 5.5 x 8.3
Weight of external version (pounds)	6.2	N/A	5.3	4.3	1.2
Requires caddies	●	○	○	●	○
Power indicator/Busy indicator	●/●	●/●	●/●	●/●	●/●
Manual eject/Software eject	●/●	●/●	●/●	●/●	●/○
Headphone jack/Volume knob	●/●	●/●	●/●	●/●	●/●
RCA jacks/Red Book audio connector	●/●	N/A/●	●/○	●/●	●/N/A
CUSTOMER SUPPORT					
Toll-free technical support	●	○	○	●	○
Telephone support hours (eastern time)	11:30–8:30 M–F	12:00–8:00 M–F	12:00–8:00 M–F	11:00–3:00, 4:00–7:00 M–F	11:00–3:00, 4:00–7:00 M–F
24-hour BBS	●	●	●	●	●
Warranty coverage	2 years	1 year	1 year	1 year	1 year

●—Yes   ○—No   N/A—Not applicable   INA—Information not available

End ■

F.2 Multimedia Upgrade Kits

(Products listed in alphabetical order by company name)	ACS/KRIS Compro Multimedia Upgrade Kit	Aztech Sound Galaxy Voyager	Creative Labs Game Blaster CD 16	Creative Labs Sound Blaster Digital Edge 3X	Creative Labs Sound Blaster Edutainment CD 16
List price	$	$	$	$	$
CD-ROM DRIVE					
CD-ROM drive included in kit	Laser Mate 562	Aztech CDA 268 OIA	Panasonic 563 (proprietary version)	NEC MultiSpin 3Xi (triple-speed)	Panasonic 563 (proprietary version)
Type	Internal	Internal	Internal	Internal	Internal
Mechanism manufacturer	Panasonic	Philips	Proprietary	NEC	Proprietary
Data-transfer rate (kilobytes per second)	300	300	300	450	300
Average access time (milliseconds)	320	350	320	195	320
Interface	Panasonic	Mitsumi	Panasonic	SCSI	Panasonic
Supports multisession Photo CD	●	●	●	●	●
Manual eject/Software-controlled eject	●/●	●/●	●/○	●/○	●/○
Disks enclosed in caddies	○	○	○	●	○
Buffer size	64K	64K	64K	256K	64K
SOUND BOARD					
Sound board included in kit	Futura 16	Sound Galaxy Nova 16	Sound Blaster 16 Basic Edition	Sound Blaster 16 SCSI-2	Sound Blaster 16 Basic Edition
Sound board chip set	Crystal	Proprietary	Yamaha OPL3	Yamaha OPL3	Yamaha OPL3
On-board DSP manufacturer	N/A	Crystal	N/A	Creative Labs	N/A
MIDI synthesizer chip	Yamaha OPL3	Yamaha OPL3	Yamaha OPL3	Yamaha OPL3	Yamaha OPL3
FM synthesis	●	●	●	●	●
Wavetable synthesis	Optional ($99)	Optional ($149)	Optional ($249)	Optional ($249)	Optional ($249)
Supports MIDI-file recording/playback	●/●	●/●	●/●	●/●	●/●
CD-ROM connector	Mitsumi, Panasonic, or Sony; SCSI optional ($24.99)	Mitsumi, Panasonic, or Sony	Proprietary	SCSI	Proprietary
Compression:					
ADPCM compression/decompression	●/●	○/●	●/●	●/●	●/●
A-Law compression/decompression	●/●	●/●	●/●	●/●	●/●
Mu-Law compression/decompression	●/●	●/●	●/●	●/●	●/●
MPEG decompression	○	○	○	○	○
Compatible with:					
Sound Blaster/Ad-Lib	●/●	●/●	●/●	●/●	●/●
Microsoft Windows Sound System	●	●	●	●	●
Connectors:					
Headphone/Powered speaker	●/●	●/●	●/●	●/●	●/●
Microphone/Mini line-in	●/●	●/●	●/●	●/●	●/●
IRQ levels supported	5, 7, 9–11	2, 3, 5, 7, 10	2, 5, 7, 10	2, 5, 7, 10	2, 5, 7, 10
Number of selectable addresses	7	4	4	4	4
OTHER COMPONENTS					
Speakers	Compro SP-681	Aztech FX20 Amplified Speakers	Labtec CT-38	Labtec CT-38 or Koss MD/1	Labtec CT-38
Headphones/microphone	●/●	○/●	○/●	○/●	○/○
CUSTOMER SERVICE					
Technical-support number	415-780-9988	800-886-8879	408-742-6622	408-742-6622	408-742-6622
Hours (eastern time)	12:00–8:30 M–F	10:00–9:00 M–F	9:00 A.M.–11:00 P.M., 7 days	9:00 A.M.–11:00 P.M., 7 days	9:00 A.M.–11:00 P.M., 7 days
Warranty	1 year parts, 2 years labor	1 year	1 year	1 year	1 year

●—Yes ○—No N/A—Not applicable

Table Continues →

■ Multimedia Upgrade Kits

	Identity IDCDKIT1	MediaMagic DSP-16 Sound System	Media Vision Super Deluxe Multimedia Kit	Media Vision Premium Deluxe Multimedia Kit	Megamedia SS20
List price	$	$	$	$	$
CD-ROM DRIVE					
CD-ROM drive included in kit	Laser Magnetic Storage (LMS)	Sony CDU-33A	Sanyo CDR H93MV	ReNO Portable	NEC CDR210
Type	Internal	Internal	Internal	External	Internal
Mechanism manufacturer	LMS	Sony	Sanyo	Panasonic	NEC
Data-transfer rate (kilobytes per second)	353	300	300	300	300
Average access time (milliseconds)	325	320	320	180	350
Interface	Proprietary	Sony	SCSI	SCSI	SCSI
Supports multisession Photo CD	●	●	●	●	●
Manual eject/Software-controlled eject	●/●	●/●	●/●	●/○	●/●
Disks enclosed in caddies	○	○	○	○	○
Buffer size	64K	64K	64K	64K	64K
SOUND BOARD					
Sound board included in kit	Identity Systems CHIC	Media Magic DSP-16	Proprietary	Media Vision Premium 3-D	Sigma Designs WinSound 16
Sound board chip set	Media Vision Jazz 16	Analog Devices 2115	Media Vision MVD101	Media Vision MVD1216	Media Vision Spectrum
On-board DSP manufacturer	N/A	Analog Devices	N/A	N/A	N/A
MIDI synthesizer chip	Media Vision Jazz 16	Analog Devices 2115	Yamaha OPL3	Yamaha OPL3	Yamaha OPL3
FM synthesis	●	●	●	●	●
Wavetable synthesis	●	○	○	Optional ($199)	○
Supports MIDI-file recording/playback	●/●	●/●	●/●	●/●	●/●
CD-ROM connector	N/A	Sony	SCSI	SCSI	SCSI
Compression:					
ADPCM compression/decompression	●/●	●/●	●/●	●/●	●/●
A-Law compression/decompression	●/●	●/●	●/●	●/●	○/○
Mu-Law compression/decompression	●/●	●/●	●/●	●/●	○/○
MPEG decompression	○	○	○	○	○
Compatible with:					
Sound Blaster/Ad-Lib	●/●	●/●	●/●	●/●	●/●
Microsoft Windows Sound System	●	●	●	●	●
Connectors:					
Headphone/Powered speaker	●/●	●/●	●/●	●/●	○/●
Microphone/Mini line-in	●/●	●/●	●/●	●/●	●/●
IRQ levels supported	2, 3, 5, 7, 10, 15	3–5, 7, 9–12	1, 3, 5, 7, 11, 15	1, 3, 5, 7, 11, 15	2, 3, 5, 7, 10–12, 15
Number of selectable addresses	3	2	1	4	4
OTHER COMPONENTS					
Speakers	Labtec CS-550	Labtec CS-150	Proprietary	Proprietary	Midi Land CP55
Headphones/microphone	○/○	○/○	●/●	●/●	○/○
CUSTOMER SERVICE					
Technical-support number	800-723-8324	800-246-7037	800-638-2807	800-638-2807	408-428-9920
Hours (eastern time)	9:00–6:00 M–F	24 hours, 7 days	9:00 A.M.–11:00 P.M., 11:00–7:00 Sat, Sun	9:00 A.M.–11:00 P.M., 11:00–7:00 Sat, Sun	8:00–5:00 M–F
Warranty	1 year	1 year	3 years	3 years	1 year

●—Yes   ○—No   N/A—Not applicable

Multimedia Upgrade Kits

	Ocean Vienna	Plextor 4PLeX Sound Chaser	Reveal Quantum	Sigma Designs ReelMagic CD-ROM Upgrade Kit	Toptek Multimedia Advanced Upgrade Kit
List price	$	$	$	$	$
CD-ROM DRIVE					
CD-ROM drive included in kit	Mitsumi FX001D	Plextor PX-43CH	Panasonic 563 (proprietary version)	Sony CDU-33A	Panasonic CR-533B
Type	Internal	Internal (external version available)	Internal	Internal	Internal
Mechanism manufacturer	Mitsumi	Plextor	Reveal	Sony	Panasonic
Data-transfer rate (kilobytes per second)	300	600	300	300	307
Average access time (milliseconds)	250	220	320	320	290
Interface	Mitsumi	SCSI	Proprietary	Sony	SCSI
Supports multisession Photo CD	●	●	●	●	●
Manual eject/Software-controlled eject	●/●	●/●	●/●	●/●	●/●
Disks enclosed in caddies	●	●	○	○	○
Buffer size	64K	1 Mb	64K	64K	256K
SOUND BOARD					
Sound board included in kit	Octek MV-16	Adaptec Mockingbird	SoundFX Wave 32	ReelMagic	Golden Sound Pro 16 Plus
Sound board chip set	Media Vision Jazz	Analog Devices 2115	Ensoniq Soundscape	Yamaha OPL2	Crystal CS4231KL
On-board DSP manufacturer	Media Vision	Analog Devices	N/A	Analog Devices	Toptek
MIDI synthesizer chip	Media Vision MVA416	Analog Devices 2115	Ensoniq Soundscape	Yamaha OPL2	Yamaha OPL4
FM synthesis	●	●	●	●	●
Wavetable synthesis	○	●	●	○	●
Supports MIDI-file recording/playback	●/●	●/●	●/●	○/●	●/●
CD-ROM connector	Mitsumi	SCSI	Mitsumi, Panasonic, or Sony; IDE	Sony	SCSI
Compression:					
ADPCM compression/decompression	●/●	●/●	○/●	○/○	●/●
A-Law compression/decompression	●/●	○/○	○/●	○/○	●/●
Mu-Law compression/decompression	●/●	○/○	●/○	○/○	●/●
MPEG decompression	○	○	○	●	○
Compatible with:					
Sound Blaster/Ad-Lib	●/●	●/●	●/●	●/●	●/●
Microsoft Windows Sound System	●	●	●	○	●
Connectors:					
Headphone/Powered speaker	●/●	●/●	●/●	●/●	●/●
Microphone/Mini line-in	●/○	●/●	●/●	○/○	●/●
Compression:	2, 3, 5, 7, 10, 15	3, 5, 7, 9–12	2, 5, 7, 15	5, 7, 9–12, 15	2, 5, 7, 10–12
Number of selectable addresses	4	4	4	5	2
OTHER COMPONENTS					
Speakers	Midi Land multi-media speakers	N/A	Reveal RS380	Sigma Designs WS-35	Midi Land CP28
Headphones/microphone	○/○	●/●	●/●	○/○	○/●
CUSTOMER SERVICE					
Technical-support number	818-339-8888	800-886-3935	800-473-8325	510-770-0100	800-416-8889
Hours (eastern time)	11:00–8:00 M–F	11:30–8:30 M–F	24 hours, 7 days	11:00–8:00 M–F	11:30–8:30 M–F
Warranty	1 year	2 years	90 days	5 years	1 year

●—Yes   ○—No   N/A—Not applicable   **Table Continues** →

■ Multimedia Upgrade Kits

	Turtle Beach MultiSound Monterey Multimedia Upgrade Kit
List price	$
CD-ROM DRIVE	
CD-ROM drive included in kit	Sony CDU-33A
Type	Internal
Mechanism manufacturer	Sony
Data-transfer rate (kilobytes per second)	300
Average access time (milliseconds)	320
Interface	Sony
Supports multisession Photo CD	●
Manual eject/Software-controlled eject	●/●
Disks enclosed in caddies	○
Buffer size	64K
SOUND BOARD	
Sound board included in kit	MultiSound Monterey
Sound board chip set	Motorola 56001
On-board DSP manufacturer	Motorola
MIDI synthesizer chip	ICS WaveFront
FM synthesis	○
Wavetable synthesis	●
Supports MIDI-file recording/playback	●/●
CD-ROM connector	None
Compression:	
ADPCM compression/decompression	●/●
A-Law compression/decompression	○/○
Mu-Law compression/decompression	○/○
MPEG decompression	○
Compatible with:	
Sound Blaster/Ad-Lib	○/○
Microsoft Windows Sound System	○
Connectors:	
Headphone/Powered speaker	○/●
Microphone/Mini line-in	○/●
IRQ levels supported	5, 7, 9–12, 15
Number of selectable addresses	8
OTHER COMPONENTS	
Speakers	N/A
Headphones/microphone	○/○
CUSTOMER SERVICE	
Technical-support number	717-764-5265
Hours (eastern time)	9:00–8:00 P.M. M–F
Warranty	1 year

●—Yes   ○—No   N/A—Not applicable

End ■

F.3 Portable Sound Devices

(Products listed in alphabetical order by company name)	DSP Solutions Inc.	InterActive	Logitech Inc.	New Media Corp.	Video Associates Labs Inc.
	DSP PortAble Sound Plus	InterActive SoundXchange Model B	Logitech AudioMan	New Media WAVjammer	Video Associates MicroKey/Audioport
List price	$	$	$	$	$
Travel weight	1 lb. 13 oz.	2 lbs. 6 oz.	13 oz.	3 oz.	13 oz.
Number and type of batteries	6 AA	N/A	2 AA	N/A	1 9-volt
Interface	Parallel	Parallel	Parallel	PCMCIA	Parallel
Maximum sampling size for recording/playback	16-bit, 16-bit	8-bit, 16-bit	8-bit, 16-bit	16-bit, 16-bit	16-bit, 16-bit
Maximum sampling rate for recording/playback (kHz)	11, 44.1	11, 44.1	11, 44.1	44.1, 44.1	44.1, 44.1
Sound chip	TI C25325	Intel 8751	AudioMan	Yamaha OPL 3	MSM 6388
DSP	●	○	○	●	●
Synthesizer type	FM	N/A	FM	FM	N/A
Line-in/Line-out connector	●/●	○/●	●/●	●/●	○/●
Separate microphone connector/Built-in speaker	○/○	○/●	○/●	○/○	●/○
Warranty coverage	90 days	1 year	Lifetime	Lifetime	1 year
Telephone number for inquiries	415-494-8086	800-292-2112	800-231-7717	800-227-3748	800-331-0547
Number to circle on reader service card	523	524	525	526	527

●—Yes ○—No N/A—Not applicable

Table Continues →

Portable Sound Devices

VocalTec Inc.

VocalTec's The CAT

List price	$
Travel weight	10 oz.
Number and type of batteries	1 9-volt
Interface	Parallel
Maximum sampling size for recording/playback	13-bit, 16-bit
Maximum sampling rate for recording/playback (kHz)	11 at 8-bit, 8 at 13-bit; 44.1
Sound chip	VocalTec
DSP	●
Synthesizer type	N/A
Line-in/Line-out connector	○/●
Separate microphone connector/Built-in speaker	●/○
Warranty coverage	1 year
Telephone number for inquiries	201-768-9400
Number to circle on reader service card	528

F.4 Portable CD-ROM Drives

(Products listed in alphabetical order by company name)	CD Porta-Drive Model T3401	Liberty 115CDP	Media Vision Reno	Micro Solutions backpack (standard speed)	Micro Solutions backpack (double speed)
Price	$	$	$	$	$
Case dimensions (HWD, in inches)	2.8 x 8.8 x 9.4	1.8 x 6.9 x 9.5	1.4 x 6 x 10.3	2.3 x 6 x 10.5	2.3 x 6 x 10.5
Travel weight	3 lbs. 6 oz.	4 lbs. 3 oz.	2 lbs. 13 oz.	4 lbs. 2 oz.	4 lbs. 2 oz.
Number and type of batteries	N/A	N/A	4 AA	N/A	N/A
AC power supply	External	Internal	External	External	External
Interface	SCSI-2	Parallel/SCSI	SCSI-2	Parallel	Parallel
Mechanism model	Toshiba XM-3401B	Toshiba XM-3401B	Matsushita (custom)	Mitsumi CMRC-FX001	Mitsumi CMRC-FX001
Claimed data-transfer rate (kilobytes per second)	330	330	306	150	300
Average access time (milliseconds)	200	200	180	280	250
Buffer size (kilobytes)	256	256	64	128	32
Supports audio CDs	●	●	●	●	●
Supports single-session and multisession Photo CD	●	●	●	●	●
Warranty coverage	1 year	1 year	1 year	1 year	1 year
Telephone number for inquiries	408-752-8500	408-983-1127	800-845-5870	800-890-7227, ext. 200	800-890-7227, ext. 200
Number to circle on reader service card	517	518	519	520	520

●—Yes ○—No N/A—Not applicable

Table Continues →

■ Portable CD-ROM Drives

	NEC MultiSpin 3Xp	Toshiba TXM-3401P
Price	$	$
Case dimensions (HWD, in inches)	2.2 x 6.1 x 10.1	2.1 x 8.7 x 9.5
Travel weight	3 lbs.	3 lbs. 14 oz.
Number and type of batteries	N/A	1 nickel cadmium pack
AC power supply	External	External
Interface	SCSI-2	SCSI-2
Mechanism model	NEC proprietary	Toshiba XM-3401
Claimed data-transfer rate (kilobytes per second)	450	330
Average access time (milliseconds)	250	200
Buffer size (kilobytes)	256	256
Supports audio CDs	●	●
Supports single-session and multisession Photo CD	●	●
Warranty coverage	2 years	1 year
Telephone number for inquiries	800-388-8888	714-457-0777
Number to circle on reader service card	477	469

●—Yes   ○—No   N/A—Not applicable

End ■

COMPARISON CHART

INPUT
DEVICES

G.1   Replacement Keyboards

(Products listed in alphabetical order by company name)	ALPS MDS101	Cherry G80-1000	Cherry G80-3000	Chicony KB-5181	DataDesk Switchboard
Price	$	$	$	$	$
PHYSICAL FEATURES					
Case material	Plastic	Plastic	Plastic	Plastic	Plastic
Cord length (inches)	72	72	72	72	96
Number of angle settings	1	1	1	2	2
Pencil-tray depth (inches)	2	2	N/A	2	N/A
KEY DESIGN					
Key-switch type	Conductive rubber-dome	Mechanical	Mechanical	Mechanical	Mechanical
Operating force required (ounces)	2	2.1	2.1	2	2.5
Key travel distance (mm)	3.5	4	4	4.5	3.5
KEYBOARD DESIGN					
Special keys (beyond the usual 101)	○	○	○	○	●
Exchangeable Ctrl and CapsLock (with extra key caps provided)	○	○	○	○	●
SYSTEM COMPATIBILITIES					
IBM-XT	●	●	●	●	●
IBM AT/Enhanced AT	●	●	●	●	●
IBM PS/2 (Model 50 or later)	●	●	●	●	●
Stated incompatibilities	None	None	None	None	None
PROGRAMMABILITY					
Software-programmable	○	○	○	○·	○
Hardware-programmable	○	○	○	○	●
MISCELLANEOUS					
Stated current drain	300 mA	200 mA	200 mA	100 mA	150 mA
Optional Dvorak keyboard models	○	○	○	○	○
Optional keyboard connectors	Mini-DIN adapter	Mini-DIN adapter	Mini-DIN adapter	Mini-DIN adapter	None
PC manufacturers that bundle this keyboard	INA	INA	INA	Amkly, AST, Insight	INA

●—Yes   ○—No   N/A—Not applicable   INA—Information not available

Table Continues →

Replacement Keyboards

	DataDesk Turbo-101	Honeywell 101 WN	IBM Enhanced 101 Key Keyboard	Key Tronic MB101 PLUS	Maxi Switch MaxiPRO
Price	$	$	$	$	$
PHYSICAL FEATURES					
Case material	Plastic	Plastic	Plastic	Plastic	Plastic
Cord length (inches)	96	84	72	72	72
Number of angle settings	1	2	1	1	1
Pencil-tray depth (inches)	N/A	N/A	1.7	1.6	1
KEY DESIGN					
Key-switch type	Mechanical	Membrane	Membrane	Membrane	Conductive rubber-dome
Operating force required (ounces)	2.5	1.9	2.5	1.8	1.9
Key travel distance (mm)	3.5	3.8	4	3.8	3.8
KEYBOARD DESIGN					
Special keys (beyond the usual 101)	○	○	○	○	●
Exchangeable Ctrl and CapsLock (with extra key caps provided)	○	○	○	○	○
SYSTEM COMPATIBILITIES					
IBM-XT	●	●	○	●	●
IBM AT/Enhanced AT	●	●	●	●	●
IBM PS/2 (Model 50 or later)	●	●	●	●	●
Stated incompatibilities	None	None	None	AT&T 6300, IBM AT 286/6, Tandy 1000	None
PROGRAMMABILITY					
Software-programmable	○	○	●	○	●
Hardware-programmable	○	○	○	○	●
MISCELLANEOUS					
Stated current drain	150 mA	125 mA	275 mA	350 mA	200 mA
Optional Dvorak keyboard models	○	○	○	●	○
Optional keyboard connectors	None	Mini-DIN adapter	None	Mini-DIN adapter	None
PC manufacturers that bundle this keyboard	INA	Philips, Unisys, Wang, Zenith	IBM	None	INA

●—Yes   ○—No   N/A—Not applicable   INA—Information not available

Replacement Keyboards ■

	Maxi Switch Tuscon-101	NMB RT-101+ Mechanical	NMB RT-101+ Membrane	Northgate OmniKey/101	Northgate OmniKey/Ultra-T
Price	$	$	$	$	$
PHYSICAL FEATURES					
Case material	Plastic	Plastic	Plastic	Plastic with metal base	Plastic with metal base
Cord length (inches)	96	72	72	84	84
Number of angle settings	1	1	1	1	1
Pencil-tray depth (inches)	2	2	2	1	1
KEY DESIGN					
Key-switch type	Conductive rubber-dome	Mechanical	Membrane	Mechanical	Mechanical
Operating force required (ounces)	1.9	2	2	2.5	2.5
Key travel distance (mm)	3.8	3.6	3.6	3.5	3.5
KEYBOARD DESIGN					
Special keys (beyond the usual 101)	○	○	○	●	●
Exchangeable Ctrl and CapsLock (with extra key caps provided)	○	○	○	●	●
SYSTEM COMPATIBILITIES					
IBM-XT	●	●	●	●	●
IBM AT/Enhanced AT	●	●	●	●	●
IBM PS/2 (Model 50 or later)	●	●	●	●	●
Stated incompatibilities	None	None	None	IBM PS/2 Model 25	IBM PS/2 Model 25
PROGRAMMABILITY					
Software-programmable	○	○	○	●	●
Hardware-programmable	○	○	○	●	●
MISCELLANEOUS					
Stated current drain	200 mA	300 mA	300 mA	200 mA	200 mA
Optional Dvorak keyboard models	○	○	○	●	●
Optional keyboard connectors	Mini-DIN adapter	None	None	Mini-DIN adapter	Mini-DIN adapter
PC manufacturers that bundle this keyboard	ACMA, California Microsystems, Digicom, DynaSystems, Gateway 2000, IDS, Informix, Micro Express, Mini Micro, National Microsystems, PC Craft, Tandon	INA	INA	Northgate	Northgate

●—Yes   ○—No   N/A—Not applicable   INA—Information not available

Table Continues →

■ Replacement Keyboards

	Tandy 101-Key Enhanced Keyboard
Price	$
PHYSICAL FEATURES	
Case material	Plastic with metal base
Cord length (inches)	72
Number of angle settings	1
Pencil-tray depth (inches)	1.3
KEY DESIGN	
Key-switch type	Membrane
Operating force required (ounces)	2
Key travel distance (mm)	3.8
KEYBOARD DESIGN	
Special keys (beyond the usual 101)	○
Exchangeable Ctrl and CapsLock (with extra key caps provided)	○
SYSTEM COMPATIBILITIES	
IBM-XT	●
IBM AT/Enhanced AT	●
IBM PS/2 (Model 50 or later)	●
Stated incompatibilities	None
PROGRAMMABILITY	
Software-programmable	●
Hardware-programmable	●
MISCELLANEOUS	
Stated current drain	500 mA
Optional Dvorak keyboard models	○
Optional keyboard connectors	Mini-DIN adapter
PC manufacturers that bundle this keyboard	Tandy

●—Yes ○—No N/A—Not applicable INA—Information not available

End ■

G.2 Mice and Trackballs

(Products listed in alphabetical prder by company name)	Antec Mouse AM-21 Plus	CalComp Wiz Mouse System	Chicony Keyboard KB-5581	CH Products RollerMouse	CMS Mini Mouse (Hi-res)
Price	$	$	$	$	$
HARDWARE FEATURES					
Type of device	Mouse	Mouse	Keyboard with built-in trackball	Trackball	Mouse
Manufacturer	Artec	CalComp	Chicony America	CH Products	INA
Interfaces supported	Serial	Serial, PDP	Serial	Serial, bus, PS/2	Serial, bus
IRQs supported	3, 4	2, 3, 4, 5	4	3, 4	2, 3, 4, 5
Base (hardware) resolution (ppi)	356	1,000	200	100, 200, 400	340
Number of buttons	3	6	3	4	3
Position sensor used	Optomechanical	Electromagnetic	Mechanical	Optomechanical	Mechanical
Mouse pad included	●	●	N/A	N/A	N/A
Ball removable for cleaning	●	N/A	○	●	●
Warranty	Five years parts and labor	Five years parts and labor	One year parts and labor	One year parts and labor	Lifetime parts and labor
Cord length (inches)	81	32	81	60	71
Weight of device only (pounds)	0.25	0.17	3.41	0.8	0.25
SOFTWARE FEATURES					
Number of bytes in CONFIG.SYS device driver	4,927	N/A	12,242	10,976	10,768
Number of bytes in command line driver	N/A	30,720	12,366	10,496	10,288
Disk format of supplied driver	5.25	5.25, 3.5	5.25	5.25	5.25
Version of tested driver	1.01	1.0.1.1	1.0	6.24A	6.11
Driver can be uninstalled from DOS	N/A	●	●	●	●
Ballistic tracking supported	○	○	○	●	○
Minimum resolution supported	N/A	N/A	N/A	1	N/A
Maximum resolution supported	N/A	N/A	N/A	2,880	N/A
Driver upgrades available	○	●	●	●	●
Other mouse emulations included	Microsoft, Mouse Systems	○	Microsoft, Mouse Systems	Microsoft	Mouse Systems
Supports Microsoft Mouse driver in Microsoft Windows	●	●	●	●	●
Mouse driver supports interrupt 33	●	●	●	●	●
Driver for Microsoft Windows included	○	●	○	●	○
Driver for AutoCAD included	○	●	○	●	○

●—Yes ○—No N/A—Not applicable INA—Information not available

Table Continues →

■ Mice and Trackballs

	CMS Mini Mouse (Standard)	Commax Fancy Mouse	Commax Witty Ball	Commax Witty Mouse	Dell Serial Mouse
Price	$	$	$	$	$
HARDWARE FEATURES					
Type of device	Mouse	Mouse	Trackball	Mouse	Mouse
Manufacturer	INA	Commax	Commax	Commax	Logitech
Interfaces supported	Serial, bus	Serial	Serial	Serial	Serial
IRQs supported	2, 3, 4, 5	0, 3, 7, 8	0, 3, 7, 8	0, 3, 7, 8	4
Base (hardware) resolution (ppi)	250	360	300	360	200
Number of buttons	3	3	3	3	2
Position sensor used	Mechanical	Optomechanical	Optomechanical	Optomechanical	Optomechanical
Mouse pad included	N/A	●	N/A	○	N/A
Ball removable for cleaning	●		○		●
Warranty	Lifetime parts and labor	One year parts and labor	One year parts and labor	One year parts and labor	One year parts and labor
Cord length (inches)	71	62.25	62	62.25	72
Weight of device only (pounds)	0.25	0.22	0.52	0.22	0.19
SOFTWARE FEATURES					
Number of bytes in CONFIG.SYS device driver	10,768	N/A	N/A	N/A	14,336
Number of bytes in command line driver	10,288	19,526	19,526	19,526	14,336
Disk format of supplied driver	5.25	5.25	5.25	5.25	5.25, 3.5
Version of tested driver	6.11	4.1	4.1	4.1	3.43
Driver can be uninstalled from DOS	●	●	●	●	●
Ballistic tracking supported	○	●	○	●	○
Minimum resolution supported	N/A	360	N/A	360	N/A
Maximum resolution supported	N/A	1,050	N/A	1,050	N/A
Driver upgrades available	●	●	●	●	●
Other mouse emulations included	Mouse Systems	Microsoft, Mouse Systems	Microsoft, Mouse Systems	Microsoft, Mouse Systems	Microsoft
Supports Microsoft Mouse driver in Microsoft Windows	●	●	●	●	●
Mouse driver supports interrupt 33	●	●	●	●	○
Driver for Microsoft Windows included	○	●	●	●	●
Driver for AutoCAD included	○	●	●	●	●

●—Yes ○—No N/A—Not applicable INA—Information not available

Mice and Trackballs

	DFI Inc. DMS-200 Mouse	DFI Inc. DMS-200H Mouse	Focus FT-100 Tracker	Fulcrum Computer Products Trackball Plus	IBM PS/2 Mouse
Price	$	$	$	$	$
HARDWARE FEATURES					
Type of device	Mouse	Mouse	Trackball	Trackball	Mouse
Manufacturer	DFI	DFI	Focus	Fulcrum	Alps
Interfaces supported	Serial	Serial	Serial	Serial	PS/2
IRQs supported	3, 4	3, 4	1, 2	1, 2	12
Base (hardware) resolution (ppi)	200	200	160	100	200
Number of buttons	3	3	3	6	2
Position sensor used	Optomechanical	Optomechanical	Optomechanical	Optomechanical	Mechanical
Mouse pad included	●	●	N/A	N/A	N/A
Ball removable for cleaning	●	●	●	○	●
Warranty	One year parts and labor	One year parts and labor	One year parts and labor	Six months parts and labor	One year parts and labor
Cord length (inches)	71	71	59.5	48	108
Weight of device only (pounds)	0.24	0.24	0.75	0.86	0.11
SOFTWARE FEATURES					
Number of bytes in CONFIG.SYS device driver	15,657	15,657	817,152	11,120	N/A
Number of bytes in command line driver	15,569	15,569	272,384	16,888	10,384
Disk format of supplied driver	5.25	5.25	5.25	5.25, 3.5	3.5
Version of tested driver	3.0	3.0	1.02	6.24B	1.1
Driver can be uninstalled from DOS	○	○	●	●	○
Ballistic tracking supported	○	●	●	●	○
Minimum resolution supported	N/A	5	160	100	N/A
Maximum resolution supported	N/A	700	500	25,000	N/A
Driver upgrades available	●	●	○	●	○
Other mouse emulations included	Microsoft, Mouse Systems	Microsoft, Mouse Systems	Microsoft, Mouse Systems	Microsoft, Mouse Systems	○
Supports Microsoft Mouse driver in Microsoft Windows	●	●	●	●	●
Mouse driver supports interrupt 33	●	●	●	●	●
Driver for Microsoft Windows included	○	○	○	○	○
Driver for AutoCAD included	○	○	○	○	○

●—Yes ○—No N/A—Not applicable INA—Information not available

Table Continues →

■ Mice and Trackballs

	IMSI Mouse	International Machine Control Systems The MousePen	International Machine Control Systems The MousePen	ITAC Systems Mouse-Trak (2 button)	ITAC Systems Mouse-Trak (3 button)
Price	$	$	$	$	$
HARDWARE FEATURES					
Type of device	Mouse	Mouse	Mouse	Trackball	Trackball
Manufacturer	Z-Nix	IMCS	IMCS	ITAC Systems	ITAC Systems
Interfaces supported	Serial, bus	Serial	PS/2	Serial, bus PS/2, InPort	Serial, bus PS/2, InPort
IRQs supported	4	0, 3, 4	0, 3, 4	3, 4, 5, 7, 10, 11, 12, 15	3, 4
Base (hardware) resolution (ppi)	250	100	100	200	200
Number of buttons	2	2	2	2	3
Position sensor used	Mechanical	Optomechanical	Optomechanical	Optomechanical	Optomechanical
Mouse pad included	N/A	N/A	N/A	N/A	N/A
Ball removable for cleaning	●	●	●	●	●
Warranty	Lifetime parts and labor	Unconditional one year parts and labor, lifetime afterward	Unconditional one year parts and labor, lifetime afterward	One year parts and labor	One year parts and labor
Cord length (inches)	69	118	118	60	60
Weight of device only (pounds)	0.25	0.06	0.06	0.94	0.94
SOFTWARE FEATURES					
Number of bytes in CONFIG.SYS device driver	10,544	10,960	10,496	11,000	11,000
Number of bytes in command line driver	9,952	10,480	10,000	10,000	10,000
Disk format of supplied driver	5.25	5.25, 3.5	5.25, 3.5	5.25	5.25
Version of tested driver	6.11	6.24A	6.24A	6.11	6.11
Driver can be uninstalled from DOS	○	●	●	●	●
Ballistic tracking supported	○	●	●	● (bus only)	● (bus only)
Minimum resolution supported	N/A	50	50	20	20
Maximum resolution supported	N/A	1,000	1,000	800	800
Driver upgrades available	●	●	●	●	●
Other mouse emulations included	Microsoft	Microsoft	Microsoft	Microsoft, Mouse Systems	Microsoft, Mouse Systems
Supports Microsoft Mouse driver in Microsoft Windows	●	●	●	●	●
Mouse driver supports interrupt 33	●	●	●	●	●
Driver for Microsoft Windows included	○	○	○	○	○
Driver for AutoCAD included	○	○	○	○	○

●—Yes　○—No　N/A—Not applicable　INA—Information not available

Mice and Trackballs ▉

	Kensington Expert Mouse	Key Tronic Professional Series Mouse	Kraft Trackball	KYE International Genius Mouse GM-6X	KYE International Genius Mouse GM-6000
Price	$	$	$	$	$
HARDWARE FEATURES					
Type of device	Trackball	Mouse	Trackball	Mouse	Mouse
Manufacturer	Kensington Microware	Key Tronic	Kraft Systems	KYE International	KYE International
Interfaces supported PS/2	Serial, bus	Serial, bus	Serial	Serial	Serial
IRQs supported	2, 3, 4, 5, 7, 10, 11, 12, 15	2, 3, 4, 5	3, 4	1, 2, 3, 4, 5	1, 2, 3, 4, 5
Base (hardware) resolution (ppi)	200	200	200	200	350
Number of buttons	2	2	3	3	3
Position sensor used	Optomechanical	Mechanical	Optomechanical	Optomechanical	Optomechanical
Mouse pad included	N/A	○	N/A	○	●
Ball removable for cleaning	●	●	●	●	●
Warranty	One year parts and labor	One year limited	Five years parts and labor	Lifetime parts and labor	Lifetime parts and labor
Cord length (inches)	72	58	96	70	71
Weight of device only (pounds)	0.89	0.32	0.75	0.26	0.26
SOFTWARE FEATURES					
Number of bytes in CONFIG.SYS device driver	15,392	10,688	11,887	N/A	13,083
Number of bytes in command line driver	20,894	10,224	13,525	12,649	13,664
Disk format of supplied driver	5.25, 3.5	5.25	5.25	5.25	5.25
Version of tested driver	2.03	1.1	1.06	8.20	9.03
Driver can be uninstalled from DOS	●	○	●	●	●
Ballistic tracking supported	●	○	○	●	●
Minimum resolution supported	20	N/A	10*	50	87.5
Maximum resolution supported	10,000	N/A	1,150*	800	1,400
Driver upgrades available	●	●	●	●	●
Other mouse emulations included	Microsoft, IBM PS/2	Microsoft	○	Microsoft, Mouse Systems	Microsoft, Mouse Systems
Supports Microsoft Mouse driver in Microsoft Windows	●	●	●	●	●
Mouse driver supports interrupt 33	●	●	●	●	●
Driver for Microsoft Windows included	●	○	○	○	○
Driver for AutoCAD included	○	○	●	○	○

●—Yes ○—No N/A—Not applicable INA—Information not available   **Table Continues** →

Mice and Trackballs

	KYE International Genius Mouse GM-F302/F303	Liuski International ProCorp Mouse (serial)	Liuski International ProCorp Mouse (bus)	Logitech Dexxa Mouse	Logitech TrackMan Stationary Mouse
Price	$	$	$	$	$
HARDWARE FEATURES					
Type of device	Mouse	Mouse	Mouse	Mouse	Trackball
Manufacturer	KYE International	P.R.O. Corp.	P.R.O. Corp.	Logitech	Logitech
Interfaces supported	Serial, PS/2	Serial	Bus	Serial, bus	Serial, bus
IRQs supported	1, 2, 3, 4, 5	3, 4	2, 3, 4, 5	2, 3, 4, 5	2, 3, 4, 5
Base (hardware) resolution (ppi)	350	250	340	200	320
Number of buttons	3	3	3	2	3
Position sensor used	Optomechanical	Mechanical	Mechanical	Optomechanical	Optomechanical
Mouse pad included	●	●	●	●	N/A
Ball removable for cleaning	●	●	●	●	●
Warranty	Lifetime parts and labor	One year parts and labor	One year parts and labor	Limited lifetime	Limited lifetime
Cord length (inches)	70	70	69.75	72	108
Weight of device only (pounds)	0.87	0.27	0.27	0.16	0.5
SOFTWARE FEATURES					
Number of bytes in CONFIG.SYS device driver	13,659	10,768	10,768	13,312	14,336
Number of bytes in command line driver	13,664	10,288	10,288	13,312	14,336
Disk format of supplied driver	5.25	5.25	5.25	5.25	5.25, 3.5
Version of tested driver	9.03	6.11	6.11	3.43	4.10
Driver can be uninstalled from DOS	●	●	●	○	●
Ballistic tracking supported	●	○	○	●	●
Minimum resolution supported	87.5	N/A	N/A	50	50
Maximum resolution supported	1,400	N/A	N/A	750	15,000
Driver upgrades available	●	●	●	●	●
Other mouse emulations included	Microsoft, Mouse Systems	○	○	○	Microsoft, Mouse Systems
Supports Microsoft Mouse driver in Microsoft Windows	●	●	●	○	●
Mouse driver supports interrupt 33	●	●	●	●	●
Driver for Microsoft Windows included	○	●	●	○	○
Driver for AutoCAD included	○	●	●	○	○

●—Yes ○—No N/A—Not applicable INA—Information not available

Mice and Trackballs

	Lynx Turbo Trackball	Marconi Marcus RB2-305/306	Microsoft Mouse	MicroSpeed FastTRAP	MicroSpeed PC-Trac
Price	$	$	$	$	$
HARDWARE FEATURES					
Type of device	Trackball	Trackball	Mouse	Trackball	Trackball
Manufacturer	Lynx	Marconi	Alps	MicroSpeed	MicroSpeed
Interfaces supported	Serial, bus, PS/2	Serial, bus	Serial, bus, PS/2, InPort	Serial, bus	Serial, bus, PS/2, InPort
IRQs supported	2, 3, 4, 5	2, 3, 4, 5	2, 3, 4, 5	2, 3, 4, 5, 7	2, 3, 4, 5, 7
Base (hardware) resolution (ppi)	250	76	400	200	200
Number of buttons	2	3	2	3	3
Position sensor used	Mechanical	Optomechanical	Mechanical	Optomechanical	Optomechanical
Mouse pad included	N/A	N/A	○	N/A	N/A
Ball removable for cleaning	●	○	●	●	●
Warranty	Lifetime replacement	One year parts and labor	One year parts and labor	One year parts and labor	One year parts and labor
Cord length (inches)	72	45.75	104	69	67
Weight of device only (pounds)	0.5	1.3	0.28	0.82	0.75
SOFTWARE FEATURES					
Number of bytes in CONFIG.SYS device driver	10,544	3,163	14,336	17,378	18,055
Number of bytes in command line driver	9,952	13,119	14,336	17,234	17,911
Disk format of supplied driver	5.25	5.25, 3.5	5.25, 3.5	5.25	5.25 or 3.5
Version of tested driver	6.11	6.21	7.04	2.06A	2.1
Driver can be uninstalled from DOS	●	●	●	○	○
Ballistic tracking supported	●	●	●	●	●
Minimum resolution supported	50	10	0	50	50
Maximum resolution supported	960	76	Infinite	1,000	1,000
Driver upgrades available	●	●	●	●	●
Other mouse emulations included	○	Microsoft	○	Microsoft, Mouse Systems	Microsoft, Mouse Systems
Supports Microsoft Mouse driver in Microsoft Windows	●	●	●	●	●
Mouse driver supports interrupt 33	●	●	●	●	●
Driver for Microsoft Windows included	○	●	●	●	●
Driver for AutoCAD included	○	●	○	●	●

●—Yes ○—No N/A—Not applicable INA—Information not available

Table Continues →

■ Mice and Trackballs

	Mouse Systems OmniMouse II	Mouse Systems PC Mouse	Mouse Systems PC Mouse III	Mouse Systems PC Trackball	Mouse Systems The White Mouse
Price	$	$	$	$	$
HARDWARE FEATURES					
Type of device	Mouse	Mouse	Mouse	Trackball	Mouse
Manufacturer	Mouse Systems	Mouse Systems	Mouse Systems	Mouse Systems	Mouse Systems
Interfaces supported	Serial, bus	Serial, bus, PS/2	Serial, bus, PS/2	Serial, PS/2	Serial, bus, PS/2
IRQs supported	2, 3, 4, 5, 7	2, 3, 4, 5, 7	2, 3, 4, 5, 7	2, 3, 4, 5, 7	2, 3, 4, 5, 7
Base (hardware) resolution (ppi)	200	100	300	200	350
Number of buttons	2	3	3	3	3
Position sensor used	Optomechanical	Optical	Optical	Optomechanical	Optomechanical
Mouse pad included	○	●	●	N/A	●
Ball removable for cleaning	●	N/A	N/A	●	●
Warranty	Lifetime parts and labor	Lifetime parts and labor	Lifetime parts and labor	Lifetime parts and labor	Lifetime parts and labor
Cord length (inches)	69	58.5	96	75	69
Weight of device only (pounds)	0.18	0.18	0.17	0.52	0.24
SOFTWARE FEATURES					
Number of bytes in CONFIG.SYS device driver	12,288	12,288	12,288	12,288	12,288
Number of bytes in command line driver	17,408	17,408	18,432	17,408	17,408
Disk format of supplied driver	5.25	5.25	5.25, 3.5	5.25	5.25, 3.5
Version of tested driver	6.23	6.23	7.0	6.23	6.23
Driver can be uninstalled from DOS	●	●	●	●	●
Ballistic tracking supported	●	●	●	●	●
Minimum resolution supported	20	20	30	20	20
Maximum resolution supported	11,200	11,200	30,000	11,200	11,200
Driver upgrades available	●	●	●	●	●
Other mouse emulations included	Microsoft	Mouse Systems, IBM PS/2	Microsoft, Mouse Systems, IBM PS/2	Microsoft	Microsoft, Mouse Systems, IBM PS/2
Supports Microsoft Mouse driver in Microsoft Windows	●	○	●	●	●
Mouse driver supports interrupt 33	●	●	●	●	●
Driver for Microsoft Windows included	○	●	●	○	○
Driver for AutoCAD included	○	○	○	○	○

●—Yes ○—No N/A—Not applicable INA—Information not available

Mice and Trackballs ◼

	Numonics Manager Mouse Cordless	Penny + Giles Controls TrackerMouse/TM 1	Penny + Giles Controls TrackerMouse/TM 1 Plus 16	Penny + Giles Controls TrackerMouse/TM 1 Plus 32	Practical Solutions The Cordless Mouse
Price	$	$	$	$	$
HARDWARE FEATURES					
Type of device	Mouse	Trackball	Trackball	Trackball	Mouse
Manufacturer	Numonics	Penny + Giles Computer Products	Penny + Giles Computer Products	Penny + Giles Computer Products	INA
Interfaces supported	Serial	Serial, PS/2	Serial	Serial, PS/2	Serial, PS/2
IRQs supported	1, 2, 3, 4	3, 4	3, 4	3, 4	3, 4
Base (hardware) resolution (ppi)	200	40	40	40	200
Number of buttons	3	2	16	32	3
Position sensor used	Optomechanical	Optomechanical	Optomechanical	Optomechanical	Optomechanical
Mouse pad included	○	N/A	N/A	N/A	○
Ball removable for cleaning	○	●	●	●	●
Warranty	One year parts and labor	One year parts and labor	One year parts and labor	One year parts and labor	One year parts and labor
Cord length (inches)	80.5	53	53	53	N/A
Weight of device only (pounds)	0.24	0.53	0.6	0.6	0.27
SOFTWARE FEATURES					
Number of bytes in CONFIG.SYS device driver	12,288	12,801	12,801	12,801	N/A
Number of bytes in command line driver	12,288	14,240	14,240	14,240	11,289
Disk format of supplied driver	5.25	5.25, 3.5	5.25, 3.5	5.25, 3.5	5.25, 3.5
Version of tested driver	2.06	3.1	3.1	3.1	4.2
Driver can be uninstalled from DOS	●	○	○	○	○
Ballistic tracking supported	●	●	●	●	●
Minimum resolution supported	50	40	40	40	10
Maximum resolution supported	1,000	400	400	400	1,200
Driver upgrades available	●	●	●	●	●
Other mouse emulations included	Microsoft, Mouse Systems	○	○	○	Mouse Systems
Supports Microsoft Mouse driver in Microsoft Windows	○	●	●	●	●
Mouse driver supports interrupt 33	●	●	●	●	●
Driver for Microsoft Windows included	○	●	●	●	●
Driver for AutoCAD included	○	●	●	●	●

●—Yes ○—No N/A—Not applicable INA—Information not available

Table Continues →

Mice and Trackballs

	ProHance PowerMouse 100	Qualitas Trading Co. Samurai Mouse	SmarTEAM Mouse	Suncom Technologies MouseTrac	Suncom Technologies SunMouse
Price	$	$	$	$	$
HARDWARE FEATURES					
Type of device	Programmable mouse	Mouse	Mouse	Trackball	Mouse
Manufacturer	ProHance Technologies	NEOS Electronics	TEAM Technology	INA	INA
Interfaces supported	Serial	Serial	Serial, bus	Serial	Serial
IRQs supported	All	3, 4	None	3, 4	3, 4
Base (hardware) resolution (ppi)	200	200	250	200	200
Number of buttons	40	2	3	3	3
Position sensor used	Optomechanical	Optomechanical	Mechanical	Optomechanical	Optomechanical
Mouse pad included	○	○	○	N/A	○
Ball removable for cleaning	●	●	●	●	●
Warranty	One year parts and labor	One year parts and labor	Limited lifetime	One year parts and labor	One year parts and labor
Cord length (inches)	70	58	70	104	56
Weight of device only (pounds)	0.44	0.27	0.26	0.70	0.28
SOFTWARE FEATURES					
Number of bytes in CONFIG.SYS device driver	N/A	16,976	10,704	N/A	N/A
Number of bytes in command line driver	15,913	16,784	10,224	N/A	N/A
Disk format of supplied driver	5.25, 3.5	5.25	5.25	N/A	N/A
Version of tested driver	5.23	4.0	6.11	N/A	N/A
Driver can be uninstalled from DOS	●	●	●	○	N/A
Ballistic tracking supported	●	●	○	○	○
Minimum resolution supported	200	100	N/A	N/A	N/A
Maximum resolution supported	400	1,000	N/A	N/A	N/A
Driver upgrades available	●	○	●	N/A	N/A
Other mouse emulations included	●	Microsoft	Microsoft	N/A	N/A
Supports Microsoft Mouse driver in Microsoft Windows	○	●	●	●	●
Mouse driver supports interrupt 33	●	●	●	N/A	N/A
Driver for Microsoft Windows included	●	○	○	○	○
Driver for AutoCAD included	○	○	○	○	○

●—Yes   ○—No   N/A—Not applicable   INA—Information not available

Mice and Trackballs ■

	Tandy Serial Mouse	Tandy 2-Button Mouse
Price	$	$
HARDWARE FEATURES		
Type of device	Mouse	Mouse
Manufacturer	Tandy	Tandy
Interfaces supported	Serial	PS/2
IRQs supported	3, 4	0
Base (hardware) resolution (ppi)	200	200
Number of buttons	2	2
Position sensor used	Mechanical	Optomechanical
Mouse pad included	○	○
Ball removable for cleaning	●	●
Warranty	90-day replacement	90-day replacement
Cord length (inches)	60	62
Weight of device only (pounds)	0.22	0.20
SOFTWARE FEATURES		
Number of bytes in CONFIG.SYS device driver	13,793	13,793
Number of bytes in command line driver	13,950	13,950
Disk format of supplied driver	5.25, 3.5	5.25, 3.5
Version of tested driver	6.10	6.10
Driver can be uninstalled from DOS	○	
Ballistic tracking supported	●	●
Minimum resolution supported	200	200
Maximum resolution supported	19,000	19,000
Driver upgrades available	○	○
Other mouse emulations included	Microsoft	Microsoft
Supports Microsoft Mouse driver in Microsoft Windows	●	●
Mouse driver supports interrupt 33	●	●
Driver for Microsoft Windows included	○	○
Driver for AutoCAD included	○	○

●—Yes ○—No N/A—Not applicable INA—Information not available

End ■

■ G.3 Portable Pointing Devices

(Products listed in alphabetical order by company name)	Appoint MousePen Professional	Appoint Thumbelina	GRiD Systems Corp. GRiD IsoPoint	IBM Corp. IBM PS/2 Trackpoint	Kraft Systems Inc. TopTrak
Price	$	$	$$$$$ (as part of GRiDCase)	$	$
HARDWARE FEATURES					
Type of device	Optomechanical mouse	Optomechanical mouse	Mechanical mouse	Optomechanical trackball/mouse	Optomechanical trackball
Connector	PS/2	PS/2	None	PS/2	DB-9 serial
Additional connector (adapter)	DB-9 serial	DB-9 serial	N/A	None	DB-25 serial
IRQs supported	3, 4	3, 4	3–5	None	3, 4
Base hardware resolution (points per inch)	150	150	450	200	200
Composition of ball	Delrin	Delrin	N/A	Phenolic	Phenolic
Ball removable for cleaning	●	○	N/A	○	●
Method of attaching device to laptop	N/A	Z-bracket	Built-in	N/A	N/A
BUTTONS					
Unduplicated	2	2	2	2	2
Total	2	2	4	4	2
Drag-lock	None	1	None	2	1
Other switches	Fixed/ballistic	None	None	None	Simultaneous left/right
PHYSICAL SPECIFICATIONS					
Length of interface cable (inches)	56	45	N/A	44	95
Weight (ounces)	2	2	N/A	5	11
Ball diameter (inches)	0.4	0.3	N/A	1.3	1.5
OTHER FEATURES					
Size of CONFIG.SYS device driver	15K	15K	14K	N/A	10K
Size of command line driver	15K	15K	14K	14K	10K
Disk format of supplied drivers	5.25, 3.5	5.25, 3.5	3.5	3.5	5.25, 3.5
Version number of tested driver	2.00	7.04	7.4	7.04	6.24
Driver can be disabled from DOS	●	●	●	●	●
Driver supports ballistic tracking	●	●	●	●	●
AutoCAD driver	○	○	○	○	●
Resolutions supported (points per inch)	150–1,000	150–1,000	100–1,000	N/A	10–1,150
Other mouse emulations included	None	None	None	Microsoft	Microsoft
Software bundled	None	None	None	None	LCS's Telepaint

●—Yes   ○—No   N/A—Not applicable   INA—Information not available

Portable Pointing Devices ■

	Logitech Inc. TrackMan Portable	Microsoft Corp. BallPoint Mouse	Mouse Systems The Little Mouse/PC	Suncom Technologies ICONtroller
Price	$	$	$	$
HARDWARE FEATURES				
Type of device	Optomechanical trackball	Mechanical trackball	Optical mouse	Mini-joystick
Connector	DB-9 serial	DB-9 serial	DB-9 serial	DB-9 serial
Additional connector (adapter)	DB-25 serial	PS/2	DB-25 serial, PS/2	DB-25 serial
IRQs supported	3, 4	All (0–15)	2–15	3, 4
Base hardware resolution (points per inch)	200	400	300	(approximately) 200
Composition of ball	Polycarbonate	Compression-molded plastic	N/A	N/A
Ball removable for cleaning	●	●	N/A	N/A
Method of attaching device to laptop	Detachable clip	Detachable clip	N/A	Duo-Lock
BUTTONS				
Unduplicated	3	2	2	3
Total	3	4	2	4
Drag-lock	2	None	None	1
Other switches	None	○	○	Resolution, compatibility, joystick button
PHYSICAL SPECIFICATIONS				
Length of interface cable (inches)	26	52 (coiled)	70	36 (coiled)
Weight (ounces)	4	6	5	3
Ball diameter (inches)	1	1.1	N/A	N/A
OTHER FEATURES				
Size of CONFIG.SYS device driver	16K	N/A	13K	13.5K
Size of command line driver	34K	16K	12K	13K
Disk format of supplied drivers	3.5	3.5	5.25, 3.5	5.25, 3.5
Version number of tested driver	6.0	1.00	7.01	1.00
Driver can be disabled from DOS	●	●	●	●
Driver supports ballistic tracking	●	●	●	○
AutoCAD driver	○	○	○	○
Resolutions supported (points per inch)	50–10,000	0.75–22,400	300–30,000	N/A
Other mouse emulations included	Microsoft	None	Microsoft, PS/2	Microsoft
Software bundled	Windows hotkeys	Mouse menus	Pop-up menus, utilities	Testing and tutor programs

●—Yes ○—No N/A—Not applicable INA—Information not available   **End ■**

COMPARISON CHART

MODEMS

H.1   V.34 Modems

(Products listed in alphabetical order by company)	Archtek America Corp. SmartLink 2834A V.34 Fax Modem	AT&T Paradyne Comsphere 3810Plus	Best Data Products Inc. Smart One 2834FX	Boca Research Inc. V.34 28,000bps External BocaModem
List price	$	$	$	$
GENERAL FEATURES				
Signal-converter (data-pump) manufacturer and model	AT&T 1633 F08 AB	Motorola 68302FC25C	Rockwell R6682-21	Rockwell RC288DPi
Controller-chip manufacturer and model	AT&T C882-29Q-5	AT&T DSP 16A	Rockwell L3902-57	Rockwell L39/U
Firmware version or date of firmware tested	005A	A01.02.00	1.000-V34	1.000-V34
AT firmware version command	ATi3	AT&V	AT&V	AT&V
Supports flash ROM	●	●	○	○
Supports Caller ID	○	○	○	○
PHYSICAL CHARACTERISTICS				
Dimensions (HWD, in inches)	1 x 7 x 5	2 x 8 x 12	2 x 6 x 10	1 x 6 x 8
Location of power switch	Back	Back	Back	Back
Location of voice-operation switch	N/A	N/A	N/A	N/A
Location of volume control	N/A	N/A	N/A	N/A
Leased-line phone jack	○	●	○	○
Alphanumeric display	○	●	○	○
Number of status indicators	9	13	8	8
Speed indicators	○	●	○	○
Includes UART serial card	●	○	○	●
Includes phone cable/serial cable	●/●	●/○	●/○	●/●
PROTOCOLS SUPPORTED				
ITU data modulation standards (2,400 bps and higher)	V.22bis, V.32, V.32bis, V.34	V.22bis, V.32, V.32bis, V.34	V.22bis, V.32, V.32bis, V.34	V.22bis, V.32, V.32bis, V.34
Other high-speed data modulation standards	V.32terbo	V.32terbo, V.34+	V.FC	V.FC
Synchronous data format	●	●	●	○
Error-control command sets	V.42, MNP 2–4	V.42, MNP 2–4	V.42, MNP 2–4	V.42, MNP 2–4
Data-compression command sets	V.42bis, MNP 5	V.42bis, MNP 5	V.42bis, MNP 5	V.42bis, MNP 5
Fax compatibility	Group 3	None	Group 3	Group 3
Fax standards	Class 1	N/A	Class 1 and 2	Class 1 and 2
TECHNICAL SUPPORT				
Command-set reference card	●	●	●	●
Quick-reference card	○	●	○	○
Technical-support number	818-912-9800	800-237-0016	818-773-9600	407-241-8088
BBS number	818-912-3980	813-532-5254	818-773-9627	407-241-1601
Warranty	2 years	2 years	2 years	5 years

●—Yes   ○—No   N/A—Not applicable

Table Continues →

■ V.34 Modems

	Cardinal Technologies Inc. Cardinal 28.8 Fax/Modem	E-Tech Research Inc. Bullet 100E	Hayes Microcomputer Products Inc. Hayes Optima 288 V.34/V.FC + FAX	Logicode Technology Inc. Quicktel 2814XV
List price	$	$	$	$
GENERAL FEATURES				
Signal-converter (data-pump) manufacturer and model	Rockwell R6682	AT&T V.34	Rockwell R6682DPi	Rockwell RC288DPi
Controller-chip manufacturer and model	Rockwell L3902	Motorola 68702	Motorola 68302	Rockwell L3902-57
Firmware version or date of firmware tested	1.000-V34	V1015	5.1	1.000-V34
AT firmware version command	ATi3	AT&V0	ATi3	ATi3
Supports flash ROM	●	●	○	○
Supports Caller ID	○	●	○	●
PHYSICAL CHARACTERISTICS				
Dimensions (HWD, in inches)	2 x 5 x 6	2 x 7 x 7	2 x 5 x 10	2 x 6 x 6
Location of power switch	Back	Back	Back	Front
Location of voice-operation switch	N/A	N/A	N/A	N/A
Location of volume control	N/A	Side	N/A	N/A
Leased-line phone jack	○	●	○	○
Alphanumeric display	○	●	○	○
Number of status indicators	8	8	8	8
Speed indicators	○	●	○	○
Includes UART serial card	○	○	Optional	●
Includes phone cable/serial cable	●/○	●/○	●/○	●/○
PROTOCOLS SUPPORTED				
ITU data modulation standards (2,400 bps and higher)	V.22bis, V.32, V.32bis, V.34	V.22bis, V.32, V.32bis, V.34	V.22bis, V.32, V.32bis, V.34	V.22bis, V.32, V.32bis, V.34A
Other high-speed data modulation standards	V.FC	V.32terbo	V.FC	V.FC
Synchronous data format	○	●	●	●
Error-control command sets	V.42, MNP 2–4	V.42, MNP 2–4	V.42, MNP 2–4	V.42; MNP 2–4, 10
Data-compression command sets	V.42bis, MNP 5	V.42bis, MNP 5	V.42bis, MNP 5	V.42bis, MNP 5
Fax compatibility	Group 3	Group 3	Group 3	Group 3
Fax standards	Class 1 and 2	Class 2.0	Class 1	Class 1 and 2
TECHNICAL SUPPORT				
Command-set reference card	●	●	●	●
Quick-reference card	○	●	○	●
Technical-support number	717-293-3124	408-988-8108	404-441-1617	805-388-9000, ext. 555
BBS number	717-293-3074	408-988-3663	404-446-6336	805-445-9633
Warranty	Lifetime	2 years	2 years	Lifetime

●—Yes   ○— No   N/A—Not applicable

V.34 Modems ■

	Motorola Information Systems Group Motorola V.3400	Multi-Tech Systems Inc. MultiModem MT2834ZDX	Multi-Tech Systems Inc. MultiModemII MT2834BA-ISI	Practical Peripherals ProClass 288MT V.34
List price	$	$	$	$
GENERAL FEATURES				
Signal-converter (data-pump) manufacturer and model	Motorola 56002	AT&T DSP 33x	AT&T DSP 33x	Rockwell R6682-21
Controller-chip manufacturer and model	Motorola 68302	Zilog 182	Zilog 182	Intel MSH S-80C32U-44
Firmware version or date of firmware tested	1.02.02	11/8/94	11/8/94	2.5
AT firmware version command	AT&V	ATL5/L7	ATL5/L7	AT&V
Supports flash ROM	○	○	●	○
Supports Caller ID	○	○	○	●
PHYSICAL CHARACTERISTICS				
Dimensions (HWD, in inches)	2 x 7 x 10	1 x 4 x 6	2 x 6 x 9	1 x 5 x 7
Location of power switch	Back	Side	Back	Back
Location of voice-operation switch	Front	N/A	Front	N/A
Location of volume control	N/A	N/A	Back	N/A
Leased-line phone jack	●	○	○	○
Alphanumeric display	●	○	○	○
Number of status indicators	6	10	13	8
Speed indicators	●	●	●	○
Includes UART serial card	●	Optional	●	○
Includes phone cable/serial cable	●/○	●/○	●/○	●/○
PROTOCOLS SUPPORTED				
ITU data modulation standards (2,400 bps and higher)	V.22bis, V.27, V.29, V.32, V.32bis, V.34	V.22bis, V.25bis, V.32, V.32bis, V.34	V.22bis, V.29, V.32, V.32bis, V.34	V.32, V.32bis, V.34
Other high-speed data modulation standards	None	V.32terbo	V.32terbo	V.FC
Synchronous data format	●	○	●	●
Error-control command sets	V.42, MNP 2–4	V.42; MNP 3, 4	V.42; MNP 2–4	V.42; MNP 2–4
Data-compression command sets	V.42bis, MNP 5	V.42bis, MNP 5	V.42bis, MNP 5	V.42bis, MNP 5
Fax compatibility	Group 3	Group 3	Group 3	Group 3
Fax standards	Class 1	Class 2	Class 2	Class 1 and 2
TECHNICAL SUPPORT				
Command-set reference card	●	●	●	○
Quick-reference card	●	○	○	●
Technical-support number	800-221-4380	800-972-2439	800-972-2439	805-496-7707
BBS number	508-261-1058	612-785-3702	612-785-3702	805-496-4445
Warranty	2 years	10 years	5 years	Lifetime

●—Yes   ○—No   N/A—Not applicable

Table Continues →

■ V.34 Modems

	Supra Corp. SupraFAX-Modem 288	U.S. Robotics Inc. Courier V. Everything	U.S. Robotics Inc. Sportster 28,800 Data/Fax	Zoom Telephonics Inc. Zoom/Fax-Modem V.34X
List price	$	$	$	$
GENERAL FEATURES				
Signal-converter (data-pump) manufacturer and model	Rockwell RC288DPi	U.S. Robotics	U.S. Robotics	Rockwell RC288DPi
Controller-chip manufacturer and model	Rockwell L390	U.S. Robotics	U.S. Robotics	Rockwell RC 288 ACi L3902-57
Firmware version or date of firmware tested	1.000.05-V34	8/26/94	9/2/94	1.000B-V34
AT firmware version command	ATi3	ATi7	ATi7	AT&V
Supports flash ROM	●	●	○	○
Supports Caller ID	●	○	○	●
PHYSICAL CHARACTERISTICS				
Dimensions (HWD, in inches)	1 x 5 x 7	2 x 7 x 11	2 x 7 x 4	2 x 6 x 9
Location of power switch	Front	Back	Top	Back
Location of voice-operation switch	N/A	Front	N/A	N/A
Location of volume control	N/A	Side	Side	N/A
Leased-line phone jack	○	○	○	○
Alphanumeric display	●	○	○	○
Number of status indicators	4	12	7	15
Speed indicators	●	●	○	●
Includes UART serial card	○	○	○	○
Includes phone cable/serial cable	●/●	● ○	● ○	● ○
PROTOCOLS SUPPORTED				
ITU data modulation standards (2,400 bps and higher)	V.22bis, V.32, V.32bis, V.34	V.22bis, V.32, V.32bis, V.34	V.22bis, V.32, V.32bis, V.34	V.22bis, V.32, V.32bis, V.34
Other high-speed data modulation standards	V.FC	V.32terbo, V.FC	V.FC	V.FC
Synchronous data format	●	●	●	●
Error-control command sets	V.42; MNP 2–4, 10	V.42, MNP 2–4	V.42, MNP 2–4	V.42, MNP 2–4
Data-compression command sets	V.42bis, MNP 5	V.42bis, MNP 5	V.42bis, MNP 5	V.42bis, MNP 5
Fax compatibility	Group 3	Group 3	Group 3	Group 3
Fax standards	Class 1 and 2	Class 1 and 2.0	Class 1	Class 1 and 2
TECHNICAL SUPPORT				
Command-set reference card	●	●	●	●
Quick-reference card	●	●	○	○
Technical-support number	503-967-2490	800-550-7800	708-982-5151	617-423-1076
BBS number	503-967-2444	708-982-5092	708-982-5092	617-423-3733
Warranty	5 years	2 years	5 years	7 years

●—Yes   ○— No   N/A—Not applicable

H.2   High Speed Modems

(Products listed in review order)	Boca Research Inc. V.Fast Class External BocaModem	Cardinal Technologies Inc. Cardinal MVP192E	CXR (Anderson Jacobson) CXR 1945-FXD1	E-Tech Research Inc. P192MX Bullet Modem	GVC Technologies Inc. Maxtech 28.8Kbps Fax Modem
List price	$	$	$	$	$
Modem type	V.FC	V.32terbo	V.32terbo	V.32terbo	V.FC
Interface	Serial	Serial	Serial	Serial	Serial
Chip set manufacturer	Rockwell	AT&T	AT&T	AT&T	Rockwell
Firmware version tested	1	E208CAMJ	69-51945-030/040	6	6.0W
Communications software included	COMit LITE for DOS and Windows	COMit for Windows	None	QuickLink II Win/DOS	COMit LITE for DOS and Windows
Fax software included	FaxWorks for DOS and Windows	FaxWorks for Windows	None	QuickLink II Win/DOS	DOSFax LITE, WinFax LITE
PHYSICAL CHARACTERISTICS					
Dimensions (inches)	1 x 5 x 7.5 (HWD)	1.3 x 5.5 x 8.6 (HWD)	1.5 x 6.8 x 11.5 (HWD)	1.3 x 4.5 (H x diameter)	1.3 x 4.8 x 7 (HWD)
Location of power switch	Back	Back	Back	Side	Back
Speed indicators	○	●	●	○	●
UART serial card	16550 UART	None	None	None	None
Phone/serial cable	●/●	●/○	●/○	●/●	●/○
PROTOCOLS SUPPORTED					
Standard data modulation	Bell 103, Bell 212, V.22bis, V.32, V.32bis	Bell 103, Bell 212, V.22bis, V.32, V.32bis	Bell 103, Bell 212, V.22bis, V.32, V.32bis	Bell 103, Bell 212, V.22bis, V.32, V.32bis	Bell 103, Bell 212, V.22bis, V.32, V.32bis
Other data modulation	V.22, V.FC	V.21, V.22, V.32terbo	V.21, V.23, V.32terbo	V.21, V.22, V.23, V.32terbo	V.21, V.22, V.FC
Data compression	V.42bis, MNP 5	V.42bis, MNP 5	V.42bis, MNP 5	V.42bis, MNP 5	V.42bis, MNP 5
Error control	V.42, MNP 2–4	V.42, MNP 2–4	V.42, MNP 4	V.42, MNP 1–4	V.42, MNP 2–4
Fax capability	Group 3	Group 3	Group 3	Group 3	Group 3
Fax standards	Class 1 and 2	Class 1 and 2	Class 1 and 2	Class 2	Class 1 and 2
MISCELLANEOUS					
Caller ID support	○	○	○	●	○
V.34 upgrade path	●	○	○	○	●
Upgrade method	Factory	N/A	N/A	N/A	Factory
TECHNICAL SUPPORT					
AT-command reference	●	●	●	●	●
Quick-reference card	○	○	○	●	○
Background information on communications	○	●	○	●	●
Technical-support number	407-241-8088	717-293-3124	800-537-5762	408-730-1399	201-579-3630
BBS number	407-241-1601	717-293-3074	None	408-730-2120	201-579-2380
Fax-back number	407-995-9456	800-775-0899	None	None	None
Free support/Toll-free number	●/○	●/○	●/●	●/○	●/○
Warranty	5 years	Lifetime	3 years	2 years	5 years

●—Yes ○—No N/A—Not applicable

Table Continues →

■ High Speed Modems

	Hayes Microcomputer Products Inc. Hayes Optima 288 V.FC + FAX	Logicode Technology Inc. Quicktel 2814XV	Microcom Inc. DeskPorte FAST	Microcom Inc. TravelPorte FAST	Multi-Tech Systems Inc. MultiModem MT1932ZDX
List price	$	$	$	$	$
Modem type	V.FC	V.FC	V.FC	V.FC	V.32terbo
Interface	Serial	Serial	Parallel or serial	Parallel or serial	Serial
Chip set manufacturer	Rockwell	Rockwell	Rockwell	Rockwell	AT&T
Firmware version tested	3.1	1	1.3/85	1.3/85	0111A
Communications software included	Smartcom LE for Windows	COMit LITE for DOS and Windows	None	None	MultiExpress for Windows
Fax software included	Smartcom Fax for Windows	DOSFax LITE, WinFax LITE	FaxWorks for Windows	FaxWorks for Windows	MultiExpressFax for Windows
PHYSICAL CHARACTERISTICS					
Dimensions (inches)	1.3 x 5.5 x 9.5 (HWD)	2 x 6 x 6 (HWD)	1.3 x 6.8 x 8.3 (HWD)	1.3 x 2.8 x 4.3 (HWD)	1 x 4.5 x 5.6 (HWD)
Location of power switch	Back	Side	Front	Back	Side
Speed indicators	●	●	●	●	●
UART serial card	None	None	N/A	N/A	None
Phone/serial cable	●/○	●/○	●/●	●/●	●/○
PROTOCOLS SUPPORTED					
Standard data modulation	Bell 103, Bell 212, V.22bis, V.32, V.32bis	Bell 103, Bell 212, V.22bis, V.32, V.32bis	Bell 103, Bell 212, V.22bis, V.32, V.32bis	Bell 103, Bell 212, V.22bis, V.32, V.32bis	Bell 103, Bell 212, V.22bis, V.32, V.32bis
Other data modulation	V.21, V.22, V.FC	V.21, V.22, V.23, V.FC	V.21, V.22, V.23, V.FC	V.21, V.22, V.23, V.FC	V.22, V.32terbo
Data compression	V.42bis, MNP 5	V.42bis, MNP 5	V.42bis, MNP 5	V.42bis, MNP 5	V.42bis, MNP 5
Error control	V.42, MNP 2–4	V.42, MNP 4	V.42; MNP 2–4, 10	V.42; MNP 2–4, 10	V.42, MNP 3–4
Fax capability	Group 3	Group 3	Group 3	Group 3	Group 3
Fax standards	Class 1	Class 1 and 2	Class 1 and 2	Class 1	Class 2
MISCELLANEOUS					
Caller ID support	○	●	○	○	○
V.34 upgrade path	●	●	●	●	○
Upgrade method	User or factory	Factory	User or factory	Factory	N/A
TECHNICAL SUPPORT					
AT-command reference	●	●	○	○	●
Quick-reference card	○	●	○	○	○
Background information on communications	○	○	●	●	●
Technical-support number	404-441-1617	805-388-9000	617-551-1313	617-551-1313	800-972-2439
BBS number	800-874-2937	800-230-8632	617-255-1125	617-255-1125	800-392-2432
Fax-back number	800-429-3739	None	800-285-2802	800-285-2802	None
Free support/Toll-free number	●/○	●/○	●/○	●/○	●/●
Warranty	2 years	Lifetime	5 years	5 years	10 years

●—Yes ○—No N/A—Not applicable

High Speed Modems ▨

	Practical Peripherals Inc. Practical Peripherals PC288MT V.FC	Practical Peripherals Inc. Practical Peripherals PM288MT II V.FC	Practical Peripherals Inc. Practical Peripherals PM288PKT V.FC	Practical Peripherals Inc. Practical Peripherals PC288LCD V.FC	Supra Corp. SupraFAX-Modem 288
List price	$	$	$	$	$
Modem type	V.FC	V.FC	V.FC	V.FC	V.FC
Interface	Serial	Serial	Serial	Serial	Serial
Chip set manufacturer	Rockwell	Rockwell	Rockwell	Rockwell	Rockwell
Firmware version tested	3.15	3.15	3.15	3.15	0.510-13-DS39F VFC
Communications software included	QuickLink II Win/DOS	QuickLink II Win/DOS	QuickLink II Win/DOS	QuickLink II Win/DOS	COMit for DOS and Windows
Fax software included	QuickLink II Win/DOS, WinFax LITE	QuickLink II Win/DOS	QuickLink II Win/DOS	QuickLink II Win/DOS, WinFax LITE	FaxTalk for Windows
PHYSICAL CHARACTERISTICS					
Dimensions (inches)	1.1 x 4.6 x 6.8 (HWD)	1.1 x 4.6 x 6.8 (HWD)	1.2 x 2.3 x 4 (HWD)	6.3 x 2.8 x 3.8 (HWD)	1 x 4.6 x 6.5 (HWD)
Location of power switch	Back	Back	Side	Front	Front
Speed indicators	○	○	○	●	●
UART serial card	None	None	None	None	None
Phone/serial cable	●/○	●/○	●/○	●/○	●/●
PROTOCOLS SUPPORTED					
Standard data modulation	Bell 103, Bell 212, V.22bis, V.32, V.32bis	Bell 103, Bell 212, V.22bis, V.32, V.32bis	Bell 103, Bell 212, V.22bis, V.32, V.32bis	Bell 103, Bell 212, V.22bis, V.32, V.32bis	Bell 103, Bell 212, V.22bis, V.32, V.32bis
Other data modulation	V.21, V.22, V.FC	V.21, V.22, V.FC	V.21, V.22, V.FC	V.21, V.22, V.FC	V.21, V.22, V.23, V.FC
Data compression	V.42bis, MNP 5	V.42bis, MNP 5	V.42bis, MNP 5	V.42bis, MNP 5	V.42bis, MNP 5
Error control	V.42, MNP 2–4	V.42, MNP 2–4	V.42, MNP 2–4	V.42, MNP 2–4	V.42; MNP 2–4, 10
Fax capability	Group 3	Group 3	Group 3	Group 3	Group 3
Fax standards	Class 1 and 2	Class 1 and 2	Class 1 and 2	Class 1 and 2	Class 1 and 2
MISCELLANEOUS					
Caller ID support	●	●	●	●	●
V.34 upgrade path	●	●	●	●	●
Upgrade method	Factory	Factory	Factory	Factory	Factory
TECHNICAL SUPPORT					
AT-command reference	●	●	●	●	●
Quick-reference card	●	●	●	●	●
Background information on communications	○	○	○	○	●
Technical-support number	805-496-7707	805-496-7707	805-496-7707	805-496-7707	800-774-4965
BBS number	805-496-4445	805-496-4445	805-496-4445	805-496-4445	503-967-2444
Fax-back number	800-225-4774	800-225-4774	800-225-4774	800-225-4774	503-967-0072
Free support/Toll-free number	●/○	●/○	●/○	●/○	●/●
Warranty	Lifetime	Lifetime	Lifetime	Lifetime	5 years

●—Yes   ○—No   N/A—Not applicable

Table Continues →

■ High Speed Modems

	U.S. Robotics Inc. Courier V.34 Ready Fax with V.FC and V.32bis	Zoom Telephonics Inc. Zoom/Fax-Modem VFX 28.8	Zypcom Inc. Zypcom Z32t-SE	Zypcom Inc. Zypcom Z32t-SX	ZyXEL ZyXEL U-1496 Plus
List price	$	$	$	$	$
Modem type	V.FC, V.32terbo	V.FC	V.32terbo	V.32terbo	ZyX 19.2
Interface	Serial	Serial	Serial	Serial	Serial
Chip set manufacturer	U.S. Robotics	Rockwell	AT&T	AT&T	ZyXEL
Firmware version tested	5/11/94	1.000b-FVCX-32	1.06	1.06	6.12 P
Communications software included	QuickLink II Win/DOS	COMit for DOS and Windows	None	None	Cybersoft for Windows
Fax software included	QuickLink II Win/DOS	DOSFax LITE, WinFax LITE	None	None	ZFAX with Voice Software (DOS)
PHYSICAL CHARACTERISTICS					
Dimensions (inches)	1.5 x 6.4 x 10.4 (HWD)	1.6 x 8.5 x 6.1 (HWD)	1.5 x 4.5 x 7.5 (HWD)	1.5 x 4.5 x 7.5 (HWD)	1.8 x 8.8 x 10.5 (HWD)
Location of power switch	Back	Back	Side	Side	Back
Speed indicators	●	●	●	●	●
UART serial card	None	None	None	None	None
Phone/serial cable	●/○	●/○	●/○	●/○	●/○
PROTOCOLS SUPPORTED					
Standard data modulation	Bell 103, Bell 212, V.22bis, V.32, V.32bis	Bell 103, Bell 212, V.22bis, V.32, V.32bis	Bell 103, Bell 212, V.22bis, V.32, V.32bis	Bell 103, Bell 212, V.22bis, V.32, V.32bis	Bell 103, Bell 212, V.22bis, V.32, V.32bis
Other data modulation	V.23, V.25, V.25bis, V.32terbo, V.FC, HST, HST Cellular	V.21, V.22, V.22 A/B, V.23, V.FC	V.13 synchronous mode, V.21, V.22, V.23, V.32terbo	V.13 synchronous mode, V.21, V.22, V.23, V.32terbo	V.21, V.22, V.23, V.26bis, V.33, 16.8Kbps, 19.2Kbps
Data compression	V.42bis, MNP 5	V.42bis, MNP 5	V.42bis, MNP 5	V.42bis, MNP 5	V.42bis, MNP 5
Error control	V.42, MNP 2–4	V.42, MNP 10	V.42, MNP 2–4	V.42, MNP 2–4	V.42, MNP 3–4
Fax capability	Group 3	Group 3	Group 3	Group 3	Group 3
Fax standards	Class 1 and 2.0	Class 1 and 2	Class 1 and 2	Class 1 and 2	Class 2 and 2.0
MISCELLANEOUS					
Caller ID support	○	○	○	●	●
V.34 upgrade path	●	●	○	●	●
Upgrade method	User	Factory	N/A	Factory	Factory
TECHNICAL SUPPORT					
AT-command reference	●	●	●	●	●
Quick-reference card	●	○	○	○	●
Background information on communications	●	●	○	○	●
Technical-support number	800-550-7800	617-423-1076	510-783-2501	510-783-2501	714-693-0808
BBS number	708-982-5092	617-423-3733	None	None	714-693-0762
Fax-back number	800-762-6163	None	None	None	None
Free support/Toll-free number	●/●	●/○	●/○	●/○	●/○
Warranty	2 years	7 years	2 years	2 years	5 years

●—Yes   ○— No   N/A—Not applicable

High Speed Modems ■

	ZyXEL ZyXEL U-1496E	ZyXEL ZyXEL U-1496E Plus
List price	$	$
Modem type	ZyX 16.8	ZyX 19.2
Interface	Serial	Serial
Chip set manufacturer	ZyXEL	ZyXEL
Firmware version tested	6.12 EP	6.12 EP
Communications software included	Cybersoft for Windows	Cybersoft for Windows
Fax software included	ZFAX with Voice Software (DOS)	ZFAX with Voice Software (DOS)
PHYSICAL CHARACTERISTICS		
Dimensions (inches)	1.5 x 6.5 x 10.5 (HWD)	1.5 x 6.5 x 10.5 (HWD)
Location of power switch	Back	Back
Speed indicators	●	●
UART serial card	None	None
Phone/serial cable	●/○	●/○
PROTOCOLS SUPPORTED		
Standard data modulation	Bell 103, Bell 212, V.22bis, V.32, V.32bis	Bell 103, Bell 212, V.22bis, V.32, V.32bis
Other data modulation	V.21, V.22, V.23, 16.8Kbps	V.21, V.22, V.23, 16.8Kbps, 19.2Kbps
Data compression	V.42bis, MNP 5	V.42bis, MNP 5
Error control	V.42, MNP 3–4	V.42, MNP 3–4
Fax capability	Group 3	Group 3
Fax standards	Class 2 and 2.0	Class 2 and 2.0
MISCELLANEOUS		
Caller ID support	●	●
V.34 upgrade path	●	●
Upgrade method	Factory	Factory
TECHNICAL SUPPORT		
AT-command reference	●	●
Quick-reference card	●	●
Background information on communications	●	●
Technical-support number	714-693-0808	714-693-0808
BBS number	714-693-0762	714-693-0762
Fax-back number	None	None
Free support/Toll-free number	●/○	●/○
Warranty	5 years	5 years

●—Yes ○—No N/A—Not applicable

E n d ■

■ H.3   PCMCIA 14.4-Kbps Modems

(Products listed in alphabetical order by company name)	AT&T KeepInTouch Card	Megahertz 14.4Kbps PCMCIA Modem with XJack	Motorola CELLect 14.4 PCMCIA Modem	Practical Peripherals ProClass PCMCIA 144	U.S. Robotics Sportster 14.4 Data/Fax PCMCIA 2.1
List price	$	$	$	$	$
Cable					
Connector type	Two-pin with RJ-11	N/A	15-pin with RJ-11	15-pin with RJ-11	15-pin with two RJ-11s
Locking	●	N/A	○	●	●
Polarized	N/A	N/A	●	●	●
Extra coupler	○	N/A	●	○	●
Card and socket services	Enabler only	Award Software, Databook, Phoenix, SystemSoft	Enabler only	Enabler only	CardSoft, System-Soft
Included fax software	QuickLink II FAX	FaxWorks Data 3.0	FaxTalk Plus	QuickLink II FAX, WinFax Lite 3.0	QuickLink II FAX
Cellular support	Optional	Optional	●	○	○
Security	○	●	○	○	○
Remote configuration	○	●	●	○	○
Caller ID support	○	○	○	○	○
Flash memory	○	●	●	●	○
Leased-line mode	○	●	○	●	○
Hayes AutoSync mode	●	●	○	●	○
Warranty	5 years	5 years	2 years	5 years	5 years

●—Yes   ○—No   N/A—Not applicable

COMPARISON CHART

16-BIT SOUND BOARDS

16-Bit Sound Boards

(Products listed in alphabetical order by company name)	ACS LaserWave Nucleus 16	Adaptec AudioEdge	Adaptec SCSI AudioMachine	Advanced Gravis UltraSound Max	Antex Z1e
List price	$	$	$	$	$
GENERAL FEATURES					
Maximum sampling rate (kHz)	44.1	44.1	44.1	48	48
Sound chip set	ESS 688F	Crystal Semiconductor 4248	Crystal Semiconductor 4248	ICS GF1	Crystal Semiconductor 4216
Manufacturer of on-board DSP	N/A	Analog Devices	Analog Devices	ICS	Texas Instruments
Amplifier (watts per channel)	4	4	4	4	N/A
IRQ levels supported	2, 5, 7, 10	2 or 9, 3, 5, 7, 10–12	2 or 9, 3, 5, 7, 10–12	2–5, 7, 9–11, 12, 15	2, 3, 5, 7, 10, 11
Number of selectable addresses	4	4	4	6	4
User can set all IRQs and DMAs via software	○	○	○	●	●
Compatibility built into hardware or software:					
Ad Lib	Hardware	Hardware	Hardware	Software	Hardware
Creative Labs Sound Blaster	Hardware	Hardware	Hardware	Software	N/A
Microsoft Windows Sound System	Both	Hardware	Hardware	Software	Software
Roland MPU-401	N/A	Hardware	Hardware	Software	Hardware
Compression support built into hardware or software:					
ADPCM	Hardware	Software	Software	Hardware	Hardware
A-Law	N/A	N/A	N/A	Hardware	N/A
Mu-Law	N/A	N/A	N/A	Hardware	N/A
MPEG compression	N/A	N/A	N/A	N/A	Hardware
MPEG decompression	N/A	N/A	N/A	N/A	Hardware
MIDI SYNTHESIZER					
MIDI synthesizer chip	Yamaha OPL3	Analog Devices DSP 2115	Analog Devices DSP 2115	ICS GF1	Yamaha OPL3
Synthesizer type	FM (wavetable option, $99)	FM, wavetable	FM, wavetable	Wavetable	FM (wavetable option, $195)
Number of operators for FM synthesis	4	2	2	N/A	4
Provides MIDI interface/ Supports General MIDI	●/●	●/●	●/●	●/●	●/●
Number of channels for recording/playback	16, 16	16, 16	16, 16	2, 34	16, 16
Number of MIDI instruments provided	175	128	128	192	128
Storage location	Hard disk	On-board ROM	On-board ROM	Hard disk	On-board ROM
Number of simultaneously supported instruments	20	32	32	32	16
Number of voices	20	32	32	32	20
3-D sound technology	None	None	None	None	None
MIXING CAPABILITIES					
Mixes audio from:					
CDs/Microphone	●/●	●/●	●/●	●/●	●/●
PC internal speaker/Stereo DAC	●/●	○/○	○/○	○/●	○/●
Stereo line-in/Stereo synthesizer	●/●	●/●	●/●	●/●	●/●
CONNECTORS AND PORTS					
CD-ROM drive interfaces	Proprietary Mitsumi, Panasonic, Sony; optional SCSI connector, $29	SCSI-2	SCSI-2	Proprietary Mitsumi, Panasonic, Sony	SCSI-1
Joystick/Variable line-out	●/●	●/●	●/●	●/●	●/○
Microphone/Low-level line-out	●/●	●/●	●/●	●/●	●/○
Low-level line-in	●	●	●	●	●

●—Yes   ○—No   N/A—Not applicable

Table Continues →

■ 16-Bit Sound Boards

	Aztech WaveRider 32+	Best Data ACE 5000	Boca Sound-Expression 14.4VSp	Creative Labs Sound Blaster 16 Value Edition	Creative Labs Sound Blaster AWE32 Value Edition
List price	$	$	$	$	$
GENERAL FEATURES					
Maximum sampling rate (kHz)	48	44.1	44.1	44.1	44.1
Sound chip set	Aztech AZT2316A	IBM Mwave	Crystal Semiconductor 4231, Opti Media 929	Proprietary Creative Labs	E-mu 8000
Manufacturer of on-board DSP	N/A	IBM	N/A	Creative Labs	E-mu
Amplifier (watts per channel)	4	N/A	4	4	4
IRQ levels supported	2, 5, 7, 10	3–5, 10, 11, 15	5, 7, 10, 11	2, 5, 7, 10	2, 5, 7, 10
Number of selectable addresses	2	2	4	4	4
User can set all IRQs and DMAs via software	●	○	○	○	○
Compatibility built into hardware or software:					
Ad Lib	Hardware	N/A	Both	Hardware	Hardware
Creative Labs Sound Blaster	Hardware	Software	Both	Hardware	Hardware
Microsoft Windows Sound System	Hardware	Software	N/A	N/A	N/A
Roland MPU-401	Hardware	N/A	Hardware	Hardware	Hardware
Compression support built into hardware or software:					
ADPCM	Hardware	Software	Hardware	Software	Software
A-Law	Hardware	N/A	Hardware	Software	Software
Mu-Law	Hardware	N/A	Hardware	Software	Software
MPEG compression	N/A	N/A	N/A	N/A	N/A
MPEG decompression	Software	N/A	N/A	N/A	N/A
MIDI SYNTHESIZER					
MIDI synthesizer chip	ICS WaveFront, Yamaha OPL3	IBM Mwave	Yamaha OPL3	Yamaha OPL3	E-mu 8000, Yamaha OPL3
Synthesizer type	FM, wavetable	Wavetable	FM	FM	FM, wavetable
Number of operators for FM synthesis	4	N/A	4	4	4
Provides MIDI interface/Supports General MIDI	●/●	○/●	●/●	●/●	●/●
Number of channels for recording/playback	16, 16	2, 2	16, 16	16, 16	16, 16
Number of MIDI instruments provided	128	128	128	128	128
Storage location	On-board ROM	Hard disk	Hard disk	Hard disk	On-board ROM
Number of simultaneously supported instruments	32	8	20	20	16
Number of voices	32	8	20	20	32
3-D sound technology	Optional SRS, $39	None	None	None	Q-Sound
MIXING CAPABILITIES					
Mixes audio from:					
CDs/Microphone	●/●	●/●	●/●	●/●	●/●
PC internal speaker/Stereo DAC	●/●	●/●	○/●	●/●	●/●
Stereo line-in/Stereo synthesizer	●/●	●/●	●/●	●/●	●/●
CONNECTORS AND PORTS					
CD-ROM drive interfaces	IDE; proprietary Mitsumi, Panasonic, Sony	Proprietary Panasonic; TEAC SuperQuad 4X	IDE; proprietary Mitsumi, Panasonic, Sony	Proprietary Panasonic	Proprietary Mitsumi, Panasonic, Sony
Joystick/Variable line-out	●/●	○/○	●/●	●/●	●/●
Microphone/Low-level line-out	●/●	●/●	●/●	●/●	●/●
Low-level line-in	●	●	●	●	●

●—Yes   ○—No   N/A—Not applicable

16-Bit Sound Boards

	Creative Labs Sound Blaster AWE32	Ensoniq Soundscape	Genoa AudioBlitz 3D	KYE Genius SoundMaker 16E/ Value Edition	Logitech SoundMan Wave
List price	$	$	$	$	$
GENERAL FEATURES					
Maximum sampling rate (kHz)	44.1	44.1	48	44.1	44.1
Sound chip set	E-mu 8000	Ensoniq OTTO	Opti Media 929	ESS 688F	Media Vision Jazz 16
Manufacturer of on-board DSP	E-mu	N/A	N/A	N/A	N/A
Amplifier (watts per channel)	4	N/A	4	2	4
IRQ levels supported	2, 5, 7, 10	2, 5, 7, 10	5, 7, 11	5, 7, 9, 10	2, 3, 5, 7, 10, 15
Number of selectable addresses	4	5	2	4	4
User can set all IRQs and DMAs via software	○	○	○	○	●
Compatibility built into hardware or software:					
Ad Lib	Hardware	Both	Both	Hardware	Hardware
Creative Labs Sound Blaster	Hardware	Both	Both	Hardware	Hardware
Microsoft Windows Sound System	N/A	Both	N/A	N/A	N/A
Roland MPU-401	Hardware	Both	Both	N/A	Hardware
Compression support built into hardware or software:					
ADPCM	Hardware	Software	Software	Hardware	Hardware
A-Law	Hardware	Hardware	Software	N/A	Hardware
Mu-Law	Hardware	Hardware	Software	N/A	Hardware
MPEG compression	N/A	N/A	N/A	N/A	N/A
MPEG decompression	N/A	N/A	N/A	N/A	N/A
MIDI SYNTHESIZER					
MIDI synthesizer chip	E-mu 8000, Yamaha OPL3	Ensoniq OTTO	Yamaha OPL3	Yamaha OPL3	Yamaha OPL4
Synthesizer type	FM, wavetable (wavetable upgrade, $249)	FM, wavetable	FM (wavetable option, $99)	FM	FM, wavetable
Number of operators for FM synthesis	4	4	4	4	4
Provides MIDI interface/ Supports General MIDI	●/●	●/●	●/●	●/●	●/●
Number of channels for recording/playback	16, 16	16, 16	2, 2	4, 4	5, 5
Number of MIDI instruments provided	128	128	128	128	128
Storage location	On-board ROM	On-board ROM	Hard disk	On-board ROM	On-board ROM
Number of simultaneously supported instruments	16	16	20	4	20
Number of voices	32	32	20	16	44
3-D sound technology	Q-Sound	None	SRS	None	None
MIXING CAPABILITIES					
Mixes audio from:					
CDs/Microphone	●/●	●/●	●/●	●/●	●/●
PC internal speaker/Stereo DAC	●/●	○/●	●/●	○/●	●/●
Stereo line-in/Stereo synthesizer	●/●	●/●	●/●	●/●	●/●
CONNECTORS AND PORTS					
CD-ROM drive interfaces	Proprietary Mitsumi, Panasonic, Sony	Proprietary Mitsumi, Panasonic, Sony	IDE; proprietary Mitsumi, Panasonic, Sony	Proprietary Mitsumi, Panasonic, Sony	Proprietary SCSI
Joystick/Variable line-out	●/●	●/○	●/●	●/●	●/●
Microphone/Low-level line-out	●/●	○/●	●/●	●/●	●/●
Low-level line-in	●	●	●	●	●

●—Yes ○—No N/A—Not applicable

Table Continues →

■ 16-Bit Sound Boards

	MediaMagic Telemetry-32	Mediatrix Audiotrix Pro	Media Vision Premium 3-D	Media Vision Pro 3-D	miroSound PCM 1 PRO
List price	$	$	$	$	$
GENERAL FEATURES					
Maximum sampling rate (kHz)	44.1	48	48	48	44.1
Sound chip set	AT&T 3210	Crystal Semiconductor 4231	Media Vision MVD1216	Media Vision MVD1216	Crystal Semiconductor 4231
Manufacturer of on-board DSP	AT&T	Crystal Semiconductor	N/A	N/A	N/A
Amplifier (watts per channel)	4	4	1–4	1–4	4
IRQ levels supported	5, 7, 9–11, 15	7, 9–11	1, 3, 5, 7, 11, 15	1, 3, 5, 7, 11, 15	7, 9–11
Number of selectable addresses	4	4	6	6	4
User can set all IRQs and DMAs via software	●	●	●	●	●
Compatibility built into hardware or software:					
Ad Lib	Both	Hardware	Software	Software	Hardware
Creative Labs Sound Blaster	Software	Hardware	Software	Software	Hardware
Microsoft Windows Sound System	Software	Hardware	Software	Software	Hardware
Roland MPU-401	Hardware	Hardware	Software	Software	Software
Compression support built into hardware or software:					
ADPCM	Software	Hardware	Hardware	Hardware	Hardware
A-Law	Software	Hardware	Hardware	Hardware	Hardware
Mu-Law	Software	Hardware	Hardware	Hardware	Hardware
MPEG compression	Software	N/A	N/A	N/A	N/A
MPEG decompression	Software	N/A	N/A	N/A	N/A
MIDI SYNTHESIZER					
MIDI synthesizer chip	AT&T 3210	Yamaha OPL4	Yamaha OPL3	Korg wavetable, Yamaha OPL3	Yamaha OPL4
Synthesizer type	FM, wavetable	FM, wavetable	FM (wavetable option, $199)	FM, wavetable	FM, wavetable
Number of operators for FM synthesis	4	4	4	4	4
Provides MIDI interface/ Supports General MIDI	●/●	●/●	●/●	●/●	●/●
Number of channels for recording/playback	10, 10	32, 32	16, 16	16, 16	32, 32
Number of MIDI instruments provided	128	128	128	128	128
Storage location	On-board ROM	On-board ROM	On-board ROM	On-board ROM	On-board ROM
Number of simultaneously supported instruments	24	32	20	20	32
Number of voices	20	44	20	32	44
3-D sound technology	None	Optional SRS, $90	SRS	SRS	None
MIXING CAPABILITIES					
Mixes audio from:					
CDs/Microphone	●/●	●/●	●/●	●/●	●/●
PC internal speaker/Stereo DAC	○/○	○/○	○/○	○/○	●/●
Stereo line-in/Stereo synthesizer	●/●	●/●	●/●	●/●	●/●
CONNECTORS AND PORTS					
CD-ROM drive interfaces	IDE; proprietary Mitsumi, Panasonic, Sony	Optional connectors: proprietary Mitsumi, Panasonic, Sony, $30; SCSI-2, $48; Philips CM206, $55	SCSI-2; proprietary Mitsumi, Panasonic, Sony	SCSI-2	IDE; proprietary Mitsumi, Panasonic, Sony
Joystick/Variable line-out	●/●	●/●	●/●	●/●	●/●
Microphone/Low-level line-out	●/●	●/●	●/●	●/●	●/●
Low-level line-in	●	●	●	●	●

●—Yes ○—No N/A—Not applicable

16-Bit Sound Boards ■

	Multiwave Audiowave Green 16	New Media .WAVjammer	Orchid SoundWave 32 Pro SCSI	Orchid SoundWave 32+ Studio	Reveal SoundFX
List price	$	$	$	$	$
GENERAL FEATURES					
Maximum sampling rate (kHz)	44.1	44.1	48	48	44.1
Sound chip set	ESS 688F	Crystal Semiconductor 4248	Analog Devices DSP-2115	Analog Devices DSP-2115	Reveal proprietary
Manufacturer of on-board DSP	N/A	N/A	Analog Devices	Analog Devices	N/A
Amplifier (watts per channel)	4	N/A	4	4	4
IRQ levels supported	2, 5, 7, 10	0–15	3–5, 7, 9–12	3–5, 7, 9–12	2, 5, 7, 9, 11, 15
Number of selectable addresses	4	N/A	8	8	2
User can set all IRQs and DMAs via software	○	●	●	●	●
Compatibility built into hardware or software:					
Ad Lib	Hardware	Software	Both	Both	Both
Creative Labs Sound Blaster	Hardware	N/A	Hardware	Hardware	Both
Microsoft Windows Sound System	Both	Software	Hardware	Hardware	Both
Roland MPU-401	N/A	N/A	Both	Both	N/A
Compression support built into hardware or software:					
ADPCM	Hardware	Both	Both	Both	Hardware
A-Law	N/A	Both	Hardware	Hardware	Hardware
Mu-Law	N/A	Both	Hardware	Hardware	Hardware
MPEG compression	N/A	N/A	N/A	N/A	N/A
MPEG decompression	N/A	N/A	N/A	N/A	N/A
MIDI SYNTHESIZER					
MIDI synthesizer chip	Yamaha OPL3	Yamaha OPL3	Analog Devices DSP 2115	Analog Devices DSP 2115	Reveal proprietary
Synthesizer type	FM (wavetable option, $79)	FM	FM, wavetable (wavetable upgrade, $129–$219)	FM, wavetable	FM
Number of operators for FM synthesis	4	4	8	2	4
Provides MIDI interface/ Supports General MIDI	●/●	○ ●	●/●	●/●	● ○
Number of channels for recording/playback	16, 16	6, 6	16, 16	16, 16	4, 4
Number of MIDI instruments provided	175	128	208	722	128
Storage location	Hard disk	On-board ROM	On-board ROM	On-board ROM	On-board ROM
Number of simultaneously supported instruments	20	20	16	32	4
Number of voices	20	20	32	56	20
3-D sound technology	None	None	Q-Sound	Q-Sound	None
MIXING CAPABILITIES					
Mixes audio from:					
CDs/Microphone	●/●	●/●	●/●	●/●	●/●
PC internal speaker/Stereo DAC	●/●	○/●	○/○	○/○	●/●
Stereo line-in/Stereo synthesizer	●/●	●/○	●/●	●/●	●/●
CONNECTORS AND PORTS					
CD-ROM drive interfaces	Proprietary Mitsumi, Panasonic, Sony; optional SCSI connector, $25	None	439	439	Proprietary Mitsumi, Panasonic, Sony
Joystick/Variable line-out	●/●	○/○	●/●	●/●	●/●
Microphone/Low-level line-out	●/●	●/●	●/●	●/●	●/●
Low-level line-in	●	●	●	●	●

●—Yes   ○—No   N/A—Not applicable

Table Continues →

■ 16-Bit Sound Boards

	Reveal SoundFX Wave	Turtle Beach Monte Carlo	Turtle Beach MultiSound Monterey	Turtle Beach Tropez
List price	$	$	$	$
GENERAL FEATURES				
Maximum sampling rate (kHz)	44.1	48	44.1	48
Sound chip set	Reveal proprietary	Crystal Semi-conductor 4231	Turtle Beach proprietary	Crystal Semi-conductor 4231
Manufacturer of on-board DSP	N/A	N/A	Motorola	N/A
Amplifier (watts per channel)	N/A	4	N/A	N/A
IRQ levels supported	2, 5, 7, 9–11	2, 5, 7, 9, 11	5, 7, 9–12, 15	2, 5, 9–12, 15
Number of selectable addresses	4	5	6	5
User can set all IRQs and DMAs via software	●	●	●	●
Compatibility built into hardware or software:				
Ad Lib	Both	Hardware	N/A	Hardware
Creative Labs Sound Blaster	Both	Hardware	N/A	Hardware
Microsoft Windows Sound System	Both	Hardware	Hardware	Hardware
Roland MPU-401	Both	N/A	N/A	Hardware
Compression support built into hardware or software:				
ADPCM	Hardware	Hardware	Hardware	Hardware
A-Law	Hardware	Hardware	N/A	Hardware
Mu-Law	Hardware	Hardware	N/A	Hardware
MPEG compression	N/A	N/A	N/A	N/A
MPEG decompression	N/A	N/A	N/A	N/A
MIDI SYNTHESIZER				
MIDI synthesizer chip	Reveal proprietary	Yamaha OPL3	ICS WaveFront	ICS WaveFront, Yamaha OPL3
Synthesizer type	FM, wavetable	FM	Wavetable	FM, wavetable
Number of operators for FM synthesis	4	4	N/A	4
Provides MIDI interface/ Supports General MIDI	●/●	●/●	●/●	●/●
Number of channels for recording/playback	4, 4	16, 32	16, 48	32, 48
Number of MIDI instruments provided	228	128	128	128
Storage location	On-board ROM	Hard disk	On-board ROM	On-board ROM
Number of simultaneously supported instruments	24	32	32	32
Number of voices	24	32	32	32
3-D sound technology	None	None	None	None
MIXING CAPABILITIES				
Mixes audio from:				
CDs/Microphone	●/●	●/●	●/●	●/●
PC internal speaker/Stereo DAC	●/●	○/●	○/●	○/●
Stereo line-in/Stereo synthesizer	●/●	●/●	●/●	●/●
CONNECTORS AND PORTS				
CD-ROM drive interfaces	IDE, proprietary Mitsumi, Panasonic, Sony	Proprietary Mitsumi, Panasonic, Sony	None	IDE
Joystick/Variable line-out	●/○	●/●	○/○	●/○
Microphone/Low-level line-out	●/●	●/●	○/●	●/●
Low-level line-in	●	●	●	●

●—Yes ○—No N/A—Not applicable

End ■

COMPARISON CHART

SURGE
SUPPRESSORS

Surge Suppressors

(Products listed in alphabetical order by company name)	AESI/ StediWatt Diagnostic Power Refinery, Model 718	American Power Conversion Surge Arrest Plus with telephone suppression	Brooks Surge Reactor BN6-6	Brooks Power Systems Surge Stopper BPS-BN6-6	Control Concepts Supertrac ST6D
List price	$	$	$	$	$
PHYSICAL CHARACTERISTICS					
Power cord length (inches)	75	72	72	72	60
Case material	Aluminum	Plastic	Metal	Aluminum	Plastic
Number of outlets	7	7	6	6	6
Socket arrangement	Single row	Single row	Single row	Single row	Two rows
TECHNOLOGY					
Capacitators	●	●	●	●	●
Inductors	●	●	●	●	●
Gas tubes	○	○	○	○	○
Numbers of MOVs (metal oxide varistors)	6	7	3	5	6
Size (mm)	22	20	20	20	20
Silicon avalanche diodes	○	○	●	●	○
UL ratings (pass-through voltage):					
Hot-to-neutral line	330V	330V	330V	330V	330V
Neutral-to-ground line	330V	330V	330V	330V	400V
Hot-to-ground line	330V	330V	330V	330V	400V
Phone jack	$20.00	●	○	○	●
GENERAL FEATURES					
Separate on/off switches for individual outlets	○	○	○	○	○
Suppression light	●	●	●	●	●
Circuit breaker	15 amps	15 amps	15 amps	15 amps	15 amps
Technical support hours (Eastern time)	8:00–6:00 M–F	8:00–8:00 M–F	8:00–5:00 M–F	9:00–7:00 M–F	8:00–5:00 M–F
Standard warranty	5 years	Lifetime	Lifetime	Lifetime	10 years
Warranty covers damage to equipment plugged in	●	●	○	●	○

●—Yes ○—No N/A—Not applicable INA—Information not available

Table Continues →

Surge Suppressors

	Current Technology Power Siftor Pro 15	Curtis Manufacturing Ruby Plus	Datashield S100	EFI PowerTrax 2000	Electripak Model 6SSU
List price	$	$	$	$	$
PHYSICAL CHARACTERISTICS					
Power cord length (inches)	72	72	72	72	48
Case material	Aluminum	Plastic	Plastic	Plastic	Metal
Number of outlets	6	6	6	6	6
Socket arrangement	Single row	Two rows	Two rows	Single row	Single row
TECHNOLOGY					
Capacitators	○	●	●	●	●
Inductors	○	●	●	●	○
Gas tubes	○	○	●	○	○
Numbers of MOVs (metal oxide varistors)	14	6	4	6	3
Size (mm)	20	14	22	18	20
Silicon avalanche diodes	○	○	○	●	○
UL ratings (pass-through voltage):					
Hot-to-neutral line	330V	400V	400V	330V	330V
Neutral-to-ground line	330V	400V	400V	330V	330V
Hot-to-ground line	330V	400V	400V	400V	330V
Phone jack	●	●	○	●	○
GENERAL FEATURES					
Separate on/off switches for individual outlets	○	○	○	○	● (4 switched, 2 unswitched)
Suppression light	○	●	○	●	●
Circuit breaker	15 amps	15 amps	10 amps	15 amps	15 amps
Technical support hours (Eastern time)	7:00–4:00 M–F	8:00–5:00 M–F	7:00–5:30 M–F	9:00–6:00 M–F	8:00–5:00 M–F
Standard warranty	Lifetime	Lifetime	Lifetime	Lifetime	5 years
Warranty covers damage to equipment plugged in	○	○	●	●	○

●—Yes ○—No N/A—Not applicable INA—Information not available

Surge Suppressors ◼

	GC-Thorsen Power Management System 64-631	Geist Ultimate SRF-6MO/S-DP	GE Wiring Devices SurgePro SP-6000NS	General Semiconductor Industries 1206K6	Hubbell Circuit Guard SS6
List price	$	$	$	$	$
PHYSICAL CHARACTERISTICS					
Power cord length (inches)	72	72	72	72	72
Case material	Steel	Plastic	Plastic	Metal	Steel
Number of outlets	6	6	6	6	6
Socket arrangement	Single row	Two rows	Two rows	Single row	Single row
TECHNOLOGY					
Capacitators	●	●	●	○	○
Inductors	○	●	●	○	○
Gas tubes	○	○	○	○	○
Numbers of MOVs (metal oxide varistors)	3	4	2	8	4
Size (mm)	14.5	20	14	20	20
Silicon avalanche diodes	○	●	○	●	○
UL ratings (pass-through voltage):					
Hot-to-neutral line	330V	330V	600V	330V	330V
Neutral-to-ground line	330V	330V	600V	330V	330V
Hot-to-ground line	330V	330V	600V	330V	330V
Phone jack	●	●	○	○	○
GENERAL FEATURES					
Separate on/off switches for individual outlets	○	○	○	○	○
Suppression light	●	●	●	●	●
Circuit breaker	15 amps	15 amps	15 amps	15 amps	15 amps
Technical support hours (Eastern time)	7:00–4:00 M–F	7:00–4:00 M–F	8:00–5:00 M–F	7:00–4:00 M–F	8:00–4:30 M–F
Standard warranty	5 years	Lifetime	None	5 years	1 year
Warranty covers damage to equipment plugged in	○	●	N/A	○	○

●—Yes ○—No N/A—Not applicable INA—Information not available

Table Continues →

■ Surge Suppressors

	Inland 3 Mode Surge Protector	Innovative Technology SPIU-6	Jayco Electronics Supress-All AC-6	Joslyn Model 1203-03 Surge Suppressor	Kensington Microware Ltd. Power Tree 50
List price	$	$	$	$	$
PHYSICAL CHARACTERISTICS					
Power cord length (inches)	48	60	72	72	108
Case material	Plastic	Plastic	Plastic	Aluminum	Plastic and steel
Number of outlets	6	6	6	6	6
Socket arrangement	Single row	Two rows	Two rows	Two rows	Two rows
TECHNOLOGY					
Capacitators	●	●	●	●	●
Inductors	○	●	○	●	●
Gas tubes	○	INA	○	●	○
Numbers of MOVs (metal oxide varistors)	3	INA	6	10	3
Size (mm)	14	INA	20	20	23
Silicon avalanche diodes	○	INA	●	○	○
UL ratings (pass-through voltage):					
Hot-to-neutral line	400V	330V	330V	330V	330V
Neutral-to-ground line	400V	330V	330V	330V	500V
Hot-to-ground line	400V	330V	330V	330V	500V
Phone jack	○	$20.00	○	○	●
GENERAL FEATURES					
Separate on/off switches for individual outlets	○	○	○	○	○
Suppression light	●	●	●	●	●
Circuit breaker	15 amps	10 amps	10 amps	15 amps	15 amps
Technical support hours (Eastern time)	8:30–5:30 M–F	8:00–5:00 M–F	9:00–5:00 M–F	10:30–7:30 M–F	11:00–8:30 M–F
Standard warranty	Lifetime	5 years	10 years	5 years	5 years
Warranty covers damage to equipment plugged in	○	○	●	○	●

●—Yes ○—No N/A—Not applicable INA—Information not available

Surge Suppressors

	L.E.A. Dynatech CS-615	L.E.A. Dynatech Transient Tamer TT 415	NCR Pyramid	NCR Series 4000 Model 4070	Pacific Electricord XP
List price	$	$	$	$	$
PHYSICAL CHARACTERISTICS					
Power cord length (inches)	72	72	72	72	72
Case material	Plastic	Plastic	Plastic	Plastic	Plastic
Number of outlets	6	4	6	7	6
Socket arrangement	Two rows	Two rows	Two rows	Horseshoe	Single row
TECHNOLOGY					
Capacitators	○	●	○	●	●
Inductors	○	●	●	●	○
Gas tubes	○	○	●	●	○
Numbers of MOVs (metal oxide varistors)	5	7	3	6	3
Size (mm)	20	20	20	20	15
Silicon avalanche diodes	●	○	●	○	○
UL ratings (pass-through voltage):					
Hot-to-neutral line	330V	330V	330V	330V	400V
Neutral-to-ground line	330V	330V	330V	330V	400V
Hot-to-ground line	330V	330V	330V	330V	400V
Phone jack	○	●	○	●	○
GENERAL FEATURES					
Separate on/off switches for individual outlets	○	○	○	○	○
Suppression light	●	●	●	○	●
Circuit breaker	15 amps	15 amps	15 amps	15 amps	15 amps
Technical support hours (Eastern time)	7:00–6:00 M–F	7:00–6:00 M–F	24 hours a day	8:00–5:00 M–F (local time)	10:00–8:00 M–F
Standard warranty	Lifetime	Lifetime	2 years	5 years	2 years
Warranty covers damage to equipment plugged in	●	●	○	●	●

●—Yes ○—No N/A—Not applicable INA—Information not available

Table Continues →

■ Surge Suppressors

	Panamax Max 6	Pass & Seymour/Legrand SpecGuard C6L	Perma Power RS-610	Power Sentry Surge Protector 300 Plus Model 106	ProTek Devices Surgebuster Model 1206K6
List price	$	$	$	$	$
PHYSICAL CHARACTERISTICS					
Power cord length (inches)	72	72	72	48	72
Case material	Plastic	Plastic	Steel	Plastic	Metal
Number of outlets	6	6	6	6	6
Socket arrangement	Two rows	Two rows	Single row	Single row	Single row
TECHNOLOGY					
Capacitators	●	●	○	●	●
Inductors	●	●	●	●	●
Gas tubes	○	○	○	○	○
Numbers of MOVs (metal oxide varistors)	6	6	3	3	8
Size (mm)	20	20	22	17	20
Silicon avalanche diodes	○	○	●	○	●
UL ratings (pass-through voltage):					
Hot-to-neutral line	330V	400V	330V	400V	330V
Neutral-to-ground line	330V	400V	330V	400V	330V
Hot-to-ground line	330V	400V	330V	400V	330V
Phone jack	○	○	○	○	○
GENERAL FEATURES					
Separate on/off switches for individual outlets	○	○	○	○	○
Suppression light	●	●	●	●	○
Circuit breaker	15 amps	15 amps	15 amps	15 amps	15 amps
Technical support hours (Eastern time)	10:30–8:00 M–F	8:00–5:30 M–F	9:00–7:00 M–F	10:00–10:00 M–F	10:00–7:00 M–F
Standard warranty	Lifetime	Lifetime	Lifetime	2 years	2 years
Warranty covers damage to equipment plugged in	●	○	●	●	○

●—Yes ○—No N/A—Not applicable INA—Information not available

Surge Suppressors

	Proxima Network-Grade Surge Protector Model S500	Proxima ProLine 30	SL Waber Surge Sentry DL6D	SL Waber Wave Tracker WT6SS	SRW Computer Components SRW GS-2
List price	$	$	$	$	$
PHYSICAL CHARACTERISTICS					
Power cord length (inches)	72	72	72	72	72
Case material	Plastic	Plastic	Plastic	Aluminum	Plastic
Number of outlets	7	6	6	6	6
Socket arrangement	Single row	Single row	Single row	Two rows	Single row
TECHNOLOGY					
Capacitators	●	●	○	●	●
Inductors	●	○	○	●	○
Gas tubes	○	○	○	●	○
Numbers of MOVs (metal oxide varistors)	6	6	1	5	3
Size (mm)	18	18	20	20	25
Silicon avalanche diodes	○	○	○	●	○
UL ratings (pass-through voltage):					
Hot-to-neutral line	330V	330V	330V	330V	340V
Neutral-to-ground line	330V	330V	330V	330V	340V
Hot-to-ground line	330V	330V	330V	330V	340V
Phone jack	○	●	○	○	○
GENERAL FEATURES					
Separate on/off switches for individual outlets	○	○	○	○	○
Suppression light	●	●	●	●	●
Circuit breaker	15 amps	15 amps	15 amps	15 amps	15 amps
Technical support hours (Eastern time)	11:00–9:00 M–F	11:00–9:00 M–F	8:00–5:00 M–F	8:00–5:00 M–F	11:00–7:30 M–F
Standard warranty	Lifetime	Lifetime	Lifetime	Lifetime	Lifetime
Warranty covers damage to equipment plugged in	●	●	●	●	○

●—Yes ○—No N/A—Not applicable INA—Information not available

Table Continues →

■ Surge Suppressors

	Tandy 6-Outlet Power Center	Tripp Lite Isobar 6 Ultra	Tripp Lite Isobar 8	Woods 5623 Surge Suppressor	Zaptech Model MSS-206	Zero Surge ZS1800 Surge Eliminator
List price	$	$	$	$	$	$
PHYSICAL CHARACTERISTICS						
Power cord length (inches)	72	72	144	48	72	72
Case material	Plastic	Steel and aluminum	Metal	Plastic	Plastic	Steel
Number of outlets	6	6	8	6	6	6
Socket arrangement	Two rows	Two rows	Single row	Single row	Two rows	Two rows
TECHNOLOGY						
Capacitators	●	●	●	●	●	●
Inductors	INA	●	○	●	○	●
Gas tubes	○	○	○	○	●	○
Numbers of MOVs (metal oxide varistors)	3	8	8	7	3	None
Size (mm)	INA	20	22	14	15	N/A
Silicon avalanche diodes	○	○	○	○	○	○
UL ratings (pass-through voltage):						
Hot-to-neutral line	340V	330V	330V	330V	400V	330V
Neutral-to-ground line	340V	330V	330V	330V	400V	N/A
Hot-to-ground line	340V	330V	330V	330V	400V	N/A
Phone jack	○	●	○	●	○	○
GENERAL FEATURES						
Separate on/off switches for individual outlets	○	○	○	○	●	○
Suppression light	●	●	○	●	○	○
Circuit breaker	15 amps	12 amps	15 amps	15 amps	15 amps	15 amps
Technical support hours (Eastern time)	9:00–6:30 M–F	7:00–5:30 M–F	8:00–6:30 M–F	8:00–5:00 M–F	12:00–9:00 M–F	9:00–5:00 M–F
Standard warranty	1 year	Lifetime	Lifetime	Lifetime	2 years	10 years
Warranty covers damage to equipment plugged in	○	●	●	○	○	●

●—Yes   ○—No   N/A—Not applicable   INA—Information not available

End ■

DIRECTORY OF MANUFACTURERS

THIS DIRECTORY IS a comprehensive listing of manufacturers of computers, mice and miscellaneous peripherals, modems and telecommunications equipment, monitors and video-related equipment, and printers, scanners, and related equipment.

This table was produced using Computer Select™, a comprehensive computer products database for buyers of hardware, software, and communications products. Computer Select is a first-rate, easy-to-use reference for current computer product specifications and reviews. Each monthly CD-ROM contains over 70,000 articles from the most recent year's worth of issues of over 140 computer, business, and technical periodicals. Computer Select also includes specifications for over 70,000 hardware, software, and data communications products and profiles of the over 12,000 companies that make those products. The product specifications and reviews are taken from Data Sources™, the most comprehensive directory of the computer industry in print.

Computer Select and Data Sources are products of the Computer Library division of Ziff Communications Company. For more information or to subscribe to Computer Select or Data Sources, contact Computer Library at 212–503–4400.

Computers

Able Technologies, Inc. (Abletec Division)
46791 Fremont Blvd.
Fremont, CA 94538
510-659-1544

ACCTON Technology Corp.
46750 Fremont Blvd., Ste. 104
Fremont, CA 94538
510-226-9800
fax: 510-226-9833

Acer America Corp.
401 Charcot Ave.
San Jose, CA 95131
800-258-6787
Technical support: 800-637-7000

ACMA Computers, Inc.
117 Fourier Ave.
Fremont, CA 94539
510-623-1212
fax: 510-623-0818

A.C.T. International
10772 Noel St.
Los Alamitos, CA 90720
714-952-8999
fax: 714-952-3804

Advance Electronic Diagnostics, Inc.
10850 North 24th Ave., Ste. 101
Phoenix, AZ 85029
602-861-9359
fax: 602-678-4471

Advanced Computer Products, Inc.
1310C E. Edinger Ave.
Santa Ana, CA 92705
800-366-3227; 714-558-8813
fax: 714-558-1603

Advanced Logic Research, Inc.
9401 Jeronimo
Irvine, CA 92718
800-444-4257; 714-581-6770
fax: 714-581-9240
Technical support: 714-458-0863

Allbest International Corp.
45-03 Junction Blvd.
Corona, NY 11368
718-760-2210
fax: 718-760-1937

ALR—Advanced Logic Research, Inc.
9401 Jeronimo
Irvine, CA 92718
800-444-4257; 714-581-6770
Technical Support: 714-458-0863

Altima Systems, Inc.
1390 Willow Pass Rd., Ste. 1050
Concord, CA 94520
800-356-9990; 510-356-5600
fax: 510-356-2408

Amax Applied Technology, Inc.
3001-A W. Mission Rd.
Alhambra, CA 91803
818-300-8828
fax: 818-282-9992

AMAX Engineering Corp.
47315 Mission Falls Court
Fremont, CA 94539
510-651-8886
fax: 510-651-3720

American Research Corp.
1101 Monterey Pass Rd.
Monterey Park, CA 91754
800-346-3272; 213-265-0835
fax: 213-265-1973
Technical support: 213-265-0523

American Systec Corp.
2860 E. Imperial Hwy.
Brea, CA 92621
714-993-0882
fax: 714-996-3903

AMI (American Micronics, Inc.)
3002 Dow Ave., Ste. 224
Tustin, CA 92680
714-573-9005
fax: 714-573-9008

Amkly Systems, Inc.
60 Technology Dr.
Irvine, CA 92718
800-367-2655; 714-768-3511

Amplicom
7985 Dunbrook Rd., Ste. H
San Diego, CA 92126
619-693-9127
fax: 619-693-3368

AMREL Technology, Inc.
9952 E. Baldwin Place
El Monte, CA 91731
800-88-AMREL; 818-575-5110
fax: 818-575-0801

AMT International
2393 Qume Dr.
San Jose, CA 95131
408-432-1790
fax: 408-944-9801

A-Plus Computer, Inc.
10016 Pioneer Blvd., Ste. 102
Santa Fe Springs, CA 90670
800-443-5373; 310-949-9345
fax: 310-949-4125

Apple Computer, Inc.
20525 Mariani Ave.
Cupertino, CA 95014
408-996-1010
Technical support: 800-776-2333

Applied Digital Data Systems, Inc. (ADDS)
100 Marcus Blvd., P.O. Box 18001
Hauppauge, NY 11788
800-231-5445; 516-231-5400
fax: 516-231-7378

Apricot in Canada
111 Granton Dr. #401
Richmond Hill, Ontario
Canada L4B 1L5
416-492-2777; 416–492–2513

Arche Technologies, Inc.
48881 Kato Rd.
Fremont, CA 94539
510-623-8100
fax: 510-683-6754
Technical support: 800-322-2724

Ares Microdevelopment, Inc.
23660 Research Dr., Unit A
Farmington Hills, MI 48335
800-322-3200; 313-473-0808

Computers

Ariel Design, Inc.
45 Pond St.
Norwell, MA 02061
800-55ariel; 617-982-8800
fax: 617-982-9095

Associates Mega Sub-System, Inc.
4801 Little John St., Unit A
Baldwin Park, CA 91706
800-886-2671; 818-814-8851
fax: 818-814-0782

AST Research Inc.
P.O. Box 19658, 16215 Alton Pkwy.
Irvine, CA 92718
800-727-1278; 714-727-4141
fax: 714-727-9355
Technical support: Use 800 number

Astarte Computer Systems, Inc.
1035 Pearl St., 5th Fl.
Boulder, CO 80302
303-449-9970
fax: 303-449-2773

Atari
1196 Borregas
Sunnyvale, CA 94088
408-745-2000
fax: 408-745-4306
Technical support: 408-745-2004

Austin Computer Systems
10300 Metric Blvd.
Austin, TX 78759
800-752-1577; 512-339-3500
fax: 512-454-1357
Technical support: 512-339-7932

Axik Computer Inc.
1031 F E. Duane Ave.
Sunnyvale, CA 94086
408-735-1234
fax: 408-735-1437

BCC
1610 Crane Court
San Jose, CA 95112
800-827-4222; 408-944-9000
fax: 408-944-0657
Technical Support: 800-827-4333

Benchmarq Corp.
2611 Westgrove, Ste. 101
Carrollton, TX 75006
800-966-0011; 214-407-0011
fax: 214-407-9845

Bi-Link Computer, Inc.
11606 E. Washington Blvd., Ste. A
Whittier, CA 90606
800-888-5369; 310-692-5345
fax: 310-695-9623

Binary Technology, Inc.
17120 Dallas Pkwy., Ste. 212
Dallas, TX 75248
800-776-7990

Bioanalytical Systems, Inc. (BAS)
2701 Kent Ave.
West Lafayette, IN 47906
317-463-4527
fax: 317-497-1102

Bi-Tech Enterprises, Inc.
10 Carlough Rd.
Bohemia, NY 11716
516-567-8155
fax: 516-567-8266

Blackship Computer Systems, Inc.
2031 O'Toole Ave.
San Jose, CA 95131
800-531-7447; 408-432-7500
fax: 408-432-1443
Technical support: Use toll-free number

Blue Star Computer, Inc.
2312 Central Ave., NE
Minneapolis, MN 55418
800-950-8884; 612-788-1404
fax: 612-788-3442
Technical support: 800-950-8894

Bondwell Industrial Co., Inc.
47485 Seabridge Dr.
Fremont, CA 94538
510-490-4300
fax: 510-490-5897
Technical support: 800-288-4388

Broadax Systems, Inc. (BSI)
9440 Telstar Ave., Ste. 4
El Monte, CA 91731
800-872-4547; 818-442-0020
fax: 818-442-4527

BRYSIS Data, Inc.
17431 E. Gale Ave.
City of Industry, CA 91748
818-810-0355
fax: 818-810-4555

BSM Corp.
1355 Glenville Dr.
Richardson, TX 75081
800-888-3475
fax: 214-699-8404

Burham Computer Center
908 E. Main St.
Alhambra, CA 91801
818-570-0396
fax: 818-570-0936

Burr-Brown Corp.
P.O. Box 11400
Tucson, AZ 85734
800-548-6132; 602-746-1111
fax: 602-741-3895
Cache Computers, Inc.

46714 Fremont Blvd.
Fremont, CA 94538
510-226-9922
fax: 510-226-9911

Caliber Computer Corp.
1500 McCandless Dr.
Milpitas, CA 95035
408-942-1220
fax: 408-942-1345

Canon U.S.A., Inc.
One Canon Plaza
Lake Success, NY 11042
516-488-6700
fax: 516-354-5805
Technical support: 800-423-2366

Cardinal Technologies, Inc.
1827 Freedom Rd.
Lancaster, PA 17601
717-293-3000
fax: 717-293-3055
Technical support: 717-293-3124

CBM Associates, Inc.
1500 Jerusalem Ave.
North Merrick, NY 11566
516-483-5300
fax: 516-483-3924

CDS Systems, Inc.
14050 21st Ave., N
Minneapolis, MN 55447-4686
612-559-7459

Chaplet Systems, Inc.
252 N. Wolf Rd.
Sunnyvale, CA 94086
408-732-7950
fax: 408-732-6050

Chaumont & Associates
805 Bayou Pines, Ste. A
Lake Charles, LA 70601
800-673-2271; 318-436-2294

Northgate Computer Systems, Inc.
7075 Flying Cloud Dr.
Eden Prairie, MN 55344
800-243-3824
fax: 612-943-8790

Chicony America, Inc.
3002 Dow Ave., Ste. 122
Tustin, CA 92680
fax: 714-573-0673
Technical support: 714-380-0928

Clone Technologies, Inc.
1213 Bittersweet Rd.
Lake Ozark, MO 65049
314-365-2050
fax: 314-365-2080

CNet Technology, Inc.
2199 Zanker Rd.
San Jose, CA 95131
408-954-8000
fax: 408-954-8866

Colby Systems Corp.
2991 Alexis Dr.
Palo Alto, CA 94304
415-941-9090
fax: 415-949-1019

Comex Computer Corp.
3450 S. Broadmont, Ste. 110
Tucson, AZ 85713
800-826-9577; 602-792-3609

Commax Technologies, Inc.
2031 Concourse Dr.
San Jose, CA 95131
800-526-6629; 408-435-5000
fax: 408-435-5005

Commodore Business Machines, Inc.
(Computer Systems Division)
1200 Wilson Dr.
Brandywine Industrial Park
West Chester, PA 19380
215-431-9100
fax: 215-431-9156

Compaq Computer Corp.
P.O. Box 692000
Houston, TX 77269-2000
800-231-0900; 713-370-0670
fax: 713-374-1402
Technical support: 800-345-1518

CompuAdd Corp.
12317 Technology Blvd.
Austin, TX 78727
800-531-5475; 512-250-1489
fax: 512-250-5760
Technical support: 800-999-9901

DIRECTORY OF MANUFACTURERS

Compudyne, Inc.
15167 Business Ave.
Dallas, TX 75244
800-932-2667; 214-888-5700
fax: 214-888-5742
Technical Support: 800-447-3895

Compulan Technology, Inc.
1630 Oakland Rd.
San Jose, CA 95131
408-922-6888
fax: 408-954-8299

CompUSER, Inc.
15151A Surveyor
Addison, TX 75244
800-932-COMP; 214-484-8500
fax: 214-702-0300

Computer Creations, Inc.
88 Westpark Rd.
Dayton, OH 45459
513-438-2777

Computer Expo Superstore, Inc.
11312 Westheimer Rd.
Houston, TX 77077
800-229-3976; 713-531-0990
fax: 713-496-4600

Computer Extension Systems, Inc.
16850 Titan Dr.
Houston, TX 77058
800-562-1699; 713-488-8830
fax: 713-488-7631

Computer Peripherals, Inc.
667 Rancho Conejo Blvd.
Newbury Park, CA 91320
800-854-7600; 805-499-5751
fax: 805-498-8848
Technical support: 800-235-7618

Computer Products Corp.
14315 S. Cherry Vale Rd.
Boulder, CO 80303
800-338-4273; 303-442-4747
fax: 303-442-7985
Technical support: Use main number

Computer Systems Corp.
205 W. Grand Ave., Ste. 112
Bensenville, IL 60106
800-284-7746; 708-860-5807

Computop, Inc.
14634 Firestone Blvd.
La Mirada, CA 90638
714-994-0605
fax: 714-994-0658

CompuTrend
1306 John Reed Court
City of Industry, CA 91745
818-333-5121
fax: 818-369-6803

Comtek Solutions, Inc.
2316 NorthWest 23rd St.
Oklahoma City, OK 73107
800-767-0668; 405-524-0668
fax: 405-525-9154

Continental Resources, Inc.
175 Middlesex Tpke., P.O. Box 9137
Bedford, MA 01730
800-937-4688; 617-275-0850
fax: 617-275-6563

Continental Technology, Inc.
300 McGaw Dr.
Edison, NJ 08837
908-255-1166
fax: 908-225-8999

Copam Electronics Corp.
45875 Northport Loop East
Fremont, CA 94538
800-326-4567; 510-623-8911
fax: 510-623-8551

Cordata Technologies, Inc.
1055 W. Victoria St.
Compton, CA 90220
800-233-3602; 800-524-2671 (in California);
310-603-2901
fax: 310-763-0447

Corman Technologies, Inc.
75 Bathurst Dr.
Waterloo, Ontario
Canada N2V 1N2
519-884-4430
fax: 519-884-0204

CSS Laboratories, Inc.
1641 McGaw Ave.
Irvine, CA 92714
714-852-8161
fax: 714-852-9464

C2 Micro Systems, Inc.
47448 Fremont Blvd.
Fremont, CA 94538
510-683-8888
fax: 510-683-8893

CTXT Systems, Inc.
9205 Alabama Ave., Ste. E
Chatsworth, CA 91311
800-872-2898; 800-438-2898 (in California);
818-341-4227

CUBE Computer Corp.
150 Clearbrook Rd.
Elmsford, NY 10523
800-522-2823; 914-592-8282
fax: 914-592-3482

CUI
1680 Civic Center Dr. #101
Santa Clara, CA 95050
800-458-6686; 408-241-9170
fax: 408-241-2487

Cyber Research, Inc.
25 Business Park Dr.
Banford, CT 06405
800-341-2525; 203-483-8815
fax: 203-483-9024

D.A.P. Technologies
5401 W. Kennedy Blvd., Ste. 480
Tampa, FL 33609
800-363-1993
fax: 813-969-3334

Darius Technology, Ltd.
2808 Ingleton Ave.
Burnaby, BC
Canada V5C 6G7
604-436-1027
fax: 604-436-0882

Data General Corp.
4400 Computer Dr.
Westboro, MA 01580
800-328-2436; 508-366-8911
fax: 508-366-1299
Technical support: 800-537-6084

Data Technology Products
P.O. Box 3497
Costa Mesa, CA 92628
800-336-7060; 714-650-7060
fax: 714-650-0346

Datalux Corp.
2836 Cessna Dr.
Winchester, VA 22601
800-328-2589; 703-662-1500
fax: 703-662-1682

Datavue
One Meca Way
Norcross, GA 30093-2919
404-564-5555
fax: 404-564-5528

Dauphin Technology, Inc.
1125 E. St. Charles Rd.
Lombard, IL 60148
800-782-7922; 708-627-4004
fax: 708-627-7618
Technical support: Use main number

DCS/Fortis
1820 West 220th St., Ste 220
Torrance, CA 90501
800-736-4847; 310-782-6090
fax: 310-782-6134

Decision Data
One Progress Ave.
Horsham, PA 19044
800-523-5357; 215-674-3300
fax: 215-675-1931

Dee Van Enterprise USA, Inc.
3817 Spinnaker Court
Fremont, CA 94538
800-878-0691; 510-623-0628
fax: 510-623-0529

Dell Computer Corp.
9505 Arboretum Blvd.
Austin, TX 78759-7299
800-426-5150; 512-338-4400
fax: 512-338-8421
Technical support: 800-624-9896

DerbyTech Computers, Inc.
718 15th Ave.
East Moline, IL 61244
800-24-DERBY; 309-755-2662

DFI, Inc.
2544 Port St.
Sacramento, CA 95691
916-373-1234
fax: 916-373-0221
Technical support: Use main number

Diamond Micro Solutions
1615 Alvarado St.
San Leandro, CA 94577
800-366-4367; 510-351-4700
fax: 510-352-1089

Digital Equipment Corp.
146 Main St.
Maynard, MA 01754-2571
508-493-5111
fax: 508-493-8780
Technical support: 800-332-8000

Digital Technology Exchange
1800 Penn St., Ste.1
Melbourne, FL 32901
407-728-0172
fax: 407-722-2216

Computers

Dolch Computer Systems
372 Turquoise St.
Milpitas, CA 95035
800-538-7506; 408-957-6575
fax: 408-263-6305
Technical support: Use main number

DTK Computer, Inc.
17700 Castleton St., Ste. 160
City of Industry, CA 91748
818-810-8880
fax: 818-810-5233
Technical support: 818-810-0098

Dyna Micro, Inc.
30 W. Montague Expy.
San Jose, CA 95134
800-336-DYNA; 408-943-0100
fax: 408-943-0714

Dynamic Decisions, Inc.
134 West 26th St.
New York, NY 10001
800-869-9888; 212-242-0108

Edge Technologies, Inc.
47963 Warm Springs Blvd.
Fremont, CA 94539
510-249-1999
fax: 510-490-3966

ELCO Computers
215 S. Raymond Ave.
Alhambra, CA 91803
818-284-3281
fax: 818-284-4871

Eltech Research, Inc.
47266 Benicia St.
Fremont, CA 94538
510-438-0990
fax: 510-438-0663

Emerald Computers
16100 S.W. 72nd Ave.
Portland, OR 97224
503-620-6094

EMPAC International Corp.
47448 Fremont Blvd.
Fremont, CA 94538
510-683-8800
fax: 510-683-8662

Engineering Systems, Inc.
1511 Natalie Lane
Ann Arbor, MI 48105
313-668-8154

EPS Technologies, Inc.
P.O. Box 278
Jefferson, SD 57038
800-447-0921; 605-966-5586
fax: 605-966-5482

Epson America, Inc.
20770 Madrona Ave.
Torrance, CA 90509-2842
800-289-3776; 310-782-0770
Technical support: 800-922-8911

Ergo Computing, Inc.
One Intercontinental Way
Peabody, MA 01960
800-633-1925

Everex Systems, Inc.
48431 Milmont Dr.
Fremont, CA 94538
800-821-0806; 510-498-1111
fax: 510-651-0728
Technical support: 510-498-4411

Evergreen Systems, Inc.
120 Landing Ct., Ste.A
Novato, CA 94945
415-897-8888
fax: 415-897-6158

Expo Tech Computers
800 N. Church St.
Lake Zurich, IL 60047
800-284-3976
fax: 800-947-3976

Federal Data Corp.
4800 Hampden Lane, Ste. 1100
Bethesda, MD 20814
301-986-0800
fax: 301-961-3892

Fifth Force (ELLO Computers)
229 S. Raymond Ave.
Alhambra, CA 91803
818-281-6956
fax: 818-281-3449

First Computer Systems, Inc.
3951 Pleasantdale Rd., Ste. 224
Atlanta, GA 30340
800-325-1911; 404-441-1911
fax: 404-441-1856
Technical support: 404-447-8324

First International Computer of America, Inc.
980A Mission Ct.
Fremont, CA 94539
510-252-7777

Flash Technology, Inc.
55 W. Hoover Ave., Ste. 9
Mesa, AZ 85210
800-448-2031; 602-464-9272
fax: 602-464-9856

Flytech Technology (U.S.A.), Inc.
3008 Scott Blvd.
Santa Clara, CA 95054
408-727-7373
fax: 408-727-7375

Fora, Inc.
3081 N. First St.
San Jose, CA 95134
408-944-0393
fax: 408-944-0392

Fountain Technologies, Inc.
12K Worlds Fair Dr.
Somerset, NJ 08873
908-563-4800
fax: 908-563-4999

Franklin Datacom
733 Lakefield Rd.
Westlake Village, CA 91361
805-373-8688
fax: 805-373-7373

FutureTech Systems, Inc.
Six Bridge St., Bridge Plaza
Hackensack, NJ 07601
800-275-4414; 201-488-4414
fax: 201-488-4405

Gateway 2000
610 Gateway Dr.
North Sioux City, SD 57049
800-523-2000; 605-232-2000
fax: 605-232-2023
Technical support: 800-248-2031

GCH Systems, Inc.
777 E. Middlefield Rd.
Mountain View, CA 94043
800-366-4560; 415-968-3400
fax: 415-964-9747

GEM Computer Products
3624 Pierce Rd.
Bakersfield, CA 93308
805-323-0707
fax: 805-323-9747

GenTech
205 Hallene Rd.
Warwick, RI 02886
800-444-3683; 401-732-5556
fax: 401-732-5518

GoldStar Technology, Inc.
1000 Sylvan Ave.
Englewood Cliffs, NJ 07632
201-816-2000
fax: 201-816-0636
Technical support: 800-777-1192

GST, Inc.
17707 Valley View Ave.
Cerritos, CA 90701
800-821-2792; 714-739-0106
fax: 714-670-6404

GVC Technologies, Inc.
376 Lafayette Rd.
Sparta, NJ 07871
800-289-4821; 201-579-3630
fax: 201-579-2702
Technical support: Use main number

Heath Co.
P.O. Box 1288
Benton Harbor, MI 49022
800-253-0570; 616-925-6000
fax: 616-925-4876

Hertz Computer Corp.
325 Fifth Ave.
New York, NY 10016
800-232-8737; 212-684-4141
fax: 212-684-3685

Hewlett-Packard Co.
3000 Hanover St.
Palo Alto, CA 94304
800-752-0900; 415-857-1501
Technical support: Use 800 number

HiQuality Systems, Inc.
740 N. Mary Ave.
Sunnyvale, CA 94086
800-827-5836; 408-245-5836

Husky Computers, Inc.
13921 ICOT Blvd.
Clearwater, FL 34620
813-530-4141
fax: 813-536-9906

Hyundai Electronics America
166 Baypointe Pkwy.
San Jose, CA 95134
408-473-9200
fax: 408-943-9567
Technical support: 800-234-3553

i Corp Computers, Inc.
398 Columbus Ave., Ste. 395
Boston, MA 02116-6008
617-424-7080
fax: 617-345-9632

DIRECTORY OF MANUFACTURERS

IBM (International Business Machines)
Old Orchard Rd.
Armonk, NY 10504
800-426-2468; 914-765-1900
Technical support: Use 800 number

ICL Business Systems
9801 Muirlands Blvd.
Irvine, CA 92718
714-458-7282
fax: 714-458-6257

Identity Systems Technology, Inc.
1235 W. Trinity Mills Rd.
Carrollton, TX 75006
800-723-8258;
fax: 214-446-8062

IMC Computer, Inc.
11160 Shelton Ct.
Houston, TX 77099
713-561-8857

Infomatic Power Systems Corp.
9832 Alburtis Ave.
Santa Fe Springs, CA 90670
310-948-2217
fax: 310-948-5264

Insight Computers
1912 West 4th St.
Tempe, AZ 85281
800-776-7600; 602-350-1176
fax: 602-829-9193
Technical support: 800-488-0007

Intelligence Technology Corp.
P.O. Box 671125
Dallas, TX 75367
214-250-4277

Intelligent MicroSystems
1633 Babcock, Ste. 424
San Antonio, TX 78229
800-777-7757

International Instrumentation, Inc.
2282 Townsgate Rd.
Westlake Village, CA 91361
800-543-DISK; 800-346-DISK (in
California); 818-991-9614
fax: 805-379-0701

**International Systems Marketing, Inc.
(ISM)**
943 A Russell Avenue
Gaithersburg, MD 20879
301-670-1813

Isotropic Computer, Inc.
East 5920 Seltice Way
Post Falls, ID 83854
208-667-1447
fax: 208-765-8130

Iverson Computer Corp.
1356 Beverly Rd., P.O. Box 6250
McLean, VA 22106-6250
703-749-1200
fax: 703-893-2396
Technical support: 800-677-7881

Jade Computer Products, Inc.
4901 W. Rosecrans Ave., Box 5046
Hawthorne, CA 90251-5046
800-421-5500; 800-262-1710 (in California)
fax: 310-675-2522

Jameco Electronics
1355 Shoreway Rd.
Belmont, CA 94002
415-592-8097
fax: 415-592-2503

Jawin Computer Products
565 W. Lambert, Ste. C
Brea, CA 92621
800-543-5107; 714-990-2097

JC Information Systems
44036 S. Grimmer
Fremont, CA 94538
510-659-8440
fax: 510-659-8449

Jetta International, Inc.
51 Stouts Lane, Ste. 3
Monmouth Junction, NJ 08852
800-445-3882; 908-329-9651
fax: 908-329-0105

Jinco Computers, Inc.
5122 Walnut Grove Ave.
San Gabriel, CA 91776
818-309-1108
fax: 818-309-1107

Join Data Systems, Inc.
14838 Valley Blvd., Ste. C
City of Industry, CA 91746
818-330-6553
fax: 818-330-6865

Kanix, Inc.
13111 Brooks Dr., Ste. F
Baldwin Park, CA 91706
818-814-3997
fax: 818-814-0248

Keydata International, Inc.
111 Corporate Blvd.
South Plainfield, NJ 07080
800-486-4800; 908-755-0350
fax: 908-756-7359
Technical Support: 800-756-7410

KFC Computek Components Corp.
31 E. Mall
Plainview, NY 11803
516-454-0262
fax: 516-454-0265

KISS Computer Corp.
2604 Washington Rd.
Kenosha, WI 53140-2375
800-GET-KISS; 414-652-5477

KRIS Technologies
260 E. Grand Ave.
South San Francisco, CA 94080
800-282-5747; 415-875-6729
fax: 415-877-8048
Technical support: Use main number

Laguna Systems, Inc.
731 E. Ball Rd., Ste. 101
Anaheim, CA 92805
714-758-9943

Leading Edge Products, Inc.
117 Flanders Rd.
Westboro, MA 01581-5020
800-874-3340; 508-836-4800
fax: 508-836-4501
Technical support: 900-370-4800

Link Computer, Inc.
560 S. Melrose St.
Placentia, CA 92670
818-968-8668
fax: 714-993-0705

Linus Technologies, Inc.
11130 Sunrise Valley Dr.
Reston, VA 22091
703-476-1500
fax: 703-264-0389

LONGSHINE Technology, Inc.
2013 N. Capitol Ave.
San Jose, CA 95132
408-942-1746
fax: 408-942-1745

LSE Electronics, Inc.
77 W. Nicholai St.
Hicksville, NY 11801
516-931-1670
fax: 516-931-2565

Lucky Computers
1701 N. Greenville, Ste. 602
Richardson, TX 75081
214-690-6110
Technical support: 800-966-5825

L&W MicroComputing Corp.
278 D W Hwy.
Nashua, NH 03060
800-882-7830; 603-888-8288
fax: 603-888-8289

Mag Computronic (USA) Inc.
17845-E Skypark Circle
Irvine, CA 92714
714-927-3998
fax: 714-827-5522

Magitronic Technology, Inc.
10 Hub Dr.
Melville, NY 11747
516-454-8255
fax: 516-454-8268

Mandax Computer, Inc.
14935 Northeast 95th St.
Redmond, WA 98052
206-867-1973

Marathon Computers
4915 Prospect, NE
Albuquerque, NM 87110
800-525-8363; 505-881-0077
fax: 505-889-9575

Martec Associates, Inc.
1510 Jarvis Ave.
Elk Grove Village, IL 60007
708-956-8090

Mascot Computer Corp.
42-20 College Point Blvd.
Flushing, NY 11355
718-321-1944
fax: 718-321-0136

Master Computer, Inc.
10742 5th Ave., NE
Seattle, WA 98125
206-365-1156

Matrix Digital Products, Inc.
1811 N. Keystone St.
Burbank, CA 91504
800-227-5723; 818-566-8567
fax: 818-566-1476

Computers

Maxtron
1825A Durfee Ave.
South El Monte, CA 91733
800-266-5706; 818-350-5706
fax: 818-350-4965

ME—Micro Express
1801 E. Carnegie Ave.
Santa Ana, CA 92705
800-989-9900; 714-852-1400
fax: 714-852-1225
Technical support: 800-762-3378

Mead Computer Corp.
1000 Nevada Hwy., Ste. 101
Boulder City, NV 89005
800-654-7762; 702-294-0204
fax: 702-294-1168

Mega Computer Systems
16980 Via Tazon
San Diego, CA 92127
619-487-8888
fax: 619-485-1518

Megadata Corp.
35 Orville Dr.
Bohemia, NY 11716-2598
800-634-2827; 516-589-6800
fax: 516-589-6858

Memorex Telex Corp.
6422 East 41st St.
Tulsa, OK 74135
800-950-3465; 918-627-1111
fax: 918-624-4581
Technical support: Use main number

Metra Information Systems, Inc.
657 Pastoria Ave.
Sunnyvale, CA 94086
800-733-9188; 408-730-9188
fax: 408-730-5933

Micro Base Technologies
3000 Scott Blvd., Ste. 203
Santa Clara, CA 95054
800-345-4479; 408-727-6276
fax: 408-727-7307

Micro Experts
2055 Beaver Ruin Rd.
Norcross, GA 30071
404-368-9176

Micro Express
1801 E. Carnegie Ave.
Santa Ana, CA 92705
800-642-7621; 714-852-1400
fax: 714-852-1225
Technical support: 800-762-3378

Micro 1 Inc.
557 Howard St.
San Francisco, CA 94105
800-338-4061; 415-974-5439

Micro Palm Computers
13773-500 ICOT Blvd.
Clearwater, FL 34620
813-530-0128
fax: 813-530-0738

Micro Smart, Inc.
200 Homer Ave.
Ashland, MA 01721
800-333-8841; 508-872-9090
fax: 508-881-1520

Micro-Technology Concepts, Inc.
258 Johnson Ave.
Brooklyn, NY 11206
800-366-4860; 718-456-9100
fax: 718-456-1200

Micro Telesis, Inc.
1260 A Logan Ave., Ste. A2
Costa Mesa, CA 92626
714-557-2003
fax: 714-557-9729

Microage-Bay Area Computers
130 Sansome St.
San Francisco, CA 94104
800-233-2778; 415-393-9600
fax: 415-393-9640

Micronics Computers, Inc.
232 E. Warren Ave.
Fremont, CA 94539
800-234-4386; 510-651-2300
fax: 510-651-5612
Technical support: Use main number

MicroServe Corp.
2504 BuildAmerica Dr.
Hampton, VA 23666
804-827-1604
fax: 804-827-7464

MicroSlate, Inc.
9625 Ignace St., Ste. D
Brossard, Quebec
Canada J4Y 2P3
514-444-3680
fax: 514-444-3683

Microsystems Group
2500 W. Higgins Rd., Ste. 450
Hoffman Estates, IL 60195
708-882-5666

Microwriter, Inc.
1101 N. Elm St., Ste. 1002
Greensboro, NC 27401
919-274-6040
fax: 919-274-6022

Midern Computer, Inc.
18005 Cortney Court
City of Industry, CA 91748
800-669-1624; 818-964-8682
fax: 818-964-2381

Mini-Micro Supply Co., Inc.
2050 Corporate Court
San Jose, CA 95131
800-628-3656; 408-456-9500
fax: 408-434-9242

Minta Technologies Co.
11 Deerpark Dr., Ste. 116, Princeton Corp. Plaza IV
Monmouth Junction, NJ 08852
800-82-MINTA; 908-329-2020
fax: 908-329-2219

Mitsuba Corp.
1925 Wright Ave.
La Verne, CA 91750
800-648-7822; 714-392-2000
fax: 714-392-2021
Technical support: 714-392-2019 (Laptop);
714-392-2018 (Desktop)

Mitsubishi Electronics America, Inc.
991 Knox St.
Torrance, CA 90502
800-556-1234, ext. 54M; 800-441-2345, ext. 54M (in California); 310-515-3993
fax: 310-527-7693
Technical support: Use main number

Modgraph, Inc.
83 Second Ave.
Burlington, MA 01803
800-327-9962; 617-938-4488
fax: 617-272-3062

MSO Computers, Inc.
463 Montague Expwy.
Milpitas, CA 95035
800-YES-4-MSO; 408-945-4270
fax: 408-945-1742

M2 Lab
315 Cloverleaf Dr., Ste. 1D
Baldwin Park, CA 91706
818-968-0643
fax: 818-968-8848

Multi Connection Technology
3518 Arden Rd.
Hayward, CA 94545
510-670-0633
fax: 510-670-0790

Multi-Pal International, Inc.
17231 E. Railroad St., Ste. 500
City of Industry, CA 91748
818-913-4188
fax: 818-912-9149

Myoda, Inc.
1053 Shore Rd.
Naperville, IL 60563
800-562-1071; 708-369-5199
fax: 708-369-6068

National Computer
9823 Mira Mesa Blvd.
San Diego, CA 92131
619-530-2446

NCR Corp.
1700 S. Patterson Blvd.
Dayton, OH 45479
513-445-5000
fax: 513-445-2008
Technical support: 800-CALL-NCR

NEC Technologies, Inc.
1414 Massachusetts Ave.
Boxborough, MA 01719
800-826-2255; 508-264-8000
fax: 508-264-8673
Technical support: 508-264-4300

Neotech Systems
8125 Catalpa, Ste. A
El Paso, TX 79925
915-779-1722

Netis Technology Inc.
1544 Century Pointe Dr.
Milpitas, CA 95035
408-263-0368

Network & Communication Technology, Inc.
24 Wampum Rd.
Park Ridge, NJ 07656
201-307-9000
fax: 201-307-9404

DIRECTORY OF MANUFACTURERS

The Network Connection, Inc.
1324 Union Hill Rd.
Alpharetta, GA 30201
800-327-4853; 404-751-0889
fax: 404-751-1884

Network Interface Corp.
15019 West 95th St.
Lenexa, KS 66215
800-343-2853; 913-894-2277
fax: 913-894-0226

New MMI Corp.
2400 Reach Rd.
Williamsport, PA 17701
800-221-4283; 717-327-9575
fax: 717-327-1217

Norand Corp.
550 Second St., SE
Cedar Rapids, IA 52401
800-553-5971; 319-369-3100

Northgate Computer Systems, Inc.
P.O. Box 59080
Minneapolis, MN 55459-0080
800-548-1993; 612-361-5000
fax: 612-943-8336
Technical support: 800-446-5037

NoteStar
5A Joanna Court
East Brunswick, NJ 08816
908-254-0555
fax: 908-254-5218

Novacor, Inc.
1841 Zanker Rd.
San Jose, CA 95112
800-486-6682; 408-441-6500
fax: 408-441-6811

Nycom Technologies Distribution, Inc.
3 Riverview Dr.
Somerset, NJ 08873
908-469-7800
fax: 908-757-6334
Technical support: 800-477-8776

Oak Microsystems, Ltd.
13 Technology Dr.
Setauket, NY 11733
516-434-7001
fax: 516-689-6081

Ocean Interface Co.
515 Spanish Lane
Walnut, CA 91789-3042
909-595-1212
fax: 714-595-9683

Octave Systems, Inc.
1715 Dell Ave.
Campbell, CA 95008
408-866-8424
fax: 408-866-4252

Olivetti USA
P.O. Box 6945, 765 U.S. Hwy. 202, S
Bridgewater, NJ 08807-0945
800-527-2960; 908-526-8200
fax: 908-526-8405
Technical support: 908-704-6501

Omnidata International, Inc.
750 West 200 North, P.O. Box 3489
Logan, UT 84321
801-753-7760
fax: 801-753-6756

ONYX Computer, Inc.
30799 Pinetree Rd., Ste. 303
Cleveland, OH 44124
800-486-5005; 216-591-0489

Osicom Technologies, Inc.
198 Green Pond Rd.
Rockaway, NJ 07866
800-922-0881; 310-315-4979
fax: 201-586-9740

Pacific Computer
9945 Lower Azusa
Temple City, CA 91780
800-346-7207; 800-421-1102 (California);
818-442-9112

**Panasonic Communications & Systems Co.
(Office Automation Group)**
2 Panasonic Way
Secaucus, NJ 07094
201-348-7000
Technical support: 800-222-0584

Pan-United Corp.
2 Ethel Rd., Ste. 203B,
Durham Business Center
Edison, NJ 08817
908-424-2212
fax: 908-248-0498

Paravant Computer Systems
305 East Dr.
Melbourne, FL 32904
800-848-8529; 407-727-3672
fax: 407-725-0496

PC Brand, Inc.
954 W. Washington St.
Chicago, IL 60607
800-722-7263; 312-226-5200
fax: 312-226-6841
Technical support: Use 800 number

PC & C Research Corp.
1100 Avenida Acaso
Camarillo, CA 93012
800-843-1239; 805-484-1685
fax: 805-987-8088

PC Craft, Inc.
640 Puente St.
Brea, CA 92621
800-733-6666; 909-869-6133
fax: 714-256-5025

PC Designs, Inc.
2504 N. Hemlock Circle
Broken Arrow, OK 74012
800-322-4872; 918-251-5550
fax: 918-251-7057

PC-Ease, Inc.
67 Melrose Rd.
Amherst, NY 14221
716-626-0315

PC Link Corp.
29 West 38th St.
New York, NY 10018
800-221-0343; 212-213-0050
fax: 212-221-7132

PC MAX
8025 Deering Ave.
Canoga Park, CA 91304
818-888-8880
fax: 818-888-5309

PC-Plus Technologies
Loft Plaza, 65 Southbridge St.
Auburn, MA 01501
800-422-4947; 508-831-9826
fax: 508-799-9941

PC Time Data
43038 Christy St.
Fremont, CA 94538
800-878-3868; 510-623-8862
fax: 510-623-8865

PCA Personal Computer Associates, Inc.
85 Chambers Dr., Ste. 7
Ajax, ON, CD L1Z 1E2
800-263-7535; 905-427-6612
fax: 416-427-0934

PCI Systems, Inc.
5690 Sonoma Dr. Ste. D
Pleasanton, CA 94566
510-484-2818
fax: 510-484-3088

Philips Consumer Electronics Co.
One Philips Dr., P.O. Box 14810
Knoxville, TN 37914-1810
615-521-4316
fax: 615-521-4406
Technical support: 800-722-6224

Philips Information Systems Co.
1435 Bradley Lane, Ste. 100
Carrollton, TX 75007
800-527-0204; 214-323-8238
fax: 214-991-6572

Polywell Computers, Inc.
61-C Airport Blvd.
South San Francisco, CA 94080
800-999-1278; 415-583-7222
fax: 415-583-1974

Poqet Computer Corp.
5200 Patrick Henry Dr.
Santa Clara, CA 95054
800-624-8999; 408-982-9500
Technical support: 408-764-9400

Positive Corp.
P.O. Box 2101
Chatsworth, CA 91313-2101
800-452-6345; 800-252-6345 (in California);
818-341-5400

Precision Systems Group
3728-48 Phillips Hwy.
Jacksonville, FL 32207
800-326-4774

Premier Computer Innovations
10310 Harwin Dr.
Houston, TX 77036
800-347-1777; 713-995-4433
fax: 713-995-4751

President Micro Systems Corp.
1300 Pioneer, Ste. C
Brea, CA 92621
213-691-1553
fax: 213-691-2151

Primax Data Products
52 Bramwin Court
Brampton, Ontario
Canada L6T 5G2
905-792-7330
fax: 905-792-6537

Computers

Private Label PCs, Inc.
1356 Beverly Rd.
McLean, VA 22101
800-666-PVLB; 703-790-4690
fax: 703-893-2396

Proteus Technology Corp.
377 Rt. 17, S, Airport Center
Hasbrouck Hgts., NJ 07604
800-878-6427; 201-288-2041
fax: 201-288-2045

Proton Corp.
5630 Cerritos Ave.
Cypress, CA 90630
714-952-6900

PSION, Inc.
118 Echo Lake Rd.
Watertown, CT 06795
800-548-4535; 508-371-0310
fax: 203-274-7976

QANTEL Business Systems, Inc.
4142 Point Eden Way
Hayward, CA 94545-3781
800-227-1894; 510-887-7777
fax: 510-782-6195

QIC Research, Inc.
3401 W. Warren Ave.
Fremont, CA 94539
510-623-2050

QSI Corp.
95 Rockwell Place
Brooklyn, NY 11217
718-834-4545
fax: 718-834-5318

Quadrant Components
4378 Enterprise St.
Fremont, CA 94538
510-656-9988
fax: 510-656-2208

Quick Technology Corp.
1642 McGaw Ave.
Irvine, CA 92714
714-660-4948
fax: 714-660-8809

Quill Corp.
P.O. Box 4700
Lincolnshire, IL 60197-4700
708-634-4800
fax: 708-634-5708
Technical support: 708-634-6650

Qume Corp.
500 Yosemite Dr.
Milpitas, CA 95035
408-942-4000
fax: 408-942-4052
Technical support: 408-942-4138 (Monitors, Terminals); 408-942-4100 (Printers)

Racore Computer Products, Inc.
170 Knowles Dr., Ste. 204
Los Gatos, CA 95030
800-635-1274; 408-374-8290
fax: 408-374-6653

Radix II, Inc.
(Sophos Integrated Systems Division)
6230 Oxon Hill Rd.
Oxon Hill, MD 20745
800-334-SISI; 301-567-5200
fax: 301-839-0836

RALPH Associates
305 Wilson Rd.
Cherry Hill, NJ 08002

Reason Technology
290 Coon Rapids Blvd.
Minneapolis, MN 55433
800-800-4860; 612-780-4792; 612-780-4797

Recortec, Inc.
1290 Lawrence Station Rd.
Sunnyvale, CA 94089
800-729-7654; 408-734-1290
fax: 408-734-2140

Reply Corp.
4435 Fortran Dr.
San Jose, CA 95134
800-955-5BY5; 408-942-4804
fax: 408-942-4897
Technical support: Use 800 number

Republic Technology Corp.
1161 Headway Circle, Bldg. 3
Austin, TX 78754
800-622-2177; 512-834-2222
fax: 512-834-1111

Research, Development & Innovations, Inc.
6696 Mesa Ridge Rd., Bldg. A
San Diego, CA 92121
619-944-6381
fax: 619-558-4720

Rio Computers
8900 San Pedro, Ste. 127
San Antonio, TX 78216
512-878-7774
fax: 512-828-1155

SAI Systems Laboratories, Inc.
911 Bridgeport Ave.
Shelton, CT 06484
800-331-0488; 203-929-0790
fax: 203-929-6948

St. Croix Computer Corp.
6640 Shady Oak Rd., 3rd Fl.
Eden Prairie, MN 55344
800-950-0174; 612-943-8618
fax: 612-943-3854

Sampo Corp. of America
(Industrial Products Division)
5550 Peachtree Industrial Blvd.
Norcross, GA 30071
404-449-6220
fax: 404-447-1109

Samsung Information Systems America, Inc.
3655 N. First St.
San Jose, CA 95134-1708
800-446-0262; 408-434-5400
fax: 408-434-5653
Technical support: Use main number

Sanyo Business Systems Corp.
(Computer Division)
51 Joseph St.
Moonachie, NJ 07074
800-524-0047; 818-998-7322
fax: 201-440-1775
Technical support: Use main number

Scantech Computer Systems, Inc.
12981 Ramona Blvd., Units H&I
Irwindale, CA 91706
818-960-2999
fax: 818-962-4819

Scenario, Inc.
260 Franklin St., Ste. 520
Boston, MA 02110
617-439-6611
fax: 617-439-6644

SCI/Fortune
2000 Ringwood Ave.
San Jose, CA 95131
800-443-7072; 408-943-6200
fax: 408-943-6249

Semi-Tech Microcomputers, Ltd.
131 McNabb St.
Markham, Ontario
Canada L3R 5V7
905-475-2670
fax: 905-475-1552

SF Micro, Inc.
1143 Post St.
San Francisco, CA 94109
800-237-5631; 415-929-1505
fax: 415-922-1187

Sharp Electronics Corp.
(Professional Products Division)
Sharp Plaza, P.O. Box 650
Mahwah, NJ 07430
201-529-8200
fax: 201-529-9636
Technical support: 800-732-8221

Sherwood/Kimtron
4181 Business Center Dr.
Fremont, CA 94538-6355
800-777-8755; 510-623-8900
fax: 510-623-8945

Siemens Nixdorf Information Systems, Inc.
200 Wheeler Rd.
Burlington, MA 01803
800-225-1484; 617-273-0480
fax: 617-221-0231
Technical support: Use main number

SIIG, Inc.
5369 Randall Place
Fremont, CA 94538
510-657-0567
fax: 510-657-5962

Silicon Electronics
3350 Scott Blvd., Ste. 1201
Santa Clara, CA 95054
408-738-8235
fax: 408-988-4431

Sirex U.S.A., Inc.
132-14 11th Ave.
College Point, NY 11356
800-722-0404; 718-746-7500
fax: 718-746-0882

Softworks Development Corp.
5985 N. Lilly Rd.
Menomonee Falls, WI 53051
800-332-3475; 414-252-2020

Soyo USA, Inc.
148 Eighth Ave., Ste. H
City of Industry, CA 91746
818-330-1712
fax: 818-968-4161

SST—Sirus Systems Technology, Inc.
4344 Young St.
Pasadena, TX 77504
800-424-0724; 713-946-0724
fax: 713-946-5451

DIRECTORY OF MANUFACTURERS

Standard Computer Corp.
12803 Schabarum Ave.
Irwindale, CA 91706
818-338-4668
Technical support: 800-662-6111

Sun Moon Star
(North America Personal Computer
Division)
1941 Ringwood Ave.
San Jose, CA 95131
800-545-4SUN; 408-452-7811
fax: 408-452-1411

SunnyTech, Inc.
17 Smith St., Ste. 7
Englewood, NJ 07631
800-367-1132; 201-569-7773
fax: 201-569-6279

Suntronics, Inc.
12603 Crenshaw Blvd.
Hawthorne, CA 90250
800-545-9777; 310-644-1140

Super Computer, Inc.
17910 S. Adria Maru Lane
Carson, CA 90746
310-532-2133
fax: 310-532-6342

Swan Technologies
3075 Research Dr.
State College, PA 16801
800-468-9044; 814-238-1820
fax: 814-237-4450
Technical support: 800-468-7926

Syntax Manufacturing Co.
5680 Bandini Blvd.
Bell, CA 90201
800-552-8900; 310-262-1300
fax: 310-261-1300

Syntrex, Inc. (Network Systems Division)
246 Industrial Way, W
Eatontown, NJ 07724
800-526-2829; 908-919-1500
fax: 908-542-3957

Sys Technology, Inc.
10655 Humbolt St.
Los Alamitos, CA 90720
310-493-6888
fax: 310-493-2816

Systems Integration Associates
222 E. Pearson, Ste. 502
Chicago, IL 60611
312-440-1275

Tadpole Technology, Inc.
8310 Capital of Texas Hwy., N, Ste. 375
Austin, TX 78731
512-338-4221

Tandem Computers, Inc.
19333 Vallco Pkwy., Location 4-40
Cupertino, CA 95014-2599
800-538-3107; 408-725-6000
fax: 408-285-0505
Technical support: Use main number

Tandon Corp.
301 Science Dr.
Moorpark, CA 93021
805-523-0340
fax: 805-529-4450
Technical support: 800-487-8324

Tandy Corp.
1800 One Tandy Center
Ft. Worth, TX 76102
817-390-3011
fax: 817-390-2774
Technical support: 817-390-3861

Tangent Computer, Inc.
197 Airport Blvd.
Burlingame, CA 94010
800-223-6677; 415-342-9388
fax: 415-342-9380
Technical support: Use 800 number

Tatung Co. of America, Inc.
2850 El Presidio St.
Long Beach, CA 90810
800-827-2850; 310-979-7055
fax: 310-637-8484
Technical support: Use main number

TECO Information Systems, Inc.
24 E. Harbor Dr.
Lake Zurich, IL 60047
708-438-3998
fax: 708-438-8061

Teconomics, Inc.
755 5th Ave., SW
Calgary, Alberta
Canada T2P 0N2
403-265-0707
fax: 403-265-1067

Telemart
8804 North 23rd Ave.
Phoenix, AZ 85021
800-426-6659; 602-944-0402
Technical support: Use 800 number

TeleVideo Systems, Inc.
550 E. Brokaw Rd., P.O. Box 49048
San Jose, CA 95161-9048
800-835-3228; 408-954-8333
fax: 408-954-0623

Tenex Computer Express
56800 Magnetic Dr.
Mishawaka, IN 46545
800-776-6781; 219-259-7051
fax: 219-255-1778

Texas Instruments, Inc.
P.O. Box 655012, M/S 57
Dallas, TX 75265
800-527-3500; 214-995-2011
fax: 214-995-4360
Technical support: 512-250-7407

3Com Corp.
P.O. Box 51845, 5400 Bayfront Plaza
Santa Clara, CA 95052-8145
800-638-3266; 408-764-5000
fax: 408-764-5032
Technical support: 800-876-3266

Top-Link Computer, Inc.
48810 Kato Rd.
Fremont, CA 94538
510-226-1403
fax: 510-623-7132

Topline Technologies, Inc.
330 E. Orangethorpe Ave.
Placentia, CA 92670
714-524-6900
fax: 714-572-3784

TOPPCs International, Inc.
648 N. Eckhoff
Orange, CA 92668
714-939-1416
fax: 714-939-0103

**Toshiba America Information Systems,
Inc. (Computer Systems Division)**
9740 Irvine Blvd.
Irvine, CA 92718
800-334-3445; 714-583-3000
Technical support: 800-999-4273

Trans PC System, Inc.
11849 E. Firestone Blvd.
Norwalk, CA 90650
310-868-6930
fax: 310-864-2249

Transource Services Corp.
2033 W. North Lane #18
Phoenix, AZ 85021
800-235-8191; 602-997-8101

Triton Technology Laboratory, Corp.
1804 Plaza Ave., Ste. 4
New Hyde Park, NY 11040
516-488-8852
fax: 516-488-8856

Tussey Computer Products, Inc.
P.O. Box 1006
State College, PA 16804
800-468-9044

TW Casper Corp.
47430 Seabridge Dr.
Fremont, CA 94538
510-770-8500
fax: 510-770-8509

Twinhead Corp.
1537 Centre Pointe Dr.
Milpitas, CA 95035
408-945-0808
fax: 408-945-1080

Ultra-Comp
11988 Dorsett Rd.
Maryland Heights, MO 63043
800-435-2266; 314-298-1998
fax: 314-991-0437
Technical support: Use main number

Unisys Corp.
P.O. Box 500
Blue Bell, PA 19424-0001
215-542-4011
Technical support: 800-448-1424

United Electronics Systems, Inc.
601 N. Vermont Ave., Ste. 100
Los Angeles, CA 90004
213-669-1234
fax: 213-668-1234

Unitek Systems Corp.
7540 Quincy St., Ste. D
Willowbrook, IL 60521
708-323-3395
fax: 708-887-0448

Unitron, Inc.
736 Stimson Ave.
City of Industry, CA 91749
818-333-0280
fax: 818-968-1388

Input Devices

US Integrated Technologies (USIT)
3023 Research Dr.
Richmond, CA 94806
510-223-1001
fax: 510-223-2766

U.S. Micro Engineering, Ltd.
P.O. Box 17728
Boulder, CO 80308
303-939-8700
fax: 303-939-8791

USA Flex
471 Brighton Dr.
Bloomingdale, IL 60108
800-876-5607; 708-351-7334
fax: 708-351-7204
Technical Support: 800-441-5416

UTI Computers
3640 Westchase Dr.
Houston, TX 77042
800-237-4961

Vector Computer Research, Inc.
803 S. Adams
Fredericksburg, TX 78624
512-997-6001

Vector Computers Corp.
3901 E. Blanche St.
Pasadena, CA 91107
818-946-0879

Vektron International
1841 Wilderness Trail
Grand Prairie, TX 75052
214-606-0280
fax: 214-606-1278

Veridata Research, Inc.
11901 Goldring Rd., Ste. A&B
Arcadia, CA 91006
818-303-0613
fax: 818-303-0626

Vertex Advanced Research, Inc.
1111 Town and Country Rd., Ste. 50
Orange, CA 92668
800-521-4892; 714-835-1919
fax: 714-835-3238

VIPC Computers
384 Jackson, Ste. 1
Hayward, CA 94544
800-222-5657; 510-881-1772

VNS America Corp.
910 Boston Post Rd., Ste. 270
Marlboro, MA 01752
800-252-4212; 508-481-7192
fax: 508-481-2218

Wang Laboratories, Inc.
One Industrial Way, M/S 014-A1B
Lowell, MA 01851
800-835-9264; 508-459-5000
Technical support: 800-247-9264

Wedge Technology, Inc.
1587 McCandless Dr.
Milpitas, CA 95035
408-263-9888
fax: 408-263-9886

Wells American Corp.
3243 Sunset Blvd.
West Columbia, SC 29169
803-796-7800

West Coast Peripherals
48521 Warm Springs Blvd., Ste. 306
Fremont, CA 94539
510-226-1844
fax: 510-226-1848

Win Laboratories, Ltd.
11090 Industrial Rd.
Manassas, VA 22110
703-330-1426

WLT Systems, Inc.
800 Chelmsford St.
Lowell, MA 01851
800-272-9771; 508-656-8590
fax: 508-656-8540

WYSE Technology
3471 N. First St.
San Jose, CA 95134
800-438-9973; 408-473-1200
fax: 408-473-1222
Technical support: 408-922-5700

Xerox Corp. (U.S. Marketing Group)
P.O. Box 24
Rochester, NY 14692
800-832-6979

Xtron Computer Equipment Corp.
716 Jersey Ave.
Jersey City, NJ 07302
800-854-4450; 201-798-5000
fax: 201-798-4322

YKE International, Inc.
76-16 Jamaica Ave.
Woodhaven, NY 11421
718-296-0101
fax: 718-296-0070

Zenith Data Systems (ZDS)
2150 E. Lake Cook Rd.
Buffalo Grove, IL 60088
800-533-0331; 708-808-5000
Technical support: Use main number

Zeno Computer Products, Inc.
P.O. Box 3518
Ontario, CA 91761
714-923-4841
fax: 714-923-6519

Zeny Computer Systems
4033 Clipper Court
Fremont, CA 94538
510-659-0386
fax: 510-659-0468

Zeos International, Ltd.
530 5th Ave., NW
St. Paul, MN 55112
800-423-5891; 612-633-4591
fax: 612-633-1325
Technical support: Use 800 number

Input Devices

Abaton
48431 Milmont Dr.
Fremont, CA 94538
800-444-5321; 510-498-1111
fax: 510-683-2870
Technical support: 510-498-4433

Acco International, Inc.
770 S. Acco Plaza
Wheeling, IL 60090-6070
800-222-6462; 708-541-9500
fax: 708-541-9638

Adaptec, Inc.
691 S. Milpitas Blvd.
Milpitas, CA 95035
408-945-8600
fax: 408-262-1845
Technical support: 408-945-2550

ADI Systems, Inc.
2121 Ringwood Ave.
San Jose, CA 95131
800-228-0530; 800-232-8282 (in California);
408-944-0100
fax: 408-944-0300

Adobe Systems, Inc.
1585 Charleston Rd., P.O. Box 7900
Mountain View, CA 94039-7900
800-922-3623; 415-961-4400
fax: 415-961-3769
Technical support: 415-961-4992

Advanced Digital Corp.
5432 Production Dr.
Huntington Beach, CA 92649
714-891-4004
fax: 714-893-1546

Advanced Gravis Computer Technology, Ltd.
7033 Antrim Ave.
Burnaby, BC
Canada V5J 4M5
800-663-8558; 604-431-5020
fax: 604-434-7809

Aedex Corp.
1070 Ortega Way
Placentia, CA 92670
714-632-7000
fax: 714-632-1334

Alarmcard Co.
14700 N.E. Eight St., Ste. 205
Bellevue, WA 98007
800-635-9083; 206-747-0824
fax: 206-644-2190

ALPS America
3553 N. First St.
San Jose, CA 95134
800-828-2577; 408-432-6000
fax: 408-432-6035
Technical support: 800-950-2577

AlteCon Data Communications, Inc.
1333 Strad Ave.
North Tonawanda, NY 14120
800-888-8511; 716-693-2121
fax: 716-693-9799

AMAC South, Inc.
2055 S. Congress Ave.
Delray Beach, FL 33445
407-243-2405
fax: 407-243-2408

American Advantech Corp.
1310 Tully Rd., Ste. 115
San Jose, CA 95122
408-293-6786
fax: 408-293-4697

AMKLY Systems, Inc.
60 Technology Dr.
Irvine, CA 92718
800-367-2655; 714-768-3511

DIRECTORY OF MANUFACTURERS

AMX Remote Control Systems
12056 Forestgate Dr.
Dallas, TX 75243
800-222-0193; 214-644-3048
fax: 214-907-2053

Anacom General Corp.
1335 S. Claudina St.
Anaheim, CA 92805-6235
714-774-8080
fax: 714-774-7388

Anakin Research, Inc.
100 Westmore Dr.
Rexdale, Ontario
Canada M9V 5C3
416-744-4246
fax: 416-744-4248

Analog Devices, Inc.
P.O. Box 9106, One Technology Way
Norwood, MA 02062-9106
617-329-4700
fax: 617-326-8703

Analog Technology Corp.
1859 Business Center Dr.
Duarte, CA 91010
818-357-0098
fax: 818-303-4993

Antec Inc.
4555 Cushing Pkwy.
Fremont, CA 94538
510-770-1200

Apollo Audio Visual
60 Trade Zone Court
Ronkonkoma, NY 11779
800-777-3750; 516-467-8033
fax: 516-467-8996

Apple Computer, Inc.
20525 Mariani Ave.
Cupertino, CA 95014
408-996-1010
Technical support: 800-776-2333

Applied Computer Sciences, Inc.
11711 Northcreek Pkwy., S, Ste. 107
Bothell, WA 98011
800-525-5512; 206-486-2722
fax: 206-485-4766

Appoint
1332 Vendels Circle
Paso Robles, CA 93446
800-448-1184; 805-237-6262
fax: 805-239-8978
Technical support: Use main number

Arche Technologies, Inc.
48502 Kato Rd.
Fremont, CA 94538
800-437-1688; 510-623-8100
fax: 510-683-6754
Technical support: 510-623-8162

Ark International, Inc.
1950 Ohio St.
Lisle, IL 60532
800-232-6221; 708-960-7463
fax: 708-960-7472

ASP Computer Products, Inc.
1026 W. Maude Ave., Ste. 305
Sunnyvale, CA 94086
800-445-6190; 408-746-2965
fax: 408-746-2803
Technical support: Use main number

Asuka Technologies, Inc.
17145 Von Karman Ave., Ste. 110
Irvine, CA 92714
714-757-1212
fax: 714-757-1288

Aten Research, Inc.
340 Thor Place
Brea, CA 92621
714-255-0566
fax: 714-255-0275

Aydin Controls
414 Commerce Dr.
Ft. Washington, PA 19034
800-347-4001; 215-542-7800
fax: 215-628-4372

Az-Tech Software, Inc.
305 E. Franklin
Richmond, MO 64085
800-227-0644; 816-776-2700
fax: 816-776-8398

Bay Technical Associates, Inc.
200 N. Second St., P.O. Box 387
Bay St. Louis, MS 39520
800-523-2702; 601-467-8231
fax: 601-467-4551

Behavior Tech Computer (USA) Corp.
46177 Warm Spring Blvd.
Fremont, CA 94539
510-657-3956
fax: 510-657-3965

Biopac Systems
275 S. Orange Ave., Ste. E
Goleta, CA 93117
805-967-6615
fax: 805-967-6043

Bitstream, Inc.
215 First St.
Cambridge, MA 02142
800-522-FONT; 617-497-6222
fax: 617-868-4732
Technical support: 617-497-7514

Black Box Corp.
P.O. Box 12800
Pittsburgh, PA 15241
412-746-5500
fax: 412-746-0746

Bondwell Industrial Co., Inc.
47485 Seabridge Dr.
Fremont, CA 94538
510-490-4300
fax: 510-490-5897
Technical support: 800-288-4388

Boxlight Corp.
19689 7th Ave., NE, Ste. 143
Poulsbo, WA 98370
800-762-5757; 206-697-4008
fax: 206-779-3299

Brady Office Machine Security, Inc.
11056 S. Bell Ave.
Chicago, IL 60643
312-779-8349

Brown & Co., Inc.
P.O. Box 2443
South Hamilton, MA 01982
508-486-7464

Buffalo Products, Inc.
2805 19th Ave., SE
Salem, OR 97302-1520
800-345-2356; 503-585-3414
fax: 503-585-4505

Burham Computer Center
908 E. Main St.
Alhambra, CA 91801
818-570-0396
fax: 818-570-0936

Burr-Brown Corp.
P.O. Box 11400
Tucson, AZ 85734
800-548-6132; 602-746-1111
fax: 602-741-3895

CalComp Plotter Products Group
P.O. Box 3250, 2411 W. La Palma Ave.
Anaheim, CA 92803
800-932-1212; 714-821-2000
fax: 714-821-2832
Technical support: Use main number

Camintonn Corp.
22 Morgan St.
Irvine, CA 92718-2022
800-843-8336; 714-454-1500
fax: 714-454-6599
Technical support: Use main number

Canon U.S.A., Inc.
One Canon Plaza
Lake Success, NY 11042
516-488-6700
fax: 516-354-5805
Technical support: 800-423-2366

Cardinal Technologies, Inc.
1827 Freedom Rd.
Lancaster, PA 17601
800-722-0094; 717-293-3000
fax: 717-293-3055
Technical support: 717-293-3124

Carroll Touch
P.O. Box 1309
Round Rock, TX 78680
512-244-3500
fax: 512-244-7040

CDCE, Inc.
2992 E. LaPalma, Ste. D
Anaheim, CA 92806
800-373-5353; 714-630-4633
fax: 714-630-5022

CH Products
970 Park Center Dr.
Vista, CA 92083
619-598-2518
fax: 619-598-2524

Chaplet Systems, Inc.
252 N. Wolf Rd.
Sunnyvale, CA 94086
408-732-7950
fax: 408-732-6050

The Cherry Corp.
3600 Sunset Ave.
Waukegan, IL 60087
708-662-9200
fax: 708-360-3566

Chicony America, Inc.
3002 Dow Ave., Ste. 122
Tustin, CA 92680
714-573-0456
fax: 714-573-0673
Technical support: 714-380-0928

Input Devices

Chisholm
910 Campisi Way
Cambell, CA 95008
800-888-4210; 408-559-1111
fax: 408-559-0444

CMS Enhancements, Inc.
2722 Michelson Dr.
Irvine, CA 92715
714-222-6000
fax: 714-549-4004
Technical support: 714-222-6058

Cole-Parmer Instrument Co.
7425 N. Oak Park Ave.
Chicago, IL 60648
800-323-4340; 708-647-7600
fax: 708-647-9660

Commax, Inc.
15 Shire Way
Middletown, NJ 07748
908-671-0775
fax: 908-671-0804

Communications Specialties, Inc.
89A Cabot Court
Hauppauge, NY 11788
516-273-0404
fax: 516-273-1638

CompuAdd Corp.
12303 Technology Blvd.
Austin, TX 78727
800-531-5475; 512-250-1489
fax: 512-250-5760
Technical support: 800-999-9901

Computer Friends, Inc.
14250 N.W. Science Park Dr.
Portland, OR 97229
800-547-3303; 503-626-2291
fax: 503-643-5379
Technical support: Use main number

Computer Peripherals, Inc.
667 Rancho Conejo Blvd.
Newbury Park, CA 91320
800-854-7600; 805-499-5751
fax: 805-498-8848
Technical support: 800-235-7618

Computer Support Corp.
15926 Midway Rd.
Dallas, TX 75244
214-661-8960
fax: 214-661-5429

Computer System Associates, Inc.
7564 Trade St.
San Diego, CA 92121
619-566-3911
fax: 619-566-0581

Comspec Communications, Inc.
74 Wingold Ave.
Toronto, ON
Canada M6B 1P5
416-785-3553
fax: 416-785-3668

Connect Computer Co., Inc.
9855 West 78th St., Ste. 270
Eden Prairie, MN 55344
612-944-0181
fax: 612-944-9298

Consolink
600 S. Sunset
Longmont, CO 80501
303-651-2642
fax: 303-678-8360

Contek International Corp.
66 Field Crest Rd.
New Canaan, CT 06840
203-972-3406
fax: 203-972-0156

Covid, Inc.
2400 West 10th Place, Ste. 4
Tempe, AZ 85281
800-638-6104; 602-966-2221
fax: 602-966-6728

CPT Corp.
8100 Mitchell Rd.
Eden Prairie, MN 55344-9833
800-447-1189; 612-937-8000
fax: 612-937-1858

Creative Computer Products, Inc.
6369 Nancy Ridge Dr.
San Diego, CA 92121
800-231-5413; 800-523-5441 (in California);
619-458-1965
fax: 619-458-9024

CTI Electronics Corp.
200 Benton St.
Stratford, CT 06497
203-386-9779
fax: 203-378-4986

Cubix Corp.
2800 Lockheed Way
Carson City, NV 89706
800-829-0550; 702-883-7611
fax: 702-882-2407

Curtis Manufacturing Co., Inc.
30 Fitzgerald Dr.
Jaffrey, NH 03452-1931
800-548-4900; 603-532-4123
fax: 603-532-4116

Cyber Research, Inc.
25 Business Park Dr.
Banford, CT 06405
800-341-2525; 203-483-8815
fax: 203-483-9024

Cybex Corp.
2800-H Bob Wallace Ave.
Huntsville, AL 35805
205-430-4000
fax: 205-534-0010

Daisy Data, Inc.
333 S. Enola Dr.
Enola, PA 17025-2897
717-732-8800
fax: 717-732-8806

Data General Corp.
4400 Computer Dr.
Westboro, MA 01580
800-328-2436; 508-366-8911
fax: 508-366-1299
Technical support: 800-537-6084

DataDesk International
9330 Eton Ave.
Chatsworth, CA 91311
800-328-2337; 818-998-4200
fax: 818-998-0330
Technical support: Use main number

Data-Doc Electronics, Inc.
4903 Commercial Park Dr.
Austin, TX 78724-2638
800-328-2362; 512-928-8926
fax: 512-928-8210

Dataflow Technologies, Inc.
1300 York Rd., Ste. 30
Lutherville, MD 21093
301-296-2630
fax: 301-321-6524

Dataworld
3733 San Gabriel River Pkwy.
Pico Rivera, CA 90660-1495
800-736-8080; 310-695-3777
fax: 310-695-7016
Technical support: 800-776-8088

Dell Computer Corp.
9505 Arboretum Blvd.
Austin, TX 78759-7299
800-426-5150; 512-338-4400
fax: 512-338-8421
Technical support: 800-624-9896

Designs By Royo
320 H St.
Marysville, CA 95901
916-741-3937
fax: 916-743-0427

DFI, Inc.
2544 Port St.
Sacramento, CA 95691
916-373-1234
fax: 916-373-0221

Dickerson Enterprises, Inc.
8101 N. Milwaukee Ave.
Niles, IL 60648
800-247-5419; 708-966-4884
fax: 708-966-0294

Digital Communications Associates, Inc. (DCA)
1000 Alderman Dr.
Alpharetta, GA 30201-4199
800-348-3221; 404-442-4000
fax: 404-442-4361
Technical support: 404-740-0300 (Micro Products)

DP-Tek, Inc.
3031 W. Pawnee St.
Wichita, KS 67213
800-727-3130; 316-945-8600
fax: 316-945-8629

Dragoon Corp.
1270 Avenida Acaso, Unit F
Camarillo, CA 93010
805-987-4911
fax: 805-987-4358

Dresselhaus Computer Products
8560 Vineyard Ave., Ste. 405
Rancho Cucamonga, CA 91730
800-368-7737; 909-945-5600
fax: 714-989-2436

Dual Group, Inc.
P.O. Box 13944
Torrance, CA 90503
310-542-0788
fax: 310-214-0697

Dunamis, Inc.
3620 Hwy. 317
Suwanee, GA 30174
800-828-2443; 404-932-0485
fax: 404-932-0486

Edimax Computer Co.
3350 Scott Blvd., Bldg. 9A
Santa Clara, CA 95054
408-496-1105
fax: 408-980-1530

DIRECTORY OF MANUFACTURERS

Edmark Corp.
14350 Northeast 21st St.
Bellevue, WA 98007
800-426-0856; 206-556-8400
fax: 206-746-3962

Educational Systems, Inc.
3175 Commercial Ave.
Northbrook, IL 60062
800-333-0551; 708-498-3780
fax: 708-498-0185

Eiki International, Inc.
27882 Camino Capistrano
Laguna Niguel, CA 92677-8000
714-582-2511

Elesys, Inc.
528 Weddell Dr.
Sunnyvale, CA 94089
800-637-0500; 408-747-0233
fax: 408-747-0131

Eliashim Microcomputers, Inc.
520 W. Hwy. 436, Ste. 1180-30
Altamonte Springs, FL 32714
800-771-SAFE; 407-682-1587
fax: 407-869-1409
Technical support: Use main number

Elite Business Applications, Inc.
36-J Rt. 3, N, P.O. Box 593
Millersville, MD 21108
800-942-0018; 301-987-9050
fax: 301-987-9098
Technical support: Use main number

Elographics, Inc.
105 Randolph Rd.
Oak Ridge, TN 37830
615-482-4100
fax: 615-482-4943

EMAC
48431 Milmont Dr.
Fremont, CA 94538
800-821-0806; 510-683-2585
fax: 510-651-0728
Technical support: 510-498-4440

EuroComm, Inc.
629 S. Rancho Santa Fe Rd., Ste. 394
San Marcos, CA 92069
619-471-9362, ext. 5
fax: 619-471-5054

Everex Systems, Inc.
48431 Milmont Dr.
Fremont, CA 94538
800-821-0806; 510-498-1111
fax: 510-651-0728
Technical support: 510-498-4411

Evergreen Systems
31336 Via Colinas, Dept. 3/336
Westlake Village, CA 91362
818-991-7835
fax: 818-991-4036

Excellink, Inc.
1430 Tully Rd., Ste. 415
San Jose, CA 95122
408-295-9000
fax: 408-295-9011

ExecRak, Inc.
115 Gun Ave.
Pointe Claire, Quebec
Canada H9R 3X2
514-697-8855
fax: 514-697-8763

Extended Systems
5777 N. Meeker Ave.
Boise, ID 83704
800-235-7576; 208-322-7575
fax: 208-377-1906

Extron Electronics
13554 Larwin Circle
Sante Fe Springs, CA 90670
800-633-9876; 310-802-8804
fax: 310-802-2741

EZ-Tek Industries
500 Hidden Valley Rd.
Grants Pass, OR 97527
503-474-2192
fax: 503-474-0787

Fifth Generation Systems, Inc.
10049 N. Reiger Rd.
Baton Rouge, LA 70809
800-873-4384; 504-291-7221
fax: 504-295-3268
Technical support: 504-291-7283

Fischer International Systems Corp.
P.O. Box 9107, 4073 Mercantile Ave.
Naples, FL 33942
800-237-4510; 800-331-2866 (in Florida);
813-643-1500
fax: 813-643-3772

Flytech Technology (U.S.A.), Inc.
3008 Scott Blvd.
Santa Clara, CA 95054
408-727-7373
fax: 408-727-7375

Forte Communications, Inc.
1050 E. Duane Ave., Ste. J
Sunnyvale, CA 94086
800-331-3903; 408-733-5100
fax: 408-733-5600

4G Data Systems, Inc.
96 Fulton St.
New York, NY 10038
212-233-4300
fax: 212-233-2627

Johnathon Freeman Technologies
P.O. Box 880114
San Francisco, CA 94188
800-288-4357; 415-822-8451
fax: 415-822-8611

FTG Data Systems
P.O. Box 615, 10801 Dale St., Ste. J-2
Stanton, CA 90680
800-962-3900; 714-995-3900
fax: 714-995-3989

FuncKey Enterprises
Rt. 1, Box 639G
Sanger, TX 76266
800-777-WORX; 817-482-6613

Galil Motion Control, Inc.
575 Maude Court
Sunnyvale, CA 94086
408-746-2300
fax: 408-746-2315

GEC-Marconi Software Systems
12110 Sunset Hills Rd., Ste. 450
Reston, VA 22090
703-648-1551
fax: 703-476-8035

Generation Systems
1185-C Bordeaux Dr.
Sunnyvale, CA 94089
800-325-5811; 408-734-2100
fax: 408-734-4626
Technical support: 800-323-9825

Genovation, Inc.
17741 Mitchell, N
Irvine, CA 92714
714-833-3355
fax: 714-833-0322

Gentek International, Inc.
305 Trapper Circle
Windsor, CT 06095
203-683-1160
fax: 203-683-2146

Glenco Engineering, Inc.
270 Lexington Dr.
Buffalo Grove, IL 60089
800-562-2543; 708-808-0300
fax: 708-808-0313

Grimes
115 S. Arovista Circle
Brea, CA 92621
714-671-3931
fax: 714-671-1426

GW Instruments
35 Medford St.
Somerville, MA 02143
617-625-4096
fax: 617-625-1322

HEI, Inc.
P.O. Box 5000, 1495 Steiger Lake Lane
Victoria, MN 55386
800-776-6688; 612-443-2500
fax: 612-443-2668

Hertz Computer Corp.
325 Fifth Ave.
New York, NY 10016
800-232-8737; 212-684-4141
fax: 212-684-3685

Hewlett-Packard Co.
3000 Hanover St.
Palo Alto, CA 94304
800-752-0900; 415-857-1501
Technical support: Use 800 number

HMW Enterprises, Inc.
604 Salem Rd.
Etters, PA 17319
717-938-4691
fax: 717-938-4095

Honeywell, Inc. (Keyboard Division)
4171 N. Mesa, Bldg. D
El Paso, TX 79902
800-445-6939; 509-928-8000
fax: 915-543-5126

Hooleon Corp.
Page Springs Rd., P.O. Box 230
Cornville, AZ 86325
800-937-1337; 602-634-7515
fax: 602-634-4620

Hornet Technology U.S.A. Corp.
330 E. Orangethorpe Ave., Ste. D-E
Placentia, CA 92670
714-572-3781
fax: 714-572-3784

Input Devices

Houston Computer Services, Inc.
11331 Richmond Ave., Ste. 101
Houston, TX 77082
713-558-9900

IBM (International Business Machines)
Old Orchard Rd.
Armonk, NY 10504
800-426-2468; 914-765-1900
Technical support: Use 800 number

ICD, Inc.
1220 Rock St.
Rockford, IL 61101-1437
815-968-2228
fax: 815-968-6888

Idea Courier/Servcom, Inc.
P.O. Box 29039
Phoenix, AZ 85038
800-528-1400; 602-894-7000

Identix, Inc.
510 N. Pastoria Ave.
Sunnyvale, CA 94086
408-739-2000
fax: 408-739-3308

IMSI
1938 Fourth St.
San Rafael, CA 94901
800-833-4674; 415-454-7101
fax: 415-454-8901

In Focus Systems, Inc.
7770 S.W. Mohawk St.
Tualatin, OR 97062
800-327-7231; 503-692-4968
fax: 503-692-4476

In Touch Systems
11 Westview Rd.
Spring Valley, NY 10977
914-354-7431

Infogrip, Inc.
812 North Blvd.
Baton Rouge, LA 70802
504-766-8082
fax: 504-336-0063

Information Strategies, Inc.
888 S. Greenville Ave., Ste. 121
Richardson, TX 75081
214-234-0176

Inmac Corp.
P.O. Box 58031, 2465 Augustine Dr.
Santa Clara, CA 95054
800-547-5444; 408-727-1970
Technical support: 800-446-6224

Intel Corp. (Personal Computer Enhancement Operation)
5200 N.E. Elam Young Pkwy., M/S CO3-07
Hillsboro, OR 97124
503-696-8080
Technical support: 503-629-7000

Intellicom
20415 Nordhoff St.
Chatsworth, CA 91311
800-992-2882; 818-407-3900
fax: 818-882-2404
Technical support: Use main number

Interaction Systems, Inc.
86 Coolidge Ave.
Watertown, MA 02172
617-923-6001
fax: 617-923-2112

Intercon Associates, Inc.
1850 Winton Rd., S, 1 Cambridge Place
Rochester, NY 14618
800-422-3880; 716-244-1250
fax: 716-473-4387

International Data Acquisition & Control, Inc.
The Meeting Place, P.O. Box 397
Amherst, NH 03031
603-673-0765
fax: 603-673-0767

International Machine Control Systems (IMCS)
1332 Vendels Circle
Paso Robles, CA 93446
800-448-1184; 805-239-8976 (in California)

Intertech Marketing, Inc.
8820 Six Forks Rd., NCNB Bank Bldg., Ste. 100
Raleigh, NC 27615
800-762-7874; 919-870-8404
fax: 919-870-8343

IOLINE Corp.
12020-113th Ave., NE
Kirkland, WA 98034
206-821-2140
fax: 206-823-8898

IQ Engineering
685 N. Pastoria
Sunnyvale, CA 94086
800-765-3668; 408-733-1161
fax: 408-733-2585
Technical support: Use 800 number

ITAC Systems, Inc.
3121 Benton St.
Garland, TX 75042
800-533-4822; 214-494-3073
fax: 214-494-4159

Jasco Products Co., Inc.
P.O. Box 466
Oklahoma City, OK 73101
800-654-8483; 405-752-0710
fax: 405-752-1157

JLCooper Electronics
13478 Beach Ave.
Marina del Rey, CA 90292
213-306-4131
fax: 213-822-2252

Don Johnston Developmental Equipment, Inc.
P.O. Box 639, 1000 N. Rand Rd., Bldg. 115
Wauconda, IL 60084-0639
800-999-4660; 708-526-2682
fax: 708-526-4177

JOYCE Associates
215 Franklin St.
Clayton, NJ 08312

K & C Technologies, Inc.
5075 Moorpark Ave.
San Jose, CA 95129
408-257-1445
fax: 408-259-2490

K. S. Brotherbox (U.S.A.) Co.
14140 Live Oak Ave., Unit D
Baldwin Park, CA 91706
818-814-0516
fax: 818-814-0323

Kansai International, Inc.
2005 Hamilton Ave., Ste. 220
San Jose, CA 95125
800-733-3374; 408-377-7062
fax: 408-782-8559

KDS Corp.
934 Cornell St.
Wilmette, IL 60091
708-251-2621
fax: 708-251-6489

KEA Systems, Ltd.
3738 N. Fraser Way, Unit 101
Burnaby, BC
Canada V5J 5G1
800-663-8702; 604-431-0727
fax: 604-431-0818

Keithley Instruments, Inc.
(Instruments Division)
28775 Aurora Rd.
Cleveland, OH 44139
800-552-1115; 216-248-0400
fax: 216-248-6168

Kennect Technology
120-A Albright Way
Los Gatos, CA 95030
800-552-1232; 408-370-2866
fax: 408-370-0484

Kensington Microware, Ltd.
2855 Campus Dr.
San Mateo, CA 94403
800-535-4242; 415-572-2700
fax: 415-572-9675
Technical support: Use main number

Key Concepts, Inc.
316 S. Eddy St.
South Bend, IN 46617
800-526-6753; 219-234-4207
fax: 219-234-6414

Key-Tech
7315 Lahser
Birmingham, MI 48010
800-383-1210; 313-644-4993
fax: 313-644-5901

Key Tronic Corp.
P.O. Box 14687
Spokane, WA 99214
800-262-6006; 509-928-8000
fax: 509-927-5216
Technical support: Use 800 number

Keytime
3147 Fairview, E, Ste. 200
Seattle, WA 98102
206-522-8973
fax: 206-323-6494

Kingston Technology Corp.
17600 Newhope St.
Fountain Valley, CA 92708
800-835-2545; 714-435-2600
fax: 714-435-2699
Technical support: Use main number

Kofax Image Products, Inc.
3 Jenner St.
Irvine, CA 92718
714-727-1733
fax: 714-727-3144

DIRECTORY OF MANUFACTURERS

Kraft Systems, Inc.
450 W. California Ave.
Vista, CA 92083
619-724-7146
fax: 619-941-1770
Technical support: Use main number

Kurta Corp.
3007 E. Chambers St.
Phoenix, AZ 85040
800-445-8782; 602-276-5533
fax: 602-276-7823

KYE International, Inc.
2605 E. Cedar St.
Ontario, CA 91761
800-456-7593; 714-923-3510
fax: 714-923-1469

Laser Storage & Graphics Co.
644 Forest Ridge Dr.
Marietta, GA 30067
404-973-3860

LaserGo, Inc.
9369 Carroll Park Dr., Ste. A
San Diego, CA 92121
619-450-4600
fax: 619-450-9334

Lasergraphics
20 Ada
Irvine, CA 92718
714-727-2651
fax: 714-727-2653

LaserPlex Corp.
304 S. Abbott Ave.
Milpitas, CA 95035
408-946-2298
fax: 408-946-0232

LaserTools Corp.
1250 45th St., Ste. 100
Emeryville, CA 94608-2907
800-767-8004; 510-420-8777
fax: 510-420-1150
Technical support: 800-767-8005

Lightek
11000 Three Chopt Rd., Ste. B
Richmond, VA 23233
804-270-4291

Lite-On, Inc.
720 S. Hillview Dr.
Milpitas, CA 95035
408-946-4873
fax: 408-942-1527

Liuski International
10 Hub Dr.
Melville, NY 11747
516-454-8220

The Lock Box
22546 Summit Rd.
Los Gatos, CA 95030
408-685-1000
fax: 408-353-1007

Logitech, Inc.
6505 Kaiser Dr.
Fremont, CA 94555
800-999-8846; 510-795-8500
fax: 510-792-8901
Technical support: 510-795-8100

Lucas Deeco Corp.
31047 Genstar Rd.
Hayward, CA 94544
510-471-4700
fax: 510-489-3500

The Lyra Group
P.O. Box 4297
Brick, NJ 08723
908-920-9667

MacSema
29383 Lamb Dr.
Albany, OR 97321
800-344-7228; 503-757-1520
fax: 503-754-7189

Mandrill Corp.
P.O. Box 33848
San Antonio, TX 78265
800-531-5314; 512-341-6155

Mark of the Unicorn, Inc.
222 Third St.
Cambridge, MA 02142
617-576-2760

Market Central, Inc.
600 N. Main St.
Houston, PA 15342-1615
412-746-6000

Marstek
17795-F Skypark Circle
Irvine, CA 92714
800-366-4620; 714-833-7740
fax: 714-833-7813
Technical support: Use main number

Maxi Switch Inc.
2901 E. Elvira Rd.
Tucson, AZ 85706
602-294-5450
fax: 602-294-6890

Merak Industries
8704 Edna St.
Warren, MI 48093
800-231-4310 ext. 768; 313-562-9768

Meridian Data, Inc.
5615 Scotts Valley Dr.
Scotts Valley, CA 95066
408-438-3100
fax: 408-438-6816
Technical support: 800-755-TECH

Merlan Scientific, Ltd.
247 Armstrong Ave.
Georgetown, ON, CD L7G 4X6
800-387-2474; 905-877-0171
fax: 416-877-0929

Mextel, Inc.
159 Beeline Dr.
Bensenville, IL 60106
800-888-4146; 708-595-4146
fax: 708-595-4149

Micro Security Systems, Inc.
4750 Wiley Post Way, Ste. 180
Salt Lake City, UT 84116
800-456-2587; 801-575-6600
fax: 801-575-6621

Micron Technology, Inc.
2805 E. Columbia Rd.
Boise, ID 83706-9698
800-642-7661; 208-368-4000
fax: 208-368-4558
Technical support: 208-368-3900

Microsafe Products Co.
P.O. Box 2393
Kirkland, WA 98083-2393
206-881-6390

Microsoft Corp.
One Microsoft Way
Redmond, WA 98052-6399
800-426-9400; 206-882-8080
fax: 206-883-8101
Technical support: 206-454-2030

MicroSpeed
44000 Old Warm Springs Blvd.
Fremont, CA 94538
800-232-7888; 510-490-1403
fax: 510-490-1665
Technical support: Use main number

MicroTouch Systems, Inc.
55 Jonspin Rd.
Wilmington, MA 01887
508-694-9900
fax: 508-694-9980

Minatronics Corp.
3046 Penn Ave.
Pittsburgh, PA 15201
412-281-5050

Mitchell Pacific
10303 Jasper Ave., Ste. 1050
Edmonton, Alberta
Canada T5J 3N6
403-425-0100
fax: 403-420-0900

Mitsumi Electronics Corp., Inc.
35 Pinelawn Rd.
Melville, NY 11747
516-752-7730
fax: 516-752-7490

Mobius Technologies, Inc.
5835 Doyle St.
Emeryville, CA 94608
800-669-0556; 510-654-0556
fax: 510-654-2834

Modular Instruments, Inc.
81 Great Valley Pkwy.
Great Valley Corp. Center
Malvern, PA 19355
215-640-9292
fax: 215-644-0190

Monterey Electronics, Inc.
2355 Paragon Dr., Ste. B
San Jose, CA 95131
408-437-5496

Mouse Systems Corp.
47505 Seabridge Dr.
Fremont, CA 94538
510-656-1117
fax: 510-770-1924

Msound International, LP
550 Kirkland Way, Ste. 100
Kirkland, WA 98033
800-366-1794; 206-821-8313
fax: 206-828-2149

Multi-Pal International, Inc.
17231 E. Railroad St., Ste. 500
City of Industry, CA 91748
818-913-4188
fax: 818-912-9149

Input Devices

NEFF Instrument Corp.
700 S. Myrtle Ave.
Monrovia, CA 91016
800-423-7151; 818-357-2281
fax: 818-303-2286

Neotec International
20468 Carrey Rd.
Walnut, CA 91789
909-595-0509
fax: 909-594-1968

Netcor/Giltronix, Inc.
850 Auburn Court
Fremont, CA 94538
800-531-1300; 510-623-3700
fax: 510-623-3717

Network Technologies, Inc.
7322 Pettibone Rd.
Chagrin Falls, OH 44022
800-742-8324; 216-543-1646
fax: 216-543-5423

NewCo Technology, Inc.
3243 Sunset Blvd.
West Columbia, SC 29169
800-662-9005; 803-794-4300
fax: 803-794-0810

NMB Technologies, Inc.
9730 Independence Ave.
Chatsworth, CA 91311
800-321-3536; 818-341-3355
fax: 818-341-8207

Northgate Computer Systems, Inc.
P.O. Box 59080
Minneapolis, MN 55459-0080
800-548-1993; 612-361-5000
fax: 612-943-8336
Technical support: 800-446-5037

Numonics Corp.
101 Commerce Dr.
Montgomeryville, PA 18936
800-247-4517; 215-362-2766; 215-361-0167

Nutmeg Systems, Inc.
25 South Ave.
New Canaan, CT 06840
800-777-8439; 203-966-7972

NVIEW Corp.
11835 Canon Blvd.
Newport News, VA 23606
800-736-8439; 804-873-1354
fax: 804-873-2153

Office Automation Systems, Inc.
9940 Barnes Canyon Rd.
San Diego, CA 92121
619-452-9400
fax: 619-452-2427

OIS Optical Imaging Systems, Inc.
1896 Barrett St.
Troy, MI 48084
313-362-2738
fax: 313-362-4866

Orange Micro, Inc.
1400 N. Lakeview Ave.
Anaheim, CA 92807
800-223-8029; 714-779-2772
fax: 714-779-9332

Our Business Machines, Inc.
12901 Ramona Blvd., Unit J
Irwindale, CA 91706
800-443-1435; 818-337-9614
fax: 818-960-1766

Pacific Data Products, Inc.
9125 Rehco Rd.
San Diego, CA 92121
619-552-0880
fax: 619-552-0889
Technical support: 619-587-4690

Pacific Rim Data Sciences
47307 Rancho Hiquera Dr.
Fremont, CA 94539
510-651-7935
fax: 510-226-9691

PC Craft, Inc.
640 Puente St.
Brea, CA 92621
800-733-6666; 909-869-6133
fax: 714-256-5025

PC Guardian
118 Alto St.
San Rafael, CA 94901
800-288-8126; 415-459-0190
fax: 415-459-1162

PC House
841 E. Artesia Blvd.
Carson, CA 90746
818-854-2140
fax: 310-324-8654

PC/M Inc.
6800 Sierra Court
Dublin, CA 94568
510-829-8700
fax: 510-829-9796

The Pendulum Group, Inc.
333 W. Hampden Ave., Ste. 1015
Englewood, CO 80110
800-772-6483; 303-781-0575
fax: 303-761-2440

Penny & Giles Controls, Inc.
163 Pleasant St., Ste. 4
Attleboro, MA 02703
508-226-3008
fax: 508-226-5208

Personal Computer Card Corp.
5151 S. Lakeland Dr.
Lakeland, FL 33813
800-336-6644; 813-644-5026
fax: 813-644-1933
Technical support: Use main number

Personal Computer Products, Inc. (PCPI)
10865 Rancho Bernardo Rd.
San Diego, CA 92127
800-225-4098; 800-262-0522 (in California);
619-485-8411
fax: 619-487-5809

Pointer Systems, Inc.
1 Mill St.
Burlington, VT 05401
800-537-1562; 802-658-3260
fax: 802-658-3714

Polytel Computer Products Corp.
1287 Hammerwood Ave.
Sunnyvale, CA 94089
800-245-6655; 408-745-1540
fax: 408-745-6340

Power Source Computer Systems, Inc.
10020 San Pablo Ave.
El Cerrito, CA 94530
510-527-6908
fax: 510-527-3823

Preh Electronics Industries, Inc.
470 E. Main St.
Lake Zurich, IL 60047-2578
708-438-4000
fax: 708-438-5522

Presentation Electronics, Inc.
4320 Anthony Court, Ste. 8
Rocklin, CA 95677
800-888-9281; 916-652-9281
fax: 916-652-9286

The Printer Works
3481 Arden Rd.
Hayward, CA 94545
800-235-6116; 510-887-6116
fax: 510-786-0589

ProCorp
10 Hub Dr.
Melville, NY 11747
516-454-8220
fax: 516-454-8266

ProTech Marketing, Inc.
9600 J Southern Pines Blvd.
Charlotte, NC 28217
800-843-0413; 704-523-9500
fax: 704-523-7651

Proxima Corp.
6610 Nancy Ridge Dr.
San Diego, CA 92121-9639
800-582-2580; 800-582-0852 (in California);
619-457-5500
fax: 619-457-9647
Technical support: Use main number

QMS, Inc.
P.O. Box 81250
Mobile, AL 36689
800-631-2692; 205-633-4300
fax: 205-633-0013
Technical support: 205-633-4500

Qualitas Trading Co.
6907 Norfolk Rd.
Berkeley, CA 94705
510-848-8080
fax: 510-848-8009

Qualtec Data Products, Inc.
47767 Warm Springs Blvd.
Fremont, CA 94539
800-628-4413; 510-490-8911
fax: 510-490-8471

QuaTech, Inc.
662 Wolf Ledges Pkwy.
Akron, OH 44311
800-553-1170; 216-434-3154
fax: 216-434-1409

Qumax Corp.
2380 Qume, Ste. D
San Jose, CA 95131
408-954-8040
fax: 408-954-8043

Radius, Inc.
1710 Fortune Dr.
San Jose, CA 95131
800-227-2795; 408-434-1010
fax: 408-434-0770
Technical support: 408-434-1012

Radix II, Inc.
(Sophos Integrated Systems Division)
6230 Oxon Hill Rd.
Oxon Hill, MD 20745
800-334-SISI; 301-567-5200
fax: 301-839-0836

DIRECTORY OF MANUFACTURERS

Rainbow Technologies, Inc.
9292 Jeronimo Rd.
Irvine, CA 92718
800-852-8569; 714-454-2100
fax: 714-454-8557

Rapid Systems
433 North 34th St.
Seattle, WA 98103
206-547-8311
fax: 206-548-0322

Reactive Systems, Inc.
222 Cedar Lane
Teaneck, NJ 07666
201-907-0100
fax: 201-907-0270

Recortec, Inc.
1290 Lawrence Station Rd.
Sunnyvale, CA 94089
800-729-7654; 408-734-1290
fax: 408-734-2140

Reflection Technology
240 Bear Hill Rd.
Waltham, MA 02154
617-890-5905
fax: 617-890-5918

Remote Measurement Systems, Inc.
2633 Eastlake Ave., E, Ste. 200
Seattle, WA 98102
206-328-2255
fax: 206-328-1787

Renton Products
P.O. Box 16271
Seattle, WA 98116
206-682-7341
fax: 206-624-5610

George Risk Industries, Inc.
802 S. Elm St., GRI Plaza
Kimball, NE 69145
800-445-5218; 308-235-4645

Roland Digital Group
1961 McGaw Ave.
Irvine, CA 92714
714-975-0560
fax: 714-975-0569

Rose Electronics
P.O. Box 742571
Houston, TX 77274
800-333-9343; 713-933-7673
fax: 713-933-0044
Technical support: Use main number

SAI Systems Laboratories, Inc.
911 Bridgeport Ave.
Shelton, CT 06484
800-331-0488; 203-929-0790
fax: 203-929-6948

Sam Systems, Inc.
P.O. Box 2339
Hammond, IN 46323
219-844-2327

Sarasota Technologies, Inc.
2215 Stickney Point Rd.
Sarasota, FL 34231
813-923-9504

Sayett Technology, Inc.
100 Kings Hwy., Ste. 1800
Rochester, NY 14617
800-836-7730; 716-264-9250
fax: 716-342-1621

Seasoned Systems, Inc.
P.O. Box 3720
Chapel Hill, NC 27515-3720
800-334-5531; 919-732-9391
fax: 919-732-9392

Second Wave, Inc.
9430 Research Blvd., Echelon II, Ste. 260
Austin, TX 78759
512-343-9661
fax: 512-343-9663

Secure-It, Inc.
18 Maple Court
East Longmeadow, MA 01028
800-451-7592; 413-525-7039

Security Microsystems, Inc.
215 Cromwell Ave.
Staten Island, NY 10305
800-345-7390; 718-667-1019
fax: 718-667-0131

Se-Kure Controls, Inc.
5685 N. Lincoln Ave.
Chicago, IL 60659
800-322-2435; 312-728-2435
fax: 312-728-6464

Selectech, Ltd.
P.O. Box 100
Williston, VT 05495
802-655-9600
fax: 802-655-5149

Sharp Electronics Corp.
(Professional Products Division)
Sharp Plaza,
Mahwah, NJ 07430
201-529-8200
fax: 201-529-9636
Technical support: 800-732-8221

Simgraphics Engineering Corp.
1137 Huntington Dr.
South Pasadena, CA 91037
213-255-0900
fax: 213-255-0987

Singular Solutions
959 E. Colorado Blvd.
Pasadena, CA 91106
818-792-9567
fax: 818-792-0903

Software Security, Inc.
1011 High Ridge Rd.
Stamford, CT 06905
800-333-0407; 203-329-8870
fax: 203-329-7428

Softworks Development Corp.
5985 N. Lilly Rd.
Menomonee Falls, WI 53051
800-332-3475; 414-252-2020

Sophisticated Circuits, Inc.
19017 120th Ave., NE, Ste. 106
Bothell, WA 98011
206-485-7979

Spark International, Inc.
1939 Waukegan Rd., Ste. 107
Glenview, IL 60025
708-998-6640
fax: 708-998-8840

Spatial Systems, Inc.
900 Middlesex Tpke., Bldg. 8
Billerica, MA 01821
508-670-2720

Spies Laboratories
4040 Spencer St., Bldg. Q
Torrance, CA 90503
800-255-9433; 800-992-9433 (in California);
310-214-2345
fax: 310-214-0751

Staff Computer Technology Corp.
440 San Lucas Dr.
Solana Beach, CA 92075
619-259-1313

Suncom Technologies
6400 Gross Point Rd.
Niles, IL 60648
708-647-4040
fax: 708-459-8095

Sunland Micro Systems
11 Musick, Fairbanks Business Park
Irvine, CA 92718
714-380-1958
fax: 714-380-0918

Support Systems International Corp.
150 S. Second St.
Richmond, CA 94804
800-777-6269; 510-234-9090
fax: 510-233-8888

Swan Technologies
3075 Research Dr.
State College, PA 16801
800-468-9044; 814-238-1820
fax: 814-237-4450
Technical support: 800-468-7926

Syncomp International Corp.
1400 W. Lambert Rd., Ste. D
Brea, CA 92621
213-690-1011
fax: 213-690-6380

System General Corp.
244 S. Hillview Dr.
Milpitas, CA 95035
408-263-6667
fax: 408-262-9220

Tall Tree Systems
P.O. Box 50690, 2585 E. Bayshore Rd.
Palo Alto, CA 94303
415-493-1980
fax: 415-493-7639

Talton/Louley Engineering
9550 Ridge Haven Court
San Diego, CA 92123
619-565-6656

Tandy Corp.
1800 One Tandy Center
Ft. Worth, TX 76102
817-390-3011
fax: 817-390-2774
Technical support: 817-390-3861

Tash, Inc.
70 Gibson Dr., Unit 12
Markham, Ontario
Canada L3R 4C2
905-475-2212
fax: 416-475-2422

TeleSensory Systems, Inc.
P.O. Box 7455, 455 N. Bernardo Ave.
Mountain View, CA 94039-7455
800-227-8418; 415-960-0920
fax: 415-969-9064

Modems and Telecommunications Equipment

Telex Communications, Inc.
9600 Aldrich Ave., S
Minneapolis, MN 55420
800-828-6107; 612-884-4051
fax: 612-884-0043

Texas Instruments, Inc.
P.O. Box 655012, M/S 57
Dallas, TX 75265
800-527-3500; 214-995-2011
fax: 214-995-4360
Technical support: 512-250-7407

ThumbScan, Inc.
1919 S. Highland Ave., Ste. 118C
Lombard, IL 60148
708-932-8844
fax: 708-495-0279

Thunderware, Inc.
21 Orinda Way
Orinda, CA 94563
510-254-6581
fax: 510-254-3047

Toshiba America Information Systems, Inc.
9740 Irvine Blvd.
Irvine, CA 92718
800-334-3445; 714-583-3000
Technical support: 800-999-4273

Total Technologies, Ltd.
2110 S. Anne St.
Santa Ana, CA 92704
800-669-4885; 714-241-0406
fax: 714-557-5838

Touchstone Technology, Inc.
955 Buffalo Rd.
Rochester, NY 14624
800-828-6968; 716-235-8358
fax: 716-235-8345

Transcend Information, Inc.
9159 La Rosa Dr.
Temple City, CA 91780
818-287-7892
fax: 818-287-5782

Trantor Systems, Ltd.
5415 Randall Place
Fremont, CA 94538
408-945-8600
fax: 510-770-9910

Trend Micro Devices, Inc.
2421 West 205th St., Ste. D-100
Torrance, CA 90501
800-228-5651; 310-782-8190
fax: 310-328-5892
Technical support: Use main number

T. S. MicroTech, Inc.
12565 Crenshaw Blvd.
Hawthorne, CA 90250
800-356-5906; 310-644-0859
fax: 310-644-0567

T&t Research
44 George St.
Etobicoke, Ontario
Canada M8V 2S2
416-252-4789

UCI Corp.
948 Cherry St.
Kent, OH 44240
216-673-5155
fax: 216-673-1811

UDP Data Products, Inc.
2908 Oregon Court, Unit I2
Torrance, CA 90503
800-888-4413; 310-791-4117
fax: 310-782-1577

Ultima Electronics Corp.
1156 Aster Ave., Ste. A
Sunnyvale, CA 94086
408-246-9208
fax: 408-246-9207

Unisys Corp.
P.O. Box 500
Blue Bell, PA 19424-0001
215-542-4011
Technical support: 800-448-1424

Unit Technology America
15237 Texaco Ave.
Paramount, CA 90723
310-602-2392
fax: 310-602-2497

Universal Vectors Corp.
580 Herndon Pkwy., Ste. 400
Herndon, VA 22070
703-435-2500
fax: 703-435-9638

Vatell Corp.
P.O. Box 66
Christiansburg, VA 24073
703-961-2001

Vernier Software
2920 Southwest 89th St.
Portland, OR 97225
503-297-5317
fax: 503-297-1760

Vertex Industries, Inc.
23 Carol St., P.O. Box 996
Clifton, NJ 07014-0996
201-777-3500
fax: 201-472-0814

Visualon, Inc.
9000 Sweet Valley Dr.
Cleveland, OH 44125
216-328-9000
fax: 216-328-9099

Wang Laboratories, Inc.
One Industrial Way, M/S 014-A1B
Lowell, MA 01851
800-835-9264; 508-459-5000
Technical support: 800-247-9264

Warp Speed Light Pens, Inc.
1086 Mechem Dr.
Ruidoso, NM 88345
800-874-4315; 505-258-5713
fax: 505-258-5744

Wen Technology Corp.
11 Clearbrook Rd.
Elmsford, NY 10523
800-377-4WEN; 914-347-4100
fax: 914-347-4128

Western Telematic, Inc.
5 Sterling
Irvine, CA 92718
800-854-7226; 714-586-9950
fax: 714-583-9514

Wink Data
720 132nd St., SW, Ste. 202
Everett, WA 98204
800-624-2101; 206-742-4145
fax: 206-742-3666

Winner Products (U.S.A.), Inc.
821 S. Lemon Ave., Ste. A-9
Walnut, CA 91789
909-595-2490
fax: 714-595-1483

Xante Corp.
23800 Hwy. 98, P.O. Box 518
Montrose, AL 36559
800-926-8839; 205-990-8189
fax: 205-990-8489

XCP, Inc.
40 Elm St.
Dryden, NY 13053
800-647-7020; 607-844-9143
fax: 607-844-8031

Z-Nix Co., Inc.
211 Erie St.
Pomona, CA 91768
909-629-8050
fax: 714-629-4792
Technical support: 909-629-3018

Zenion Industries, Inc.
5430 Commerce Blvd.
Rohnert Park, CA 94928
800-477-5297; 707-584-3663
fax: 707-584-4664

Zeny Computer Systems
4033 Clipper Court
Fremont, CA 94538
510-659-0386
fax: 510-659-0468

ZEOS International, Ltd.
530 5th Ave., NW
St. Paul, MN 55112
800-423-5891; 612-633-4591
fax: 612-633-1325
Technical support: Use 800 number

Zoltrix, Inc.
41394 Christy St.
Fremont, CA 94538
510-657-1188
fax: 510-657-1280

Modems and Telecommunications Equipment

ACCTON Technology Corp.
1962 Zanker Rd.
San Jose, CA 95112
408-452-8900
fax: 408-452-8988

Adtech Micro Systems, Inc.
48430 Milmont Dr.
Fremont, CA 94538
510-659-0756
fax: 510-659-9364

Advanced Microcomputer Systems, Inc.
1460 SW 3rd St.
Pompano Beach, FL 33069
800-972-3733; 305-784-0900
fax: 305-784-0904
Technical support: Use main number

DIRECTORY OF MANUFACTURERS

Ameriquest Technologies
2722 Michelson Dr.
Irvine, CA 92715
714-222-6000
fax: 714-261-0556
Technical support: Use main number

Apple Computer, Inc.
20525 Mariani Ave.
Cupertino, CA 95014
408-996-1010
Technical support: 800-767-2775

Aprotek
9323 W. Evans Creek Rd.
Rogue River, OR 97537
503-582-2120
fax: 503-582-2149

ATI Technologies, Inc.
33 Commerce Valley Dr. East
Toronto, ON
Canada L3T 7N6
905-882-2600
fax: 905-882-2620
Technical support: 905-882-2626

AT&T Paradyne
8545 126th Ave., N, P.O. Box 2826
Largo, FL 34649-2826
800-482-3333, ext. 448; 813-530-2000
fax: 813-530-2109

Barr Systems, Inc.
4131 Northwest 28 Lane
Gainesville, FL 32606
800-227-7797; 904-371-3050
fax: 904-491-3141
Technical support: Use 800 number

Bay Technical Associates, Inc.
200 N. Second St., P.O. Box 387
Bay St. Louis, MS 39520
800-523-2702; 601-467-8231
fax: 601-467-4551

BCH Equipment Corp.
6864 Cochron Rd.
Solon, OH 44139
800-237-8121; 216-498-1512

Best Data Products, Inc.
21800 Nordoff
Chatsworth, CA 91311
800-632-BEST; 818-773-9600
fax: 818-773-9619
Technical support: Use main number

Black Box Corp.
P.O. Box 12800
Pittsburgh, PA 15241
412-746-5500
fax: 412-746-0746

Calculus, Inc.
1050 Independence Ave.
Mountain View, CA 94043
415-390-8770

Cardinal Technologies, Inc.
1827 Freedom Rd.
Lancaster, PA 17601
717-293-300
fax: 717-293-3055
Technical support: 717-293-3124

Cardkey Systems, Inc.
101 W. Cochran St.
Simi Valley, CA 93065
805-522-5555
fax: 805-522-5407

Cermetek Microelectronics, Inc.
1308 Borregas Ave.
Sunnyvale, CA 94088
800-882-6271; 408-752-5000
fax: 408-752-5004

CLEO Communications
3796 Plaza Dr.
Ann Arbor, MI 48108
800-233-2536; 313-662-2002
fax: 313-662-1965
Technical support: 313-662-4194

CNet Technology, Inc.
2199 Zanker Rd.
San Jose, CA 95131
408-954-8000
fax: 408-954-8866

ComData Corp.
7900 N. Nagle Ave.
Morton Grove, IL 60053
800-255-2570; 708-470-9600

Compulan Technology, Inc.
1630 Oakland Rd. Ste.A111
San Jose, CA 95131
408-922-6888
fax: 408-432-8699

Compuquest, Inc.
801 Morse Ave.
Schaumburg, IL 60193
800-722-2353; 708-529-2552
fax: 708-894-6048

Computer Friends, Inc.
14250 N.W. Science Park Dr.
Portland, OR 97229
800-547-3303; 503-626-2291
fax: 503-643-5379
Technical support: Use main number

Computer Peripherals, Inc.
667 Rancho Conejo Blvd.
Newbury Park, CA 91320
800-854-7600; 805-499-5751
fax: 805-499-5742
Technical support: 805-499-6021

Computer Products, Inc.
(Measurement & Control Division)
2900 Gateway Dr.
Pompano Beach, FL 33069
305-974-5500
fax: 305-979-7371

COMSPEC Digital Products, Inc.
2313 W. Sam Houston Pkwy., N, Ste. 141
Houston, TX 77043
713-461-4487
fax: 713-461-8846

Comstat DataComm Corp.
1720 Spectrum Dr., NW
Lawrenceville, GA 30243
800-248-9496; 404-822-1962
fax: 404-822-4886

Connect, Inc.
10161 Bubb Rd.
Cupertino, CA 95014
800-262-2638; 408-973-0110
fax: 408-973-0497

Continental Resources, Inc.
175 Middlesex Tpke., P.O. Box 9137
Bedford, MA 01730
800-937-4688; 617-275-0850
fax: 617-275-6563

CXR Telcom Corp.
2040 Fortune Dr., Ste.102
San Jose, CA 95131
800-537-5762; 408-435-8520
fax: 408-435-1276

Data Race, Inc.
11550 IH 10, W, Ste. 395
San Antonio, TX 78249
210-558-1900
fax: 210-558-1929

DCB of Champaign, Inc.
807 Pioneer
Champaign, IL 61820
800-637-1127; 217-352-3207
fax: 217-352-0350

DigiBoard
10000 W. 76th St.
Eden Prarie, MN 55344
800-344-4273; 612-943-1055
fax: 612-943-0599
Technical support: 612-943-0579

Digicom Systems, Inc.
188 Topaz St.
Milpitas, CA 95035
800-833-8900; 408-262-1277
fax: 408-262-1390

Digital Equipment Corp.
146 Main St.
Maynard, MA 01754-2571
508-493-5111
fax: 508-493-8780
Technical support: 800-332-8000

Duracom Computer Systems
1425 Greenway Dr., Ste. 650
Irving, TX 75038
214-518-1200
fax: 214-518-1090

E-Tech Research, Inc.
3525 Ryder St.
Santa Clara, CA 95051
408-730-1388
fax: 408-730-2488

Edimax Computer Co.
3350 Scott Blvd., Bldg. 62
Santa Clara, CA 95054
408-496-1105
fax: 408-980-1530

Eicon Technology Corp.
2196 32nd Ave.
Montreal, Quebec
Canada H8T 3H7
514-631-2592
fax: 514-631-3092

Elec & Eltek (USA) Corp.
1183 Weddell Dr.
Sunnyvale, CA 94089
408-734-4223
fax: 408-734-8352

Everex Systems, Inc.
5020 Brandin Ct.
Fremont, CA 94538
800-821-0806; 510-498-1111
fax: 510-683-3398
Technical support: 510-498-4411

Farallon Computing, Inc.
2470 Mariner Sq. Loop
Alameda, CA 94501
510-814-5100
fax: 510-814-5026

Modems and Telecommunications Equipment

FastComm Communications Corp.
45472 Holiday Dr.
Sterling, VA 22170
800-521-2496; 703-318-7750
fax: 703-878-4625
Technical support: 800-282-9642

Franklin Datacom
733 Lakefield Rd.
Westlake Village, CA 91361
805-373-8688
fax: 805-373-7373

Galacticomm, Inc.
4101 Southwest 47th Ave., Ste. 101
Ft. Lauderdale, FL 33314
305-583-5990
fax: 305-583-7846

Galaxy Networks, Inc.
9348 DeSoto Ave.
Chatsworth, CA 91311
818-998-7851
fax: 818-998-1758

Gandalf Data, Inc.
130 Colonnade Sq.
Nepan, Ont. KZE 7M4
800-426-3253; 613-723-6500
fax: 613-226-1717
Technical support: Use 800 number

GCH Systems, Inc.
777 E. Middlefield Rd.
Mountain View, CA 94043
800-366-4560; 415-968-3400
fax: 415-964-9747

General DataComm, Inc.
1579 Straits Tpke.
Middlebury, CT 06762-1299
800-777-4005; 203-574-1118
fax: 203-758-8507
Technical support: 203-598-7526

G.I.S.
1700 S. Patterson Dr.
Dayton, OH 45479
908-221-2000
Technical support: Use main number

Global Village Communication, Inc.
685 E. Middlefield Rd.
Mountain View, CA 94043
415-329-0700
fax: 415-390-8282

GoldStar Electronics, Inc.
1000 Sylvan Ave.
Englewood Cliffs, NJ 07632
201-816-2000
fax: 201-816-2188
Technical support: 800-777-1192

GVC Technologies, Inc.
376 Lafayette Rd.
Sparta, NJ 07871
800-289-4821; 201-579-3630
fax: 201-579-2702
Technical support: Use main number

Holmes Microsystems, Inc.
2620 South 900 West
Salt Lake City, UT 84119
800-648-7488; 801-975-9929
fax: 801-975-9726
Technical support: Use main number

Hyundai Electronics America
166 Baypointe Pkwy.
San Jose, CA 95134
800-544-7808; 408-473-9200
fax: 408-943-9567
Technical support: 800-234-3553

IBM (International Business Machines)
Old Orchard Rd.
Armonk, NY 10504
800-426-2468; 914-765-1900
Technical support: Use 800 number

Inmac Corp.
P.O. Box 58031, 2465 Augustine Dr.
Santa Clara, CA 95054
800-547-5444; 408-727-1970
Technical support: 800-547-5444

Intel Corp. (Personal Computer Enhancement Operation)
5200 N.E. Elam Young Pkwy., M/S CO3-07
Hillsboro, OR 97124
503-696-8080
Technical support: 503-629-7000

Intelligence Technology Corp.
P.O. Box 671125
Dallas, TX 75367
214-250-4277

Intelligent Modem Corp.
435 W. Universal Circle
Sandy, UT 84070
801-561-8080
fax: 801-561-0117

ITS, Inc. (MI)
205 Hillbrady Rd.
Battle Creek, MI 49015
800-999-9ITS; 616-969-0500

Join Data Systems, Inc.
15336 Easter Valley Blvd.
City of Industry, CA 91746
818-330-6553
fax: 818-330-6865

Kasten Chase Applied Research
100 Millplain Rd.
Danbury, CT 06811
203-791-3885
fax: 203-791-3884

Lava Computers
28A Dansk Court
Rexdale, Ontario
Canada M9W 5V8
416-674-5942

Leading Edge Products, Inc.
117 Flanders Rd.
Westboro, MA 01581-5020
800-874-3340; 508-836-4800
fax: 508-836-4501
Technical support: 900-370-4800

LONGSHINE Technology, Inc.
2013 N. Capitol Ave.
San Jose, CA 95132
408-942-1746
fax: 408-942-1745

Megahertz Corp.
605 N. 5600 W.
Salt Lake City, UT 84116
800-527-8677; 801-320-7000
fax: 801-320-6010
Technical support: Use 800 number or
fax 801-320-6020

Memotec Data, Inc.
600 McCaffrey St.
Montreal, Quebec
Canada H4T 1N1
800-361-1962; 514-738-4781
fax: 514-738-4436

MICOM Communications Corp.
4100 Los Angeles Ave.
Simi Valley, CA 93063-3397
805-583-8600
fax: 805-583-1997

Micro Electronic Technologies
35 South St.
Hopkinton, MA 01748
800-766-SIMM; 508-435-9057
fax: 508-435-6481

Micro Integrated Communications Corp. (MiCC)
3270 Scott Blvd., Ste. 101
Santa Clara, CA 95054
408-980-8061
fax: 408-980-9568
Technical support: Use main number,
ext. 109

Micro-Technology Concepts, Inc.
258 Johnson Ave.
Brooklyn, NY 11206
800-366-4860; 718-456-9100
fax: 718-456-1200

Microcom, Inc.
500 River Ridge Dr.
Norwood, MA 02062-5028
800-822-8224; 617-551-1000
fax: 617-551-1968
Technical support: 617-551-1313

MicroGate Corp.
9501 N. Capitol of Texas Hwy., Ste 105
Austin, TX 98759-6374
800-444-1982; 512-345-7791
fax: 512-343-9046

Mirror Technologies, Inc.
5198 W. 76th St.
Edina, MN 55439
800-654-5294; 612-832-5622
fax: 612-832-5709
Technical support: 800-323-9285

Misco
One Misco Plaza
Holmdel, NJ 07733
800-876-4726; 908-264-1000
fax: 908-264-5955

Mitsuba Corp.
1925 Wright Ave.
La Verne, CA 91750
800-648-7822; 909-392-2000
fax: 909-392-2021
Technical support: 909-392-2019 (Laptop);
909-392-2018 (Desktop)

Morton Management, Inc.
12079 Tech Rd.
Silver Spring, MD 20904
301-622-5600
fax: 301-622-5438

Motorola Codex
20 Cabot Blvd.
Mansfield, MA 02048
800-446-6336; 508-261-4000
fax: 508-261-1203
Technical support: 800-544-0062

DIRECTORY OF MANUFACTURERS

Motorola UDS
5000 Bradford Dr.
Huntsville, AL 35805-1993
800-451-2369; 205-430-8000
fax: 205-830-5657
Technical support: Use 800 number

Multi-Tech Systems, Inc.
2205 Woodale Dr.
Mounds View, MN 55112
800-328-9717; 612-785-3500
fax: 612-785-9874
Technical support: Use main number

NetQuest Corp.
523 Fellowship Rd., Ste. 205
Mt. Laurel, NJ 08054
609-866-0505
fax: 609-866-2852

**Network Equipment Technologies, Inc.
(N.E.T.) (Access Products Division)**
800 Saginaw Dr.
Redwood City, CA 94063
415-366-4400
fax: 415-366-5675

Network Software Associates, Inc.
39 Argonaut
Laguna Hills, CA 92656
714-768-4013
fax: 714-768-5049

Okidata Corp.
532 Fellowship Rd.
Mt. Laurel, NJ 08054
800-654-3282; 609-235-2600
fax: 609-778-4184
Technical support: 609-273-0300

Packard Bell
8285 W. 3500 South
Magma, UT 84044
801-579-0160

Patton Electronics Co.
7622 Rickenbacker Dr.
Gaithersburg, MD 20879
301-975-1000
fax: 301-869-9293

PCS Performance Computer Systems, Inc.
35520 Mound Rd.
Sterling Heights, MI 48310
800-473-7369; 313-795-9209
fax: 313-268-3313

Penril DataComm Networks
1300 Quince Orchard Blvd.
Gaithersburg, MD 20878
301-921-8600
fax: 301-921-8376
Technical support: Use main number

Practical Peripherals, Inc.
375 Conejo Ridge Ave.
Thousand Oaks, CA 91361
800-442-4774; 805-497-4774
fax: 805-374-7200
Technical support: 805-496-7707

Processing Innovations, Inc.
10471 S. Brookhurst
Anaheim, CA 92804
714-535-8161

Prodatel Communications, Inc.
720 Montgolfier, Ste. 201
Ville de Laval, Quebec
Canada H7W 4Z2
514-689-8663
fax: 514-686-0239

Prometheus Products, Inc.
9524 S.W. Tualatin Sherwood Road
Tualatin, OR 97062
800-477-3473; 503-692-9600
fax: 503-692-9601
Technical support: 503-624-0953

Racal-Milgo
1601 N. Harrison Pkwy.
Sunrise, FL 33323-2899
800-722-2555; 305-846-1601
fax: 305-846-4942
Technical support: 305-846-4600

Racal-Datcom
1708 McCarthy Blvd.
Milpitas, CA 95035
408-432-8008
fax: 408-432-8311
Technical support: 408-456-7806

Reliable Communications, Inc.
P.O. Box 816, 4868 Hwy. 4
Angels Camp, CA 95222
800-222-0042; 209-736-0421
fax: 209-736-0425

SAI Systems Laboratories, Inc.
911 Bridgeport Ave.
Shelton, CT 06484
800-331-0488; 203-929-0790
fax: 203-929-6948

Sharp Digital Information Products, Inc.
16841 Armstrong Ave.
Irvine, CA 92714-4979
800-562-7427; 714-261-6224
fax: 714-261-9321

Sharp Electronics Corp.
(Professional Products Division)
Sharp Plaza, P.O. Box 650
Mahwah, NJ 07430
201-529-8200
fax: 201-529-9636
Technical support: 800-732-8221

Shiva Corp.
N.W. Park 63 3rd Ave.
Burlington, MA 01803
800-458-3550; 617-270-8300
fax: 617-270-8599
Technical support: 617-270-8400

Sprint Products Group, Inc
600 Industrial Pkwy.
Industrial Airport, KS 66031
913-791-7700

Star Logic, Inc.
234 E. Caribbean Dr.
Sunnyvale, CA 94089
408-747-0903
fax: 408-747-0954

Sunhill, Inc.
500 Andover Park, E
Seattle, WA 98188
800-544-1361; 206-575-4131
fax: 206-575-3617

Supra Corp.
7101 Supra Dr. S.W.
Albany, OR 97321
800-727-8772; 503-967-2400
fax: 503-967-2401
Technical support: Use 800 number

Swan Technologies
3075 Research Dr.
State College, PA 16801
800-468-9044; 814-238-1820
fax: 814-237-4450
Technical support: 800-468-7926

Tandy Corp.
1800 One Tandy Center
Ft. Worth, TX 76102
817-390-3011
fax: 817-390-2774
Technical support: 817-390-3861

Telcor Systems Corp.
4 Strathmore Rd.
Natick, MA 01760
800-826-2938; 508-653-3995
fax: 508-651-0065

Telebit Corp.
1315 Chesapeake Terr.
Sunnyvale, CA 94089
800-835-3248; 408-734-4333
fax: 408-734-3333
Technical support: 408-734-5200

Terminal Data Corp.
15733 Crabbs Branch Way
Rockville, MD 20855
301-921-8282
fax: 301-921-8353

TIL Systems, Inc.
225 Stedman St., Ste. 27
Lowell, MA 01851
508-970-1189
fax: 508-970-1295

**Toshiba America Information Systems,
Inc. (Computer Systems Division)**
9740 Irvine Blvd.
Irvine, CA 92718
800-334-3445; 714-583-3000
Technical support: 800-999-4273
(Computers)

Universal Data Systems, Inc.
5000 Bradford Dr.
Huntsville, AL 35805-1993
800-631-4869; 205-430-8000

US Robotics, Inc.
3100 N. McCormick Blvd.
Skokie, IL 60076
800-342-5877; 708-982-5001
fax: 708-982-5235
Technical support: 800-982-5151

Ven-Tel, Inc.
2121 Zanker Rd.
San Jose, CA 95131
800-538-5121; 408-436-7400
fax: 408-436-7451
Technical support: Use 800 number

Vocal Technologies, Ltd.
3032 Scott Blvd.
Santa Clara, CA 95054
408-980-5181
fax: 408-980-8709

Monitors and Video-Related Equipment

Wang Laboratories, Inc.
One Industrial Ave., M/S 027-39B
Lowell, MA 01851
800-247-9264; 508-459-5000
Technical support: Use 800 number

Western DataCom Co., Inc.
P.O. Box 45113
Westlake, OH 44145-0113
800-262-3311; 216-835-1510
fax: 216-835-9146

X-Alt, Inc.
42 Digital Dr.
Novato, CA 94949
800-899-9258; 415-883-9611
fax: 415-883-9628

Xecom, Inc.
374 Turquoise St.
Milpitas, CA 95035
408-945-6640
fax: 408-942-1346

Xpra Com Inc.
P.O. Box 235
Ajax, Ontario
Canada L1S 3C3
905-427-6612
fax: 905-427-0934

Yang Automatic Machines
4920 E. La Palma Ave.
Anaheim, CA 92807
800-233-4208; 714-693-0333
fax: 714-693-0705

Zenith Data Systems
2150 E. Lake Cook Rd.
Buffalo Grove, IL 60089
708-808-5000
fax: 708-808-4434

Zoltrix, Inc.
47273 Fremont Blvd.
Fremont, CA 94538
510-657-1188
fax: 510-657-1280

Zoom Telephonics, Inc.
207 South St.
Boston, MA 02111
800-631-3116; 617-423-1072
Technical support: 617-423-1076

Monitors and Video-Related Equipment

AccuSys, Inc.
3695 Kings Row
Reno, NV 89503
702-746-1111
fax: 702-746-2306

Actix Systems, Inc.
3350 Scott Blvd.
Santa Clara, CA 95054
800-927-5557; 408-986-1625
fax: 408-986-1646

Ad Lib, Inc.
350 Franquet St., Ste 80
St.-Fay, Quebec
Canada G1P 4P3
418-656-8742
fax: 418-656-1646

ADI Systems, Inc.
2115 Ringwood Ave.
San Jose, CA 95131
800-228-0530; 408-944-0100
fax: 408-944-0300

Advanced Digital Imaging
1250 N. Lakeview Ave., Ste O
Anaheim, CA 92807
714-779-7772
fax: 714-779-7773

Advanced Logic Research, Inc.
9401 Jeronimo
Irvine, CA 92718
800-444-4257; 714-581-6770
fax: 714-581-9240
Technical support: 714-458-0863

Aedex Corp.
1070 Ortega Way
Placentia, CA 92670
714-632-7000
fax: 714-632-1334

Ahead Systems, Inc.
44244 Fremont Blvd.
Fremont, CA 94538
510-623-0900
fax: 510-623-0960

Alacrity Systems, Inc.
43 Newburg Rd.
Hackettstown, NJ 07840
800-252-2748; 908-813-2400
fax: 908-813-2490

Alacron, Inc.
71 Spitbrook Rd., Ste. 204
Nashua, NH 03060
603-891-2750
fax: 603-891-2745

Allen Communication, Inc.
5225 Wiley Post Way, Ste. 140
Salt Lake City, UT 84116
800-325-7850; 801-537-7800
fax: 801-537-7805

Alloy Computer Products, Inc.
25 Porter Rd.
Littleton, MA 01460
508-486-0001
fax: 508-486-3755

Alpha Microsystems
3511 W. Sunflower Ave.
Santa Ana, CA 92704
714-957-8500
fax: 714-957-8705

Amdek Corp.
3471 N. First St.
San Jose, CA 95134
800-722-6355; 408-473-1200
fax: 408-473-2845

Answer Software Corp.
20045 Stevens Creek Blvd., Ste. 1E
Cupertino, CA 95014-2353
408-253-7515
fax: 408-253-8430

Antex Electronics Corp.
16100 S. Figueroa St.
Gardena, CA 90248
800-338-4231; 310-532-3092
fax: 310-532-8509

Appian Technology, Inc.
477 N. Matilda Ave.
Sunnyvale, CA 94088
408-730-8800
fax: 408-730-5456

Apple Computer, Inc.
20525 Mariani Ave.
Cupertino, CA 95014
408-996-1010
Technical support: 800-767-2775

Applied Data Sciences, Inc.
P.O. Box 814209
Dallas, TX 75381
214-243-0113
fax: 214-243-0217

Applied Data Systems, Inc.
409A E. Preston St.
Baltimore, MD 21202
800-541-2003; 410-576-0335

Ara-Tech, Inc.
7523 Van Alden Ave.
Reseda, CA 91335
818-996-8801
fax: 818-996-8850

Ariel Corp.
433 River Rd.
Highland Park, NJ 08904
908-249-2900
fax: 908-249-2123

Artic Technologies
55 Park St., Ste. 2
Troy, MI 48083
313-588-7370
fax: 313-588-2650

Artist Graphics
2675 Patton Rd.
St. Paul, MN 55113
800-627-8478; 612-631-7800
fax: 612-631-7802
Technical support: 612-631-7888

AST Research Inc.
P.O. Box 19658, 16215 Alton Pkwy.
Irvine, CA 92713-9658
800-727-1278; 714-727-4141
fax: 714-727-9355
Technical support: Use 800 number

ATI Technologies, Inc.
33 Commerce Valley Dr. East
Thornhill, Ontario
Canada L3T 7N6
905-882-2600
fax: 905-882-2620
Technical support: 905-882-2626

Atlaz International, Ltd.
616 Burnside Ave., P.O. Box 110
Inwood, NY 11096
516-239-1854
fax: 516-239-1939

Autrec, Inc.
4305-40 Enterprise Dr., Ste. A
Winston-Salem, NC 27106
919-759-9493

Barco, Inc.
1000 Cobb Place Blvd.
Kennesaw, GA 30144
404-590-7900
fax: 404-590-8836

DIRECTORY OF MANUFACTURERS

Beaver Computer Corp.
1610 Crane Ct.
San Jose, CA 95112
408-944-9000
fax: 408-944-9001

Behavior Tech Computer (USA) Corp.
4180 Business Center Dr.
Fremont, CA 94538
510-657-3956
fax: 510-657-3965

Bell & Howell Quintar Co.
370 Amapola Ave., Ste. 106
Torrance, CA 90501
800-223-5231; 310-320-5700
fax: 310-618-1282

Bit 3 Computer Corp.
8120 Penn Ave., S
Minneapolis, MN 55431-1393
612-881-6955
fax: 612-881-9674

Boca Research, Inc.
6413 Congress Ave.
Boca Raton, FL 33487-2839
407-997-6227
fax: 407-997-0918

**Business Technology Manufacturing, Inc.
(BTM)**
42-20 235th St.
Douglaston, NY 11363
718-229-8080

CalComp Plotter Products Group
P.O. Box 3250, 2411 W. La Palma Ave.
Anaheim, CA 92803
800-932-1212; 714-821-2000
fax: 714-821-2832
Technical support: Use main number

Cardinal Technologies, Inc.
1827 Freedom Rd.
Lancaster, PA 17601
717-293-3000
fax: 717-293-3055
Technical support: 717-293-3124

Carroll Touch
P.O. Box 1309
Round Rock, TX 78680
512-244-3500
fax: 512-244-7040

CCSI/The Voice Connection
8258 Kingslee Rd.
Bloomington, MN 55438
612-944-1334

Chaplet Systems, Inc.
252 N. Wolf Rd.
Sunnyvale, CA 94086
408-732-7950
fax: 408-732-6050

Chugai Boyeki (America) Corp.
55 Mall Dr.
Commack, NY 11725
800-422-6707; 516-864-9700
fax: 516-543-5426

Colorgraphic Communications Corp.
5980 New Peachtree Rd.
Atlanta, GA 30341
404-455-3921
fax: 404-458-0616

Command Corp., Inc.
3761 Venture Dr., Ste. 270
Duluth, GA 30136
404-813-8030

Commax Technologies, Inc.
2031 Concourse Dr.
San Jose, CA 95131
800-526-6629; 408-435-5000
fax: 408-435-5005

**Communication Automation & Control,
Inc.**
1642 Union Blvd., Ste. 200
Allentown, PA 18103-1510
800-367-6735; 610-776-6669
fax: 610-770-1232

Compaq Computer Corp.
P.O. Box 692000
Houston, TX 77269-2000
800-231-0900; 713-370-0670
fax: 713-374-1402

Comprehensive Video Supply
148 Veterans Dr.
Northvale, NJ 07647
800-526-0242; 201-767-7990
fax: 201-767-7377

CompuAdd Corp.
12303 Technology Blvd.
Austin, TX 78727
800-531-5475; 512-250-1489
fax: 512-250-5760
Technical support: 800-999-9901

Computer Friends, Inc.
14250 N.W. Science Park Dr.
Portland, OR 97229
800-547-3303; 503-626-2291
fax: 503-643-5379
Technical support: Use main number

Comy Technology Multi-Micro Systems
2124 Zanker Rd.
San Jose, CA 95131
408-437-1555
fax: 408-437-1583

Conrac Display Products, Inc.
1724 S. Mountain Ave.
Duarte, CA 91010
818-303-0095
fax: 818-303-5484

Control Vision
P.O. Box 596
Pittsburg, KS 66762
800-292-1160; 316-231-6647

Cordata Technologies, Inc.
1055 W. Victoria St.
Compton, CA 90220
310-603-2901
fax: 310-763-0447

Cornerstone Technology
1990 Concourse Dr.
San Jose, CA 95131
800-562-2552; 408-435-8900
fax: 408-435-8998

CSP, Inc.
40 Linnell Circle
Billerica, MA 01821
508-663-7598
fax: 508-663-0150

CSS Laboratories, Inc.
1641 McGaw Ave.
Irvine, CA 92714
714-852-8161
fax: 714-852-0414

Cubix Corp.
2800 Lockheed Way
Carson City, NV 89706
800-829-0550; 702-883-7611
fax: 702-882-2407

Data Translation, Inc.
100 Locke Dr.
Marlboro, MA 01752
508-481-3700
fax: 508-481-8620

Dell Computer Corp.
9505 Arboretum Blvd.
Austin, TX 78759-7299
800-426-5150; 512-338-4400
fax: 512-728-3653
Technical support: 800-624-9896

DFI, Inc.
135 Main Ave.
Sacramento, CA 95838
916-568-1234
fax: 916-568-1233
Technical support: Use main number

Diamond Computer Systems, Inc.
1130 E. Arques Ave.
Sunnyvale, CA 94086
408-736-2000
fax: 408-730-5750

Diaquest, Inc.
1440 San Pablo Ave.
Berkeley, CA 94702
510-526-7167
fax: 510-526-7073

Digidesign, Inc.
1360 Willow Rd., Ste. 101
Menlo Park, CA 94025
800-333-2137; 415-327-8811
fax: 415-327-0777
Technical support: Use main number

Digital Vision, Inc.
270 Bridge St.
Dedham, MA 02026
800-346-0090; 617-329-5400
fax: 617-329-6286

Dragon Systems, Inc.
320 Nevada St.
Chapel Bridge Park
Newton, MA 02160
617-965-5200
fax: 617-527-0372

DSP Technology, Inc.
48500 Kato Rd.
Fremont, CA 94538-7385
510-657-7555
fax: 510-657-7576

DTK Computer, Inc.
17700 Castleton St., Ste. 160
City of Industry, CA 91748
818-810-8880
fax: 818-810-5233
Technical support: 818-810-0098

Monitors and Video-Related Equipment

**Du Pont Electronics Imaging Division
(Computing Products Group)**
P.O. Box 6099
Newark, DE 19714-6099
302-733-9692
Technical support: 800-225-8414

Electrograph Systems, Inc.
175 Commerce Dr.
Hauppauge, NY 11788
800-776-5768; 516-436-5050
fax: 516-436-5227

Electrohome, Ltd.
809 Wellington St., N.
Kitchener, Ontario
Canada N2G 4J6
519-744-7111
fax: 519-749-3151

Electronics, Inc.
1000 Sylvan Ave.
Englewood Cliffs, NJ 07632
201-816-2000
fax: 201-816-2188
Technical support: 800-777-1192

Elite Business Applications, Inc.
8324 Veterans Hwy., P.O. Box 728
Millersville, MD 21108
800-576-2349; 410-987-3048
fax: 410-987-3258
Technical support: Use main number

ELSA America, Inc.
400 Oyster Point Blvd., Ste. 109
South San Francisco, CA 94080
800-272-3572; 415-615-7799
fax: 415-588-0113

Epson America, Inc.
20770 Madrona Ave.
Torrance, CA 90509-2842
800-289-3776; 310-782-0770
Technical support: 800-922-8911

ER&S Computer Solutions, Inc.
12727 N.E. 20th St., Ste. 25
Bellevue, WA 98005
206-881-1789
fax: 206-883-7136

Everex Systems, Inc.
5020 Brandin Ct.
Fremont, CA 94538
800-821-0806; 510-498-1111
fax: 510-683-3398
Technical support: 510-498-4411

Extended Systems
P.O. Box 4937, 6123 N. Meeker Ave.
Boise, ID 83704
800-235-7576; 208-322-7575
fax: 208-377-1906

Falco Data Products, Inc.
440 Potrero Ave.
Sunnyvale, CA 94086-4117
800-325-2648; 408-745-7123
fax: 408-745-7860
Technical support: Use main number

Focus Information Systems, Inc.
46713 Fremont Blvd.
Fremont, CA 94538
510-657-2845
fax: 510-657-4158

Fora, Inc.
30 Montague Expy.
San Jose, CA 95134
800-FOR-FORA; 408-944-0393
fax: 408-944-0392

FTG Data Systems
P.O. Box 615, 10801 Dale St., Ste. J-2
Stanton, CA 90680
800-962-3900; 714-995-3900
fax: 714-995-3989

Genoa Systems Corp.
75 E. Trimble Rd.
San Jose, CA 95131
408-432-9090
fax: 408-434-0997

G.I.S.
1700 S. Patterson Dr.
Dayton, OH 45479
908-221-2000
Technical support: Use main number

Golden Dragon
3330 McNicoll Ave.
Scarborough, Ontario
Canada M1V 2L2
416-297-1202
fax: 416-754-2240

GoldStar Technology, Inc.
3003 N. First St.
San Jose, CA 95134-2004
408-432-1331
fax: 408-432-6053
Technical support: 800-777-1192

Hercules Computer Technology, Inc.
3839 Spinnaker Ct.
Fremont, CA 94538
800-532-0600; 510-623-6030
fax: 510-623-1112
Technical support: 510-623-6050

Hewlett-Packard Co.
3000 Hanover St.
Palo Alto, CA 94304
800-752-0900; 415-857-1501
Technical support: 800-544-9976

High Res Technologies
16 English Ivy Wy. No. York, Ontario
Canada M2H 3M4
416-497-6493
fax: 416-497-1636

Hitachi America, Ltd. (OAS Division)
110 Summit Ave.
Montvale, NJ 07645
201-573-0774
fax: 201-573-7660

HNC, Inc.
5930 Cornerstone Ct.
San Diego, CA 92121-3728
619-546-8877
fax: 619-452-6524

HYPERSPEED Technologies, Inc.
10225 Barnes Canyon Rd.
San Diego, CA 92121-2736
619-578-4893
fax: 619-271-6717

Hyundai Electronics America
166 Baypointe Pkwy.
San Jose, CA 95134
800-544-7808; 408-473-9200
fax: 408-943-9567
Technical support: 800-234-3553

IBM (International Business Machines)
Old Orchard Rd.
Armonk, NY 10504
800-426-2468; 914-765-1900
Technical support: Use 800 number

IDEAMATICS, Inc.
1364 Beverly Rd., Ste. 101
McLean, VA 22101
800-247-4332; 703-903-4972
fax: 703-903-8949

IDEC, Inc.
1195 Doylestown Pike
Quakertown, PA 18951
215-538-2600
fax: 215-538-2665

Idek North America
650 Louis Dr. #120
Warminster, PA 18974
800-594-7478; 215-957-6543
fax: 215-957-6551

IEV Corp.
3595 S. 500 West
Salt Lake City, UT 84115
800-438-6161; 801-263-6042
fax: 801-263-9980

Ikegami Electronics (U.S.A.), Inc.
37 Brook Ave.
Maywood, NJ 07607
201-368-9171
fax: 201-569-1626

Image Processing Systems, Inc.
3440 Pharmacy Ave.
Scarborough, Ontario
Canada M1W 2P8
416-492-4000
fax: 416-492-4001

Image Systems Corp.
11595 K-Tel Dr.
Hopkins, MN 55343
800-462-4370; 612-935-1171
fax: 612-935-1386

Imaging Technology, Inc.
55 Middlesex Turnpike
Bedford, MA 01730
800-335-3035; 617-275-2700
fax: 617-275-9590

Imagraph Corp.
11 Elizabeth Dr.
Chelmsford, MA 01824
508-256-4624
fax: 508-250-9155

Imtec, Inc.
P.O. Box 809 Imtec Lane
Bellows Falls, VT 05101
802-463-9502
fax: 802-463-4334

Infotronic America, Inc.
8834 N. Capital of Texas Hwy., Ste. 200
Austin, TX 78759
512-345-9646
fax: 512-345-9895

Intecolor Corp.
2150 Boggs Rd., Bldg. 200
Duluth, GA 30126
404-623-9145
fax: 404-623-9163

DIRECTORY OF MANUFACTURERS

Intel Corp.
2200 Mission College Blvd.
Santa Clara, CA 95054-1537
408-765-8080
fax: 408-765-1821

International Meta Systems, Inc.
23842 Hawthorne Blvd., Ste 200
Torrance, CA 90505
310-375-4700
fax: 310-378-7643

International PowerSystems Corp.
3400 Britannia Dr. East
Tucson, AZ 85706
602-889-7600
fax: 602-294-1808

Jodan Technology, Inc.
133 Massachusettes Ave., P.O. Box 362
Lexington, MA 02173-0362
617-863-8898
fax: 617-863-0462

Jovian Logic Corp.
47929 Fremont Blvd.
Fremont, CA 94538
510-651-4823
fax: 510-651-1343

JOYCE Associates
215 Franklin St.
Clayton, NJ 08312

JVC Information Products Co. of America
17811 Mitchell Ave.
Irvine, CA 92714
714-261-1292
fax: 714-261-9690

Keithley MetraByte
440 Myles Standish Blvd.
Taunton, MA 02780
508-880-3000
fax: 508-880-0179

KFC Computek Components Corp.
31 E. Mall
Plainview, NY 11803
516-454-0262
fax: 516-454-0265

Korea Data Systems Co., Ltd.
6 Blackstone Valley Pl.
Lincoln, RI 02865
401-334-0100
fax: 401-334-0103

LaserMaster Technologies Corp.
7156 Shady Oak Rd.
Eden Prairie, MN 55344
612-944-9330
fax: 612-944-0522
Technical support: 612-944-9331

Lava Computers
28A Dansk Court
Rexdale, Ontario
Canada M9W 5V8
416-674-5942

Lazerus
2821 Ninth St.
Berkeley, CA 94710
510-339-6263
fax: 510-339-6265, press *

Liebert Corp.
1050 Dearborn Dr.
Columbus, OH 43229
800-BACK-UPS; 614-888-0241
fax: 614-841-6022

Link Computer, Inc.
16800 E. Gale
City of Industry, CA 91745
818-968-8669
fax: 818-968-2188

Lite-On, Inc.
720 S. Hillview Dr.
Milpitas, CA 95035
408-946-4873
fax: 408-942-1527

Logitech, Inc.
6505 Kaiser Dr.
Fremont, CA 94555
510-795-8500
fax: 510-792-8901

Logos Systems International
100 Royal Oak Ct.
Scotts Valley, CA 95066
408-438-5012
fax: 408-439-9440

LSI Logic Corp.
1551 McCarthy Blvd.
Milpitas, CA 95035
800-433-8778; 408-433-8000
fax: 408-434-6457

MacSema
94 S.E. Wilson
Bend, OR 97702
503-389-1122
fax: 503-389-1888

Magni Systems, Inc.
9500 S.W. Gemini Dr.
Beaverton, OR 97005
800-624-6465; 503-626-8400
fax: 503-626-6225

Mass Microsystems, Inc.
1582 Centrepoint Dr.
Milpitas, CA 95035
800-522-7970; 408-956-5999
fax: 408-956-5995
Technical support: 800-442-7979

Matrox Electronic Systems, Ltd.
1055 St. Regis Blvd.
Dorval, Quebec
Canada H9P 2T4
800-361-4903; 514-685-2630
fax: 514-685-2853

Media Vision, Inc.
47300 Bayside Pkwy.
Fremont, CA 94538
800-348-7116; 510-770-8600
fax: 510-770-8648

Memory Technologies, Tx Inc.
3007 N. Lamar
Austin, TX 78705
800-950-8411; 512-451-2600
Technical support: Use main number

Metheus Corp.
1600 N.W. Compton Dr.
Beaverton, OR 97006-6905
800-547-5315; 503-690-1550
fax: 503-690-1525

Micro Express
1801 E. Carnegie Ave.
Santa Ana, CA 92705
800-989-9900; 714-852-1400
fax: 714-852-1225
Technical support: 800-899-4832

Micro-Labs, Inc.
204 Lost Cyn. Ct.
Richardson, TX 75080
214-234-5842
fax: 214-234-5896

Micro Solutions Computer Products
132 W. Lincoln Hwy.
DeKalb, IL 60115
815-756-3411
fax: 815-756-2928

The Micro Works, Inc.
1942 S. El Camino Real
Encinitas, CA 92024
619-942-2400

Microdyne Corp.
491 Oak Rd.
Ocala, FL 34472
904-687-4633
fax: 904-687-3392

Microfield Graphics, Inc.
9825 S.W. Sunshine Court
Beaverton, OR 97005
800-334-4922; 503-626-9393
fax: 503-641-9333

Micron Technology, Inc.
2805 E. Columbia Rd.
Boise, ID 83706-9698
208-368-4000
fax: 208-368-4558
Technical support: 208-368-3900

Microtek Lab, Inc.
3715 Dolittle Dr.
Redondo Beach, CA 90278
800-654-4160; 310-297-5000
fax: 310-297-5050
Technical support: 310-297-5100

MicroWay, Inc.
P.O. Box 79, Research Park
Kingston, MA 02364
508-746-7341
fax: 508-746-4678

Mirage Computer Systems
119 S. Bundy Dr.
Los Angeles, CA 90048
800-228-3349; 310-440-1460
fax: 310-476-6839

Mirror Technologies, Inc.
5198 W. 76th St.
Edina, MN 55439
800-654-5294; 612-832-5622
fax: 612-832-5709
Technical support: 800-323-9285

Mitsuba Corp.
1925 Wright Ave.
La Verne, CA 91750
800-648-7822; 909-392-2000
fax: 909-392-2021
Technical support: 909-392-2019 (Laptop);
909-392-2018 (Desktop)

Mitsubishi Electronics America, Inc.
(Professional Electronics Division)
800 Cottontail Lane
Somerset, NJ 08873
908-563-9889
fax: 908-563-9196
Technical support: Use main number

Monitors and Video-Related Equipment

Mobius Technologies, Inc.
5835 Doyle St.
Emeryville, CA 94608
800-800-4334; 510-654-0556
fax: 510-654-2834

Modgraph, Inc.
6 Gill
Burlington, MA 01803
800-327-9962; 617-938-4488
fax: 617-938-4455

Monitor Technology Corp.
2864 Vicksburg Ln.
Plymouth, MN 55447
612-551-1478
fax: 612-551-1587
Technical support: Use main number

Music Quest, Inc.
P.O. Box 260963
Plano, TX 75026
800-876-1376; 214-881-7408

Mylex Corp.
34551 Ardenwood Blvd.
Fremont, CA 94555-3607
800-77-MYLEX; 510-796-6100
fax: 510-745-7564
Technical support: Use main number

Nanao USA Corp.
23535 Telo Ave.
Torrance, CA 90505
800-800-5202; 310-325-5202
fax: 310-530-1679
Technical support: Use main number

National Instruments Corp.
6504 Bridge Point Pkwy.
Austin, TX 78730-5039
800-433-3488; 512-794-0100
fax: 512-794-8411
Technical support: Use 800 number

NCD-PCX Division
9590 S.W. Gemini Dr.
Beaverton, OR 97005
503-641-2200
fax: 503-643-8642

NEC Technologies, Inc.
1414 Massachusetts Ave.
Boxborough, MA 01719
508-264-8000
fax: 508-264-8673
Technical support: 800-388-8888

Nemonix, Inc.
25 South St.
Hopkinton, MA 01748
800-435-8650; 508-435-9087
fax: 508-435-6127

New Media Graphics Corp.
780 Boston Rd.
Billerica, MA 01821
508-663-0666
fax: 508-663-6678

Newbridge Microsystems
603 March Rd.
Kanata, Ontario
Canada K2K 2M5
800-267-7231; 613-592-0714
fax: 613-592-1320

NewVoice
8500 Leesburg Pike, Ste. 409
Vienna, VA 22182-2409
703-448-0570
fax: 703-448-1078

Nissei Sangyo America, Ltd. (NSA)
800 South St.
Waltham, MA 02154
617-893-5700

Novacor, Inc.
780 Montague Expy., Ste. 104
San Jose, CA 95131
800-486-6682; 408-441-6500
fax: 408-441-6811

Nth Graphics
11500 Metric Blvd., Ste. 210
Austin, TX 78758
800-624-7552; 512-832-1944
fax: 512-832-5954
Technical support: Use main number

Number Nine Computer Corp.
18 Hartwell Ave.
Lexington, MA 02173
800-438-6463; 617-674-0009
fax: 617-674-2919

Nuvo Star, Inc.
2488 Townsgate Rd., Ste. C
Westlake Village, CA 91361
805-446-6175
fax: 805-446-6194

Omnicomp Graphics Corp.
1734 W. Sam Houston Pkwy., N
Houston, TX 77043
713-464-2990
fax: 713-827-7540

Omnitronix, Inc.
760 Harrison St.
Seattle, WA 98109
206-624-4985
fax: 206-624-5610

Online Products Corp.
20251 Century Blvd.
Germantown, MD 20874
800-922-9204; 301-428-3700
fax: 301-428-2903

Optiquest
20490 Business Pkwy.
Walnut, CA 91789
800-THE-OPTI; 909-468-3750
fax: 909-468-3770

Orange Micro, Inc.
1400 N. Lakeview Ave.
Anaheim, CA 92807
714-779-2772
fax: 714-779-9332

Orchid Technology, Inc.
45365 Northport Loop West
Fremont, CA 94538
800-767-2443; 510-683-0300
fax: 510-490-9312

Our Business Machines, Inc.
12901 Ramona Blvd., Unit J
Irwindale, CA 91706
800-443-1435; 818-337-9614
fax: 818-960-1766

**Panasonic Communications & Systems Co.
(Office Automation Group)**
2 Panasonic Way
Secaucus, NJ 07094
201-348-7000
Technical support: 800-222-0584

Parallax Graphics, Inc.
2500 Condensa St.
Santa Clara, CA 95051
408-727-2220
fax: 408-980-5139

Parsytec, Inc.
245 W. Roosevelt Rd., Bldg. 9, Unit 60
West Chicago, IL 60185
708-293-9500
fax: 708-293-9525

PC Craft, Inc.
163 University Pkwy.
Pomona, CA 91768
909-869-6133
fax: 909-869-6128

PC Tech, Inc.
980 W. Lakewood Ave.
Lake City, MN 55041
612-345-4555
fax: 612-345-5514

The Periscope Co., Inc.
1475 Peachtree St., Ste. 100
Atlanta, GA 30361
800-722-7006; 404-888-5335
fax: 404-888-5520

Personal Computer Graphics Corp.
1646 17th St.
Santa Monica, CA 90035
310-452-8470

Personal Computer Peripherals Corp.
4710 Eisenhower Blvd., Bldg. A
Tampa, FL 33634
800-622-2888; 813-884-3092
fax: 813-886-0520

Philips Consumer Electronics Co.
One Philips Dr., P.O. Box 14810
Knoxville, TN 37914-1810
615-521-4316
fax: 615-521-4406
Technical support: 800-722-6224

Pinnacle Micro, Inc.
19 Technology
Irvine, CA 92718
800-553-7070; 714-727-3300
fax: 714-727-1913

Pixelworks, Inc.
7 Park Ave.
Hudson, NH 03051
800-247-2476; 603-880-1322
fax: 603-880-6558

Pixielink Corp.
8 Kane Industrial Dr.
Hudson, MA 01749
508-562-4803

PKI Pao-Ku InH
1053 Shore Rd.
Napierville, IL 60563
800-676-9632; 708-369-5199
fax: 708-369-5935

Portable Storage Solutions
2616 Willow Bend Pl.
El Cajon, CA 92019
800-257-1666
fax: 619-441-6999
Technical support: Use 800 number

DIRECTORY OF MANUFACTURERS

Powercard Supply
12231 Southwest 129 Court
Miami, FL 33186
800-63-PCPWR; 305-251-5855
fax: 305-251-2334

Poynting Products, Inc.
P.O. Box 1227
Oak Park, IL 60304
312-489-6638

Princeton Graphic Systems
P.O. Box 100040, 1100 Northmeadow
Pkwy., Ste. 150
Roswell, GA 30076
800-221-1490; 404-664-1010
fax: 404-664-1510
Technical support: Use main number

Princeton Publishing Labs
101 Business Park Dr., Ste. 100
Skillman, NJ 08558
609-924-1153
fax: 609-924-6465

Processor Sciences, Inc.
180 Bear Hill Rd.
Waltham, MA 02154
617-890-0292
fax: 617-890-3345

Progressive Image Technology
120 Blue Ravine Rd., Ste. 2
Folsom, CA 95630
916-985-7501
fax: 916-985-7507

Prometa USA, Inc.
5929 Southwest 36th Way
Gainesville, FL 32608
800-283-6382; 904-335-6382

Proton Corp.
16826 Edwards Rd.
Cerritos, CA 90701
714-952-6900

PSI Integration, Inc./Supra
851 E. Hamilton Ave., Ste. 200
Campbell, CA 95008
800-774-4965

Purart, Inc.
P.O. Box 189
Hampton Falls, NH 03844
603-772-9907

QANTEL Business Systems, Inc.
4142 Point Eden Way
Hayward, CA 94545-3781
800-227-1894; 510-887-7777
fax: 510-782-6195

Q/Cor
One Quad Way
Norcross, GA 30093-2919
800-548-3420; 404-923-6666
fax: 404-564-5528
Technical support: Use main number

QDI Computer, Inc.
11552 E. Washington Blvd., Unit D
Whittier, CA 90606
213-908-1029
fax: 213-908-1033

Quadtel
3190-J Airport Loop Dr.
Costa Mesa, CA 92626
714-754-4422
fax: 714-754-4426

Questel, Inc.
10175 Joerschke Dr., P.O. Box 752
Grass Valley, CA 95945
916-477-5000

Qume Corp.
500 Yosemite Dr.
Milpitas, CA 95035
408-942-4000
fax: 408-942-4052
Technical support: 408-942-4138 (Monitors,
Terminals); 408-942-4100 (Printers)

RangerTechnologies, Inc.
313 2nd St. E.
Hastings, MN 55033
612-437-2233
fax: 612-437-7325

Radius, Inc.
1710 Fortune Dr.
San Jose, CA 95131
800-227-2795; 408-434-1010
fax: 408-434-0770
Technical support: 408-434-1012

Rapid Systems
433 North 34th St.
Seattle, WA 98103
206-547-8311
fax: 206-548-0322

Rasterex USA
1908 Cliff Valley Way, Ste. 2010
Atlanta, GA 30329
800-648-7249; 404-320-0800
fax: 404-315-7645

RasterOps Corp.
2500 Walsh Ave.
Santa Clara, CA 95051
408-562-4200
fax: 408-562-4065
Technical support: 800-729-2656

Redlake Corp.
15005 Concord Circle
Morgan Hill, CA 95037
800-543-6563; 408-779-6464
fax: 408-778-6256

REDMS Group, Inc.
20160 Paseo Del Prado, Ste. D
Walnut, CA 91789
714-598-8209
fax: 714-598-7321

Relax Technology
3101 Whipple Rd., Ste. 22
Union City, CA 94587
510-471-6112
fax: 510-471-6267
Technical support: Use main number

Reliable Communications, Inc.
P.O. Box 816,
Angels Camp, CA 95222
800-222-0042; 209-736-0421
fax: 209-736-0425

Relisys
320 S. Milpitas Blvd.
Milpitas, CA 95035
408-945-9000
fax: 408-945-0587

Renaissance GRX, Inc.
2265 116th Ave. Northeast
Bellevue, WA 98004
206-454-8086

Sampo Corp. of America
(Industrial Products Division)
5550 Peachtree Industrial Blvd.
Norcross, GA 30071
404-449-6220
fax: 404-447-1109

**Samsung Information Systems America,
Inc.**
3655 N. First St.
San Jose, CA 95134-1708
800-423-7364; 408-434-5400
fax: 408-434-5447
Technical support: 800-726-7864

Samtron
14251 E. Firestone Blvd., Ste. 101
La Mirada, CA 90638
310-802-8425
fax: 310-802-8820

SANYO/ICON International, Inc.
18301 Von Karman, Ste. 750
Irvine, CA 92715
800-US-SANYO; 714-440-3100
fax: 714-263-3758

SCION Corp.
152 W. Patrick St.
Frederick, MD 21701
301-695-7870
fax: 301-695-0035

Seawell Microsystems, Inc.
3808 39th Ave., SW
Seattle, WA 98116
206-938-5420

Sefco East
41-37 24th St.
Long Island City, NY 11101
718-786-2001

Seiko Instruments U.S.A., Inc.
(PC Products Division)
1130 Ringwood Court
San Jose, CA 95131
408-922-5900
fax: 408-922-5835
Technical support: 800-757-1011

Sherwood
4181 Business Center Dr.
Fremont, CA 94538-6355
800-777-8755; 510-623-8900
fax: 510-623-8945

Sigma Designs, Inc.
46501 Landing Pkwy.
Fremont, CA 94538
510-770-0100
fax: 510-770-2640

Signal Analytics Corp.
440 Maple Ave., E, Ste. 201
Vienna, VA 22180
703-281-3277
fax: 703-281-2509

Silicon Graphics, Inc.
2011 N. Shoreline Blvd., P.O. Box 7311
Mountain View, CA 94039-7311
415-960-1980
Technical support: 800-800-4744

SiliconSoft, Inc.
5131 Moorpark Ave., Ste. 303
San Jose, CA 95129
408-446-4521
fax: 408-446-5196

Monitors and Video-Related Equipment

Sirex U.S.A., Inc.
132-14 11th Ave.
College Point, NY 11356
718-746-7500
fax: 718-746-0882

**SONY Corporation of America
(Component Peripheral Products Co.)**
3300 Zanker Rd.
San Jose, CA 95134
408-432-0190
fax: 408-943-0740

**SONY Corporation of America
(Information Products Division)**
#1 Sony Dr.
Park Ridge, NJ 07656
800-222-7669; 201-930-1000
fax: 201-573-8608
Technical support: Use 800 number

**SONY Corporation of America
(Microcomputer Products Division)**
#1 Sony Dr.
Park Ridge, NJ 07656
201-930-1000
fax: 201-573-8608

Spark International, Inc.
1939 Waukegan Rd., Ste. 107
Glenview, IL 60025
708-998-6640
fax: 708-998-8840

Spectragraphics Corp.
9707 Waples St.
San Diego, CA 92121
800-821-4822; 619-450-0611
fax: 619-450-0218
Technical support: 619-587-6853

Spectral Innovations, Inc.
1885 Lundy Ave., Ste. 208
San Jose, CA 95131
408-955-0366
fax: 408-955-0370

Spectrum Signal Processing, Inc.
8525 Baxter Pl., Ste.100
Burnaby, BC
Canada V5A 4V7
604-421-5422
fax: 604-421-1764
Technical support: 800-500-7557

Stac Electronics
5993 Avenida Encinas
Carlsbad, CA 92008
800-522-7822; 619-431-7474
Technical support: 619-929-3900

STB Systems, Inc.
1651 N. Glenville, Ste. 210
Richardson, TX 75081
214-234-8750
fax: 214-234-1306

Strobe Data, Inc.
13240 Northup Way, Ste. 19A
Bellevue, WA 98005-2077
206-641-4940
fax: 206-641-1303

SunRiver Corp.
2600 McHale Ct., Ste. 125
Austin, TX 78758
512-835-8001
fax: 512-835-8026
Technical support: 512-835-8082

SuperMac Technology
215 Moffit Park Dr.
Sunnyvale, CA 94089-1374
800-624-8999; 408-541-6100
fax: 408-735-7250
Technical support: 408-541-7680

Swan Technologies
3075 Research Dr.
State College, PA 16801
800-468-9044; 814-238-1820
fax: 814-237-4450
Technical support: 800-468-7926

Symmetric Research
15 Central Way, Ste. 9
Kirkland, WA 98033
206-828-6560

Syscom, Inc. (CA)
2362-D Qume Dr.
San Jose, CA 95131
800-624-8007; 408-432-8153

Systran Corp.
4126 Linden Ave.
Dayton, OH 45432-3068
513-252-5601
fax: 513-258-2729

Tandy Corp.
1800 One Tandy Center
Ft. Worth, TX 76102
817-390-3011
fax: 817-390-2774
Technical support: 817-390-3861

Tatung Co. of America, Inc.
2850 El Presidio St.
Long Beach, CA 90810
800-827-2850; 310-637-2105
fax: 310-637-8484
Technical support: Use 800 number

Taxan America, Inc.
2880 San Tomas Expy., Ste. 101
Santa Clara, CA 95051
800-829-2641; 408-748-0200
fax: 408-748-9190
Technical support: 714-979-3001

Technical Solutions, Inc.
P.O. Box 1148
Mesilla Park, NM 88047
505-524-2154

Technicon
112 W. Marvin Ave.
Longwood, FL 32750
407-834-7777
fax: 407-834-1542

Tecmar
6225 Cochran Rd.
Solon, OH 44139
800-624-8560; 216-349-0600
fax: 216-349-0851
Technical support: 800-344-4463

Tektronix, Inc.
Howard Vollum Park, P.O. Box 500
Beaverton, OR 97077-0001
800-835-9433; 503-627-7111
fax: 503-627-5502
Technical support: 800-835-6100

Ten X Technology, Inc.
4807 Spicewood Springs Rd.
Bldg. 3, Ste. 3200
Austin, TX 78759
800-922-9050; 512-346-8360
fax: 512-346-9580

Texas Instruments, Inc.
P.O. Box 655012, M/S 57
Dallas, TX 75265
800-848-3927; 214-995-2011
fax: 214-995-4360
Technical support: Use 800 number

Texas Microsystems, Inc.
P.O. Box 42963
Houston, TX 77242-2963
800-627-8700; 713-541-8200
fax: 713-541-8226
Technical support: Use main number

TIMESLIPS Corp.
239 Western Ave.
Essex, MA 01929
800-285-0999; 508-768-6100
fax: 508-768-7660
Technical support: 508-768-7490

**Toshiba America Electronic Components,
Inc.**
One Parkway, N, Ste. 500
Deerfield, IL 60015-2547
800-843-2108; 708-945-1500
fax: 708-945-1044

TrueVision, Inc.
7340 Shadeland Station
Indianapolis, IN 46256-3921
800-858-8783; 317-841-0332
fax: 317-576-7700
Technical support: 317-577-8788

Tseng Laboratories, Inc.
6 Terry Dr.
Newtown, PA 18940
215-968-0502
fax: 215-860-7713

TTX Computer Products, Inc.
8515 Parkline Blvd.
Orlando, FL 32809
407-826-0186
fax: 407-826-0267

Turtle Beach Systems
52 Grumbackerr Rd.
York, PA 17402
717-767-0200
fax: 717-767-6033

TVM Professional Monitor Corp.
4260 E. Brickell st.
Ontario, CA 91761
800-822-8168; 909-988-3368
fax: 909-986-3188

Unisys Corp.
P.O. Box 500
Blue Bell, PA 19424-0001
215-542-4011
Technical support: 800-448-1424

Univision Technologies, Inc.
Three Burlington Woods
Burlington, MA 01803
617-221-6700
fax: 617-221-6777

Vectrix Corp.
204 S. Olive St.
Rolla, MO 65401
314-364-7500
fax: 314-364-9533

Vermont Microsystems, Inc.
11 Tigan St., P.O. Box 236
Winooski, VT 05404-0236
800-354-0055; 802-655-2860
fax: 802-655-9058

DIRECTORY OF MANUFACTURERS

Video Associates Labs
4926 Spicewood Springs Rd.
Austin, TX 78759
800-331-0547; 512-346-5781
fax: 512-346-9407

VideoLogic, Inc.
245 First St.
Cambridge, MA 02142
617-494-0530
fax: 617-494-0534

Visionetics International
21311 Hawthorne Blvd., Ste. 300
Torrance, CA 90503
310-316-7940
fax: 310-316-7457

V Tech Industries
800 N. Church St.
Lake Zurich, IL 60047
708-540-8086
fax: 708-540-8335
Technical support: 708-540-5022

Wang Laboratories, Inc.
One Industrial ave., M/S 027-39B
Lowell, MA 01851
800-639-9204; 508-459-5000
Technical support: 800-247-9264

Ward Systems Group, Inc.
Executive Park West
5 Hillcrest Dr.
Frederick, MD 21702
301-662-7950
fax: 301-662-5666

Warp Speed Light Pens, Inc.
1086 Mechem Dr.
Ruidoso, NM 88345
800-874-4315; 505-258-5713
fax: 505-258-3911

Western Digital Imaging
800 E. Middlefield Rd.
Mountain View, CA 94043
415-960-3353
fax: 415-335-2533
Technical support: 800-832-4778

Willow Peripherals, Inc.
190 Willow Ave.
Bronx, NY 10454
800-444-1585; 718-402-9500
fax: 718-402-9603

Workstation Technologies, Inc.
18010 Sky Park Cir., Ste 155
Irvine, CA 92714
714-250-8983

Wyse Technology
3471 N. First St.
San Jose, CA 95134
800-438-9973; 408-473-1200
fax: 408-473-1222
Technical support: 408-922-4390

Xerox Corp.
1960 East Grand Ave.
El Segundo, CA 90245
800-832-6979

Xtron Computer Equipment Corp.
716 Jersey Ave.
Jersey City, NJ 07302
201-798-5000
fax: 201-798-4322

Xycom, Inc.
750 N. Maple Rd.
Saline, MI 48176
800-AT-XYCOM; 313-429-4971
fax: 313-429-1010

YARC Systems Corp.
975 Business Center Cir.
Newbury Park, CA 91320
805-499-9444
fax: 805-499-4048

Zenith Data Systems
2150 E. Lake Cook Rd.
Buffalo Grove, IL 60089
708-808-5000

Printers and Related Equipment

AcuPrint, Inc.
6954 La Place Ct.
Carlsbad, CA 92008
619-931-9316
fax: 619-931-1671

Advanced Matrix Technology, Inc.
765 Flynn Rd.
Camarillo, CA 93010
800-992-2264; 805-388-5799
fax: 805-494-3087
Technical support: Use main number

Advanced Technologies International
361 Sinclare-Frontage Rd.
Milpitas, CA 95035
408-942-1780
fax: 408-942-1260

Agfa Compugraphic
200 Ballardbale St.
Wilmington, MA 01887
508-658-5600
fax: 508-658-6285

ALPS Electric
3553 N. First St.
San Jose, CA 95134
800-825-2577; 408-432-6000
fax: 408-432-6035
Technical support: Use 800 number

American Computer Hardware Corp.
2205 S. Wright St.
Santa Ana, CA 92705
800-447-1237; 714-549-2688
fax: 714-662-0491

Apple Computer, Inc.
20525 Mariani Ave.
Cupertino, CA 95014
408-996-1010
Technical support: 800-767-2775

ATT Global Info Solutions.
1700 S. Patterson Blvd.
Dayton, OH 45479
513-445-5000
fax: 513-445-2008
Technical support: 800-543-9935

Autographix, Inc.
45 Manning Rd.
Billerica, MA 01821
800-548-8558; 508-663-2766

Autologic, Inc.
1050 Rancho Conejo Blvd.
Newbury Park, CA 91320
805-498-9611
fax: 805-499-1167

Axis Communications, Inc.
99 Rosewood Dr., Ste. 170
Danvers, MA 01923
508-777-7957
fax: 508-777-9905

Axonix Corp.
1214 Wilmington Ave.
Salt Lake City, UT 84106
800-866-9797; 801-466-9797
fax: 801-485-6204

BDT Products, Inc.
17152 Armstrong Ave.
Irvine, CA 92714
800-346-3238; 714-660-1386
fax: 714-474-0480

BGL Technology Corp.
451 Constitution Ave.
Camarillo, CA 93012
805-987-7305
fax: 805-987-7346

Bren Instruments, Inc.
(Printing Systems Division)
308 Century Court
Franklin, TN 37064
800-826-3991; 615-794-6825
fax: 615-794-7478

Brother International Corp.
(Office Systems Division)
200 Cottontail Lane
Somerset, NJ 08875-6714
908-356-8880
fax: 908-469-5167

Bull HN Information Systems, Inc.
2 Technology Park
Billerica, MA 01821-4199
508-294-6000
fax: 508-294-6440

C-Tech Electronics, Inc.
2701 Dow Ave.
Tustin, CA 92680
800-347-4017; 714-573-4604
fax: 714-757-4533

CalComp Plotter Products Group
P.O. Box 3250
2411 W. LaPalma Ave.
Anaheim, CA 92803
800-932-1212; 714-821-2000
fax: 714-821-2832

Canon U.S.A., Inc.
One Canon Plaza
Lake Success, NY 11042
516-488-6700
Technical support: 800-423-2366

Citizen America Corp.
2450 Broadway Ave., Ste. 600
Santa Monica, CA 90404-3060
310-453-0614
fax: 310-453-2814

C. Itoh Electronics Co.
615 Hawaii Ave.
Torrance, CA 90503
800-347-2484; 714-573-2942

Printers and Related Equipment

Colorocs Corp.
5600 Oakbrook Pkwy, Ste.24D
Norcross, GA 30093
800-242-2579; 404-447-3570
fax: 404-447-3590

Computer Communications, Inc.
369 Van Ness Wy
Torrance, CA 90501
800-421-1178; 310-320-9101
fax: 310-533-8502

Computer Language Research, Inc.
2395 Midway Rd.
Carrollton, TX 75006
800-FORM-FREE; 214-250-7000
fax: 214-250-1014

Computer Products Plus, Inc.
16351 Gothard St.
Huntington Beach, CA 92647
800-274-4277; 714-847-1799
fax: 714-848-6850

CSS Laboratories, Inc.
1641 McGaw Ave.
Irvine, CA 92714
714-852-8161
fax: 714-852-0410

Data General Corp.
4400 Computer Dr.
Westboro, MA 01580
800-328-2436; 508-366-8911
fax: 508-366-1299
Technical support: 800-344-3577

Data Systems Hardware
22560 Glenn Dr., Ste. 112
Sterling, VA 22170
703-450-1700
fax: 703-450-5726

Dataproducts Corp.
6219 De Soro Ave., P.O. Box 746
Woodland Hills, CA 91365-0746
818-887-8000
fax: 818-887-4789
Technical support: 818-888-4102

Datasouth Computer Corp.
4216 Stuart Andrew Blvd.
Charlotte, NC 28217
800-476-2120; 704-523-8500
fax: 704-523-9298

DCS/Fortis
1820 West 220th St., Ste 220
Torrance, CA 90501
800-736-4847; 310-782-6090
fax: 310-782-6134

Decision Data
One Progress Ave.
Horsham, PA 19044
800-933-9897; 215-674-3300
fax: 215-675-1931

DeRex, Inc.
546 NW 77 St.
Boca Raton, FL 33487
800-245-7282; 407-994-6993
fax: 407-994-6996

Dianachart, Inc.
101 Round Hill Dr.
Rockaway, NJ 07866
201-625-2299
fax: 201-625-2449

Digital Design, Inc.
7596 Centurion Pkwy. N.
Jacksonville, FL 32256
800-733-0908; 904-645-9390
fax: 904-645-8886

Digital Equipment Corp.
146 Main St.
Maynard, MA 01754-2571
508-493-5111
fax: 508-493-8780
Technical support: 800-332-8000

Digitec
959 Cheney Ave.
Marion, OH 43302
614-387-3444
fax: 614-383-6254

DSI, Inc.
1 Inverness Dr. E.
Englewood, CO 80112
800-641-5215; 303-754-2000
fax: 303-754-2009

Eastman Kodak Co.
(Copy Products Division)
343 State St.
Rochester, NY 14650
800-242-2424; 716-724-4000
fax: 716-724-0663
Technical support: Use 800 number

Epson America, Inc.
20770 Madrona Ave.
Torrance, CA 90509-2842
800-289-3776; 310-782-0770
Technical support: 800-922-8911

Everex Systems, Inc.
5020 Brandin Ct.
Fremont, CA 94538
800-821-0806; 510-498-1111
fax: 510-651-0728
Technical support: 510-498-4411

Exabyte Corp.
1685 38th St.
Boulder, CO 80301
800-825-4727; 303-442-4333

Facit, Inc.
400 Commercial St., Manchester, NH
03101-1107
800-798-3224; 603-647-2700
fax: 603-647-2724
Technical support: Use main number

Florida Digital, Inc.
6953 Sonny Dale Unit G.
Melbourne, FL 32904
407-952-2842
fax: 407-952-0815

Fujitsu America, Inc.
(Computer Products Group)
2904 Orchard Pkwy
San Jose, CA 95134-2022
800-626-4686; 408-432-1300
fax: 408-894-1709
Technical support: 408-894-3950

General Parametrics Corp.
1250 Ninth St.
Berkeley, CA 94710
800-223-0999; 510-524-3950
fax: 510-524-9954

Genicom Corp.
Genicom Dr.
Waynesboro, VA 22980
800-443-6426; 703-949-1000
fax: 703-949-1392
Technical support: 703-949-1031

Gulton Graphic Instruments
1900 S. County Trail
East Greenwich, RI 02818
800-343-7929; 401-884-6800
fax: 401-884-4872

Hewlett-Packard Co.
3000 Hanover St.
Palo Alto, CA 94304
800-752-0900; 415-857-1501
Technical support: 208-323-2551

Howtek, Inc.
21 Park Ave.
Hudson, NH 03051
800-44-HOWTEK; 603-882-5200
fax: 603-880-3843
Technical support: Use main number

Hyundai Electronics America
166 Baypointe Pkwy.
San Jose, CA 95134
408-894-9751
fax: 408-894-9751
Technical support: 800-289-4986

IBM (International Business Machines)
Old Orchard Rd.
Armonk, NY 10504
800-736-6268; 914-765-1900
Technical support: 800-453-9872

Idea Courier/Servcom, Inc.
P.O. Box 29391
Phoenix, AZ 85038
800-528-1400; 602-894-7000

IDEAssociates, Inc.
29 Dunham Rd.
Billerica, MA 01821
800-257-5027; 508-663-6878
fax: 508-663-8851

Interface Systems, Inc.
5855 Interface Dr.
Ann Arbor, MI 48103
800-544-4072; 313-769-5900
fax: 313-769-1047

JOYCE Associates
215 Franklin St.
Clayton, NJ 08312

Kentek Information Systems, Inc.
2945 Wilderness Place
Boulder, CO 80301
303-440-5500

Konica Business Machines USA, Inc.
500 Day Hill Rd.
Windsor, CT 06095
800-456-6422; 203-683-2222
fax: 203-688-0700

Kyocera Electronics, Inc.
1321 Harbor Bay Pkwy.
Alameda, CA 94501
800-367-7437; 510-748-6680
fax: 510-748-6963

DIRECTORY OF MANUFACTURERS

Laser Computer, Inc.
(a Video Technology Co.)
800 Church St.
Lake Zurich, IL 60047
708-540-8086
fax: 708-540-8335
Technical support: 708-540-5022

LaserMaster Technologies Corp.
7156 Shady Oak Rd.
Eden Prairie, MN 55344
612-944-9330
fax: 612-944-0522
Technical support: 612-944-9331

Lexi Computer Systems Corp.
242 Neck Rd., P.O. Box 8183
Ward Hill, MA 01835-0483
800-222-5394; 508-521-1118
fax: 508-521-0851

Linotype-Hell
425 Oser Ave.
Hauppauge, NY 11788-9890
800-633-1900; 516-434-2000

Magnetec Corp.
61 W. Dudleytown Rd.
Bloomfield, CT 06092
203-243-8941
fax: 203-243-5152

Mannesmann Tally Corp.
8301 South 180th St.
Kent, WA 98032-0413
800-843-1347; 206-251-5500
fax: 206-251-5520
Technical support: 206-251-5593

Memorex Telex Corp.
6422 East 41st St.
Tulsa, OK 74135
800-333-2623; 918-627-1111
fax: 214-444-3588
Technical support: 800-522-0822

Microtek Lab, Inc.
3715 Doolittle Dr.
Redondo Beach, CA 90278
800-654-4160; 310-297-5000
fax: 310-297-5050
Technical support: 310-297-5100

Miltope Business Products Corp.
1770 Walt Whitman Rd.
Melville, NY 11747
516-420-0200
fax: 516-756-7606

Minolta Corp.
(Document Imaging Systems Division)
101 Williams Dr.
Ramsey, NJ 07446
201-825-4000
fax: 201-444-8736

Mirror Technologies, Inc.
5198 W. 76th St.
Edina, MN 55439
800-654-5294; 612-270-2718
fax: 612-832-5709
Technical support: 800-323-9285

Mosier, Scott and Associates, Inc.
(Protocol Division)
9839 Whithorn Dr.
Houston, TX 77095
713-550-4550
fax: 713-550-5037

Motorola Commercial Systems
1299 E. Algonquin Rd.
Shaumburg, IL 60196
800-759-1107; 602-438-3000
fax: 408-366-4402
Technical support: 800-759-1107

National Computer Systems, Inc.
9940 Barnes Canyon Rd.
San Diego, CA 92121
800-328-6290
fax: 619-452-2427

NBS Southern, Inc.
11451 S. Belcher Rd.
Largo, FL 34643
800-327-5602; 813-541-2200
fax: 813-546-8042

NEC Information Systems, Inc.
1414 Massachusetts Ave.
Boxborough, MA 01719
508-264-8000
fax: 508-264-8673
Technical support: 800-388-8888

NewGen Systems Corp.
17550 Newhope St.
Fountain Valley, CA 92708
714-641-8600
fax: 714-641-2800

NeXT, Inc.
900 Chesapeake Dr.
Redwood City, CA 94063
800-848-NEXT; 415-366-0900
fax: 415-780-3714
Technical support: Use 800 number

Nissho Electronics (U.S.A.) Corp.
1801 Von Karman Ave. Ste.350
Irvine, CA 92715
800-233-1837; 714-261-8811
fax: 714-261-8819

Novatek Corp.
3700 Northwest 124th Ave., Ste. 137
Coral Springs, FL 33065
305-341-7700
fax: 305-345-9334

Océ Bruning
1800 Bruning Dr. W.
Itasca, IL 60143
800-545-5445; 708-351-6000
fax: 708-351-6005 (supplies only)

Okidata Corp.
532 Fellowship Rd.
Mt. Laurel, NJ 08054
800-654-3282; 609-235-2600
fax: 609-778-4184
Technical support: 609-273-0300

Olivetti Office USA
P.O. Box 6945, 765 U.S. Hwy. 202, S
Bridgewater, NJ 08807-0945
800-527-2960; 908-526-8200
fax: 908-526-8405
Technical support: 908-704-6501

Olympus Image Systems, Inc.
15271 Barranca Pkwy
Irvine, CA 92718-2201
800-347-4027; 714-753-5935
fax: 714-453-4418

OWEN Associates, Inc.
22 Princeton Dr.
Delran, NJ 08075
Packard Bell
9425 Canoga Ave.
Chatsworth, CA 91311
Technical support: 800-733-4411

Panasonic Communications & Systems Co.
(Office Automation Group)
2 Panasonic Way
Secaucus, NJ 07094
201-348-7000
Technical support: 800-222-0584

Pentax Technologies Corp.
100 Technology Dr.
Broomfield, CO 80021
800-543-6144; 303-460-1600
fax: 303-460-1628

Personal Computer Products, Inc. (PCPI)
10865 Rancho Bernardo Rd.
San Diego, CA 92127
800-262-0522 (in California); 619-485-8411
fax: 619-487-5809

Prepress
11 Mt. Pleasant Ave.
East Hanover, NJ 07936
800-631-8134; 201-887-8000

Printek, Inc.
1517 Townline Rd.
Benton Harbor, MI 49022
800-368-4636; 616-925-3200
fax: 616-925-8539

Printer Systems Corp. (PSC)
207 Perry Pkwy.
Gaithersburg, MD 20877
800-638-4041; 301-258-5060
fax: 301-926-7333

Printronix, Inc.
P.O. Box 19559, 17500 Cartwright Rd.
Irvine, CA 92713-9559
800-826-3874; 714-863-1900
fax: 714-660-8682

Printware, Inc
1270 Eagan Idust. Rd.
St. Paul, MN 55121
800-456-1616; 612-456-1400

QMS, Inc.
P.O. Box 81250
Mobile, AL 36689
800-631-2692; 205-633-4300
fax: 205-633-0013
Technical support: 205-633-4500

Remanco Systems, Inc.
264 Fordham Rd.
Wilmington, MA 01923
508-658-7400
fax: 508-658-8111

Ricoh Corp.
5 Dedrick Place
West Caldwell, NJ 07006
800-327-8349; 201-882-2000
fax: 201-882-2506

Rosetta Technologies Corp.
9417 Princess Palm Ave.
Tampa, FL 33619
800-937-4224; 813-623-6205
fax: 813-620-1107

Backup and Storage

The ScanSoft Group, Inc.
1531 Sam Rittenberg Blvd.
Charleston, SC 29407
803-571-2430
fax: 803-571-6230

Seiko Instruments U.S.A., Inc.
(PC Products Division)
1130 Ringwood Court
San Jose, CA 95131
408-922-5900
fax: 408-922-5835
Technical support: 800-757-1011

Seikosha America, Inc.
10 Industrial Ave.
Mahwah, NJ 07430
800-338-2609; 800-477-7468 (NJ);
201-327-7227
fax: 201-818-9135
Technical support: 800-825-5349

Sharp Electronics Corp.
(Professional Products Division)
Sharp Plaza, P.O. Box 650
Mahwah, NJ 07430
201-529-8200
fax: 201-529-9636
Technical support: 800-237-4277

Singer Data Products
790 Maple Lane
Bensenville, IL 60106
708-860-6500
fax: 708-860-3672

Star Micronics America, Inc.
70-D Ethel Rd. W.
Piscataway, NJ 08854
800-447-4700; 212-572-5550
fax: 212-286-9063
Technical support: 908-572-3300

Storage Technology Corp.
2270 South 88th St.
Louisville, CO 80028-4310
303-673-5151

Stratus Computer, Inc.
55 Fairbanks Blvd.
Marlboro, MA 01752
508-460-2000
fax: 508-481-8945

Sun Microsystems, Inc.
2550 Garcia Ave.
Mountain View, CA 94043
800-821-4643; 800-821-4642 (in California);
415-960-1300
fax: 415-969-9131
Technical support: 800-USA-4SUN

Synergystex International, Inc.
3065 Nationwide Pkwy.
Brunswick, OH 44212
216-225-3112
fax: 216-225-0419

Syntest Corp.
40 Locke Dr.
Marlboro, MA 01752
508-481-7827
fax: 508-481-5769

Talaris Systems, Inc.
P.O. Box 261580,
11339 Sorrento Valley Rd.
San Diego, CA 92196
619-587-0787
fax: 619-587-6788

Tandem Computers, Inc.
19333 Vallco Pkwy., Location 4-40
Cupertino, CA 95014-2599
800-538-3107; 408-725-6000
Technical support: 800-255-5010

Tandy Corp.
1800 One Tandy Center
Ft. Worth, TX 76102
817-390-3011
fax: 817-390-2774
Technical support: 817-390-3861

Taneum Computer Products, Inc.
203 Southwest 41st St.
Renton, WA 98055
800-829-7768; 206-251-0711
fax: 206-251-6332

TEC America Electronics, Inc.
2710 Lakeview Court
Fremont, CA 94538
510-651-5333
fax: 510-651-6914

Tektronix, Inc.
Howard Vollum Park, P.O. Box 500
Beaverton, OR 97077-0001
800-835-9433; 503-627-7111
fax: 503-627-5502
Technical support: 800-835-6100

Terminal Data Corp.
5898 Condor Dr.
Moorpark, CA 93021
805-529-1500
fax: 805-529-6538

Texas Instruments, Inc.
P.O. Box 655012, M/S 57
Dallas, TX 75265
800-348-3927; 214-995-2011
fax: 214-995-4360
Technical support: Use 800 number

Toshiba America Information Systems, Inc. (Computer Systems Division)
9740 Irvine Blvd.
Irvine, CA 92718
714-583-3000
Technical support: 800-456-8649

Troy
2331 S. Pullman St.
Santa Ana, CA 92705
800-332-MICR; 714-250-3280
fax: 714-250-8972

Unisys Corp.
P.O. Box 500
Blue Bell, PA 19424-0001
215-542-4011
Technical support: 800-448-1424

Wang Laboratories, Inc.
One Industrial Ave., 021-39B
Lowell, MA 01851
800-639-9264; 508-459-5000
Technical support: 800-247-9264

Xerox Corp. (U.S. Marketing Group)
P.O. Box 24
Rochester, NY 14692
800-832-6979

Xpoint Corp.
3100 Medlock Rd., Ste. 370
Norcross, GA 30071
404-446-2764
fax: 404-446-6129

Xtron Computer Equipment Corp.
716 Jersey Ave.
Jersey City, NJ 07302
201-798-5000
fax: 201-798-4322

Backup and Storage

Chinon America, Inc.
615 Hawaii Ave.
Torrance, CA 90503
800-441-0222; 310-533-0274
fax: 310-533-1727
Technical support: Use main number ext.811

Colorado Memory Systems, Inc.
800 S. Taft Ave.
Loveland, CO 80537
303-635-1500
fax: 800-368-9673

COREtape
CORE International, Inc.
7171 N. Federal Hwy.
Boca Raton, FL 33487
800-688-9910; 407-997-6055

Everex Systems
5020 Brandin Ct.
Fremont, CA 94538
800-821-0806; 510-498-1111
fax: 510-651-0728
Technical support: 510-498-4411

Hitachi America, Ltd. (OAS Division)
110 Summit Ave.
Montvale, NJ 07645
800-448-2244; 201-573-0774
fax: 201-573-7660

IBM (International Business Machines)
Old Orchard Rd.
Armonk, NY 10504
800-736-6268; 914-765-1900
Technical support: 800-453-9872

Micro Solutions Computer Products
132 W. Lincoln Hwy.
DeKalb, IL 60115
815-756-3411
fax: 815-756-2928

Mountain Network Solutions, Inc.
360 El Pueblo Rd.
Scotts Valley, CA 95066
800-458-0300

NEC Technologies, Inc.
1414 Massachusetts Ave.
Boxborough, MA 01719
508-264-8000
fax: 508-264-8673
Technical support: 800-388-8888

PLI—Peripheral Land, Inc.
47421 Bayside Pkwy.
Fremont, CA 94538
800-288-8754

Procom Technology, Inc.
2181 Dupont Dr.
Irvine, CA 92715
800-800-8600; 714-549-9449

DIRECTORY OF MANUFACTURERS

**SONY Corporation of America
(Microcomputer Products Division)**
1 Sony Dr.
Park Ridge, NJ 07656
201-930-1000
fax: 201-573-8608

Tandy Corp.
1800 One Tandy Center
Ft. Worth, TX 76102
817-390-3011
fax: 817-390-2774
Technical support: 817-390-3861

Tecmar
6225 Cochran Rd.
Solon, OH 44139
800-624-8560; 216-349-0600
fax: 216-249-0851
Technical support: 800-344-4463

Todd Enterprises, Inc.
224-49 67th Ave.
Bayside, NY 11364
800-445-8633; 718-343-1040

**Toshiba America Information Systems,
Inc. (Computer Systems Division)**
9740 Irvine Blvd.
Irvine, CA 92718
714-583-3000
Technical support: 800-456-8649

Wangtek, Inc.
41 Moreland Rd.
Simi Valley, CA 93065
800-992-9916

Accessories

Acme Electric Corp.
20 Water St.
Cuba, NY 14727
800-325-5848; 716-968-2400

Advanced Gravis Computer Technology, Ltd.
3750 N. Fraser Way, Ste. 101
Burnaby, BC
Canada V5J 5E9
800-663-8558; 604-431-5020
fax: 604-431-5155
Technical support: 604-431-1807

AESI (Advanced Electronics Systems, Inc.)
2005 Lincoln Way, E
Chambersburg, PA 17201
800-345-1280; 717-263-5681
fax: 717-263-1040
Technical Support: 800-733-3155

Alpha Technologies Inc.
3767 Alpha Way
Bellingham, WA 98226
206-647-2360

American Power Conversion Corp.
132 Fairgrounds Rd.
P.O. Box 278
West Kingston, RI 02892
800-788-2208; 401-789-5735
fax: 401-789-3710
Technical Support: 800-800-4272

AVM Technology, Inc.
655 East 9800 South
Sandy, UT 84070
800-880-0041; 801-571-0967
fax: 801-566-2952

Best Power Technology Inc.
P.O. Box 280
Necedah, WI 54646
800-356-5794; 608-565-7200

Brooks Electronics, Inc.
4001 N. American St.
Philadelphia, PA 19140
800-523-0130; 215-228-4433
fax: 215-227-7687

Brooks Power Systems
1400 Adams Rd., Unit E
Bensalem, PA 19020
800-523-1551; 215-244-0264
fax: 215-244-0160

Chinon America, Inc.
615 Hawaii Ave.
Torrance, CA 90503
800-441-0222; 310-533-0274
fax: 310-533-1727

Clary Corp.
1960 S. Walker Ave.
Monrovia, CA 91016
800-442-5279

Control Concepts
328 Water St.
P.O. Box 1380
Binghamton, NY 13902-1380
800-288-6169; 607-724-2484
fax: 607-722-8713

Controlled Power Co.
1955 Stephenson Hwy.
Troy, MI 48083
800-521-4792; 313-528-3700

C-Power Products Inc.
2007 Industrial Blvd.
Rockwall, TX 75087
800-800-2797; 214-771-2179

Curtis Manufacturing Co., Inc.
30 Fitzgerald Dr.
Jaffrey, NH 03452-1931
800-955-5544; 603-532-4123
fax: 603-532-4116

Deltec Electronics Corp.
2727 Kurtz St.
San Diego, CA 92110
800-854-2658; 619-291-4211

EFI Electronics Corp.
2415 South 2300 West
Salt Lake City, UT 84119
800-877-1174; 801-977-9009
fax: 801-977-0200

Electripak
1555 Lynnfield Rd., Ste. 250
Memphis, TN 38119
800-888-0211; 901-682-7766

EPE Technologies Inc.
1660 Scenic Ave.
Costa Mesa, CA 92626
714-557-1636

Exide Electronics Corp.
8521 Six Forks Rd.
Raleigh, NC 27615
800-554-3448; 919-872-3020

GC Electronics Co.
1801 Morgan St.
Rockford, IL 61102
800-435-2931; 815-968-9661
fax: 815-968-9731

Geist, Inc.
P.O. Box 83088
Lincoln, NE 68501
800-432-3219; 402-474-3400
fax: 402-474-4369

GE Wiring Devices
225 Service Ave.
Warwick, RI 02886
401-886-6200
fax: 401-886-6250

Golden Pacific Electronics Inc.
560 S. Melrose St.
Placentia, CA 92670
714-993-6970

Hitachi America, Ltd. (OAS Division)
110 Summit Ave.
Montvale, NJ 07645
800-448-2244; 201-573-0774
fax: 201-573-7660

Hubbell, Inc.
(Wiring Device Division)
1613 State St.
Bridgeport, CT 06605-0933
203-337-3100
fax: 203-579-2892

IBM (International Business Machines)
Old Orchard Rd.
Armonk, NY 10504
800-736-6268; 914-765-1900

Inland Datapak
1210 E. Whitcomb
Madison Heights, MI 48071
800-969-3705; 313-588-9057
Technical Support: Use 800 number

Innovative Technology, Inc.
15470 Flight Path Dr.
Brooksville, FL 34609
904-799-0713

IntelliPower Inc.
10-A Thomas St.
Irvine, CA 92718
714-587-0155

ITT Constant Power
Commerce Park
14 Commerce Dr., P.O. Box 222
Danbury, CT 06813-0222
800-348-8797; 203-790-7790

Joslyn Electronic Systems Corp.
P.O. Box 817
Goleta, CA 93116
800-752-8068; 805-968-3551
fax: 805-968-0922

Kensington Microware, Ltd.
2855 Campus Dr.
San Mateo, CA 94403
800-535-4242; 415-572-2700
fax: 415-572-9675

L.E.A. Dynatech, Inc.
6520 Harney Rd.
Tampa, FL 33610
800-654-8087; 813-621-1324
fax: 813-621-8980

Liberty Systems, Inc.
375-A Saratoga Ave.
San Jose, CA 95129-1339
408-983-1127
fax: 408-243-2885

Accessories

Liebert Corp.
9650 Jeronimo Rd.
Irvine, CA 92718
800-222-5877; 714-457-3600

MacProducts USA, Inc.
608 West 22nd Street
Austin, TX 78705-5116
800-622-3475;512-472-8881
Direct sales: 800-622-3475
fax: 512-499-0888

Meirick Inc.
420 S. Hickory St.
Mt. Vernon, MO 65712
800-735-5069; 417-466-3941

MIDI Land, Inc.
440 S. Lone Hill Ave.
San Dimas, CA 91773
909-592-1168
fax: 909-592-6159

Minuteman UPS
P.O. Box 815188
Dallas, TX 75381
800-238-7272; 214-446-7363

NCR Corp.
1334 S. Patterson Blvd.
Dayton, OH 45479
800-262-7782

NEC Technologies, Inc.
1414 Massachusetts Ave.
Boxborough, MA 01719
508-264-8000
fax: 508-264-8673
Technical support: 800-388-8888

Network Security Systems Inc.
9401 Waples St.
San Diego, CA 92121
800-755-7078; 619-587-7950

Oneac Corp.
27944 N. Bradley Rd.
Libertyville, IL 60048
800-327-8801, ext.5; 708-816-6000

Pacific Electricord Co.
747 W. Redondo Beach Blvd.
P.O. Box 10
Gardena, CA 90247
800-326-8887; 310-532-6600
fax: 310-532-5044

Panamax
150 Mitchell Blvd.
San Rafael, CA 94903-2057
800-472-5555; 415-499-3900
fax: 415-472-5540

Pass & Seymour/Legrand
P.O. Box 4822
Syracuse, NY 13221
800-776-4035; 315-468-6211
fax: 315-468-6296

Perma Power Electronics, Inc.
4001 N. American St.
Philadelphia, PA 19140
800-323-4255
fax: 215-227-7687
Technical Support: 800-523-0130

Philips Consumer Electronics Co.
One Philips Dr.
P.O. Box 14810
Knoxville, TN 37914-1810
615-521-4316
Direct sales: 615-475-8869
fax: 615-521-4406
Technical support: 900-555-5500

PLI—Peripheral Land, Inc.
47421 Bayside Pkwy.
Fremont, CA 94538
800-288-8754

Powercom America Inc.
17155 Von Karman Ave. #108
Irvine, CA 92714
714-252-8241

Power Sentry, Inc.
6271 Bury Dr., Ste. A
Eden Prarie, MN 55346
800-852-4312; 612-949-1100

Procom Technology, Inc.
2181 Dupont
Irvine, CA 92715
800-800-8600; 714-549-9449

ProTek Devices Inc.
2001 N. Tenth Place
Tempe, AZ 85281
602-968-6060
fax: 602-921-3760

Proxima Corp.
9440 Carroll Pk. Dr.
San Diego, CA 92121-2298
800-447-7694; 619-457-5500
fax: 619-558-1408

SL Waber, Inc.
520 Fellowship Rd., Ste. 306
Mt. Laurel, NJ 08054
800-634-1485; 609-866-8888
fax: 609-866-1945

SOLA
1717 Busse Rd.
Elk Grove Village, IL 60007-5666
800-289-7652; 708-439-2800

**SONY Corporation of America
(Microcomputer Products Division)**
1 Sony Dr.
Park Ridge, NJ 07656
201-930-1000
fax: 201-573-8608

SRW Computer Components Co., Inc.
1402 Morgan Circle
Tustin, CA 92680
800-331-7248 (NC); 800-547-7766 (CA);
714-259-7500
fax: 714-259-8037

Storage Devices, Inc.
6800 Orangethorpe Ave.
Buena Park, CA 90620
714-562-5500
fax: 714-562-5505

Superior Electric
383 Middle St.
Bristol, CT 06010-7488
800-227-6469; 203-585-4500

Tandy Corp.
1800 One Tandy Center
Ft. Worth, TX 76102
817-390-3011
fax: 817-390-2774
Technical support: 817-390-3861

Todd Enterprises, Inc.
224-49 67th Ave.
Bayside, NY 113643
800-445-8633; 718-343-1040

**Toshiba America Information Systems,
Inc. (Computer Systems Division)**
9740 Irvine Blvd.
Irvine, CA 92718
714-583-3000
Technical support: 800-456-8649

Tripp Lite
500 N. Orleans
Chicago, IL 60610-4188
312-329-1777
fax: 312-644-6505
Technical Support: 312-329-1601

TSi Power Inc.
3055 Northwoods Circle
Norcross, GA 30071
800-874-3160; 404-263-6063

Unison
500 N. Orleans St.
Chicago, IL 60610-4188
312-329-1601

Upsonic
1392 Industrial Dr.
Tustin, CA 92680
800-877-6642; 714-258-0808

Woods Wire Products, Inc.
510 Third Ave.
Carmel, IN 46032
800-428-6168; 317-844-7261
fax: 317-843-1675

Zero Surge
103 Clairmont Rd.
Bernardsville, NJ 07924
908-766-4220

GLOSSARY

adapter   Also known as an add-on card, controller, or I/O card. Adapters are installed in expansion slots to enhance the processing power of the computer or to communicate with other devices. Examples of adapters include asynchronous communication, floppy disk-controller, and expanded memory.

address   A unique memory location permitting reading or writing of data to/from that location. Network interface cards and CPUs often use shared addresses in RAM to move data between programs.

alpha channel   The upper 8 bits of a 32-bit data path in some graphics adapters. The alpha channel is used by some software for controlling the color information contained in the lower 24 bits.

Alt key   The alternate key on the keyboard is similar to the control key. It is like a Shift key in that when used simultaneously with another key it creates a command or, in certain applications, a graphics character. The Alt key is more common in telecommunications programs and TSR (terminate and stay resident) programs than in regular programs. It is often used in multitasking enviroments (OS/2, Windows, DESQview X).

analog-to-digital converter (ADC)   A device that converts analog input signals to digital output signals used to represent the amplitude of the original signal.

ANSI (American National Standards Institute)   An organization that develops and publishes standards for codes, alphabets, and signaling schemes.

API (application program interface)   A set of standard software interrupts, calls, and data formats that application programs use to initiate contact with network services, mainframe communications programs, or other program-to-program communications.

application software   A computer program designed to help people perform a certain type of work. An application can manipulate text, numbers, graphics, or a combination of elements. Some application packages focus on a single task and offer greater computer power while others, called integrated software, offer less power but include several applications, such as word processing, spreadsheet, and database programs. An application may also be referred to as *software, program, instructions,* or *task.*

GLOSSARY

areal density   The amount of data that can be stored in one area of a disk—hard or floppy.

ASCII (American Standard Code for Information Interchange)   The data alphabet used in the IBM PC to determine the composition of the 7-bit string of 0s and 1s that represents each character (alphabetic, numeric, or special). It is a standard way to transmit characters.

aspect ratio   A video term that refers to the proportion of a pixel's width to its height. In VGA and Super VGA mode, this ratio is 1:1, which means the pixels are as tall as they are wide.

asynchronous communication   A type of serial communication by which data is passed between devices. "Asynchronous" means that the timing of each character transmitted is independent of other characters. Also known as ASYNC.

AT command set   Commands used by Hayes and Hayes-compatible modems. Every command starts with the letters *AT,* for ATtention. The most common commands include ATDT (dial a number), ATA (manually answer the phone), ATZ (reset modem), ATS0=0 (disable auto-answer), and ATH (hang up the phone). You can use several commands on one line; you only need "AT" before the first one. Some modems require commands typed in capital letters. The AT command set is an industry standard set of commands.

autosizing   True autosizing occurs when a monitor maintains a constant image size when moving across low and high resolutions.

average access time   The time (in milliseconds) that a disk drive takes to find the right track in response to a request (the seek time), plus the time it takes to get to the right place on the track (the latency).

back up   To make a copy of a file, group of files, or the entire contents of a hard disk.

barrel distortion   Barrel distortion occurs in monitors at the edges of the screen. The sides of the affected image seem to bow out—like a funhouse mirror—and resemble a barrel. It is the inverse of *pincushioning*.

baud rate   A measure of the actual rate of symbols transmitted per second, which may represent more than one bit. A given baud rate may have

GLOSSARY

more than one bps (bits per second) rate. Baud rate is often used interchangeably with bps, although this is technically incorrect.

binary   A numbering system with two digits, 0 and 1, used by computers to store and process information.

BIOS (basic input/output system)   A collection of primitive computer routines (stored in ROM in a PC) that control peripherals such as the video display, disk drives, and keyboard.

bisynchronous   Computer communications in which both sides simultaneously transmit and receive data. Also called BISYNC.

bit   A binary digit: the smallest piece of information that can be recognized and processed by a computer. A bit is either 0 or 1. Bits can form larger units of information called nibbles (4 bits), bytes (8 bits), and words (usually 16 bits).

bit-BLT (bit-block transfer)   A video term to identify the operation in which a block of pixel data in one area of the frame buffer is copied to another area of the frame buffer through the computer's video memory. By performing bit-block transfers, graphics coprocessors can dramatically improve video display speeds, since a displayed object is treated as one unit rather than as many individual pixels.

bits per second (bps)   The number of data bits sent per second between two modems. Used as a measure of the rate at which digital information is handled, manipulated, or transmitted. Similar, but not identical, to baud rate.

buffer   An area of RAM (usually 512 bytes plus another 16 for overhead) in which DOS stores data temporarily.

bulletin board system (BBS)   A computer (generally a microcomputer) set up to receive calls and act as a host system. BBSs allow users to communicate through message bases and to exchange files.

bus   A group of wires used to carry a set of related signals or information within a computer from one device to another.

business software   Any computer application designed for use in business (as opposed to scientific use or entertainment). These applications include word processing, spreadsheets, databases, and communications as

GLOSSARY

well as accounting, payroll, financial planning, project management, support systems, PIMs, and office management.

byte　A sequence of adjacent binary digits that the computer considers a unit. A byte consists of 8 bits.

C　A programming language used predominantly by professional programmers to write applications software.

cache　An amount of RAM set aside to hold data that is expected to be accessed again. The second access, which finds the data in RAM, is very fast. (Pronounced like "cash.")

CAD/CAM (computer-aided design/computer-aided manufacturing) A term describing the use of computers in both the design and manufacturing of a product, such as a machine part, in which the product is designed with a CAD program and the finished design is translated into a set of instructions to be used by machines in the fabrication, assembly, and process control stages.

CGA　IBM's first color graphics standard, capable of 320 by 320 resolution at four colors (or gray shades on laptops), or 640 by 200 at two colors (black and white). CGA-only laptops are behind the times.

chip　An integral part of the PC. These are very tiny, square or rectangular slivers of material (usually silicon) with electrical components built in. Some of the chips in a computer aid in memory, but the most important chip is the microprocessor. This is the "8088", "286", "386", or "486" that every salesperson will speak of when talking about a specific machine's features.

clone　An IBM PC/XT- or AT-compatible computer made by another manufacturer.

cluster　A hard-disk term that refers to a group of sectors, the smallest storage unit recognized by DOS. On most modern hard disks, four 512-byte sectors make up a cluster, and one or more clusters make up a track.

CMOS (complementary metal oxide semiconductor)　An integrated circuit requiring low power. Most laptop CPUs use CMOS.

GLOSSARY

coding   The act of programming a computer; specifically, generating source code in the language of the program's choice. The most popular languages used by programmers are Pascal, C, and C++.

COM   Communications port or serial port used by modems, mice, and some printers. DOS assigns these ports as COM1, COM2, and sometimes COM3 and COM4. DOS also lets you refer to the first communications port as AUX. Note: Some programs count communications ports starting with 0, so "Port 0" or "Communications Port 0" would be COM1, and "Port 1" would be COM2.

communications parameters   Settings that define how your communications software will handle incoming data and transmit outgoing data. Parameters include bits per second, parity, data bits, and stop bits.

control key (Cntrl or Ctrl)   This is like a Shift key or Alt key in that when used simultaneously with another key it makes a new graphic character or command.

convergence   A video term that describes the way in which the three beams that generate the three color dots (red, green, blue) should meet. When all three dots are excited at the same time and their relative distance is perfect, the result is pure white. Deviation from this harmony (due to an incorrect relationship of the beams to each other) results in poor convergence. This causes white pixels to show bits of color and can decrease image sharpness and resolution.

CPU (central processing unit)   The functional "brain" of a computer; the element that does the actual adding and subtracting of 0s and 1s and the manipulation and moving of data that is essential to computing.

database   A file consisting of a number of records or tables, each of which is constructed of fields (in column format) of a particular type, together with a collection of operations that facilitate searching, sorting, recombination, and similar acts.

data bits   The bits sent by a modem. These bits make up characters and don't include the bits that make up the communications parameters.

DB-9   A 9-pin connector, usually for serial ports. The connector attached to your laptop is typically a male DB-9. The device at the other end (an external modem, most likely) almost always has a 25-pin (DB-25) connector and is always female. This means the cable you want to buy is 9-pin

GLOSSARY

female (computer end) to 25-pin male (modem end). Some older laptops with EGA video connectors will have a 9-pin female connector on the laptop.

DB-15   A 15-pin connector stuffed in the space of a DB-9 connector, used to connect VGA monitors to the laptop.

DB-25   A 25-pin connector for parallel ports and some serial ports (mostly on desktop PCs). At the computer end, the parallel port is female and the serial port is male. At the other end, the connector is a 36-pin Centronics male (parallel) or 25-pin female (serial). For printers, specify a DB-25 male to a Centronics cable. For serial devices, specify a DB-25 female to a DB-25 male cable.

Del (Delete key)   In most word-processing programs, this key will delete the characters to the right of the cursor.

device   Any piece of computer hardware.

device-level interface   An interface that uses an external controller to connect the disk drives to the PC. Among its other functions, the controller converts the serial stream of data read from the drive into parallel data for the host computer's bus. ST506 and ESDI are device-level interfaces.

dial-up line   A communications circuit established with a modem by dialing a destination over a commercial telephone system.

digital-to-analog converter (DAC)   A circuit that accepts digital input signals and converts them to analog output signals. Sometimes called DAC chips, they are used in VGA video cards, for example.

DIN connector   Plug and socket conforming to the DIN (Deutsche Industrie Norm) standard. Many keyboard connectors are DIN.

directory   A list of file names and locations of files on a disk.

disk   A circular metal platter or mylar diskette with magnetic material on both sides that stores programs and data. Disks are rotated continuously so that read/write heads mounted on movable or fixed arms can read or write programs or data to and from the disk.

GLOSSARY

disk cache   A portion of a computer's RAM set aside for temporarily holding information read from a disk. The disk cache does not hold entire files as does a RAM disk, but information that has either been recently requested from a disk or has previously been written to a disk.

disk defragmenter   Defragmentation is the rewriting of all the parts of a file on contiguous sectors. When files on a hard disk drive are being updated, the information tends to be written all over the disk, causing delays in file retrieval. Defragmentation reverses this process, and is often achieved with special defragmentation programs that provide up to 75 percent improvement in the speed of disk access and retrieval.

disk drive   The motor that actually rotates the disk, plus the read/write heads and associated mechanisms, usually in a mountable housing. Sometimes used synonymously to mean the entire disk subsystem.

disk format   Refers to the method in which data is organized and stored on a floppy or hard disk.

DOS (disk operating system)   A set of programs that control the communications between components of the computer. Examples of DOS functions are: displaying characters on the screen, reading and writing to a disk, printing, and accepting commands from the keyboard. DOS is a widely used operating system on IBM-compatible personal computers (PCs).

dot matrix   A type of printer technology using a print head with pins to poke out arrays of dots that form text and graphics.

dot pitch   A monitor characteristic; specifically, the distance between the holes in the *shadow mask*. It indirectly describes how far apart the individual dots are on screen. The smaller the dot pitch, the finer the image's "grain." Some color monitors, such as the Sony Trinitron, use a slot mask (also known as an aperture grille) that is perforated by strips, not holes, in the shadow mask. In this case, the dots are arranged in a linear fashion, and their density is called striped dot pitch. (Monochrome monitors do not use a shadow mask and therefore do not have a dot pitch.)

download   To receive information from another modem and computer over the telephone lines. It is the opposite of upload.

GLOSSARY

DRAM (dynamic random-access memory)   The most commonly used type of memory, found on video boards as well as on PC system boards. DRAM is usually slower than VRAM (video random-access memory), since it has only a single access pathway.

drift   Together with jitter and swim, describes unwanted motion in a line of text displayed on a monitor. The three terms refer to different periods of time between on-screen wavers.

drive array   A storage system composed of several hard disks. Data is divided among the different drives for greater speed and higher reliability.

DSDD (double-sided, double-density)   On PCs and laptops, DSDD means 720K $3^1/_2$-inch diskettes or 360K $5^1/_4$-inch diskettes.

DSHD (double-sided, high-density)   On PCs and laptops, DSHD means 1.44Mb $3^1/_2$-inch diskettes or 1.2Mb $5^1/_4$-inch diskettes.

EGA   IBM's second graphics standard (1984), capable of 640 by 300 resolution at 16 colors.

EIA (Electronic Industries Association)   Standards-setting body of manufacturers. Sets the RS-232C standard, now technically the EIA 232D standard.

EISA (Extended Industry Standard Architecture)   Primarily a desktop specification for high-performance computers. Competes with IBM's Micro Channel architecture (MCA). EISA computers can use existing PC, XT, and AT add-in cards; MCA computers can't.

E-mail (electronic mail)   The exchange of messages via a bulletin board or on-line service. One user leaves the message on the service "addressed" to another user. The other user later connects to the same service and can read the message and reply to it.

EMM (expanded memory manager)   The software driver used to implement the Expanded Memory Specification. Drivers written for the 80386 and 80486 microprocessors usually allow you to use extended memory to simulate expanded memory.

EMS (expanded memory specification)   A description of a technique for expanding memory in an IBM-compatible microcomputer. Also called LIM EMS because it was developed by Lotus, Intel, and Microsoft.

GLOSSARY

ESDI (enhanced small device interface)   A device-level interface designed for a disk drive as a successor to ST-506 but with a higher transfer rate (1.25Mb to 2.5Mb per second).

Enter   When pressed, this key lets the computer know a command has been issued; in a word processing document, this key is used like a typewriter's Return key to add a line feed. Also called the Return key.

Esc (Escape key)   A key that will usually back you out of a program, a menu, a dialog box, or a command.

expanded memory   Memory that can be used by some DOS software to access more than the normal 640K (technically, more than 1Mb). 80386, 80386SX, and 80486 computers can create expanded memory readily by using an EMS (expanded memory specification) driver provided with DOS, through Microsoft Windows, or through a memory manager such as Quarterdeck QEMM or Qualitas 386 To The Max. To use expanded memory, a program must be EMS-aware or run under an environment such as Microsoft Windows. 8088- and 80286-based computers often need special hardware to run expanded memory.

extended memory   Memory above 1Mb in 80286 and higher computers. Can be used for RAM disks, disk caches, or Microsoft Windows, but requires the processor to operate in a special mode (protected mode or virtual real mode). With a special driver, you can use extended memory to create expanded memory.

file   A collection of related records treated as a unit. In a computer system, a file can exist on magnetic tape, disk, or as an accumulation of information in system memory. A file can contain data, programs, or both.

fixed disk   Also called an internal disk, a hard disk, or a Winchester. An early IBM disk drive was called the 30–30 (like the rifle), hence the nickname "Winchester." A bulk storage system with nonremovable, rotating, rigid, magnetic storage disks. There are some types of hard disk with removable rigid media in the form of disk packs.

flicker   A monitor term that describes two different effects. True flicker, where the screen seems to blink rapidly on and off, is caused by a slow refresh rate or low vertical frequency. This means the screen isn't rewritten quickly enough to fool the eye into seeing a steady image. The second kind of flicker looks more like a jiggling of horizontal lines, caused by interlacing. To avoid both kinds of flicker you need a high

GLOSSARY

vertical frequency (at least 60 Hz, but often more) and a noninterlaced video scheme—currently an expensive combination.

floppy disk   A removable, rotating, flexible magnetic storage disk. Floppy disks come in a variety of sizes, but 3^1/$_2$-inch and 5^1/$_4$-inch are the most popular. Storage capacity is usually between 360K and 1.44Mb. Also called flexible disk or diskette.

floppy drive   A disk drive designed to read and write data to a floppy disk for transfer to and from a computer.

form factor   Fancy way of saying size (width, depth, height).

format   A DOS command that records the physical organization of tracks and sectors on a disk.

frame buffer   A large section of memory used to store an image to be displayed on-screen as well as parts of the image that lie outside the limits of the display.

function   An operation, a set of tasks for a computer to do.

function keys (F-keys)   Keys numbered from F1 to F12 that are used to perform special functions. They are used to standardize software interfaces. For example, F1 in most software will activate the help screen. Function keys also make word processing packages easier to use by serving as shortcuts for often-used commands.

gateway   An ad hoc connection between two on-line services. A gateway exists when you are provided with a means of accessing one on-line service through another. For instance, users of CompuServe can access MCI Mail through a gateway.

GCR (group coded recording)   A hard-disk term for a storage process where bits are packaged as groups, with each group assigned to and stored under a particular code. Used by RLL drives.

graphics coprocessor   Similar to a math coprocessor in concept, a programmable chip that can speed video performance by carrying out graphics processing independently of the microprocessor. Graphics coprocessors can speed up performance in two ways: by taking over tasks the main processor would lose time performing and by optimizing for graphics. Video adapter cards with graphics coprocessors are expensive

GLOSSARY

compared to those without them, but they speed up graphics operations considerably. Among the coprocessor's common abilities are drawing graphics primitives and converting vectors to bitmaps.

handshaking A modem term that describes the initial exchange between modems. It's like "are you there?" with the response "I am here."

hard disk A mass storage device that transfers data between the computer's memory and the disk storage media.

hardware The physical components of a computer.

head actuator In a disk drive, the mechanism that moves the read/write head radially across the surface of the platter of the disk drive.

high-speed modem A modem operating at speeds from 9,600 to 19,200 bits per second.

Home This key is supposed to move the cursor to the upper-left corner of the screen. In reality, it does a number of different things, depending on how the software program has been written to use it. Sometimes it will work as it's supposed to, other times it will move the cursor to the top of the current page, but often it does nothing.

horizontal scan frequency The frequency per second at which a monitor repaints the horizontal lines that make up an image. This frequency is measured in kHz (kilohertz). A standard VGA signal requires a 31.5-kHz horizontal scan frequency.

host system In telecommunications, the system that you have called up and to which you are connected, such as a BBS (bulletin board system) or an on-line service such as CompuServe.

Hz (Hertz) A unit of measurement. This used to be called cycles per second.

IDE (integrated drive electronics) A disk drive with its own controller electronics built in to save space and money. Many laptops use IDE drives.

IEEE (Institute of Electrical and Electronic Engineers) A standards-setting group.

GLOSSARY

Ins (Insert key)   A key that in many instances is a "toggle." (This means that if you press the key it will turn a function on or off.) The Insert key will turn the insert mode on or off. If you turn off the insert mode, move your cursor to within a line of text, and begin to type, you will write over existing text instead of adding text. With the insert mode on you would place new text between existing text.

Intel   A major manufacturer of integrated circuits used in computers. Intel makes the 8086 family of microprocessors and its derivatives: the 8088, 80286, 80386SX and DX, and 80486SX and DX. These are the chips used in the IBM PC family of computers and all the computers discussed in this book.

integrated circuit (IC)   A tiny complex of electronic components and their connections that is produced in or on a slice of material (such as silicon). A single IC can hold many electronic elements. Also called a chip.

interlaced and noninterlaced scanning   Two monitor schemes with which to paint an image on the screen. Interlaced scanning takes two passes, painting every other line on the first pass and filling in the rest of the lines on the second pass. Noninterlaced scanning paints all the lines in one pass and then paints an entirely new frame. Noninterlaced scanning is preferable because it reduces screen flicker, but it's more expensive.

interleaving   A hard-disk term that describes a method of arranging disk sectors to compensate for relatively slow computers. Spreads sectors apart instead of arranging them consecutively. For example, 3:1 interleaving means your system reads one out of every three tracks on one rotation. The time required for the extra spin lets the read/write head catch up with the disk drive, which might otherwise outrun the head's ability to read the data. Thanks to track buffering and the speed of today's PCs, interleaving is obsolete. Look for a "1:1 interleaving," which indicates a noninterleaved drive.

I/O (input/output)   Input is the data flowing into your computer. Output is the data flowing out. I/O can refer to the parallel and serial ports, keyboard, video display, and hard and floppy disks.

IRQ (interrupt request)   A request for attention and service made to the CPU. The keyboard and the serial and parallel ports all have interrupts. Setting two peripherals to the same IRQ is a cause of hair pulling among desktop PC users; laptops don't suffer the problem as badly because they have few, if any, add-on products that need interrupts set.

GLOSSARY

ISA (Industry Standard Architecture)   Computers using the same bus structure and add-in cards as the IBM PC, XT, and AT. Also called classic bus. It comes in an 8-bit and 16-bit version. Most references to ISA mean the 16-bit version. Many machines claiming ISA compatibility will have both 8- and 16-bit connectors on the motherboard.

JPEG (Joint Photographic Experts Group)   The image compression standard developed by an international committee of the same name. JPEG was developed to compress large still images, such as photographs, single video frames, or scanned pictures, to reduce the amount of memory required to store them.

kilo   One thousand, but in computers, it's typically 1,024 (2 to the tenth power).

kilobyte   1,024 bytes. Sometimes abbreviated as k (lowercase), K-byte, K, or KB for kilobyte and Kb for kilobit (1,024 bits). When in doubt about whether an abbreviation refers to kilobytes or kilobits, it's probably kilobytes, with these exceptions: the speed of a modem (as in 2.4 kilobits per second) and the transfer rate of a floppy disk (as in 500 kilobits per second).

local area network (LAN)   A small- to moderate-size network in which communications are usually confined to a relatively small area, such as a single building or campus.

logical drive   A drive that has been created by the disk operating system (DOS). This is done either at the preference of the user or because the DOS version does not allow a formatted capacity in excess of 32Mb. A user with a 100Mb hard disk will want to use more than 32Mb, so a program will tell DOS there are a bunch of "logical" drives that add up to 100Mb. DOS 5.0 eliminates this need.

log on or log off   The process of connecting or disconnecting your computer to another system by modem.

LPT Printer port (short for line printer)   LPT1 is the first printer port. DOS also allows you to use PRN to describe the printer port.

mega   One million, but with computers it typically means 1,048,576 (1,024 times 1,024).

GLOSSARY

megabyte (Mb)   1,048,576 bytes (1,024 times 1,024). Used to describe the total capacity of a hard or floppy disk or the total amount of RAM. Sometimes abbreviated as Mb, M, MB, or meg for megabyte; and Mb, M-bit, or Mbit for megabit. When in doubt, it's probably megabyte, not megabit, with these exceptions: the capacity of a single memory chip (a 1-megabit chip; you need eight chips plus an optional ninth parity-checking chip to get 1 megabyte of memory), the throughput of a network (4 megabits per second), and the transfer speed of a hard disk (5 megabits per second).

memory   A device that stores data in a computer. Internal memories are very fast and are either read/write random-access memory (RAM) or read-only memory (ROM). Bulk storage devices are either fixed disk, floppy disk, tape, or optical memories; these hold large amounts of data, but are slower to access than internal memories.

MFM (modified frequency modulation)   A hard-disk method of magnetically encoding information that creates a one-to-one correspondence between data bits and flux transitions (magnetic changes) on a disk. It uses smaller storage densities and lower transfer speeds than RLL.

MHz (megahertz)   One million cycles per second, typically used in reference to a computer's clock rate. Both the clock rate and the processor type (80286, 80386, etc.) determine the power and speed of a computer.

Micro Channel architecture (MCA)   The basis for the IBM Micro Channel bus, used in high-end models of IBM's PS/2 series of personal computers.

microprocessor   An integrated circuit (IC) that communicates, controls, and executes machine language instructions.

microsecond   1/1,000,000 (one-millionth) of a second.

millisecond (ms)   1/1,000 (one-thousandth) of a second. Hard disks are rated in milliseconds. Modern laptop hard disks have drives of 20 to 40 milliseconds, meaning they can find the average piece of data in $1/25$ to $1/30$ of a second. Older hard disks were about 100 milliseconds. Higher numbers mean slower performance.

MNP (Microcom Network Protocol)   MNP classes (or levels) 1–4 cover error correction. MNP 5 covers data compression and can compress data up to 2:1, providing twice the effective speed (4,800 bps on a 2,400-bps

GLOSSARY

modem). MNP levels 6–10 are less widely accepted, although MNP 10 may gain ground as an error-correcting protocol for cellular communications. MNP is likely to be superseded by V.42 error correction and V.42bis data correction. V.42 incorporates MNP 1–4; V.42bis does not incorporate MNP 5, but many V.42bis modems include it anyway.

modem   A combination of the words *modulate* and *demodulate.* A device that allows a computer to communicate with another computer over telephone lines.

MTBF (mean time between failures)   How long your computer or other equipment runs before it breaks, based on component testing.

multimedia   The presentation of information on a computer using sound, graphics, animation, video, and text.

nanosecond   1/1,000,000,000 (one-billionth) of a second. Memory chips are rated in nanoseconds, typically 80 to 150 nanoseconds. Higher numbers indicate slower chips.

NetWare   A popular series of network operating systems and related products made by Novell.

network   A continuing connection between two or more computers that facilitates sharing files and resources.

OEM (original equipment manufacturer)   This is a company that puts parts from other companies together and sells the resultant product under its own brand name.

online/offline   When connected to another computer via modem and telephone lines, a modem is said to be online. When disconnected, it is offline.

operating system (OS)   A set of programs residing in ROM and/or on disk that controls communications between components of the computer and the programs run by the computer. MS-DOS is an operating system.

OS/2 (Operating System/2)   An operating system developed by IBM and Microsoft for use with Intel's microprocessors. Unlike its predecessor, DOS, OS/2 is a multitasking operating system. This means many programs can run at the same time.

GLOSSARY

OS/2 Extended Edition   IBM's proprietary version of OS/2; it includes built-in communications and database-management facilities.

parallel port   A port that transmits or receives 8 bits (1 byte) of data at a time between the computer and external devices. Mainly used by printers. LPT1 is a parallel port, for example.

PCL (printer command language)   Usually refers to Hewlett Packard laser printers. Most HP compatibles support PCL 4. HP's newest printers (the III series) use PCL 5, which includes scalable fonts and monochrome support for HPGL.

PEL   Picture element or pixel. It represents one dot on your computer screen.

peripheral   A device that performs a function and is external to the system board. Peripherals include displays, disk drives, and printers.

PgUp and PgDn keys   Move the cursor up or down 25 lines—usually a full page. In telecommunications programs these keys are used to begin to send or to get ready to receive files.

PIM (personal information manager)   A program that manages a person's collection of personal information, keeping track of notes, memos, time planning, telephone numbers, and addresses.

pincushioning   A monitor term that describes an unwanted curve of an image that usually occurs at the edges of the screen. The sides of an image appear to curve inward.

Piracy   The act of making or distributing an unauthorized copy of a copyrighted software product for financial gain. In most countries such an act is prohibited by law.

pixel   (See *PEL.*) A pixel is the smallest information building block of an on-screen image. On a color monitor screen, each pixel is made of one or more triads (red, green, and blue). Resolution is usually expressed in terms of the number of pixels that fit within the width and height of a complete on-screen image. In VGA, the resolution is 640 by 480 pixels; in SuperVGA, it is 800 by 600 pixels.

platter   The actual disk inside a hard-disk drive; it carries the magnetic recording material. All but the thinnest disk drives have multiple platters,

GLOSSARY

most of which have two sides that can be used for data storage. (On multiple-platter drives, one side of each platter is usually reserved for storing control information.)

port   The channel or interface between the microprocessor and peripheral devices.

print server   A computer on the network that makes one or more attached printers available to other users. The server usually requires a hard disk, to spool the print jobs while they wait in a queue for the printer.

print spooler   The software that holds print jobs sent to a shared printer over a network when the printer is busy. Each file is saved in temporary storage and then printed when the shared printer is available.

programming language   Any artificial language that can be used to define a sequence of instructions that can ultimately be processed and executed by the computer.

PROM (programmable read-only memory)   A (usually) permanent memory chip programmed after manufacture (unlike a ROM chip). EPROMs (erasable PROMs) and EEPROMs (electrically erasable PROMs) can be erased and reprogrammed several times.

protocol   Rules governing communications, including flow control (start-stop), error detection or correction, and parameters (data bits, stop bits, parity). If they use the same protocols, products from different vendors can communicate.

QWERTY   The keyboard arrangement on computers and typewriters, after the Q-W-E-R-T-Y layout of the top row of the alphabet keys.

RAM (random-access memory)   Also known as read-write memory; the memory used to execute application programs.

RAM disk   VDISK (virtual disk) that can be used in place of a hard or floppy disk for frequently accessed files. A RAM disk is dangerous for storing data because the contents are lost if the computer crashes or if power is turned off. Most users with extra RAM use it for a disk cache rather than as a RAM disk.

GLOSSARY

read/write head   The part of the hard disk that writes data to or reads data from a platter. It functions like a coiled wire that reacts to a changing magnetic field by producing a minute current that can be detected and amplified by the electronics of the disk drive.

restore   To replace files on a disk from a backup copy.

RF (radio frequency)   A generic term referring to the technology used in cable television and broadband networks. It uses electromagnetic waveforms, usually in the megahertz (MHz) range, for transmission. It can also refer to the emissions coming from a computer that cause interference with TV reception.

RGB (red, green, blue)   The triad, the three colors that make up one pixel of a color monitor.

RJ-11/RJ-45   Designations for commonly used modular telephone connectors. RJ-11 is the 8-pin connector used in most voice connections. RJ-45 is the 8-pin connector used for data transmission over twisted-pair telephone wire.

RLL (run length limited)   A hard-disk method of encoding information magnetically that uses a scheme (GCR) to store blocks of data instead of single bits of data. It allows greater storage densities and higher transfer speeds than the other method in use (MFM).

ROM (read-only memory)   The memory chip(s) that permanently store computer information and instructions. Your computer's BIOS (basic input/output system) information is stored in a ROM chip. Some laptops even have the operating system (DOS) in ROM.

roping   A video term to describe image distortion that gives solid, straight lines a helical or twisted appearance. The problem is caused by poor convergence.

RS-232C   An electrical standard for the interconnection of equipment established by the Electrical Industries Association; the same as the CCITT code V.24. RS-232C is used for serial ports.

SCSI (small computer system interface)   A system-level interface designed for general purpose applications that allows up to seven devices to be connected to a single host adapter. It uses an 8-bit parallel connection

GLOSSARY

that produces a maximum transfer rate of 5Mb per second. The term is pronounced "scuzzy."

sector   The basic storage unit on a hard disk. On most modern hard disks, sectors are 512 bytes each, four sectors make up a cluster, and there are 17 to 34 sectors in a track—although newer drives may have a different number of sectors.

serial port   The "male" connector (usually DB-9 or DB-25) on the back of your computer. It sends out data one bit at a time. It is used by modems and, in years past, for daisy-wheel and other printers. The other port on your computer is the parallel port, which is a "female" connector. It is used for printers, backup systems, and mini-networking (LANs). See also *COM* port.

shadow mask   Inside the color monitor just behind the screen, it is drilled with small holes, each of which corresponds to a triad. The shadow mask helps guide the electron beams so that each beam hits only one phosphor dot in the triad.

shareware   Copyrighted software that is distributed free of charge but is usually accompanied by a request for a small payment from satisfied users to cover costs and registration for documentation and program updates. These programs range from fully functional programs to ones having only limited features.

shell   A piece of software providing direct communication between the user and the operating system. The main inner part of the system, called the kernel, is enclosed by the shell program, as in a nut.

slot mask   Also known as an aperture grille, serves the same function as the shadow mask on a monitor.

spindle   One part of a hard disk, around which the platters rotate.

software   Programming tools such as languages, assemblers, and compilers; control programs such as operating systems; or application programs such as electronic spreadsheets and word processors. Software instructs the computer to perform tasks.

spreadsheet   An application commonly used for budgets, forecasting and other finance-related tasks. Data and formulas to calculate those data

GLOSSARY

are entered into ledger-like forms (spreadsheets or worksheets) for analysis, tracking, planning, and evaluation of impacts on economic strategy.

ST-506   A hard-disk device-level interface (a connection between the hard disk and the computer system); the first interface used with PCs. It provides a maximum data-transfer rate of less than 1Mb per second (625k per second with MFM encoding, or 984k per second with RLL encoding.)

start bit   A data bit used in asynchronous transmission to signal the start of a character and indicate that the channel is active. It signifies that what follows is the data.

stop bit   A data bit used in asynchronous transmission to signal the end of a character and indicate that the channel is idle. It is a mark signal lasting at least for the duration of 1 bit.

street price   The real or typical selling price of computers, hardware, and software. Most laptop and desktop computers sell for about 25 percent below list price. Software may be discounted even more.

synchronous communication   Fixed-rate serial communication, eliminating the need for transmitting inefficient start-stop information. PC-to-mainframe communication may be synchronous; most PC-to-PC communication is asynchronous. Most laptop modems are asynchronous only. If you're not sure whether you need a synchronous-asynchronous modem, you probably don't.

system-level interface   A connection between the hard disk and its host system that puts control and data-separation functions on the drive itself (and not on the external controller). SCSI and IDE are system-level interfaces.

SysReq (System request key)   The seldom-used key used to get attention from another computer.

telecommunication   Using your computer to communicate with another computer via telephone lines and your modem.

TMS 34010   A popular graphics coprocessor chip from Texas Instruments that is one of the leading choices for coprocessed video adapter boards.

GLOSSARY

track   The circular path traced across the spinning surface of a disk platter by the read/write head inside the hard-disk drive. The track consists of one or more clusters.

track buffer   Memory sometimes built into disk-drive electronics, sufficient to store the contents of one full track. This allows the drive to read the entire track quickly, in one rotation, then slowly send the information to your CPU. It eliminates the need for interleaving and can speed up drive operation.

transfer rate   The speed at which a disk drive can transfer information between its platters and your CPU. The transfer rate is typically measured in megabytes per second, megabits per second, or megahertz.

triad   Three phosphor-filled dots (one red, one green, one blue) arranged in a triangular fashion within a monitor. Each of the three electron guns is dedicated to one of these colors. As the guns scan the screen, each active triad produces a single color, which is determined by the combination of excited color dots and by how active each dot is.

TTL (transistor-transistor logic)   Another way of saying digital, as in TTL monitor. CGA and EGA monitors are TTL. VGA monitors are analog.

TTY (teletype terminal or dumb terminal)   In communications or printing, the simplest form of terminal or printer. If you choose a TTY printer, you don't get any boldfacing, underlining, or other print enhancements. TTY is also the name of a DOS device referring to the keyboard and display.

UART (universal asynchronous receiver transmitter)   The circuit that controls the serial port, converting bytes to bits and bits to bytes, and adding and stripping start and stop bits. Buying tip: Look for a computer with a 16550A or 16550AF UART instead of the older, slower 16450 or 8250 UARTs if you're planning to do high-speed data communications (19,200 bps between your computer and modem).

UNIX   An operating system used mostly by minicomputers.

utility program   A program designed to perform maintenance work on a system or on system components, e.g. a storage backup program, a disk and file recovery program, or a resource editor.

GLOSSARY

V. The CCITT international communications standards, pronounced "vee-dot." Various V. standards cover speed (modulation), error correction, data compression, and signaling characteristics. The ones listed in this glossary are the most important.

V.22 1,200-bps modem speed, about 120 characters per second. Most 1,200-bps communication in the United States uses the Bell 212A standard instead. Above 1,200 bps, all standards are the same around the world.

V.22bis 2,400-bps modem speed.

V.29 9,600-bps data communications (also 4,800 and 7,200) used by Group III fax machines and PC fax modems. Fax modems, at least of the same brand, can exchange nonfax data at 9,600 bps, usually in half-duplex mode (one way at a time).

V.32 9,600-bps data communications (also 4,800). Most but not all 9,600-bps modems support V.32 or V.32bis.

V.32bis A follow-on to V.32 that allows 14,400-bps (also 4,800, 7,200, 9,600, and 12,000) data communications. V.29 is 9,600 bps, but it can't talk to V.32.

V.42 Emerging error-control standard. Uses a protocol called LAPM or LAP-M (link access protocol-modem). Incorporates MNP error-control levels 1–4 for compatibility with existing modems. If you have a V.42 modem, it has MNP 1–4 error correction whether the specifications say it or not.

V.42bis Emerging data-compression standard, better than MNP 5 data compression because it compresses data up to 4:1 (versus 2:1). Includes the V.42 error-control standard, so even if a modem is listed as having V.42bis but not V.42, it has both. Buying caution: A "V.42bis-compatible" modem may only have MNP 5, not LAPM; a "V.42bis-compliant" modem should have both. Ask before you buy.

VAR (value-added retailer) Similar to a dealer, but VARs take a computer, add special software to run on it, and price it higher than a dealer would since it has "value added."

vertical frequency This is also called the vertical refresh rate, or the vertical scan frequency. It is a monitor term that describes how long it

GLOSSARY

takes to draw an entire screenful of lines, from top to bottom. Monitors are designed for specific vertical and horizontal frequencies. Vertical frequency is a key factor in image flicker. Given a low enough vertical frequency (53 Hz, for example) nearly everyone will see a flicker because the screen isn't rewritten quickly enough. A high vertical frequency (70 Hz on a 14-inch monitor) will eliminate the flicker for most people.

VESA (Video Electronics Standards Assoication)   A consortium of manufacturers formed to establish and maintain industry-wide standards for video cards and monitors. VESA is responsible for establishing the Super VGA recommendations that many manufacturers follow today.

video bandwidth   The highest input frequency a monitor can handle. It determines the monitor's resolution capabilities. Video bandwidth is measured in MHz (megahertz).

VGA   IBM's third (1987) and current mainstream graphics standard, capable of 640-by-480-pixel resolution at 16 colors or gray shades. SuperVGA (800 by 600) resolution is important on desktop PCs. A handful of laptops support SuperVGA when connected to an external monitor; they use regular VGA when driving the built-in display. Caution: Some laptop vendors use "text mode" VGA, which means the monitor displays only 400 pixels, not 480, vertically, and uses either EGA (640 by 350) or double-scan CGA (640 by 400) for graphics.

VLSI (very large scale integration)   A group of a bunch of different chips and their functions jammed onto a single silicon chip. Over 100,000 transistors can be integrated into one, and the amazing thing is that as one chip they consume little power and can perform extremely complex functions.

VRAM (video random-access memory)   Special-purpose RAM with two data paths for access, rather than the one path in conventional RAM. The two paths let a VRAM board handle two functions at once: display refresh and processor access. VRAM doesn't force the system to wait for one function to finish before starting the other, so it permits faster operation for the video subsystem.

wide area network (WAN)   Usually a moderate to large network in which communications are conducted over the telephone lines using modems.

GLOSSARY

window   An area of a screen that displays information. Some programs support several windows that can be viewed simultaneously or sequentially.

write protection   Keeping a file or disk from being written over or deleted. $3^1/_2$-inch floppy disks use a sliding write-protect tab in the lower-left corner (diagonally across from the beveled corner of the disk) to keep the computer from writing to the disk. When the opening is hidden by the tab (no light passes), you can write to the disk; tab open, you can't write. This can be confusing because it's the exact opposite of how a $5^1/_4$-inch disk works. Most file management utilities allow you to write-protect individual files.

XMA (extended memory specification)   Interface that lets DOS programs cooperatively use extended memory in 80286 and higher computers. One such driver is Microsoft's HIMEM.SYS, which manages extended memory and HMA (high memory area), a 64K block just above 1Mb.

X Window   A network-based windowing system that provides a programmatic interface for graphic window displays. X Window permits graphics produced on one networked workstation to be displayed on another.

INDEX

INDEX

INDEX

INDEX

INDEX

INDEX

INDEX

INDEX

INDEX

INDEX

INDEX

The Quick and Easy Way to Learn.

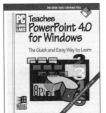

Ziff-Davis Press Survey of Readers

Please help us in our effort to produce the best books on personal computing.
For your assistance, we would be pleased to send you a FREE catalog
featuring the complete line of Ziff-Davis Press books.

1. How did you first learn about this book?

Recommended by a friend . . . . ☐ -1 (5)

Recommended by store personnel . . . . ☐ -2

Saw in Ziff-Davis Press catalog . . . . ☐ -3

Received advertisement in the mail . . . . ☐ -4

Saw the book on bookshelf at store . . . . ☐ -5

Read book review in: _____ ☐ -6

Saw an advertisement in: _____ ☐ -7

Other (Please specify): _____ ☐ -8

2. Which THREE of the following factors most influenced your decision to purchase this book? (Please check up to THREE.)

Front or back cover information on book . . . ☐ -1 (6)

Logo of magazine affiliated with book . . . . . ☐ -2

Special approach to the content . . . . ☐ -3

Completeness of content . . . . ☐ -4

Author's reputation. ☐ -5

Publisher's reputation . . . . ☐ -6

Book cover design or layout . . . . ☐ -7

Index or table of contents of book . . . . ☐ -8

Price of book . . . . ☐ -9

Special effects, graphics, illustrations . . . . . . ☐ -0

Other (Please specify): _____ ☐ -x

3. How many computer books have you purchased in the last six months? _____   (7-10)

4. On a scale of 1 to 5, where 5 is excellent, 4 is above average, 3 is average, 2 is below average, and 1 is poor, please rate each of the following aspects of this book below. (Please circle your answer.)

Depth/completeness of coverage   5   4   3   2   1   (11)

Organization of material   5   4   3   2   1   (12)

Ease of finding topic   5   4   3   2   1   (13)

Special features/time saving tips   5   4   3   2   1   (14)

Appropriate level of writing   5   4   3   2   1   (15)

Usefulness of table of contents   5   4   3   2   1   (16)

Usefulness of index   5   4   3   2   1   (17)

Usefulness of accompanying disk   5   4   3   2   1   (18)

Usefulness of illustrations/graphics   5   4   3   2   1   (19)

Cover design and attractiveness   5   4   3   2   1   (20)

Overall design and layout of book   5   4   3   2   1   (21)

Overall satisfaction with book   5   4   3   2   1   (22)

5. Which of the following computer publications do you read regularly; that is, 3 out of 4 issues?

Byte . . . . ☐ -1 (23)

Computer Shopper . . . . ☐ -2

Home Office Computing . . . . ☐ -3

Dr. Dobb's Journal . . . . ☐ -4

LAN Magazine . . . . ☐ -5

MacWEEK . . . . ☐ -6

MacUser . . . . ☐ -7

PC Computing . . . . ☐ -8

PC Magazine . . . . ☐ -9

PC WEEK . . . . ☐ -0

Windows Sources . . . . ☐ -x

Other (Please specify): _____ ☐ -y

Please turn page.

6. What is your level of experience with personal computers? With the subject of this book?

	With PCs	With subject of book
Beginner	☐ -1 (24)	☐ -1 (25)
Intermediate	☐ -2	☐ -2
Advanced	☐ -3	☐ -3

7. Which of the following best describes your job title?

Officer (CEO/President/VP/owner)........ ☐ -1 (26)
Director/head......................... ☐ -2
Manager/supervisor..................... ☐ -3
Administration/staff................... ☐ -4
Teacher/educator/trainer.............. ☐ -5
Lawyer/doctor/medical professional....... ☐ -6
Engineer/technician.................... ☐ -7
Consultant............................ ☐ -8
Not employed/student/retired........... ☐ -9
Other (Please specify): _____ ☐ -0

8. What is your age?

Under 20............................. ☐ -1 (27)
21-29................................ ☐ -2
30-39................................ ☐ -3
40-49................................ ☐ -4
50-59................................ ☐ -5
60 or over........................... ☐ -6

9. Are you:

Male................................. ☐ -1 (28)
Female............................... ☐ -2

Thank you for your assistance with this important information! Please write your address below to receive our free catalog.

Name: _____

Address: _____

City/State/Zip: _____

Fold here to mail.

3431-06-07